Contreras & Leutwyler

Spanish-English Compendium of Law

This book is intended to assist legal professionals in better communicating with, and understand of, the legal and social needs of the Spanish speaking community.

It is not intended to replace language instruction, nor is it intended to be a substantive legal text.

Bonifacio Contreras
Brad Leutwyler

WWW.SPANISHLAWBOOKS.COM

Contreras & Leutwyler: Spanish-English Compendium of Law

Publisher	Global Publishingr
Cover and design	Christine Lord
Editors	*English* - Christine Lord *Spanish* - Joshua Alexander
Webmaster	Brad Leutwyler www.voteforbrad.com
Marketing	C&L Publishing, Inc. Ed News En Español *www.spanishlawbooks.com* *www.ednewsenespanol.com*

Library of Congress Cataloging–in-Publication Data
Contreras, Bonifacio & Leutwyler, Brad
Contreras & Leutwyler Spanish-English Compendium of Law

ISBN 1-881050-20-3

1. Dictionary, Spanish 2. Spanish legal phrases
3. Spanish law phrases 4. Law terms 5. Spanish grammar

First Edition 2005, second printing 2008
Printed in the United States of America

DEDICATION

First and foremost, my efforts in this endeavor are dedicated to all of the Spanish speaking people who have been denied fair representation and/or treatment by the American legal system due to a communication barrier. It is my sincere hope that this work will, in some small way, contribute to remedying their plight.

Next, I wish to thank and recognize Prof. Carlton J. Snow, Prof. Leroy Tornquist, Prof. Dean Richardson, Prof. Claudia Burton, Prof. Richard Breen, Hon. Sigurd Murphy, W. Brad Coleman, Esq, Hon. Gregory Motyka and Hon. James Wanamaker. More important than any title or standing that any may hold, each one of these individuals serves as an oasis of humanity, compassion and open-minded reason on a legal landscape which is more often than not parched and lifeless in such respects. I thank them for being such fine examples.

Additionally, there is a discrete group of people who, no matter how hard I try, I cannot begin to thank enough. I thank my wife and daughter for their infinite patience, not just in relation to this book. I thank my parents for their unexplainably steadfast and continued support, even when, in the middle of a semester of astrophysics study, I decided to write this book.

Last but not least, I thank Bonifacio Contreras. You are brilliant, and this labor of love has been relatively simple because of your dedication and hard work. It has been an honor, an education and a pleasure.

Brad Leutwyler, 2008

I wish to thank and recognize Prof. Richard Gonzales and Prof. April Land, both of the University of New Mexico Law school, for their encouragement and suggestion that I write a legal dictionary after having seen my medical dictionary.

A special word of gratitude to Christine Lord who has always been a source of hope and encouragement. I express my heartfelt thanks and gratitude to my niece Rose Anaya and her daughter Maria Anaya for the support during the writing of the book. A special thanks is also in order for my nephew, Pablo Garcia, for the tech and moral support during this endeavor.

Finally, a very special "gracias" to Brad Leutwyler, whose gentle reminders and insightful comments kept me on track throughout the preparation of the manuscript.

Bonifacio Contreras, 2005

Table of contents

TOPICAL SECTIONS 561

SPANISH-ENGLISH PHRASES AND VERNACULAR DICTIONARY

A

a *(indefinite article which is not always translated into Spanish)* un, una; unas; unos; **I have a car** tengo un coche; **do you have a question?** ¿tienes una pregunta?; **I have a question** tengo una pregunta; **I'm a lawyer** soy abogada; soy abogado; **half an hour** media hora; **she's a famous lawyer** es una abogada famosa; **you have a problem** usted tiene un problema

a week from today dentro de una semana; de aquí a una semana

A.B.A *abbrev of* **American Bar Association** Asociación Norteamericana de Abogados; Asociación Estadounidense de Abogados

abandon abandonar; desamparar; **the baby was found abandoned** encontraron al bebé abandonado; **she abandoned the baby at the entrance to the hospital** abandonó al bebé en la puerta del hospital; **to abandon hope** abandonar las esperanzas; perder las esperanzas

abandoned *(child)* abandonada; abandonado; desamparada; desamparado; *(house, property)* abandonada; abandonado; desierta; desierto

abandoned property propiedad abandonada

abandonment abandono; *(neglect)* desamparo; **the state of neglect in which this old lady lives** el desamparo en que vive esta anciana

abandonment by husband abandono del hogar conyugal por el marido

abandonment by wife abandono del hogar conyugal por la mujer

abandonment of action caducidad de la instancia; desistimiento de la acción

abandonment of appeal deserción del recurso; deserción de la apelación

abandonment of child abandono de un menor

abandonment of children abandono de menores

abandonment of claim renuncia a un derecho; renuncia a una acción

abandonment of contract rescisión unilateral del contrato

abandonment of copyright abandono de derecho de autor

abandonment of domicile abandono de domicilio; abandono del hogar

abandonment of rights renuncia de derechos

abandonment of spouse abandono del cónyuge

abandonment of suite abandono de la instancia

abate *(anger)* aplacarse; calmarse; *(violence)* disminuir; *(pollution)* poner término a; acabar con

abatement *(anger)* aplacamiento; disminución; reducción; *(termination)* supresión; **tax abatement** disminuir la carga fiscal; disminuir la carga presupuestaria

abatement of action extinción de la acción

abatement of debts la reducción de deudas

abatement notice intimación *(generalmente de origen municipal)*

abatement of taxes remisión de impuestos; reducción de impuestos

abbreviate *(word, title)* abreviar; *(account)* resumir

abdicate *(rights)* abdicar; renunciar

abdication *(of duty, responsibility)* abdicación; *(of rights)* renuncia

abduct plagiar; raptar; secuestrar

abduction plagio; rapto; secuestro

abductor raptor; raptora; secuestrador; secuestradora

aberrant *(adj: behavior)* aberrante; *(in statistics)* anómala; anómalo; atípica; atípico

abet *(crime)* inducir; instigar; **aid and abet** ayudar y encubrir

abetment apoyo; incitación; instigación

abettor alentador en la comisión de un crimen; alentadora en la comisión de un crimen; asistente en la comisión de un crimen; incitador en la comisión de un crimen; incitadora en la comisión de un crimen

abeyance *(activity; project)* **hold something in abeyance** suspender algo; dejar algo en suspenso; **inheritance in abeyance** herencia yacente; **lands in abeyance** bienes mostrencos; **to be in abeyance** estar suspendida; estar suspendido; estar en suspenso

abeyant expectante; suspenso

abhor aborrecer; detestar

abhorrence aborrecimiento; aversión

abide *(verb)* respetar; soportar; tolerar

abide by *(verdict, rules, law)* acatar; atenerse a; obrar de acuerdo a; *(promise)* cumplir; cumplir con; **they did not abide by the terms of the contract** no respetaron los términos del contrato; **he was willing to abide by the ruling** estaba dispuesto a acatar la sentencia

abide by a rule someterse a una regla

abide by the constitution acatar la Constitución

ability *(talent)* aptitud; capacidad; *(faculty, power)* capacidad; **a lawyer of great ability** un abogado muy capaz; una abogada muy capaz; **people's ability to pay** los recursos de la gente; los recursos de que dispone la gente; **to the best of one's ability** lo mejor que uno pueda

ability to act capacidad de actuar

ability to pay debts capacidad de pagar las deudas; solvencia

ability to support capacidad de sostener a otra persona

ability to walk movimiento

abject *(adj: contemptible)* abyecta; abyecto; vil; *(condition)* lamentable; **an act of abject cowardice** un acto de abyecta cobardía; un acto de vil cobardía; **live in abject poverty** vivir en la mayor miseria

abjure *(activities, claims)* renunciar a

able *(adj)* poder; **to be able to** + *infin* poder + *infin*; saber + *infin*; ser capaz de + *infin*; lograr + *infin;* **to be able to pay** ser capaz de pagar

able-bodied sana; sano; no discapacitada; no discapacitado

able buyer comprador con capacidad financiera de pagar su compra; compradora con capacidad financiera de pagar su compra

able-minded inteligente

ably con mucha habilidad; de una manera capaz; hábilmente

abnegate abnegar; renunciar

abnegation abnegación; renuncia

abnormal anómala; anómalo; anormal; de modo anormal

abnormal behavior comportamiento anormal; conducta anormal

abnormal risk riesgo anormal; riesgo atípico

abnormality anomalía; anormalidad

abnormality of the mind deficiencia mental; enfermedad mental

abnormally anormalmente; de modo anormal

abnormally dangerous de peligrosidad atípica; de peligrosidad inusual

aboard a bordo de

aboard the plane a bordo del avión

aboard the ship a bordo del barco

abode *(noun: dwelling-place)* morada; habitación; **place of abode** *(law)* domicilio; residencia; **right of abode** derecho de residencia; **of no fixed abode** sin domicilio fijo

abolish *(law)* derogar; abolir; eliminar por completo

abolition *(of law)* derogación; abolición; **the Abolition** *(in US history)* la abolición de la esclavitud

abolitionist *(noun)* abolicionista

abort *(medical)* abortar; *(negotiations, efforts, plans)* malograr; *(abandon mission)* abandonar

abortion *(termination of pregnancy)* aborto; **illegal abortion** aborto ilegal; **to have an abortion** hacerse un aborto; **to perform an abortion** practicar un aborto

abortion clinic clínica donde se practican abortos

abortion laws leyes sobre el aborto

abortion on demand libre aborto; aborto libre y gratuito

abortion pill píldora abortiva

abortive *(attempt, project, efforts)* frustrada; frustrado; **negotiations proved abortive** las negociaciones fracasaron; las negociaciones malograron

about *(approximately)* más o menos; a eso de; aproximadamente; alrededor de; *(with numbers)* unos; unas; *(theme, books, etc.)* acerca de; tratarse de; **¿about how many?** ¿cuántos aproximadamente?; **at about two o'clock** a eso de las dos; alrededor de las dos; **in about three hours** en unas tres horas; **in about four weeks** en unas cuatro semanas; **she must be about 40** debe tener alrededor de 40 años; **be about to** estar a punto de

about face *(reversal of policy)* cambio radical de postura; **to do an about face** cambiar radicalmente de postura

above encima de; anterior; superior; **as shown above** como se demostró anteriormente; como se demostró más arriba; **for the above reasons** por dichas razones; por lo antedicho; **he's above that sort of thing** no se rebaja a hacer semejantes cosas; **he's above suspicion** está por encima de toda sospecha; **she's above suspicion** está por encima de toda sospecha; **in the paragraph above this one** en el párrafo anterior a éste; *(facts, text)* **the above** lo anterior; *(persons)* dichas personas; **the above remarks** las observaciones anteriores; **they're not above the law** no están por encima de la ley

above all sobre todo

above board a la vista de todos; abiertamente

above board *(adj)* legítima; legítimo; limpia; limpio; **open and above board** sin tapujos

above-mentioned *(fact, name, person)* antedicho; citado anteriormente; **the above-mentioned** *(singular person)* el antedicho; la antedicha; *(plural persons)* las antedichas; los antedichos

abreast *(up to date)* **be abreast of something** estar al día en algo; estar al corriente de algo; **to keep abreast of something** mantenerse al día en algo; mantenerse al corriente de algo; **to keep somebody abreast of something** mantener a alguien al día en algo; mantener a alguien al corriente de algo; **to stay abreast of something** mantenerse al día en algo; mantenerse al corriente de algo

abridge *(verb)* resumir; condensar un texto; abreviar un texto; **abridge a right** disminunir un derecho; **abridged edition** edición condensada; edición abreviada

abridgement resumen; compendio

abroad *(in other countries)* en el extranjero; en el exterior; **to go abroad** irse al extranjero; irse al exterior

abrogate *(law, treaty, constitution)* abrogar; anular; *(formal)* derogar

abrogation *(of law, treaty, agreement)* abrogación; derogación

abscond *(verb)* fugarse; huir; desaparecer

absconder *(noun)* fugitiva; fugitivo; prófuga; prófugo

absence *(noun: of person)* ausencia; **after an absence of six weeks** después de una ausencia de seis semanas; *(law)* **be sentenced in one's absence** ser juzgada en rebeldía; ser juzgado en rebeldía; **in her/his absence** en su ausencia; **there was absence of intention** no hubo intención; **there was absence of malice** no hubo dolo

absence of intention no hubo intención

absence of malice no hubo dolo

absence of something falta de algo

absence of wrong doing ausencia de daño

absent *(adj: person)* ausente; **be absent from something** faltar a algo

absent without leave ausente sin permiso; ausente sin licencia

absentee *(noun: person)* ausente

absentee ballot voto por correo; voto en ausencia; voto por correspondencia

absentee landlord propietaria ausentista; propietario ausentista; propietaria ausente de su inmueble; propietario ausente de su inmueble; arrendador ausente; arrendadora ausente

absentee voting voto por correo por las personas ausentes de su domicilio

absenteeism *(noun)* ausentismo

absentia *(noun)* ausencia

absolute *(trust; confidence)* absoluta; absoluto; plena; pleno; **with absolute certainty** con absoluta certeza; **with absolute truth** la pura verdad; **it's an absolute necessity** es absolutamente imprescindible

absolute acceptance aceptación absoluta; aceptación incondicional

absolute conveyance transmisión total de la propiedad; transmisión incondicional de la propiedad

absolute covenant estipulación incondicional

absolute guarantee garantía absoluta; garantía completa; garantía incondicional

absolute liability responsabilidad civil sin necesidad de probar culpa o negligencia

absolute nuisance prejuicio absoluto; daño absoluto

absolute obligation obligación absoluta

absolute owner propietaria absoluta; propietario absoluto

absolute ownership propiedad absoluta; propiedad plena

absolute pardon indulto absoluto

absolute possession posesión permanente; posesión absoluta; posesión plena

absolute privilege privilegio absoluto

absolute property propiedad absoluta; propiedad plena

absolute right derecho absoluto

absolute sale venta en la que se transfiere el dominio pleno del bien vendido

absolute title título de propiedad absoluta sobre un inmueble; título de propiedad plena sobre un inmueble

absolute warranty garantía absoluta

absolutely *(adv)* rotundamente; totalmente; **I trust her absolutely** tengo plena confianza en ella; **I trust him absolutely** tengo plena confianza en él; **the jury is not absolutely convinced** el jurado no está totalmente convencido; **It's absolutely true** es la pura verdad

absolutely void afectado por una nulidad absoluta

absolve *(verb)* absolver; eximir; liberar; **to absolve someone for something** absolver a alguien de algo; eximir a alguien de algo; **he was absolved of guilt** fue absuelto de culpa; fue eximido de culpa

absorb *(immigrants)* integrar; asimilar

absorbed tax impuesto absorbido por una de las partes

absortion la continuación de la existencia de una compañía al ser incorporada a otra compañía

abstain *(verb)* abstenerse; privarse

abstain from something abstenerse de algo + *infinitive*; **abstain from sexual relations** abstenerse de las relaciones sexuales

abstract *(theory)* abstracta; abstracto; *(summary)* resumen; sumario

abstract idea idea abstracta

abstract instruction instrucción al jurado que sólo supone la enunciación de una regla abstracta de derecho, sin referirse adecuadamente a los presupuestos fácticos del caso

abstract of article resumen; sumario; compendio; extracto

abstract of judgement resumen de un fallo

abstract of record resumen de un caso; resumen de un expediente judicial

abstract of title resumen del título

abstract thing cosa abstracta

abstraction substracción ilegal; apropiación ilegal; hurto; tomar algo con la intención de cometer un fraude

absurd absurda; absurdo; ridícula; ridículo; **don't be absurd!** ¡no seas ridícula!; ¡no seas ridículo!

absurdity lo absurdo; absurdez; absurdidad; disparate; contrasentido

absurdly de manera absurda

abundant abundante

abundantly abundantemente; en abundancia; **to make something abundantly clear** no dejar ningún lugar a dudas al respecto

abuse *(verb: power, person, hospitality)* abusar; *(verb: child, woman)* maltratar; abusar de; *(noun)* abuso; **abuse of a child** abuso de un menor; aprovecharse sexualmente de un menor; **alcohol abuse** alcoholismo; **child abuse** malos tratos a la infancia; **drug abuse** toxicomanía; **physical abuse** malos tratos; **sexual abuse** abusos sexuales; abusos deshonestos; **be open to abuse** prestarse al abuso

abuse of power abuso de autoridad; abuso de poder *(in some countries it is used without the article)*; abuso del poder *(in some countries it is used with the article, which is contracted)*

abuse of children malos tratos a la infancia

abuse of process abuso malicioso del proceso legal por una parte con un fin ilegal

abuse of the elderly malos tratos a la anciana; malos tratos al anciano

abusive *(adj)* insultante; grosera; grosero; **to use abusive language** lanzar improperios

abusive home hogar abusivo

abusively *(speak)* groseramente; **to start yelling abusively** empezar a gritar groserías

abut colindar; tener los linderos uno al lado del otro; predios contiguos; *(land)* **to abut on something** colindar con algo; *(building)* **to abut against** colindar con

abutter colindantes; dueña colindante; dueño colindante; personas que poseen fincas vecinas; personas que poseen fincas que colindan

abutting contigua; contiguo; colindante

abutment machón; contrafuerte

academic académica; académico; **that's academic now** eso ya no tiene ninguna trascendencia

academic question punto legal innecesario e inaplicable para resolver un caso; punto hipotético

academic training estudios superiores

academic year año académico

acceed acceder; acordar; conceder

accelerated depreciation varios métodos de depreciar activos, con deducciones mayores en los primeros años de vida del activo

acceleration acortar el período de tiempo para fijar un interés anticipado; reducir el período de tiempo para fijar un interés anticipado

accelerated clause cláusula de aceleración

accent acento; **he speaks with a Spanish accent** habla con acento español; **she has a Spanish accent** tiene acento español; **she has a funny accent** tiene acento raro

accept *(receive willingly)* recibir; aceptar; *(of evidence)* aceptar; admitir

accept a bribe aceptar un soborno

accept liability aceptar responsabilidad

accept responsibility aceptar responsabilidad

acceptable *(conduct)* aceptable; *(tolerable)* admisible; **would that be acceptable to you?** ¿eso le resultaría aceptable?

acceptable evidence *(conduct)* prueba admisible

acceptance *(of a contract)* aceptación de una oferta; acto mediante el cual se origina un contrato; acto mediante el cual surge un contrato; **banker's acceptance** carta mediante el cual el banco promete pagar una suma cierta de dinero en una fecha próxima; documento mediante el cual el banco promete pagar una suma cierta de dinero en una fecha próxima

accepted practice la práctica establecida

access *(verb)* obtener acceso a; entrar a *(noun: of a contract or document)* acceso; *(to a street through a lot)* acceso; **multiple access** acceso múltiple

access to health care acceso a la atención médica

access to the courts acceso a la justicia

accessibility accesibilidad; asequible; susceptible

accessible accesible; asequible; susceptible

accession toma de posesión

accessory cómplice *(una persona que ayuda a contribuir a un delito sin estar presente al momento del mismo)*

accessory after the fact encubridor; encubridora *(persona que ayuda a encubrir un delito)*

accessory before the fact instigador; instigadora *(persona que ayuda a preparar la comisión de un delito)*

accessory charge cargo accesorio

accessory to the crime cómplice en el crimen

accessory to the murder cómplice en el asesinato

accident accidente; acontecimiento inesperado; **by accident** *(by chance)* por casualidad; *(unintentionally)* sin querer; **industrial accident** accidente laboral; accidente de trabajo; **road accident** accidente de tránsito; accidente de tráfico; accidente de circulación; **traffic accident** accidente de circulación; accidente de tránsito; accidente de tráfico; **to have an accident** tener un accidente; sufrir un accidente

accident and health insurance seguro contra accidentes y enfermedades

accident benefits beneficio por accidente

accident insurance seguro de accidentes

accident policy póliza contra accidentes

accident report informe de accidente

accidental bodily injury lesión corporal accidental

accidental damage daño accidental

accidental death muerte accidental

accidental death benefit beneficio por muerte accidental

accidental drowning ahogamiento accidental; ahogamiento producido por accidente

accidental fire fuego accidental

accidental injury lesión accidental

accidental killing homicidio accidental

accidental overdose sobredosis accidental; sobredosis producida por accidente

accidental poisoning envenenamiento accidental; envenenamiento producido por accidente

acclaim *(verb)* aclamar; proclamar

accomodate acomodar; alojar; hospedar; *(have room for)* tener cabida para; *(contain, house)* albergar; contener

accomodation *(agreement, compromise)* acuerdo; **to reach an accomodation with somebody over something** llegar a un acuerdo con alguien sobre algo; *(lodgings)* alojamiento; hospedaje

accomodation papers carta de acomodación

accompanied by acompañada de; acompañado de

accompany acompañar

accompanying adjunta; adjunto; **the accompanying note** las notas adjuntas; **the accompanying instructions** las instrucciones adjuntas

accompanying relative *(for green card)* familiar acompañante

accomplice cómplice; **he was an accomplice to amurder** era cómplice en un asesinato

accomplish *(task)* llevar a cabo; realizar; *(goal)* lograr; conseguir

accomplishment *(aim, objective, success)* logro; *(skill)* habilidad

accord *(agreement)* acuerdo; **be in accord with somebody** estar de acuerdo con alguien; **be in accord with something** estar de acuerdo con algo

accord and satisfaction *(agreement)* acuerdo transaccional; transacción

accord executory *(agreement)* acuerdo transaccional aún no cumplido

accordance *(agreement)* acuerdo; **in accordance with** de acuerdo con; de acuerdo a; conforme; según; **in accordance with my instructions** conforme a mis instrucciones; de acuerdo con mis instrucciones; según mis instrucciones; **in accordance with the instructions of the judge** de acuerdo con las instrucciones del juez

according *(depending on whether)* según + *subjunctive*; *(depending to what extent)* en la medida en que + *subjunctive*; **it all went according to plan** todo salió tal como se había planeado; todo salió conforme a lo planeado; todo salió según lo planeado

according to *(as said, given by)* según; *(as determined by)* según

according to contract de acuerdo al contrato

according to custom de acuerdo a los costumbres

according to facts de acuerdo a los hechos

according to his lawyer según su abogada; según su abogado

according to law conforme a derecho; legal

according to the decision según el fallo

according to the judge según el juez; según la jueza

according to the ruling según el auto

accordingly *(correspondingly)* en consecuencia; **you must accept the responsibility and act accordingly** debe asumir la responsabilidad y obrar en consecuencia

accost abordar; importunar; **he was accosted by a man in the street** un hombre lo acostó en la calle; **the women complain of being accosted in the street** las mujeres se quejan de ser importunadas en la calle

account *(explanation)* explicación; *(version)* versión; *(report)* informe; *(with bank)* cuenta; cuenta corriente; lista detallada de los créditos y deudas entre las partes; **account for** dar cuentas de; **by all accounts** a decir de todos; por lo que dicen todos; **by her own account** según ella misma; **by his own account** según él mismo; **no satisfactory account of why it happened has been given** nunca se ha dado una explicación satisfactoria de por qué ocurrió; **on no account** de ninguna manera; **savings account** cuenta de ahorros; **she gave me a very different account of the events** me dio una versión muy distinta de los hechos; **to settle one's account** pagar su cuenta; saldar su cuenta; *(consideration)* **to take something into account** tener algo en cuenta; tomar algo en cuenta

account balance saldo de una cuenta

account balanced and rendered cuenta presentada a la contraparte

account book libro contable

account closed cuenta cerrada

account debtor persona deudora bajo una cuenta corriente

account for *(provide record of, justify)* dar cuenta de

account holder titular de una cuenta

account in trust cuenta fideicomisaria, abierta en beneficio de una tercera persona

account number número de cuenta

account payable cuenta por pagar

account receivable cuenta por cobrar

account rendered cuenta presentada al deudor

account stated cuenta convenida; cuenta cuyo saldo, y las condiciones de su pago, han sido acordadas entre las partes

account settled cuenta saldada

account statement estado de cuenta

accountability responsabilidad

accountability to somebody responsabilidad ante alguien

accountable responsable; **be accountable to somebody** ser responsable ante alguien

accountancy *(noun)* contabilidad

accountant *(noun)* contador; contadora

accounts contabilidad; **to keep the accounts** llevar la contabilidad; llevar las cuentas

accounting *(business, finance)* contabilidad; teneduría de libros

accounting documents documentos de contabilidad

accounting records registros de contabilidad

accounting year ejercicio

accredit *(verb)* acreditar

accretion *(noun)* adición; aditamiento; acrecentamiento; aumento en la superficie de un terreno por causas naturales; aumento en la superficie de un predio por causas naturales; aumento en los bienes de un fideicomiso; *(verb)* acrecer; aumentar

accroach *(noun)* usurpación; tomar o ejercitar un poder o autoridad sin derecho a ello

accrual basis *(noun)* base devengada

accrue *(verb)* acumular; acumularse

accrue cause of action acumulación de acción *(momento en el cual un pleito puede ser procesado)*

accrued dividend dividendo devengado; dividendo que ha sido declarado pero aún no pagado

accrued interest interés acumulado; interés devengado

accumulate *(wealth, interest)* acumular; amontonar; atesorar; *(information, evidence)* reunir; acumular

accumulated earnings tax impuesto federal sobre las ganancias acumuladas y no distribuidas como dividendos de una sociedad anónima

accumulated interest interés acumulado

accumulated profits ganancias acumuladas en exceso del capital inicial y las obligaciones existentes

accumulated surplus ganancias acumuladas en exceso del capital inicial y las obligaciones existentes

accumulation *(wealth, interest)* acumulación; amontonamiento; hacinamiento

accumulation trust fideicomiso

accuracy *(translation, description)* exactitud; fidelidad

accurate *(adj) (translation, description)* exacta; exacto; fiel

accusation acusación; **to make an accusation** hacer una acusación; **what is the accusation against him?** ¿de qué se lo acusa?

accusation brief escrito de acusación

accusatorial procedure procedimiento legal; juicio legal

accusatory body gran jurado

accuse *(law)* acusar; denunciar; delatar; **the accused** el acusado; la acusada; el inculpado; la inculpada; **to accuse somebody of something** acusar a alguien de algo; **they stand accused of** se les acusa de; **they were accused of racial discrimination** los acusaron de discriminación racial; **they were accused of distorting the facts** los acusaron de tergiversar los hechos; **two executives of the company were accused of stealing nearly $600 million from the company's funds** dos ejecutivos de la empresa fueron acusados de robar cerca de 600 millones de dólares de los fondos de la compañía

accuse falsely acusar falsamente

accused, the el acusado; la acusada; las acusadas; los acusados

accused party parte acusada

accusor *(noun)* acusador; acusadora

accustom acostumbrar; habituar; **to accustom somebody to something** acostumbrar a alguien a algo; habituar a alguien a algo

accustomed *(adj)* acostumbrada; acostumbrado; **be accustomed to something** estar acostumbrada a algo; estar acostumbrado a algo; **to become accustomed to something** acostumbrarse a algo; habituarse a algo; **to get accustomed to something** acostumbrarse a algo; habituarse a algo

acid test ratio método de análisis financiero que compara la relación entre el efectivo y las cuentas por cobrar contra los pasivos

achievable alcanzable; **it will only be achievable with great difficulty** sólo con gran dificultad se podrá lograr

achieve *(accomplish)* llevar a cabo; ejecutar; realizar; lograr; *(attain)* conseguir; obtener; *(ambition)* hacer realidad

achievement *(feat)* logro; *(success)* éxito; logro; hazaña

acknowledge *(admit)* admitir; reconocer; **an acknowledged fact** un hecho reconocido

acknowledgement reconocimiento; confirmación

acknowledgement of debt reconocimiento de deuda

acknowledgement of guilt reconocimiento de culpabilidad

acknowledgement of paternity reconocimiento de paternidad

acquaint informar; familiarizar con

acquaint oneself with ponerse al corriente de; **perhaps you are not fully acquainted with the facts** quizás usted no esté totalmente al tanto de los hechos; quizás usted no esté totalmente al corriente de los hechos; **be acquainted** conocerse; **be acquainted with** conocer; estar al corriente de; **be acquainted with something** estar al corriente de algo; estar al tanto de algo; estar familiarizado con algo

acquaintance *(person)* conocida; conocido; **they are old acquaintances** se conocen desde hace tiempo; **strike up an acquaintance with** entablar una relación con; **to make the acquaintance of** conocer; **we are old acquaintances** nos conocemos desde hace tiempo

acquest adquirido; algo comprado

acquiesce consentir; asentir; aceptar

acquiescence consentimiento; conformidad

acquire adquirir; obtener; conseguir

acquired citizenship ciudadanía adquirida

Acquired Immune Deficiency Syndrome (AIDS) Síndrome de Inmunodeficiencia Adquirida (sida) *or* (SIDA)

acquired rights derechos adquiridos

acquisition adquisición

acquisition by purchase adquisición mediante compra

acquisition of property adquisición de propiedad

acquit *(verb)* absolver; exonerar; liberar de una culpa u obligación

acquit on all counts solicitar la total absolución; **he asked the court to acquit his client on all counts** solicitó la total absolución de su cliente

acquit somebody of something absolver a alguien de algo; **she was acquitted** la absolvieron de toda culpa

acquittal absolución; finiquitar; descargo

acquittal by jury absolución mediante jurado

acquittance pago; recibo; finiquito; convenio escrito liberando una obligación de pagar dinero

across *(from one side to another)* cruzar; atravesar; a través; al otro lado

across the board incluyendo todo

act *(deed)* acto; acción; **an act of agression** una agresión; **an act of Congress** una ley aprobada por el Congreso; **an act of treason** una traición; **by an act of God** *(law)* por caso fortuito; por acto de la naturaleza; **criminal act** un delito; acto criminal; **legislative act** ley pasada por una o ambas cámaras de la legislatura; **private act** actos de personas particulares en relación a sus asuntos; **public act** acto público; **get one's act together** organizarse; **pass an act** aprobar una ley; **the government's latest act** la última acción del gobierno

act *(take action, do something)* actuar; hacer de; tomar medidas; **I'm acting on behalf of my client** actúo en representación de mi cliente;

we must act now tenemos que tomar medidas inmediatamente; **act as** servir de; **this will act as a warning** esto servirá de advertencia

act against actuar contra

act alone actuar sola; actuar solo; **the charges show that the defendant acted alone** las acusaciones consideran que el procesado actuó solo; las acusaciones consideran que la procesada actuó sola

act as a joint sponsor for compartir la responsabilidad de

act as an agent actuar como agente

act as a mediator actuar como mediador; actuar como mediadora

act as a moderator actuar como moderador; actuar como moderadora

act illegally actuar ilegalmente

act improperly actuar impropiamente

act in bad faith actuar de mala fe

act in collusion actuar en colusión

act in concert actuar en concierto

act in good faith actuar de buena fe

act in opposition actuar en oposición

act jointly actuar conjuntamente

act of agression acto de agresión

act of betrayal traición

act of cruelty acto de crueldad

act of hostility acto de hostilidad

act of law efecto jurídico

act of violence acto de violencia

act on behalf of actuar de parte de

acting actuando; en funciones; efectuando o desempeñando los poderes de otro

acting judge juez interino

action acción; actuación; conducta; comportamiento; demanda formal ante la corte; medida; **civil action** acción civil; **my first action would be** lo primero que haría sería + *infinitive*; **no further action will be taken** no se tomará ninguna otra medida; **to bring an action against** entablar juicio; entablar pleito; hacer causa; demandar a alguien; ejercitar un acción contra alguien; **they took disciplinary action against her** le aplicaron medidas disciplinarias; fue sancionada; **to take action** tomar medidas; **what course of action do you recommend?** ¿qué medidas recomienda?; **wrongful death action** acción jurídica a consecuencia de una muerte; *(law)* **to aggravate an action** acriminar una causa; **legal action** acción judicial

action brought acción iniciada

action for bodily injury acción por lesión corporal

action for breach of contract acción por incumplimiento de contrato

action for damage to property acción por daño a la propiedad

action for damages acción por daños y perjuicios

action for debt acción por cobro de deuda

actionable accionable; procesable; capaz de motivar una acción; **an actionable fraud** *(in civil law)* un fraude justiciable; **an actionable negligence** *(in civil law)* una negligencia procesable; ser enjuiciable; ser materia de juicio; *(in criminal law)* ser procesable; **be actionable** *(in civil law)* ser enjuiciable; ser materia de juicio; *(in criminal law)* ser procesable

active *(adj)* activa; activo; que implica acción; *(noun: market, trading)* activa; activo; *(practicing)*; **be politically active** militar políticamente; **sexually active person** persona que mantiene relaciones sexuales

active file archivo activo

actively *(adv)* activamente; **be actively involved in** tomar parte activa en

activism activismo

activist activista

activity actividad; **the activities of drug dealers** las actividades de los narcotraficantes

activities of daily living funciones básicas de la vida diaria; actividades diarias

actor actor, **he's a good actor** disimula muy bien; **the main actors in the crime** los principales protagonistas del crimen; **the main actors in the scandal** los principales protagonistas del escándalo

actual *(adj)* real; **he cited actual cases** citó casos reales; **in actual fact** en realidad; **the actual owner** el verdadero dueño; la verdadera dueña; **there was no actual written agreement** no hubo un acuerdo escrito propiamente dicho; **this is the actual spot where it happened** ocurrió aquí mismo; **those were her actual words** ésas fueron sus palabras textuales

actual authority autorización real

actual cash value valor real en efectivo; el valor que tendría un objeto, un bien o una mercancía en el mercado

actuality realidad; **in actuality** en realidad

actually en realidad; **actually he'd rather not talk** la verdad es que prefiere no hablar; **she's actually very bright** en realidad es muy inteligente; la verdad es que es muy inteligente

actuarial actuarial

actuarial method método actuarial; forma de llevar la contabilidad en un libro para tal fin

actuary actuario; persona que se especializa en las ciencias actuariales basadas en estadísticas y poblaciones; en las compañías de segoros, especialista en cuestiones de estadísticas

adapt adaptar; *(oneself)* adaptarse; amoldarse; **adapt oneself to something** adaptarse a algo

adaptable *(person)* adaptable; **be very adaptable** *(person)* ser muy adaptable

addict adicta; adicto; **drug addict** drogadicta; drogadicto; toxicómana; toxicómano; **heroin addict** heroinómana; heroinómano

addicted adicta; adicto; **addicted to** adicta a; adicto a; **he is addicted to heroin** es adicto a la heroína; **she is addicted to crack** es adicta al crack

addiction adicción; **drug addiction** drogadicción; toxicomanía; **heroin addiction** adicción a la heroína; **this drug can produce addiction** esta droga puede crear dependencia; **physical addiction** dependencia física

addictive que crea adicción; que crea dependencia

addictive drug droga que crea adicción; droga que crea dependencia

addictive substance sustancia que crea adicción; sustancia que crea dependencia

additional information información supletoria

address *(noun)* dirección; **home address** domicilio; domicilio particular; **the letter is addressed to you** la carta está dirigida a usted; la carta viene a su nombre; *(verb: to speak to)* dirigirse a; **are you speaking to me?** ¿se dirige usted a mí?; **has your addressed changed?** ¿te has mudado?; ¿has cambiado de dirección?; **how long have you been at this address?** ¿Desde cuándo vives aquí?

address book librito de direcciones

address it to my office mándamela a mi oficina; mándamelo a mi oficina

address label etiqueta con la dirección

address the court dirigirse al tribunal

addressee *(noun)* destinataria; destinatario

adduce evidence rendir prueba

ademption revocación de una herencia; anulación de una herencia

adequate *(adj)* suficiente; adecuada; adecuado; **we didn't get adequate notice** no se nos avisó con la suficiente anticipación

adequately suficientemente; de forma aceptable; de forma acuedable

adequate notice suficiente aviso

adhere *(stick to something, principle, cause)* adhersirse a algo; *(regulations)* atenerse a; cumplir con algo; observar algo; **adhere to the rules** atenerse al reglamento

adherence *(principles, cause)* adhesión a algo; *(to law, rule)* observancia; **adherence to the law** observancia de la ley

adjoin *(be adjacent to)* lindar con; colindar con

adjoining *(houses, rooms)* contigua; contiguo; colindante; de al lado; **we are going to meet in the adjoining room** nos vamos a reunir en el cuarto de al lado

adjourn *(verb)* suspender; levantar la sesión; aplazar; **the court adjourned for lunch** el tribunal levantó la sesión para ir a comer; **we are going to adjourn for lunch** vamos a levantar la sesión para ir a comer; **the court is adjourned** se levanta la sesión

adjournment suspensión

adjudge declarar

adjudicate *(give judgement)* adjudicar; arbitrar; fallar; *(law, to abjudicate on something)* **he was asked to adjudicate on the dispute** le pidieron que arbitrara en el conflicto

adjudication adjudicación

adjudication process proceso de adjudicar un caso entre las partes; proceso de adjudicar un pleito entre las partes

adjudicator *(in dispute)* árbitra; árbitro; *(in competition)* juez; jueza

adjunct adjunta; adjunto; unir una cosa con otra

adjunction adjunción; unir una cosa a otra permanentemente

adjuration juramento

adjust *(modify)* ajustar; arreglar; regular; transar; *(in money matters)* ajustar; llegar a un acuerdo; *(in insurance)* tasar; liquidar

adjust a claim liquidar un siniestro; tasar un siniestro

adjustable life insurance seguro de vida ajustable

adjusted gross income renta bruta ajustada

adjuster *(noun)* ajustador; ajustadora; **claims adjuster** persona que actúa en nombre de una compañía de seguros para decidir si un reclamo será pagado

adjustment *(noun)* ajuste

administer *(verb)* administrar; juramentar; *(punishment, drug)* administrarle algo a alguien; **she administered the oath to the witness** le tomó juramento al testigo; juramentó al testigo

administrative agency agencia administrativa

administrative board junta administrativa

administrative fee cargo administrativo

administrative law judge juez de ley administrativa; juez de derecho administrativo

admissible evidence *(law)* prueba admisible

admission *(confession)* admisión; reconocimiento; *(hospital)* ingreso; internación; **he was, by his own admission, a poor father** él mismo admitía que no era un buen padre; él mismo reconocía que no era un buen padre

admission of evidence admisión de evidencia

admission of guilt admisión de culpabilidad

admission to bail admisión de fianza

admissions admisiones; confesiones

admit *(confession: crime, mistake, failure)* admitir; confesar; reconocer; **he admitted having lied** admitió que había mentido; reconoció que había mentido; **to admit something to somebody** confesarle algo a alguien

admittance form formulario de entrada

admit to *(crime)* confesarse culpable; confesar haberlo hecho; **she admits to doing it** confiesa haberlo hecho

admonish amonestar; regañar; reprender; **to admonish someone for something** amonestar a alguien por algo; reprender a alguien por algo

admonishment *(scolding)* admonestación; *(warning)* advertencia

adolescence adolescencia

adolescent *(noun)* adolescente; *(adj)* adolescente; *(years)* de adolencia; *(immature)* de adolescente; infantil

adopt *(law: child)* adoptar

adopted adoptada; adoptado; adoptiva; adoptivo; **she's adopted** es adoptada

adopted children niños adoptados

adopted daughter hija adoptiva

adopted son hijo adoptivo

adoption certificate certificado de adopción

adoptive admission admisión adoptiva; aprobación de lo afirmado por otra persona mediante el silencio al no negar lo afirmado

adult adulta, adulto; persona mayor de edad; **all of her adult life** toda su vida de adulto; **all of his adult life** toda su vida de adulto

adult day-care center centro de cuidado diurno para adultos

adult education educación para adultos

adulterate adulterar

adulteration adulteración; cambiar algo puro mezclando o añadiendo algo de calidad inferior

adulterer adúltera; adúltero

adultery adulterio; **commit adultery** cometer adulterio; **he committed adultery** cometió adulterio; **she committed adultery** cometió adulterio

adulthood edad adulta; adultez

advance *(noun)* avance; progreso; adelanto; **to make advances to somebody** *(general)* entrar en contacto con alguien; *(amorously)* insinuarse con alguien; **in advance** por adelanto; de antemano; *(threateningly)* **advance on somebody** acercarse a alguien en forma amenazante; **let somebody know a week in advance** avisar a alguien con ocho días de anticipación; **pay in advance** pagar por delantado

advance filing reclamación por adelantado; solicitud por adelantado

advance loan anticipo

advance notice *(law)* preaviso; aviso previo

advance payment pago anticipado; pago por adelantado; pago adelantado

advance sheet panfleto que contiene una decisión judicial que aún no ha sido codificada

advance warning *(law)* preaviso; aviso previo

advancement *(noun)* avance de herencia; anticipación de herencia

advantage ventaja; *(exploit)* **to take advantage of someone** aprovecharse de alguien

advantageous *(adj)* ventajosa; ventajoso; favorable

adventure *(noun)* aventura; riesgo comercial; empresa comercial

adversarial *(law)* adversarial

adversarial procedure procedimiento contradictorio

adversarial proceedings proceso contradictorio

adversary *(noun)* adversaria; adversario; contraria; contrario

adverse *(adj)* adversa; adverso; opuesta; opuesto

adverse claim reclamación adversa, solicitud adversa

adverse interest interés contrario; conflicto de interés que tiene un testigo contra una parte

adverse party parte adversa

adverse possession posesión adversa; prescripción adquisitiva

adverse witness testigo adverso

advice *(counsel)* consejo; aviso; **a piece of advice** un consejo; **ask for advice** pedir consejos; **follow my advice** hazme caso; **take legal advice** consultar a un abogado; consultar a una abogada; **take my advice** hazme caso; **they should take legal advice** deberían asesorarse con un abogado; deberían asesorarse con una abogada; deberían consultar a un abogado; deberían consultar a una abogada

advisable *(adj)* aconsejable; conveniente; **if you think it advisable** si le parece bien

advise *(noun)* consejo; asesoría

advise *(verb: recommend)* aconsejar; recomendar; **have you been advised of your rights?** ¿le han informado de sus derechos? **I advise on immigration matters** asesoro en los aspectos inmigratorios; **you would be well advised to get a lawyer** haría bien en asesorarse con un abogado; sería aconsejable que se asesorara con un abogado

advise and consent consulta y consentimiento

advise somebody to + *infin* aconsejarle a alguien que + *subj*;

advisement *(noun)* consulta; deliberación

advisory *(body, board, service)* consultiva; consultivo; **in an advisory capacity** en calidad de asesor; en calidad de asesora

advisory jury jurado de consulta

advocacy group grupos de presión, intercesión; apoyo

affair *(case, event)* acción que puede originar una demanda; acontecimiento; asunto; demanda; evento que puede originar un juicio; *(liason)* aventura; **he had an affair with her years ago** tuvo un lío con ella hace muchos años; **he's having an affair** tiene amante; **she's having an affair** tiene amante; **they're having an affair** tienen relaciones; tienen un lío

affect *(have an affect on)* afectar; *(have an affect on a person)* afectar a; influir en; **it did not affect the jury's decision** no influyó en la decisión del jurado

affected class clase afectada

affection *(noun)* afecto; cariño; **the children are in need of affection** las niñas están necesitadas de afecto; los niños están necesitados de afecto; las niñas están necesitadas de cariño; los niños están necesitados de cariño

affidavit *(noun)* affidávit; declaración hecha bajo juramento; declaración jurada; **swear an affidavit** hacer una declaración jurada

affidavit of support declaración jurada de manutención

affiliate afiliada; afiliado; asociada; asociado

affiliated company empresa filial; empresa subsidiaria

affiliated member miembro afiliado

affiliated union sindicato afiliado

affiliation *(noun)* afilación; asociación; **her political affiliations** su filiación política; **her political affiliations** su filiación sindical

affiliation proceedings juicio de filiación; procedimiento judicial para determinar si una persona es el padre de un menor

affinity *(noun)* afinidad; parentesco contraído por matrimonio

affirm *(verb)* afirmar; confirmar; *(innocence)* declarar; hacer firme; *(law: contract, judgement)* ratificar

affirmation *(assertion)* afirmación; *(law)* testimonio

affirmative *(reply, statement)* afirmitiva; afirmitivo; **answer in the affirmative** dar una respuesta afirmativa; **he answered in the affirmative** respondió affirmativamente

affirmative action *(US)* discriminación positiva; medidas a favor de las minorías

affirmative defense defensa afirmativa *(en una demanda por lesiones, el demandado puede afirmar, en su defensa, que el demandante fue negligente y que eso provocó la lesión)*

affirmatively *(adv)* afirmativamente

afford *(spare, risk)* **an opportunity you cannot afford to miss** una ocasión que no es para desperdiciar; **can we afford the risk?** ¿podemos arriesgarlo? **we can afford to wait** nos podemos permitir esperar; **you can't afford not to sue him for damages** no puedes permitirte el lujo de no demandarlo por daños y perjuicios

affordable *(price)* asequible; razonable

affordable housing vivienda asequible

affray *(law)* ateración del orden público

affront *(noun)* afrenta; *(verb)* ofender; **be affronted** ofenderse, **this affronts your dignity** esto constituye una afrenta a su dignidad

aforementioned *(adj)* antedicha; antedicho; anteriormente dicha; anteriormente dicho; **the aforementioned person** el susodicho; la susodicha

aforethought pensado con anticipación; premeditada; premeditado

afoul *(in idiom)* **run afoul of the law** cometer un delito

afraid *(frightened)* **be afraid** tener miedo; **be afraid** *(person)* temer a; tener miedo a; **there's nothing to be afraid of** no tienes nada que temer

African-Americans Africano-Americanos

after *(afterwards)* después; *(place, order)* después de; tras; *(time, order)* después de; luego; **the meeting is after four** la reunión es luego de las cuatro; **the meeting is after three** la reunión es después de las tres; **the police are after him** la policía le está buscando

after a few days después de unos días; unos días más tarde; pasado algunos días

after a few months después de unos meses

after all con todo; después de todo

after birth placenta; secundinas

aftercare *(noun: after prison)* asistencia durante el período de reinserción; asistencia durante el período de readaptación

after dark después del anochecer

after days of negotiating tras días de negociaciones

after hours of negotiating tras horas de negociaciones

after long deliberations tras largas deliberaciones

after months of negotiating tras meses de negociaciones

after-tax neto de impuestos

after the fact después de los hechos

after waiting around for 20 minutes después de una antesala de 20 minutos

after work después del trabajo

A.G. *abbrev for* **Attorney General** Fiscal General; *(in US at national level)* Ministro (que está al mando del Departamento de Justicia y es además miembro del gabinete presidencial); Procurador General

again *(adv)* otra vez; de nuevo; *(often translated by)* volver a + *infin*; **now and again** de vez en cuando

against *(prep)* contra; **it's against the law** la ley lo prohíbe; es ilegal

against all medical advice contra todo criterio médico

against medical advice contra criterio médico

against the evidence contra la evidencia

against the law contra la ley

age *(gen)* edad; *(old)* vejez; **at the age of** a la edad de; **be under age** ser menor de edad; **come of age** llegar a la mayoría de edad; **from an early age** desde pequeña; desde pequeño; desde temprana edad; **under age** menor de edad

age at the moment of the crime edad en el momento del crimen

age of consent edad núbil; edad para consentir

age of majority mayoría de edad

age of reason edad de razón

aged, blind, or disabled anciana, ciega, o incapacitada; anciano, ciego, o incapacitado

agency *(noun)* agencia; delegación; organismo

agency shop acuerdo entre patrón y sindicato

agenda *(noun)* orden del día; **the first item on the agenda** el primer orden del día

agent *(noun)* agente; persona autorizada para actuar por cuenta de otra; representante; **be the sole agent for** tener la representación exclusiva de

aggravate *(verb)* agravar

aggravated assault agresión mayor

aggravated burglary robo calificado; robo con agravantes

aggravated felony delito grave con agravantes

aggravated manslaughter homicidio agravado

aggravating circumstance circunstancia agravante

aggravation *(noun)* agravante

aggressive *(hostile person)* agresiva; agresivo

aggressively *(behave, react)* agresivamente

aggressor *(noun)* agresor; agresora; la persona que primero usa fuerza; la persona que primero usa violencia

aggrieved *(adj)* ofendida; ofendido

aggrieved party parte demandante; parte perjudicada

ago *(adv)* **a week ago** hace una semana; **as long ago as 1995** ya en 1995; **how long ago was it?** ¿cuánto tiempo hace?; ¿hace cuánto tiempo? **long ago** hace mucho tiempo

agree *(verb: be in agreement over)* estar de acuerdo; **are we agreed on that point?** ¿estamos de acuerdo en ese punto? **they agreed to meet this afternoon** quedaron en encontrarse esta tarde; quedaron en verse esta tarde; **to agree that** estar de acuerdo; estar de acuerdo en que; quedar en que; **to agree to do something** consentir en hacer algo; estar de acuerdo con; **to agree with** estar de acuerdo con

agree on ponerse de acuerdo en; quedar en; **a date to be agreed on later** una fecha que se decidirá más adelante; una fecha que se concertará más adelante

agree to notify estar de acuerdo en notificar

agree with estar de acuerdo con

agreed case caso acordado *(caso en que los hechos importantes son establecidos por las partes y el juez no tiene que resolver cuestiones de hecho, sino decidir solamente los puntos legales controversiales)*

agreement *(understanding)* acuerdo; arreglo; *(consent)* acuerdo; *(treaty, etc.)* acuerdo; pacto; **by mutual agreement** por acuerdo mutuo; de común acuerdo; **be in agreement with** estar de acuerdo con; **come to an agreement** llegar a un acuerdo; **to reach an agreement** llegar a un acuerdo; **written agreement** acuerdo escrito; **verbal agreement** acuerdo verbal

agreement between a businessman and a worker acuerdo entre empresario y trabajador

agricultural equipment equipo agrícola; maquinaria agrícola

agricultural labor trabajo agrícola

agricultural work trabajo agrícola

aid *(noun)* ayuda; auxilio; **with the aid of** con la ayuda de; *(verb)* ayudar

aid and abet ayudar y encubrir; *(law)* **aid and abet somebody** ser cómplice de alguien en la comisión de un delito; instigar y secundar a alguien en la comisión de un delito; **aided and abetted by his partner** instigado y secundado por su socio; **come to the aid of** acudir en ayuda de; acudir en auxilio de

aid and advice to appellant ayuda y consejo al apelante

aid and comfort ayudar y confortar *(ayudar y confortar al enemigo es un delito de traición bajo la Constitución de Estados Unidos)*

Aid to Families With Dependent Children (AFDC) Ayuda a Familias con Niños Dependientes (AFDC)

aid to the aged ayuda a los ancianos

aider and abettor una persona que ayuda a otra a cometer un delito

AIDS *(noun)* sida; SIDA

AIDS Related Complex (ARC) Complejo Relacionado con SIDA

aim *(noun)* objetivo; propósito; **do you have a main aim in life?** ¿tiene usted un norte en la vida? ¿tiene usted un objetivo en la vida? **with the aim of** con la intención de; con el propósito de; *(verb: weapon)* apuntar; **aim at somebody** apuntarle a alguien

ajudication *(noun)* decisión judicial mediante la cual se le quita algo a alguien

aka = also known as alias

alcohol alcohol; **I never touch alcohol** soy abstemio

alcohol abuse el abuso en la bebida

alcoholic *(adj)* alcohólica; alcohólico

alcoholic husband esposo alcohólico

alcoholic wife esposa alcohólica

alcometer medidor de alcohol *(see breathalyzer)*

alias alias; **she traveled under an alias** viajaba usando un alias; viajaba bajo un nombre falso

alibi *(excuse)* excusa; pretexto; *(law)* coartada

alien *(adj: of foreign country)* extranjera, extranjero; *(noun: foreigner)* extranjera, extranjero; **enemy alien** extranjero enemigo; **illegal alien** inmigrante ilegal

alien lawfully admitted extranjera legalmente admitida; extranjero legalmente admitido

alien registration card tarjeta de inscripción de extranjeros; tarjeta de registro de extranjero; tarjeta de residencia

alien registration number número de inscripción de extranjeros

alien status estado legal de extranjera; estado legal de extranjero

alienate *(law: property)* enajenar; alienar; *(pol, psych)* alienar; **alienate oneself from somebody** alejarse de alguien; **alienate oneself from something** alejarse de algo; **this has alienated all his friends** esto ha hecho que todos sus amigos se alejen de él; esto ha hecho que todos sus amigos se distancien de él

alienation *(law: property)* enajenación; alienación; *(of friend)* alejamiento

alienation clause cláusula de enajenación *(cláusula de un contrato de seguro sobre el traspaso de la propiedad asegurada: de ser vendida o transferida la propiedad, la póliza de seguro termina)*

alienation from society marginación social

alimony *(law)* alimenticia; alimenticio; pensión alimenticia

alimony payments pagos de manutención

all *(adj)* toda, todas, todo, todos; *(adj)* **above all** sobre todo; **after all** con todo; **of all the stupid things to do** ¡qué estupidez!; **of all the times to choose** ¡no podía haber sido en peor momento!

all afternoon toda la tarde

all day todo el día

all day long todo el día

all-important de fundamental importancia; de primera importancia; de suma importancia

all kinds of people todo tipo de gente

all morning toda la mañana

all of the laws regulating la legislación que regula

all-points bulletin boletín dirigido al público en general

all right *(don't worry)* **are you all right?** ¿estás bien?; **it's all right** no se preocupe; *(satisfactory)* **it's all right** todo está bien; todo va bien; **it's all right with me** yo, de acuerdo; lo que es por mí, no hay problema; **yes, that's all right** sí, de acuerdo

all sorts of people todo tipo de gente

allegation *(noun)* acusación; alegación; imputación; **to make an allegation** hacer una acusación

allege *(verb)* afirmar; alegar; declarar; presentar hechos en una demanda

alleged *(criminal)* presunta; presunto *(fact, claim)* supuesta; supuesto

alleged offender *(law)* presunto delincuente; presunta infractora; presunto infractor

alleged offense *(law)* presunta infracción; presunto acto antijurídico

allegedly *(adv)* supuestamente; según se dice; según se afirma

allegiance *(noun)* lealtad; **all political allegiances** todas las filiaciones políticas; **to swear allegiance to** jurar lealtad a; rendir homenaje a

allergist *(noun)* alergista; especialista en alergias

alley *(noun)* callejón

alleyway *(noun)* callejón

alliance *(noun)* alianza

almost *(adv)* casi

allocate *(resources)* adjudicar; asignar; **within the allocated time** dentro del plazo concedido; dentro del plazo establecido

allocation *(distribution)* distribución; reparto

allotment *(noun)* asignación; repartición; porción

allow *(law: admit; appeal)* admitir; *(permit)* permitir; **allow me!** !permítame! **was he allowed to speak with a lawyer?** ¿se le permitió hablar con un abogdo? **were you allowed to see a lawyer?** ¿se le permitió ver a un abogdo? **you shouldn't have allowed yourself to get angry** se debería haber controlado

allowance letter carta de pensión (asignación); carta de aprobación

already*(adv)* ya

also *(adv: as well)* también; *(moreover)* además

alter *(verb: change)* amañar; **he altered the official report** amañó el informe oficial; **that doesn't alter the fact that you lied to us** el hecho es que nos mentiste

alter ego *(woman)* amiga íntima; *(man)* amigo íntimo

alter the official report amañar el informe oficial

altercation *(noun)* altercado

alternate *(verb)* oscilar; **do you often alternate between hope and despair?** ¿oscila usted a menudo entre la esperanza y la desesperación?

alternate juror jurado supernumerario; jurado supletorio

although *(conj)* aunque

always *(adv)* siempre; **as always** como siempre; **nearly always** casi siempre

ambulance *(noun)* ambulancia

ambulatory surgical center centro de cirugía ambulatoria

amend *(verb)* enmendar; cambiar

amended birth certificate certificado de nacimiento enmendado; acta de nacimiento enmendada

amendments *(noun)* enmiendas

American *(noun & adj)* Estadounidense; **Americans** *(noun)* los Estadounidenses

American Council Savings Education Consejo de Educación para el Ahorro.

American judicial system sistema judicial estadounidense

amnesty amnestía; **to grant an amnesty to someone** amnistiar a alguien; conceder la amnestía a alguien; declarar la amnestía a alguien

among *(prep)* entre

among friends entre amigos

among other things entre otras cosas

among social equals entre gente de la misma clase

amortization amortización *(pagar una deuda en forma periódica y regular con pagos iguales)*

amount *(noun)* cantidad; *(bill)* suma; importe; **a bill for the amount of** una cuenta por el valor de; **for the amount of** por importe de; **any amount of** cualquier cantidad de; **no amount of arguing will change their minds** por más que discutamos no van a cambiar de opinión; **the total amount** la totalidad; la cantidad total; *(of money)* suma total

amount to *(verb; figurative)* equivaler; **this amounts to a refusal** esto equivale a una negativa; venir a ser

amply *(adv)* abundantemente; *(sufficiently)* bastante; **you were amply justified** usted tuvo plena razón

amputate *(noun)* amputar

amputation *(noun)* amputación

an out-of-court settlement un arreglo extrajudicial; una transacción extrajudicial

ancestry ascendencia

and *(conj: the usual translation* y *becomes* e *when it precedes a word beginning with* i, h, *or* y*)* y; *(in numbers)* **an hour and five minutes** una hora y cinco minutos; **one and a half** uno y medio; *(showing continuation, repetition)* **better and better** cada vez mejor; **easier and easier** cada vez más fácil; **faster and faster** cada vez más rápido

and/or y/o *(término vago)*

anger cólera; enfado; enojo; **are you easily angered?** ¿se enoja con facilidad?; **red with anger** furiosa; furioso; enfurecida; enfurecido; **to lash out in anger** arremeter con ira; **to speak in anger** hablar indignada; hablar indignado; **words spoken in anger** palabras dichas en momento de ira

angrily con ira

angry *(person)* enfadada; enfadado; enojada; enojado; **are you very angry at the way youv'e been treated?** ¿estás muy enfadada por cómo te han tratada?; ¿estás muy enojado por cómo te han tratado?; **do these sort of things make you angry?** ¿le enfurecen estas cosas?; **there's no point getting so angry about it** no vale la pena enojarse tanto por eso; no vale la pena enfadarse tanto por eso; **to be angry** estar enfadada; estar enfadado; **to be angry with someone** estar enfadada con alguien; estar enfadado con alguien; **to get angry** enfadarse; enojarse

anguish *(mental)* agonía; angustia; **the anguish of indecision** la agonía de la indecisión; **the anguish of waiting** la agonía de la espera; **to cause anguish to somebody** angustiar a alguien

anguished *(mental)* angustiada; angustiado; acongojada; acongojado

ankle *(anat)* tobillo

announce anunciar; comunicar; dar a conocer; declarar; hacer saber

announcement anuncio; declaración

annoy *(bother, irritate)* fastidiar; irritar; molestar; **are you very annoyed?** ¿está usted muy enojada?; ¿está usted muy enojado?; ¿está usted muy enfadada?;¿está usted muy enfadado?; **to be annoyed about something** estar enfadada por algo; estar enfadado por algo; estar molesta por algo; estar molesto por algo; **to be annoyed with somebody** estar enfadada con alguien; estar enfadado con alguien; **to be annoyed with something** estar molesta por algo; estar molesto por algo; **to get annoyed** enfadarse

annoyance *(irritation)* fastidio; irritación; **to cause annoyance to somebody** irritar a alguien

annual anual

annual earnings test límite anual de ganancias

annual income ingresos anuales

annual leave vacaciones acumuladas (anuales)

annual report of earnings informe anual de ganancias

annuitant *(noun)* pensionista; pensión vitalicia

annuity *(noun)* anualidad

annuity benefit beneficio de la anualidad

annulment *(noun)* anulación

anonymous *(adj)* anónima; anónimo

another *(additional)* otra, otro; *(diffferent)* distinta; distinto; **another one** otra, otro; *(in phrases)* **another time** en otra ocasión; **in another five minutes** en cinco minutos más; **only another 15 minutes** sólo faltan 15 minutos; **that's quite another matter** eso es otra cosa; eso es otra cuestión; eso es distinto; **we've hit yet another problem** nos hemos topado con otro problema

answer *(law)* contestación

answer *(noun: reply)* contestación; razón; respuesta; **by way of an answer** como toda respuesta; **he has an answer for everything!** ¡tiene una respuesta para todo! **I can't get an answer out of him** no consigo que me dé una contestación; no consigo que me dé una respuesta; **in answer to your question** para contestar su pregunta; en respuesta a su pregunta; **there must be an answer** debe haber una explicación; debe haber una razón; **what is your answer?** ¿cuál fue su contestación? ¿cuál fue su respuesta?

answer *(verb)* contestar; responder; **we must answer their letter** tenemos que contestar su carta

answer for ser responsable de; **he's got a lot to answer for** nos debe muchas explicaciones; **she will have to answer for what she did** va a tener que dar cuentas de lo que hizo; va a tener que responder de lo que hizo

answerable responsable; **to be answerable to somebody for something** ser responsable ante alguien de algo

answering machine contestador automático; gravadora telefónica

answerphone teléfono con contestador automático

antenuptial antes del matrimonio

antenuptial agreement capitulaciones matrimoniales

anti-abortion *(adj)* antiabortista

anti-abortionist *(noun)* antiabortista

anticipate prever; esperar; **as anticipated** como esperábamos; según se esperaba; **I don't anticipate any problems** no creo que vaya a haber ningún problema; **this is better than I anticipated** esto es mejor de lo que esperaba; **this is worse than I anticipated** esto es peor de lo que esperaba; **the trial was more difficult than I anticipated** el juicio resultó más difícil de que se había previsto; el juicio resultó más difícil de que se esperaba; **I don't anticipate making any major changes in your defense** no tengo previsto hacer ningún cambio importante en su defensa

anxiety *(concern, distress)* preocupación; ansiedad; inquietud; **is it a great anxiety to you?** ¿le preocupa mucho?; **it is a great anxiety to me** me preocupa mucho

anxious inquieta; inquieto; preocupada; preocupado

anxiously *(worry)* con inquietud; con preocupación; *(eagerly)* ansiosamente; con ansiedad

any *(adv: comparative)* **do you feel any better now?** ¿se siente mejor?; **it doesn't seem to have affected you any** no parece haberle afectado en absoluto

any *(in questions)* **are there any questions?** ¿alguien teine alguna pregunta?; **are there any problems?** ¿alguien teine algún problema?; **is she in any danger?** ¿corre peligro?; **do you have any brothers and sisters?** ¿tiene hermanos?; **do you have any children?** ¿tiene hijos?; **do you need any help?** ¿necesita ayuda?; **have you had any news?** ¿has tenido alguna noticia?

any *(no matter which)* **any one of them could be the murderer** cualquiera de ellas podría ser la asesina; cualquiera de ellos podría ser el asesino; **call me any time** llámame cuando quieras; **it could be for any of the following reasons** podría ser por cualquiera de las siguientes razones

any *(with uncountable nouns and in if clauses and suppositions)* **call me if there are any changes** llámame si hay algún cambio; **call me if there is any trouble** llámame si hay algún problema; **if any laywer can help you, she can** si hay un abogado que le pueda ayudar, es ella

anybody *(everybody, whoever)* **anybody could do it** cualquiera podría hacerlo; **ask anybody** pregúntale a cualquiera; **before anybody could stop her** antes de que nadie pudiera detenerla; **before anybody could stop him** antes de que nadie pudiera detenerlo; **anybody else would have done the same** cualquier otra persona habría hecho lo mismo; cualquier otro habría hecho lo mismo; **anybody will tell you the same** cualquiera le dirá lo mismo; **that's anybody's guess** ¡quién lo sabe! **the same as anybody else** igual que todo el mundo; lo mismo que todo el mundo

anyhow de todas formas; de todos modos; **anyhow, you are here** de todas formas estás aquí; de todos modos estás aquí

anything *(something)* algo; **anything else?** ¿algo más?; ¿alguna cosa más?; **anything missing?** ¿falta algo?; **before anything is decided** antes de decidir nada; **call me if anything goes wrong** llámame si algo sale mal; **don't say anything!** ¡no digas nada!; **get professional advice before you do anything** antes de hacer nada, asesórate con un profesional; **is there anything you don't understand?** ¿hay algo que no entiende usted?; **should we call his parents or anything?** ¿deberíamos llamar a sus padres o hacer algo?; **this will persuade her if anything will** si hay algo que la pueda convencer, es esto; **what, if anything, should we do?** ¿qué deberíamos hacer, si es que deberíamos hacer algo?

anything *(whatever)* **anything but that** todo menos eso; **anything could happen** podría pasar cualquier cosa; **anything is possible** todo es possible; **anything urgent should be brought to my attention** se me debe informar inmediatamente de cualquier caso urgente; se me debe informar inmediatamente de cualquier problema urgente; **anything you say!**; ¡lo que usted diga!; **anything will do** cualquier cosa sirve; **can't anything be done?** ¿no se puede hacer nada?; **I'd give anything to know** daría cualquier cosa para saberlo; **if anything it's much better** es mejor si cabe; **I'll do anything I can to help** hare todo lo que pueda para ayudarle; **we can't do anything else** no podemos hacer otra cosa

anyway *(in any case)* **thanks, anyway, but ...** gracias de todos modos, pero ...; **who's this Juan Torres, anyway?** ¿y quién es el tal Juan Torres?

anywhere *(no matter where)* **you can sit anywhere you like** se puede sentar donde quiera; **that won't get you anywhere** con eso no vas a conseguir nada; con eso no vas a lograr nada

anywhere *(pronoun)* **she hasn't anywhere to stay** no tiene donde quedarse

apart *(adv: in pieces; separate)* **keep them apart** manténgalos separados; **they have lived apart for six months** viven separados desde seis meses; **they have lived apart for some years** hace ya algunos años que viven separados; **to fall apart** deshacerse; hacerse pedazos

apathy apatía; indiferencia; **extreme apathy** abulia; **to be sunk in apathy** estar hundida en la apatía; estar hundido en la apatía; estar sumida en la apatía; estar sumido en la apatía

apolitical apolítica; apolítico

apologetic de disculpa; **he was very apologetic** estaba lleno de disculpas; **to be apologetic** deshacerse en disculpas

apologetically con aire de disculpa

apologize disculparse; pedir perdón; **he didn't even apologize** ni siquiera pidió perdón; ni siquiera se disculpó; **you must apologize to her** tienes que pedirle perdón; **you must apologize to him for** tienes que pedirle perdón por

apology disculpa; excusa; **I owe you an apology** le debo una disculpa; **please accept my apologize** le ruego me disculpe; **to offer one's apology** disculparse; excusarse; presentar sus disculpas

appall consternar; horrorizar; **I'm appalled by their attitude** me horroriza su actitud; **I was appalled by the news** me horrorizó la noticia

appalling atroz; espantosa; espantoso; horrorosa; horroroso; terrible

apparent *(adj)* aparente; clara; claro; manifiesta; manifiesto; **for no apparent reason** sin motivo alguno; **it's apparent that** astá claro que; **it's apparent to me that ...** me resulta evidente que ...; me resulta obvio que ...; **there's no apparent difference** no se advierte ninguna diferencia; no se nota ninguna diferencia; **to become apparent** quedar claro

apparent authority permiso tácito; autoridad aparente

apparent consent consentimiento aparente

apparent danger peligro aparente

apparent defect defecto aparente

apparently al parecer; aparentemente; por lo visto; según parece

appeal *(noun: law)* apelación; recurso de apelación; recurso de alzada; **he was acquitted on appeal** su condena fue revocada en la apelación; **right of appeal** derecho de apelación; **to lodge an appeal** apelar; presentar una apelación; **to lodge an appeal against a decision** interponer un recurso de apelación en contra de una decisión; **to lodge an appeal against a sentence** interponer un recurso de apelación en contra de una sentencia; **to lose on appeal** perder en la apelación; perder en segunda instancia; **to have no right of appeal** no tener derecho a apelar; **to have the right of appeal** tener derecho a apelar; **to win on appeal** ganar en la apelación; ganar en segunda instancia; *(plea)* petición, súplica; **an appeal for help** una petición de socorro

appeal *(verb: law)* apelar; **he will appeal to the Supreme Court** apelará ante el Tribunal Supremo; **to appeal against a decision** apelar contra un decisión; **to appeal against a sentence** apelar contra una sentencia; **to appeal the court's decision** apelar contra la decisión del tribunal; **to appeal the judge's decision** apelar contra la decisión del juez

appeal for annulment recurso de casación

appeal lodged by recurso de apelación interpuesto por

appeal on the grounds of unconstitutionality recurso de amparo

appeal rights derechos de apelación

Appeals Council Consejo de Apelaciones

Appeals Council Process Improvement (ACPI) Mejoramiento del Proceso de Consejo de Apelaciones

appeals court tribunal de apelación

appeals hearing vista de apelación

appeals procedure procedimiento de apelación

appear *(law, defendant)* comparecer; personarse; apersonarse; **she's appearing on a charge of murder** comparece acusada de asesinato; **to appear before a judge** comparecer ante un juez; *(lawyer)* **to appear for the defense** comparecer por la defensa; **to appear for the prosecution** comparecer por la acusación; **to appear on a charge of murder** comparecer acusada de homicidio; comparecer acusado de homicidio

appear *(verb: seem)* parecer; **everyone appears to be here** parece que ya está aquí todo el mundo; **he appeared to have understood** pareció haber entendido; dio la impresión de que había entendido; **it now appears he was lying** ahora resulta que estaba mintiendo; **that's how he appears to a lot of people** ésa es la impresión que le da a mucha gente; **the questioning did not appear difficult** el interrogatorio no parecía difícil; **there appears to be a misunderstanding** parecería que hay un malentendido; **this would appear to be what happened** parecería que esto fue lo que pasó

appearance *(law)* comparecencia; comparición; apersonamiento; **a court appearance** una comparecencia ante el tribunal; **to make an appearance in court** comparecer ante el tribunal

appellant *(noun)* apelante; recurrente

appellate court tribunal de apelación; tribunal de segunda instancia

applicable aplicable; pertinente; **a rule applicable to all** una regla que se extiende a todos; **this law is also applicable to foreigners** esta ley se refiere también a extranjeros; **this part is not applicable to you** esta parte no te atañe; **this part is not applicable to us** esta parte no nos atañe

applicant *(noun)* aplicante; solicitante

application *(noun)* solicitud; petición

Application for a Social Security Card (SS-5-FS) — Foreign Service Solicitud para una Tarjeta de Seguro Social — Servicio al Extranjero

application for employment authorization solicitud de autorización de empleo

application for naturalization solicitud de naturalización

application form solicitud; impreso de solicitud

Application to Register Permanent Residence or Adjust Status Solicitud para Registrar la Residencia Permanente o Cambiar el Estado

apply for solicitar algo; pedir algo

apply for and receive financial assistance solicitar y recibir ayuda económica; solicitar y recibir prestaciones económicas; pedir y recibir ayuda económica; pedir y recibir prestaciones económicas

appoint *(verb: name, choose)* nombrar; designar; *(date)* fijar; *(task)* asignar

appointment *(noun: with lawyer, doctor, hairdresser)* cita; hora; **I have to make an appointment with my lawyer** tengo que concertar una cita con mi abogado

apportion *(verb)* repartir; prorratear

appraisal *(noun: situation, employee)* evaluación; *(property)* tasación; valoración; *(fig)* apreciación; estimación

appraise *(verb: situation, employee)* evaluar; *(property)* tasar; avaluar

appraiser *(noun)* perito catastral; evaluador; evualadora; perito que fija el precio de una cosa

appreciate *(be grateful for)* apreciar; agradecer; **I'd appreciate your cooperation** agradecería su cooperación; **I'd appreciate your help** agradecería su ayuda; *(to understand)* **yes, I appreciate that** sí, lo comprendo; *(property)* aumentar en valor; aumentarse en valor

appreciation *(gratitude)* agradecimiento; reconocimiento; **as a token of my appreciation** en señal de mi gratitud; **to show one's appreciation for something** *(gratitude)* mostrar su agradecimiento por algo; *(property rise in value)* aumento en valor

appreciative *(grateful)* de agradecimiento; **he wasn't very appreciative** no se mostró muy agradecido; **to be appreciative of something** estar agradecida por algo; estar agradecido por algo

apprehend *(arrest)* arrestar; detener; aprehender; *(understand)* comprender

apprehension *(arrest)* detención; *(anxiety, fear)* aprensión; temor

apprehensive *(look)* aprensiva; aprensivo; de aprensión; recelosa; receloso

approach *(to talk to)* **have you approached her about it?** ¿ya se lo ha planteado?; ¿ya ha hablado con ella del asunto?; **he approached me for a loan** se dirigió a mí para pedirme un préstamo

appropriate *(convenient)* adecuada; adecuado; apropiada; apropiado; conveniente; oportuna; oportuno; **assess the situation and take the appropiate action** evalúe la situación y tome las medidas pertinentes; **complete as appropiate** rellenar lo que corresponda; **delete as appropiate** tachar lo que no corresponda; **whichever seems more appropriate** el que sea más appropiado; **you should take all appropriate precautions** usted debe tomar todas las precauciones del caso

appropriate for apropiada para; apropiado para; **it would not be appropriate for me to comment** no sería apropiado que hiciera algún comentario

appropriately de manera apropiada; apropiadamente

approval *(agreement, consent)* abrobación; consentimiento; el visto bueno; **does it meet with your approval?** ¿merece su aprobación; **I've drafted a letter for your approval** he escrito una carta para que usted le dé el visto bueno; **on approval** a prueba; **to get somebody's approval** conseguir la aprobación de alguien; **to have somebody's approval** tener la aprobación de alguien; **to seek somebody's approval for something** tratar de obtener la aprobación de alguien para algo

approve *(agree)* aprobar; dar el visto bueno; **do you approve?** ¿le parece bien?

approved school escuela aprobada

approximate *(adj)* aproximada; aproximado

approximately *(adv)* aproximadamente; más o menos; **it happened approximately five days ago**; ocurrió hace aproximadamente cinco días; **approximately ten weeks ago** hace aproximadamente diez semanas; hace diez semanas aproximadamente; hace unas diez semanas

April Abril *(see* **July** *for usage)*

arbitration arbitraje; **to go to arbitration** recurrir al arbitraje; someterse al arbitraje

arbitrator árbitra; árbitro

area *(noun)* área; zona; región; **in the area that divides Mexico and the US** en la zona que divide a México y Estados Unidos; **the area we live in** el barrio en el que vivimos; **in the Albuquerque area** en la zona de Albuquerque; en el área de Albuquerque; *(fig)* **an area of concern** un tema que procupa; **in all the areas of life** en todos los ámbitos de la vida

Area Agency on Aging Agencia de Ancianidad en su área local; Agencia de Envejecimiento

area code código de la zona; prefijo

Argentinian *(adj)* Argentina; Argentino

arguable discutible; **it is arguable whether ...** es discutible que ...; **it is arguable that ...** se puede decir que ...; podría decirse que ....

argue *(debate)* alegar; debatir; discutir; persuadir; **a well argued point** un argumento buen presentado; **he argued against doing it** se manifestó en contra de hacerlo; **he argued that it couldn't be done** argumentó que no se podía hacer; *(dispute)* discutir; pelearse; **the lawyer argued provocation** el abogado alegó provocación; **to argue about something** pelearse por algo; **to argue with somebody** pelearse con alguien; *(reason)* argumentar; razonar; **to argue against** oponerse a; **to argue for** abogar por

argument *(disagreement, quarrel)* discusión; *(more heated)* pelea; riña; **they had an argument about money** tuvieron una discusión por una cuestión de dinero; *(debate)* polémica; **to have an argument with someone** tener una discusión con alguien; discutir con alguien; *(more heated)* pelearse con alguien; reñir con alguien

argument presented in the sentencing hearing *(law)* alegato presentado en la vista de sentencia; alegato presentado en la instrucción de cargos

arguments *(law)* alegatos

arguments during the hearing *(law)* alegatos durante la vista; alegatos durante la instrucción de cargos

arise *(debate)* presentarse; surgir; **difficulties have arisen** han surgido dificultades; **if the need arises** si fuera necesario; **should the need arise** de ser necesario; **should the question arise** si se plantea la ocasión; **the disagreement arose from a misunderstanding** el desacuerdo surgió de un malentendido

arm *(weapon)* arma; *(anatomy)* brazo; *(verb)* armar; **to arm oneself** armarse; **they armed themselves with knives and clubs** se armaron con porras y cuchillos; se armaron de porras y cuchillos

armed *(weapon)* armada; armado; a mano armada; **to be armed** estar armada; estar armado

armed escort escolta armada

armed robbery robo a mano armada; atraco a mano armada; asalto a mano armada

armed with a knife armada con un cuchillo; armado con un cuchillo

arms *(noun: weapon)* armas

arms cache alijo de armas

arms deal venta de armas

army ejército; **to join the army** alistarse; engancharse

around *(approximately)* alrededor de; a eso de; aproximadamente; **around 2 o'clock** a eso de las 2; **around 50** 50 más o menos; **he must be around 50** debe tener unos 50; debe andar por los 50; *(in the vicinity)* **he's around somewhere** anda por ahí; **he must be somewhere around here** debe estar por aquí; **is John around?** ¿anda John por ahí?; ¿está John por ahí?; **there is no one around** aquí no hay nadie

arraign *(law: suspect)* celebrar la vista incoatoria; hacer comparecer ante un tribunal; **the suspect will be arraigned tomorrow** el sospechoso comparecerá ante el juez mañana; la sospechosa comparecerá ante el juez mañana

arraignment *(law)* comparecencia ante el juez; lectura de acusación

arraignment notice to appear *(law)* aviso de comparecencia

arrange *(set up a meeting, etc.)* concertar; fijar; *(loan)* tramitar; **I've arranged an appointment for Tuesday** he concertado cita para el martes

arranged marriage *boda concertada por las familias de los contrayentes*

arrangement *(agreement)* **we made an arrangement to meet the following day** quedamos en encontrarnos al día siguiente; **what's the arrangement for tomorrow?** ¿cuál es el plan para mañana?

arrangement with creditors arreglo con los acreedores

arrears atrasos; mora; **to be in arrears with the rent** estar atrasada en el pago del alquiler; estar atrasado en el pago del alquiler; estar atrasada en el pago de la renta; estar atrasado en el pago de la renta; **to get into arrears** atrasarse en los pagos

arrest *(noun)* detención; arresto; **he's under arrest on a robbery charge** ha sido arrestado acusado de robo; ha sido detenido acusado de robo; **to be under arrest** estar detenida; estar detenido; quedar detenida; quedar detenido; **to make an arrest** hacer un arresto; hacer una detención; **to place someone under arrest** arrestar a alguien; detener a alguien; **to put someone under arrest** arrestar a alguien; detener a alguien; **the arresting officer** el oficial de policía que hizo el arresto; el oficial de policía que hizo la detención; **to resist arrest** resistirse a la autoridad; **you're under arrest** queda arrestada; queda arrestado; queda detenida; queda detenido; *(verb: criminal)* detener; **he was arrested hours later** fue arrestado horas más tarde

arrest order pedido de detención; **the arrest order was signed by** el pedido de detención fue firmado por

arrest record reporte de arresto

arrest warrant orden de arresto

arrested on suspicion of detenida como; detenido como

arrested on suspicion of having carried out illegal abortions detenida como presunta autora de prácticas abortivas ilegales; detenido como presunto autor de prácticas abortivas ilegales

arresting officer el oficial de la policía que hace el arresto; el oficial de la policía que hace la detención; el oficial de la policía que hizo el arresto; el oficial de la policía que hizo la detención;

arrival arribo; llegada; **we expect his arrival any tme** estamos esperando su llegada de un momento a otro

arrive llegar; *(baby)* nacer; **they've arrived!** ¡han llegado!; ¡ya están aquí!; **to arrive at a conclusion** llegar a una conclusión; **to arrive at a desicion** llegar a una decisión; **to arrive home** llegar a casa; **to arrive late** llegar tarde; **to arrive on time** llegar a tiempo; **when they arrived on the scene** cuando aparecieron; cuando llegaron en el lugar

arrogate *(law)* **to arrogate something to oneself** arrogagarse algo

arrogation *(law)* arrogación

arson incendiarismo; incendio premeditado; **it was arson** el incendio fue provocado

arson of an occupied structure incendio de un inmueble habitado

arthritis *(noun)* artritis; inflamación de las coyunturas

article *(law, newspaper)* artículo; cláusula; *(clothing)* **an article of clothing** una prenda de vestir; **articles of clothing** prendas de vestir; **luxury articles** artículos de lujo

articles of incorporation pacto social

as a child de pequeña; de pequeño

as always como siempre

as far as I know que yo sepa

as far as I'm concerned en lo que a mí se refiere

as for en cuanto a

as for me en cuanto a mí

as from desde una fecha superior

as if como si

as instructed de acuerdo a las instrucciones recibidas

as it is tal y como están las cosas

as it were por así decirlo

as I've said before como he dicho antes

as long as mientras

as of tomorrow a partir de mañana

as of yesterday a partir de ayer

as per de acuerdo con

as quickly as possible lo más rápido posible

as soon as tan pronto como

as soon as possible cuanto antes; lo más pronto posible

as things stand tal y como están las cosas

as though como si

as well también

as yet hasta ahora

ascertain *(verb)* cerciorarse; establecer; averiguar; determinar

Ash Wednesday Miércoles de Ceniza

ashamed avergonzada; avergonzado; apenada; apenado; **it's nothing to be ashamed of** no hay por qué apenarse; no hay por qué avergonzarse; **to feel ashamed** sentir vergüenza; tener vergüenza; **you ought to be ashamed of yourself!** ¡debería darle vergüenza!; ¡no le da vergüenza!

ash-blond *(hair)* rubio ceniza; **she's ash-blond** tiene el pelo rubio ceniza

aside from aparte de

ask preguntar; pedir; **to ask about something** preguntar acerca de algo; **to ask somebody something** preguntarle algo a alguien; **there's no harm in asking** con preguntar no se pierde nada

ask a question hacer una pregunta

ask after preguntar por

ask around preguntar por ahí

ask why preguntar por qué

asocial *(behavior)* asocial; *(existence)* con limitado contacto social

assail *(verb)* acometer; atacar

assailant *(noun)* agresor; agresora; asaltador; asaltadora; atacante

assassin *(noun)* asesina; asesino

assassinate asesinar; **to assassinate somebody's character** acabar con la reputación de alguien; arruinar la reputación de alguien

assassination *(noun)* asesinato; **character assassination** difamación

assassination attempt atentado; tentativa de asesinato

assault *(noun)* agresión; *(verb)* agredir; atacar

assault and battery agresión con lesiones

assault rifle rifle de asalto

assault with a deadly weapon agresión con arma mortífera; agresión con arma de fuego

assault with intent to commit a violent felony agresión con ánimo de cometer un delito violento

assault with intent to commit mayhem agresión con ánimo de cometer los delitos de mutilación

assault with intent to kill agresión con ánimo de matar

assault with intent to poison agresión con ánimo de envenenar

assault with intent to rape agresión con ánimo de violar

assemble *(gather, crowd)* congregarse; juntarse; reunirse; *(gather facts, evidence)* recoger; recopilar; reunir

assemble evidence against somebody reunir pruebas contra alguien

assembly *(noun)* asamblea; reunión; **freedom of assembly** libertad de reunión; **the right to assembly** el derecho de reunión; **unlawful assembly** reunión no autorizada

assent *(noun)* asentimiento; *(verb)* asentir; consentir; expresar su conformidad

assert *(declare)* afirmar; aseverar; **to assert oneself** imponerse

assertion *(noun)* afirmación; aseveración

assess *(damages)* fijar; *(price)* valorar; tasar; *(tax)* gravar

assessment *(judgement)* juicio; *(of performance)* evaluación; valoración; *(of worth, value)* valoración; tasación; *(tax)* gravamen

assessor *(law)* asesor; asesora; *(tax)* tasador; tasadora

assets *(noun)* activos; bienes

assets and liabilities activo y pasivo

assign *(task)* asignar; *(attribute)* atribuir; *(law: property)* ceder; **to assign somebody to something** cederle algo a alguien; *(appoint)* **to assign somebody to** designar a alguien para; nombrar a alguien para

assign number asignar número

assigned counsel *(law)* abogada de oficio; abogado de oficio; defensor de oficio; defensora de oficio

assignee *(law)* cesionaria; cesionario

assignor *(law)* cedente

assignment *(mission)* misión; *(task)* tarea; trabajo; asignación

assist *(verb)* ayudar; asistir; **to assist somebody with something** ayudar a alguien en algo

assistance *(noun)* ayuda; asistencia; **can I be of any assistance?** ¿puedo ayudarle?; ¿le puedo servir en algo?; **to give assistance to somebody** prestarle asistencia a alguien; prestarle ayuda a alguien

assisted living vida asistida

assisted living facilities instituciones de vida asistida

association *(organization)* asociación; sociedad; **in association with** conjuntamente con; *(partnership)* asociación

assume *(verb)* suponer; **assuming that ...** suponiendo que ...; **under an assumed name** bajo un nombre falso; **we may therefore assume that ...** así, es de suponer que ...

assumption *(noun)* suposición; supuesto; asunción; **on the assumption that ...** suponiendo que ...; **that's only an assumption** es una suposición

assumption of risk asunción del riesgo

assurance *(guarantee)* garantía; promesa; **I give you my assurance that ...** le puedo asegurar que ...

assure *(make certain)* asegurar; **I assured him of my support** le aseguré mi apoyo

asthma *(noun)* asma

asylee *(noun)* asilada; asilado

asylum *(refuge)* asilo; **to seek political asylum** pedir asilo político; solicitar asilo político; *(lunatic asylum)* manicomio; psiquiátrico

asylum seeker solicitante de asilo

at a bad moment en un mal momento

at a disadvantage en desventaja

at a later date en fecha posterior; más adelante

at an early stage en una etapa temprana

at Colleen's en casa de Colleen

at gunpoint a punta de pistola

at her insistance porque ella insistió

at his insistance porque él insistió

at issue en cuestión; disputa; de lo que se trata; **the matter at issue is ...** de lo que se trata es de ...

at knifepoint a punta de navaja

at large *(prisoner: at liberty)* **to be at large** andar suelta; andar suelto; *(country, society)* en general; **the country at large** el país en general; **society at large** la sociedad en general

at night de noche; por la noche

at noon a medio día

at school en la escuela

at that very moment en ese mismo momento

at the age of 20 a los 20 años

at the earliest cuanto antes

at the end of the street al final de la calle

at the last count en el último recuento

at the latest a más tardar

at the time to a la hora de

at this time a esta hora; a estas horas

at your disposal a su disposición

ATM *acrónimo en inglés de* cajero automático permanente

attach *(law: property, salary)* embargar; **the attached letter** la carta adjunta

attachment *(law: property, salary)* embargo; secuestro

attachment of earnings retención de ingresos

attack *(noun)* asalto; ataque

attain insured status obtener suficientes créditos; estar asegurada; estar asegurado; trabajar lo suficiente

attained age edad cumplida

attainment of age cumplimiento de edad

attempt *(law)* tentativa de delito

attempt *(noun)* intento; **to make an attempt on somebodys life** atentar contra la vida de alguien; **at least they made the attempt** al menos lo intentaron; al menos hicieron la tentativa

attempted coup asonada; **the attempted coup began around 4 o'clock in the afternoon** la asonada comenzó sobre las 4

attempted kidnapping tentativa de secuestro

attempted murder tentativa de asesinato; homicidio frustrado; homicidio imperfecto

attempted rape tentativa de violación

attempted robbery tentativa de robo

attempted suicide intento de suicida

attend asistir a; ir a

attending school asistiendo a la escuela; asistiendo al colegio

attention *(noun)* atención; **to attract somebody's attention** llamar la attención de alguien; **to call somebody's attention to something** hacerle notar a alguien de algo; **it has come to my attention that ...** me he enterado de que ...; **to pay attention to** prestar atención a ...; **to pay no attention to** no prestar atención a

attention span capacidad de concentración

attest *(certify a fact)* atestiguar; dar fe de; *(signature)* autenticar; autorizar

attestation *(certification of fact)* testimonio; *(certification of signature)* autenticación; autorización; *(evidence)* prueba; testimonio

attitude *(noun)* actitud; **very negative attitude** actitud muy negativa

attorney *(noun)* abogada; abogado; letrada; letrado

attorney-at-law abogada; abogado

attorneys-at-law abogada; abogado

attorney client privilege secreto profesional entre abogado y cliente

attorney fees honorarios para abogado

Attorney General *(US at national level)* Ministra de Justicia; Ministro de Justicia; *(US at state level)* Fiscal General

attorney of record abogado del caso *(abogado registrado en el tribunal y que representa a una persona)*

attorney's name nombre de la abogada; nombre del abogado

auction remate; subasta; **to put something up for auction** rematar algo; subastar algo

auction off rematar; subastar

audit *(noun: inspection)* auditoria

audit report informe de auditorio

auditor *(noun)* auditor; auditora

August Agosto *(see July for usage)*

aunt *(noun)* tía; **my aunt and uncle** mis tíos

aunt by marriage tía política

auntie *(colloquial)* tía; tiíta

aunty *(colloquial)* tía; tiíta

authentic *(adj)* autentíca; autentíco

authenticate *(declare genuine)* autenticar; autentificar; *(confirm, prove)* corroborar; probar

author autor; autora

authority *(noun)* autoridad; **apparent authority** permiso tácito; **express authority** poder expreso; **general authority** derecho legal a actuar; derecho legal para actuar; **I have it on good authority that ...** me ha dicho una fuente de máxima confianza que ...; me ha dicho una fuente fidedigna que ...; **I have no authority in the matter** no tengo competencia en el asunto; **I'm not in a position of authority** no tengo autoridad; **those in authority** los que mandan; los que tienen la autoridad; **to give somebody the authority to do something** autorizar a alguien para que haga algo; **to have the authority to do something** estar autorizada para hacer algo; estar autorizado para hacer algo; tener autoridad para hacer algo

authorize *(empower)* autorizar; *(approve)* aprobar; **to authorize somebody to do something** autorizar a alguien que haga algo

authorized health agency agencia autorizada de salud

auto insurance seguro de auto; seguro de coche; seguro automovilístico

auto stripping desmantelamiento de vehículo; desmantelamiento de auto; desmantelamiento de coche

auto tampering desmantelamiento de vehículo; desmantelamiento de auto; desmantelamiento de coche

automated telling machine cajero automático permanente

automatic enrollment inscripción automática

automatic entitlement derecho automático

automatic increase aumento automático

automatic recomputation recomputación automática

automobile accident accidente de auto; accidente de coche

autopsy *(noun)* autopsia; **to carry out an autopsy on somebody** hacerle la autopsia a alguien; **to perform an autopsy on somebody** hacerle la autopsia a alguien

autumn *(noun)* otoño; **in the autumn** en otoño; en el otoño

avail *(in phrases)* **to avail oneself of** aprovechar algo; **it is of no avail** es inútil; no sirve de nada; **to no avail** en vano

availability of funds disponibilidad de fondos; fondos disponibles

avenge *(verb)* vengar; **to avenge oneself** vengarse

avenue *(noun)* avenida

average *(noun)* promedio; **an average of** un promedio de; **he is of average height** es de estatura mediana; **on average** por regla general; **the average man** el hombre común

average indexed monthly earnings promedio de ganancias mensuales ajustadas

average premium prima promedio

averse *(in phrases)* **to be averse to something** ser reacio a algo; tener pocas ganas de hacer algo; **would you be averse to answering some questions?** ¿tendría inconveniente en contestar unas preguntas?

avoid *(verb)* eludir; evitar; **to avoid doing something** evitar hacer algo

avow *(verb)* confesar; reconocer

await *(verb)* aguardar; esperar; estar a la espera; **she is awaiting trial** está a la espera de ser procesada; **prisoners awaiting trial** detenidos a la espera de juicio

await further instructions espere a recibir nuevas instrucciones

awaiting trial a la espera de juicio

award *(honor)* conferir; *(law)* **damages were awarded against her ex husband** su ex-marido fue condenado a indemnizarla por daños y perjuicios

awared a contract otorgar un contrato

aware *(adj)* consciente; **not that I am aware of** que yo sepa; **to be aware of** ser consciente de; **to become aware of** darse cuenta de; enterarse de; **I'm fully aware that ...** tengo plena consciencia de que ...

awkward age edad del pavo; **they're at that awkward age** están en la edad del pavo

B

baby *(noun)* bebé; niña; niño

baby-battering maltrato de los hijos

baby boomers niños de la posguerra, persona nacida en la época de posguerra (entre 1946-1960)

baby boy nene; niño

baby girl nena; niña

baby sitter baby sitter; cangura; canguro; niñera

baby-snatcher secuestrador de bebés; secuestradora de bebés

back *(adv: indicating return, repetition)* **I'll be back by 2 o'clock** estaré de vuelta para las 2; volveré antes de las 2; **Juan is back in Mexico** Juan ha vuelto a México

back *(verb: support)* apoyar; respaldar

back *(anat)* espalda

back door puerta trasera

back pay atrasos; pago retroactivo

back up *(verb: support)* apoyar; confirmar; respaldar; **her account is backed up by evidence** hay pruebas que confirman su versión; hay pruebas que respaldan su versión

background *(of person, knowledge)* educación; formación; **he comes from a poor background** él es de familia pobre; **she comes from a wealthy background** ella es de familia rica; **they come from a working-class background** ellos son de la clase obrera

background information *(phrases)* **he'll give you some background information** él le informará sobre la situación; él le informará sobre los antecedentes

backing *(noun)* apoyo; respaldo

backlash *(adverse reaction)* reacción violenta; reacción en contra; **there are fears of a backlash on the part of** se teme una reacción en contra por parte de

backstreet abortion aborto clandestino

bad *(adj)* malo *(the usual translation* **malo** *becomes* **mal** *when it is used before a masculine singular noun)*; **I feel bad** me siento mal; **I feel bad about it** lo lamentó; *(ill)* **to be in a bad way** estar grave; estar mal; **to be in bad with somebody** estar de malas con alguien

bad blood animosidad; mala sangre; resentimiento; **there was bad blood between them after their argument** quedaron resentidos a raíz de la discusión *(see* **blood***)*

bad boy malo

bad check talón sin fondos

bad debt cuenta mala; deuda incobrable

bad example mal ejemplo

bad faith mal fe; **to act in bad faith** actuar de mala fe

bad for your health mala para la salud; malo para la salud; perjudicial para la salud

bad girl mala

bad habit vicio; mala costumbre; mal hábito

bad idea mala idea

bad language palabrotas; malas palabras

bad-mannered *(person)* maleducada; maleducado

bad-tempered *(temporarily)* de mal humor; *(permanently)* de mal carácter; de mal genio

badge of fraud fuerte indicio de fraude

badger *(verb)* acosar; atormentar

badly *(adv)* mal; **he was badly hurt** estaba gravementa herido; **he badly needs help** le urge la ayuda; necesita ayuda urgentemente; **to treat somebody badly** maltratar a alguien

badly explained mal explicada; mal explicado

badly injured gravemente herida; gravemente herido; herida de gravedad; herido de gravedad

badly made mal hecha; mal hecho

badly mistaken muy equivocada; muy equivocado

badly organized mal organizada; mal organizado

baffle *(verb: experts, investigators)* confundir; desconcertar; **it baffles me how they escaped** no me explico cómo se escaparon

baffling *(crime)* de difícil solución; desconcertante; incomprensible

bail *(law)* caución; fianza judicial; **he was released on bail** fue puesto en libertad bajo fianza; **to grant bail to somebody** conceder la libertad bajo fianza a alguien; **to post bail for somebody** pagar la fianza de alguien; **to refuse bail to somebody** denegarle la libertad bajo fianza a alguien; **to stand bail for somebody** pagar la fianza de alguien

bail bond contrato de fianza; **secured bail bond** caución real; **unsecured bail bond** caución sin garantía real

bail bondsman fiador judicial; fiadora judicial; garante

bail out obtener la libertad de alguien bajo fianza; **to bail somebody out** pagarle la fianza a alguien

bailee *(noun)* depositaria; depositario

bailiff alguacil; guarda de sala *(funcionario que custodia al acusado en el juzgado)*

balance balance; saldo; **on balance** a fin de cuentas; tomando todo en cuenta

balance carried forward remanente a cuenta nueva; **the balance of the evidence** las pruebas consideradas en su conjunto

balance due saldo deudor

balance outstanding saldo pendiente

bald *(adj)* calva; calvo; **he's bald** es calvo; **to go bald** quedarse calvo; **he's gone bald** se ha quedado calvo

balding *(adj)* **he's balding** se está quedando calvo

balloon loan préstamo balloon

balloon payment pago balloon

ballot *(noun)* votación; **to decide by ballot** decidir por votación

ban *(verb)* prohibir; proscribir; vedar; *(noun)* prohibición

bandages *(noun)* vendajes

banish *(verb)* desterrar; expulsar; prohibir

banishment *(exhile)* destierro

bank *(verb)* **I bank with** tengo la cuenta en; *(noun)* banco

bank account cuenta bancaria; cuenta de banco

bank balance saldo

bank book libreta de banco

bank loan préstamo bancario; crédito bancario

bank rate tipo de interés bancario

bank robber ladrón de banco; ladrona de banco

bank robbery asalto a un banco; atraco a un banco

bank statement estado de cuenta

bankcard *(noun)* tarjeta de crédito

bankrupt *(company, person)* en bancarrota; en quiebra; *(law)* en quiebra; **to be bankrupt** estar en bancarrota; estar en quiebra; **to go bankrupt** ir a la bancarrota; quebrar

bankruptcy *(law)* bancarrota; quiebra; **to file for bankruptcy** presentar una solicitud de declaración de quiebra

bankruptcy court tribunal de bancarrota

bankruptcy order orden de quiebra

bankruptcy proceedings juicio de insolvencia; juicio de quiebra

bankruptcy stay suspensión del cumplimiento de la bancarrota

baptismal certificate certificado de bautismo; certificado de bautizo; fe de bautismo

bar *(law: profession)* abogacía

bar *(law: physical barrier in courtroom)* barra

bar association *(law: profession)* colegio de abogados

bare *(adj: meager)* escasa; escaso; **the bare minimum** lo indispensable; lo justo; **the bare essentials** las necesidades básicas; **the bare necessities** las necesidades básicas

barely *(hardly)* apenas; **I can barely hear you** apenas te oigo; casi no te oigo

bargain *(noun; deal agreement)* negocio; trato; acuerdo; *(cheap purchase)* ganga; pichincha; *(verb)* regatear; negociar

barrier *(noun)* barrera; **cultural barrier** barrera cultural; **language barrier** barrera idiomática

barter *(noun)* trueque; permuta; *(verb)* cambiar; trocar; **to barter something for something** cambiar algo por algo; trocar algo por algo; hacer trueques

base *(verb: found)* **to base something on something** basar algo en algo; fundamentar algo en algo

baseball cap gorra de béisbol; **he was wearing a baseball cap** llevaba una gorra de béisbol; tenía puesto una gorra de béisbol

based on the evidence basada en la evidencia

basic *(adj)* básica; básico; fundamental; elemental; **the basics** los fundamentos

basically *(adv)* fundamentalmente

basis *(noun)* fundamento; base; **on the basis of** en base a; **on the basis that ...** partiendo de la base de que ...

bat *(noun)* palo de béisbol

bathroom *(noun)* baño; **where is the bathroom?** ¿dónde está el baño?

batter *(child, wife)* maltratar; pegarle a *(opponent, victim)* apalear, aporrear

batter in destrozar a golpes; **his skull had been battered in** le habían partido el cráneo a golpes

battered *(beaten: baby, child, wife)* maltratada; maltratado; que recibe malos tratos

battered child niña que sufre abuso físico y emocional; niño que sufre abuso físico y emocional

battered spouse esposa que sufre abuso físico y emocional; esposo que sufre abuso físico y emocional; esposa que ha recibido malos tratos; esposo que ha recibido malos tratos

battered spouse petition petición por parte de un esposo que ha recibido malos tratos; petición por parte de una esposa que ha recibido malos tratos

battering *(noun)* paliza

battery *(noun)* lesiones; agresión

BCIS Form I-130 Petition for Alien Relative Formulario I-130 del CIS de Petición para Familiar Extranjero; Forma I-130 del CIS de Petición para Familiar Extranjero

be a joint sponsor for compartir la responsabilidad de

be afraid tener miedo

be heard by the court ser oído por el tribunal

be on a first-name basis tutearse

be under age ser menor de edad

be under arrest quedar detenida; quedar detenido

bear *(in phrases)* **policeman bearing riot shields** policías con escudos antidisturbios; **the right to bear arms** el derecho a portar armas

bear market *caída general de los precios de las acciones o valores*

bear with tener paciencia con

bear witness to dar fe de que; **I bear witness to the authenticity of the document** doy fe de que el documento es auténtico

beard *(noun)* barba; **a man with a beard** un hombre con barba; **to have a beard** tener barba; **to wear a beard** tener barba

bearded *(man)* con barba; de barba; barbudo

bearing *(relevance)* relación; **this has no bearing on the matter** esto no tiene nada que ver con el asunto

beat *(hit repeatedly)* golpear; *(inflict blows on)* **he beats his children** les pega a sus hijos; maltrata a sus hijos; **he was beaten to death** lo mataron a golpes; **she nearly beat the life out of him** casi lo mata a golpes

beat up *(person)* dar una paliza a; **they stole his wallet and beat him up** le robaron la cartera y le dieron una paliza

beat up on *(person)* darle una paliza a

beating *(punishment)* golpes; golpiza; paliza; **to give somebody a beating** darle una paliza a alguien

because *(conj)* porque; **because of** por; a causa de; debido a; **he left because he wanted to** se fue porque quiso

become *(make oneself)* hacerse; llegar a ser; *(turn into)* ponerse; volverse; **to become a lawyer** hacerse abogada; hacerse abogado; llegar a ser abogada; llegar a ser abogado; **to become arrogant** volverse arrogante; **to become distant** volverse distante

become a citizen hacerse ciudadana; hacerse ciudadano; llegar a ser ciudadana; llegar a ser ciudadano; convertirse en ciudadana; convertirse en ciudadano

become a lawyer hacerse abogada; hacerse abogado; llegar a ser abogada; llegar a ser abogado

become effective entrar en vigor

become of *(in questions)* ser de; **whatever became of Juan?** ¿qué fue de Juan?; **what's to become of the house if he dies?** ¿qué va a pasar con la casa si él muere?; **what's to become of me?** ¿qué va a ser de mí?

beeper *(conj)* localizador; busca

before *(in order, rank, time,)* antes de; dentro de; **long before** mucho antes; *(place)* ante; delante de; *(earlier than)* antes de; antes de que + *subj*; *(preceeding)* antes

before and after antes y después

before going antes de marcharse

before he was 30 antes de cumplir los 30

before its due date antes de su fecha de vencimiento

before long dentro de poco

before midday antes del mediodía

before questioning antes del interrogatorio

before Roe antes de Roe

before supper antes de la cena

before the court ante los tribunales; ante la corte; **they spoke with dignity and courage before the court** ellos hablaron con dignidad y coraje ante la corte

before the fact antes de los hechos

before three antes de las tres

beforehand *(adv)* con anticipación; de antemano; previamente

befriend *(verb)* hacerse amiga de; hacerse amigo de; ofrecer amistad a

beg *(entreat; person)* pedir; rogar; suplicar; **he begged me to help him** me suplicó que le ayudara; **on that point, I beg to differ** si me permite, en ese punto no estoy de acuerdo; **to beg somebody for something** pedir algo a alguien

beggar *(noun)* mendiga; mendigo

begin *(verb)* comenzar; empezar; *(discussion)* entablar; *(set in motion)* iniciar; *(undertake)* emprender; **he began talking** empezó a hablar; **he began to talk** empezó a hablar; **I don't know where to begin** no sé por dónde comenzar; no sé por dónde empezar; **let's begin at the beginning** empecemos por el principio; **to begin doing something** empezar a hacer algo; **to begin with** para empezar; **to begin work on something** comenzar a trabajar en algo; empezar a trabajar en algo

beginning *(in time, place)* comienzo; principio; **at the beginning of** al principio de; **from beginning to end** de principio a fin; desde el principio hasta el final; **right from the beginning of** desde el principio de

behalf *(noun)* **on behalf of** de parte de; en nombre de

behave *(verb)* comportarse; portarse; **behave yourself!** ¡compórtate!; ¡pórtate bien!; **he's very badly behaved** se porta muy mal; **to behave oneself** comportarse bien; portarse bien

behavior *(conduct)* comportamiento; conducta; **to be on one's best behavior** comportarse lo mejor posible

behest *(phrases)* **at his behest** a petición suya; por orden de él; **at the behest of somebody** a instancia de alguien

behind *(in the rear of)* detrás de; *(fig)* **what's behind all of this?** ¿qué hay detrás de todo esto?; *(fig)* **his family is behind him** tiene el apoyo de su familia

behind bars entre rejas

belief *(noun)* creencia; **contrary to general belief** contrariamente a lo que en general se cree; contrariamente a la opinión generalizada; **it is my belief that ...** creo que ...; **it's beyond belief** es increíble; **she acted in the belief that ...** actuó convencida de que ...; actuó en la creencia de que ...

believe *(verb)* creer; **believe you me!** ¡te lo juro!; **he is believed to be in Mexico** se cree que está en México; **I believe not** creo que no; **I believe so** creo que sí; **I don't believe a word she says** no le creo ni una palabra; **the police believe him to be dangerous** la policía cree que es peligroso

belittle *(achievements)* despreciar; menospreciar; *(person)* denigrar; rebajar; *(minimize)* restar importancia a; **to belittle oneself** menospreciarse; tenerse en menos

belittling *(achievements)* denigrante

bell *(fig)* **he was saved by the bell** lo salvó la campana; se salvó de milagro; *(fig)* **to ring a bell** sonarse; **Carlos Rodriguez? does that ring a bell with you?** ¿Carlos Rodriguez? ¿te suena de algo?; **that rings a bell** eso me suena

belligerent *(person, tone)* agresiva; agresivo

belligerently *(person, tone)* agresivamente

belong *(property)* **to belong to somebody** petenecerle a alguien; ser de alguien; **does this belong to you?** ¿esto es tuyo?; **it belongs to her** es de ella; le pertenece a ella; **who does that car belong to?** ¿de quién es ese coche?; **who does this belong to?** ¿a quién pertenece esto? ¿de quién es esto?; *(have rightful or usual place)* **I feel I belong here** aquí me siento en casa; **I still feel I don't belong here** todavía no me siento en casa; **these figures belong under the heading of expenses** esas cifras deben ir en el apartado de gastos

belongings *(noun)* pertenencias; **personal belongings** efectos personales; objetos personales

below *(less than)* **below average** inferior a la media; por debajo de la media; **below standard** por debajo del nivel exigido; **he earns below $20,000 a year** gana menos de 20.000 dólares al año; *(under)* abajo de; debajo de; **the floor below** el piso de abajo; **the room directly below** la pieza justo abajo de ésta; la pieza justo debajo de ésta

belt *(noun)* cinturón; **seat belt** cinturón de seguridad; *(verb: colloquial, clout, punch, slap)* **to belt someone** darle una paliza a alguien; **he belted me one** me dio un mamporro; me dio una torta; me dio una paliza

belting *(noun: colloquial)* paliza; **to give somebody a belting** darle una paliza a alguien

bemuse *(person, puzzeled)* desconcertar; **I'm still bemused with your answer** sigo desconcertada con tu respuesta; sigo desconcertado con tu respuesta; *(adj)* aturdida; aturdido; confusa; confuso; desconcertada; desconcertado

bench *(law: judges collectively)* **the bench** *or* **the Bench** el tribunal; la judicatura; los juezes que forman el tribunal; **to appear before the bench** comparecer ante el tribunal *(see* **appearance***)*; *(person)* juez; jueza; *(place where a judge is)* estrado

bench conference consulta en el estrado *(reunión del juez con los abogados de ambas partes a su banco y fuera del oído del jurado)*

bench trial juicio ante un juez y sin jurado

bench warrant orden de detención; orden de arresto *(orden de dentención emitida directamente por el juez para que la policía arreste a una persona)*

bend the rules acomodar las reglas

beneath *(unworthy of)* **it's beneath her** es indigno de ella; **it's beneath him** es indigno de él; **it's beneath him to do such a thing** hacer tal cosa es indigno de él

beneath contempt despreciable

beneficial *(advantageous, good)* beneficiosa; beneficioso; **to be beneficial to somebody** ser beneficiosa para alguien; ser beneficioso para alguien; *(law)* **she has the beneficial interest in the property** tiene el usufructo de la propiedad; **he has a beneficial interest in the deal** es parte interesado en la transacción; **she has a beneficial interest in the deal** es parte interesada en la transacción

beneficiary *(noun)* beneficiaria; beneficiario

beneficiary designation form formulario de designación de beneficiarios

beneficiary's behalf en nombre, a favor del beneficiario; por parte del beneficiario

benefit *(noun)* beneficio; bien; provecho; ventaja; **a change will be of benefit to you** un cambio le resultará beneficioso; un cambio le resultará provechoso; **for the benefit of** a beneficio de; en provecho de; **for the benefit of your children** por el bien de sus hijos; **the benefits of a good education** las ventajas de una buena educación; *(verb)* aprovechar; beneficiar; sacar partido de; sacar provecho de

benefit amount cantidad de beneficio

Benefit Eligibility Screening Tool (BEST) Programa para Determinar Elegibilidad a Beneficios

benefit estimate cálculo de beneficio; estimado de beneficio; presupuesto de beneficio

benefit increase aumento de beneficio

benefit of the doubt beneficio de la deuda; **to give somebody the benefit of the doubt** darle a alguien el beneficio de la deuda; **to have the benefit of** tener la ventaja de

benefit payments pagos de beneficios

benefit period período de beneficios

benefit statement estado de beneficios; declaración de beneficios

benefits *(noun)* beneficios; prestaciones

bent *(determined)* **to be bent on doing something** estar empeñada en hacer algo; estar empeñado en hacer algo; estar resuelta en hacer algo; estar resuelto en hacer algo

bequeath *(verb)* legar; **to bequeath something to somebody** legarle algo a alguien

bequest *(noun)* legado

berserk *(adj)* frenética; frenético; **to go berserk**; perder los estribos; ponerse hecha una furia; ponerse hecho una furia; volverse loca; volverse loco; **she'll go berserk when she finds out** se va a poner hecha una furia cuando se entere

beside *(anger)* **to be beside oneself** estar fuera de sí; **he was beside himself with anger** estaba fuera de sí con rabia; *(at the side of)* al lado de; junto a; *(extraneous to)* **that's beside the point** eso no tiene nada que ver; eso no viene al caso

besides *(in addition to)* además de; aparte de; **there are five other witnesses, besides you** además de ti, hay otros cinco testigos; aparte de ti, hay otros cinco testigos; *(apart from)* **no one knows besides you** nadie lo sabe aparte de ti

best *(adj)* mejor; **all the best!** ¡buena suerte! ¡que le vaya bien!; **as best I could** lo mejor que pude; **at her best** en sus mejores momentos; **at his best** en sus mejores momentos; **do whatever you think is best** haz lo que mejor te parezca; **for the best part of the year** durante la mayor parte del año; **he testified for the best part of an hour** prestó declaración durante casi una hora; **he's the best judge** es el mejor juez; **I know what's best for you** yo sé qué es lo que más le conviene; **the best thing to do is to wait** lo mejor es esperar; **to know what is best for somebody** saber lo que más le conviene a alguien; **to the best of your recollection, he wasn't there?** ¿si la memoria no le falla, no estaba?; **your best bet is to stay here** lo mejor que puede hacer es quedarse aquí

best evidence mejor evidencia; mejor prueba

betrayal *(noun)* traición; **a betrayal of trust** un abuso de confianza; **an act of betrayal** una traición

betrayal of trust abuso de confianza

better *(adj)* mejor; **he's changed — and for the better!** ha cambiado — ¡y para bien!; **for better or worse** para bien o mal; **I've got an even better idea** tengo una idea aún mejor; **so much the better** tanto mejor; **things couldn't be better** todo va de maravilla; **things took a turn for the better** las cosas dieron un giro positivo; **we get along better than we used to** nos llevamos mejor que antes; **you'd better not complain!** ¡más te vale no quejarte!

Better Business Bureau Oficina para Mejores Negocios; Oficina de Mejores Transacciones

better off mucho mejor; **they're far better off without him** están mucho mejor sin él

between *(prep)* entre; **between now and then** de aquí a allá; **between now and Thursday** de aquí al Jueves; **just between ourselves** entre nosotros; **just between you and me** entre nosotros; **she's between jobs at the moment** en este momento no está trabajando; **they divided the money between them** se dividieron el dinero entre ellos; **we did it between the two of us** lo hicimos entre los dos

between consenting adults entre personas de edad para consentir

bewilder *(confuse)* desconcertar; dejar perpleja; dejar perplejo; *(overwhelm)* apabullar; **they bewildered me with facts and figures** me apabullaron con datos y cifras

bewildered *(adj)* apabullada; apabullado; desconcertada; desconcertado; perpleja; perplejo; **I was utterly bewildered by what she said** lo que dijo me dejó absolutamente perpleja; lo que dijo me dejó absolutamente perplejo

bewildering *(adj)* apabullante; desconcertante

bewilderment *(noun)* desconcierto; perplejidad

beyond *(apart from)* además de; *(exceeding)* superior a; *(further than)* más allá de; **try to think beyond the immediate future** trata de pensar más allá del futuro inmediato; *(longer than)* **I can't tell you anything beyond that** no le puedo decir nada más que eso; **it won't last much beyond an hour** no durará mucho más de una hora; *(on the other side of)* del otro lado de; *(outside)* fuera de; **circumstances beyond our control** circunstancias ajenas a nuestra voluntad; **she told us little beyond what we already knew** no nos dijo gran cosa fuera de lo que ya sabíamos; *(surpassing)* **it's beyond belief** es increíble; **it's beyond dispute** es indiscutible; **to live beyond one's means** vivir por encima de sus posibilidades

beyond a reasonable doubt fuera de toda duda razonable; más allá de toda duda fundada; más allá de una duda razonable; sin que quede lugar a duda

beyond the reach of the law fuera del alcance de la ley

beyond our control ajena a nuestra voluntad; **for reasons beyond our control** por causas ajenas a nuestra voluntad

bias *(noun)* parcialidad; sesgo

bias against prejuicio en contra de

bid *(noun)* oferta; propuesta; **he made one last bid for freedom** hizo un último intento de escapar; **make a bid** hacer una oferta

big *(adj)* grande; importante; *(phrases)* **a big decision** una decisión importante; una gran decisión; **a big successes** un gran éxito; **big deal!** ¡y qué!; **big talk** fanfarronada; **his big brother** su hermano mayor; **it was a big mistake** fue un gran error; fue un grave error; **it was big of her** fue muy generosa de su parte; **that's big of you!** ¡qué amable!;

¡qué generosa eres!; ¡qué generoso eres!; **there's a big difference** hay una gran diferencia; **to act big** fanfarronear; **to do things in a big way** hacer las cosas a lo grande; **to make it big** tener un gran éxito; **to talk big** darse importancia; fanfarronear; **to think big** ser ambiciosa; ser ambicioso; planear las cosas a lo grande; **what's the big idea?** ¿a qué viene eso?

big-hearted generosa; generoso

bigamist *(noun)* bígama; bígamo

bigamous *(adj)* bígama; bígamo

bigamous marriage matrimonio bígamo

bigamy *(adj)* bigamia

bigot *(noun)* fanática; fanático; intolerante

bigoted *(adj)* fanática; fanático; intolerante; prejuiciada; prejuiciado

bigotry *(noun)* fanatismo; intolerancia

bill *(noun)* cuenta; **to pay the bill** pagar la cuenta

bill of health certificado de sanidad; patente de sanidad

bill of indictment auto de procesamiento

bill of particulars exposición revelatoria

Bill of Rights Declaración de Derechos

bill of sale contrato de venta; escritura de venta

billing statement cuenta de cobro; factura

billy club (el) garrote

bind over *(law: transfer)* entregar

binding *(adj: law)* vinculante

binding agreement laudo de obligado cumplimiento; acuerdo vinculante

binding arbitration decision laudo de obligado cumplimiento

binding contract contrante vinculante

binding instructions *instrucciones que debe seguir el jurado en cuanto a la decisión a tomar si encuentra probados ciertos hechos*

binding law in all of the states ley vinculante en todos los estados

binge *(colloquial)* borrachera; juerga; parranda; **to go out on a binge** irse de juerga; irse de farra; irse de parranda

biopsy *(noun)* biopsia

birth *(noun)* nacimiento; *(childbirth)* parto; **the country of birth** su país de nacimiento

birth certificate acta de nacimiento; certificado de nacimiento; partida de nacimiento

birth control control de la natalidad

birth defect defecto de nacimiento

birth record inscripción de nacimiento

birthdate *(noun)* fecha de nacimiento

birthday *(noun)* cumpleaños

birthright *(noun)* derecho de nacimiento; *(fig)* patrimonio

black *(color)* negra; negro; **a black man** un negro; **a black woman** una negra; **her arms were black with bruises** tenía los brazos llenos de moretones; **she was dressed in black** iba vestida de negro; **to beat somebody black and blue** darle una tremenda paliza a alguien; **to see everything in black and white** ver las cosas en blanco y negro; *(fin)* **in the black** en el haber

black coffee café solo

black eye ojo morado; **to give somebody a black eye** ponerle un ojo morado a alguien

black eye law ley de ojos morados

blacklist *(noun)* lista negra; *(verb)* poner en la lista negra

black lung disease enfermedad pulmonar minera

blackmail *(noun)* chantaje; *(verb)* chantajear; **that's emotional blackmail** eso es un chantaje afectivo

blackmailer *(noun)* chantajista

black market mercado negro

black out *(noun: loss of consciousness)* desmayo; desvanecimiento; **to have a black out** sufrir un desvanecimiento; *(failure of memory)* laguna; pérdida temporal de la memoria; *(power failure)* apagón; *(verb: lose consciousness)* perder el conocimiento

bladder *(noun)* vejiga

blade *(noun)* navaja

blame *(noun)* culpa; **the blame for what happened lies entirely with them** la culpa de lo que pasó la tienen sólo ellos; *(verb)* **he's to blame** él tiene la culpa; **she's to blame** ella tiene la culpa; **to be to blame for something** ser responsable de algo; tener la culpa de algo; **to lay the blame on somebody** echarle la culpa a alguien; **to blame somebody for something** culpar a alguien de algo; echarle la culpa de algo a alguien; **you have only yourself to blame** usted tiene toda la culpa; la culpa es sólo suya

blank *(noun: empty space)* espacio en blanco; **fill in the blanks** rellene los espacios en blanco; **my mind was a complete blank** me quedé totalmente en blanco; **my mind went blank** me quedé en blanco

blank bullet bala de fogueo; cartucho sin bala

blank check cheque en blanco

bleak *(future, prospect)* poco prometador; poco prometadora

bleed *(verb: from cut, wound)* sangrar; **she bled to death** se desangró; murió desangrada; **to bleed to death** desangrarse; morir desangrada; morir desangrado

blind *(adj: medical)* ciega; ciego; **to be blind in one eye** ser tuerta; ser tuerto; **to go blind** quedarse ciega; quedarse ciego; **he was blinded in the accident** se quedó ciego en un accidente; perdió la vista en un accidente; **to be blind drunk** estar más borracha que una cuba; estar más borracho que una cuba

blind alley callejón sin salida

blind date cita a ciegas; cita con un desconocido; cita con una desconocida

blind man ciego

blind woman ciega

blindness ceguera

block (on claim form) encasillado (en un formulario)

blood *(noun)* sangre; **bad blood** animosidad; mala sangre; resentimiento; **in cold blood** a sangre fría; **there was bad blood between them after their argument** quedaron resentidos a raíz de la discusión; **to lose blood** perder sangre

blood bath baño de sangre; masacre

blood evidence evidencia de sangre; **the blood evidence points directly to her** la evidencia de sangre apunta directamente hacia ella

blood group grupo sanguíneo

blood sample muestra de sangre

blood spatter evidence evidencia de sangre de salpicadura

blood spatter pattern patrón de sangre de salpicadura

blood-stained *(adj)* manchada de sangre; manchado de sangre

blood test análisis de sangre

blood transfusion transfusión de sangre

blood type grupo sanguíneo

bloodline *(noun)* línea de sangre

bloodstain *(noun)* mancha de sangre

blow *(setback; shock, strike)* golpe; **to come to blows** llegar a las manos

blue *(adj & noun)* azul; **dark blue** azul oscuro; **light blue** azul claro; **he's got the blues** está triste; tiene pena; **to feel blue** estar tristón; tener pena

blue-collar *(job)* manual; *(union)* obrera; obrero

blue-collar workers los obreros; trabajadores manuales

blue jeans blue jeans; tejanos; vaqueros; **he was wearing blue jeans** llevaba vaqueros; tenía puesto vaqueros

blue law *ley que prohíbe la realización de ciertas actividades los domingos*

blues *(colloquial: depression)* **the blues** la depre; **to have the blues** tener la depre

blunt trauma trauma contundente

blur *(adj)* borrosa; borroso; *(fig)* **my mind was a blur** todo se volvió borroso en mi mente; **the memory is just a blur** el recuerdo está impreciso

Board of Pardons and Paroles Junta de Perdones y Libertades Condicionales

boardinghouse *(noun)* casa de huéspedes

boat people balseras; balseros

bodily harm daños graves; daños personales

body *(animal, person)* cuerpo; tronco; *(dead)* cadáver; *(mass, collection)* conjunto; *(of people)* grupo; **a dead body** un cadáver; *(fig)* **a large body of evidence** un conjunto de pruebas; una recopilación importante de datos

body bag bolsa para restos humanos

body blow golpe duro

body count número de muertos

body guard *(single person)* guardaespaldas; *(group)* escolta

body language gestualidad; lenguaje gestual

body of evidence conjunto de pruebas

body of law cuerpo de leyes; cuerpo legal

body search cacheo

body size estatura

body type tipo somático

body weight peso

bogus *(adj)* falsa; falso; fraudulenta; fraudulento; **a bogus company** una empresa fantasma

Bolivian Boliviana; Boliviano

bomb *(noun)* bomba

bomb scare amenaza de bomba

bombproof a pruebas de bomba

bona fide auténtica; auténtico; genuina; genuino; **a bona fide offer** una oferta seria

bona fide purchaser comprador de buena fe; compradora de buena fe

bond *(fin)* bono; obligación; *(link)* lazo; vínculo; **a bond had formed between them** entre ellos se había creado un vínculo; **the bond between mother and child** el vínculo afectivo entre madre e hijo

bond of friendship vínculo de amistad

bonded *(adj: person)* protegida por seguro de infidelidad; protegido por seguro de infidelidad

bonds of friendship lazos de amistad; vínculos de amistad

bondsman *(law)* fiador judicial; fiadora judicial; garante; aval; fiador; fiadora

book *(law: to book someone)* fichar

book *(printed work)* libro; *(record charge against)* multar; ponerle multa a; **he was booked for speeding** le pusieron una multa por exceso de velocidad; lo multaron por exceso de velocidad; **to throw the book at somebody** echar un rapapolvo a alguien

booking *(law: recording an arrest)* ficha policial; inscripción del arresto

booze *(noun)* bebida; trago

border *(noun)* frontera; **to cross the border** cruzar la frontera; pasar la frontera; *(verb: pol)* limitar con

border crosser crusadora de frontera; crusador de frontera

border crossing card tarjeta para cruzar la frontera

border patrol patrulla de fronteras; patrulla fronteriza

border patrol agent agente de la Patrulla Fronteriza

border security seguridad en la frontera

border town pueblo fronterizo

born *(adj)* **a child was born to them** tuvieron un hijo; **born into poverty** nacida en la pobreza; nacido en la pobreza; **she was born of middle class parents** nació en una familia de clase media; sus padres eran de clase media; **to be born** nacer; **when was she born?** ¿cuándo nació?

borrow *(to have on loan)* pedir prestada; pedir prestado; tomar prestada; tomar prestado; **he had to borrow some money** tuvo que pedir dinero prestado

borrower *(noun)* prestataria; prestatario

borrowing *(noun)* prestámos

borrowing capacity capacidad de endeudamiento

boss *(employer, owner)* patrón; patrona; *(superior)* jefa; jefe; **you decide, you're the boss** decídelo tú, que eres el que manda; decídelo tú, que eres la que manda

both *(adj)* ambas; ambos; las dos; los dos; **both you and I were there** lo vimos tanto tú como yo; lo vimos los dos; **they were both there** estaban allí los dos

bother *(noun: nuisance)* lata; molestia; *(trouble)* aprieto; dificultad; **I'm sorry to bother you** perdona la molestia; **it isn't any bother** no es ninguna molestia; **it isn't worth the bother** no vale la pena; *(verb: annoy, irritate)* **don't bother me!** ¡no me molestes!; **nothing seems to bother her** nada parece preocuparla; **what's bothering you?** ¿qué es lo que te preocupa?; ¿qué te pasa?

bottle *(noun: container)* botella; *(of perfume, medicine, ink)* frasco; *(alcohol colloquial)* **to go on the bottle** darse a la bebida; **to come off the bottle** dejar la bebida; **to hit the bottle** darle a la bebida; darle al trago

bottom *(phrases)* **at the bottom of** al fondo de; detrás de; **he's at the bottom of it** él está detrás de esto; **to get to the bottom of** llegar al fondo de

bound *(obliged)* obligada; obligado; **he felt bound to tell the truth** se sintió obligado a decir la verdad; **the police are bound to prosecute in such cases** la policía está obligada a remitir tales casos a la justicia; **you are still bound by your promise** sigues estando obligada a cumplir con lo que prometiste; sigues estando obligado a cumplir con lo que prometiste; *(tied up)* amarrada; amarrado; atada; atado; **my hands were bound** tenía las manos atadas

boy*(noun)* chico; niño; **she has three boys** tiene tres chicos; tiene tres niños

boycott *(noun)* boicot; boicoteo; **to mount a boycott** organizar un boicot; *(verb)* boicotear; hacerle el boicot a

boyfriend*(noun)* novio; **live-in boyfriend** compañero

boyish *(enthusiasm, smile)* de chico; de niño; **his boyish looks** su aspecto de chico; su aspecto juvenil

bracket *(category)* **income bracket** nivel de ingresos; **tax bracket** banda impositiva

braces (**limbs**) abrazaderas

braces (**dental**) frenos; ganchos dentales

brain *(noun)* cerebro

brain-damaged con lesión cerebral

brain dead clínicamente muerto

brain death muerte cerebral; muerte clínica

brain scan escanografía cerebral

branch manager director de sucursal; directora de sucursal

brandish *(verb)* esgrimir

brandishing knives esgrimiendo cuchillos

brass knuckles *(noun)* manoplas; nudilleras de metal

brawl *(noun)* pelea; reyerta; gresca; *(verb)* pelearse; **street brawl** reyerta callejera

Brazilian *(adj)* Brasileña; Brasileño

breach *(of code, law)* incumplimiento; violación

breach of confidence un abuso de confianza; una infidencia

breach of contract incumplimiento de contrato

breach of faith un abuso de confianza; una infidencia

breach of the peace alteración del orden público; **she was arrested for breach of the peace** la detuvieron por alterar el orden público

breach of trust un abuso de confianza; una infidencia

bread winner proveedor de la familia; la que mantiene a la familia; el que mantiene a la familia; **he's the only bread winner of the family** es el único sostén de la familia

break *(verb)* **to break the law** contravenir la ley; infringir la ley; violar la ley; *(intermission)* **to take a break** descansar; **let's take a break** tomémonos un descanso; hagamos una pausa; paremos para descansar; **we have a coffee break at 11** a las 11 paramos para tomar un café; *(separation)* **he made a break for cover** corrió a refugiarse; **he made a break with his past** cortó con su pasado; rompió con su pasado; **lucky break** golpe de suerte; racha de buena suerte

break away *(become free)* **to break away from somebody** desprenderse de alguien; soltarse; **she tried to break away from him** trató de soltarse

break-in*(noun)* robo; **they had a break-in next door** entraron a robar en la casa de al lado; entraron ladrones en la casa de al lado

break into *(force entry)* entrar para robar; meterse para robar; entrar por fuerza; **our house was broken into** nos entraron a robar; nos entraron ladrones; **a thief broke into my office** un ladrón entró por fuerza en mi oficina

break the law contravenir la ley; infringir la ley; violar la ley

break up *(disperse)* disolver; separar; **come on, break it up!** ¡vamos, basta ya!; **he broke up the fight between the boys** separó a los niños que se estaban peleando; *(ruin, wreck)* **he felt responsable for breaking up their marriage** se sentía responsable de su separación; se sentía responsable del fracaso de su matrimonio; **their marriage broke up** se separaron; su matrimonio fracasó

break up with acabar con; **I've broken up with her** he acabado con ella; **I've broken up with him** he acabado con él

breakdown *(lose control)* perder el control; **he broke down and cried** perdió el control y se echó a llorar; *(fail: health, negotiations, talks)* fracasar; **his health broke down** perdió la salud; se enfermó

breakdown of negotiations ruptura de las negociaciones

breakdown of talks ruptura de las negociaciones

breakfast *(noun)* desayuno; **to have breakfast** desayunar; **to skip breakfast** no desayunar; *(verb)* desayunar

breakfast time hora del desayuno

breaking and entering allanamiento de morada; allanamiento de vivienda; escalamiento

breakout *(prison)* fuga

breakup *(marriage)* separación

breast *(anat)* seno; pecho

breath test prueba del alcohol

breathalyzer*(noun)* alcohómetro; **breathalyzer test** prueba del alcohol; **to fail the breathalyzer test** no pasar la prueba del alcohol; **to pass the breathalyzer test** pasar la prueba del alcohol

breathing test examen respiratorio

breathlessness falta de respiración

bribe *(noun)* cohecho; coima; mordida; soborno; **as a bribe** como coima; **to accept a bribe** aceptar un soborno; dejarse sobornar; **to take a bribe** aceptar un soborno; dejarse sobornar; *(verb)* cohechar; coimear; morder; sobornar

bribery *(noun)* cohecho; coima; soborno; **they are open to bribery** se los puede comprar; se los puede morder; se los puede sobornar

bribery and corruption el soborno y la corrupción

bride *(noun)* novia; **the bride and bridegroom** los novios; *(after ceremony)* los recién casados

bridegroom *(noun)* novio

bridesmaid *(noun)* dama de honor

bridge *(noun)* puente

bridge loan crédito puente; préstamo puente

brief *(adj: statement, summary)* breve; sucinta; sucinto; **his report was brief and to the point** su informe era breve e iba al grano; **in brief** en resumen; **please be brief** sea breve, por favor

brief *(noun: law)* escrito; **twelve page brief** escrito de doce páginas; **it's a very complicated brief** es un caso muy complicado; *(verb: lawyer)* instruir

bright *(hopeful)* brillante; halagüeña; halagüeño; prometedor; prometedora; **he has a bright future ahead of him** tiene un brillante porvenir por delante; **the prospects are not very bright** las perspectivas no son muy prometedoras

bring *(verb)* traer; **bring your passport with you** traiga consigo el pasaporte

bring a lawsuit against somebody iniciar una demanda en contra de alguien; interponer una demanda en contra de alguien; entablar un pleito contra alguien

bring an action against somebody iniciar una demanda en contra de alguien; interponer una demanda en contra de alguien; hacer causa; entablar un pleito contra alguien

bring charges against somebody formular cargos en contra de alguien; formularle cargos a alguien; presentar cargos contra alguien

bring in for questioning ser interrogada; ser interrogado; ser sometida a un interrogatorio; ser sometido a un interrogatorio

bring in the police pedir la intervención de la policía; **they had to bring in the police** tuvieron que hacer intervenir a la policía

bring the lawsuit to an end poner término a la causa

bring trouble traer problemas

broadside a car chocar contra un auto de lado

broken *(adj)* rota; roto; fracturada; fracturado

broken English mal Inglés; **in broken English** en mal Inglés; **he speaks broken English** chapurrea el Inglés

broken home hogar deshecho; hogar roto; familia dividida

broken marriage matrimonio deshecho

broker *(noun)* corredor

bronchitis *(noun)* bronquitis

broomstick *(noun)* palo de escoba

brothel *(noun)* burdel; casa de tolerancia

brother *(noun)* hermano; **do you have any brothers and sisters?** ¿tienes hermanos?; **older brother** hermano mayor; **younger brother** hermano menor

brother-in-law *(noun)* cuñado

brown *(adj: clothes, shoes,)* café; marrón; *(hair)* castaño; *(skin)* morena; moreno

bruise *(noun: contusion)* magulladura; moretón; moradura

brutality *(noun)* brutalidad; sevicia; **the brutality of the murder** el salvajismo del asesinato; **they complained about police brutality** se quejaron de la dureza de la represión policial

brutally *(adv)* brutalmente; **were you brutally beaten?** ¿le golpearon brutalmente?

buckteeth *(phrase)* **to have buckteeth** tener dientes de conejo; tener los dientes salidos

bucktoothed *(adj)* con los dientes salidos; dientuda; dientudo

buddy *(noun)* amiga; amigo; compinche; cuate; **they're good buddies** son muy compinches; son muy cuates

budget *(noun)* presupuesto

build *(establish, develop)* **he tried to build a new life in America** intentó empezar de nuevo en América

building *(edifice)* edificio; inmueble; *(construction)* construcción

building code código de construcción

building contractor contratista de obras

building materials materiales para la construcción

building permit permiso de obras

building site *(under construction)* obra

bullet *(noun)* bala; **blank bullet** bala de fogueo; **random bullet** bala perdida; **rubber bullet** bala de goma; **stray bullet** bala perdida

bullet-riddled abaleada; abaleado

bullet-riddled body cuerpo abaleado

bullet wound balazo; herida de bala

bully *(noun: thug)* bravucón; bravucona; matón; matona; **the class bully** el bravucón de la clase; el matón de la clase; *(verb)* intimidar; matonear; **she bullied him into doing it** lo acosó hasta que lo hizo

bully around intimidar

bullying *(noun)* intimidación; acoso

burden *(noun)* carga; peso; **financial burden** una carga económica; **tax burden** carga fiscal; **the burden of proof lies with him** él lleva la carga de la prueba; **the burden of responsibility** el peso de la responsibilidad; *(verb)* cargar con; **don't burden me with your troubles** no me vengas con tus problemas

burden of proof carga de la prueba; peso de la prueba

burdensome *(adj)* gravosa; gravoso; onorosa; onoroso

bureau *(noun)* oficina

Bureau of Citizenship and Immigration Services (BCIS) Oficina de Ciudadanía y Servicios Inmigratorios (OCSI)

Bureau of Vital Statistics Registro Demográfico

burglar *(noun)* ladrón; ladrona

burglar alarm alarma antirrobo

burglar tools instrumentos para allanamiento con fines delictivos; herramientas para allanamiento con fines delictivos

burglarize *(verb)* robar

burglarproof *(adj)* a prueba de robos

burglary *(noun)* robo; robo en una casa

burglary of vehicles allanamiento de vehículos

burial *(noun)* entierro

burial expenses gastos de funeral, gastos funerarios

bury*(verb)* sepultar; enterrar

bus driver conductor de autobús; conductora de autobús; chofer de autobús

bus stop parada de autobús

business *(noun)* negocios; comercio; **to do business with** negociar con; **he's in business** se dedica al comercio; **to go into business** dedicarse al comercio; **I'm here on business** estoy de negocios; estoy en viaje de negocios; **to go out of business** quebrar; **to put somebody out of business** hacer que alguien quiebre; **to set up in business as** montar un negocio de; **to set somebody up in business** montar un negocio a alguien; **it's a family business** es una empresa familiar; **what business are you in?** ¿a qué se dedica usted?

business address dirección comercial; dirección profesional

business associate socia; socio

business day día laboral

business deal acuerdo comercial; trato comercial

business expenses gastos comerciales

business hours horas de oficina

business insurance seguro comercial

business law derecho empresarial

business letter carta comercial

business lunch comida de negocios

business people gente de negocios

business premises local comercial

business school escuela de comercio

business suit traje de calle

businessman *(noun)* empresario; hombre de negocios

businesswoman empresaria; mujer de negocios

buy *(noun)* compra; *(verb)* comprar

buying and selling comraventa

by birth por nacimiento

by coercion bajo coacción; por la fuerza

by law por ley

by mail por correo

bystander *(noun)* espectador; espectadora transeúente; *(witness)* testigo

C

cache alijo; **arms cache** alijo de armas; *(hiding place)* escondite

cache away meter en un escondite; esconder

cadaver *(noun)* cadáver

cahoots *(phrase)* **to be in cahoots with somebody** estar conchabada con alguien; estar conchabado con alguien

calendar *(law)* calendario de juicios; lista de juicios; tabla de juicios; **fix the calendar** fijar el calendario; **put it on the calendar** apuntarlo en el calendario; **jot it down on the calendar** apuntarlo en el calendario

calendar month mes; mes del calendario

calendar year año calendario; año natural; año civil

caliber *(diameter)* calibre; **a 44 caliber bullet** una bala de calibre 44; *(ability, quality)* **a lawyer of his caliber** un abogado de su calibre; una abogada de su calibre

calf *(anat)* pantorrilla

call *(by telephone)* llamada; **an 800 call** una llamada gratuita; **I have to return his call** tengo que devolverle la llamada; **local call** llamada urbana; **long distance call** llamada interurbana; llamada internacional; **there is a call for you on line one** lo llaman por la línea uno; tiene una llamada por la línea uno; **to give somebody a call** llamar a alguien por teléfono; **to make a call** llamar por teléfono; hacer una llamada telefónica; **will you take the call?** ¿le paso la llamada?; *(cry of person)* grito; llamada; llamado; **a call for help** un grito de socorro; una llamada de socorro; *(verb: doctor, police)* llamar; **I'll call you tomorrow** te llamaré mañana; te llamo mañana; **to call somebody as a witness** citar a alguien como testigo; **whose calling, please?** ¿de parte de quién, por favor?

call back *(by telephone)* **can I call you back?** ¿puedo llamarte más tarde?; **she never calls you back** nunca te devuelve la llamada.

call 911 llame al 911

calm *(person)* calmada; calmado; tranquila; tranquilo; **keep calm!** ¡calma!; ¡tranquilo!; **she remained calm throughout** no perdió la calma en ningún momento; **we'll discuss it when you feel calmer** lo hablaremos cuando estés más calmada; lo hablaremos cuando estés más calmado

can *(allow oneself to)* **I couldn't very well tell him just then** no se lo podía decir justo en ese momento; **you can't blame her** no puedes echarle la culpa

can *(indicating ability)* poder; saber; **can you answer the question?** ¿puedes contestar la pregunta?; **I cannot believe she said that** no puedo cree que dijera eso; **I'll do what I can** haré lo que pueda; **I'll tell you what I can** te diré todo lo que pueda; **she couldn't answer the question.** no pudo contestar la pregunta; **they did all they could** hicieron todo lo que pudieron; **you can do it if you try hard** puedes hacerlo si te esfuerzas

can *(indicating disbelief, puzzelment)* **this can't be true!** ¡esto no puede ser!; **how could you lie to me?** ¿cómo pudiste mentirme?; **they can't have left already!** ¡no es posible que ya se han ido!

can *(indicating mental activity)* **can you remember her name?** ¿te acuerdas de cómo se llama?; **can't you tell he's lying?** ¿no te das cuenta de que está mintiendo?; **I can't understand it** no lo entiendo; no puedo entenderlo

can *(indicating perception)* **as you can see, there's a lot of work to be done** como puedes ver, hay mucho que hacer; **can you hear me?** ¿me puedes oyer?; **I could hear every word they said** oía todo lo que decían

can *(indicating possibility, suggestion)* **anything can happen in a preliminary hearing** puede pasar cualquier cosa en una audiencia preliminar; **he can't be her husband** no puede ser su marido; **he could have forgotten** puede ser que se haya olvidado; **it can't be true!** ¡no puede ser!; ¡no es posible!; **you can't be serious!** ¡no lo dirás en serio!; **you could have told me!** ¡podías habérmelo dicho!; **you could try telephoning his office** ¿por qué no le llamas a su despacho?

cancel *(meeting, trip)* cancelar; suspender; **he cancelled at the last moment** a último momento canceló la cita; **what will we do if they cancel the appointment?** ¿qué vamos a hacer si cancelan la cita?

cancel a default judgement cancelar un fallo por falta de comparecencia

cancellation *(noun)* cancelación; rescisión

cancellation clause cláusula de rescisión

cancelled check cheque cancelado

candid *(adj)* abierta; abierto franca; franco; sincera; sincero; **what's your candid opinion?** dime francamente lo que opinas

candidly *(adv)* con franqueza; sinceramente

candor *(noun)* franqueza; **with perfect candor** con absoluta franqueza

cane *(noun)* bastón

cap *(upper limit)* tope; **to put a cap on something** poner un tope a algo; *(baseball, schoolboy's, etc)* gorra; *(judges)* birrete

capability *(noun)* capacidad; competencia

capable *(able to)* capaz; *(competent)* competente

capacity *(noun)* capacidad

capital *(law: crime, offense)* que está sancionado con la pena de muerte

capital case caso que está sancionado con la pena de muerte

capital gain plusvalía

capital murder *(law: killing of peace officer)* homicidio con pena capital

capital offense delito capital; delito punible con pena capital

capital punishment pena capital; pena de muerte

capital punishment as a means of crime punishment pena capital como modo de castigar delitos

capitalize on aprovechar; sacar partido de; sacar provecho de

Capitol Hill Congreso de Estados Unidos

capricious *(adj: person)* caprichosa; caprichoso; antojadiza; antojadizo

capture *(seize a person by force)* capturar; apresar; aprehender; **the police managed to capture one of the kidnappers** la policía logró capturar a uno de los plagiarios

car *(noun)* automóvil; carro; coche; **to go by car** ir en coche

car accident accidente de auto; accidente de coche

car bomb coche bomba

car chase persecución de un coche

car insurance seguro de auto; seguro automovilístico

car pool lane carril de transporte en grupo

car title título de automóvil

cardiac arrest ataque de corazón, fallo cardíaco

care *(noun: uneasiness, worry)* **he hasn't a care in the world** no le preocupa nada

care *(verb: attention, carefulness; look after)* cuidarse; **he can take care of himself** él sabe cuidarse; **I can take care of myself** yo sé cuidarme; **take care!** ¡ten cuidado!; **to take care of somebody** atender a alguien; cuidar de alguien; **you must take better care of yourself** debes cuidarte más; **in his/her care** a su cuidado; a su cargo

care *(verb: feel concern)* importarle a uno; **I couldn't care less what he does** no me importa en absoluto lo que haga; **who cares what she says?** ¿a quién le importa lo que ella diga?

care *(wish)* **to care to** + *inf*; **would you care to join us for a coffee?** ¿le gustaría tomar un café con nosotros?; **would you care to step this way?** ¿tendría la bondad de pasar por aquí?

care and welfare cuidado y bienestar

care giver persona que cuida de un incapacitado; persona que cuida de una incapacitada

care worker asistente social; cuidador; cuidadora

career *(noun)* carrera

career guidance orientación profesional; orientación vocacional

career path trayectoria profesional

career woman mujer de carrera

careful *(cautious)* cuidadosa; cuidadoso; prudente; **be careful!** ¡ten cuidado!; **be careful what you say to him** cuidado con lo que le dices; **he was careful not to offend her** tuvo cuidado de no ofenderla; **to be careful to** + *infin* procurar; **be careful not to upset the witness** procure no disgustar al testigo; **to be careful with something** tener cuidado con algo; **you can't be too careful** toda prudencia es poca; todos los cuidados son pocos; **you should be more careful in the future** tendrás que tener más cuidado en el futuro

carefully *(adv)* con cuidado; cautelosamente; cuidadosamente

careless *(gen)* descuidada; descuidado; *(inattentive)* poco atenta; poco atento; *(thoughtless)* imprudente

careless driving conducción negligente

careless mistake descuido; error por descuido; **you made some careless mistakes** cometiste errores por descuido

carelessly *(adv)* descuido; despreocupación; falta de atención; sin la debida atención

carelessness *(noun)* falta de atención; falta de cuidado

caretaker *(noun)* cuidador de paciente; cuidadora de paciente

carrier *(company)* compañía; empresa; agencia de seguros; *(of disease)* portador; portadora

carry *(entail, involve responsibility)* acarrear; conllevar; traer aparejado; **crimes of this nature carry a high penalty** este tipo de delito trae aparejada una pena grave

carry *(have on oneself, transport)* llevar; traer; **are you carrying any money?** ¿traes dinero?; **he always carries a gun** siempre lleva pistola; **the offense carries a $50 fine** la infracción será penalizada con una multa de 50 dólares

carrying concealed weapons portar armas ocultas

case *(law)* causa; caso; **the Romero case** el caso Romero; **the police are investigating several cases of fraud** la policía está investigando varios casos de estafa; **to dismiss a case** sobreseer una causa; **to hear a case** conocer de una causa; **to lose a case** perder un juicio; perder un pleito; **to win a case** ganar un juicio; ganar un pleito; *(argument)* **the case for the prosecution** la acusación; **the case for the defense** la defensa; **she has a good case** sus argumentos son buenos; **she has a strong case** sus argumentos son poderosos; **there is a case for leniency** hay razones para ser indulgente; **there is a case for doing nothing** hay razones para no hacer nada; **I rest my case** a las pruebas me remito; **in some cases** en algunos casos

case *(instance, situation)* **a clear case of bias** un caso claro de parcialidad; **in her case** en su caso; **in most cases** en la mayoría de los casos; **as the case may be** según el caso; según sea el caso; **in no case** bajo ninguna circunstancia; en ninguna circunstancia; **in that case** en ese caso

case *(in phrases)* **in any case** de todas formas; de todas maneras; en cualquier caso; de cualquier modo; **just in case** por si acaso; **in case of** en caso de; **to case the joint** reconocer el terreno *(antes de cometer un delito)*

case argued before the high court actos probatorios

case in chief actos probatorios

case in point precedente legal de un mismo tribunal u otro superior que decide un caso similar

case law jurisprudencia; derecho jurisprudencial; precedentes judiciales

case load número de casos

case number número del caso

case of fraud caso de estafa

case record expediente

case worker asistente social *(trabajador social asignado a trabajar con clientes en comunidades de bajos recursos económicos)*

cash *(noun)* dinero en efectivo; **do you have $100 in cash?** ¿tienes 100 dólares en efectivo?

cash a check cobrar un cheque

cash bail fianza en dinero efectivo

cash benefits beneficios en efectivo

cash dividend dividendo en efectivo

cash gifts regalos en efectivo

cash in hand *(in accounting)* pagar en efectivo

cash offer oferta de pago en efectivo

cash value valor en efectivo

cash wages sueldo en efectivo; pago en efectivo; salario en efectivo

cashier's check cheque bancario; cheque de cajero

cast *(plaster)* yeso; enyesada; enyesado; **he's got a cast on his leg** tiene la pierna enyesada

casual *(adj* superficial; **a casual glance** una ojeada rápida; **it's just a casual relationship** es una relación superficial; **a casual acquaintance** un conocido; una conocida; **to do casual work** trabajar como eventual

casual sexual encounters relaciones sexuales fuera de una pareja estable

casual worker *(farm)* jornalera; jornalero; *(factory)* obrera; obrero

casually *(informally)* de manera informal; informalmente; *(wihout concern)* con toda tranquilidad

casualty *(injured person)* herida; herido; *(dead person)* víctima

catastrophic coverage protección contra catástrofe

catastrophic illness enfermedad catastrófica

cause *(law: case)* causa; **to plead somebody's cause** abogar por alguien; **to show cause** fundamentar

cause of action *(law: case)* causa de demanda

cause *(of accident, event)* causa; origen; **the cause of death is unknown** se desconoce la causa de la muerte; **there's good cause for concern** existen motivos para preocuparse; existen razones para preocuparse; **there's no cause for concern** no hay por qué preocuparse; **to be the cause of** ser causa de; **in the cause of justice** por la justicia; **to make common cause with** hacer causa común con

cause for concern motivo de preocupación

cause damage to dañar; causar daño a

caution *(noun: care, prudence)* cautela; prudencia; **to act with caution** actuar con cautela; *(verb: warn)* advertir; *(law)* **caution somebody for something** amonestar a alguien por algo

cautionary remarks advertencias

cautionary words advertencias

cavity *(dental)* carie

CD disco compacto; disco para almacenar información digitalizada

ceiling *(upper limit)* límite; tope; *(of building)* techo

center lane only *(traffic sign)* carril central exclusivamente

cerebral palsy parálisis cerebral

certain *(sure: fact, opinion)* cierta; cierto; segura; seguro; **it is certain that ...** es seguro que ...; **I am certain of it** estoy segura de ello; estoy seguro de ello; **be certain to tell her** no dejes de decírselo; no te olvides de decírselo; **I'll make certain that he understands** me aseguraré de que entienda

certificate *(document)* **birth certificate** partida de nacimiento; certificado de nacimiento; acta; certificado; **death certificate** acta de defunción; certificado de defunción; **marriage certificate** acta de matrimonio; certificado de matrimonio

certificate of citizenship certificado de ciudadanía

certificate of deposit certificado de depósito

certified check cheque certificado; cheque conformado

certified letter carta certificada

certified mail correo certificado

certified to teach habilitada para ejercer la docencia; habilitado para ejercer la docencia; **he is not certified to teach in this state** no está habilitado para ejercer la docencia en este estado

certify *(verb)* certificar; **I certify that the document is authentic** doy fe de que el documento es auténtico; **this is to certify that ...** por la presente certifico que ...; doy fe de que ...

certifying of payments certificación de pagos

cessation because of medical improvement suspensión por causa de mejoramiento médico; terminación por causa de mejoramiento médico; cese por causa de mejoramiento médico

cessation following trial work period (TWP) suspensión al completar el período probatorio de trabajo; terminación al completar el período probatorio de trabajo; cese al completar el período probatorio de trabajo

cessation of disability suspensión de incapacidad; terminación de incapacidad; cese de incapacidad

chain of custody custodia continua

chair *(verb)* silla; asiento; **take a chair, please** siéntese, por favor; tome asiento, por favor; **electric chair** silla electríca

challenge *(law)* recusación *(see **peremptory challenge**)*

challenge *(noun)* desafío; reto; *(verb)* desafiar; retar

challenge for cause recusación con causa

champion *(verb)* abogar por; **he championed immigrants' rights** abogaba por los derechos de los inmigrantes

chance witness testigo circunstancial

change *(verb)* cambiar; *(noun)* cambio; **a change for the worse** un cambio para peor; **for a change** para variar

change in income, resources, composition of family, and living arrangements cambio de ingresos, recursos, composición de familia y tipo de alojamiento

change in public opinion cambio en la opinión pública

change in the law cambio en la ley

change jobs cambiar de trabajo

change lawyers cambiar de abogada; cambiar de abogado

change machine máquina de cambio

change of address cambio de domicilio; cambio de dirección

change of clothes una muda; cambiarse de ropa

change of life menopausia

change of ownership cambio de dueña; cambio de dueño

change of payee cambio de tutor; cambio de representante

change of plan cambio de plan

change of residence cambio de residencia

change of scene cambio de aires

change of venue cambio de competencia territorial; traslado de competencia territorial; **request for a change of venue** presentar una solicitud de cambio de competencia territorial

change one's mind cambiar de opinión

change one's name cambiar de apellido

change one's opinion cambiar de opinión

change the subject cambiar de tema

character *(noun)* carácter; personalidad; **a man of good character** un hombre de buena reputación; **it was completely out of character for him** no era nada típico de él; **he's quite a character** es todo un personaje

character assassination difamación

character evidence prueba concerniente a la reputación de una persona

character trait rasgo de personalidad

character witness testigo de solvencia moral; testigo sobre el carácter de una persona

charge *(noun: law)* acusación; cargo; imputación; **a crime for which no one has ever been charged** un crimen sobre el cual no existe ninguna acusación formal; **he denied the charge** negó la acusación; **reduced charge** acusación de gravedad reducida; **related charge** delito conexo; **what is the charge against me?** ¿cuál es el cargo que se me hace? ¿cuál es la acusación que se me hace?; **what is the charge against you?** ¿cuál es el cargo que se le hace? ¿cuál es la acusación que se le hace?; **he's being tried on a charge of murder** se lo juzga por homicidio; **to bring a charge of theft against somebody** formular cargos de robo contra alguien; presentar cargos de robo contra alguien; **to lay a charge of theft against somebody** formular cargos de robo contra alguien; presentar cargos de robo contra alguien; **to bring charges gainst somebody** formular cargos contra alguien; presentar cargos contra alguien; **to press charges gainst somebody** formular cargos contra alguien; presentar cargos contra alguien; **to drop charges**

retirar los cargos; retirar la acusación; **he denies all the charges against him** niega todos los cargos que se le imputan

charge *(verb: law)* **to charge somebody with something** acusar a alguien de algo; **he was charged with murder** fue acusado de asesinato; **the crimes with which he is charged** los delitos que se le imputan; los delitos de los que se le acusa; **they charged him with stealing** lo acusaron de robar; **to appear on a charge of** comparecer acusado de; **he was arrested on a charge of murder** le detuvieron bajo acusación de asesinato

charge card tarjeta de cargo

charge of crime *(law)* acusación de crimen

charge to the jury *(law)* pautas sobre la ley para el jurado

charges contained in the indictment cargos contenidos en la acusación

charges made by the government cargos presentados por el gobierno

charging document *(law)* documento acusatorio

charitable organization organización de caridad; organización caritativa; asociación de beneficencia

chase *(pursuit)* persecución; **car chase** persecución en coche; **to give chase** salir en persecución de alguien; ir tras alguien; **he ran off and we gave chase** se echó a correr y nosotros salimos en su persecución; **we chased after the thief** salimos tras el ladrón; fuimos tras el ladrón

chat *(noun)* charla; conversación; plática; **to have a chat with somebody** charlar con alguien; conversar con alguien; hablar con alguien; **it's time we had a serious chat** es hora que hablemos seriamente; **I'll have a chat with him about his behavior** hablaré con el sobre su comportamiento

chat *(verb)* charlar; hablar; conversar; platicar

cheap labor mano de obra barata

cheat *(verb: deceive)* estafar; engañar; timar

check *(noun: financial)* cheque; *(passport, inspection)* control; revisión; *(facts, information)* verificación; *(verb: passport, ticket)* revisar; controlar; checar; *(verify facts, information)* comprobar; verificar

check stub talón de cheque; talonario

checking account cuenta corriente

checklist lista de control; lista de comprobación

checkpoint *(noun)* punto de control; punto de inspección de vehículos; retén

checks and balances mecanismo de equilibrio de poderes; la división del poder gubernamental entre las tres ramas

chemotherapy *(noun)* quimoterapia

chest wound herida en el pecho

chief *(head)* jefa; jefe; líder

chief of police jefa de policía; jefe de policía

Chief Justice *(US)* Presidente del Tribunal Supremo

child *(boy)* niño; *(girl)* niña

child abuse malos tratos a un menor; malos tratos a la infancia; *(sexual)* abusos deshonestos

child alimony manutención de los hijos

child benefit subsidio familiar por hijos

child care cuidado de niños

child custody guarda de un niño; patria potestad; custodia de menores

child labor trabajo de menores

child molester *persona que somete a un niño a abusos deshonestos*

child support obligación de los padres de suministrar alimentos y cuidados a sus hijos menores; alimentos para menores; obligación alimentaria; mantenimiento de hijos

child welfare protección a la infancia; bienestar infantil

childbirth *(noun)* parto; alumbramiento; **she died in childbirth** murió de parto

childcare cuidado de los niños; puericultura

childcare facilities guarderías

childhood *(noun)* niñez; infancia

childhood disability benefits beneficios de incapacidad en la niñez

childless *(adj)* sin hijos

children from low income families niños de familias de bajos ingresos

children of school age niños en edad escolar

children's home asilo de niños

children's term insurance rider anexo de término (temporal) para hijos

chiropractor quiropráctica; quiropráctico

choose *(decide)* **to choose to** + *infin* decidir + *infin*; optar por + *infin*; **he chose to appear in court** optó por comparecer ante el tribunal

Christmas *(noun)* Navidad

Christmas eve *(noun)* Nochebuena

chronic kidney failure insuficiencia renal permanente; fallo crónico del riñón; fallo permanente del riñón

circuit *(law)* distrito jurisdiccional

circuit court tribunal superior; corte de circuito

circuit court of appeals corte de apelaciones

circumstance *(condition, fact)* **the circumstances surrounding his death** las circunstancias que rodearon su muerte; **owing to circumstances beyond our control** debido a circunstancias ajenas a nuestra voluntad;

aggravating circumstances circunstancias agravantes; **extenuating circumstances** circunstancias atenuantes; **exonerating circumstances** circunstancias eximentes; **under the circumstances** dadas las circunstancias; **under no circumstances** bajo ninguna circunstancia

circumstantial evidence prueba circunstancial; evidencia circunstancial; pruebas indiciarias

circumvention *(law)* **circumvention of the law** el burlar la ley

cirrhosis of the liver cirrosis del hígado; cirrosis hepática; enfermedad del hígado

citation *(law)* citación; emplazamiento

cite *(law)* citar; invocar; **he was cited to appear in court** lo citaron para que se presentara en el tribunal de justicia

citizen *(noun)* ciudadana; ciudadano

citizenry *(noun)* ciudadanía; ciudadanos

citizen's arrest *detención llevada a cabo por un ciudadano común*

citizenship *(noun)* ciudadanía

Citizenship and Immigration Services (CIS) Cuidandnia y Servicio Inmigratorios de Estados Unidos

city *(noun)* ciudad

city block cuadra

city hall ayuntamiento; municipio

city life vida en la ciudad; vida urbana

city street calle de la ciudad; calle urbana

citywide *(adj)* que abarca toda la ciudad

civil *(adj)* civil

civil action acción civil

civil capacity capacidad civil

civil court sala de lo común

civil criminal law derecho civil; derecho penal

civil disobedience resistencia pasiva

civil jury trial *juicio civil donde el jurado resuelve toda disputa sobre los hechos en cuestión*

civil law derecho civil

civil lawsuit pleito civil

civil liability responsabilidad civil

civil liberties derechos civiles

civil matters asuntos civiles

civil rights derechos civiles

civil servant funcionaria; funcionario

civil service administración pública

civil status estado civil

civil unrest malestar social

civilians *(noun)* población civil

claim *(law)* demanda; **to file a claim** presentar una demanda; **to put in a claim for something** entablar demanda de algo; *(verb)* reclamar

claim compensation reclamar una indemnización

claim damages from somebody reclamar a alguien por daños y perjuicios

claim for disability allowance solicitud de una prestación por invalidez; **my claim for disability allowance was rejected** rechazaron mi solicitud de una prestación por invalidez

claim for Medicare payment reclamación de pago de Medicare

Claim for State Disability Insurance Benefits Formulario para Beneficios del Seguro Estatal de Incapacidad

claim form *(for benefit)* solicitud; formulario; formulario para solicitar prestaciones sociales, reembolsos de gastos etc

claim number número de reclamación

claimant *(in court)* demandante; reclamante; *(to social benefit)* solicitante

claims adjuster persona que actúa en nombre de una compañía de seguros para decidir si un reclamo será pagado

clamp down *(verb + adverb)* **to clamp down on somebody** tomar medidas drásticas contra alguien; **to clamp down on something** tomar medidas drásticas contra algo

clampdown *(noun: colloquial)* medidas drásticas contra; ristringir severamente; **there's been clampdown on loans** se ha restringido severamente la concesión de créditos

clampdown on illegal immigrants medidas drásticas contra los inmigrantes ilegales

clarification *(explanation)* aclaración; **this requires clarification** esto requiere una aclaración; esto hay que aclararlo; **I'd like some further clarification on this point** quisiera que se me aclarara este punto

clarify *(verb)* aclarar

clash *(noun)* choque; enfrentamiento; **a clash with the police** un choque con la policía; un enfrentamiento con la policía; **police clashed with demonstrators** hubo choque entre la policía y los manifestantes

class action court case acción colectiva de la corte

class action suit acción popular; demanda colectiva; pleito de clase

clean bill of health certificado de salud

clean hands inocente

clean-shaven *(face)* bien afeitado; bien rasurado; **a clean-shaven man** un hombre sin barba ni bigote

clear *(adj) (easily understood, explanation; instructions)* clara; claro; **is that clear?** ¿está claro?; ¿queda claro?; **it's not entirely clear to me why it's necessary** no me queda muy claro por qué es necesario; **let's get this clear** entendámonos bien; **a clear case of murder** un caso evidente de homicidio; **to make oneself clear** explicarse claramente; *(declare innocent, etc.)* **he was cleared of murder** fue absuelto de asesinato; **she was cleared of the murder charge** fue absuelta del cargo de asesinato

clear and convincing evidence prueba clara y contundente; prueba clara y convincente

clear and present danger peligro claro e inmediato

clear of all charges absolver de todos los cargos

clear one's name limpiar su nombre

clear title título limpio

clearly establishes that ... establece claramente que ...

clerk of the court actuaria; actuario

clergyman *(priest)* clérigo; sacerdote; cura; padre

climate of violence experienced within the family el clima de violencia vivido en el ámbito de la familia

clinic *(in state hospital)* consultorio; *(private)* clínica; **law clinic** consultorio legal; consultorio jurídico

clinical psychologist psicológa clínica; psicológo clínico

clinical records expedientes; registros; récords

close *(link, connection)* ; **they are close friends** son muy amigos; son amigos íntimos; **his closest friends and family** sus amigos y familiares más allegados; **they've always been very close** siempre han sido muy unidos; **they were close collaborators** mantenían una estrecha colaboración

close friends and family amigos y familiares más allegados

close relative cercano pariente

close the file archivar el expediente

closing arguments alegatos de clausura; alegatos finales

closing balance balance de cierre; balance final

closing costs costos de cierre

closing date la fecha de caducidad del plazo; fecha tope; fecha límite

closing statements alegatos de clausura; alegatos finales; informe final

clothes *(noun)* ropa

clothing *(noun)* ropa

coat *(men, women)* abrigo

cocaine *(noun)* cocaína

cocaine adiction cocainomanía

code *(law)* código

code of behavior *(law)* código de conducta

code of practice *(law)* código profesional

co-defendant *(law)* codemandada; codemandado; coacusada; coacusado; coprocesada; coprocesado

coercion *(law)* coacción; **by coercion** bajo coacción; por la fuerza

coercive *(adj)* coactiva; coactivo; coercitiva; coercitivo

cohabitation*(noun)* cohabitación

coherent *(argument)* lógica; logíco; *(account, speech, person)* coherente

coincide *(happen at the same time)* coincidir; **to coincide with** coincidir con; *(agree)* **to coincide with** estar de acuerdo con

coincidence *(chance happening)* casualidad; coincidencia; **what a coincidence!** ¡qué casualidad!; ¡qué coincidencia!; **by coincidence he was there;** dio la casualidad de que estaba allí; **it was pure coincidence that ...** fue pura casualidad que ...; **it was no coincidence that ...** no fue casualidad que ...

coincidentally *(adv)* por casualidad; casualmente

cold *(adj)* **in cold blood** a sangre fría

cold-blooded *(murder)* a sangre fría; *(killer)* despiadada; despiadado; cruel; desalmada; desalmado

cold-hearted *(adj)* insensible; cruel; fría; frío

cold turkey *(slang)* **he went cold turkey for three months** estuvo con el síndrome de abstinencia durante tres meses; **he quit heroin cold turkey** cortó en seco con la heroína; paró en seco con la heroína

colitis *(noun)* colitis; inflamación del colón

collaborate *(verb)* colaborar; **to collaborate on something**; colaborar en algo; **to collaborate with somebody**; colaborar con alguien

collar *(clothing)* cuello

collar *(verb)* agarrar; **they were collared by the police** la policía les echó el guante; **he collared me as I was leaving** me agarró cuando salía

collarbone *(anat)* clavícula

collateral *(fin)* garantía; subsidiaria

collateral evidence prueba inmaterial; prueba colateral

collateral issues *(law: matters not directly related to the main issues of the case)* cuestiones accesorias; cuestiones incidentales

collateral facts hechos collaterales

collateral loan préstamo collateral

collect a debt cobrar una deuda

collect rent cobrar alquiler

collect the evidence recopilar la evidencia

collection charges gastos de cobro

collection of evidence recopilación de evidencia

collective bargaining negociación del convenio colectivo; negociación colectiva

collector *(noun)* cobrador; cobradora; albacea

collusion *(noun)* confabulación; connvivencia; **to be in collusion with somebody** estar coludida con alguien; estar coludido con alguien; estar en colusión con alguien; estar en connvivencia con alguien

Colombian *(adj)* Colombiana; Colombiano

color-blind daltónica; daltónico; daltoniana; daltoniano

color blindness daltonismo

color prejudice prejuicio racial

combat *(noun)* combate; *(verb)* combatir; luchar; **to combat terrorism** combatir contra el terrorismo

combination of impairments combinación de impedimentos

come *(in phrases)* **how come you don't know?** ¿cómo es que no sabes?; **how come you didn't know?** ¿cómo es que no sabías?

come about *(happen)* **it came about that ...** ocurrió que...; sucedió que ...; **how does that come about?** ¿cómo es eso?; **how does it come about that ...?** ¿cómo es que ...?

come at atacar; asaltar; **she was coming at me with a knife** se me venía encima con un cuchillo

come by *(get, acquire)* **how did you come by that scar?** ¿cómo te hiciste esa cicatriz?

come down *(judge, court: decide)* **to come down in favor of somebody** fallar en favor de alguien; **to come down in favor of something** fallar en favor de algo

come from *(originate from)* venir de; ser de; **where do you come from?** ¿de dónde eres?; *(family line)* descender de

come in! it's open ¡entra! está abierto

come off *(take place, come to pass, turn out)* tener lugar; realizarse; **to come off badly** salir mal; **to come off well** salir bien

come up to acercarse; **two policemen came up to him** se le acercaron dos policías

comfort *(mental)* consuelo; **words of comfort** palabras de consuelo; **to give comfort to somebody** consolar a alguien; **to give aid and comfort to terrorists** cooperar con terroristas

coming *(approaching: days, weeks, months, years)* **this coming Monday** este Lunes; el Lunes que viene; **this coming month**; el mes que viene; **this coming year**; el año que viene; **in the coming weeks** en las semanas venideras

command *(language)* **his command of English** su dominio del Inglés; **to have a good command of English** dominar el Inglés

comment *(noun: remark)* comentario; observación; **to make a comment about something** hacer un comentario sobre algo; hacer una observación sobre algo; **to comment on** hacer un comentario de; **he made some nasty comments about her** habló muy mal de ella; **no comment** sin comentario; **I have no further comment to make** no tengo nada que agregar

commit *(law: confine, remand custody)* encerrar; internar; recluir

commit *(law: crime)* cometer; **to commit suicide** suicidarse; **to commit somebody for trial** remitir a alguien al tribunal; **to commit somebody to prison** encarcelar a alguien; **he was committed to prison** fue encarcelado; **she was committed for trial** se dictó auto de procesamiento; **to commit somebody to a mental hospital** internar a alguien en un manicomio; **to commit murder** cometer un asesinato

commit *(pledge)* **he is committed to change** está dedicado a buscar el cambio; **to commit oneself to** comprometerse a; **I can't commit myself** no puedo comprometerme

commit adultery cometer adulterio

commit to trial enjuiciar; **he has not been commited to trial yet** todavía no ha sido enjuiciado

commitment *(noun)* responsabilidad; obligación; **a familiy is a major commitment** una familia es una gran responsabilidad; **he has no family commitments** no tiene obligaciones familiares; no tiene cargas familiares; **to meet one's commitments** hacer frente a sus obligaciones

common *(affecting many, mutual)* común; corriente; **the common people** la gente común y corriente; **he was treated like a common criminal** le trataron como a un vulgar delincuente; **it's common decency** es una cuestión de buena educación; **it's common knowledge** todo el mundo lo sabe; **it's common knowledge that ...** es del dominio público que ...; **to have something in common with somebody** tener algo en común con alguien

common ground *(fig)* puntos comunes; puntos en común

common knowledge de conocimiento común

common language lengua común

common law derecho consuetudinario; derecho común

common-law husband concubino; esposo en un matrimonio por consentimiento mutuo y cohabitación

common-law marriage concubinato; matrimonio por consentimiento mutuo y cohabitación

common-law wife concubina; esposa en un matrimonio por consentimiento mutuo y cohabitación

common pleas acciones civiles

common pleas court tribunal de acciones civiles

common sense sentido común

common sense will prevail se impondrá el sentido común

common thief ladrón habitual

communication *(verbal or written contact)* contacto; *(exchange of information)* comunicación; **to be in communication with** estar en contacto con

community center centro cívico; centro social

community college *establecimiento donde se imparten cursos de nivel terciario de dos años de duración*

community property copropiedad

community relations relaciones con la comuinidad

community service trabajo comunitario *(prestado en lugar de cumplir una pena de prisión)*

community service work trabajo comunitario

commute *(law: reduce sentence or punishment)* conmutar; **the death sentence was commuted to one of life imprisonment** le conmutaron la pena de muerte por la de cadena perpetua

company *(companionship)* compañía; **in somebody's company** en compañía de alguien; **to part company with somebody** separarse de alguien

company *(noun)* compañía; empresa

company address dirección de la compañía; dirección de la empresa

company car coche de empresa; coche de compañía

company name nombre de la compañía; nombre de la empresa

compensate *(verb)* compensar; indemnizar; **to compensate somebody for something** compensar a alguien por algo

compensation *(award)* compensación; *(damages)* indemnización; *(reward)* recompensa; resarcimiento; **in compensation for damages** en compensación por daños

compensation package paquete salarial

compensatory damages indemnización por daños y perjuicios; resarcimiento de daños y perjuicios

compensatory payment indemnización

competence *(law)* aptitud; idoneidad; *(judicial authority)* competencia; **legal competence** aptitud legal

competency *(law)* capacidad mental

competency to stand trial *(law)* capacidad mental para ser juzgada; capacidad mental para ser juzgado

competent *(law)* competente; capaz; **to be competent to** estar capacitada para + *infin*; estar capacitado para + *infin*; **he's competent to stand trial** está capacitado para ser juzgado; está capacitado para ser procesado; *(witness)* hábil; **a competent knowledge of a language** un conocimiento suficiente del idioma

competent evidence *(law)* prueba relevante para demostrar el punto en controversia y adecuada para tal fin

competition court *(law)* tribunal de defensa de la competencia

competitive medical plans planes médicos competitivos

complain *(verb)* quejarse; reclamar; **to complain of something** quejarse de algo

complainant *(law)* actor; actora; demandante

complaining witness *(law)* querellante

complaint *(law: a charge against a person)* denuncia; *(law: formal document)* queja; querrella

complaint *(statement of displeasure)* queja; reclamo; **to make a complaint** quejarse; reclamar; **to lodge a complaint** presentar una queja; hacer una reclamación; **they have no cause for complaint** no tienen motivo de queja; **they have no grounds for complaint** no tienen motivo de queja; **reason for complaint** motivo de queja

complaint form formulario de queja

complaint proceedings recurso de queja

complete *(verb: building, education)* acabar; terminar; *(prison sentence)* cumplir; *(fill in form, questionaire)* llenar; rellenar

complete *(adj: entire, set)* completa; completo; *(finished)* terminada; terminado; concluida; concluido; *(thorough, absolute)* total; completa; completo

complete an application llenar una solicitud; completar una solicitud

complete and sign llenar y firmar

completely *(adv)* completamente; totalmente; por completo; **I completely forgot** me olvidé completamente; me olvidé totalmente; me olvidé por completo; **it's completely and utterly false** es completa y absolutamente falso; **we completely failed to convince them** no logramos convencerlos en absoluto

completely and utterly untrue completa y absolutamente falso

complex case caso complejo

complexion *(skin type)* cutis; *(in terms of color)* tez; **a good complexion** un buen cutis; **a dark complexion** una tez oscura; **a light complexion** una tez clara

compliance *(acquiescence)* acatamiento; conformidad; **compliance with something** conformidad con algo; **in compliance with the law** acatamiento de la ley; en conformidad con la ley; conforme a la ley

compliance with the law acatamiento de la ley

complicity *(noun)* complicidad; estar envuelto en la ejecución de un crimen

comply *(verb)* acatar; cumplir; **to comply with an order** acatar una orden; cumplir una orden; **to comply with the judge's instructions** seguir las instrucciones del juez; **she refused to comply with the order**

se negó a acatar la orden; **to comply with the wishes of the majority** acatar la voluntad de la mayoría

comply with the Constitution acatar la Constitución

comply with the law acatar la ley

composite picture *(law)* retrato robot; retrato hablado

comprehend *(understand)* comprender; **I don't think you fully comprehend the situation** me parece que no acabas de comprender la situación

comprehensive insurance seguro a todo riesgo

comprehensive outpatient rehabilitation rehabilitación completa de pacientes externos; rehabilitación completa de pacientes ambulatorios

compromise *(agreement)* acuerdo mutuo; arreglo; compromiso; **to reach a compromise** llegar a un acuerdo mutuo

compulsive gambler un jugador emperdenido; una jugadora emperdenida; ludópata

compulsive gambling ludopatía

computer crime delitos informáticos

con *(law: prisoner, convict)* presa; preso

con *(law: verb)* timar; estafar; **I've been conned!** ¡me han estafado!; **to con somebody into doing something** engañar a alguien para que haga algo

con man estafador

concealed weapon arma ocultada

concealment *(law)* ocultación; encubrimiento

concealment, detention, taking and retaining of child in violation of custody *(law)* quebrantamiento de las normas de tutela

conceive *(child, to become pregnant)* concebir

concerning *(prep)* sobre; acerca de; concerniente a; tocante a; **I'd like a word with you concerning the case** quisiera hablar con usted sobre el caso; quisiera hablar con usted acerca del caso

conclusive evidence *(law)* prueba concluyente; prueba decisiva

concurrent sentence pena simultánea

concurrently *(adv)* simultáneamente; **the two sentences are to run concurrently** las dos condenas se cumplirán simultáneamente

condemn *(sentence, reprimand)* condenar; **he was condemned to death** lo condenaron a muerte; fue condenado a muerte; **he was condemned to a life of poverty** estaba condenado a vivir en la miseria; **such conduct is to be condemned** tal conducta es censurable

condemnation condena; repulsa; *(sentencing)* condena a algo; *(of property)* declaración de ruinoso; *(of meat; food product)* declaración de no apto para el consumo

condition *(stipulation, requirement)* condición; **under the conditions of the contract** bajo las condiciones del contrato; **she made it a condition that ...** puso como condición que ...; **on condition that ...** con la condición de que; a condición de que ...

conditional *(adj)* condicional

conditional discharge libertad condicional

conditions of employment las condiciones de empleo; las condiciones de trabajo

condone *(adj)* aprobar; consentir; tolerar; **I'm not condoning them** no apruebo su conducta

conduct *(behavior)* conducta; comportamiento; actuación; **disorderly conduct** alteración del orden público; **she was arrested for disorderly conduct** la detuvieron por alteración del orden público; **he criticized the conduct of the police** criticó la actuación de la policía

conduct *(carry out)* llevar a cabo; realizar

confess *(admit)* confesar; **he confessed to five murders** confesó haber cometido cinco asesinatos; **to confess that** confesar que; **to confess one's guilt** reconocer su cupabilidad; **to confess oneself guilty of** confesarse culpable de

confession *(statement)* confesión; **to make a confession** confesar; hacer una confesión; **I have a confession to make** tengo que confesar; tengo que hacerte una confesión

confide *(secret)* confiar; **he confided to me that ...** me dijo en confianza que ...; **he confided his troubles to me** me confió sus problemas; **he confided to me that he was scared** me confió que estaba asustado

confidential informant *(law)* confidente; delator; delatora; soplón; soplona

confidential record expediente confidencial

confidentiality *(noun)* confidencialidad

confine *(imprison)* encerrar; confinar; recluir

confinement *(imprisonment)* arresto; prisión; encarcelamiento; detención; reclusión; **to be in solitary confinement** estar incomunicada; estar incomunicado

confiscate *(verb)* confiscar; decomisar; incautar

confiscated possessions bienes privados

confiscation *(noun)* confiscación; decomiso

conflict *(noun)* conflicto; **to come into conflict with somebody** entrar en conflicto con alguien; **to come into conflict with something** entrar en conflicto con algo; **a conflict of opinions** una discrepencia de opiniones; **in conflict with** en conflicto con

conflict of interest conflicto de intereses

conflicting evidence *(law)* prueba contradictoria; prueba contraria; prueba en contrario

confrontation *(noun: conflict)* enfrentamiento; confrontación; *(of witness in court)* careo

Congressional Hispanic Caucus (CHC) Comité Hispano del Congreso

connected *(ideas, events)* relacionada; relacionado; **the two murders are connected** los dos asesinatos están relacionados entre sí; hay una conexión entre los dos asesinatos

connection *(in phrases)* **she is wanted in connection with the killing** se la busca en conexión con el asesinato; se la busca en relación con el asesinato; **in connection with** con respecto a; en relación a; **in this connection** a este respecto

conscience *(noun)* conciencia; **to have a clear conscience** tener la conciencia tranquila; tener la conciencia limpia; **my conscience is clear!** ¡yo tengo la conciencia tranquila!; **she has a guilty conscience** no tiene la conciencia tranquila

conscience clause *(law) cláusula que salvaguarda la libertad de conciencia*

conscientious objector objetor de conciencia; objetora de conciencia

conscious *(awake, alert)* consciente; **he was fully conscious** estaba totalmente consciente; *(aware)* **to be conscious of something** ser consciente de algo; estar consciente de algo; tener consciencia de algo; **I'm fully conscious of it's importance** estoy plenamente consciente de su importancia

consciousness *(state of being awake, alert)* conocimiento; **to lose consciousness** perder el conocimiento; **to regain consciousness** recobrar el conocimiento

consecutive sentences sentencias consecutivas

consensual oral sex sexo oral consensuado

consensual sex sexo consensuado

consent *(noun)* consentimiento; **with the consent of** con el consentimiento de; **by mutual consent** de mutuo acuerdo; **by common consent** de común acuerdo; **without his consent** sin su consentimiento; *(law)* **age of consent** edad núbil

consent search *(law)* registro con permiso del sujeto

consenting adult *(law) adulto que realiza un acto por su propia y libre voluntad*

consequential damages daño emergente

conserved funds fondos conservados

consideration *(thought, reflection)* consideración; **the matter is under consideration** la cuestión se está estudiando; **after due consideration** después de un detenido examen de la cuestión; **to take something into consideration** tener en cuenta; tomar en consideración

conspiracy *(law: to commit a crime)* asociación delectiva; conspiración de delito

conspiracy to commit a crime conspiración para delinquir

conspiracy to defraud conspiración para defraudar

conspirator *(law)* conspirador; conspiradora

construction ahead *(traffic sign)* Zona de construcción adelante

constructive payment pago implícito

consulate *(noun)* consulado

consultation *(with a lawyer)* consulta

consultative examination examen consultativo

consulting physician médica consultora; médico consultor

Consumer Affairs Office Oficina de Asuntos del Consumidor

Consumer Credit Protection Act (CCPA) Ley de Protección al Crédito del Consumidor

consumer rights derechos del consumidor

constitutional law derecho político

constitutional right derecho constitucional

construe *(verb)* deducir; interpretar

contact *(noun)* contacto; *(verb)* **get in contact** ponerse en contacto; **have contact with** relacionarse con

contact lenses lentes de contacto

contact's name nombre del contacto

contained in the indictment contenido en la acusación

contempt *(scorn)* desprecio; desdén; **he felt nothing but contempt for them** no sentía más que desprecio por ellos; no sentía más que desdén por ellos; **hold in contempt** *(law)* juzgar en rebeldía

contempt of court *(law)* desacato al tribunal; contumacia; **he was in contempt of court** había cometido desacato al tribunal; **to hold somebody in contempt** despreciar a alguien

contend *(verb)* argumentar; mantener; sostener

contention *(noun)* argumento; **it is our contention that ...** pretendemos que ...; sostenemos que ...

contest *(verb)* impugnar; refutar

contested facts *(noun)* hechos contenciosos; hechos controvertidos

contesting paternity impugnación de paternidad

contingent fee honorario de contingencia

contingent of police dispositivo policial

continuance *(law)* aplazamiento; postergación

continuance of eligibility continuación de elegibilidad

continuing disability incapacidad continua

continuing disability reviews revisión de continuación de incapacidad

continuing education educación para adultos

contraband *(noun)* contrabando

contraception on demand libre acceso a los anticonceptivos

contract *(agreement)* contrato; **to sign a contract** firmar un contrato; **to enter into a contract with somebody** hacer un contrato con alguien; **to be under contract to do something** estar bajo contrato para hacer algo; **breach of contract** incumplimiento de contrato

contract *(for murder)* **to put out a contract on somebody** ponerle precio a la cabeza de alguien

contract between sponsor and household member contrato entre el patrocinador y el miembro de la unidad familiar

contract killer asesina a sueldo; asesino a sueldo; sicaria; sicario

contract negotiations negociaciones de contrato

contract of sale contrato de contraventa

contract work trabajo bajo contrato

contracting party pactante

contractor contratista

contractually *(noun)* contractualmente; **a contractually binding agreement** un acuerdo vinculante según contrato; **we are contractually bound to finish it** estamos obligados por contrato a terminarlo

contradict *(verb)* contrar

contrary to general belief contrariamente a lo que en general se cree; contrariamente a la opinión generalizada

contravention *(noun)* contravención; infracción; **to be in contravention of the law** estar en contravención de la ley; **to act in contravention of the law** obrar en contravención de la ley

contribution *(noun)* contribución; *(to social security fund)* cotización; aporte

controlled substance sustancia regulada; **criminal possession of a controlled substance** tenencia ilícita de sustancias reguladas

contusion *(noun)* contusión

convalescent home clínica de reposo; casa de convalecencia

convalescent hospital hospital para convalescientes

convenience items artículos de conveniencia

conversion *(law)* apropiación indebida; conversión; transformación

conveyance *(law: transfer of property)* traspaso; transferencia; **deed of conveyance** escritura de compraventa

convict *(found guilty; pled guilty)* condenada; condenado; convicta; convicto; rea; reo; penada; penado

convict *(serving prison term)* presidiaria; presidiario; presa; preso

convict *(verb)* declarar culpable; condenar; juzgar culpable; **she was convicted on eight charges of espionage** fue declarada culpable de ocho acusaciones de espionaje; **a convicted rapist** un violador convicto; **a convicted murderer** un asesino convicto; una asesina convicta; **to be convicted of something** ser condenada por algo; ser condenado por algo; **he was convicted for murdering his wife** fue condenado por el asesinato de su esposa; **he was convicted of drunk driving** fue condenado por conducir en estado de embriaguez; **he was convicted of stealing** lo condenaron por robo

convicted felon criminal convicto que ha cometido un delito grave

convicted rapist violador convicto; violadora convicta

convicted murderer asesina convicta; asesino convicto

conviction *(law)* condena; fallo condenatorio; sentencia condenatoria; **with that evidence they were able to secure a conviction** con esas pruebas lograron que se la condenara; con esas pruebas lograron que se lo condenara; **he had several previous convictions for theft** tenía varias condenas previas por robo; **there were 12 convictions for theft** hubo 12 condenas por robo; **to have no previous convictions** no tener antecedentes penales

conviction *(strong belief)* convicción; **it is my conviction that** creo firmamente que; **he spoke without much conviction** habló sin mucha convicción

conviction upheld convicción confirmada

convince *(verb)* convencer; **that doesn't convince me** eso no me convence; **to convince somebody of something** convencer a alguien de algo; **he failed to convince them of his innocence** no logró convencerlos de su inocencia; **to convince somebody that** convencer a alguien de que

convinced *(persuaded)* **to be convinced of something** estar convencida de algo; estar convencido de algo; **to be convinced that** estar convencida de que; estar convencido de que

convincing *(adj)* convincente

convincingly *(adv)* convincentemente

cook *(noun)* cocinera; cocinero

cook the books *(alter, doctor)* amañar los libros; amañar el informe oficial

cool *(person, calm)* **keep cool!** ¡tranquila!; ¡tranquilo!; no te pongas nerviosa; no te pongas nervioso; no perder la calma *(set phrase)* **cool, calm and collected** tranquila y serena; tranquilo y sereno; **to keep a cool head** no perder la calma; **to play it cool** tomarse las cosas con calma; tomársela con calma; tomárselo con calma

cool down *(become less angry)* calmarse

cool off *(become less angry)* calmarse

cooling off period *(between two parties)* período de enfriamiento durante el cual ninguna parte en el litigio debe tomar acción alguna

cooperate *(verb)* cooperar; colaborar; **to cooperate with the authorities** cooperar con las autoridades

cop *(colloquial: policeman)* poli; tira; cana; paca; paco; **the cops** la poli; la plasma; la cana

copycat *(noun)* imitador; imitadora

copycat crime crimen de imitación

copyright *(noun)* derechos de reproducción

copyright right dereccho de autor

cordless telephone teléfono inalámbrico; teléfono sin hilos

corner *(noun: of street)* esquina

coroner *(noun)* médica forense; médico forense

corporal punishment pena corporal

correct *(adj)* correcta; correcto; exacta exacto; **that's correct!** ¡correcto!; **you are correct** tiene razón; usted está en lo cierto; **I stand corrected** reconozco el error

corrective lenses lentes correctivos

corroborate *(verb)* corroborar

corroboration *(noun)* corroboración; **they produced evidence in corroboration of her story** presentaron pruebas que corroboraban su versión

corroborative *(law: information, facts, statement)* corroborante

corroborative evidence pruebas corroborantes; **for want of corroborative evidence** a falta de pruebas corroborantes

corrupt *(person)* corrupta; corrupto; corrumpida; corrumpido

corrupt practices *(law)* corrupción; corruptela

corruption *(of morals; person)* corrupción; **he was accused of bribery and corruption** lo acusaron de soborno y corrupción

cost efficient rentable

cost of living, the el costo de la vida

cost of living adjustment ajuste del costo de la vida

costs *(noun)* costos

could *(in phrases)* **I would help if I could** te ayudaría si pudiera; **you could be right** puede ser que tengas razón; **that could be the case, but we have no evidence** pudiera ser, pero no tenemos pruebas; **we couldn't possibly agree to that** de ninguna manera podríamos acceder a eso

counsel *(law, advice)* abogada; abogado; consejo; asesora legal; asesor legal; **opposing counsel** abogada de la parte contraria; abogado de la parte contraria; **retained counsel** abogada contratada; abogado contratado; **to hold counsel with somebody** asesorarse con alguien; **to take counsel with somebody** aconsejarse con alguien; **to have the right to counsel** tener el derecho a ser representado por un abogado en el tribunal; derecho a tener un abogado

counsel *(verb)* aconsejar; recomendar; **to counsel somebody to** + *infin* aconsejarle a alguien que + *subj*; **he counseled against taking legal action** aconsejo no entablar demanda; aconsejo que no entablara demanda

counsel for the defense abogada defensora; abogado defensor

counsel for the prosecution fiscal

counsel of record abogada patrocinante; abogado patrocinante

counseling *(noun)* terapia

counseling services servicios de asesoramiento; servicios de orientación; servicios de consejo

counselor *(law)* abogada; abogado

counselor-at-law *(law)* abogada; abogado

counselors-at-law *(law)* abogada; abogado

count *(law; particular, point)* capítulo; punto; **to be found guilty on all counts** ser declarado culpable de todos los cargos; **they're right on the first count** en el primer punto tienen razón

countable resources recursos incluíbles; recursos contables

counter offer contra oferta

counterproductive *(adj)* contraproducente

country *(noun)* país; *(native land)* patria

country of birth país de nacimiento

country of last residence país de su última residencia

county *(noun)* condado

county court juzgado comarcal; juzgado de primera instancia

county road *(traffic sign)* vía municipal; vía del condado

couple *(two people)* pareja; **a married couple** un matrimonio

course of action *(law)* acción de la justicia; **interfere with the course of justice** entorpecer la acción de la justicia

court *(law)* tribunal; corte; juzgado; **the court will arise** pónganse de pie; **to appear in court** comparecer ante el tribunal; comparecer ante los tribunales; **I'll see you in court!** ¡te voy a demandar!; **to go to court** acudir a los tribunales; **to take somebody to court** demandar a alguien; llevar a alguien a juicio; llevar a alguien a los tribunales; **in open court** en audiencia pública; **the court is adjourned** se levanta la sesión; **to settle out of court** transigir extrajudicialmente; llegar a una transacción extrajudicial; **district court** tribunal de distrito

court appearance comparecencia ante el tribunal; comparición; apersonamiento

court appointed attorney abogada nombrada por la corte; abogado nombrado por la corte; abogada de oficio; abogado de oficio

court calendar lista de causas; orden del día

court case causa; juicio

court clerk actuaria; actuario; secretaria de actas; secretario de actas

court date fecha de corte; **first court date** primera fecha de corte

court docket lista de causas; orden del día

court hearing vista

court injunction *(law)* mandamiento judicial

court of appeals corte de apelación; tribunal de apelación; tribunal de segunda instancia

court of claims tribunal de reclamaciones

court of inquiry comisión de investigación

court of justice tribunal de justicia

court of law tribunal de justicia; tribunal judicial; juzgado

court official funcionaria del juzgado; funcionario del juzgado

court order mandamiento judicial; orden judicial; orden del tribunal; providencia

court proceedings proceso; autos procesales

court records actas del tribunal

court reporter taquígrafa de actas; taquígrafo de actas; persona que transcribe lo secedido en un proceso judicial

court stenographer taquígrafa de actas; taquígrafo de actas; persona que transcribe lo secedido en un proceso judicial

court trial juicio sin jurado

courthouse *(noun)* juzgado

courtroom sala de un tribunal

cousin *(noun)* prima; primo; **first cousin** prima hermana; primo hermano; **second cousin** prima segunda; primo segundo; *(cousin to one's parents)* **cousin once removed** tía segunda; tío segundo

cover *(insurance)* cobertura; **the policy provides third party cover** la póliza cubre contra terceros; **to take out cover against something** asegurarse contra algo; *(envelope)* **under separate cover** por separado; **under plain cover** sobre sin membrete; **to take cover** ponerse a cubierto; **to run for cover** correr a ponerse a cubierto

cover up *(noun)* encubrimiento de actvidades ilícitas; maniobra para encubrir; *(verb: facts, truth)* ocultar; tapar; *(mistake)* disimular; *(conceal error)* disimular; **to cover up for somebody** encubrir a alguien

coverage *(insurance)* cobertura; **the policy provides third party coverage** la póliza cubre contra terceros; **to take out coverage against something** asegurarse contra algo

coverage of prenatal care cobertura de atención prenatal

covered *(adj)* cubierta; cubierto

covered by Social Security cubierta por la Ley de Seguro Social; cubierto por la Ley de Seguro Social

co-worker *(noun)* colega; compañera de trabajo; compañero de trabajo

crack *(drug)* crack

crack down *(adv)* **to crack down on somebody** tomar medidas energéticas contra alguien; **to crack down on something** tomar medidas energéticas contra algo

crackhead *(slang)* adicta al crack; adicto al crack

cradle robber *(colloquial)* corruptor de menores; corruptora de menores

cradle snatcher *(colloquial)* corruptor de menores; corruptora de menores

credentials *(noun: ambassador)* cartas credenciales; referencias; **she has excellent credentials** tiene excelentes referencias

credibility *(noun)* credibilidad; **to lack credibility** carecer de credibilidad

credible *(adj)* creíble

credible evidence *(law)* prueba creíble

credit card tarjeta de crédito

credit line línea de crédito

creditor *(noun)* creedor; creedora

creditworthiness *(noun)* capacidad de pago; solvencia

creditworthy *(adj)* con capacidad de pago; solvente

crew leader jefe de cuadrilla, capataz; troquero, contratista

crib death muerte de cuna

crime *(wrongful act)* delito; *(murder)* crimen; **to commit a crime** cometer un crimen; cometer un delito; **the scene of the crime** el lugar del delito; el lugar del crimen; la escena del crimen; **a life of crime** una vida de delincuencia; **an increase in crime** un aumento de la delincuencia; un aumento de la criminalidad

crime laboratory laboratorio criminológico

crime of passion crimen passional

crime prevention la prevención del crimen; la prevención de la delincuencia

crime punishable by death un delito castigado con la pena de muerte

crime report informe sobre delitos

crime scene lugar del crimen; lugar del delito

crime victim víctima de un crimen; víctimas de delitos criminales

crime wave ola delictiva

crimes of violence delitos violentos

criminal *(noun)* delincuente; *(serious offender)* criminal

criminal *(adj: of crime)* delictiva; delictivo; *(case)* criminal; *(bankruptcy)* fraudulente

criminal act acto criminoso; hecho delictivo; hecho delictuoso

criminal and social history information información sobre los antecedentes penales y sociales

criminal case causa penal

criminal charge acusación; cargo; imputación

criminal code código penal

criminal conviction condena criminal

criminal court juzgado de lo penal; tribunal que sólo trata con asuntos criminales; sala de lo penal

criminal damage to property daños en propiedad ajena

criminal defense lawyer abogada de defensa penal; abogado de defensa penal

criminal judgement fallo criminal

criminal law derecho penal

criminal lawyer abogada criminalista; abogado criminalista; abogada penalista; abogado penalista

criminal matters asuntos penales; cuestiones penales

criminal negligence negligencia criminal; imprudencia temeraria

criminal offense delito

criminal offense report informe sobre delitos

criminal possession tenencia

criminal possession of a controlled substance tenencia ilícita de sustancias reguladas

criminal possession of a dangerous weapon tenencia ilícita de armas peligrosas

criminal possession of a weapon tenencia ilícita de armas

criminal possession of receiving stolen goods tenencia ilícita de bienes hurtados

criminal possession of receiving stolen property tenencia ilícita de bienes hurtados

criminal possession of stolen property tenencia ilícita de bienes hurtados

criminal proceedings causa criminal; acto procesal penal; proceso criminal; actuaciones penales; **it could give rise to criminal proceedings** podría dar lugar a actuaciones penales

criminal procedure law derecho procesal penal

criminal record antecedentes penales; **to have a criminal record** tener antecedentes penales

criminal responsibility responsabilidad criminal; responsabilidad penal

criminal restraint constreñimiento ilegal

criminal sale of a controlled substance venta ilícita de sustancias reguladas

criminal sanctions sanción penal

criminal sexual contact abuso deshonesto

criminal sexual contact of a minor abuso deshonesto de un menor

criminal sexual penetration acceso carnal violento

criminal trial causa criminal

criminally *(law)* **they're criminally liable** se les puede imputar delito; **an institution for the criminally insane** una institución penitenciaria para delincuentes psicóticos

criminologist *(noun)* criminóloga; criminólogo

criminology *(noun)* criminología

crippled *(adj)* lisiada; lisiado; impedida; impedido; tullida tullido

criteria *(noun)* criterios

critical condition estado crítico

critically *(crucially)* fundamentalmente; **critically important** de importancia fundamental

crony *(colloquial)* compinche

crook *(thief)* ladrona; ladrón; sinvergüenza; pilla; pillo

crooked *(colloquial: dishonest)* deshonesta; deshonesto; chueca; chueco

cross *(noun: relig)* cruz; *(verb)* cruzar; atravesar

cross-examination repreguntas; contrainterrogación; **under cross-examination** durante las repreguntas; durante la contrainterrogación

cross-examine repreguntar; contrainterrogar

cross out *(on form)* tachar

cross-refer referir; **to cross refer somebody to something** remitir a alguien a algo; **cross refer something to something** remitir de algo a algo

cross-reference remisión

cross road *(traffic sign)* cruce de caminos; Intersección

cross the border cruzar la frontera

crossing *(traffic sign)* cruce

crosswalk *(noun)* cruce de peatones

cruel and unusual punishment penas crueles e inusuales

cruelty *(noun)* crueldad

crutches *(noun)* muletas

Cuban *(noun & adj)* cubana; cubano

culpability *(noun)* culpabilidad

culpable *(adj: person)* culpable; imputable; **to hold someone culpable for something** considerar a alguien culpable de algo

culpable negligence negligencia culposa

culprit *(noun)* culpable; *(law)* inculpada; inculpado

cumulative evidence evidencia acumulativa

cumulative sentence pena sucesiva

cumulative sentences penas sucesivas; acumulación de penas

curfew *(noun)* toque de queda; **to be under curfew** estar bajo toque de queda; **they went out after curfew** salieron después del toque de queda

current account cuenta corriente

current assets activo circulante; activo corrienta

current liabilities pasivo circulante

current market value valor actual en el mercado

current year año actual; el presente año

currently insured actualmente asegurada; actualmente asegurado

curriculum *(range of courses)* plan de estudios; *(for single courses)* programa de estudio; currículo

curve ahead *(traffic sign)* curva adelante

custodial care cuidado custodial

custodial sentence pena de prisión; pena privativa de libertad

custodian *(noun)* guardían; guardiana

custody *(detention)* **to be in police custody** estar detenida; estar detenido; **to take somebody into custody** detener a alguien; **he was taken into custody and turned over to the juvenile court** fue detenido y entregado al tribinal de menores; *(of child)* custodia; guarda; **he was given custody of the children** le dieron la custodia de los niños; le otorgaron la custodia de los niños; **in the custody of** al cargo de; al cuidado de

custody *(of children)* patria potestad; custodia

custody arrangement arreglos de custodia

custody cases casos de custodia

custody of the children custodia de los niños

custom *(noun)* costumbre

customs *(noun)* aduana; **to go through customs** pasar por la aduana

customs agent agente de aduanas

customs declaration declaración de aduana

customs duty derechos de aduana

customs official oficial de aduanas

cystic fibrosis fibrosis cística

D

dad *(colloquial: father)* papá

daddy *(colloquial: father)* papi

dagger *(weapon)* daga; puñal

daily maintenance manutención diaria; mantenimiento diario

damage *(to object)* daño; *(to reputation, cause)* daño; perjuicio; *(phrases)* **the damage is done** el daño ya está hecho; **what's the damage?** ¿cuánto va a ser?; ¿por cuánto salió?; **minor damages** daños menores

damage *(verb: harm)* dañar; perjudicar

damages *(law)* daños y perjuicios

danger *(noun)* peligro; **to be in danger** estar en peligro; **there's no danger of that** no hay peligro de que eso suceda; **her life is in danger** su vida está en peligro; su vida está en riesgo; **the doctor said he is out of danger** el médico dijo que está fuera de peligro

dangerous *(adj)* peligrosa; peligroso

dangerous driving conducción con imprudencia temeraria

dangerous weapon arma peligrosa

dangerously *(adv)* peligrosamente; **to live dangerously** llevar una vida arriesgada

dark glasses gafas oscuras

dark-skinned morena; moreno

date *(noun)* fecha; **closing date** la fecha de caducidad del plazo; **what's the date today?** ¿qué fecha es hoy?; ¿a qué fecha tenemos?; **to date** hasta la fecha; **the letter was dated May 12** la carta estaba fechada el doce de mayo

date of birth fecha de nacimiento

date of crime fecha del crimen; fecha del delito

date of deposition fecha de la deposición

date rape violación durante una cita

daughter *(noun)* hija

daughter-in-law *(noun)* nuera

dawn *(daybreak)* amanecer; **at dawn** al amanecer

dawn on *(phrase)* **it dawned on me that ...** caí en la cuenta de que ...

day *(noun)* día; **two days ago** hace dos días; **in two days** dentro de dos días; **all day** todo el día; **during the day** durante el día; **the day before** el día anterior; **on the following day** al día siguiente; **the day before yesterday** anteayer

day care *(for children)* servicio de guardería infantil

day care provider *(for children)* proveedor de servicio de guardería infantil

day in court *expresión que indica el derecho que tiene toda persona de ser notificada sobre el proceso en el cual se involucra su interés, así de ser escuchada en audiencia*

day laborer jornalera; jornalero; bracera; bracero

day nursery guardía infantil

daylight *(phrase)* **in broad daylight** en plena luz del día

daylight saving time hora de verano

days leading up to his death días precedentes a su muerte; **the days leading up to his death** los días precedentes a su muerte

days preceding his death días precedentes a su muerte; **the days preceding his death** los días precedentes a su muerte

dead *(no longer alive)* muerta; muerto; **he's dead** está muerto; **to shoot somebody dead** matar a alguien a tiros; **to strike somebody dead** matar a alguien a golpes

dead body cadáver; cuerpo sin vida

dead drunk completamente borracha; completamente borracho

dead on arrival ingresar cadáver

deadlocked jury jurado en desacuerdo; jurado sin veredicto

deadly force uso de fuerza letal; fuerza mortal

deaf *(adj)* sorda; sordo; **to be deaf in one ear** ser sorda de un oído; ser sordo de un oído; **he's deaf and dumb** es sordomudo

deaf and dumb sordomuda; sordomudo

deal *(noun)* acuerdo; trato; transacción; **it's a deal!** ¡trato hecho!

deal with abordar; **they will have to deal with these problems** tendrán que abordar estos problemas

dealing in stolen property tráfico de bienes hurtados

death *(noun)* muerte; fallecimiento; **an early death** una muerte prematura; una muerte temprana; **he was stabbed to death** lo mataron a puñaladas; **he was beaten to death** lo mataron a golpes; **he was sentenced to death** lo condenaron a muerte; **to freeze to death** morirse de frío; **to starve to death** morirse de hambre; **to bleed to death** morir desangrada; morir desangrado; **he drank himself to death** el alcohol acabó con él; el alcohol lo mató; **to die a natural death** morir de muerte natural; **to put somebody to death** ejecutar a alguien; dar muerte a alguien

death blow golpe mortal

death by misadventure *(law)* muerte accidental

death certificate acta de defunción; certificado de defunción

death penalty pena de muerte

death pension beneficios de pension por fallecimiento

death row corredor de la muerte

death sentence pena de muerte

death warrant orden de ejecución; sentencia de muerte

death wish *(psych)* pulsión de muerte

debit card tarjeta de débito

debt *(noun)* deuda; **bad debt** deuda incobrable; **to be in debt** tener deudas; estar endeuada; estar endeuado; **to get into debt** contraer deudas; cargarse de deudas; llenarse de deudas; **to be out of debt** tener las deudas saldadas; **to be deeply in debt** estar muy cargada de deudas; estar muy cargado de deudas; **he's hopelessly in debt** está agobiado de deudas

debt-collection agency agencia de cobro

debt collector cobrador de deudas; cobradora de deudas

debt-ridden agobiada por las deudas; agobiado por las deudas

decayed tooth diente cariado

deceased *(adj)* difunta; difunto; **her deceased husband** su difunto marido

decedent outside of U.S. fallecida fuera de Estados Unidos; fallecido fuera de Estados Unidos

deceit *(noun)* engaño; fraude; trampa; mentira; **she is full of deceit** es muy falsa; **he obtained the money by deceit** se hizo con el dinero mediante engaños

deceitful *(adj: person)* falsa; falso; embustera; embustero; engañosa; engañoso

deceitful crime delito doloso

deceive *(verb)* engañar; defraudar; **she deceived me into thinking that ...** me engañó, haciéndome pensar que ...

December*(noun)* Diciembre *(see* **July** *for usage)*

deception *(noun)* engaño; trampa; mentira; fraude

The Deceptive Mailings Prevention Act La Ley de Prevención de Correspondencia Fraudulenta

decide *(verb: person)* decidir; **you must decide what to do** tú tienes que decidir qué vas a hacer; **you must decide when to act** tú tienes que decidir cuándo debes actuar; **you must decide where to go** tú tienes que decidir adónde vas a ir; **have you decided anything yet?** ¿ya has decidido algo? ¿ya has resuelto algo?

decision *(law)* fallo; resolución; *(selection, choice)* decisión; **it's your decision** es tu decisión; **to make a decision** tomar una decisión

declaration *(law: finding)* pronunciamiento; *(law: statement)* declaración

declare *(state; announce)* declarar; *(opinion)* manifestar

decrease *(noun)* disminución; descenso; **crime is on the decrease** la delincuencia está disminuyendo

decree *(noun)* decreto; **to issue a decree** promulgar un decreto; *(verb)* decretar

deductible *(adj)* deducible

deduction *(noun)* deducción; descuento; **he gets $12 a week after deductions** gana doce dólares semanales netos

deed *(law)* escritura; **the deed to the house** la escritura de la casa

deed of conveyance escritura de compraventa

deed to the house la escritura de la casa

deed to the land la escritura del terreno

deem *(verb)* considerar; atribuir

deemable income ingreso atribuible

deemed child hija atribuída; hijo atribuído

deemed income ingreso atribuído

deep *(in phrases)* **it is with deep regret that ...** es con gran pesar que ...; es con profundo pesar que ...; **there is deep suspicion that ...** existen grandes sospechas de que ...; existen graves sospechas de que ...; **to be in deep trouble** estar en un serio apuro; estar en un buen lío; **it left a deep impression on me** me causó una profunda impresión; **deep down you know I'm right** en el fondo sabes que tengo razón

deeper interrogation of the client más profundo interrogatorio del cliente

deeper interrogation of the witness más profundo interrogatorio del testigo

deface *(verb)* disfigurar

defamation *(noun)* difamación; **to sue somebody for defamation of character** demandar a alguien por difamación

default *(on payments)* mora; *(failure to appear in court)* incomparecencia; *(law)* rebeldía; **he won his case by default** ganó el caso en rebeldía del demandado; **she is in default of her mortgage** está en mora en los pagos de la hipoteca

default interest interés de mora

default judgement fallo por falta de comparecencia

defect *(noun)* defecto; **a speech defect** un defecto en el habla; **a birth defect** un defecto de nacimiento

defend *(law)* defender; **she hired a lawyer to defend her** contrató a un abogado para que la defendiera; **Jones was defending and Ríos prusecuting** Jones actuaba por la defensa y Ríos por la acusación

defend the legal rights of the accused defender los derechos legales de la acusada; defender los derechos legales del acusado

defending counsel abogada defensora; abogado defensor

defendant *(in civil case)* demandada; demandado; *(in criminal case)* acusada; acusado; imputada; imputado; inculpada; inculpado; procesada; procesado

defendant's seat in court banquillo

defending *(law)* abogada defensora; abogado defensor

defense *(law)* defensa; descarga; **the accused will conduct his own defense** el acusado se hará cargo de su propia defensa; el acusado llevará su propia defensa; **ignorance of the law is no defense** la ignorancia de la ley no exime de su cumplimiento; **the defense** la defensa; **the case for the defense** el argumento de la defensa; **witness for the defense** testigo de cargo; testigo de la defensa

defense counsel abogada defensora; abogado defensor

defense lawyer abogada defensora; abogado defensor

defense witness testigo de la defensa

deferment *(noun)* aplazamiento; diferimiento

deferred *(law)* aplazada; aplazado; *(charges)* diferida; diferido

deferred compensation compensación aplazada; compensación diferida

deferred fine *(law)* multa aplazada

deferred inspection inspección diferida

deferred payment pago a plazos

defiance *(noun)* desafío; **in defiance of the law** desafiando la ley; en desafío a la ley; **an act of defiance** un desafío; un acto de rebeldía; **in defiance of her orders** haciendo caso omiso de sus órdenes; a despecho de sus órdenes; **he acted in defiance of the regulations** no respetó el reglamento

defiance of authority desfiando la autoridad

defiant *(attitude, tone, answer)* desafiante; *(person)* rebelde

defiantly *(adv)* con actitud desafiante; insolentemente

definitely *(without doubt)* **it's definitely true** no hay deuda de que es cierto; **it's definitely better** es mucho mejor; **I'll definitely go** seguro que iré

defraud *(person)* estafar; **to defraud somebody of something** estafarle algo a alguien; **he defrauded the firm of 100,000 dollars** estafó cien mil dólares de la compañía

defy *(challenge: person)* desafiar; retar; **I defy you to do it** te desafío a hacerlo; *(refuse to obey: person)* resistir; oponerse a

degree *(law)* **first degree murder** asesinato en primer grado; homicidio en primer grado; **second degree murder** asesinato en segundo grado; homicidio en segundo grado

degree *(level, amount)* grado; nivel; **it's a matter of degree** es cuestión de grados; depende de hasta que punto; **it's a question of degree** es cuestión de grados; depende de hasta que punto; **to such a degree that**

... hasta tal punto que ...; **to a certain degree** hasta cierto punto; **to some degree** hasta cierto punto; **to the highest degree** en sumo grado; **a high degree of uncertainty** un alto grado de incertidumbre

dejected *(adj)* abatida; abatido; desalentada; desalentado; con el ánimo por el suelo

dejection *(noun)* abatimiento; desánimo

delay *(make late, hold up)* **the judge delayed the start of the trial** el juez demoró el comienzo del juicio; **I was delayed by the traffic** me retrasé por el tráfico; me demoré por el tráfico

delayed retirement credits créditos por jubilación aplazada; créditos por jubilación demorada

deliberate *(verb)* deliberar; **the jury is deliberating** el jurado está deliberando

deliberation *(law)* deliberación; **after long deliberations** tras largas deliberaciones

delinquency *(law)* delincuencia; *(fin)* mora

delinquency charge recargo de mora

delinquent *(noun)* delincuente

delivery room sala de parto

demand *(noun: claim)* exigencia; *(request)* petición; pedido; **to comply with somebody's demand** satisfacer las exigencias de alguien; **the trial made enormous demands on his health** el juicio puso a prueba su salud; **abortion on demand** libre aborto; **contraception on demand** libre acceso a los anticonceptivos

demand *(verb: call for, insist)* exigir; preguntar; **I demand a fair trial** exijo un juicio imparcial; **they're demanding immediate payment of the debt** exijen el pago inmediato de la deuda; **the unions are demanding better working conditions** los sindicatos reclaman mejores condiciones de trabajo; **to demand money with menaces** *(law)* exigir dinero con intimidación; **she demanded to know the reason** quiso saber el por qué; exijió que se le dijera por qué; **to demand something of somebody** exigirle algo a alguien

demand for payment aviso de pago; **last demand for payment** último aviso de pago

demise *(law)* transferencia en arrendamiento; *(death)* fallecimiento; **upon his demise** tras su fallecimiento

demonstrate *(verb: show)* demostrar; manifestarse

denial *(law: of justice, rights)* denegación; **a denial of justice** una denegación de justicia; *(of accusation, fact);* **to issue a denial** publicar un desmentido; **to issue a denial of something** desmentir algo; **he issued a written denial** publicó un desmentido; lo desmintió por escrito; **his denial was pointless as we had proof** era absurdo que lo negara ya que teníamos prueba

denial letter carta de denegación

denial notice aviso de denegaci

denounce *(inform against)* denunciar; **they denounced him to the police as a thief** lo denunciaron a la policía por ladrón

dental care cuidado dental

dental cavity diente cariado

dentures *(noun)* dentadura postiza

deny *(law: charge)* rechazar; *(report)* desmentir; *(accusation, fact)* **to deny having done ...** negar haber hecho ...; **to deny that ...** negar que ...; **there's no denying it** no se puede negar; **there's no denying that** es innegable que; no se puede negar que; **he denies having said it** niega haberlo dicho; **to deny somebody something** negarle algo a alguien; **to deny oneself something** privarse de algo; **he denied that other people had been present** negó que hubiera habido alguien más presente; **she denied stealing it** negó haberlo robado; **she denied having stolen it** negó haberlo robado; **justice has been denied us** no se nos ha hecho justicia

deny a motion denegar el pedimento

depart *(deviate from)* **to depart from something** apartarse de; alejarse de; **his version departs from the truth on several points** su versión se aparte de la verdad en varios puntos; su versión se aleja de la verdad en varios puntos

Department of Corrections Departamento de Correcciones

Department of Health and Human Services (HHS) Departamento de Salud y Servicios Sociales

Department of Homeland Security (DHS) Departamento de Seguridad de la Patria; Departamento de Seguridad Nacional

Department of Housing and Urban Development (HUD) Departamento de Vivienda y Desarrollo Urbano

Department of Human Resources Departamento de Recursos Humanos

Department of Justice Departamento de Justicia

Department of Labor Departamento del Trabajo

Department of Labor's Wage & Hour Division Departamento del Trabajo, División de Salarios y Horarios

Department of Public Welfare Departamento de Bienestar Público

Department of Public Works of the County of ... Departamento de Obras Públicas del Condado de ...

Department of the Youth Authority Dirección de Juventud

Department of Veterans Affairs Departamento de Asuntos del Veterano

dependency *(noun)* dependencia; dominio; **drug dependency** drogadependencia

dependency and support dependencia y mantenimiento

depend *(verb: rely on)* **to depend on** contar con; depender de; **you can depend on it!** ¡tenlo por seguro!; **you can depend on me!** ¡cuenta conmigo!; **you can depend on her support** puedes contar con su apoyo; **some people just can't be depended on** no se puede contar con ciertas personas; no se puede confiar en ciertas personas; **I'll be there, you can count on it** estaré allí, cuenta con ello; estaré allí, tenlo por seguro; **you can't depend on him to tell the truth** no puedes estar seguro de que va a decir la verdad

dependent *(noun)* dependiente; how many dependents does he have? ¿cuántas personas tiene a su cargo?

dependence *(addiction)* dependencia; **drug dependence** drogadependencia

deport *(expel from country)* deportar; expulsar del país; desterrar

deportation *(noun)* deportación

depose *(law)* declarar; deponer

deposit *(leave)* depositar; **I deposited my will with my lawyer** dejé el testamento en manos de mi abogado

deposit *(noun)* arras

deposit account cuenta de ahorros

deposit slip hoja de ingreso; comprobante de depósito; resguardo de ingreso; volante de depósito

deposition *(law)* deposición; declaración jurada extrajudicial; **to take a deposition** tomar una deposición; **date of deposition** fecha de la deposición; **time of deposition** hora de la deposición

deposition details *(law)* detalles de la deposición

depressed *(adj)* deprimida; deprimido; abatida; abatido; **she's feeling a bit depressed** anda un poco deprimida; **to become depressed** deprimirse; dejarse abatir; **to get depressed about something** deprimirse por algo

depressing *(adj)* deprimente

depression *(despondency)* depresión; abatimiento; **to suffer from depression** sufrir depressiones

deprive *(verb)* privar; **he was deprived of his freedom** se vio privado de su libertad

deputy Commissioner comisionada adjunta; comisionado adjunto

deputy sheriff ayudante del sheriff

derelict *(adj: ruined, building, area)* abandonadas y en ruinas; abandonados y en ruinas

dereliction of duty negligencia en el cumplimiento del deber

describe *(person, scene)* describir; **describe him for us** descríbenoslo; **describe it for me** descríbemelo; **could you describe the thief to me?** ¿me podría describir al ladrón?; **how would you describe yourself** ¿cómo se definiría?; ¿cómo te definirías?

description *(of person, scene, event)* descripción; **I was able to identify the car from his description** pude identificar el coche gracias a su descripción; **I know no one answering that description** no conozca a nadie que responda a esa descripción; **she gave an accurate description of events** hizo una fiel descripción de los hechos; **give a short description of the crime** dé una breve descripción del delito

description of the charges descripción de los cargos

desert *(verb)* abandonar; huir; **they deserted their children** abandonaron a sus hijos; **she deserted the baby at the entrance to the hospital** abandonó al bebé en la puerta del hospital

designer drug droga de laboratorio

desk job empleo de oficina; trabajo de oficina

despair *(noun)* desesperación; **she was in despair** estaba desesperada; **in despair** desesperada; desesperado

despair *(verb)* perder las esperanzas; desesperar

desperate *(adj: person, attempt)* desesperada; desesperado; **to be desperate** estar desesperada; estar desesperado; **they're getting desperate** se están empezando a desesperar; **I'm afraid he'll do something desperate** tengo miedo de que haga alguna locura; **we are getting desperate** estamos al borde de la desesperación

desperation *(noun)* desesperación; **in desperation** en la desesperación

despite *(prep)* a pesar de; **he appeared in court despite his illness** compareció ante el tribunal a pesar de su enfermedad; compareció ante el tribunal a pesar de estar enfermo

despondency *(noun)* abatimiento; desaliento

despondent abatida; abatido; desanimada; desanimado; descorazonada; descorazonado

destitute *(adj: very poor)* indigente; **she was left destitute** quedó en la indigencia; quedó en la miseria

destroy *(verb)* destruir; **destroy the lives of many people** destruir muchas vidas; **detail** *(noun)* detalle; pormenor; **in detail** detallamente; **to go into detail** entrar en detalles; **down to the last detail** hasta en los menores detalles; **he asked for further details** pidió más información detallada; **there's no need to go into detail** no es necesario entrar en detalles; **he went into great detail** lo contó con todos los detalles; lo contó con todos los pormenores; **to describe something in detail** describir algo detalladamente; **to explain something in detail** explicar algo detalladamente

detain *(suspect, criminal)* detener

detective *(private)* detective; *(in police force)* agente; oficial

detective agency agencia de detectives

detective work pesquisas; investigaciones

detention *(in custody)* detención; arresto; **he spent three weeks in detention** estuvo detenido tres semanas

detention center centro de rehabilitación; reformatorio de menores; correccional de menores; centro de detención

detention center for minors centros de detención de menores

detention for questioning detención hecha por la policía u otros oficiales para interrogar a una persona

detention home centro de rehabilitación; reformatorio de menores; correccional de menores

detention of a material witness detención de un testigo esencial

detention of minors detención de menores

detention order orden de arresto

deter *(discourage)* desalentar; *(dissuade)* disuadir; *(prevent)* impedir

determinate sentencing sentencia fija

determined period of time período de tiempo determinado

deterrence *(noun)* disuasión

development *(noun)* desarrollo; **housing development** urbanización; complejo habitacional

developmental *(adj)* del desarrollo

deviance *(noun)* desviación

deviant *(noun)* un individuo de conducta desviada

deviant *(adj: practices, conduct)* desviada; desviado; que se aparta de la norma

device *(noun)* aparato; dispositivo; artefacto

devil's advocate abogado del diablo

diabetic *(adj)* diabética; diabético

diagnosis *(noun)* diagnóstico; diagnosis

diagnosis related group classification (DRG's) clasificación de grupos de diagnosis relacionada

diagnostic test prueba diagnóstica; examen diagnóstico; análisis diagnóstico

dialysis *(noun)* diálisis

dialysis machine dializador

die *(verb)* fallecer; morir; matarse; **to die instantly** morir en el acto; fallecer en el acto; **he died in an accident** murió en un accidente

die from old age morir de vieja; morir de viejo; **she died from old age** murió de vieja; **he died from old age** murió de viejo

difference of opinion desavenencia

difficult *(adj: not easy)* difícil; **I find it difficult to believe that ...** me cuesta cree que ... ; **the difficult part is ...** lo difícil es ...; **it is difficult to know whom to believe** es difícil saber a quién creerle; **to make life difficult for somebody** hacer la vida imposible a alguien

difficulty *(noun: of situation, task)* dificultad; **with difficulty** con dificultad; **without difficulty** sin dificultad; **he has difficulty in understanding English** tiene dificultad para entender el Inglés; **to get into difficulties with** meterse en problemas con

diminish *(verb)* disminuir; reducirse

diminished capacity disminución de capacidad

diminished responsibility disminución de responsabilidad

direct deposit depósito directo

direct evidence *(law)* prueba testifical directa

direct examination *(law)* examen del testigo por la parte citante

Direct Loan Program Programa de Préstamo Directo

directed verdict *(law)* veredicto por instrucción judicial

directly connected to the case directamente relacionado con el caso

dirt road camino sin pavimiento

disability *(noun)* invalidez; discapacidad; minusvalía; *(particular handicap)* problema; **she managed to overcome her disability** consiguió superar su problema; *(law; disqualification)* incapacidad legal

disability compensation benefits beneficios de compensacion por incapacidad

disability denial notice aviso de denegación de incapacidad

Disability Determination Services Agencias de Determinación de Incapacidad

disability evaluation specialist especialista en evaluación de incapacidad

disability freeze período de incapacidad inactivo

disability insurance seguro de incapacidad

disability pension beneficios de pension por incapacidad

disability rights derechos de discapacidad

disable *(verb: illness, accident, injury)* dejar inválida; dejar inválido

disabled *(adj: physically handicapped)*; discapacitada; discapcitado; minusválida; minusválido

disabled widow viuda incapacitada

disabled widower viudo incapacitado

disadvantage *(noun: hindrance, drawback)* desventaja; inconveniente; **to be at a disadvantage** estar en desventaja; **this put him at a disadvantage** esto lo dejó en situación desventajosa

disagree *(verb: differ in opinion)* **to disagree with somebody** no estar de acuerdo con alguien; **to disagree with something** no estar de acuerdo con algo; **I disagree** yo no estoy de acuerdo; **I disagree with you** no estoy de acuerdo con usted; discrepamos

disagreement *(noun: difference of opinion)* desacuerdo; **to be in disagreement with** estar en desacuerdo con

disagreement of opinion desavenencia

disallow *(law: claim, evidence)* rechazar; desestimar; *(goal)* anular

disallow *(verb)* denegar

disallowance *(noun)* denegación

disappointed *(adj)* **to be disappointed** estar desilusionada; estar desilusionado; estar decepcionada; estar decepcionado; **he is disappointed with the verdict** el veredicto lo ha decepcionado

disappointed *(adj)* decepcionante; **the verdict was very disappointing** el veredicto fue muy decepcionante; **how disappointing!** ¡qué desilusión!

disappointment *(noun)* desilusión; decepción; pesar; **much to my disappointment, our defense fell through** para mi gran desilusión, nos falló nuestra defensa; **to our disappointment** a nuestro pesar; **he is a big disappointment to us** nos ha decepcionado mucho

disaster area zona de desastre

disaster fund fondo para los damnificados; fondo de ayuda para casos de desastres

disaster relief auxilio a las víctimas de una catástrofe

disavow *(verb)* negar; **he disavowed all knowledge of the matter** negó tener conocimiento del asunto; **she disavowed any connection with the terrorists** negó tener ninguna relación con los terroristas

disbar *(verb)* inhabilitar para el ejercicio de la abogacía

discharge *(verb: release from prison)* liberar; poner en libertad; *(juror)* dispensar; *(soldier)* dar de baja del ejército; puesta en libertad; *(law)* **conditional discharge** libertad condicional; *(from hospital)* dar de alta

discharge a contract *(law)* terminar un contrato

discharge a court order *(law)* revocar una orden judicial

discharge a jury *(law)* dispensar a un jurado

discharge a prisoner liberar a un prisionero

disclaim *(law: property, trust)* renunciar a

disclaim *(verb)* negar; **he disclaimed all responsibility for the accident** negó toda responsabilidad en el accidente; **he disclaimed ownership of the knife** negó que el cuchillo fuera suyo; **she disclaimed all knowledge of his whereabouts** negó conocer su paradero

disclaimer *(law)* descargo de responsabilidad; cláusula de protección; **to put in a disclaimer** negarlo; rechazarlo

disclose *(verb)* revelar

disclosure *(noun)* revelación

disclosure of information revelación de información

discount *(noun)* descuento; **I got a 10% discount** me hicieron un diez de descuento; *(verb: amount)* descontar; *(price)* reducir; *(disregard, claim, criticism)* descartar; pasar por alto; no tener en cuenta

discourage *(verb)* desalentar; desanimar; **to become discouraged** desanimarse; *(deter crime)* poner freno a; *(deter burglary)* disuadir; *(frighten away)* ahuyentar

discover *(verb: find)* descubrir; darse cuenta de; *(find out)* descubrir; hallar

discovery *(law)* proposición de prueba; descubrimiento *(métodos para obtener e intercambiar información entre las partes con el objeto de establecer los hechos de un caso)*

discredit *(verb)* desacreditar; desprestigiar; poner en duda

discrepancy *(noun)* discrepancia

discriminate *(verb)* discriminar; **to discriminate against somebody** discriminar a alguien; **to discriminate in favor of somebody** favorecer a alguien

discrimination *(noun)* discriminación; **racial discrimination** discriminación racial; **sexual discrimination** discriminación sexual

discuss *(verb)* hablar de; discutir; deliberar; cambiar opiniones sobre; analizar; **we discussed what to do next** estuvimos deliberando sobre qué debíamos hacer a continuación

discussion *(noun: of plan, problem;)* discusión; debate; deliberacicón; **after much discussion** después de largas deliberaciones; **it's still under discussion** todavía se está discutiendo; **when does it come up for discussion?** ¿cuándo se va a discutir?; cuándo se va a tratar?; **under discussion** en discusion

dishonest *(adv: person, answer)* deshonesta; deshonesto; *(dealing, means)* fraudulente; deshonesta; deshonesto

dishonestly *(adv)* deshonestamente; con deshonestidad

dishonorable discharge *(mil)* licencia deshonrosa

dishonorably *(adv)* de manera deshonrosa; **to be dishonorably discharged** ser dada de baja con deshonor; ser dado de baja con deshonor

dismiss *(law: case)* sobreseer; anular; *(charge, appeal)* rechazar; desestimar; *(employee)* despedir; destituir; **he was dismissed from his job** lo despidieron del trabajo; *(possibility, suggestion)* rechazar; descartar; **he immediately dismissed the thought** inmediatamente descartó la idea; **with that he dismissed the matter** con eso dio por concluido el asunto

dismissal *(law: case)* sobreseimiento; *(rejection)* desestimación

dismissal by court sobreseimiento por la corte

dismissal letter carta de despido

dismissed worker trabajador despedido; trabajadora despedida

disobey *(person)* desobedecer; *(rule)* infringir

disobey the law desobedecer la ley

disorderly conduct alteración del orden público; **he was arrested for disorderly conduct** lo detuvieron por alteración del orden público

disposable assets activos disponibles

disposable income renta disponible

displaced person desplazada; desplazado

disprove *(verb: claim, assertion, charge)* desmentir; refutar

dispute *(noun: controversy, clash)* polémica; controversia; *(debate)* discusión; conflicto; *(quarrel)* disputa; **it is open to dispute whether he acted reasonably** si actuó razonable o no es discutible; si actuó razonable o no se presta a discusión; **the matter is still in dispute** aún no se ha llegado a un acuerdo sobre el asunto; **the matter is still under dispute** aún no se ha llegado a un acuerdo sobre el asunto; *(verb: contest)* discutir, cuestionar; rechazar; negar; **I don't dispute the fact that it was a mistake** no discuto que fue un error; **it cannot be disputed that ...** no se puede negar que ...

disqualify *(verb)* inhabilitar; descalificar; **to disqualify somebody from something** inhabilitar a alguien para algo; **he was disqualified from holding public office** fue inhabilitado para ocupar cargos públicos; **a criminal record disqualifies you from jury duty** tener antecedentes criminales inhabilita para ser miembro de un jurado

disqualify oneself *(judge)* inhibirse; **she disqualified herself from the case** se inhibió de conocer el asunto

disregard *(verb: danger, difficulty)* ignorar; despreciar; *(advice, wishes)* hacer caso omiso de; no prestar atención; **you disregard everything I tell you** haces caso omiso de todo lo que te digo; **he disregarded my advice** hizo caso omiso de mis consejos; **they disregarded his criminal past and gave him the job** no tuvieron en cuenta sus antecedentes penales y le dieron el puesto

disrespect *(noun)* falta de respeto; **disrespect for something** falta de respeto hacia algo; **I meant no disrespect** no fue mi intención ofenderlo; **with disrespect** con poco respeto

disruptive *(adj: influence)* perjudicial; negativa; negativo; *(factor)* perturbador; perturbadora; **all these interruptions are very disruptive to the case** todas estas interrrupciones perjudican el desarrollo del caso; **he has a record of disruptive behavior** siempre ha causado problemas de disciplina

dissatisfaction *(noun)* descontento; insatisfacción

dissatisfied *(adj)* descontenta; descontento; insatisfecha; insatisfecho; **to be dissatisfied with somebody** estar descontenta con alguien; estar descontento con alguien; **dissatisfied with something** descontenta con algo; descontento con algo

dissolution of contract terminación de un contrato

dissolution of a marriage terminación de un matrimonio

distinction *(noun: difference)* distinción; **you shouldn't make a distinction between them** no deberías hacer distinciones entre ellos; **we must make a distinction between ...** debemos distinguir entre ...; **we must draw a distinction between ...** debemos distinguir entre ...; **without distinction of race or creed** sin distinción de raza o credo

distinguishing marks señas particulares

distort *(verb: of facts)* desvirtuar; tergiversar

distortion *(noun: of facts)* distorsión; tergiversación; **a gross distortion of the truth** una total distorsión de la verdad

distress *(adj)* angustia; preocupación; afflicción

distressed *(adj)* angustiada; angustiado; consternada; consternado; **he is distressed** está angustiado

district attorney fiscal del distrito

district attorney's office fiscalía

district court tribunal de distrito

district manager gerente de distrito

distrust *(verb)* desconfiar de; no fiarse de

distrust *(noun)* desconfianza; recelo; **distrust of somebody** falta de confianza en alguien; **distrust of something** falta de confianza en algo

disturbing the peace alterar el orden público; alteración del orden público; **he was arrested for disturbing the peace** lo detuvieron por alterar el orden público

divided highway *(traffic sign)* carretera dividida; vía dividida

divided highway begins *(traffic sign)* comienza vía dividida

divided highway ends *(traffic sign)* termina vía dividida

divorce *(noun: law)* divorcio; **to get a divorce from his wife** conseguir el divorcio de su esposa; **to obtain a divorce from her husband** conseguir el divorcio de su esposo; **he was granted a divorce** le concedieron el divorcio; **divorce is on the increase** el número de divorcios está aumentando; **divorce is on the rise** el número de divorcios está aumentando

divorce *(verb: law)* divorciarse; **to get divorced** divorciarse; **they'll end up divorcing** van a terminar divorciándose

divorcé *(noun)* divorciado

divorce court tribunal de pleitos matrimoniales

divorce proceedings *(law)* pleito de divorcio; trámites de divorcio; tramitación de divorcio

divorced *(adj: law)* divorciada; divorciado; **a divorced man** un divorciado; **a divorced woman** una divorciada; **his parents are divorced** sus padres están divorciados

divorcee *(noun)* divorciada; divorciado

divorcée *(noun)* divorciada

DMV Departamento de Vehículos Motorizados

do *(auxiliary verb)* hacer; **he's doing eight years for armed robbery** está cumpliendo ocho años por atracado a mano armada; **they can do you for possession** te pueden agarrar por posesión; **the other car was doing one hundred miles an hour** el otro coche iba a cien millas por hora; **do something!** ¡haz algo!; **and do you know what she did?** ¿sabes lo que hizo?; **you did the right thing** hiciste lo correcto; **it was**

a silly thing to do** fue una estupidez; **can I do anything to help?** ¿puedo ayudar en algo?; **let me do the talking** déjame hablar a mí

Do Not Enter *(traffic sign)* Prohibido Entrar

Do Not Pass *(traffic sign)* Prohibido Pasar

docket *(noun)* expediente

docket number número de causa

doctor *(noun: medical)* médica; médico

doctor *(verb: alter, change)* amañar; alterar; falsificar; **he doctored the official report** amañó el informe oficial

doctor bills cuentas de doctor; cuentas de médico

doctor and other medical bills cuentas de doctor y otros gastos médicos

doctor's office consultorio médico

doctor the official report amañar el informe oficial

document *(noun)* documento; **are your documents in order?** ¿tiene los documentos en regla? ¿tiene los papeles en regla? *(verb)* documentar

document of title documento de resguardo

document subject to verification documento sujeto a verificación

documentary evidence prueba documental; prueba escrita

dodge *(verb)* evadir; **to dodge the issue** evadir el tema

doing business efectuar negocios; realizar negocios

doing business as efectuar negocios como; realizar negocios como

domestic partner compañera doméstica; compañero doméstico

domestic services servicios domésticos

domestic violence violencia en el hogar; violencia doméstica

domestic workers trabajadores dómesticos

domicile *(noun)* domicilio

done *(pred)* hecha; hecho; terminada; terminado

don't hang up! ¡no cuelgues!

don't you know that ...? ¿acaso no sabes que ...?; **don't you know that what you have done is a crime?** ¿acaso no sabes que lo que has hecho es un delito?

door *(noun)* puerta; **open the door** abrir la puerta; **shut the door** cerrar la puerta; **front door** puerta principal; **back door** puerta trasera

door-to-door de puerta a puerta

doorbell *(noun)* timbre

dope *(noun: drugs, slang)* droga; pichicata; **to do dope** doparse; drogarse

dope dealer camella; camello

dopehead *(noun: slang)* drogata; drogato; pichicatera; pichicatero; flapera; flapero

double chin papada

double indemnity indeminización doble

double jeopardy prohibición contra doble enjuiciamiento

doubt *(noun: law)* duda; **beyond reasonable doubt** más allá de toda duda fundada; *(noun)* duda; incertidumbre; **there's no room for doubt** no hay lugar a duda; no cabe duda; **I have no doubt whatsoever that ...** no tengo la menor duda de que ...; **the result is still in doubt** aún se desconoce el resultado; **his integrity is not in doubt** su integridad no está en duda; **I have my doubts** tengo mis dudas; **I doubt he'll agree** dudo que vaya a acceder; **there is no doubt that ...** no cabe duda de que ...

doubt *(verb: fact, truth)* dudar de; **do you doubt my word?** ¿dudas de mi palabra? **I doubt his story** dudo de que su historia sea verdad; **I very much doubt it** lo dudo mucho

down *(of position)* abajo

down payment depósito; pago al contado; desembolso inicialenganche; **no down payment** sin anticipo

down the street calle abajo

Down's Syndrome síndrome de Down

downtown *(noun)* centro; *(adv)* **to go downtown** ir al centro; **to live downtown** vivir en el centro

downtown Albuquerque el centro de Albuquerque

dragnet *(noun: police operation)* operación policial de captura; operativo policial de captura

draw up *(law)* redactar; **draw up laws regarding citizenship of the country** redactar leyes con respecto a la ciudadanía del país

drawl *(noun) acento caracterizado por la longitud de las vocales*; voz cansina; **a Southern drawl** un acento sureño; un acento del sur

dress *(for girl, woman)* vestido; **short dress** vestido corto; *(past the knee)* **long dress** vestido largo; **evening dress** traje largo; traje de gala; traje de noche; **formal dress** traje de etiqueta

dressing *(surgical)* vendajes; vendas

drinking *(noun: alcohol)* consumo; **his drinking is causing concern** lo mucho que bebe está causando preocupación; **he has given up drinking** ha dejado la bebida; **to take up drinking** darse a la bebida

drink *(verb)* beber; tomar; **his problems drove him to drink** sus problemas lo llevaron al alcohol

drinking problem beber demasiado; **he has a drinking problem** su problema es la bebida; **she has a drinking problem** su problema es la bebida

drive-by shooting disparar desde adentro del auto; al disparar desde adentro del auto; **in a drive-by shooting** cuando dispararon desde adentro del auto

driver's license permiso de conducción; carnet de conducir, carné

driver's manual manual del conductor

driveway *(noun)* entrada

driving school autoescuela; escuela de manejo; academia de conductores; academia de choferes

driving test examen de manejar

driving under the influence conducir bajo la influencia del alcohol o de las drogas; manejar bajo la influencia del alcohol o de las drogas

driving while drunk manejo en estado de embriaguez

driving while intoxicated conducir bajo la influencia del alcohol o de las drogas; manejar bajo la influencia del alcohol o de las drogas

drop charges retractar una querella; retractar una denuncia

drop out of school abandonar la escuela; abandonar los estudios; **she dropped out of school** abandonó los estudios

drown *(verb: person)* ahogar; ahogarse; **to be drowned** ahogarse; morir ahogada; morir ahogado

drug *(noun: medication)* farmáco; medicamento; medicina; *(narcotic)* droga; estupefaciente; **do you do drugs?** ¿te drogas? **I don't do drugs** you no me drogo; **to be on drugs** drogarse; **hard drugs** drogas duras; **soft drugs** drogas blandas

drug abuse toxicomanía

drug abuser toxicómana; toxicómano

drug addict drogadicta; drogadicto; toxicómana; toxicómano

drug baron capa; capo

drug dealer narcotraficante; vendedor de drogas; vendedora de drogas

drug dependence drogadependencia

drug dependency drogadependencia

Drug Enforcement Administration (DEA) Administración Antinarcóticos

drug habit drogadicción

drug peddler narcotraficante; traficante de drogas

drug pusher narcotraficante; traficante de drogas

drug-related relacionada con drogas; relacionado con drogas

drug-related crime drogodelincuencia

drug runner narcotraficante; traficante de drogas

drug smuggler traficante de drogas

drug squad brigada antidrogas

drug trafficker narcotraficante, traficante de drogas

drug trafficking narcotráfico, trafíco de drogas

drug use consumo de drogas

drug user consumidor de drogas; consumidora de drogas

druggist *(noun)* farmacéutica; farmacéutico

drunk *(prep)* borracha; borracho; **to be drunk** estar borracha; estar borracho

drunk and disorderly *(law)* en estado de embriaguez y alternando el orden público

drunk and incapable *(law)* en estado de embriaguez e irresponsabilidad

drunk driver conductor en estado de embriaguez; conductora en estado de embriaguez

drunk driving *(law)* delito de conducir en estado de embriaguez; delito de conducir bajo la influencia de alcohol; **he was convicted of drunk driving** fue condenado por conducir en estado de embriaguez; **it was his second drunk driving offense** era la segunda vez que lo detenían por conducir borracho

drunkard *(adj)* borracha; borracho; beoda; beodo

drunken *(adj)* borracha; borracho; **in a drunken stupor** en un sopor etílico

due date fecha de vencimiento; **before its due date** antes de su fecha de vencimiento

due notice notificación debida

due process debidas garantías procesales; debido procedimiento de ley

due process of law debido proceso de ley

due to debida a; debido a

duly sworn debidamente juramentada; debidamente juramentado

dumb *(adj: unable to speak)* muda; mudo; **she's deaf and dumb** es sordomuda

dump *(colloquial: boyfriend, girlfriend)* botar; *(colloquial: leave a body)*; **they dumped his body in a field outside of Phoenix** dejaron su cuerpo tirado en un camino fuera de Phoenix

duplicate claim reclamación duplicada

duration *(noun)* duración; **for the duration of the trial** mientras dure el juicio; mientras dure el proceso

duration and continuity duración y continuidad

duress *(noun)* coacción; compulsión; **under duress** bajo coacción

during the day durante el día

during the day of durante el día de

during the hearing durante la audiencia; durante la instrucción de cargos

during the hearing of durante la audiencia de; durante la instrucción de cargos de

during the month durante el mes

during the month of durante el mes de

during the trial durante el juicio

during the week durante la semana; entre semana

during the week of durante la semana de

during the year durante el año

dusk *(noun)* anochecer; **at dusk** al anochecer

duty *(noun: obligation)* deber; obligación

E

each *(adj invar)* **each question** cada pregunta; **each one** cada una; cada uno; **each one of us** cada uno de nosotros; **each one of them** cada uno de ellos

each *(pron)* cada una; cada uno; **each day** cada día; **each of them blamed the other** se echaron la culpa mutualmente; **he questioned each of them in turn** les preguntó uno por uno; **they hate each other** se odian; **they are always criticizing each other** siempre se están criticando el uno al otro; **we give each other advice** nos aconsejamos mutuamente

ear *(anat)* oído; *(outer part)* coreja

early *(adj: before expected)* temprana; temprano; prematura; prematuro; primera; primero; **an early death** una muerte temprana; una muerte prematura; **at an early stage** en una etapa temprana; **it's too early to tell** es demasiado pronto para saber; **in early childhood** en la primera infancia; **in the early hours of the morning** en las primeras horas de la mañana; en las primeras horas de la madrugada; **in the early afternoon** a primeras horas de la tarde; **in early June** a principios de junio; a comienzos de junio; **from an early age** desde pequeña; desde pequeño; **he was released earlier than expected** lo pusieron en libertad antes de lo esperado; **he is in his early twenties** tiene poco más de veinte años; **as early as possible** lo más pronto posible; cuanto antes; **you're early!** ¡llegaste temprano!

early retirement jubilación anticipada

earn *(verb: money, wages)* ganar; **to earn one's living** ganarse la vida; **he earns very good money** gana mucho dinero

earn *(verb: degree)* licenciarse; **he earned a degree in mechanical engineering** se licenció en ingeniería mecánica

earned income ingresos en concepto de salario; ingresos en concepto de sueldo; ingresos devengados; renta devengada

earned income credit crédito de renta ganada; crédito de ingreso ganado

earnest money fianza; pago a cuenta de precio; capacidad remunerativa

earning capacity potencial de ingreso

earnest payment fianza

earning potential potencial ganador

earning power potencial de ingreso; capacidad de ganancia

earnings *(noun: wages)* sueldo; salario; *(income)* ingreso; *(profits)* ganancias; **his earnings are not enough to support himself** no gana lo suficiente para mantenerse

earnings record registro de ganancias

earnings test límite de ganancias

easement servidumbre

Easter Semana Santa; Pascua

Easter Sunday Domingo de Pascua

easy *(in phrases)* **to take the easy way out** optar por el camino fácil; **that's easy for you to say** se dice muy fácil; es fácil hablar; **she's easy to get along with** es fácil llevarse bien con ella

easy money dinero fácil; plata fácil

education educación; formación; **higher education** estudios superiores; **primary education** enseñanza primaria; **secondary education** enseñanza secundaria; **he doesn't have a university education** no cursó estudios universitarios; **a man of considerable education** un hombre muy culto; **a man of little education** un hombre poco culto

effective *(adj: law)* **to become effective** entrar en vigor; entrar en vigencia; **the new law becomes effective as of May 14** la nueva ley entrará en vigor a partir del catorce de mayo; la nueva ley entrará en vigencia a partir del catorce de mayo

effective date fecha de vigencia; fecha vigente

effective date of final judgement fecha efectiva de una sentencia definitiva

effort *(noun: attempt)* esfuerzo; **to make an effort** hacer un esfuerzo; **please make an effort to get here before ten** por favor traten de llegar antes de las diez; por favor intenten llegar antes de las diez; **it's not worth the effort** no vale la pena

eight *(adj & noun)* ocho; **he is eight years old** él tiene ocho años de edad; **they live at number eight** viven en el número ocho; **there are eight of us** somos ocho; **all eight of them came** vinieron los ocho; **it costs eight dollars** cuesta ocho dólares; vale ocho dólares; **it's eight o'clock** son las ocho

eighteen *(adj & noun)* dieciocho

eighteenth *(adv)* decimoctava; decimoctavo

eighth *(adj)* octava; octavo

eightieth *(adj)* octagésima; octagésimo

eighty *(adj & noun)* ochenta

either *(adj: one or other, positive)* cualquiera de los dos; **either day would suit me** cualquiera de los dos días me conviene; *(each)* **on either side** en los dos lados; **in either hand** en cada mano; **either one would be suitable** cualquiera de los dos servirá

elapsed years años transcurridos

elbow *(anat)* codo

electric chair silla electríca

electric shock descarga electríca

electrocardiogram electrocardiograma

electronic monitoring bracelet pulsera de seguimiento electrónica

electronic newsletter noticiero electrónico

electronic transfer account (ETA) cuenta de transferencia electrónica

element *(noun: component part)* elemento; base; **it may be an element of her decision** puede que haya sido un elemento que influyera en su decisión; **the element of surprise** el factor sorpresa; **there's an element of truth in what he says** hay algo de verdad en lo que dice; **lawless elements in society** elementos rebeldes de la sociedad; *(rudiments)* **we have the elements for an agreement** tenemos las bases de un acuerdo; **we have the elements for a solution** tenemos las bases de una solución

elementary *(adj)* elemental; básica; básico

elementary education enseñanza primaria

elementary school escuela de enseñanza primaria

elementary school teacher maestra de enseñanza primaria; maestro de enseñanza primaria

elementary teacher maestra de enseñanza primaria; maestro de enseñanza primaria

elevator *(noun)* ascensor

eleven *(adj & noun)* once

eleventh *(adj)* undécima; undécimo

eligibility *(noun)* elegibilidad

eligible *(adj: applicant, candidate)* que reúne los requisitos necesarios; **he's eligible for a grant** tiene derecho a solicitar una beca; **he's now legally eligible for US citizenship** ahora cumple con los requisitos para solicitar la ciudadanía Estadounidense; ahora reúne los requisitos para solicitar la ciudadanía estadounidense; **to be eligible for** reunir los requisitos para

eligible for citizenship elegible para la ciudadanía

eligible for an immigrant visa elegible para recibir una visa de inmigración

eligible individual individuo elegible

eligible to submit their citizenship applications elegibles para someter sus solicitudes de ciudadanía

elope *(adj)* fugarse con un amante; fugarse para casarse

elopement *(noun)* fuga

else *(adv)* **all else** todo lo demás; **if all else fails** si todo lo demás falla; como último recurso; **was anybody else there?** ¿estaba alguien más?; **I can't think of anything else** no se me ocurre nada más; **I have nothing**

else to say no tengo nada más que decir; **what else did he say?** ¿qué más dijo?; **who else knows?** ¿quién más lo sabe?; **anything else** cualquier otra cosa; **how else?** ¿de qué otra manera?

E-mail *(noun)* correo electrónico

E-mail address *(noun)* dirección de correo electrónico

emancipated *(adj: law)* emancipada; emancipado; **to become emancipated** emanciparse

emancipation *(noun)* emancipación; *(fig)* liberación

embezzle *(verb: funds, money)* malversar; desfalcar

embezzelment *(noun)* malversación; desfalco; peculado

embezzelment of funds malversación de fondos

embryo *(noun)* embrión; **at the embryo stage** en estado embrionario

emerge *(verb: become evident, known)* surgir; aparecer; revelarse; **when the facts began to emerge** cuando los hechos empezaron a salir a luz; **it has now emerged that this was not true** ahora se ha revelado que esto no era cierto; **it emerged from the interview that he already knew** en la entrvista salió a relucir que ya lo sabía; en la entrvista se reveló que ya lo sabía; *(come into being)* **no agreement has emerged from the discussions** no ha surgido ningún acuerdo de las discussiones; **it emerges that ...** resulta que ...

emergency *(noun)* emergencia; crisis; **in an emergency** en caso de emergencia; **in case of emergency** en caso de emergencia; **it's an emergency** es una situación de emergencia

emergency childbirth parto repentino

emergency exit salida de emergencia

emergency medical technician técnica de emergencia médica; técnico de emergencia médica; técnica en urgencia médica; técnico en urgencia médica

emergency room sala de urgencias

emergency service servicio de emergencia; servicio de urgencia

emigrant *(noun)* emigrante

emigrate *(verb)* emigrar

emigration *(noun)* emigración

emotion *(noun: feeling)* sentimiento; **he was torn by conflicting emotion** se debatía entre sentimientos contradictorios; **he said it with no apparent emotion** lo dijo sin mostrar ninguna emoción

emotional *(adj: disorder, block)* emocional; afectiva; afectivo; *(moving speech, experience)* emotiva; emitivo; conmovedor; conmovedora

emotional crisis crisis emocional

emotional decision decisión impulsiva; **it was a purely emotional decision** fue una decisión totalmente impulsiva; **to get emotional** emocionarse; exaltarse

emotional distress angustia mental

emotional disturbance daño emocional

emotional state muy emocionada; muy emocionado; muy exaltada; muy exaltado; **he came to me in an emotional state** vino a verme muy emocionado

emotional vulnerability vulnerabilidad emocional

emotionally involved envuelta sentimentalmente; envuelto sentimentalmente; **they are emotionally involved** tienen una relación sentimental; **they were emotionally involved** tenían una relación sentimental

emotionless *(adj)* sin emoción; impasible

empanel *(verb)* formar; **to empanel a jury** confeccionar la lista de un jurado; **he was empanelled for the trial** lo inscribieron para formar parte del jurado del caso

emphasis *(noun)* énfasis; **she repeated her words for emphasis** repitió las palabras para darles mayor énfasis; **to speak with emphasis** hablar con énfasis; **to lay emphasis on something** hacer hincapié en algo; **to put emphasis on something** hacer hincapié en algo

emphasize *(verb: phrase, word)* enfatizar; poner énfasis en; *(fact, point, warning)* recalcar; hacer hincapié en; enfatizar; repetirse bastante; **it cannot be too strongly emphasized that ...** no puede repetirse bastante que ...; **I must emphasize that ...** debo insistir en que ...

employ *(verb: take on, hire)* contratar; emplear; **we cannot employ him without a work permit** no podemos contratarlo si no tiene permiso de trabajo; *(have working)* **the company employs hundreds of workers** la compañía emplea a cientos de trabajadores; la compañía da empleo a cientos de trabajadores; **he's employed as a nightwatchman** trabaja de vigilante nocturno

employ *(noun:)* emplear; **to be in somebody's employ** trabajar para alguien; **to be in the employ of somebody** trabajar para alguien; ser empleada de alguien; ser empleado de alguien

employable *(adj)* que se puede emplear; **at his age you cease to be employable** a su edad ya nadie quiere emplearlo; **a second language would make you more employable** si pudieras hablar otro idioma, tendrías más posibilidades de conseguir trabajo

employed *(adj: in work)* empleada; empleado; **how long were you employed by them?** ¿cuánto tiempo estuvo empleado allí?; ¿cuánto tiempo trabajó allí?; **she's currently employed in research** en este momento se dedica a la investigación

employee *(noun:)* empleada; empleado; trabajador; trabajadora; **she's an employee in an insurance company** está empleada en una compañía de seguros; **management and employees reached an agreement** la dirección y los trabajadores llegaron a un acuerdo

employee benefit plan plan de beneficios para empleados

employer *(noun: manager, boss)* empleador; empleadora; *(of domestic work)* patrón; patrona; **she's a fair employer** es justa con sus empleados; **unions and employers** sindicatos y la patronal; sindicatos y los empresarios; **list your three most recent employers** indique las últimas tres empresas para las que ha trabajo; **one of the biggest employers in the country** uno de los mayores empleadores del país; **one of the biggest employers in the state** uno de los mayores empleadores del estado

employer's contributions aportes del empleador; aportes de la empresa; cotizaciones por parte de la empresa

employer's quarterly tax return declaración de impuestos trimestrales del patrono; declaración de impuestos trimestrales del patrono empleador

employment *(noun: work)* trabajo; empleo; **to find employment** encontrar trabajo; tener trabajo; **to seek employment** buscar empleo; buscar trabajo; **conditions of employment** condiciones de empleo; **full employment** pleno empleo; **place of employment** lugar de trabajo

employment agency agencia de trabajo; agencia de colocación

Employment Development Department Departamento del Desarrollo del Empleo

employment opportunities oportunidades de empleo

employment relationship relación de empleo

employment support ayuda de empleo

empower *(noun: police, lawyer, etc.)* conferirle poderes a; otorgarle poderes a; autorizar; **to empower somebody to do something** autorizar a alguien para hacer algo; **she is empowered to sign the contract on my behalf** está autorizada a firmar el contrato en mi nombre; está autorizada para firmar el contrato en mi nombre

enclosed *(adj)* adjunta; adjunto

enclosure *(noun)* contenido, adjunto

encounter *(verb: faced with danger, difficulty, opposition)* encontrar; encontrarse con; tropezar con

encounter *(noun: meeting)* encuentro; **a chance encounter** un encuentro casual; un encuentro fortuito; **casual sexual encounters** relaciones sexuales fuera de una pareja estable; **his first encounter with the law** su primer tropiezo con la ley; **her second encounter with the law** su segundo tropiezo con la ley

encounter group grupo de encuentro

encourage *(verb: give hope, courage)* animar; alentar; **she encouraged me to carry on** me alentó a seguir adelante; **she encouraged me to try again** me alentó para que volviera a intentarlo; **to encourage somebody to do something** animar a alguien a hacer algo; **I tried to encourage him to carry on** traté de animarlo a que continuara

encouragement *(noun: heartening)* ánimo; aliento; **to give encouragement to** dar ánimo a; animar; **she doesn't need any encouragement** no le hace falta que la animen a hacerlo

encouraging *(adj: news, progress)* alentador; alentadora; esperanzador; esperanzadora; **she has always been very encouraging** siempre me ha alentado mucho; siempre nos ha alentado mucho

encumber *(law: levy tax on titles, deeds)* gravar

encumber *(verb: burden)* cargar; **to be encumbered with something** estar cargada de algo; estar cargado de algo; **she is encumbered with a large family** tiene la carga de una familia numerosa; **he's encumbered with a large mortgage** tiene la carga de una fuerte hipoteca

encumbrance *(law: burden)* gravamen; carga; **the encumbrances on the property** las cargas que gravan la propiedad; **free from encumbrances** libre de gravamen

end *(in phrases)* **for weeks on end** durante semanas y semanas; durante semanas enteras; **toward the end of the summer** hacia finales del verano; **at the end of the month** a fin de mes; **by the end of the week** para el fin de semana; **to the very end** hasta el fin; hasta el final; **in the end** al final; **a violent end** un final violento; un fin violento; **I was with him at the end** estuve con él en sus últimos momentos; **to make ends meet** hacer llegar el dinero; hacer alcazar el dinero

end a pregnancy poner fin a un embarazo

end-stage renal disease enfermedad renal en etapa final

end the lawsuit poner término a la causa

end up in jail acabar en la cárcel

endanger *(verb: life, health, position)* poner en peligro; **she endangered her own life** puso en peligro su propia vida

endangerment *(noun)* imprudencia temeraria

endorse *(verb: a check)* endosar

endorsement *(signature)* endoso

enemy alien extranjero enemigo

enforce *(verb: law, regulation)* hacer respetar; cumplir; obedecer

enforce her/his rights hacer valer sus derechos

enforcement *(noun: law, regulation)* hacer cumplir; hacer respetar; **they are responsible for the enforcement of the law** son responsables de hacer cumplir la ley; son responsables de hacer respetar la ley; **law enforcement agency** agencia jurídica; **law enforcement officers** agentes de la ley

engage *(verb: hire a lawyer)* contratar

English *(noun)* Inglés; *(adj)* Inglés; Inglesa

English as a Second Language Inglés como Segundo Idioma

English-speaking de habla Inglesa

enjoin *(verb: law)* prohibir; **to enjoin somebody from** prohibirle a alguien que + *subj*

enjoyment *(noun: law)* goce; **the enjoyment of a right** el goce de un derecho; **the enjoyment of a title** el goce de un título

enjoyment *(noun: pleasure)* placer; **to do something for pleasure** hacer algo por placer

enlisted man soldado raso

enlisted woman soldado raso

enough evidence pruebas suficientes

enroll *(verb)* inscribirse

enrollee *(noun)* inscrita; inscrito

enrollment period período de inscripción

enrollment register registro de inscripción

enter *(verb: law)* **to enter an appeal** interponer un recurso de apelación; apelar; **to enter a writ of habeas corpus** presentar un recurso de habeas corpus; **to enter a plea of not guilty** declararse inocente; **to enter a protest** formular una protesta

enter a judgement asentar una sentencia; registrar un fallo en los libros del tribunal; registrar una sentencia en los libros del tribunal

enter a plea *(a judge)* asentar una declaración judicial del acusado con respecto a las acusaciones

enter a plea *(a defendant)* declararse oficialmente

enter a plea of guilty declararse culpable

enter a plea of not guilty declararse inocente

enter into contract with entrar en contacto con

enter into force entrar en vigor

enterprise *(noun: company)* empresa; **free enterprise** la libre empresa; **private enterprise** el sector privado

entirely *(in phrases)* **I agree entirely** estoy totalmente de acuerdo; **I entirely agree** estoy totalmente de acuerdo; **I'm not entirely surprised** no me sorprende del todo; **It's entirely up to you** como tu quieras; **he did it entirely for the money** lo hizo únicamente por el dinero; **it wasn't entirely his fault** no fue únicamente culpa suya; no fue exclusivamente culpa suya

entitled *(adj)* tener derecho a; calificar; ser elegible

entitlement *(noun)* derecho a; *(program)* de ayuda social

entitlement to something derecho a algo

entity *(noun)* entidad; **legal entity** persona jurídica

entrap *(verb: law)* incitar a la comisión de un delito

entrapment *(noun: law)* incitación por agentes de la ley a la comisión de un delito

entrepreneur *(noun)* empresaria; empresario

entry of judgement *(law)* asentamiento de fallo; asentamiento de sentencia

entry procedures requisitos para la entrada entrada

entry visa visa de entrada

epileptic *(adj)* epiléptica; epiléptico

epilepsy *(noun)* epilepsia

equal *(in phrases)* **everyone is equal before the law** todos somos iguales ante la ley; **to be on equal terms with somebody** estar en igualdad de condiciones con alguien; **all things being equal** si todo sigue igual

Equal Access to Justice Act Ley de Igualdad de Acceso a la Justicia

equal opportunities igualdad de oportunidades

Equal Employment Opportunity Commission Comisión de Igualdad de Oportunidades de Empleo

equal opportunity employer empresa que practica una política de igualdad de oportunidades *(sin distinción de raza, credo ni orientación sexual)*; patrono no discriminatorio

equal pay igualdad de retribución para hombres y mujeres

equal right to education el mismo drecho a la enseñanza; **everyone has an equal right to education** todo el mundo tiene el mismo derecho a la enseñanza

equal rights igualdad de derechos

equality *(noun)* igualdad

equally *(adv: to an equal degree)* igualmente; **they are equally guilty** son igualmente culpables; **they are equally valid** son igualmente válidas; son igualmente válidos

equip *(verb)* equipar

equitable *(adj)* equitativa; equitativo

equity value valor líquido

escape *(verb: flee)* escaparse; *(prisoner)* fugarse; escaparse; **to escape from prison** fugarse de la prisión; **to escape from jail** fugarse de la cárcel; **they are looking for an escaped convict** están buscando a un preso que se ha fugado de la cárcel; **to escape from** huirse de; **an escaped prisoner** un fugativo; una fugativa

escape *(verb: from an accident, danger)* salvarse; escaparse; *(prisoner)* **he escaped unscathed** escapó ileso; **she escaped with minor injuries** sólo sufrió heridas leves; **he escaped with a few bruises** salió sin daños mayores

escape *(noun: from prison, jail)* fuga; huida; **an attempted escape** un intento de fuga; **there's been an escape** alguien se ha fugado; **to make one's escape** escaparse; lograr huir

escape attempt intento de fuga

escape plan plan de escape

escaped convict presa que se ha fugado de la cárcel; preso que se ha fugado de la cárcel

escaped prisoner fugativa; fugativo

escort *(noun: guard)* escolta; **armed escort** escolta armada; **under police escort** escoltada por la policía; escoltado por la policía; **to travel under escort** viajar bajo escolta

escrow *(noun)* fideicomiso; **to be in escrow** estar en depósito; estar bajo la custodia de un tercero

essential *(adj)* esencial; **the essential thing** lo esencial; imprescindible; **to be essential to somebody** ser imprescindible para alguien; **she's become essential to me** se me ha hecho imprescindible; **to be essential to something** ser imprescindible para algo; **it is essential that ...** es imprescindible que ...

essential person persona indispensable

establish *(verb)* establecer; fundar

estate *(noun: land, property)* finca; propiedad; estancia; hacienda

estate *(noun: law)* patrimonio; *(of deceased person)* sucesión; herencia; **she left a large estate** dejó una gran herencia; **real estate** bienes raíces

estimate *(verb)* calcular; estimar; *(noun)* cálculo

estimated value valor estimado; valor calculado

estranged *(adj)* separada; separado; **his estranged wife** su mujer que vive separada de él; **her estranged husband** su marido que vive separada de ella; **to become estranged** separarse; **they're estranged now** ahora están separados

estrangement *(noun)* separación; alejamiento

ethnic *(adj: concerning race, origin, group makeup)* étnica; étnico; **an ethnic minority** una minoría étnica; **the conflicts are ethnic in origin** los conflictos son de origen racial

ethnic cleansing limpieza étnica

ethnic minority minoría étnica

evade *(verb: capture, arrest, pursuers)* evadir; eludir; *(punishment)* evitar; *(questions, issue)* evadir; *(taxes)* evadir

evaluate *(verb: assess value)* valorar; calcular el valor de; *(judge)* evualar; **to evaluate evidence** evaluar las evidencias; *(property)* tasar; valorar

even *(in phrases)* **even as I speak** en este mismo momento; **even as he had predicted** exactamente como había predicho; **you're not even trying** ni siquiera lo estás intentando; **don't even think about it** ¡ni se te ocurra!; **even though I don't agree with you** aunque no estoy de acuerdo con usted; **even I know that** eso lo sé hasta yo

evening *(noun: before dark)* tarde; *(nightfall)* anochecer; **in the evening** por la tarde; **this evening** esta tarde; **tomorrow evening** mañana por la tarde; **yesterday evening** ayer por la tarde

event *(noun: happening, incident)* acontecimiento; suceso; **events proved us right** el desarrollo de los acontecimientos demostró que estábamos en lo cierto; **the events of that night** los acontecimientos de aquella noche; **the event took place when** el suceso se produjo cuando

event *(in phrases)* **in any event** en todo caso; **in either event** en cualquier de los casos; **in the event of ...** en caso de ... **in the event that ...** en caso de que ...

every *(adj: each);* **we've every reason to doubt her word** tenemos razones de sobra para dudar de su palabra

every now and then de tanto en tanto

every one of you todo y cada uno de ustedes

every room was searched se registraron todas las habitaciones; se registró cada una de las habitaciones

every time that ... cada vez que ...

every year todos los años; cada año

evict *(verb)* desahuciar; desalojar

eviction *(noun)* desahucio; desalojo; **eviction for lack of payment** desahucio por falta de pago

eviction notice apercibimiento de desahucio; apercibimiento de desalojo

eviction order orden de desalojo

evidence *(noun: law, proof)* pruebas; **circumstantial evidence** evidencia circunstancial; prueba circunstancial; pruebas indiciarias; **the evidence for the defense** el descargo de la defensa; **the evidence for the prosecution** el cápitulo de cargos; **to give evidence for** declarar a favor de; prestar declaración a favor de; **to give evidence** prestar declaración; **to give evidence against** declarar en contra de; prestar declaración en contra de; **to destroy the evidence** destruir las pruebas; **the revolver was produced as evidence** el révolver fue presentado como prueba; **there is no evidence against him** no hay evidencia en contra suya; **to turn state's evidence** declarar como testigo de la acusación *(con el propósito de obtener una reducción de la propia pena)*

evidence based on evidencia basada en

evidence heard by jury evidencia audible por el jurado

evidence or witnesses *(law)* pruebas o testigos

evidentiary evidence *(law)* hecho probatorio

evidentiary hearing vista probatoria

evidentiary material *(law)* material probatorio

evidentiary proceedings diligencia probatoria

evil *(adj)* malvada; malvado; **an evil killer** un malvado asesino

evildoer *(noun)* malhechor; malhechora

exact *(adj: precise)* exacta; exacto; precisa; preciso **this is the exact spot** éste es el sitio exacto; éste es el lugar preciso; **those were her exact words** ésas fueron sus palabras textuales

exact words palabras textuales

examination of witness interrogatorio del testigo

exception *(noun)* objeción firme

excess income ingreso en exceso; ingreso excesivo

exchange *(noun)* intercambio; **there was an exchange of shots** hubo un tiroteo; **a heated exchange** un acalorado intercambio de palabras; **we exchanged a few words** cruzamos unas palabras

exchange of gunfire balacera; tiroteo; **there was an exchange of gunfire** hubo un tiroteo; hubo una balacera

exchange of shots balacera; tiroteo; **there was an exchange of shots** hubo un tiroteo; hubo una balacera

exclusion of wages exclusión de sueldo; exclusión salarios

ex-con *(noun)* ex convicta; ex convicto

exlcusionary rule *(law)* regla de exclusión

exculpatory evidence *(law)* evidencia exculpatoria

exculpatory statement *(law)* declaración exculpatoria

excuse *(law: to relieve from responsibility)* dispensar

excuse a juror *(law: to relieve from responsibility)* dispensar a un jurado

excuse a witness *(law: to relieve from responsibility)* dispensar a un testigo

execute *(verb: put to death)* ejecutar; *(law: sign, seal legal document)* cumplir con las formalidades; llevar a efecto; realizar

execution *(noun: putting to death)* ejecución; *(law: sign, seal legal document)* cumplimiento

exempt *(adj)* exenta; exento

exhaust *(verb)* agotar

exhausted *(adj)* agotada; agotado; exhausta; exhausto

exhibit *(law)* prueba real admitida; documento de prueba; documento u objeto que se exhibe en un juicio como prueba

exhibit *(law)* manifestar; mostrar; exhibir; exponer; poner de manifiesto

exhume *(verb)* exhumar; desenterrar

ex-husband *(noun)* ex marido

exit *(way out from building, airplane, freeway)* salida; **the rear exit** la salida de atrás

exit visa visa de salida

exonerate *(law)* exculpar

exonerating circumstance circunstancia eximente

expect *(verb)* esperar; suponer

expectant *(adj: pregnant)* expectante

expectant mother mujer encinta; futura mamá

expectant parents futuros padres

expectation *(noun)* esperanzas; expectativas

Expected Family Contribution (EFC) Contribución Familiar Esperada

expedite *(verb)* acelerar; apresurar

expenses *(noun)* gastos

expenses to be borne by claimant gastos a cuenta del reclamante

experience *(noun)* experiencia; **to learn something by experience** saber algo por experiencia; **work experience** experiencia laboral

expert *(noun)* experta; experto; perito; **ask him, he's the expert** pregúntale a él que es el experto; **I'm no expert** no soy ningún experto

expert knowledge conocimientos de experto

expert testimony prueba pericial; peritaje; prueba de peritos

expert witness testigo perito

expiration date fecha de vencimiento

expire *(verb)* vencer; caducar; finalizar

explain *(verb)* explicar; **to explain something to somebody** explicarle algo a alguien; **to explain oneself** explicarse

explain how ... explicar cómo ...

explain why ... explicar por qué ...

explanation *(noun)* explicación

express authority poder expreso

express notice notificación expresa

extended care tratamiento adicional; tratamiento prolongado, tratamiento extendido; cuidado adicional; cuidado prolongado; cuidado extendido

extended coverage protección adicional; protección prolongada; protección extendida

extenuating circumstances circunstancias extraordinarias; circunstancias atenuantes

extension *(noun)* extensión; ampliación

extort *(verb)* extorsionar; **to extort money from somebody** extorsionar a alguien; **to extort a confession from somebody** arrancarle a alguien una confesión; obtener de alguien una confesión

extortion *(noun)* extorsión; chantaje

extracurricular activities actividades extraescolares

extraditable *(adj)* extraditable

extradite *(adj)* extraditar; **to extradite somebody** conseguir la extradición de alguien

extradition *(noun)* extradición

extradition request petición de extradición

extramarital *(adj)* fuera del matrimonio

ex-wife *(noun)* ex mujer

eye *(noun)* ojo; **in the eyes of the law** a los ojos de la ley

eye examination examen de la vista

eye witness *(law)* testigo ocular; testigo presencial; testigo de vista

eye witness testimony *(law)* testimonio de testigo ocular; testimonio de testigo presencial; testimonio de testigo de vista

eyeglasses anteojos; gafas; lentes

F

fabricate *(verb: invent story, excuse)* inventar; *(document; evidence)* falsificar

fabrication *(noun: lie, invention)* invención; mentira; **this story is a complete fabrication** esto es pura mentira

face *(noun: of person)* cara; rostro; **his face was badly scarred** tenía la cara llena de cicatrices; **she has a thin face** tiene la cara delgada; **she has an oval face** tiene la cara ovalada

face to face *(adv)* cara a cara; frente a frente; **we finally met face to face** finalmente nos encontramos cara a cara; finalmente estuvimos frente a frente; **I'd rather discuss it face to face** preferiría discutirlo cara a cara

face to face interview entrevista frente a frente; entrevista en persona; entrevista cara a cara

face value *(of money, bonds)* valor nominal; **I took what she said at face value** yo me creí lo que dijo

facial hair vello facial

facilitator *(noun)* facilitador; facilitadora

facilities *(noun)* instalaciones; instituciones

fact *(law)* hecho; **before the fact** antes de los hechos; **after the fact** después de los hechos

fact *(noun)* hecho; **the fact that ...** el hecho de que ...; **the fact is that ...** el hecho es que ...; **I know for a fact that ...** sé a ciencia cierta que ...; **it is a well-known fact** todo el mundo lo sabe; **what are the facts of the case?** ¿qué se sabe en concreto sobre el caso?; **I want hard facts** quiero datos concretos; **the fact of the matter is that ...**el hecho es que ...; **it's a fact that ...** es un hecho que...; **to stick to the facts** atenerse a los hechos

fact-finding *(adj)* de investigación; investigador; investigadora; **a fact-finding committee** una comisión de investigación

fact of life realidad de la vida

facts in issue *(law)* hechos contenciosos; hechos controvertidos

factsheet *(noun)* hoja informativa; hoja de datos

fail *(verb)* fallar; fracasar; **to fail to** + *infin*; **you failed to mention the crucial point** no has mencionado el punto crucial; **she failed to keep her word** faltó a su palabra; no cumplió con su palabra; **without fail** sin falta; **I fail to understand** no logro entender

failure *(noun: business, marriage, talks)* fracaso; quiebra; **it was a complete failure** fue un fracaso total; **to end in failure** acabar mal; malograrse; **failure to keep one's word** falta de cumplimiento de la palabra

failure to disperse incumplimiento de dispersarse

failure to pay incumplimiento en el pago

failure to prosecute abandono del proceso

failure to report dejar de informar

fair *(adj: person, decision)* justa; justo; imparcial; **it's not fair!** ¡no es justo! ¡no hay derecho!; **it's only fair that ...** lo más justo sería que ...; **it's fair to say that ...** hay que reconocer que ...; **fair enough!** ¡vale!; **a fair amount of** bastante; *(complexion, hair)* rubia; rubio; güera; güero

fair competition competencia justa

fair market value valor equitativo en el mercado

fair-minded *(adj)* justa; justo; imparcial

fair trial *(law)* juicio justo; **a fair trial cannot be held in Albuquerque** un juicio justo no puede llevarse a cabo en Albuquerque

fairly *(adv: just, honestly)* con imparcialidad; justamente; **the judge dealt fairly with him** el juez fue justo con él; el juez lo trató con justicia; **I'm fairly sure** creo que sí; **fairly good** bastante bueno

fairness *(noun)* justicia; imparcialidad; equidad

fake *(noun: object)* falsificación; imitación; farsa; ser puro cuento; **this passport is a fake** este pasaporte es falso; **his limp was a fake** su cojera era una farsa; **the whole story was a complete fake** toda la historia era puro cuento

fake *(verb: document or signature)* falsificar; *(results, evidence)* falsear; amañar; **he faked the official report** amañó el informe oficial; **the kidnap was faked** el secuestro fue una farsa

false *(adj)* falsa; falso; **under false pretenses** mediante fraude; mediante engaño

false arrest detención ilegal; arresto ilegal

false hairpiece peluca

false imprisonment privación ilegal de la libertad

false police report falso informe policial; falso parte policial

false pretense apariencias falsas; pretensiones falsas; mediante fraude; mediante engaño

false pretenses de manera fraudulenta

false representation representación falsa hecha con intención de engañar

false statement declaración falsa

false teeth dentadura postiza

false witness falso testimonio

falsely accused acusada equivocadamente; acusado equivocadamente

falsify *(verb)* falsificar; falsear

fall *(season)* otoño

fall guy cabeza de turco; chivo; **Jim was the fall guy** Jim fue el que pagó el pato

family *(noun)* familia; **my son and his children** mi hijo y su familia; **my daughter and her family** mi hija y su familia; **a friend of the family** un amigo de la familia; una amiga de la familia; **he's just like one of the family** es como de la familia; **she comes from a good family** es de buena familia; **we are a very close family** somos una familia muy unida; *(relatives, children)* **do you have any family?** ¿tiene usted parientes?; ¿tiene usted hijos?; **within the family** en el ámbito de la familia; **the climate of violence experienced within the family** el clima de violencia vivido en el ámbito de la familia

family business negocio familiar

family court tribunal familiar *(el tribunal familiar atiende asuntos de familia que involucran a menores)*

family culture cultura familiar

family doctor médica de cabecera; médico de cabecera

family employment empleo de familia

family law derecho de familia; derecho familiar

family law court tribunal de derecho familiar

family life vida doméstica

family man padre de familia

family maximum benefits beneficios máximos de familia

family name apellido; nombre de familia

family planning planificación familiar

family planning clinic centro de planificación familiar

family unit núcleo familiar

family values valores tradicionales de la familia

far *(adv)* lejos; *(in phrases)* **as far as I know** que yo sepa; **as far as I'm concerned** en lo que a mí respecta

far-reaching de gran alcance; trascendental; transcendental

farm *(noun)* granja; finca

farm laborer *(noun)* jornalera; jornalero; obrera; obrero; peón

farmer *(noun)* agricultor; agricultora; granjera; granjero

farmhand *(noun)* peón de labranza

farmwork *(noun)* encofrado

farmworkers *(noun)* trabajadores agrícolas

fatality *(noun: death)* muerte *(victim)* muerta; muerto; víctima; **there were no fatalities** no hubo muertos

fatally *(adv)* mortalmente

fatally wounded herida mortalmente; herido mortalmente; herida de muerte; herido de muerte; **he was fatally wounded** fue herido de muerte; fue herido mortalmente

father *(noun: parent)* padre; **he's been like a father to me** ha sido como un padre para mí; **his father and mother** sus padres; **her father and mother** sus padres

father figure figura paterna; imagen paterna

father-in-law *(noun)* suegro

fatherland *(noun)* patria

fatherless *(adj)* huérfana de padre; huérfano de padre; **to be fatherless** ser huérfana de padre; ser huérfano de padre; no tener padre

fatherly *(adj)* paternal; **he gave him some fatherly advice** lo aconsejó como un padre

father's first name nombre de pila del padre

father's last name apellido del padre

father's middle name segundo nombre del padre

fatigue *(noun)* fatiga; cansancio

fault *(noun: responsibility; blame)* culpa; **whose fault is it?** ¿quién tiene la culpa?; ¿de quién es la culpa?; **it's your fault** tú tienes la culpa; la culpa es tuya; **it's not my fault** yo no tengo la culpa; no es culpa mía; **to be at fault** ser culpable; **they were at fault in not reporting the theft** hicieron mal al no denunciar el robo; obraron mal al no denunciar el robo; **my memory could be at fault here** en esto me podría estar fallando la memoria; **it's nobody's fault** nadie tiene la culpa

February *(noun)* Febrero *(see* **July** *for usage)*

Federal Case Registry (FCR) of Child Support Registro Federal de Casos (FCR) de Manutención de los Hijos

Federal Citizen Information Center Centro Federal de Información para Ciudadanos

federal civil rights case caso federal de derechos civiles

federal crime delito federal

federal district court tribunal federal de primera instancia; corte de distrito federal

Federal Employees Retirement System (FERS) Sistema de Retiro de Empleados Federales

federal excise tax impuestos federales sobre artículos de uso y consumo

Federal Family Education Loan (FFEL) Programa de Préstamo Federal de Educación Familiar

federal government gobierno federal

federal grants subvenciones federales; concesiones federales

Federal Housing Administration (FHA) Administración Federal de Vivienda

federal immigration laws leyes federales de inmigración

Federal Insurance Contributions Act (F.I.C.A) Impuestos de Seguro Social; Ley de Contribución al Seguro Federal

federal jurisdiction jurisdicción federal

federal offense delito federal

Federal Parent Locator Service (FPLS) Servicio Federal de Ubicación de Padres (FPLS)

federal protective officer oficial de la policía estatal federal

Federal Supplemental Educational Opportunity Grants (FSEOG) Becas Federales Suplementarias para Oportunidad Educativa

Federal Trade Commission Comisión Federal de Comercio

feedback *(noun)* reacción; feedback

feel *(verb)* sentirse; encontrarse

fellow citizen conciudadana; conciudadano

fellow countryman compatriota

felon *(noun: law)* autor de un delito; autora de un delito *(persona que ha cometido un delito grave)*

feloniuos *(adj)* criminal

feloniuos homicide homicidio por culpa

felony *(law)* delito grave; delito mayor

felony murder *(law)* homicidio preterintencional

female *(noun: in official reports)* mujer

female impersonator imitador de mujeres

female prisoner presa; prisionera; rea

fetal *(adj)* fetal; **in a fetal position** en posición fetal

fetus *(noun)* feto

feud *(noun)* contienda; enemistad; **a family feud** una disputa familiar; *(verb)* contender; pelear; **to feud with somebody** pelearse con alguien

fewer charges menos cargos

fib *(noun)* mentirijilla; **to tell a fib** decir una mentirijilla; decir mentirijillas

fibber *(noun)* mentirosilla; mentirosillo

ficticious *(adj: name, address)* ficticia; ficticio; falsa; falso

fieldwork *(noun: research)* trabajo de campo

fieldworker *(noun: researcher)* trabajador de campo; trabajadora de campo

fifteen *(adj & noun)* quince

fifteenth *(adj & noun)* decimoquinta; decimoquinto

fifth *(verb)* quinta; quinto

Fifth Amendment Quinta Enmienda

fight *(noun: between two people)* pelea; *(struggle, campaign)* lucha; *(argument)* disputa; *(law)* negar una acusación; **he's had a fight with his wife** se ha peleado con su mujer; **she's had a fight with her husband** se ha peleado con su marido; **he's had a fight with his girlfriend** se ha peleado con su novia; **she's had a fight with her boyfriend** se ha peleado con su novio; **they've had a fight with their neighbors** se han peleado con sus vecinos; **they've had a fight with each other** se han peleado; **he broke up the fight between the boys** separó a los niños que se estaban peleando

fight back defenderse; resistir

fight for abogar por; **he fought for immigrants' rights** abogaba por los derechos de los inmigrantes

fighting *(noun: in general)* el pelear; el luchar; *(in street)* disturbio; **the street fighting lasted all day** se luchó todo el día en las calles

fighting words palabras que provocan a pelea

fiftieth *(adj)* quincuagésima; quincuagésimo

file *(noun: collection of documents)* archivo; *(of a particular case)* expediente; dossier; **he discovered that they were keeping a file on him** descubrió que lo tenían fichado; **to put something on file** archivar algo; **the information is all on file** toda la información está archivada; **that file has been closed for years** ese caso se cerró hace ya muchos años

file *(verb: letters, papers)* archivar; **file this under "pending"** archiva esto en 'pendiente'; **file these letters away** archiva estas cartas

file *(law: charges)* entablar; formular; interponer; **to file a suit** entablar una demanda; formular una demanda

file a brief *(law)* interponer un escrito; presentar un escrito

file a charge *(law)* entablar cargos; presentar cargos; formular cargos

file a claim presentar una demanda

file a complaint *(law)* presentar una queja; presentar un reclamo

file a notice of appeal *(law)* formular una notificación de comparecencia

file a motion *(law)* interponer una petición; presentar un escrito al tribanal

file a petition interponer una petición

file a petition requesting that interponer una petición pidiendo que; interponer una petición solicitando que

file a police report presentar un informe policial; presentar una parte policial

file an appeal *(law)* interponer un recurso de apelación; apelar formalmente; presentar una apelación

file an application hacer una solicitud; presentar una solicitud

file an indictment *(law)* interponer un documento inculpatorio

file an objection *(law)* interponer una objeción

file card ficha

file clerk administrativa; administrativo; archivera; archivero

file charges *(law)* entablar querella

file charges against *(law)* entablar querella contra

file for civil action entablar una acción civil

file for divorce presentar una demanda de divorcio

filing *(law)* radicación

filing date fecha de radicación, fecha de solicitud

filing fees honorarios de presentación

filing of return presentación de la declaración

fill *(verb)* rellenar; **fill in the blanks** rellene los espacios en blanco

final *(adj)* última; último; **a last demand for payment** un último aviso de pago; **that's final** no hay más que hablar; **the judge's decision is final** la decisión del jurado es inapelable

final argument *(law)* alegato de clausura; alegato final

final judgement *(law)* sentencia definitiva; sentencia firme

final offer última oferta

final statement *(law)* alegato de clausura; alegato final

finality of decision finalidad de la decisión

finally *(adv: lastly)* por último; finalmente; para finalizar; *(at last)* por fin; finalmente; **he's finally been arrested** por fin lo han detenido; finalmente ha sido detenido; por fin lo han arrestado; finalmente ha sido arrestado

finance charges costos financieros

finance company sociedad financiera

financial assistance prestaciones económicas

financial assistance in cases of disability prestaciones económicas en casos de invalidez

financial backing respaldo financiero

financial burden carga económica

financial hardship privación económica; apuros económicos

financial help ayuda económica

financial security seguridad económica

financial standing capacidad financiera

financial statement estado financiero; resultado financiero

financial worth valor neto

financial year ejercicio financiero; año contable

find *(law: make a determination)* determinar; dictar sentencia; fallar; resolver

find guilty declarar culpable

find not guilty absolver; absolver de toda culpa; **she was found not guilty** la absolvieron de toda culpa; la declararon inocente; **he was found not guilty** lo absolvieron de toda culpa; lo declararon inocente

find work conseguir trabajo

finding *(law)* determinación; fallo; resolución; sentencia; laudo arbitral; **to announce one's findings** dictar laudo

finding of facts hallazgo de los hechos

finding of guilt *(law)* fallo condenatorio; sentencia condenatoria; sentencia de condena; veredicto de culpabilidad

finding of law conclusión de derecho

finding of probable cause dictarse auto de procesamiento

findings by the court determinaciones de hechos por la corte

findings of the investigation resultados de la investigación

fine *(law)* multa; pena pecuniaria; **to get a fine for something** ser multada por algo; ser multado por algo; **to get a fine for doing something** ser multada por hacer algo; ser multado por hacer algo; **I got a fine for ...** me pusieron una multa por ...; **she was fined for speeding** la multaron por exceso de velocidad; le pusieron una multa por exceso de velocidad; le aplicaron una multa por exceso de velocidad

finger *(noun: of hand)* dedo; **index finger** dedo índice; **middle finger** dedo medio; dedo corazón; **ring finger** dedo anular; **little finger** dedo meñique

fingernail *(noun)* uña

fingerprint *(noun)* huella digital; huella dactilar; impresión digital; **to take somebody's fingerprint** tomarle las huellas digitales a alguien

fingerprint *(verb)* tomarle las huellas digitales a alguien

fire *(noun)* fuego; **to be on fire** estar en llamas; estar ardiendo; **to set something on fire** prenderle fuego a algo; **to set fire to something** prenderle fuego a algo; *(accident)* incendio; **there was a fire at the factory** hubo un incendio en la fábrica; **forest fire** incendio forestal; *(of guns)* fuego; **to open fire on somebody** abrir fruego sobre alguien;

to exchange fire tirotearse; **to come under fire** entrar en la línea de fuego; **we were under fire** estaban disparando sobre nosotros

fire *(verb: gun, rifle)* disparar; hacer fuego; **to fire a gun at somebody** dispararle a alguien; **to fire a shot at somebody** dispararle un tiro a alguien; **to fire at somebody** disparar contra alguien; **the police fired on the demonstrators** la policía disparó sobre los manifestantes

fire insurance seguro de incendios; seguro contra incendios

fire exit salida de incendios

firearm *(noun)* arma de fuego

firebomb *(noun)* bomba incendiaria

firefighter bombera; bombero

fireman *(noun)* bombera; bombero

firm *(noun)* empresa; firma; compañía

firm address dirección de la compañía; dirección de la empresa

firm name nombre de la compañía; nombre de la empresa

firm offer oferta en firme

first-born *(adj)* primogénita; primogénito

First Amendment Primera Enmienda a la Constitución

first-born child *(noun)* primogénita; primogénito

first court date primera fecha de corte

first cousin prima hermana; primo hermano

first degree murder homicidio en primer grado; asesinato en primer grado

first grade primer año de la escuela primaria; primer grado

first language lengua materna

first lien primer gravamen sobre una propiedad

first mortgage primera hipoteca

first name nombre de pila; *(colloquial)* primer nombre; **to be on a first-name basis** tutearse; tratarse de tú con alguien

first offender delincuente primario; delincuente sin antecedentes penales (persona declarada culpable de un delito por primera vez)

first papers *solicitud inicial del trámite para obtener la ciudadanía estadounidense*

first responders primeros respondientes

first year of high school el primer año de la escuela secundaria

fiscal year año fiscal

fisherman *(noun)* pescador; pescadora

fishing *(noun: profession)* pesca

fist *(noun)* puño

fistfight *(noun)* pelea a puñetazos

five *(adj & noun)* cinco

five-year continuous residence residencia continua de cinco años

fix-it ticket multa de arreglo de vehículo

fixed assets activo fijo

fixed-term liabilities deudas a largo plazo

flame *(noun)* llama; **to be in flames** estar en llamas; **to go up in flames** incendiarse

flash *(verb: expose oneself)* exhibirse en público

flasher *(noun: man who exposes himself)* exhibicionista

flashing lights luces que se encienden y se apagan; luces intermitentes

flee *(noun)* huir; escapar; darse a la fuga; **to flee the country** huir del país

flight *(escape)* fuga; huida; *(airplane)* vuelo

flight attendant auxiliar de vuelo

fling *(verb: love affair)* aventura; **to have a fling** irse de juerga

flood *(noun)* inundación

flood damages daños causados por las inundaciones

flood insurance seguro contra inundaciones

flood victims los damnificados por las inundaciones

flooding *(noun)* inundación

floodwater *(noun)* crecida

flophouse *(noun)* albergue para vagabundos

fluency *(noun: in speech, writing)* fluidez; soltura; **She speaks Spanish with great fluency** habla Español con mucha fluidez; habla Español con mucha soltura

fluent *(adj: in languages)* hablar con fluidez; hablar con soltura; **to be fluent in Spanish** hablar Español con fluidez; hablar Español con soltura; **she spoke in fluent Spanish** habló con fluidez en Español; habló Español con soltura

fluently *(adv: write, express oneself)* con fluidez; con soltura

flu-shot *(noun)* vacuna de influenza; vacuna de gripe

fly-by-night *(adj: dealer, firm)* pirata, que no inspira confianza; *(noun)* pirata

fly off the handle perder los estribos

focus *(verb)* fijar; enfocar; concentrar; **it's important to focus our attention on this point** conviene fijar la atención en este punto

follow the law obedecer la ley

follow-up*(noun)* recordatorio; continuación; seguimiento

follow up *(verb)* seguir; darle seguimiento a; **to follow up a lead** seguir una pista; investigar una pista

fondle *(verb)* acariciar

fondness *(noun)* cariño; afición

food *(noun)* comida; alimento

food coupons vales de comida

food poisoning intoxicación por alimentos

food stamps vales de comida; cupones de alimentos; cupones alimenticios

Food Stamp Program Programa de Cupones para Alimentos

foot *(anat)* pie

for a change para variar

for all practical purposes a efectos prácticos

for driving under the influence of alcohol por manejar estando borracha; por manejar estando borracho

for each appeal para cada apelación

for lack of por falta de

for lack of evidence por falta de pruebas

for no reason at all sin ningún motivo

for our purposes para nuestros propósitos

for the crime of por el delito de

for the most part en general

for the time being por ahora; de momento

for years durante años

force *(noun: strength, violence)* fuerza; **use force** hacer uso de la fuerza; **resort to force** recurrir a la fuerza; **the police were out in force** había una gran presencia policial; **force of habit** la fuerza de la costumbre; **the police force** la policía; **deadly force** fuerza mortal

force *(verb)* forzar

forcible rape violación por la fuerza

foreclose *(verb: loan, mortgage)* ejecutar; **to foreclose on something** ejecutar algo

foreclosure *(noun: loan, mortgage)* ejecutación; juicio hipotecario

forcible entry usurpación de domicilio; violación de propiedad

foreign *(adj: customs, language, country)* extranjera; extranjero

foreign-born nacida en el extranjero; nacido en el extranjero

foreign legal adoption adopción legal extranjera

Foreign Work Test Límite de Trabajo en el Extranjero

foreigner *(noun)* extranjera; extranjero

foreman *(noun)* capataz; mayordomo

foreman of the jury *(law)* presidente del jurado

forensic *(adj)* forense

forensic medicine medicina legal; medicina forense

forensic report informe del médico forense

foreseeable *(adj)* previsible

forest fire incendio forestal

forewoman of the jury *(law)* presidenta del jurado

forfeit *(verb: property)* perder el derecho a; *(law: they were consficated)* le fueron consficados los bienes

forfeiture *(noun: loss)* pérdida; confiscación

forge *(verb)* falsificar

forged money moneda falsa

forgery *(noun)* falsificación

form *(noun: document)* formulario; impreso; **to fill out a form** llenar un formulario; **tax forms** formularios de impuestos; **application form** solicitud

form letter carta modelo

Form W-2 comprobante de ganancias anuales; comprobante de retención de salarios

formalize *(make official)* formalizar; dar carácter oficial; dar carácter oficial a

former *(earlier, previous)* antigua; antiguo; **my former wife** mi ex-esposa; **my former husband** mi ex-esposo

forthwith *(adv)* inmediatamente

foster *(verb: child)* criar; *(place in care of foster parents)* colocar con una familia de acogida

foster care cuidado tutelar; cuidado de crianza

foster child *(boy)* hijo de leche; *(girl)* hija de leche; *(boy)* niño adoptivo; *(girl)* niña adoptiva

foster family familia de acogida

foster home casa cuna; hogar de cuidado tutelar, hogar de crianza, hogar de familia adoptiva

foster parents padres de crianza

fostering acogimiento familiar

four *(adj & noun)* cuatro

four-way-intersection cruce de cuatro direcciones

fourteen *(adj & noun)* catorce

fourteenth *(adj)* decimocuarto

Fourteenth Amendment Decimocuarta Enmendia a la Constitución

fourth *(verb)* cuarta; cuarto

Fourth Amendment Cuarta Enmendia a la Constitución

frame of mind estado de ánimo; **to be in the right frame of mind for something** estar de humor para algo; **to be in the wrong frame of mind for something** no estar de humor para algo; **I got myself in the right frame of mind for the trial** me preparé mentalmente para el juicio

frame of reference parámetros de referencia; marco de referencia

frame up estratagema para incriminar a alguien; **it's a frame up** aquí hay trampa

framework *(noun)* marco; **we have to operate within the framework of the law** debemos operar dentro del marco de la ley

fraud *(noun)* fraude; estafa; **by fraud** fraudulentamente; por medios fraudulentos

Fraud and Abuse Hotline Línea de Emergencia para Fraude y Abuso; Línea Directa de Fraude y Abuso

fraudulence *(noun)* fraudulencia

fraudulent *(adj)* fraudulenta; fraudulento

fraudulent crime delito doloso

fraught *(adj)* **to be fraught with** ser muy peligrosa; ser muy peligroso; **the operation was fraught with danger** la operación fue muy peligrosa; **this plan is fraught with problems** este plan está lleno de problemas; este plan está erizado de problemas; **the atmosphere is fraught with tension** el ambiente estaba cargado de tensión

free *(adj: at liberty)* libre; **to be free** ser libre; **to set somebody free** poner a alguien en libertad; dejar a alguien en libertad; **to get free** escaparse; **he went free for years because of lack of witnesses** durante años no se lo pudo inculpar por falta de testigos; **they let him go free for lack of evidence** lo dejaron en libertad por falta de pruebas; **trouble free** sin problemas; **tax free** libre de impuestos

Free Application for Student Aid (FAFSA) Solicitud Gratuita de Ayuda Federal Para Estudiantes

free collective bargaining negociación colectiva entre los trabajadores y la patronal

free enterprise la libre empresa

free pamphlet folleto gratis; folleto gratuito

freedom *(noun: liberty)* libertad

freedom of assembly libertad de reunión

freedom of expression *(noun: liberty)* libertad de expresión

freedom of information libertad de información

Freedom of Information Act (FOIA) Ley de Libertad de Información

freedom of movement libertad de movimientos

freedom of religion libertad de cultos

freedom of speech libertad de expresión

freedom of the press libertad de prensa

freelance *(adj)* por cuenta propia; *(verb)* trabajar por cuenta propia

freely *(adv: without restriction)* libremente; sin trabas; **I traveled freely around the country** viajé libremente por el país; viajé sin trabas por el país

freeway *(noun)* autopista

freeze *(noun: limitation, stoppage)* congelación; **a wage freeze** una congelación salarial; **a price freeze** una congelación de precios

freeze *(verb)* congelar

Freudian slip acto fallido

Friday *(noun)* Viernes *(see* **Monday** *for usage)*

friend *(noun: close acquaintance)* amiga; amigo; **a friend of ours** un amigo nuestro; **a friend of the family** un amigo de la familia; una amiga de la familia; **she's no friend of mine** amiga mía no es; **he felt he was among friends** se sentía entre amigos; **they've been friends for years** hace años que son amigos; **we're just good friends** sólo somos amigos

friendly *(adj: person)* simpática; simpático; *(place, atmosphere)* agradable; *(welcome)* cordial; **I'll give you some friendly advice** te voy a dar un consejo de amigo; **to be on friendly terms with somebody** llevarse bien con alguien

friendly fire fuego amigo

friendship *(noun)* amistad; **he did it out of friendship for her** lo hizo por la amistad que lo unía a ella

fringe benefits *(labor relation)* incentivos; complementos; beneficios económicos

frisk *(noun)* cachear; palpar de armas

from *(prep: indicating starting place)* de; desde; **where are you from?**; ¿de dónde eres?; **where has he come from?** ¿de dónde ha venido?; *(lindicating time)* de; desde; **from now on** de aquí en adelante; **from time to time** de vez en cuando

from bad to worse de mal en peor

front door *(of a house)* puerta principal; puerta de la calle

fugitive *(law)* prófuga; prófugo

fugitive warrant *(law)* mandamiento de detención de una prófuga; mandamiento de detención de un prófugo; orden de detención de una prófuga; orden de detención de un prófugo

full employment pleno empleo

full name nombre y apellidos

full pension pensión completa

full retirement age edad de jubilación completa

full-time *(adj: employment)* a tiempo completo; **a full-time job** un puesto de plena dedicación; **to work full-time** trabajar a tiempo completo

full-time nursing care servicio de enfermería de tiempo completo; cuidado de enfermería de tiempo completo

full-time student estudiante de tiempo completo

fully comprehensive insurance seguro contra todo riesgo

fully convinced convencida del todo; convencido del todo

fully insured totalmente asegurada; totalmente asegurado

fully satisfied satisfecha del todo; satisfecho del todo

fully trained nurse enfermera diplomada; enfermero diplomado

fundamental rights derechos fundamentales *(ortorgados por la Constitución)*

funded *(adj)* costeada; costeado

funds *(noun)* fondos

funeral *(noun: burial)* funeral; entierro

furnish evidence suministrar prueba

furnished room cuarto amurblado

further hearings vistas adicionales

further questioning nuevo interrogatorio

future *(adj)* futura; futuro; venidera; venidero; próxima; próximo; **at some future date** en alguna ocasión futura; **in the near future** en fecha próxima; *(noun)* porvenir; futuro

G

gag order auto de reserva; orden de desacato; mordaza judicial

gain *(noun: business, profit)* ganancia; beneficio; *(increase)* aumento; *(verb)* conseguir; obtener; adquirir

gainfully *(adv)* **to be gainfully employed** tener un trabajo retribuido; tener un trabajo remunerado

gainful employment trabajo retribuido; trabajo remunerado

gall bladder vesícula biliar

gallstone *(anat)* cálculo de la vesícula; piedras de la vesícula

gamble *(lay wager)* jugar; *(noun: bet)* apuesta

gambler *(noun)* jugador; jugadora; **compulsive gambler** un jugador emperdenido; una jugadora emperdenida; ludópata

gambling *(noun)* juego de azar; **compulsive gambling** ludopatía

gang *(noun: of criminals)* banda; pandilla; *(of workman)* cuadrilla; brigada; *(clique)* grupo

gang of thugs pandilla de matones

gang together formar un grupo; formar una pandilla

gang up *(colloquial for to unite in opposition)* **to gang up against somebody** conspirar contra alguien; unirse contra alguien

gangbang *(noun: slang)* violación múltiple; violación colectiva *(violación de una mujer por varios individuos)*

gangland *(noun)* mundillo del crimen; mundo del crimen

gangster *(noun)* gángster; pistolera; pistolero

ganja *(noun)* marihuana

gap *(noun)* espacio; brecha; **she has a gap between her front teeth** tiene los dientes de adelante separados; **generation gap** brecha entre las generaciones

gap-toothed *(with gaps between teeth)* que tiene los dientes separados; *(with missing teeth)* desdentada; desdentado; a quien le faltan dientes

garage mechanic mécanica; mécanico

garage owner propietaria de un taller de reparaciones; propietario de un taller de reparaciones

garbage collector basurera; basurero

garbage man basurera; basurero

garbage worker basurera; basurero

gardener *(noun)* jardinera; jardinero; hortelana; hortelano

garnish wages embargar los ingresos

garnishable embargable

garnishee order orden de embargo

garnishment order sentencia de embargo; auto de embargo

garnishment proceedings procedimiento de embargo

gash *(noun)* tajo; corte profundo; **I gashed my hand on a piece of glass** me hice un tajo en la mano con un vidrio

gather *(verb: crowd)* congregarse, reunirse; juntarse; *(conclude)* deducir; **I gather from what you're saying that you don't agree** deduzco por lo que dices que no estás de acuerdo; **you don't agree, I gather** según parece no estás de acuerdo

gather facts recopilar los hechos

gather information recabar información

gather together *(people, objects)* juntar; reunir

gay *(adj: homosexual)* gay; homosexual; **lesbians and gay men** lesbianas y gays; hombres y mujeres gay; **the gay community** la comunidad gay; **the gay scene** el ambiente gay

gay *(noun)* gay; homosexual

gay rights derechos de los homosexuales

general *(adj: not detailed or specific)* en general; **in general** por lo general; **as a general rule** por regla general; **in general terms** en términos generales; **the general idea is to ...** el propósito general es de ...; **I get the general picture** me hago una idea general; **be more general** no des tantos detalles; **speaking in general terms, you are right** hablando en general, tienes razón; **as a general rule the courts don't permit it** por lo general los tribunales no lo permiten; por reglas generales los tribunales no lo permiten

general authority derecho legal a actuar; derecho legal para actuar

general damages daños efectivos

General Education Development Certificate (GED) Certificado de Desarrollo Educativo General

general enrollment period período de inscripción general

generally *(adv: usual)* por lo general; generalmente; *(for the most part)* en general; **it is generally believed that...** la mayoría cree que ...

general-purpose *(adv: tool, dictionary)* de uso general

generation *(noun: group of people)* generación; **the younger generation** los jóvenes; **the older generation** los mayores; **first generation** primera generación; **segunda generation** segunda generación

generation gap brecha entre las generaciones

general practitioner médica de cabecera; médico de cabecera

genetic fingerprint huella genética

gentleman *(noun: man)* señor; *(well-mannered, well-bred man)* caballero; **to be a perfect gentleman** ser un cumplido caballero; *(as a term of address)* **ladies and gentlemen** señoras y señores

gentleman's agreement pacto de caballeros; acuerdo entre caballeros

geriatric *(adj)* anciana; anciano

geriatric home hogar de ancianos

gesture *(noun: of body)* gesto; ademán; **a rude gesture** un gesto grosero; **a gesture of defiance** in gesto desfiante; *(verb)* hacer gestos; *(fig)* **what a nice gesture!** ¡qué detalle más amable!; **as a gesture of friendship** en señal de amistad

get *(verb: general meanings)* conseguir; obtener; lograr, recibir; traer

get *(in phrases)* **to get back to what I was saying ...** volviendo a lo que estaba diciendo ...; **she got twelve years for armed robbery** le dieron doce años por robo a mano armada; **how much were you getting in your old job?** ¿cuánto ganabas en tu trabajo anterior; **I got the impression that ...** me dio la impresión de que ...; **I got the feeling that ...** tengo la sensación de que ...; **don't get me wrong** no me malentiendas; **I didn't quite get that: could you repeat?** no entendí bien ¿podrías repetir lo que dijiste?; **I didn't get your name** no entendí tu nombre; **did you get the number?** ¿tomaste nota del número?;

when can you get the documents to us? ¿cuándo nos puede hacer llegar los documentos?; **I'll get him to help you** le diré que te ayude; le pediré que te ayude; **you'll never get them to agree to that** no vas a lograr que acepten eso

get away *(escape: prisoner, suspect)* escaparse; **don't let him get away** no dejes que se escape

get away with *(escape: prisoner, suspect)* **you won't get away with this** esto no va a quedar así; **are you going to let him get away with calling you a liar?** ¿vas a dejar que te llame mentiroso y se quede tan fresco? **don't let them get away with it** no dejes que se salgan con la suya

get drunk emborracharse

get in *(join, to be accepted)* andar con; **he got in with a bad crowd** empezó a andar con malas compañías

get into arguments entrar en disputas; **he never gets into arguments** nunca entra en disputas

get involved in an argument *(law)* meterse en una discusión

get rid of deshacerse de; **he got rid of the body** se deshizo del cadáver

getaway *(quick departure)* huida; fuga; **to make one's getaway** escaparse; huir; **the getaway car** el coche que usaron para la fuga; **the thiefs made a quick getaway** los ladrones se dieron rápidamente a la fuga

get together *(come together)* **they got together to discuss the problem** se reunieron para tratar el asunto

get work conseguir trabajo

getting involved in lawsuits *(law)* meterse en pleitos

GI Bill *(person)* proyecto de ley para excombatientes

gift *(noun: present)* regalo; obsequio; donación; *(talent)* talento; don; dote

gift tax impuesto sobre donaciones

gifted *(person)* de talento; talentosa; talentoso; **a very gifted young woman** una joven de gran talento

girl *(noun: small)* niña; nena; chiquilla; *(young woman)* chica; muchacha; chavala

girlfriend *(noun: of girl, woman)* amiga; *(of boy, man)* novia

gist *(noun)* lo esencial; **that was the gist of it** eso fue fundamentalmente lo que dijo; **just give me the gist of it** cuéntamelo en líneas generales; **to get the gist of something** comprender lo esencial de algo; captar lo esencial de algo; **the gist of what she was saying was ...** en esencia lo que estaba diciendo era ...

give *(in phrases)* **the judge has given his verdict** el juez ha dictado sentencia; **the judge gave her five years** el juez le dio cinco años; el juez la condenó a cinco años; **she gave me to understand that ...** me dio a entender que ...; **to give evidence** prestar declaración; **she gave a detailed description of the crime scene** describió el lugar del crimen detalladamente; **she gave me her word** me dio su palabra; **I'll give it a quick look** le echaré una miradita; **why not give it a try?** ¿por qué no lo intentas? **give it to me straight** dime la verdad; sé sincera conmigo; sé sincero conmigo; **give a short description of the crime** dé una breve descripción del delito

give an account of dar cuenta de

give birth dar a luz

give protection brindar protección

give up a right denunciar de un derecho

given *(adj & adv)* determinada; determinado; **given that ...** dado que ...; **at a given moment** en un momento determinado; **given the circumstances** dadas las circunstancias ...; **given name** nombre de pila; **given his good reputation** ... dada su buena reputación ...

glad *(adj: pleased)* contenta; contento; feliz; alegre; **to be glad that ...** alegrarse de que ...; **I am glad to hear it** me alegra saberlo; **you'll be glad to hear that ...** te alegrará saber que ...

glasses *(noun)* lentes; anteojos; espejuelos; gafas

glue-sniffing inhalación de pegamento

go *(in phrases)* **the court hearing went well** la vista salió bien; **how did the court hearing go?** ¿cómo te fue en la vista?; **how's it going?**; ¿qué tal?; ¿qué tal te va?; **where do we go from here?** ¿qué hacemos ahora?; **let's go!** ¡vamos!;

go ahead with llevar adelante; **we're going ahead with our defense** llevamos adelante nuestra defensa.

go in entrar; intervenir; **the police went in to break up the demonstration** la policía intervino para dispersar a los manifestantes

go into entrar en; **to go into details** entrar en detalles; **I don't want to go into that** no quiere entrar en este tema; **in this article he goes into the reasons why ...** en el artículo analiza las razones por las cuales ...

go on seguir; proseguir; durar; **the trial went on for months** el juicio duró meses; **the investigation goes on** la investigación continúa; **the jury deliberation just went on and on** la deliberación del jurado se alargó interminablemente; **what's going on?** ¿qué pasa?; **he went on to say that ...** añadió que ...

go to work ir al trabajo; ir a trabajar

godchild *(noun)* ahijada; ahijado

goddaughter *(noun)* ahijada

godfather *(noun)* padrino

godmother *(noun)* padrina

godparents *(noun)* padrinos

godson *(noun)* ahijado

good *(in phrases: the usual translation* **bueno** *becomes* **buen** *when it is used before a masculine singular noun)* **it looks good** tiene buen aspecto; **in good condition** en buen estado; **he promised to make good the damage to the car** se comprometió a hacerse cargo de la reparación del coche; **they made good their promise** cumplieron con su promesa; **they made good on their threat** cumplieron con su amenaza; **to make good on one's escape** lograr huir; **things are looking pretty good now** en este momento las cosas van muy bien; **it's a good chance for you to meet them** es una buena ocasión para que los conozcas; **it's a good thing you remembered** menos mal que te acordaste; **it seemed like a good idea at the time** en aquel momento nos pareció una buena idea; **to be in a good mood** estar de buen humor; **good for you!** ¡bien hecho!

good behavior buena conducta

good cause *(legally sufficient grounds)* justificación; motivo justificante; razón justificada

good faith buena fe

good grief! ¡Jesús!; ¡por Dios!

good time *(the amount that a given prison sentence is reduced)* remisión de la duración de la pena

government gobierno

Government Pension Offset (GPO) Ajuste por Pensión del Gobierno

government vehicle coche del gobierno

government witness testigo del gobierno

government's latest act última acción del gobierno

grace period período de gracia; **three days' grace** un plazo de tres días

graduate *(noun: education)* licenciada; licenciado; graduada; graduado; bachiller; **he is in graduate school** está haciendo un curso de posgrado; **a University of New Mexico graduate** un licenciado de la Universidad de Nuevo México; una licenciada de la Universidad de Nuevo México

graduate *(verb: from a college, university)* obtener el título; terminar la carrera; graduarse; recibirse; *(obtain a bachelor's degree)* licenciarse; *(progress to)* **to graduate from something to something** pasar de algo a algo; **they often graduate from marijuana to heroin** a menudo pasan de la marihuana a la heroína; **he graduated in history** se licenció en historia

graduate student estudiante de posgrado

grand jury jurado indagatorio; jurado de acusación *(jurado que decide si hay suficientes pruebas para procesar)*

grand jury summoned by jurado de acusación convocado por

grand larceny hurto mayor; robo de mayor cuantía; robo en mayor cuantía

grandchild *(noun)* nieta; nieto

granddad *(noun)* abuelo

granddaddy *(noun)* abuelito

granddaughter *(noun)* nieta

grandfather *(noun)* abuelo

grandfathered *(adj)* exenta; exento

grandma *(noun)* abuela

grandmother *(noun)* abuela

grandparents *(noun)* abuelos

grandson *(noun)* nieto

grand theft hurto mayor; robo de mayor cuantía; robo en mayor cuantía

granny *(noun)* abuelita

grant *(verb: desire, wish, request)* conceder; otorgar; **he was granted permission** se le concedió permiso; **granted that ...** dado que ...; **I grant him that** le concedo eso; **to take something for granted** dar algo por supuesto; dar algo por sentado; **he takes her for granted** no le hace el más mínimo caso; *(admit)* **I grant that the plan is good** reconozco que es un buen plan; **he's a fair judge, I'll grant you that** es un juez justo, eso no te lo discuto

grant *(noun: subsidy)* subvención; subsidio; *(to student)* beca

grant *(verb)* dar lugar a

grant a motion *(verb)* dar lugar al pedimento

grant a probation *(verb)* conceder condena condicional probatoria; otorgar condena condicional probatoria

grant-in-aid *(noun: subsidy)* subvención; subsidio

grass *(drug, marijuana)* maría; hierba; monte; mota

grateful *(adj)* agradecida; agradecido; *(noun)* agradecimiento; de gratitud; **I'm very grateful to you for your advice** le agradezco mucho sus consejos; le estoy muy agradecida por sus consejos; le estoy muy agradecido por sus consejos; **I'd be so grateful if you could do it** te agradecería tanto que lo hicieras; **just be grateful for what you've got!** ¡da gracias por lo que tienes!; **I am grateful to you** le estoy muy agradecida; le estoy muy agradecido; **I am most grateful to you for your help** le agradezco mucho su ayuda

gratuitous military wage credits créditos gratuitos por servicio militar

gray *(adj & noun: color)* gris; *(beard, hair)* canosa; canoso; gris; cana; cano; **a gray hair** una cana; **she has gray hair** es canosa; tiene canas

great *(in phrases)* **we discussed it in great detail** lo discutimos punto por punto; lo discutimos muy minuciosamente; **on an even greater scale** incluso a mayor escala; **with great interest** con gran interés; **with great care** con gran cuidado; **great progress has been made** se han hecho grandes progresos; **greater help is needed** se necesita más ayuda; **it's a great pity you can't come** es una verdadera lástima que no puedes venir; **I'm in no great hurry** no tengo mucha prisa; no estoy muy apurada; no estoy muy apurado; **you're a great help!** ¡valiente ayuda la tuya!; **he's a great believer in ...** es un gran partidario de ...; **the great thing is that ...** lo mejor de todo es que ...;

the important thing is that ... lo importante es que ...; **it was great!** ¡fue estupendo!; **it's of no great importance** no tiene importancia

great-aunt *(noun)* tía abuela

great-grandchild *(noun)* bisnieta; bisnieto

great-grandchildren *(noun)* bisnietos

great-granddaughter *(noun)* bisnieta

great-grandfather *(noun)* bisabuelo

great-grandmother *(noun)* bisabuela

great-grandparents *(noun)* bisabuelos

great-nephew *(noun)* sobrinonieto

great-niece *(noun)* sobrinanieta

great-uncle *(noun)* tío abuelo

green *(adj & noun)* verde

green arrow *(traffic sign)* flecha verde

green card tarjeta verde; permiso de residencia y trabajo

green light semáforo en luz verde

greenish *(adj)* verdosa; verdoso

greenish blue azul verdosa; azul verdoso

greet *(verb: welcome, receive)* recibir; darle la bienvenida a

grief *(noun: sorrow)* dolor; pena; pesar; *(cause of sorrow)* tristeza

grief-stricken *(adj: person)* consternada; consternado; acongojada; acongojado; desconsolada; desconsolado; apesadumbrada; apesadumbrado

grievance *(noun: complaint)* queja; agravio; *(ground for complaint)* motivo de queja; *(of workers)* revindicación

grievance procedure sistema de trámite de quejas; procedimiento conciliatorio

grieve *(verb)* dar pena a; causar tristeza a; afligir; **it grieves me to see ...** me da pena ver ...

gringo *(noun)* gringa; gringo

grocery store tienda de abarrotes

groom *(noun)* novio; **the bride and groom** los novios; *(after ceremony)* los recién casados

gross *(adj: extreme, flagrant)* flagrante; burda; burdo; **a gross distortion of the facts** una burda tergiversación de los hechos; **she earns $100,000 gross a year** gana en total cien mil dólares al año; **I earn $700 a week gross** ganó setecientos dólares brutos por semana

gross earnings ganancias brutas

gross ignorance ignorancia crasa; ignorancia supina

gross indecency *(law)* ultraje contra la moral pública

gross misconduct *(law)* negligencia grave

gross negligence *(law)* culpa grave

gross wage salario bruto

ground floor planta baja; primer piso

grounds *(in phrases)* **on legal grounds** por motivos legales; por razones legales; **on financial grounds** por motivos económicos; por razones económicas; **there are grounds for thinking he's dead** existen razones para pensar que ha muerto; **there are grounds for believing he's dead** existen razones para creer que ha muerto

grounds for concern motivos de preocupación

grounds for divorce causal de divorcio

group counseling terapia grupal; terapia de grupo

group life insurance seguro de vida colectivo

group therapy terapia grupal; terapia de grupo

guarantee *(law: debt, treaty)* avalar; garantizar; *(document, article)* garantía; prenda

guarantee *(on consumer goods)* garantía; **to be under guarantee** estar bajo garantía; **manufacturer's guarantee** garantía de fábrica; *(assurance)* garantía; **there's no guarantee that he'll come back** no hay ninguna garantía de que vaya a volver; **you have my personal guarantee that ...** le garantizo personalmente que ...

guarantor *(noun)* garante; fiadora; fiador; aquél que da una garantía

guardian *(noun)* tutor; tutora

guardianship *(noun)* tutela; *(awarded by a judge)* tutela dativa

Guatemalan *(adj & noun)* Guatemalteca; Guatemalteco

guideline *(noun)* pauta; directriz; **to serve as a guideline** servir de pauta; **they lack clear guidelines on this matter** carecen de pautas en esta materia; carecen de directices en esta materia; **to lay down guidelines** establecer pautas; **to issue guidelines** establecer pautas

guilt *(law)* culpabilidad; *(blame)* culpa; **to admit one's guilt** confesarse culpable

guilt complex complejo de culpa

guiltless *(adj)* inocente; libre de culpa; **I am guiltless of any crime** no he cometido ningún delito

guilty *(adj: law)* culpable; **to plead guilty** confesarse culpable; **how do you plead? — not guilty** ¿cómo se declara? — inocente; **how do you plead? — guilty or not?** ¿se confesa inocente o culpable? **he was the guilty party** él era el culpable; **to find somebody guilty** declarar a alguien culpable; **to find somebody not guilty** declarar a alguien inocente; **to be guilty of something** ser culpable de algo; *(ashamed, remorseful; shameful)* culpable; vergonzosa; vergonzosa; **to have a guilty conscience** tener remordimientos de conciencia; tener la conciencia sucia; **don't feel guilty about that** no te sientas culpable por eso; **I feel guilty about not having warned her**; me siento culpable por no habérselo advertido

guilty feelings sentimiento de culpa; sentimiento de culpabilidad

guilty party *(law)* parte culpable; el culpable; la culpable; **he was the guilty party** él era el culpable

guilty plea *(law)* declaración judicial de culpabilidad; confesión judicial de culpabilidad; **not guilty plea** *(law)* declaración judicial de no culpabilidad

gums *(anat)* encías

gun *(noun: pistol)* pistola; revólver; *(shotgun, rifle)* escopeta; fusil; rifle; **to draw a gun on somebody** apuntar a alguien con un arma; **to pull a gun on somebody** apuntar a alguien con una pistola; **to hold a gun to somebody's head** ponerle a alguien una pistola en la sien

gun battle *(noun)* tiroteo; balacera

gun crime delito con arma

gun down *(verb: shoot)* asesinar; matar; **he was gunned down** *(killed)* lo mataron a tiros; **he was gunned downed** *(injured)* lo tumbaron a tiros; lo balearon

gun law *(noun: to control firearms)* legislación para el control de armas

gun license *(noun)* licencia de armas

gun permit licencia de armas

gun shy *(adj)* que se asusta con el ruido de las escopetas

gunbattle *(noun)* tiroteo; balacera; **there was a gunbattle** hubo una balacera; hubo un tiroteo

gunfight *(noun)* tiroteo; balacera; **there was a gunfight** hubo una balacera; hubo un tiroteo

gunfire *(noun: from gun, rifle)* disparos; tiroteo; balacera; **there was an exchange of gunfire** hubo una balacera; hubo un tiroteo

gunman *(noun)* pistolera; pistolero; *(triggerman)* gatillera; gatillero; **masked gunman** pistolera enmascarada; pistolero enmascarado

gunned down abatida; abatido

gunpoint *(noun)* punta de pistola; **at gunpoin**t a punta de pistola

gunrunner *(noun)* traficante de armas

gunrunning *noun)* tráfico de armas

gunshot *(noun)* disparo; tiro

gunshot wound herida de bala

gym shoe *(adj)* zapatilla de gimnasia

H

habeas corpus hábeas corpus; **to apply for habeas corpus** presentar un recurso de hábeas corpus

habit *(noun)* costumbre; hábito; *(bad)* vicio; mala costumbre; mal hábito

habitual *(adj)* habitual; acostumbrada; acostumbrado

habitually *(adv)* por costumbre; constantemente

hack *(verb: cut roughly)* cortar a tajos; tajear; **he was hacked to death** lo mataron a hachazos; lo mataron a machetazos

hack *(noun: blow with ax)* hachazo; *(with machete)* machetazo

hacker *(noun: computer)* pirata informática; pirata informático

hail fom ser de; **he hails from Mexico** es de México

hair *(noun: on human head)* pelo; cabello; **to have long hair** tener el pelo largo; **to have short hair** tener el pelo corto; **to have black hair** tener el pelo negro; **to have brown hair** tener el pelo castaño; **white hair** canas; **a girl with long hair** una chica de pelo largo; **a good head of hair** una buena cabellera; una buena mata de pelo; **to have one's hair cut** cortarse el pelo; **to get one's hair cut** cortarse el pelo; **to lose one's hair** perder el pelo; **he' losing his hair** se le está cayendo el pelo; **his hair is getting very thin** se está quedando calvo; **to wear one's hair down** llevar el pelo suelto; **to wear one's hair up** llevar el pelo recogido; **to comb one's hair** peinarse

hair trigger *(gun trigger)* gatillo

hairless *(head)* sin pelo; calvo; pelón

hairline *(head: where hair begins)* nacimiento del pelo; **he has a receding hairline** tiene las entradas cada vez más pronunciadas

hairpiece *(noun)* postizo

hairstyle *(noun)* peinado; corte de pelo

hairy *(adj: legs, chest)* peluda; peludo; velluda; velludo

half *(noun: in phrases)* **an hour and a half** una hora y media; **it's half past ten** son las diez y media; **half of that money is mine** la mitad de ese dinero es mía; **one and a half hours** una hora y media; **half my salary goes to the mortgage** la mitad de mi sueldo se me va en la hipoteca; **he's half her age** ella le dobla la edad; **half an hour** media hora; **half of my friends** la mitad de mis amigos

half an hour media hora

half brother hermanastro; medio hermano

half day media jornada

half hour media hora

half length de medio cuerpo

half open *(adj)* entreabierta; entreabierto

half pension media pensión

half sister hermanastra; media hermana

half truth verdad a medias

halfway *(adv)* medio camino; **to meet somebody halfway** llegar a un acuerdo; hacer concesiones mutuas

halfway house *(for drug addict, criminal, mental patient)* centro de reinserción social *(institución diseñada para rehabilitar a personas que han salido recientemente de un hospital o prisión)*

halfway there a mitad de; a medio camino

half-year *(noun)* medio año; semestre

hand *(noun: anat)* mano; *(in phrases)* **to be at hand** acercarse; estar próxima; estar próximo; **help is at hand** la ayuda está en camino; **I'm always on hand when you need me** si me necesitas, aquí estoy; **the police were on hand** la policía estaba cerca; **the situation is getting out of hand** la situación se les va de la mano; **I don't have your file on hand** no tengo su archivo a mano; **to have a hand in something** tener parte en algo

hand *(in phrases)* **to have one's hands tied** tener las manos atadas; **at the hands of** a manos de; **to change hands** cambiar de dueño; cambiar de manos; **the contract is now in the hands of the lawyer** ahora el contrato está en manos del abogado; **in good hands** en buenas manos; **the matter is out of my hands** el asunto no está en mis manos

hand baggage *(noun)* equipaje de mano

hand down a decision anunciar un fallo; dictar un fallo

hand down a sentence anunciar una condena; dictar una condena

hand luggage equipaje de mano

handbag *(noun)* cartera; bolsa

handcuff *(verb)* esposar; ponerle esposas a

handcuffs *(noun)* esposas; **a pair of handcuffs** unas esposas

handgun *(noun)* révolver; pistola

handgun assault asalto a mano armada; atraco a mano armada

handicap *(disability)* impedimento

handicapped *(adj)* disminuida; disminuido; discapacitada; discapacitado; minusválida; minusválido; **he's visually handicapped** su visión es parcial

handicapped individual individuo con impedimento; con desventaja

handle *(verb: people)* tratar; *(gun, car)* conducir; manejar; *(emotion)* controlar; *(goods)* comerciar con

handling *(noun: treatment of situation)* manejo; **the police handling of the case** la manera en que la policía llevó el caso

handwriting *(noun)* escritura; letra; **he has bad handwriting** tiene muy mala letra; **he has good handwriting** tiene muy buena letra; **she has bad handwriting** tiene muy mala escritura; **she has good handwriting** tiene muy buena escritura

handwriting expert perito calígrafo

handwritten *(adj)* escrita a mano; escrito a mano; **a handwritten note** una nota escrita a mano

hanging *(law)* ejecución; la horca; la pena de muerte en la horca

hangover *(noun: after drinking)* resaca; cruda

hang-up *(noun)* complejo; trauma; **he has so many hang-ups** tiene tantos complejos; tiene tantos traumas

happen *(verb: occur)* pasar,; suceder; ocurrir; acontecer; **what's happening?** ¿qué pasa?; ¿qué sucede?; ¿qué ocurre?; **what's happened?** ¿qué ha pasado?; ¿qué ha sucedido?;¿qué ha ocurrido?; **how did it happen?** ¿cómo ocurrió esto?; **accidents will happen** son cosas que pasan; **don't let it happen again** que no vuelva a ocurrir; **what has happened to him?** ¿qué le ha pasado?; **how did the accident happen?** ¿cómo ocurrió el accidente?

harass *(verb: pestering)* acosar; hostigar

harassment *(noun: pestering)* hostigamiento; vejación; acoso; **police harassment** acoso por parte de la policía; **racial harassment** hostilidad racial; **sexual harassment** acoso sexual

harbor suspicions albergar sospechas

harboring a criminal encubrimiento de un fugitivo; encubrimiento de una fugitiva; encubriendo a un fugitivo; encubriendo a una fugitiva

hard *(adj: difficult)* difícil; **I find that hard to believe** me cuesta creerlo; **such documents are hard to come by** esos documentos son difíciles de conseguir; **the judge is difficult to please** el juez es difícil de complacer; **you'll have a hard time explaining that to the judge** te costará explicárselo al juez

hard-core pornography pornografía dura

hard-drinking *(adv)* bebedor; bebedora

hard drugs drogas duras

hard feelings resentimiento

hard labor trabajos forzados

hard liquor bebidas alcohólicas fuertes

hard porn pornografía dura

hard to believe difícil de creer

hard-working *(adj)* trabajador; trabajadora

hardened criminal criminal habitual; delincuente empedernida; delincuente empedernido

hardly *(adv: scarcely)* apenas; difícilmente; **that can hardly be true** eso difícilmente puede ser verdad; **I hardly know him** apenas lo conozco

hardship *(noun: deprivation)* privación; *(financial)* apuro; *(condition of life)* miseria; **they experienced great hardships** pasaron muchos apuros; pasaron muchas dificultades; **they suffered great hardship** pasaron muchos apuros; pasaron muchas dificultades

hardship case caso de daño irreparable; caso de privación; caso de dificultad económica

harm *(noun)* daño; **to do harm** hacer daño; **to do harm to somebody** hacerle daño a alguien; **where's the harm in that?** ¿y qué tiene eso de malo?; **I didn't mean any harm** no quería hacerle daño

harm *(verb)* hacerle daño a; hacer mal a; perjudicar

harmful *(adj: substance)* nociva; nocivo; *(influence)* perniciosa; pernicioso; dañina; dañino; perjudicial

harmful act acto dañino; acto perjudicial

harmful product producto dañino

harsh *(adj: punishment)* dura; duro; severa; severo; *(conditions, words)* dura; duro

harsh penalty penalidad severa

hat *(noun)* sombrero

hatchback *(noun)* coche con puerta trasera; coche con tres o cinco puertas

hate *(verb: loathe)* odiar; aborrecer; **to hate somebody for something** odiar a alguien por algo

hate campaign campaña de desprestigio

hate mail cartas en que se expresa odio al destinatorio

hatred *(noun)* odio

have one's roots in tener sus raíces en

hazard *(risk, danger)* peligro; riesgo; **a health hazard** un riesgo para la salud

hazard insurance seguro de personas o bienes en peligro especial

hazardous *(risk, danger)* peligrosa; peligroso

head *(noun: anat)* cabeza; *(chief)* director; directora; **a fine head of hair** una buena cabellera

head of household cabeza de familia

head-on collision choque frente a frente; choque de frente

head start program ventaja inicial; programa de educación de iniciación temprana *(education)* programa de enseñanza preescolar para niños carenciados

head wound herida en la cabeza

health *(noun)* salud; **to be in good health** estar bien de salud; **to be in bad health** estar mal de salud; **to be in poor health** estar mal de salud; **he's worried about his health** está preocupado por su salud; **on grounds of ill health** por motivos de salud; **his ill health** su mala salud

health benefit subsidio de enfermedad

health care asistencia sanitaria

Health Care Financing Administration (HCFA) Administración para el Financiamiento de Servicios de Salud

health care provider proveedor de asistencia sanitaria

health center centro médico; centro de salud

health hazard riesgo para la salud

health inspector inspector de sanidad

health insurance seguro de enfermedad

health insurance for children seguro médico para niños

Health Maintenance Orgainzation Organización de Mantenimiento de Salud

health plan plan de salud

hear *(in phrases)* **to hear that ...** oír decir que ...; **to hear about** oír hablar de; **I've never heard of him** no me suena su nombre; **I heard that ...** oí decir que ...

hear *(law: case)* ver; oír

hear a case *(law)* ver una causa; conocer de una causa; entender de una causa; oír una causa

hear of *(encounter, get to know of)* **I've heard of him** he oído hablar de él; **never heard of him** no tengo ni idea de quién es; **if you hear of anything interesting, let me know** si te enteras de algo interesante, me lo dices

hearing *(law)* vista; audiencia; instrucción de cargos; **he never got a fair hearing** en ningún momento se le permitió explicar su punto de vista; no se le juzgó imparcialmente; **preliminary hearing** audiencia preliminar; **supression hearing** audiencia de exclusión de prueba

hearing aid audífono

hearing difficulties problemas auditivos; problemas de audición

hearing of the determining factors vista de los condicionantes

hearing officer funcionario de audiencias; funcionario de vistas

hearing proceedings actuación de audiencia; actuación de vista

hearing process proceso de audiencia; proceso de vista

hearsay *(noun)* prueba de referencia; habladurías; rumores; **it's just hearsay** son rumores nada más

hearsay evidence prueba de oídas; prueba referencial; prueba testifical por referencia

hearsay exception exceptuación a la regla de prueba de oídas

hearsay witness testigo de oídas

heart *(anat)* corazón

heart attack ataque al corazón; infarto

heart murmur murmullos del corazón; soplos del corazón

heart of the matter fondo de la cuestión; el meollo de la cuestión

heat *(noun; warmth)* calor; *(excitement, passion)* calor; acaloramiento

heat of passion arrebato y obcecación; estado de emoción violenta

heavily *(adv)* muy; **he was heavily built** era corpulento; era de aspecto fornido; **she was heavily made up** iba muy maquillada; **he is heavily in debt** está muy endeudado; tiene muchas deudas; **his English is heavily accented** habla inglés con un acento muy fuerte

heavy *(adj)* pesada; pesado; **how heavy are you?** ¿cuánto pesas?; **to be a heavy drinker** beber mucho; beber en exceso; **to be a heavy smoker** fumar mucho; **a man of medium height and heavy build** un hombre fornido de estatura mediana

heavy-set *(adj)* corpulenta; corpulento; fornida; fornido

heel *(anat)* talón

height *(noun: measurement)* altura; *(person)* estatura; talla; **he's 6 feet in height** tiene seis pies de altura; tiene seis pies de alto; **of average height** de estatura mediana; de talla mediana; **what height are you?** ¿cuánto mides?; *(culmination, peak)* **at the height of his career** en la cumbre de su carrera; en el punto alto de su carrera

heir *(noun)* heredera; heredero

heiress *(noun)* heredera

help *(verb: assist)* ayudar; asistir; *(noun)* ayuda; asistencia

helpline teléfono de la esperanza

her death su muerte; **her death has left him very depressed** está muy abatido por su muerte

here *(in phrases)* **come here!** ¡ven aquí!; **here he comes** ya viene; **here I am** aquí estoy; **here are the documents** he aquí los papeles; **here you are!** ¡toma!; **my friend here will do it** este amigo mío lo hará; **that's neither here nor there** eso no viene al caso; **I left it right here** lo dejé aquí mismo; **give it here!** ¡dámelo!; **here's what you should do** esto es lo que debes hacer; he aquí lo que debes hacer; **I'd like to say here that ...** sobre este punto yo quisiera decir que ...; **here I disagree** ahí no estoy de acuerdo

hereafter *(law: in legal texts, from now on)* de aquí en adelante; a partir de ahora; *(in the future)* en el futuro

hereby *(law: in will)* por el presente testamento

hereinafter *(law: in legal texts, from now on)* de aquí en adelante; en lo sucesivo

hereof *(law)* del presente documento

hereto *(law: used in legal texts)* a esto; adjunta; adjunto; **the documents hereto appended** los documentos adjuntos

heretofore *(law)* hasta ahora; hasta este momento

hereunder *(below)* a continuación; abajo

hereupon *(law)* en ese momento

herewith *(law)* adjunta; adjunto; **we are sending you herewith a copy of ...** adjunta nos es grato remitirles una copia de

heritage *(of nation)* patrimonio; **our national heritage** nuestro patrimonio nacional; **our cultural heritage** nuestro patrimonio cultural

heroin *(noun)* heroína

heroin addict heroinómana; heroinómano

heroin user heroinómana; heroinómano

hers *(poss pron)* el suyo; la suya; las suyas; los suyos; de ella; **this notebook is hers** este cuaderno es suyo; este cuaderno es de ella; **a friend of hers** un amigo suyo; un amigo de ella

hesitate *(verb)* vacilar; titubear; no dejar de; **please don't hesitate to ask ...** no dejes de preguntar; **to hesitate to do something** no decidirse a hacer algo; **to hesitate before doing something** dudar antes de hacer algo; **to hesitate about doing something** vacilar en hacer algo; **don't hesitate to ask me** no vaciles en pedírmelo; no dejes de pedírmelo

high blood pressure alta presión sanguínea; alta presión de la sangre

high court Tribunal Supremo

high on drugs intoxicada con drogas; intoxicado con drogas

high penalty pena grave

high school colegio secundario

high security prison prisión de alta seguridad

higher education estudios superiores; enseñanza superior

Higher Education Services Corporation Corporación de Servicios de Educación Superior

higher learning estudios superiores

highway *(noun)* carretera

highway patrol policía caminera

hijack *(verb: airplane; vehicle)* secuestrar; *(noun)* secuestro

hijacker *(noun)* secuestrador; secuestradora

hijacking *(noun)* robo en tránsito; secuestrado

hire *(verb: staff, person)* contratar

hired assassin asesinos a sueldo; sicarios

hired hand jornalera; jornalero

his *(poss pron)* el suyo; la suya; las suyas; los suyos; de él; **all that is his** todo eso es suyo; todo eso es de él; **it isn't his, but hers** no es de él, sino de ella; **a friend of his** un amigo suyo; un amigo de él

his death su muerte; **his death has left her very depressed** está muy abatida por su muerte

Hispanic *(adj & noun: culture, people)* hispánica; hispánico; hispana; hispano; *(community)* hispana; hispano

hit *(in phrases)* **he was hit by a car** le pilló un coche; **a car hit him** lo pilló un coche; **he hit her across the face** le cruzó la cara; **the truck hit a tree** el camión chocó con el árbol; el camión chocó contra el árbol; **the house was hit by a bomb** una bomba cayó sobre la casa; **the bullet hit him in the leg** la bala le dio en la pierna; la bala lo alcanzó en la pierna; **I've been hit!** ¡me han dado! **thieves have hit many stores in the area** ha habido robos en muchas tiendas de la zona

hit-and-run *(driver)* que atropella y huye; *(accident)* en que el conductor se da la fuga; en que la conductora se da la fuga

hit-and-run accident accidente en el que el culpable se da a la fuga

hit by *(car, driver)* embestida por; embestido por; pillada por; pillado por; **the car was hit by a truck** el coche fue embestido por un camión; **she was hit by a truck** la pilló un camión

hit head on chocar de frente

hit list *(murder list)* lista de sentenciados

hit man *(assasin)* asesino a sueldo; sicaria; sicario; *(ruthless)* hombre duro

HMO Organización de Mantenimiento de Salud

hold *(law: make accountable)* obligar

hold *(law: detain, imprison)* detener; **she is being held at the police station for questioning** está detenida en la comisaria para ser interrogada; **the wing where terrorists are held** el ala donde tienen recluidos a los terroristas; **he was held prisoner in his own home** lo detuvieron preso en su propia casa

hold *(law: to determine, rule or adjudicate)* dictar fallo; fallar; **the court held that** la corte falló que

hold *(verb: to have, to keep in one's custody)* tener; estar en posesión de; estar en poder de; **my lawyer has the deed** mi abogado tiene la escritura; la escritura está en poder de mi abogado; **he holds the view that ...** sostiene que...; mantiene que ...; es de la opinión de que ...; *(consider, maintain)* **this is held to be the case** se considera que es así; **to hold somebody responsible for something** responsabilizar a alguien de algo; *(stop)* **hold it!** ¡espera!; **hold it right there or I'll shoot!** ¡quieto o disparo!;

hold a hearing celebrar una audiencia; celebrar una vista

hold down *(adv: keep a job)* **to hold down a job** conservar un empleo; mostrarse adecuada para un empleo; mostrarse adecuado para un empleo; **he's incapable of holding down any kind of job** es incapaz de tener un trabajo y cumplir con él

hold hostage *(law)* tener como rehén; tomar como rehén; **to hold somebody hostage** tener a alguien como rehén; tomar a alguien como rehén; **to hold a prison guard hostage** retener a un funcionario; **three prisoners held a prison guard hostage** tres reclusos retuvieron a un funcionario

hold in contempt *(law)* juzgar en rebeldía

hold somebody responsible for achacarle la responsabilidad a alguien; **he was held responsible for the accident** le achacaron la responsabilidad del accidente

hold up *(rob)* asaltar; atracar

home *(noun: of person, dwelling)* casa; hogar; **children's home** asilo de niños; **old people's home** asilo de ancianos; **to own one's own home** tener casa propia; *(in wider sense)* **Albuquerque's been my home since I was 10** he vivido en Albuquerque desde que tenía diez; **they made their home in California** se establecieron en California; **I still think of Mexico as my home** para mí México es mi patria; **to leave home** irse de casa; ausentarse de casa; **have you heard from home?** ¿te han escrito de tu casa?; **he lived away from home for a year** vivió fuera un año; **he worked away from home for a year** trabajó fuera un año; *(family environment)* hogar; **she comes from a good home** es de buena familia; se crió en un buen hogar; **a broken home** un hogar deshecho; *(in home)* **at home** en casa; **I'll be at home after 4** estaré en casa después de las cuatro; **if anybody calls, I'm not at home** si alguien llama, di que no estoy en casa; **he's got problems at home** tiene problemas familiares; *(at ease)* **sit down, make yourself at home** siéntate y ponte cómodo; estás en tu casa; **to feel at home with somebody** encontrarse a gusto con alguien; sentirse a gusto con alguien

home address domicilio; domicilio particular

home computer computadora doméstica

Home Health Agency Agencia de Servicios de Salud en el Hogar

home health aid *(concept)* ayuda médica en el hogar

home health aid *(person)* asistente para servicios de la salud en el hogar

home health care servicio de cuidado de la salud en el hogar

home health visit visita para servicios de salud en el hogar

home improvement loan préstamo de mejoras en el hogar

home loan préstamo garantizado por la residencia del deudor

home telephone number teléfono particular; teléfono de la casa

homeboy *(noun)* compinche; cuate; chico del barrio

homegirl *(noun)* chica del barrio

Homeland Security Seguridad de la Patria

homeless *(adj)* sin hogar; sin vivienda; sin techo; **the homeless** las personas sin hogar

homelessness *(noun)* falta de vivienda; el número de gente sin hogar; el número de personas sin techo

home loan *(noun)* préstamo para la vivienda

home owner *(noun)* propietaria de una vivienda; propietario de una vivienda

home ownership *(noun)* propietarios de viviendas; compra de viviendas por particulares

home town ciudad natal; pueblo natal

homeowner's insurance seguro de propietario de vivienda

homesick *(adj)* nostálgica; nostálgico; **to be homesick** tener nostalgia; echar de menos a la familia; **I feel homesick** echo de menos mi familia

homesickness *(noun)* nostálgia; añoranza; morriña

homicidal maniac maniaca homicidal; maniaco homicidal

homicide *(noun: crime, act)* homicidio

homosexual *(adj & noun)* homosexual

homosexuality *(noun)* homosexualidad

Honduran *(adj & noun)* hondureña; hondureño

honest *(adj)* honrada; honrado; sincera; sincero; franca; franco; **the honest truth is ...** la pura verdad es ...; **to be perfectly honest with you ...** para decirlo con toda franqueza; **be honest with me** sé franco conmigo; **to make an honest living** ganarse la vida honradamente; **honest to God!** ¡palabra!

honestly *(adv)* sinceramente; francamente; **I can honestly say that ...** puedo decir con toda sinceridad que ...

honor *(noun)* honor; **a man of honor** un hombre de honor; un hombre de palabra; **a point of honor** una cuestión de honor; **Her Honor** Su Señoría; **His Honor** Su Señoría; **Your Honor** Su Señoría

honor *(verb: show respect)* honrar; *(keep to agreement, obligation)* cumplir; cumplir con; **I intend to honor the contract** tengo toda la intención de cumplir con el contrato

honorable military discharge despido honorable del servicio militar

hope *(noun)* esperanza; **to be full of hope** estar lleno de esperanzas; **my hope is that ...** espero que ...; **I don't want to raise false hopes** no quiero crear falsas expectativas; **in the hope of doing something** en la esperanza de hacer algo; **there is no hope of that** no hay posibilidad de eso; **to raise somebody's hopes** dar esperanzas a alguien

hope *(verb)* esperar; **I hope so** espero que sí; **I hope not** espero que no; **to hope to ...** esperar que ...; **to hope to do something** pretender hacer algo; esperar hacer algo

hopeless *(adj)* desesperada; desesperado; sin esperanzas; imposible; perdida; perdido **it's a hopeless case** es un caso perdido

hopelessly ill estar desahuciada; estar desahuciado

hospice *(noun: for the dying)* residencia para enfermos desahuiciados

hospice care cuidado de hospicio

hospital *(noun)* hospital; **to be in the hospital** estar en el hospital; estar hospitalizada; estar hospitalizado

hospital bill factura del hospital

hospital invoice factura del hospital

hospital room cuarto de hospital

hospital stay estancia en el hospital; hospitalización; estadía en el hospital

hospital zone *(traffic sign)* zona hospitalaria

hospitalized *(adj)* hospitalizada; hospitalizado

host *(verb)* patrocinar; *(person)* anfitrión; anfitriona

hostage *(noun)* rehén; **to take somebody hostage** tomar a alguien como rehén; **to hold somebody hostage** tener a alguien como rehén

hostile witness *(law)* testigo hostil

hot line *(noun)* línea de emergencia; línea directa de ayuda; línea de ayuda

hot pursuit persecusión inminente de un delincuente

hotly *(adv)* con pasión; con vehemencia; **he was hotly pursued by the police** la policía le siguió muy de cerca

hour *(noun)* hora; **a quarter of an hour** un cuarto de hora; **three quarters of an hour** tres cuartos de hora; **an hour and a half** una hora y media; **one and a half hours** una hora y media; **50 miles per hour** cincuenta millas por hora; **to be paid by the hour** cobrar por horas; **I earn $40 an hour** ganó cuarenta dólares por hora; *(long time)* **It'll take 5 hours** llevará cinco horas; **we waited for hours and hours** esperamos horas y horas; **what hours do you work?** ¿qué horario tienes?; **on the hour** en la hora en punto; **in the early hours** en la madrugada; **visiting hours** horas de visita; **to work long hours** trabajar mucho; **to work after hours** trabajar después de hora; **after hours** fuera de horario; **she's out till all hours** se queda fuera hasta muy tarde

hours to be arranged horario a convenir

hourly cost costo horario

hourly rate sueldo por hora

hourly wage sueldo por hora

house *(noun: dwelling)* casa

house arrest arresto domiciliario; **to be under house arrest** encontrarse bajo arresto domiciliario

House of Representatives Cámara de Representantes

housecleaning *(noun)* limpieza general

household *(noun)* casa; familia; hogar

household appliances enseres domésticos

household chores tareas domésticas; quehaceres domésticos

household expenses gastos de la casa

household goods enseres de la casa; enseres domésticos

household worker empleada doméstica; empleado doméstico; trabajador doméstico; trabajadora doméstica

housekeeper *(noun: woman)* ama de llaves; *(in hotel)* gobernanta; *(man)* encargado de la casa; **she's a good housekeeper** es muy buena administradora

housemaid *(noun)* ama; criada

housing *(noun: dwellings)* viviendas; **low income housing** viviendas para familias de bajos ingresos; **poor housing conditions** viviendas inadecuadas

housing assistance ayuda para la vivienda

housing development urbanización; complejo habitacional

housing equality igualdad de vivienda; igualdad en la vivienda

housing project complejo de viviendas subvencionadas

housing shortage escasez de viviendas

how to file cómo presentar; **how to file a complaint to OSHA** cómo presentar una queja ante OSHA

how to file for your own divorce cómo solicitar para su propio divorcio

how to make your own will cómo hacer su propio testameto

human *(adj)* humana; humano; **I'm only human** todos somos humanos; **it's human nature to be jealous** es cosa natural tener celos

human being ser humano

human beings seres humanos

human remains restos humanos

human resources recursos humanos

human rights derechos humanos

human-rights organizations organizaciones defensores de los derechos humanos

human rights violation violaciones de los derechos humanos

humiliation vejación; humillación

hundred *(adj)* ciento; *(before noun)* cien; **a hundred and ten** ciento diez; **at 100 miles per hour** a cien millas por hora; **a hundred percent** el cien por ciento

hundredth *(adj)* centésima; centésimo

hung jury jurado en desacuerdo; jurado sin veredicto

hung over con resaca; con cruda

husband *(noun)* marido; esposo; **they are husband and wife** están casados; son marido y mujer

husband and wife privilege secreto matrimonial

hush money *(colloquial)* unto de rana; dinero con que se compra el silencio de alguien

hypertension *(noun)* hipertensión; alta presión sanguínea; alta presión de sangre

I

idea *(noun)* idea; **I have an idea** tengo una idea; **what a good idea!** ¡qué buena idea!; **that's not a bad idea** no es mala idea; **it seemed like a good idea at the time** en aquel momento pareció una buena idea; **to have an idea that ...** tener la impresión de que ...; **it wasn't my idea** no fue idea mía; **whatever gave you that idea?** ¿de dónde sacaste esa idea?;

identical *(adj)* identíca; identíco

identical twins gemelos identícos; *(colloquial)* cuates

identification *(noun)* identificación; **do you have any other identification?** ¿tiene algún otro documento que acredite su identidad?

identification card carnet de identidad; carné de identidad; cédula de identidad

identification papers documentos de identidad; papeles de identidad; documentación de identidad

identification tag placa de identidad

identify *(verb)* identificar; **to identify oneself** establecer su identidad; **he was identified as a member of the gang** se lo identificó como miembro de una banda; **they failed to identify the problem** no lograron identificar el problema

identikit picture *(police composite)* retrato hablado; retrato robot

identity *(noun)* identidad; **to prove one's identity** demostrar su identidad; **you'll need some proof of identity** necesitará algún documento que acredite su identidad; **it was a case of mistaken identity** fue un caso de identidad equivocada; fue un caso de identidad errónea

identity card carnet de identidad; carné de identidad; cédula de identidad

identity crisis crisis de identidad

identity theft robo de identidad

if *(in phrases)* si; **that's a big if** es un gran pero; **as if** como si; **as if by chance** como por casualidad; **let me know if you hear anything** si oyes algo, dímelo; **if for some reason** si por algún motivo; si por alguna razón; **if I were you** yo que tú; yo en tu lugar; **if necessary** si es necesario; **if only I could** ¡ojalá pudiera!; **if only I had known!** ¡de haberlo sabido!; **if the case goes to trial** si el caso va a juicio; **if you ask me** en lo que a mí se refiere

ignition interlock device dispositivo de llave de contacto interlock; dispositivo de llave del arranque interlock

ignition key llave de contacto; llave del arranque

ignorance *(noun)* ignorancia; **to show one's ignorance** manifestar su falta de educación; **I was kept in ignorance of the content of the will** me ocultaron el contenido del testamento

ignorance of something ignorancia de algo

ignorance of the law is no excuse la ignorancia de la ley no exime de su cumplimiento; el desconocimiento de la ley no exime de su cumplimiento

ignorant *(adj: lacking knowledge)* ignorante; **to be ignorant of something** ignorar algo; desconocer algo

ignore *(verb: not take notice of)* hacer caso omiso de; no hacer caso de; pasar por alto; **he chose to ignore the remark** prefirió ignorar el comentario; **we can't ignore the fact that ...** no podemos dejar de tener en cuenta el hecho de que ...

ill-advised *(hardly)* desacertada; desacertado; **you would be ill-advised to go** no sería aconsejable que fueras; **it was an ill-advised remark** fue un comentario inoportuno; **you would be ill-advised to go** harías mejor en no ir

ill afford *(hardly)* mal; **we can ill afford to lose him** mal podemos permitir que se vaya; **we can ill afford to buy it** mal podemos permitirnos el lujo de comprarlo; **I can ill afford to buy a new car** mal puedo yo permitirme comprar un coche nuevo; **we can ill afford to let such an opportunity slip** realmente no podemos dejar pasar semejante oportunidad

ill-treat *(verb)* vejar; maltratar

ill-treatment *(noun)* maltrato; malos tratos; **to suffer ill-treatment** ser víctima de malos tratos; recibir malos tratos

illegal *(adj: unlawful)* ilegal; **I've done nothing illegal** no he hecho nada ilegal; **to make something illegal** prohibir algo

illegal abortion aborto ilegal

illegal alien inmigrante ilegal

illegal entry entrada ilegal; allanamiento de vivienda illegal

illegal entry into the country entrada ilegal al país

illegal immigrant inmigrante ilegal

illegal motives móviles espurios

illegal possession tenencia ilegal

illegal possession of a controlled substance tenencia ilegal de sustancias reguladas

illegal possession of a dangerous weapon tenencia ilegal de armas peligrosas

illegal possession of a weapon tenencia ilegal de armas

illegal possession of receiving stolen goods tenencia ilegal de bienes hurtados

illegal possession of receiving stolen property tenencia elegal de bienes hurtados

illegal possession of stolen property tenencia ilegal de bienes hurtados

illegal procedure jugada antirreglamentaria

illegality *(noun)* ilegalidad

illegally *(adv: unlawful)* ilegalmente

illegally obtained evidence prueba ilegal

illegitimate child hija ilegítima; hijo ilegítimo; hija natural; hijo natural

illicit *(adj)* ilícita; ilícito

illiteracy *(noun)* analfabetismo

illiterate *(adj & noun: unable to read)* analfabeta; analfabeto

immaterial *(law: evidence, issue)* no pertinente; no esencial; *(adj)* irrelevante; **that's immaterial** eso es irrelevante; eso no tiene importancia; eso no importa; **the difference between them is immaterial to me** la diferencia entre ellos me es indiferente; **it is immaterial whether ...** no importa si ...

immediate *(adj)* inmediata; inmediato; **the law will take immediate effect** la ley entrará in vigor inmediatamente; **to take immediate action** actuar de inmediato; **the immediate area** las inmediaciones; **my immediate neighbors** mis vecinos de al lado; **it is not immediately obvious** no resulta obvio a primera vista

immediate arrest of inmediata detención de

immediate claims taking proceso de toma de solicitudes inmediatas; servicio de toma de solicitudes inmediatas

immediate family parientes cercanos

immediately *(adv)* inmediatamente; de inmediato

immigrant *(noun)* inmigrante

immigration *(noun)* inmigración

Immigration and Nationality Act Ley de Inmigración y Nacionalidad

Immigration and Naturalization Service Servicio de Inmigración y Naturalización

immigration authorities servicio de inmigración

immigration control control de inmigración

immigration laws leyes inmigratorias; leyes de inmigración

immigration police *(colloquial)* la migra *(on the US-Mexican border)*

immigration records expedientes de inmigración

immigration worker trabajador inmigrante; trabajadora inmigrante

immunity *(law)* inmunidad; **he was offered immunity from prosecution provided that he cooperated** le ofrecieron no seguirle proceso si cooperaba; transactional immunity inmunidad absoluta

immunity from prosecution inmunidad procesal penal; inmunidad judicial; ofrecerle a alguien no seguir proceso

immunity letter carta de inmunidad

impair one's health sufrir menoscabo; **his health was not impaired** su salud no sufrió menoscabo alguno

impairment *(noun)* incapacidad específica; impedimento

impairment related work expense gastos de trabajo relacionados con la incapacidad

impanel a jury *(law)* insacular un jurado; integrar un jurado

impeach *(law: to challenge the witness)* tachar; *(discredit testimony, motives)* impugnar; poner en tela de juicio

impediment *(noun: hinderance)* impedimento; **impediment to something** impedimento para algo; **lawful impediment** impedimento; **a speech impediment** un defecto del habla

imperative *(adj: essential)* imprescindible; fundamental; **it is imperative that the work be completed by Friday** es imprescindible que el trabajo esté listo para el viernes; **it is imperative that he appear in court** es imprescindible que comparezca ante el tribunal

impinge *(verb)* incidir; vulnerar; afectar; **to impinge on something** incidir en algo; afectar a algo; vulnerar algo; **to impinge on somebody's rights** vulnerar los derechos de alguien; **to impinge on somebody's privacy** vulnerar la intimidad de alguien; **to impinge on somebody's freedom** vulnerar la libertad de alguien

implement *(verb: decision, plan idea)* llevar a cabo; poner en práctica; ejecutar; implementar; *(law)* aplicar

implementation *(noun)* implementación; puesta en práctica; ejecución; *(of law)* aplicación

implicate *(verb)* implicar; involucrar; **they are implicated in the murder** están implicados en el asesinato; están involucrados en el asesinato; **to implicate somebody in something** comprometer a alguien en algo; **are you implicated in this?** ¿andas metido en esto?; **he implicated three others** acusó a tres más

implied consent *(law)* consentimiento implicado

implied notice *(law)* notificación tácita

important consideration factor importante; **his age is an important consideration** su edad es un factor importante

important source of income importante fuente de ingresos

impose *(verb: restriction, punishment, condition)* imponer; aplicar; molestar; **the judge imposed the maximum sentence** el juez aplicó la sentencia máxima; **she imposed her will on them** les impusó su voluntad; **I don't wish to impose, but ...** no quiesiera molestar, pero ...; **I think I've imposed on him enough already** me parece que ya lo he molestado bastante; me parece que ya lo he importunado bastante; **to impose on somebody's generosity** abusar de la generosidad; **to impose on somebody's goodwill** abusar de la buena voluntad; **to impose on somebody's hospitality** abusar de la hospitalidad

impose a sentence *(law)* imponer una sentencia

imposition *(noun: right)* imposición; abuso; molestia; **it's a bit of an imposition** es un abuso; **I hope you don't think it an imposition** espero que no sea una molestia; espero que no se considere un abuso;

it was really an imposition on her hospitality la verdad es que fue abuso de su hospitalidad

impound *(assets, possessions)* incautar; incautarse; *(stray dogs)* llevar a la perrera municipal; *(vehicle)* embargar; llevar al depósito municipal

impress *(verb: make impression)* **to impress somebody favorably** causarle una buena impresión a alguien; **to impress somebody unfavorably** causarle una mala impresión a alguien; **we were impressed by your testimony** tu testimonio nos causó una buena impresión; **he only did it to impress her** lo hizo sólo para impactarla; lo hizo sólo para dejarla admirada; **my excuse did not impress them** mi excusa no los convenció

impression *(noun: idea, image)* impresión **my impressions of the judge** las impresiones del juez; **it's my impression that she doesn't want to take the stand** tengo la impresión de que no quiere subir al estrado; me da la impresión de que no quiere subir al estrado; **to give somebody the impression that ...** darle a alguien la impresión de que ...; **I get the impression that he wants to plead guilty** me da la impresión de que quiere confesarse culpable; **sorry, I obviously had the wrong impression of you** lo siento, está visto que me había formado una opinión equivocada de ti; **to be under the impression that ...** creer que ..., pensar que ...; tener la impresión de que ...

imprison *(law: jail, prison)* encarcelar; meter en la cárcel; *(lock up)* encerrar; **to be imprisoned** estar encarcelada; estar encarcelado; estar en la cárcel; **she was imprisoned** fue encarcelada

imprisonment *(law: act)* encarcelamiento; *(state)* prisión; **life imprisonment** cadena perpetua; **they protested against his imprisonment** protestaron en contra de su encarcelamiento; **ten year's imprisonment** diez años de prisión; **he was sentenced to life imprisonment** fue condenado a cadena perpetua

in *(in phrases)* **in jail** en la cárcel; **in prison** en la prisión; **he's in for larceny** está preso por ladrón; **what's he in for?** ¿de qué delito se le acusa?; **she's in for theft** está en la cárcel por robo; **we must be in court before nine** debemos estar ante el tribunal antes de las nueve; **the judge isn't in yet** el juez no ha llegado todavía; **she was in on it from the start** lo supo desde el principio; estuvo al tanto desde el principio; **he's in with a really bad crowd** anda en muy malas compañías; **he's in a meeting** está en una reunión; **at four o'clock in the afternoon** a las cuatro de la tarde; **to come in the afternoon** ven por la tarde; **in January** en enero; **in years** hace años; **I haven't seen her in years** hace años que no la veo; **he's in his forties** tiene cuarenta y tantos; **in two months** dentro de dos meses; **in two hours** dentro de dos horas; **in danger** en peligro; **to be in danger** estar en peligro; **to be in difficulties** estar pasando dificultades; **to be in a good mood** estar de buen humor; **the in crowd** el grupito; **the in place** el lugar de moda; **in town** en la ciudad; **in the past** en el pasado; **in anger** con enojo; **to be in a rage** estar furiosa; estar furioso; **to be in on the plan** estar al tanto del plan

in about four weeks en unas cuatro semanas

in about three hours en unas tres horas

in **advance** por adelantado; de antelación

in **April** en abril

in **August** en agosto

in **broken English** en mal inglés

in **camara** a puerta cerrada

in **compliance with the law** en conformidad con la ley; conforme a la ley

in **criminal matters** en asuntos penales; en cuestiones penales

in **December** en diciembre

in **defense of the accused** en descargo de la acusada; en descargo del acusado

in **due course** a su debido tiempo

in **escrow** en depósito; bajo la custodia de un tercero

in **February** en febrero

in **front of** en frente de; delante de

in **front of us** por delante; **we've got a big task in front of us** tenemos una gran tarea por delante

in **her/his care** a su cuidado; a su cargo

in **her/his own name** a nombre propio

in **its entirety** en su totalidad

in **January** en enero

in **July** en julio

in **June** en junio

in **light of** en vista de; a la luz de; **in light of what the court said** en vista de lo que la corte dice; en vista de lo que el tribunal dice

in **many cases** en muchos casos

in **March** en marzo

in **May** en mayo

in **my opinión** en mi opinión; a mi parecer; a mi juicio

in **November** en noviembre

in **October** en octubre

in **recess** *(law: court)* levantar la sesión; **the court is in recess until tomorrow** el tribunal ha levantado la sesión hasta mañana

in **September** en septiembre

in **the eyes of the law** a los ojos de la ley

in **the judgement of** a juicio de

in **which he was killed** que le costó la vida; **the attack in which he was killed** el atentado que le costó la vida

in which she was killed que le costó la vida; **the attack in which she was killed** el atentado que le costó la vida

in witness hereof en fe de todo ello

inadmissible *(adj)* inadmisible; improcedente; **it is inadmissible as evidence** es inadmisible como prueba

inadvertent *(adj)* involuntaria; involuntario; **she had made an inadvertent admission of guilt** había admitido involutariamente su culpabilidad; había admitido inadvertidamente su culpabilidad

inadvertently *(adv)* sin querer; sin darse cuenta; inadvertidamente; por descuido

inadvisable *(adj)* desconsejable; poco aconsejable; poco recomendable

inappropriate *(adj)* inadecuada; inadecuado; poco apropiada; poco apropiado

inasmuch as ya que; puesto que; dado que

incapacitate *(law: disqualify)* inhabilitar; incapacitar; **to be incapacitated** estar incapacitada; estar incapacitado; **physically incapacitated** físicamente incapacitada; físicamente incapacitado

incarcerate *(verb)* encarcelar

Incarceration Verification Form formulario para una verificación de estar encarcelado

incest *(noun)* incesto

incite *(verb)* incitar a; provocar; **he incited the crowd to violence** incitó a las multitudes a la violencia; instigó a las multitudes a la violencia

inclined *(adj: disposed)* **to be inclined to do something** tener tendencia a hacer algo; **I'm inclined to agree** yo me inclino a pensar lo mismo; **I'm inclined to believe you** estoy dispuesto a creerte; **if you feel so inclined** si te llama la atención

include *(verb: contain as a part)* incluir; **her duties include looking after the children** sus obligaciones incluyen el cuidar de los niños; **does the rent include heating costs?** ¿el alquiler incluye los gastos de calefacción?; ¿en el alquiler están incluidos los gastos de calefacción?; **I'll include a note with your letter** incluiré una nota con tu carta; adjuntaré una nota con tu carta; **your name is not included on the list** tu nombre no figura en la lista

income *(noun)* ingresos; rentas; **I live within my income** vivo de acuerdo con mis ingresos; **they're living beyond their income** gastan más de lo que ganan; **taxable income** renta gravable; renta imponible; **annual income** ingresos anuales; **an important source of income** una importante fuente de ingresos; **lower income groups** grupos de bajos ingresos; **upper income groups** grupos de altos ingresos

income bracket nivel de ingresos

income gross ingreso bruto

income level nivel de ingresos

income net ingreso neto

income tax return declaración de impuestos

incompetence *(noun: ineptitude)* incompetencia; ineptitud; *(law)* incapacidad para + *infin*

incompetent *(noun: inept)* incompetente; inepta; inepto; *(law)* incapaz; **to be incompetent to** + *infin* ser incapaz para + *infin*; no tener capacidad para + *infin*

incompetent to stand trial *(law)* incapaz de ser enjuiciada; incapaz de ser enjuiciado

inconclusive evidence prueba ineficaz

incorporate *(adj)* incorporar; *(law)* constituir; constituir en sociedad; **a company incorporated in the state of New Mexico** una compañía constituida en el estado de Nuevo México

incorporation *(noun)* incorporación; *(law)* constitución en sociedad

incorrect *(adj)* incorrecta; incorrecto; errónea; erróneo; equivocada; equivocado; **it would be incorrect to say that ...** sería erróneo decir que ...; **that is incorrect** eso no es cierto;

increase *(noun)* aumento; incremento; **to be on the increase** estar en aumento; ir en aumento; **drug-taking is still on the increase** el consumo de drogas sigue en aumento; **rapid increase of** aumento rápido de

increase in crime aumento de la delincuencia

incriminate *(noun)* incriminar; **there is evidence which incriminates him;** hay pruebas que lo incriminan

incriminating evidence *(law: evidence, statements, documents)* pruebas que incriminan; **there is incriminating evidence against him** hay pruebas que lo incriminan

incur *(noun)* incurrir; *(loss; damage; injury)* sufrir

indecency indecencia; *(law)* **gross indecency** ultraje contra la moral pública

indecent assault abusos deshonestos

indecent exposure exhibición impúdica; delito de exhibicionismo

indeed *(in phrases)* efectivamente; en realidad; realmente; **there are mistakes indeed, but ...** claro que hay errores, pero ...; **if indeed he is right** si es que tiene razón; **if indeed he is wrong ...** si es que realmente se equivocó ...; **it is indeed difficult** es dificilísimo; **yes, indeed!** ¡sí, en efecto!; **no, indeed!** ¡no,por cierto!; **indeed!** ¡de veras!; **thank you very much, indeed** muchísimas gracias; **she was very late, indeed** llegó tardísimo; **this may indeed be the case, but ...** quizás sea así, pero ...; no digo que no sea así, pero ...

indemnity *(insurance)* indemnidad; *(compensation)* indemnización; reparación; **double indemnity** indeminización doble

indicate *(verb: point out)* indicar; señalar; **to indicate something to somebody** señalar algo a alguien; **there's nothing to indicate whether they approve or not** no hay nada que indique si les parece bien o no

indication *(noun)* indicio; pauta; **the judge gave us no indication of what was going to happen** el juez no nos dio ningún indicio de lo que iba a ocurrir; el juez no nos dio ninguna pauta de lo que iba a ocurrir; **there is every indication that ...** todo parece indicar que ...; todo hace suponer que ...; **there is no indication that ...** no hay señal de que ...; **this is some indication of** eso da una idea de; **all indications are that ...** todo parece indicar que ...

indict *(law)* acusar; expedir documento inculpatorio; enjuiciar; **to indict somebody for murder** acusar a alguien de homicidio; **he has been indicted on four counts of fraud** lo han acusado de cuatro delitos de estafa; **he has not been indicted yet** todavía no ha sido enjuiciado

indictable*(law)* tipificado como delito

indictable offense *(law)* delito procesable

indictment *(law)* acusación; formular documento inculpatorio; enjuiciamiento; **the indictment of Ricardo G. on a fraud charge** el enjuiciamiento de Ricardo G. acusado de estafa; **to bring an indictment against somebody** formular cargos contra alguien; *(document)* acusación; **the indictment was read out to the accused** se le leyeron los cargos al acusado; *(crtiticism)* **the report contained a damning indictment of the trial** el informe censuraba duramente al juicio; el informe criticó duramente al juicio

indignant *(adj)* indignada; indignado; **to be indignant** estar indignada; estar indignado; **he was indignant at the suggestion** la sugerencia lo indignó; **he was indignant about the way in which he was dismissed without notice** lo indignó que lo despidieron sin previo aviso

indignation *(adj)* indignación; **indignation at something** indignación ante algo; **he expressed his indignation at this suggestion** expresó su indignación ante esta sugerencia; se mostró muy indignado ante esta sugerencia

indirect evidence prueba indirecta

indirect tax impuesto indirecto

indiscriminate *(adj: attacks, killings)* sin distinción; indiscriminada; indiscriminado; impensada; impensado; *(uncritical)* hecho sin criterio

indisputable *(adj)* irrefutable; indiscutible; **it is indisputable that ...** es indiscutible que ...; es indisputable que ...

individual *(adj)* individual; **each individual juror** cada miembro del jurado por separado; cada uno de los miembros del jurado; **each case will be judged on its individual merits** cada caso se juzgará según sus propios méritos; **it can be adapted to suit individual needs** puede adaptarse según las necesidades de cada uno; puede adaptarse según las necesidades de cada caso

individual *(noun)* individua; individuo; **I am speaking as a private individual** habló a título personal

individual income ingreso individual

Individual Retirement Account (IRA) Cuenta de Jubilación Individual

individual rights derechos individuales

industrial accident accidente laboral; accidente de trabajo

industrial dispute conflicto laboral

inebriated *(adj: person)* ebria; ebrio; *(state)* de embriaguez

inebriation *(adj: person)* embriaguez

ineffective *(adj: measure, response)* ineficaz; *(attempt)* infructosa; infructoso; que no da resultado; que no surte efecto; **the plan proved wholly inefective** el proyecto no surtió efecto; *(person)* incapaz; incompetente; ineficiente

ineligible *(adj: candidate)* inelegible; no apta; no apto; **to be ineligible for something** no reunir los requisitos para algo; **I'm ineligible for a pension** no reúno las condiciones exigidas para que me den una pensión; no tengo derecho a una pensión; **she is ineligible to vote** no tiene derecho a votar

ineligible witness testigo inhábil

infancy *(noun: babyhood)* primer infancia; **from earliest infancy** desde su más tierna infancia; *(law)* menor de edad

infant *(noun: baby)* bebé; niña; niño; **while still an infant** cuando era un bebé; *(law)* menor de edad

infant mortality mortalidad infantil

infatuated *(adj)* encaprichada; encaprichado; **to be infatuated with somebody** estar encaprichada con alguien; estar encaprichado con alguien; **he became infatuated with her** se encaprichó con ella

infatuation *(noun)* encaprichamiento; **it's just infatuation** es sólo un encaprichamiento pasajero

inference *(noun)* deducción; conclusión; inferencia; **to draw an inference** hacer una deducción; **by inference we can conclude that ...** por deducción podemos concluir que ...

inferior *(adj)* inferior; **to feel inferior** sentirse inferior; **of inferior quality** de ínfima calidad; **she makes me feel inferior** me hace sentir inferior

inferior court tribunal inferior

infidelity *(noun: adulterer)* infidelidad; *(disloyalty)* deslealtad

infighting *(noun: in organization)* lucha interna; luchas internas

inflame the passion of the jury encender la pasión del jurado

inflict *(verb: pain, damage)* causar; ocasionar; inferir; *(punishment)* imponer; aplicar; infligir; **to inflict something on somebody** causar algo a alguien; **the suffering which he inflicted on his family** el sufrimiento que le causó a su familia; el sufrimiento que le ocasionó a su familia; **he would never forgive the indignities inflicted on him** nunca perdonaría las vejaciones de las que había sido objeto; nunca perdonaría las vejaciones que le habían infligido; **heavy penalties were inflicted on them** se les aplicaron penas severas; se les impusieron penas severas; **to inflict a blow** asestar un golpe; dar un golpe

influence *(noun: effect)* influencia; **to have an influence on something** influir en algo; **to be a good influence on somebody** ejercer buena influencia sobre alguien; **to be a bad influence on somebody** ejercer mala influencia sobre alguien; influir sobre algo; **the judge had a great influence on the outcome** el juez tuvo gran influencia sobre el resultado; **to be under the influence of somebody** estar bajo la influencia de alguien; **to be under the influence of something** estar bajo la influencia de algo; **he has influence, that's how he got the job** tiene influencia, por eso le dieron el puesto; *(be drunk)* **he was already under the influence** ya estaba borracho; **under the influence of drugs** drogada; drogado

influential *(adj: writer, thinker, position)* influyente; **she has very influential friends** tiene amigos muy influyentes; **he is very influential in the government** es muy influyente en círculos gubernamentales; tiene mucha influencia en círculos gubernamentales; **she was influential in persuading him to accept** influyó para que aceptara

inform *(verb: advise)* informar; notificar; **somebody informed the police** alguien informó a la policía; alguien le pasó el dato a la policía; **to keep somebody informed** mantener a alguien informado; mantener a alguien al corriente; **the judge must be informed at once** hay que informarle al juez inmediatamente; hay que avisarle al juez inmediatamente; **we've not yet been informed of any change of plan** todavía no se nos ha informado de ningún cambio de plan; **it's aim is to inform people about ...** tiene por objeto informar sobre ...; **to inform somebody that ...** informarle a alguien de algo; **I'm reliably informed that ...** me informan de buena fuente que ...; **to inform against** delatar a alguien; denunciar a alguien; **I am happy to inform you that ...** me da mucho gusto comunicarle que ...; **keep me informed** téngame al corriente; **why was I not informed?** ¿por qué no me avisaron?; **a well informed person** una persona bien informada

informal resources recursos informales

informant *(noun)* confidente; delator; delatora; soplón; soplona

information *(law)* informe acusatorio

information *(noun: facts, news)* información; **a piece of information** un dato; **they gave us a little information** nos dieron un poco de información; nos facilitaron un poco de información; **they gave us a lot of information** nos dieron mucha información; nos facilitaron mucha información; **information about** información acerca de; **we have very little information about ...** tenemos muy poca información sobre ...; **we have no information as to his whereabouts** desconocemos su paradero; **for your information** para su información

informer *(noun: police)* delator; delatora; informante; **police informer** informante de la policía

infraction *(law)* infracción; contravención; transgresión

infraction of the law *(law)* infracción de la ley

infringe *(verb: contract)* no cumplir con; incumplir; *(treaty, rule)* infringir; transgredir; violar; **to infringe on something** violar algo

infringement *(of law)* contravención; violación; vulneración; *(of contract)* incumplimiento; *(of rights)* violación

infringement of copyright no respetar los derechos de autor

infuriate *(verb)* enfurecer; poner furiosa; poner furioso; **his comments infuriated the judge** sus comentarios enfurecieron al juez

inhabitant *(noun)* habitante

inherit *(verb)* heredar; **to inherit something from somebody** heredar algo de alguien; **from their father they inherited nothing but debts** de su padre no heredaron más que deudas

inheritance *(noun: something inherited)* herencia; **to come into an inheritance** heredar; *(act)* sucesión; **she acquired the property by inheritance** adquirió la propiedad por sucesión

inheritance tax impuesto sucesorio; impuesto sobre sucesiones; impuesto a la herencia

inherited *(adj)* heredada; heredado

initial appearance vista inicial

initiate *(verb: start)* iniciar; dar comienzo a; entablar; poner en marcha

initiate an investigation of a person formar expediente a alguien

initiate proceedings against somebody entablarle juicio a alguien

initiation of the proceedings incoación del procedimiento

injunction *(law)* mandamiento judicial; entredicho; **to seek an injunction against somebody** solicitar un mandamiento judicial en contra de alguien; **to obtain an injunction against somebody** obtener un mandamiento judicial en contra de alguien

injure *(verb: person, pride, feeling)* herir; lastimar; *(interests; reputation; prospects)* dañar; *(knee, arm, etc.)* lesionar; lastimar; **she injured her knee** lesionó la rodilla; **he injured his arm** se lastimó el brazo; **he was slightly injured in the accident** resultó levemente herido en el accidente; **he was seriously injured in the accident** resultó gravemente herido en el accidente; **he was injured in the accident** fue lastimado en el accidente; **to injure oneself** hacerse daño; lastimarse

injured *(adj: person, limb)* herida; herido; lesionada; lesionado; *(law)* **the injured party** la parte perjudicada; **the injured** los heridos; **there were four injured** hubo cuatro heridos; **several people were injured in the explosion** la explosión causó varios heridos; **the injured had to be taken to the hospital** hubo que hospitalizar a los heridos; **24 people were injured in the accident** veinticuatro personas resultaron heridas en el accidente

injured party quien sufre el agravio; **I am the injured party** soy yo quien sufrió el agravio; **who is the injured party?**; ¿quien sufrió el agravio?

injurious *(adj)* perjudicial; **to be injurious to something** ser perjudicial para algo; **it's injurious to one's health** es perjudicial para la salud

injury *(noun)* herida; **to receive an injury** recibir una herida; **to sustain an injury** sufrir una herida; **injuries to the hands and face** heridas en manos y cara; **internal injuries** heridas internas; **head injuries** heridas en la cabeza; *(pride, reputation)* agravio; **an injury to somebody's reputation** un agravio a la reputación de alguien

injury case *(law)* caso por lesiones

injustice *(noun)* injusticia; **you do me an injustice** usted es injusto conmigo; **to do somebody an injustice** cometer una injusticia con alguien; ser injusto con alguien

in lieu of en lugar de

in-laws *(noun: spouses' parents)* suegros; *(spouses' family)* parientes políticos

inmate *(noun: of prison)* presa; preso; interna; interno; presidiaria; presidiario; *(of asylum)* internada; internado; interna; interno; *(of hospital)* paciente hospitalizada; paciente hospitalizado

innocent *(adj: not guilty)* inocente; **to be innocent of something** ser inocente de algo

innocent until proven guilty inocente hasta que se pruebe la culpabilidad

innuendos *(noun plural)* insinuación; indirecta; **the article is full of innuendos** el artículo hace muchas insinuaciones; **she's always making innuendos about my father** siempre está lanzando indirectas sobre mi padre; siempre está haciendo insinuaciones sobre mi padre

inquest *(law)* indagación; investigación; pesquisa judicial; **to hold an inquest on something** llevar a cabo una investigación sobre algo

inquire *(verb)* preguntar; inquirir; informarse; **to inquire about something** informarse acerca de algo; preguntar acerca de algo; informarse sobre algo; preguntar por algo; **to inquire about somebody** preguntar por alguien; **she inquired about your health** preguntó por tu salud; se interesó por tu salud; **to inquire into something** investigar algo; **to inquire for somebody** preguntar por alguien; **someone was inquiring for you** alguien preguntó por ti

inquire within infórmese aquí; se dan informaciones

inquiry *(noun)* interrogante; pregunta; averiguación; expediente informativo; indagación; **we made inquiries about his past** hicimos averiguaciones sobre su pasado; hicimos indagaciones sobre su pasado; **we made inquiries into his past** hicimos averiguaciones sobre su pasado; **to hold an inquiry into something** llavar a cabo una investigación sobre algo; montar una investigación sobre algo; **the police are making inquiries into the murder** la policía está investigando el asesinato; **the inquiry found that ...** la investigación concluyó que ...

inquiry into the deaths investigación de las muertes; expediente informativo de las muertes

insane *(adj: mad)* insana; insano; demente; loca; loco; **they drive you insane** te enloquecen; te sacan de quicio; **it's an insane idea** es una locura; es una idea descabellada; **he must be insane** él debe estar loco; él debe estar chiflado

insane asylum manicomio

insanity *(adj: mad)* demencia; locura; insensatez

insecure *(not confident)* insegura; inseguro

inside *(noun)* interior; *(adj & prep)* dentro; adentro

inside job *(crime)* crimen organizado desde dentro; **the police think the robbery was an inside job** la policía cree que alguien de la casa está implicado en el robo; la policía cree que alguien de la empresa está implicado en el robo

insider trading *(financial)* abuso de información privilegiada

insight *(noun: perceptiveness)* perspicacia; **she has great insight** es muy perspicaz; *(comprehension)* **insight into something** llegar a comprender bien algo

insofar as en la medida en que

inspector *(noun: police)* inspector de policía; inspectora de policía

installment *(payment)* plazo; cuota; **monthly installments** mensualidades; plazos mensuales; cuotas mensuales; **to pay in installments** pagar a plazos; pagar en cuotas; **to buy something on installment** comprar algo a plazos; comprar algo en cuotas

installment plan plan de financiación; **to buy something on an installment plan** comprar algo a plazos; comprar algo en cuotas

instantly *(adv)* al instante; en el acto; instantáneamente; **he died instantly** murió en el acto

instigate *(verb: provoke)* instigar a; incitar a; provocar

instigation *(noun)* instigación; incitación; **they had concealed the information at his instigation** instigados por él, habían ocultado la información; **they had concealed the information at their brother's instigation** por instigación de su hermano, habían ocultado la información; **it was carried out at the director's instigation** se llevó a cabo a instancias del director

institute proceedings against enjuiciar; **proceedings have not been instituted against him yet** todavía no ha sido enjuiciado

institution *(mental)* manicomio; asilo; institución; **she ended up in an institution** terminó en un manicomio

institutionalize *(put in an institution)* internar

instruct *(verb: law, jury)* instruir *(sobre ciertos aspectos legales)* **I have been instructed by my legal advisers that ...** mis asesores legales me han instruido que ...

instruct the jury instruir al jurado

instruction *(verb: law, jury)* instrucciones; *(general)* orden; **to give somebody instructions to do something** dar órdenes a alguien de hacer algo; **I gave clear instructions that ...** di instrucciones precisas de que ...; **they were acting on the instructions of the chief of police** cumplían órdenes del jefe de policía

instruction jury jurado de instrucción

insult *(noun)* injuria; insulto

insurance *(noun: right)* seguro; **comprehensive insurance** seguro a todo riesgo; **accident insurance** seguro de accidentes; **fire insurance** seguro de incendios; seguro contra incendios; **liability insurance** seguro contra terceros; **life insurance** seguro de vida; **medical insurance** seguro médico; seguro de enfermedad; **third party insurance** seguro contra terceros; **he works in insurance** trabaja en el ramo de los seguros; **to take out insurance** contratar un seguro; hacerse un seguro; **she took out an insurance policy;** se hizo un seguro **you can claim on the insurance** puedes reclamar al seguro

insurance against damage seguro contra daños

insurance against fire seguro contra incendios

insurance against theft seguro contra robo

insurance agent agente de seguros

insurance broker corredor de seguros; corredora de seguros

insurance certificate póliza de seguros

insurance claim demanda de seguro; reclamación de seguro; reclamación al seguro

insurance company compañía de seguros

insurance policy póliza de seguros

insurance premium prima de seguro

insure *(verb)* asegurar; **he insured his life for $1,000,000.** se hizo un seguro de vida de millon dólares; **I'm insured to drive any car** con mi seguro puedo manejar cualquier coche; **the insured sum** la cantidad asegurada; **to insure somebody against something** asegurar a alguien contra algo; **to insure something against something** asegurar a algo contra algo; **you must insure yourself** tienes que asegurarte; **you must insure your home against fire** tienes que asegurar la casa contra incendios; **we're insured against all risks** estamos asegurados contra todo riesgo; **the insured** el asegurado; la asegurada; las aseguradas; los asegurados

insured status cómo estar asegurada; cómo estar asegurado

insurer *(noun: company)* compañía de seguros; compañía aseguradora; *(person)* asegurador; aseguradora

intake interview *(law)* entrevista de entrada

integrated health care atención integrada

intent *(adj: determined)* decidida; decidido; resuelta; resuelto; **to be intent on** estar decidida a; estar decidido a; estar resuelta a; estar resuelto a; **she was intent on success** estaba resuelta a triunfar; estaba decidida a triunfar; se había propuesto triunfar

intent *(noun)* propósito; intención; **with intent to** + *infin* con el objeto de + *infin*; con el propósito de + *infin*; **with intent to kill** con intentos homicidas; **to all intents and purposes** prácticamente; en realidad; **what are your intentions?** ¿qué piensas hacer?

intention *(noun: aim, purpose)* intención; propósito; **it was not my intention to cause trouble** no fue mi intención ocasionar problemas; **I have every intention of going** tengo la firme intención de ir; **I did it**

with the best of intentions lo hice con la mejor intención del mundo; lo hice con la mejor voluntad

interdict *(noun: law)* interdicto; entredicho

interdict *(verb: law)* prohibir; **to interdict somebody from something** prohibirle algo a alguien

interdiction *(verb: law)* interdicción; prohibición

interest *(noun: felt by person)* interés; **interest in somebody** interés en alguien; **interest in something** interés en algo; **to lose interest** perder interés; **to show an interest in** demostrar interés en; mostrarse interesada en; mostrarse interesado en; **to take an interest in somebody** interesarse por alguien; **to take an interest in something** interesarse por algo; **he took no further interest in the matter** dejó de interesarse por el asunto; **his only interest seems to be drinking** parece que su único interés es la bebida; **is this of any interest to you?** ¿esto te interesa? **it's a matter of public interest** es un asunto de interés público

interfere with the course of justice entorpecer la acción de la justicia

intermarriage *(between groups)* matrimonio mixto; *(between relatives)* matrimonio entre parientes

internal affairs investigaciones internas

intermediate school escuela donde se cursa el primer ciclo de la enseñanza secundaria

Internal Revenue Service, the la Hacienda; la Dirección General Impositiva; Rentas Públicas; Servicios de Impuestos Internos; Servicios de Rentas Internas

international money order giro postal internacional; giro monetario internacional

interpret *(verb: understand)* interpretar; **how are we to interpret this?** ¿cómo debemos interpretar esto?; **how are we to interpret that remark?** ¿cómo hemos de interpretar ese comentario? **it can be interpreted in two ways** se puede interpretar de dos maneras; **that is not how I interpreted it** no lo entendí yo así; *(translate)* traducir; **to translate from Spanish into English** traducir del español al inglés

interpretation *(explanation; interpretation)* interpretación; **it's open to a number of different interpretations** se puede interpretar de muchas maneras; **it's all a question of interpretation** depende de cómo se interprete; **according to this interpretation** de acuerdo con esta interpretación; **my friend was able to provide an interpretation** mi amigo pudo hacer de intérprete

interpreter *(noun)* intérprete

Interpreter Program of the U.S. Courts Programa de Intérpretes de las Cortes de Estados Unidos

interracial *(adj: discord, harmony)* interracial; *(marriage, etc.)* mixta; mixto

interrogate *(verb: question, criminal, suspect)* interrogar; someter a un interrogatorio; **were you interrogated?** ¿te interrogaron? **were you interrogated by the police?** ¿te sometió la policía a un interrogatorio?; **were you interrogated at the police station?** ¿te interrogaron en la comisaria?

interrogating room sala de interrogatorio

interrogation *(noun: question, criminal, suspect)* interrogatorio

interrogator *(noun:)* interrogador; interrogadora

interruption of business lucro cesante

intersection *(traffic)* cruce; bocacalle

Interstate Freeway *(traffic sign)* Autopista Interestatal

interview *(noun: law)* interrogatorio; *(job, university, radio)* entrevista

intestine *(anat)* intestino

intoxicated *(adj)* en estado de embriaguez

intoxication *(noun)* embriaguez; intoxicación

introduce into evidence presentar como prueba

intruder *(noun)* intrusa; intruso

investigate *(verb: crime, murder, cause)* investigar; hacer indagaciones sobre

investigation *(verb: crime, murder, cause)* investigación; averiguación; indagación **she is under investigation by the police** la policía está haciendo averiguaciones sobre ella

investigation of the deaths investigación de las muertes

investment *(noun)* inversión

involuntary manslaughter *(law)* homicidio culposo involuntario

involve *(verb: entail, comprise)* consistir; involucrar; **what exactly does your work involve?** ¿en qué consiste exactamente tu trabajo?; **to involve somebody in something** involucrar a alguien en algo; **they tried to involve her in the scandal** trataron de involucrarla en el escándalo; trataron de implicarla en el escándalo; **don't try to involve me in your problems** no intentes mezclarme en tus problemas; **I was involved in an accident last year** el año pasado me vi envuelto en un accidente

involvement *(noun: entanglement)* participación; **that confirmed the extent of his involvement in the affair** eso confirmó su grado de participación en el asunto; **they deny any involvement in terrorists attacks** niegan estar implicados en ningún ataque terrorista; **his involvement in the plot** su participación en el complot; *(relationship)* relación; **I disapprove of your involvement with him** tu relación con él no me parece nada bien

irreconcilable differences diferencias irreconciables

irrefutable evidence pruebas fehacientes

irrelevant *(adj)* impertinente; no pertinente

issue *(law)* cuestión

issue a decision emitir una decisión

issue a ruling *(law)* dictar una providencia

issue a warrant *(law)* expedir una orden

issue an order *(law)* expedir una orden

issue guidelines establecer pautas; establecer directrices

issue of fact *(law)* cuestión de hecho

issue of law *(law)* cuestión de derecho

it is ordered that the defendant comply with se ordena que el acusado cumpla con; se ordena que la acusada cumpla con

item *(noun)* artículo; pieza

item of unclaimed property bien mostrenco

itemize *(verb)* detallar

itemized deductions deducciones detalladas

it's a deal! ¡trato hecho!

it's the law es la ley

J

jacket *(noun: clothing)* chaqueta; *(for documents)* carpeta; **sports jacket** chaqueta americana

jackknife *(noun)* navaja; *(verb: truck)* plegarse

jail *(noun)* cárcel; prisión; **she's in jail** está presa; está en la cárcel; **he went to jail** lo metieron preso; **she was sentenced to ten years in jail** fue condenada a diez años de cárcel; fue condenada a diez años de prisión

jail *(verb)* encarcelar; **he was jailed for life** lo condenaron a cadena perpetua; **she was jailed for theft** la metieron presa por robo; **to jail somebody for two months** condenar a alguien a dos meses de cárcel; **he was put in jail** fue encarcelado

jail sentence pena de prisión

jailbait *(noun)* **minor female with whom an adult man is enticed to have sexual relations.** chica menor de edad, con quien constituye delito tener relaciones sexuales

jailbird *(noun)* delincuente habitual; presa reincidente; preso reincidente; presidiaria reincidente; presidiario reincidente

jailbreak *(noun)* fuga de la cárcel

jailer *(noun)* carcelera; carcelero

jailhouse *(noun)* cárcel

jam *(noun; difficult situation)* aprieto; apuro; lío; **to be in a jam** estar en un aprieto; estar en apuros; **to get into a jam** meterse en un lío; *(traffic)* atasco; embotellamiento

janitor *(noun)* conserje; portera; portero

January enero *(see* **July** *for usage)*

jargon *(noun)* jerga

jaw *(anat)* quijada; mandíbula

jaywalk *(verb)* cruzar la calzada imprudentemente

jaywalker *(noun)* peatón imprudente

jaywalking *(noun)* cruzar la calzada con riesgo de provocar un accidente; **she was fined for jaywalking** la multaron por cruzar la calzada con riesgo de provocar un accidente

jealous *(adj: husband; wife)* celosa; celoso; **to get jealous** ponerse celosa; ponerse celoso; **he does it to make you jealous** lo hace para que te pongas celosa; *(envy)* enviosa; envioso

jealousy *(noun)* celos; envidia

jeans *(noun)* vaqueros; tejanos; jeans; **a pair of jeans** unos pantalones vaqueros; unos tejanos

jeopardize *(verb)* poner en peligro; hacer peligrar; arriesgar

jeopardy *(noun)* peligro; **in jeopardy** en peligro; **to put something in jeopardy** poner algo en peligro; arriesgar algo; hacer peligrar algo

jersey *(noun)* camiseta

jet-black *(adj)* negro azabache

jewel *(noun: gem)* piedra preciosa; *(piece of jewelry)* joya; alhaja

jewelry *(noun: gem)* joya; alhaja

job *(noun: occupation, post)* trabajo; empleo; **to be in a job** tener trabajo; **to lose one's job** perder el empleo; **he's out of a job** está sin trabajo; **a part-time job** un trabajo de medio tiempo; **a full-time job** un trabajo de tiempo completo; **to have a teaching job** trabajar en la enseñanza; **she's got a job as a hairdresser** trabaja de peluquera; **he hasn't had a job since 2000** no ha trabajado desde dos mil; **he's between jobs** actualmente está sin trabajo; **on-the-job training** cursos de capacitación para el trabajo; cursos de capacitación en el trabajo; **on the job** en horas de trabajo;

job *(in phrases)* **she's had a nose job** se ha operado la nariz; se ha hecho la cirugía estética en la nariz; *(crime)* **to pull a job** dar un golpe; **to do a job** dar un golpe; **I'm only doing my job** sólo cumplo con mi deber

job description descripción del trabajo

job hunting búsqueda de trabajo; busca de trabajo

job opportunity oportunidad de trabajo; oportunidad laboral

job seeker demandante de empleo

job security seguridad en el puesto; seguridad profesional; garantía de trabajo

job skills *(noun)* **Practical talents useful for gainful employment.** formación de tipo práctico que capacita para desenvolverse en la vida laboral

job specification especificación del trabajo

job training entrenamiento de empleo; adiestramiento de empleo

jobless *(adj)* sin trabajo; parada; parado

John Doe An average man. fulano; el típico estadounidense; el estadounidense medio; **Unknown person** *(nombre ficticio dado a una persona en juicio, porque no se permite usar su verdadero nombre, o porque se trata de un menor)*

John Q Public el hombre de la calle; el ciudadano medio; el ciudadano de a pie

join the army alistarse en el ejército; incorporarse a filas

joinder *(law)* acumulación de acciones

joint *(noun: marijuana)* porro; canuto; toque; varillo

joint account cuenta conjunta

joint effort trabajo de equipo; trabajo realizado en conjunto

joint heirs coherederos

joint liability responsabilidad solidaria

joint owner comunera; comunero; condueña; condueño; copropietaria; copropietario

joint ownership condominio; propiedad mancomunada; propiedad en conjunto

joint partner copartícipe

joint partnership empresa colectiva

joint policy póliza conjunta

joint property propiedad indivisa

joint return declaración de la renta conjunta

joint tax return declaración de la renta conjunta

joint tenancy comunidades en manos comunes

joint trial juicio conjunto contra dos o más procesados

joint venture empresa conjunta; sociedad conjunta

joints *(anat)* coyunturas; articulaciones

jot down apuntar; anotar; **jot down everything that you remember** apunta todo lo que recuerdas

jot it down on the calendar apuntarlo en el calendario

journal *(noun: periodical)* revista; publicación; periódico; *(diary)* diario; **to keep a journal** llevar un diario; *(law)* actas

joyride *(noun: leisure)* dar una vuelta; **let's go out for a joyride** vamos a dar una vuelta en coche; *(in stolen car)* **they took the car for a joyride** robaron el coche para dar una vuelta

judge *(noun: law)* juez; jueza; magistrada; magistrado; **undersigned judge** infrascrito juez; **the judge's decision is final** la decisión del juez es irrevocable; **the judge gave him the maximum sentence** el juez le impusó la máxima pena; **in accordance with the instructions of the judge** de acuerdo con las instrucciones del juez; **acting judge** juez interino; **to appeal the judge's decision** apelar contra la decisión del juez; **to appear before a judge** comparecer ante un juez; **he's the best judge** es el mejor juez; **to comply with the judge's instructions** seguir las instrucciones del juez; **the judge delayed the start of the trial** el juez demoró el comienzo del juicio; **the judge dealt fairly with him** el juez fue justo con él; el juez lo trató con justicia; **the judge has given his verdict** el juez ha dictado sentencia; **the judge gave her five years** el juez le dio cinco años; el juez la condenó a cinco años; **the judge is difficult to please** el juez es difícil de complacer; **you'll have a hard time explaining that to the judge** te costará explicárselo al juez; **the judge imposed the maximum sentence** el juez aplicó la sentencia máxima; **the judge isn't in yet** el juez no ha llegado todavía; **the judge's proposals have had a mixed reception** las propuestas del juez han sido recibidas con reservas; **the judge found that he had been negligent** el juez declaró que había sido negligente; **the judge remitted six months of his sentence** el juez le redujo la pena en seis meses; **the judge gave him a six-month sentence** el juez le condenó a seis meses de prisión

judge *(verb: law)* juzgar; *(contest)* ser el juez de; *(verb: law)* calcular; *(in phrases)* **I'm no judge of character** no entiendo de sicología; **judging from** a juzgar por; **as far as I can judge** por lo que puedo entender

judge in the case juez del caso

judgement *(law)* fallo; decisión; sentencia; **to pass judgement on somebody** juzgar a alguien; *(noun)* **I did not have enough information to form a judgement** no tenía suficiente información como para formarme una opinión; **my judgement is that ...** yo opinó que ...; juzgo que ...; **in my judgement** a mi juicio

judgement for the plaintiff sentencia al favor al demandante

judgement of acquittal *(law)* fallo absolutorio; sentencia absolutoria

judgement of conviction *(law)* fallo condenatorio; sentencia condenatoria; sentencia de condena

judgement of dismissal sentencia absolutoria

judgement of his peers juicio por jurado

judging from what you say a juzgar por lo que tú dices

judicial formalities diligencias judiciales

judicial notice aviso judicial

judicial procedures diligencias judiciales

judicial protection tutela judicial

July *(noun)* julio; **at the beginning of July** a principios de julio; **at the end of July** a finales de julio; **during July** durante el mes julio; **during the month of July** en el mes de julio; **each July** cada julio; todos los meses de julio; **early in July** a principios de julio; a primeros de julio; **every July** cada julio; todos los meses de julio; **in July** en julio; **in July of next year** en julio del año que viene; **in the middle of July** a mediados de julio; **in the month of July** durante el mes julio; en el mes de julio; **last July** julio pasado; **next July** el julio que viene; el próximo julio; **on the eleventh of July** el once de julio; **on the first of July** el primero de julio

jump bail fugarse bajo fianza; fugarse al estar bajo fianza; violar la libertad bajo fianza; huir estando en libertad bajo fianza

junkie yonqui; drogadicta; drogadicto

jurisdiction *(noun)* jurisdicción; competencia; fuero; **to have jurisdiction over** tener jurisdicción sobre; **it's within my jurisdiction** está dentro de mi competencia; **it's outside my jurisdiction** está fuera de mi competencia

juror *(noun)* jurada; jurado; miembro de un jurado; **alternate juror** jurado supernumerario; jurado supletorio

jury *(law)* jurado; **trial by jury** juicio ante jurado; **to serve on a jury** ser miembro de un jurado; **to sit on a jury** ser miembro de un jurado; **to do jury duty** ser miembro de un jurado; actuar como jurado

jury box tribuna del jurado

jury deliberation deliberación del jurado

jury duty servicio de jurado

jury fixing soborno del jurado

jury instructions *(law)* pautas sobre la ley para el jurado; instrucciones al jurado

jury list lista del jurado

jury pool reserva de jurados

jury room sala de deliberaciones

jury selection integración del jurado

jury summation declaraciones finales de los abogados al jurado

jury system sistema jurídico

jury trial juicio por jurado

jury verdict veredicto del jurado

just *(law)* justa; justo; **we must be just to them** debemos ser justos con ellos; **we must be just toward them** debemos ser justos con ellos; **our cause is just** nuestra causa es justa

just *(in recent past)* **I've just remembered that ...** me acabó de acordar de que ...; **she's just left** se acaba de ir; **she'd only just finished** acababa de terminar; *(only)* sólo; enseguida; **I'll be with you in just a moment** enseguida estoy con usted; en un segundo estoy con usted; **I went there just once** fui sólo una vez; **she was just three when her father**

died tenía sólo tres años cuando murió su padre; **they're just friends** sólo son amigos; no son más que amigos

just cause justa causa

just cause for discharge justa causa para el despido

just married recién casados

justice *(law)* justicia; **court of justice** tribunal de justicia; **justice was done** se hizo justicia; **in the end he was brought to justice** finalmente pagó sus culpas; **to bring somebody to justice** llevar a alguien ante los tribunales; *(person)* juez

justice of the peace *(law)* juez de la paz

justifiable homicide *(law)* homicidio justificable

justified *(adj)* justificada; justificado; **to be justified in doing something** tener motivo para hacer algo; tener razón al hacer algo; **am I justified in thinking that ... ?** ¿hay motivo para creer que ...?

justified homicide homicidio justificado

juvenile *(adj)* juvenil; infantil; *(law, court)* de menores

juvenile *(noun)* joven; menor

Juvenile Assessment Center Centro Juvenil de Evaluación

juvenile delinquent delincuente menor de edad; delincuente juvenil

juvenile court tribunal de menores

K

kangaroo court tribunal informal *(tribunal irregular y arbitrario)*

keep *(noun)* comida; sustento; **to earn one's keep** ganarse el sustento

keep *(verb: detain)* tener; entretener; *(restrain)* tener; retener; **to keep somebody in prison** tener a alguien presa; tener a alguien preso; mantener a alguien en la cárcel; **to keep somebody waiting** hacer esperar a alguien; *(law, rule, obligation)* observar; *(appointment)* acudir a; ir a; *(promise, vow)* cumplir; **he kept his word** cumplió su palabra; no faltó a su palabra

keep *(in phrases)* **keep her informed** manténla al tanto; **he can't keep a job** es incapaz de mantener un trabajo; **keep it, I don't need it** quédate con él, no lo necesito; **they kept his job for him** le guardaron el puesto; **he keeps a mistress** mantiene a una amante; **she keeps a diary** escribe un diario; lleva un diario; **I've kept a note of everything** he tomado nota de todo; **I've kept a record of everything** lo tengo todo anotado; **try and keep him talking** procura que siga hablando; **don't let me keep you** no te quiero entretener; **what kept you?** ¿por qué tardaste?; **they kept me at the police station for hours** me tuvieron horas en la comisaria; **you have to keep trying** tienes que seguir intentándolo

keep away *(phrases)* **keep away from me!** ¡no te me acerques!; **keep away from my family!** ¡deja en paz a mi familia!; **she can't keep away from the casino** tiene que ir al casino, es superior a ella; **you'd better keep her away from me** más vale que no dejes que se me acerque

keep books llevar libros; **he keeps books for a restaurant** lleva libros para un restaurante

keep records llevar cuentas; mantener archivos; llevar registros

Keep Right *(traffic sign)* Conserve su Derecha

keep out *(adv)* **to keep somebody out of trouble** evitar que alguien se meta en líos; **to keep somebody out of the way** sacar a alguien de en medio; **to keep out of something** no meterse en algo; **you keep out of this!** ¡no te metas en esto!

keep up sostener; sujetar; mantener viva; mantener vivo

keep up the good work! ¡bien hecho!; ¡sigue así!; ¡síguele dando!

keep up with mantenerse a la par con

keep within the law obrar legalmente

key *(noun: for lock)* llave; *(to puzzle, code)* clave; **the key to success** la clave del éxito

kickback *(noun)* soborno; mordida; coima; pago indebido

kick out *(verb: from home)* echar de casa; **his parents have kicked him out** sus padrtes lo han echado de casa; *(from university)* expulsar de la universidad

kidnap *(verb)* secuestrar; raptar; plagiar

kidnapper *(verb)* secuestrador; secuestradora; raptor; raptora

kidnapping *(noun)* secuestro; rapto; plagio

kidnapping and disappearance of secuestro y desaparición de

kidney*(anat)* riñón

kidney transplant transplante del riñón

kill *(verb: cause death of)* matar; dar muerte a; **to kill oneself** matarse; suicidarse; **you'll get yourself killed** te van a matar; **he killed himself** se suicidó; **he was killed by the rebels** lo mataron los rebeldes; fue muerto por los rebeldes; **she was killed in a car crash** se mató en un accidente de coche; murió en un accidente de coche; **nine people were killed in the fire** nueve personas resultaron muertas en el incendio; **he was killed in the war in Iraq** murió en la guerra de Iraq; **it was drink that killed him** la bebida acabó con él

kill *(in phrases)* **I went for a walk to kill time** fui a dar un paseo para matar el tiempo; **I have an hour to kill** tengo una hora sin nada que hacer; **all this work is killing me** tanto trabajo me está matando

killer *(noun: person)* asesina; asesino

killing *(noun: of person)* asesinato; *(of animal, massacre)* matanza; **to avoid the killing of civilians** para evitar que murieran civiles; para evitar la muerte de civiles; **the barbaric killing of innocent people** la sanguinaria matanza de inocentes

kin *(noun)* familia; parientes; **next of kin** parientes más cercanos

kind *(adj: person, act, word)* amable; atenta; atento; *(friendly)* amistosa; amistoso; amigable; *(treatment)* buena; bueno; cariñosa; cariñoso; **to be kind to somebody** portarse bien con alguien; tratar bien a alguien

kind *(noun)* clase; tipo; género; **all kinds of** things toda clase de cosas; **people of all kinds** gente de todas clases; **he's not the kind of person to ...** él no es de los que ...; **she's the kind that will ...** ella es de las que ...

kind-hearted *(adj: person)* de buen corazón; bondadosa; bondadoso; **he's very kind-hearted** tiene muy buen corazón

kindergarten *(noun)* jardín de infancia; jardín infantil; jardín de infantes

kinship *(noun)* parentesco

knee *(noun: anat)* rodilla

knife *(noun)* cuchillo; navaja; *(dagger)* puñal

knife fight pelea con cuchillos; pelea con navajas

knife-point *(noun)* **at knife-point** a punta de navaja

knifing *(noun)* ataque con cuchillo; ataque con navaja

knock *(in phrases)* **I got a knock on the head** me di un golpe en la cabeza; **the blow knocked her unconscious** el golpe la dejó inconsciente; **she went in without knocking** entró sin llamar; **she hit her head and knocked herself out** se dio un golpe en la cabeza y perdió el conocimiento; **he knocked the knife out of her hand** le quitó el cuchillo de la mano de un golpe; **to knock somebody to the ground** tirar a alguien al suelo; echar a alguien al suelo

knock and announce rule *regla que exige que en casos de arresto los funcionarios públicos toquen a la perta y anuncien su capacidad y propósito*

knock down atropellar; **she was knocked down by a car** la atropelló un coche

know *(verb: have knowledge, be aware)* saber; **I don't know his name** no sé cómo se llama; **I don't know how old he is** no sé cuántos años tiene; **what do you know about that?** ¿tú qué sabes de eso? **not to know the first thing about something** no saber nada de algo; no tener ni idea de algo; **I don't know that I agree** no sé si estoy de acuerdo; **I'll have you know that ...** has de saber que ...; **you know as well as I do that ...** sabes tan bien como yo que ...; **I don't know how to put this, but ...** no sé cómo decirlo, pero ...; **it is well known that ...** todo el mundo sabe que ..; **it soon became known that ...** pronto se supo que ...; **he let it be known that ...** dio a entender que ...; **how do you know?** ¿cómo lo sabes?; **when will you know?** ¿cuándo lo sabrás?

knowingly *(adv)* a sabiendas

knowledge *(noun: awareness)* conocimiento; **I had no knowledge of their activities** no estaba enterado de sus actividades; no tenía conocimiento de sus actividades; **it has come to my knowledge that ...** ha llegado a mi conocimiento que ...; **it is common knowledge that ...** todo el mundo sabe que ...; **my knowledge of Spanish is very limited** mis conocimientos de español son muy limitados; **my knowledge of law is very limited** mis conocimientos de la ley son muy limitados; **without my knowledge** sin saberlo yo; **to your knowledge** a sabiendas; a su entender

known *(adj)* conocida; conocido; sabida; sabido; **her last known address** la última dirección que se le conoce; **he likes to be known as Alex** le gusta que lo llamen Alex; **you'll need what's known as an affidavit** vas a necesitar lo que se conoce como un affidávit; **she is known to the police** la policía la tiene fichada

knowingly *(adv: smile, nod)* de manera cómplice; *(deliberately)* a sabiendas; **she had knowingly received stolen goods** había recibido objetos robados a sabiendas

L

label *(noun: on bottle, file)* etiqueta; rótulo **address label** etiqueta con la dirección; *(brand name)* marca; *(record company)* sello discográfico

label *(verb: bottle, file)* etiquetear; rotular; ponerle una etiqueta a

labor *(noun: productive work)* trabajo; **cheap labor** mano de obra barata; **organized labor** sindicalización; sindicación; **hard labor** trabajos forzados

labor *(medical, delivery);* parto; **a difficult labor** un parto difícil; **to be in labor** estar de parto; **to go into labor** entrar en trabajo de parto

labor costs costos de la mano de obra

labor dispute conflicto laboral

labor force trabajadores; mano de obra

labor law derecho laboral; ley laboral

labor leader dirigente sindical; líder sindical

labor market mercado de trabajo; mercado laboral

labor movement movimiento obrero

labor pains dolores del parto; contracciones del parto

labor shortage escasez de mano de obra

labor supply oferta de mano de obra

labor union sindicato

labor ward sala de partos

laborer *(noun: on roads, etc.)* peón; *(in construction industry)* peón de albañil; *(farm worker)* peón; trabajador agrícola; trabajadora agrícola; **day laborer** jornalera; jornalero; bracera; bracero

lack *(noun)* falta; carencia; **for lack of** por falta de; carecer de; necesitar

lack *(verb)* no tener; carecer de; faltarle; **she lacks confidence** le falta confianza en sí misma; no tiene confianza en sí misma; carece de confianza en sí misma; **we lack the time to do it** nos falta el tiempo para hacerlo; **there is no lack of money** el dinero no falta; **they lack for nothing** no les falta nada

lack of capacity falta de capacidad; no tener la capacidad para

lack of interest falta de interés

lack of resources falta de recursos; carencia de recursos

lack of severity falta de gravedad; insuficiencia de gravedad

lack of sleep falta de sueño

lack of something carencia de algo; falta de algo

lacking *(adj)* **the necessary resources are lacking** faltan los recursos necesarios; se carece de los recursos necesarios; **to be lacking in something** no tener algo; carecer de algo

lad *(noun: boy)* muchacho; chico; chaval

Ladies and Gentleman! ¡señoras y señores!

ladies room lavabo de señoras; baño de señoras; servicio de señoras

lady *(noun: woman)* señora; dama

lame *(adj)* coja; cojo; renga; rengo; **to be lame** *(temporarily)* estar coja; estar cojo; *(permanently)* ser coja; ser cojo; *(injured)* ser lisiada; ser lisiado; **to be lame in one leg** cojear de una pierna; **to go lame** quedarse coja; quedarse cojo

lame in one foot coja de un pie; cojo de un pie

lame in one leg coja de una pierna; cojo de una pierna

lance corporal soldado de primera clase

land *(noun: property)* tierra; terreno; **a plot of land** un terreno; una parcela; **to work on the land** trabajar la tierra; cultivar la tierra; **to own land** poseer tierras; *(country)* país; nación; **native land** patria

land *(in phrases)* **I have landed myself with a lot of problems** me he metido en un montón de problemas; **that venture finally landed her in prison** con aquel negocio fue a parar a la cárcel; **he is sure to land in debt** seguro que termina endeudado

landlady *(noun: of rented dwelling)* casera; dueña; propietaria; arrendadora; **my landlady** mi casera; la deuña de mi casa

landlord *(noun: of rented dwelling)* casero; dueño; arrendedor; **my landlord** mi casero; el dueño de mi casa

landmark case caso sobresaliente que marca un cambio importante en las decisiones de los tribunales

landowner *(noun)* terrateniente; hacendada; hacendado

lane *(for road; traffic)* carril; pista; **to change lanes** cambiar de carril; cambiar de pista; **a four lane highway** una autopista de cuatro carriles; una autopista de cuatro pistas; **traffic is reduced to one lane** se circula por un solo carril; se circula por un a sola pista

Lane Ends *(traffic sign)* El Carril Termina

language *(noun: speech, means of communication)* lenguaje; **bad language** palabrotas; malas palabras; **I've never heard him use such language before** nunca le había oído decir tales palabras; **watch your language!** ¡no digas palabrotas!; ¡esa boca!; **the English language** la lengua inglesa; el idioma inglés; *(native tongue)* lengua materna; *(education)* **first language** primer idioma; primera lengua; **second language** segunda lengua; segundo idioma

language barrier barrera liguística; barrera del idioma

large contingent of police fuerte dispositivo policial

lapse *(noun fault, error)* falla; fallo; **a security lapse** una falla en el sistema de seguridad; un fallo en el sistema de seguridad; un descuido en el sistema de seguridad; **a lapse of concentration** una falta de concentración; **to have a lapse of memory** tener una falla de memoria; tener un fallo de memoria; **several hours had lapsed** habían transcurrido varias horas; **his concentration lapsed** se desconcertó; perdió la concentración; **to lapse into unconsciousness** perder el conocimiento

larceny *(law)* hurto; robo; latrocinio; **petty larceny** hurto

large *(in phrases)* **to be at large** andar suelta; andar suelto; **he's a large man** es un hombre corpulento; **she has a large nose** tiene la nariz grande; **a large proportion of his income** gran parte de sus ingresos; una buena parte de sus ingresos

last *(in phrases)* **this is the last time that ...** es la última vez que ...; **to be the last person to** + *infin* ser la última persona en + *infin*; **she was last seen a year ago** hace un año que se la vio por última vez; la última vez que se la vio fue hace un año; **when did you last see him?** ¿cuándo fue la última vez que lo vio?; **this time last week** la semana pasada a estas horas; **for the last ten hours** durante las últimas diez horas; **for the last nine days** durante los últimos nueve días; **for the last three months** durante los últimos tres meses; **the week before last** la semana antepasada; **it lasted for three hours** duró tres horas; **last night** anoche; **the night before last** antenoche; **at long last** por fin; al fin

last demand for payment último aviso de pago

last-ditch *(study)* desesperada; desesperado; **a last-ditch attempt** un intento desesperado

last Friday el miércoles pasado

last-minute *(adj)* de última hora

last Monday el lunes pasado

last month el mes pasado

last resort de última instancia

last Saturday el sábado pasado

last Sunday el domingo pasado

last Thursday el jueves pasado

last Tuesday el martes pasado

last Wednesday el miércoles pasado

last week la semana pasada

last will and testament última voluntad y testamento

last year el año pasado

last year of high school el último año de la escuela secundaria

latch *(noun)* cerrojo

late *(adj: not on time)* tardía; tardío; **to be late** llegar tarde; **to arrive late** llegar tarde; **to be ten minutes late** llegar con diez minutos de retraso; **it's getting late** se está haciendo tarde; **to keep late hours** acostarse tarde; **at this late hour** a esta hora avanzada; **in late spring** hacia fines de la primavera; **to work late** trabajar hasta tarde; **late at night** entrada la noche; **late in life** a una edad avanzada; **as late as 2000** todavía en dos mil; **hurry up, it's late** date prisa, que es tarde

late at night a altas horas de la noche

law *(noun: governing actions)* ley; *(study)* derecho; **by law** según la ley; **to break the law** violar la ley; infringir la ley; contravenir la ley; **to keep within the law** obrar legalmente; **to enforce the law** imponer la ley; hacer respetar la ley; **to stay within the law** actuar dentro de la ley; **to operate within the law** operar dentro de la ley; **to operate outside the law** operar fuera de la ley; **against the law** contra la ley; **civil criminal law** derecho civil; derecho penal; **to practice law** ejercer de abogada; ejercer de abogado; **to study law** estudiar derecho; **court of law** tribunal de justicia; **an officer of the law** un agente de la ley; **to pass a law** aprobar una ley; **no one is above the law** nadie está por encima de la ley; **in accordance with the law** en conformidad con la ley; de acuerdo con la ley; **permitted by law** permitida por la ley; permitido por la ley; **required by law** exigida por la ley; exigido por la ley; **she's been in trouble wth the law before** ya ha tenido problemas con la ley; ya ha tenido problemas con la autoridad

law-abiding *(adj)* respetuosa de la ley; respetuoso de la ley

law and order orden público

law blank formulario legal en blanco

law clinic consultorio legal; consultorio jurídico

law court tribunal de justicia

law enforcement *la imposición del cumplimiento de la ley*

law enforcement agency agencia jurídica

law enforcement officer agente de la ley

law on abortion legislación sobre el aborto

law school facultad de derecho

law student estudiante de derecho

lawbreaker infractor de la ley; infractora de la ley

lawful *(adj)* legítima; legítimo; válida; válido; legal

lawful admission admisión legal; entrada legal

lawful entry ingreso lícito

lawful impediment impedimento

lawful owner propietaria legal; propietario legal

lawful permanent resident residente legal permanente

lawful purpose propósito legal

lawless *(adj)* ingobernable; que rechaza la ley

laws that govern immigration leyes que rigen la inmigración

lawsuit *(noun)* causa; causa civil

lawyer *(noun)* abogada; abogado; **the matter is in the hands of my lawyer** el asunto está en manos de mi abogado

lawyer fees honorarios de abogado; **what are your fees?** ¿cuáles son sus honorarios?

lawyer who specializes in worker's rights abogada laborista; abogado laborista

lay *(verb: present, put forward)* formular; presentar; **to lay a complaint against somebody** formular una queja contra alguien; presentar una queja contra alguien; **to lay a case before somebody** exponer un caso ante alguien; **to lay a rumor to rest** acallar un rumor

lay down guidelines establecer pautas; establecer directrices

lay off *(verb: employment)* despedir; *(colloquial)* dejar; **you should lay off drinking** debes dejar la bebida; **you should lay off gambling** debes dejar el juego; **just lay off, will you?** ¡basta ya!; **lay off me** ¡déjame en paz!; **lay off her** ¡déjala en paz!; **lay off him** ¡déjalo en paz!; **lay off them** ¡déjalos en paz!

lay opinion *(law)* opinión lega

lay witness *(law)* testigo lego

layoff *(noun: employment)* despido

lazy *(adj* perezosa; perezoso

lead *(noun: clue)* pista; **the police have a lead** la policía tiene una pista; **to investigate a lead** investigar una pista; **to follow up a lead** seguir una pista; **the Spanish police focus on the Al-Qaeda lead** la policía española se centra en la pista de Al Qaeda; **the police follow the lead of the hired assassins of a journalist** la policía le sigue la pista a los sicarios que acabaron con la vida de un periodista

lead *(noun: leading position; leadership)* delantera; ventaja

lead *(verb)* dirigir; conducir; supervisar

lead on *(verb: raise false hopes)* engañar; **to lead somebody on to something** engañar a alguien para que haga algo; **they were led on with promises of high wages** los engañaron con promesas de sueldos altos

lead up to *(noun: precede)* preceder; **the events leading up to the crime** los acontecimientos que procedieron al delito; **he was obviously leading up to something** era obvio que estaba preparando el terreno para algo; **what's all this leading up to?** ¿qué te propones con todo esto?

leadership qualities dotes de mando; dotes de liderazgo

leading question pregunta sugerente; pregunta sugestiva *(pregunta que sugiere la respuesta que se quiere obtener en un juicio)*

leak *(verb: information)* filtrar; **the report was leaked to the press** filtraron el informe a la prensa; *(pipes, roof)* gotear; perder; **the pipe leaks** la cañería pierde agua; **the roof is leaking** hay goteras en el techo; **the car is leaking oil** el coche pierde aceite

learn *(verb: gain knowledge of)* aprender; **to learn English** aprender inglés; *(become informed about)* enterarse de; **we learned that he committed the crime** nos enteramos de que el cometió el crimen

learning disabilities discapacidades de aprendizaje

lease *(noun)* alquiuler; contrato de arrendamiento; *(of real estate)* usufructo; *(verb)* arrendar; alquilar

lease out *(verb)* arrendar; dar en arriendo; *(real estate)* tener el usufructo de

leasehold *(noun)* derecho de arrendamiento

leaseholder *(noun)* arrendataria; arrendatario

leasing *(noun)* arrendamiento con opción de compra; **I leased the premises** tomé el local en arrendamiento

leave *(verb: abandon, husband, wife)* dejar; **she left her husband for another man** dejó a su marido por otro hombre; **he was left for dead** lo dieron por muerto; **they left him to die in the desert** lo abandonaron a su suerte en el desierto; **they dumped his body in a field outside of Phoenix** dejaron su cuerpo tirado en un camino fuera de Phoenix

leave for another man abandonar por otro; **she left him for another man** lo abandonó por otro

leave for another woman abandonar por otra; **he left her for another woman** la abandonó por otra

leave the area abandonar el área; **the police have started to leave the area** la policía ha comenzado a abandonar el área

leave the country abandonar el país

leave the premises abandonar el recinto; abandono del recinto; **the police ordered everyone to leave the premises** la policía ordenó el abandono del recinto

leave without paying rent irse sin pagar el alquiler; irse sin pagar el arrendamiento

left *(adj)* izquierda; izquierdo; **on the left** a la izquierda; **from left to right** de izquierda a derecha

left-handed *(person)* zurdo

left turn lane carril de viraje a la izquierda

leg *(anat)* pierna

legal *(adj: allowed)* legal; permitida por la ley; permitido por la ley; **he is the legal owner** es el legítimo propietario; **she is the legal owner** es la legítima propietaria; **the contract is legal and binding** el contrato tiene validez legal y es obligatorio para las partes; **she was below the legal age** no tenía la edad establecida por la ley; **they decided to make their relationship legal** decidieron legalizar sus relaciones; **a legal matter** cuestión jurídica; asunto jurídico

legal *(adj: relating to legal system, profession)* legal; jurídica; jurídico

legal action acción judicial; **we will be forced to take legal action** nos veremos obligados a poner el asunto en manos de nuestros abogados

legal advice *(from professionals)* **to seek legal advice** consultar a un abogado; consultar a una abogada; asesorarse con un abogado; asesorarse con una abogada

legal adviser asesor legal; asesora legal

legal age edad legal

legal aid abogacía de pobres; *asistencia legal sin cargo para las personas de bajos ingresos*

legal aid lawyer abogada de oficio; abogado de oficio; abogada de turno; abogado de turno

legal and practical issues asuntos legales y prácticos; cuestiones legales y prácticas

legal argument argumento legal

legal capacity capacidad legal

legal competence aptitud legal

legal costs costos legales

legal custody custodia legal

legal dependency dependencia legal

legal disability incapacidad legal

legal entity persona jurídica

legal ethics ética legal

legal father padre legal

legal fees honorarios legales

legal guardian tutor legal; tutora legal

legal holiday día festivo oficial

legal incapacity incapacidad legal

legal issues cuestiones legales; asuntos legales

legal loophole laguna jurídica

legal mother madre legal

legal name nombre legal

legal owner dueña legal; dueño legal

legal problems problemas legales

legal procedures trámites legales

legal proceedings procedimientos legales; **she has started legal proceedings against them** ha procedido judicialmente en contra de ellos; les ha entablado pleito

legal profession, the *(lawyers)* abogados; los letrados; *(professional activity)* la abogacía; **she entered the legal profession** se hizo abogada

legal representation representación legal

legal representative representante legal; representante judicial

legal residence residencia legal

legal resident residente legal

legal resources recursos legales

legal rights derechos legales

legal separation separación legal

legal services sevicio legal; asistencia jurídica

legal settlement acuerdo legal

legal status situación jurídica; situación legal

legal system sistema jurídico

legal tender moneda de curso legal

legalese *(noun)* jerga legal de los abogados

legalistic *(adj)* legalista

legality *(noun)* legalidad

legalization *(noun: of document)* legalización

legalize *(verb: of document)* legalizar; *(act)* despenalizar; **to legalize a drug** despenalizar el uso de una droga

legally *(noun)* legalmente; desde un punto de vista legal; **this contract is legally binding** este contrato obliga legalmente; **legally, you have no right to the money** desde un punto de vista legal, no tiene derecho al dinero

legally binding que obliga legalmente

legally speaking desde el punto de vista legal

legate *(noun)* legado

legatee *(noun)* legataria; legatario

legislate *(verb)* legislar

legislation *(noun: laws)* legislación; **under existing legislation** de acuerdo a la legislación vigente; conforme a la legislación vigente; **a new piece**

of legislation una nueva ley; un nuevo proyecto de ley; **to introduce legislation** introducir legislación; introducir leyes

legislative *(adj)* legislativa; legislativo

legislator *(noun)* legislador; legisladora

legislature *(noun)* asamblea legislativa

legitimate *(adj)* legítima; legítimo; válida; válido; justa; justo; *(verb)* dar legitimidad a

legitimize *(verb: make lawful)* legitimar; *(child, birth)* legalizar; justificar

lender *(noun)* prestamista

length *(in phrases)* **the road was lined with policeman along its entire length** había policía todo a lo largo de la carretera; **she went to great lengths to help us** se desvivió por ayudarnos; **he even went to the lengths of hiring a private detective** llegó al extremo de contratar un detective privado; **for what length of time?** ¿durante cuánto tiempo?; ¿por cuánto tiempo?; **to explain at length** explicar con mucho detalle; **to speak at length** hablar largamente

length of service duración del servicio

lenient sentence sentencia poca severa

lesbian *(noun)* lesbiana; *(adj)* lesbiana; lesbiano; lésbica; lésbico

lessen *(verb: pain)* aliviar; atenuar; *(cost, risk)* reducir; disminuir

lesser included offense infracción menor incluida

let *(in phrases)* **let her speak** déjala hablar; **let him speak** déjalo hablar; **let me help you** deja que te ayude; **let me have your answer tomorrow** dame la respuesta mañana; contéstame mañana; **let me know if there is any problem** avísame si hay algún problema; **he let it be known that ...** hizo saber que ...; **let that be a warning to you!** ¡que eso te sirva de lección!

let off *(sentence)* **he was let off lightly** se ecapó con un castigo bien leve; **he was let off with a warning** se llevó sólo una advertencia

let out *(release from jail, prison)* **he's hoping to be let out of prison soon** espera que lo dejen salir de la cárcel pronto; espera que lo suelten pronto

let the record show that ... que conste en acta que ...

letter bomb carta bomba

letter of advice carta de aviso

letter of application carta de solicitud

letter of attorney carta de poder

letter of credit carta de crédito

letter of denial carta de denegación

letter of dismissal carta de despido

letter of intent carta de intenciones

letter of introduction carta de recomendación

letter of protest carta de protesta

letter of proxy carta de poder

letter of resignation carta de dimisión

letterhead *(noun)* membrete

level *(noun)* nivel; *(adj)* llana; llano; plana; plano

level of care nivel de cuidado

level of proficiency nivel de competencia

level of severity nivel de gravedad

lewd *(adj: person)* lasciva; lascivo

lewdness *(noun)* lascivia; exhibición deshonesta

liabilities *(noun: financial)* pasivo; deudas; obligaciones; **current liabilities** pasivo circulante; **fixed-term liabilities** deudas a largo plazo; **long-term liabilities** deudas a largo plazo; **we are unable to meet our liabilities** no podemos hacer frente a nuestras obligaciones; **to meet one's liabilities** satisfacer sus deudas

liability *(noun: responsibility)* responsabilidad; **to deny liability for something** negar ser responsable de algo; **to admit liability for something** admitir ser responsable de algo; **tax liability** pasivo exigible en concepto de impuestos

liability attaches deudas que se embargan

liability in tort responsabilidad extracontractual

liability insurance seguro contra terceros; seguro contra responabilidades

liable *(adj: responsible)* responsable; **to be liable for something** ser responsable de algo; responder de algo; **to hold somebody liable** responsabilizar a alguien; considerar a alguien responsable; **any income is liable for tax** cualquier ingreso es gravable; cualquier ingreso está sujeto a impuestos; **to be liable to** + *infin* es probable que; **I'm liable to forget** es probable que me olvide

liaison *(noun)* enlace; contacto; coordinación

liaison officer oficial de enlace

liar *(noun)* mentirosa; mentiroso; embustera; embustero

libel *(noun)* calumnia; difamación; **to sue somebody for libel** demandar a alguien por calumnia; demandar a alguien por difamación; **to publish a libel** publicar un libelo

libel *(verb: law)* calumniar; difamar; injuriar

libelous *(adj: law, article, remark)* difamatoria; difamatorio; calumniosa; calumnioso

liberate *(verb: set free)* poner en libertad; dejar en libertad; liberar; libertar

liberated *(adj)* liberada; liberado

liberation *(noun: of prisoner; nation)* liberación

license *(noun)* licencia; permiso; **driver's license** carnet de conducir; permiso de conducir

license *(noun: freedom)* libertad; **the editor permitted himself considerable license** el editor se tomó bastantes libertades

license number matrícula; número de matrícula

license plate *(noun)* placa de la matrícula

license plate number número de la placa de matrícula

lie *(noun)* mentira; **that's a lie** eso es mentira; **to tell lies** decir mentiras; **to live a lie** vivir una mentira; **to catch somebody in a lie** pescar a alguien en una mentira; **to tell lies** mentir

lie detector detector de mentiras

lien *(noun: right)* derecho de retención; **to put a lien on something** embargar algo; **how can I put a lien on a debtor's personal property?** ¿cómo puedo embargar los bienes personales de un deudor?

lieutenant *(noun)* teniente

life *(plural:* **lives***)* vida; **to be sent to prison for life** ser condenada a cadena perpetua; ser condenado a cadena perpetua; **to do life** cumplir una condena de reclución perpetua; **early in life** en su juventud; **for life** de por vida; durante la vida de; **maimed for life** lisada de por vida; lisado de por vida; **for the rest of his life** el resto de sus días; **for the rest of her life** el resto de sus días; **later in life** más tarde; más adelante; **lose one's life** perder la vida; **risk one's life** arriesgar la vida; **a matter of life and death** cosa de vida o muerte

life expectancy esperanza de vida; expectativas de vida

life imprisonment pena de cadena perpetua

life in the United States vida en Estados Unidos

life insurance seguro de vida

life insurance policy póliza de seguro de vida

life of crime vida de delincuencia

life pension pensión vitalicia

life sentence pena de cadena perpetua

life term pena de cadena perpetua

lifeless *(adj: person)* sin vida; exánime

lifelong *(adj: person)* de toda la vida; **he is a lifelong friend** es un amigo de toda la vida

lifeskills *(noun)* *formación de tipo práctico que capacita para desenvolverse en la vida diaria*

lifestyle estilo de vida; tren de vida

lifetime *(noun)* vida; **in my lifetime** durante mi vida; en el curso de mi vida; **within my lifetime** mientras viva; **the chance of a lifetime** una oportunidad única

lifetime guarantee garantía para toda la vida

lifetime learning credit crédito de aprendizaje de toda la vida

lifetime reserve reserva vitalicia; reserva por vida

lifework *(noun)* trabajo de toda una vida

light-haired *(adj: person)* rubia; rubio; güera; güero

light-skinned *(adj: person)* de piel clara

light work trabajo ligero; trabajo liviano

lighter sentence sentencia más ligera

like *(in phrases)* **in like cases** en casos parecidos; **people like that** esa clase de gente; ese tipo de gente; **what's he like?** ¿cómo es él?; **what's she like?** ¿cómo es ella?; **would you like me to wait?** ¿quiere que espere?; **as you like** como quieras; **whenever you like** cuando quieras; **whether he likes it or not** quiera o no quiera

likelihood *(noun)* probabilidad; posibilidad; **is there any likelihood of her changing her mind?** ¿hay alguna probabilidad de que cambie de opinión?; **there is no likelihood of that happening** no hay ninguna probabilidad de que eso suceda; **there is little likelihood that she'll agree** es poco probable que acepte; **there is no likelihood of that** es poco probable

likely *(adj)* probable; razonable; *(believable)* verosímil; **a likely explanation** una explicación razonable; **the likely outcome** el resultado más probable; **a likely story!** ¡puro cuento!; ¡no me digas!

limbs *(anatomy)* extremidades; miembros; **to lose a limb** perder un brazolímite

limit *(noun)* límite; **don't drive if your over the limit** no manejes si has bebido demasiado; no conduzcas si has bebido demasiado; *(verb)* limitar; restringir

limited aplication aplicación limitada; **this law is very limited in its application** esta ley tiene una aplicación muy limitada

limited liability responsabilidad limitada

limp *(noun)* cojera; renquera; renguera; **she walks with a limp** cojea; renquea; **he has a bad limp** tiene una cojera muy pronunciada; tiene una renquera muy pronunciada; *(verb)* cojear; renquear; rengear; **he limped to the door** fue cojeando a la puerta

line of credit línea de crédito

lineup rueda de sospechosos; rueda de reconocimiento; rueda de presos

link *(in chain)* eslabón; *(connection)* conexión

lip *(anat)* labio

liquid *(adj)* líquida; líquido

liquid assets *(adj)* activo líquido

liquidate *(law: assets)* liquidar

liquidation *(law: assets)* liquidación; **to go into liquidation** entrar en liquidación

liquidity *(law: assets)* liquidez

liquor *(noun)* alcohol; bebidas alcohólicas; **hard liquor** bebidas alcohólicas fuertes

lisp *(noun)* ceceo; *(verb)* cecear; **to speak with a lisp** cecear

list *(include names, events, etc.)* anotar; enumerar; hacer una lista; listar; **it is not listed** no aparece en la lista; **he's not listed** no aparece en la lista; no figura en la lista; **he's listed as missing** figura en la lista de desaparecidos

listed events acontecimientos enumerados; acontecimientos listados

listen *(adj)* escuchar; **to listen to somebody** escuchar a alguien; **he wouldn't listen** no quiso escuchar; **to listen to reason** atender razones

literate *(able to read)* alfabetizada; alfabetizado

litigant *(noun)* litigante

litigate *(verb)* litigar

litigation *(noun)* litigio; pleito; **a litigation between** un litigio entre

litigous *(adj)* contenciosa; contencioso; pleiteador; pleiteadora

litmus test prueba de ácido; prueba de tornasol

little *(pron: not much)* poca; poco; **little by little** poco a poco; **he only speaks a little English** habla poco inglés; **he had little to say** poco fue lo que tenía que decir; **that has little to do with it!** ¡eso tiene poco que ver!; **to make little of something** sacar poco provecho de algo

live *(verb: be, remain alive)* vivir; *(reside)* vivir; **where do you live?** ¿dónde vives?; **he lives in Albuquerque** vive en Albuquerque; **she lives at 44 Cedar** vive en la avenuda Cedar cuarenta y cuatro; **she has three months to live** le quedan tres meses de vida; **according to doctors, she will live** según los médicos, se salvará; *(colloquial)* **you'll live** no te vas a morir

live and work in the US vivir y trabajar en Estados Unidos

live in vivir en; habitar en; radicar en

live in abject poverty vivir en la mayor miseria

live in boyfriend compañero

live in girlfriend compañera

live together *(adv: in amity)* convivir; *(as lovers)* vivir juntas; vivir juntos; vivir liadas; vivir liados

live very quietly vivir tranquila; vivir tranquilo

live with vivir con; **to live with the knowledge that ...** vivir sabiendo que ...

liver *(anat)* hígado

livelihood *(noun)* sustento; **to earn one's livelihood** ganarse la vida; ganarse el sustento

living *(noun: livelihood)* **to earn one's living** ganarse la vida; **to make one's living** ganarse la vida; **what do you do for a living?** ¿en qué trabajas?; ¿a qué te dedicas?

living arrangement tipo de alojamiento; tipo de subsistencia, tipo de arreglo de alojamiento

living conditions condiciones de vida

living expenses gastos de mantenimientos; gastos de subsistencia

living in the same household viviendo en el mismo hogar

living standards nivel de vida

living wage salario digno; sueldo vital

living with viviendo con

load *(noun)* carga; **she felt a load had been lifted from her** se sintió como si le hubieran quitado un peso de encima; **that's taken a load off my mind!** ¡eso me quita un peso de encima!

loaded *(adj: drunk, rich with money)* **to be loaded** estar borracha; estar borracho; erstar forrada de dinero; estar forrado de dinero

loaded gun pistola cargada

loan *(noun: of money)* préstamo; crédito; empréstito

loan account cuenta de crédito

loan agreement acuerdo de crédito

loan application solicitud de préstamo

loan in default incumplimiento de pago de un préstamo

local *(adj)* local; del pueblo; de la región; de la zona; **he's a local** es de aquí; **he's not a local** no es de aquí; **the local community** los vecinos

local authority municipio; ayuntamiento

local border crossing card tarjeta para cruzar la frontera local

local call llamada urbana

local Department of Education Departamento de Eucación local

local Department of Health Departamento local de Salud

local government administración municipal

located *(adj)* ubicada; ubicado; localizada; localizado; situada; situado

lock away *(person, criminal)* encerrar

lock up *(person, criminal)* encarcelar; encerrar

locksmith *(noun)* cerrajera; cerrajero

lodge *(verb: law)* interponer; *(get stuck)* **the bullet lodged in the lung** la bala se alojó en el pulmón; **the bullet had lodged itself in his thigh** la bala se le había alojado en el muslo; **the bullet had lodged in his spine** la bala se le había alojado en la columna

lodge an appeal *(law)* interponer un recurso

lodging *(noun)* alojamiento; hospedaje

loitering *(noun)* merodear con fines delectivos

long distance call llamada interurbana; llamada internacional

long hair *(noun)* melenuda; melenudo

long-haired *(adj)* de pelo largo

long-legged *(adj)* de piernas largas

long-running dispute larga disputa

long-term a largo plazo

long-term liabilities deudas a largo plazo

long-term memory memoria a largo plazo

long-waisted *(adj)* de talle largo; **she's long-waisted** es larga de talle

longtime *(adj)* de toda la vida; **his longtime enemy** su enemigo de toda la vida; **his longtime companion** su compañera de tantos años

look for *(adj)* buscar; **the police are looking for the murderer** la policía está buscando al asesino

look for work buscar trabajo

look out for *(be on the watch for)* tener cuidado con; **we were warned to look out for the thieves** nos advirtieron que tuivéramos cuidado con los ladrones

looking after children cuidado de los hijos; **he has no experience in looking after children** no tiene experiencia en el cuidado de los niños

looking after your interests velando por sus intereses

loophole *(noun: in law, contract)* **a legal loophole** una laguna jurídica; una laguna legal

loophole in the law laguna jurídica

loose ends cabos sueltos; **the investigation has left a lot of loose ends** la investigación ha dejado muchos cabos sueltos; **to leave no loose ends** no dejar ningún cabo suelto

loot *(noun: plunder)* botín; *(money, slang)* guita; lana; pasta; *(verb)* saquear; robar

looter *(noun)* saqueador; saqueadora

looting *(noun)* saqueo; pillaje

lose one's cool perder los estribos

loss *(noun)* pérdida

loss of judgment pérdida de juicio

loss of profits lucro cesante

loss of liberty privación de libertad; **to suffer loss of liberty** sufrir privación de libertad

loss of major functions pérdida de funciones básicas; pérdida de funciones principales

loss of memory pérdida de memoria

loss of speech pérdida del habla

losses *(verb)* deaths; *(military)* bajas

lost check cheque perdido

love *(noun: affection, emotional attachment)* el amor; **love for somebody** amor por alguien; **their love for each other** el amor que tenían; **to fall in love with somebody** enamorarse de alguien; **to be in love with somebody** estar enamorada de alguien; estar enamorado de alguien; **a love-hate relationship** una relación de odio amor

love *(verb: care for)* querer; amar

Low Clearance Ahead *(traffic sign)* altura restringida más adelante

low income bajos ingresos

low income families familias de bajos ingresos

low income housing viviendas de bajos ingresos; viviendas para familias de bajos ingresos

low point bajón; **a low point in his career** un bajón en su carrera

low salaries bajas remuneraciones

lower age limit edad mínima

lower back pain dolor de espalda; dolor de riñones

lower class clase baja

lower income groups grupos de bajos ingresos

lower middle class la clase media baja

lowlife *(people, environment)* bajos fondos; **the Albuquerque lowlife** los bajo fondos de Albuquerque

lucky break golpe de suerte; racha de buena suerte

lump-sum death payment pago global por muerte

lunch *(noun)* almuerzo; **to have lunch** almorzar

lunchbreak *(noun)* hora de la comida; hora de comer ; hora de comer

lunchroom *(noun)* comedor; refectorio

lunchtime *(noun)* hora del almuerzo; hora de almorzar

lung *(anat)* pulmón

luxury items artículos de lujo

M

ma *(noun: colloquial)* mamá

Mace® *(tear gas) gas para defensa personal*

machine-gun *(noun)* ametralladora

machine-gun *(verb)* ametrallar

machine-gun fire *(verb)* fuego de ametralladora

machine-pistol *(verb)* pistola automática

machismo *(noun)* machismo

mad *(adj: insane)* loca; loco; **to go mad** volverse loca; volverse loco; **are you mad?** ¿estás loca?; ¿estás loco?; **to be mad at somebody** estar furiosa con alguien; estar furioso con alguien

mad *(adj: angry)* furiosa; furioso; enfadada; enfadado; enojada; enojado

madman *(noun)* loco

madwoman *(noun)* loca

magistrate *(noun)* juez de instrucción; magistrada; magistrado; juez; jueza

Magnetic Resonance Imaging (MRI) Imagen de Resonancia Magnética

maid *(noun)* muchacha de servicio; sirvienta; criada; empleada doméstica; *(occasional housekeeper)* señora de la limpieza; limpiadora

maiden name apellido de soltera

mail *(noun)* correo

mail bomb *(noun)* paquete-bomba

mail fraud fraude por correo

mailbox *(for deliveries)* buzón; casillero; *(on street)* buzón de correos

mailing address dirección postal

mailing list lista de distribución

maim *(verb; cripple)* lisiar; *(mutilate)* mutilar; **she survived but she was maimed for life** sobrevivió pero quedó lisiada de por vida; **to be maimed for life** quedar lisiada de por vida; quedar lisiado de por vida

maimed for life lisiada de por vida; lisiado de por vida

main *(adj)* principal; fundamental; más importante; central; **the main thing** lo principal; lo fundamental; lo más importante

main door *(of a public building)* puerta principal; puerta de la calle; **I'll meet you at the main door** te espero en la puerta principal

main language spoken idioma principal que se habla en casa

main road carretera principal

main street calle principal

Main Street Calle Mayor

mainline *(verb: drugs, slang)* picarse; chutarse; inyectarse

maintain *(verb: claim)* mantener; sostener; **she maintains that John is innocent** mantiene que John es inocente; sostiene que John es inocente

maintain records mantener los archivos; mantener los registros; llevar registros

maintenance *(noun: law, money)* pensión alimenticia; alimentos

maintenance allowance pensión alimenticia

maintenance dialysis diálisis regular

maintenance of a household sostén del hogar

maintenance order obligación de pasar una pensión alimenticia al cónyuge

maintenance worker encargada del servicio de mantenimiento; encargado del servicio de mantenimiento

major *(adj: breakthrough, change, cause, etc.)* muy importante; *(setback)* seria; serio; *(revision)* a fondo; *(illness)* grave; **of major importance** de la mayor importancia

major *(noun: education, subject)* asignatura principal; *(verb)* **to major in something** especializarse en algo; estudiar algo

major damages daños mayores

major joints coyunturas principales

majority *(noun)* mayoría; **in the vast majority of the cases** en la inmensa mayoría de los casos; **to be in the majority** ser mayoría; **they won by a majority** ganaron por mayoría; **by a majority decision** por decisión mayoritaria; **majority rule**; gobierno mayoritario; **absolute majority** mayoría absoluta; *(law)* **to attain one's majority** llegar a la mayoría de edad

majority rule gobierno de la mayoría

majority verdict veredicto por mayoría

make *(in phrases)* **to make a mistake** cometer un error; equivocarse; **to make a deal** hacer un trato; **we made our escape at nightfall** nos escapamos al anochecer; **to make a speech** pronunciar un discurso; **to make a suggestion** hacer una sugerencia; **do I make myself clear?** ¿me explico?; ¿está claro?

make a difference poder influir; poder afectar; importar mucho

make a note apuntar

make a note of everything that you remember apunta todo lo que recuerdas

make a note on the calendar apuntarlo en el calendario

make a ruling that fallar que; resolver que

make a statement *(law)* prestar declaración

make a statement under oath *(law)* prestar declaración bajo juramento

make an allegation hacer una acusación

make an appointment citarse con; concertar una cita

make an official complaint *(law)* presentar una denuncia

make of car marca del vehículo; marca del coche; marca del auto

make payment pagar; hacer un pago; abonar

make sure asegurarse de; verificar, cerciorarse

maladjusted *(adj)* inadaptada; inadaptado; desadaptada; desadaptado

maladjustment *(adj)* inadaptación; desadaptación

male *(adj)* macho; masculino; *(noun)* macho; *(person)* varón; **a 27 year old male born in** un varón de veintisiete años y nacido en

male doctor médico; doctor

male chauvinism machismo

male chauvinist machista

male nurse enfermero

malice *(law)* dolo penal

malice *(grudge)* rencor; *(badness)* malicia; **out of malice** por malevolencia; **he did it without malice** lo hizo sin mala intención; *(law)* dolo; intención delictuosa; **with malice aforethought** con premiditación

malicious *(adj: person, remark, gossip)* maliciosa; malicioso; malintencionada; malintencionado

malicious destruction of property daños en propiedad ajena

malignant *(adj)* maligna; maligno; grave

malnourished *(adj)* malnutrida; malnutrido

malnutrition *(noun)* desnutrición

malpractice *(noun)* negligencia; mala práctica; conducta incorrecta

maltreatment *(noun)* malos tratos

mama *(noun)* mamá

man *(noun: adult male)* hombre; persona; **any man** cualquier hombre; cualquiera

man and wife marido y mujer

man with a past hombre con pasado

manage *(verb)* dirigir; administrar; gerenciar; *(handle, cope with)* manejar; controlar

manage to escape lograr escapar; lograr huir; lograr darse a la fuga

manage to flee lograr huir; lograr darse a la fuga; **he managed to flee the country** logró huir del país

managed care atención médica manejada; cobertura médica manejada

Managed Care Plan (Medicare) Plan de Servicios Administrados

management *(noun: business, administration)* dirección; administración; *(handling, control)* manejo; gestión

management and workers *(of a particular company)* directivos y trabajadores; directivos y empleados; patronal y trabajadores; **senior**

management altos cargos; **middle management** mandos intermedios; cuadros intermedios

manager *(noun)* director; directora; gerente; **sales manager** jefe de ventas; **branch manager** director de sucursal; directora de sucursal

managerial *(adj)* administrativa; administrativo

mandatory *(adj)* obligatoria; obligatorio

mandatory minimum sentence pena mínima obligatoria

mandatory sentence pena obligatoria

manhandle *(verb: treat roughly)* maltratar

manhunt *(noun)* persecución; búsqueda

maniac *(noun)* maniaca; maniaco; **homicidal maniac** maniaca homicidal; maniaco homicidal

manic-depressive *(adj & noun)* maníacodepresiva; maníacodepresivo

manner *(noun: mode; way, fashion)* manera; modo; **in such a manner that ...** de tal manera que ...; **in a manner of speaking** en cierto sentido; hasta cierto punto; **it's just a manner of speaking** es un decir

manners *(noun: bad, good)* modales; educación; **good manners** educación; **bad manners** falta de educación

manslaughter *(law)* homicidio culposo; homicidio involuntario

many *(in phrases)* **not many** pocas; pocos; **many people** mucha gente; **not many people** poca gente; **in many cases** en muchos casos; **he's had one too many** ha tomado uno de más; **how many are there!** ¡cuántos hay!; **many cases still remain unsolved** falta aún solucionar muchos casos; **many years ago** hace muchos años; **many a time** muchas veces

March *(noun)* marzo *(see* **July** *for usage)*

Mardi Gras martes de carnaval

marijuana marihuana; marijuana

marijuana seeds semillas de marihuana

marijuana *(noun)* marihuana

marital *(adj: problems)* matrimonial; *(bliss)* conyugal

marital problems problemas matrimoniales; problemas conyugales

marital status estado civil

marital settlement agreement acuerdo de resolución matrimonial

mark *(noun: sign; symbol)* marca; *(stain)* mancha; *(imprint)* huella; **scratch mark** rasguño; **distinguishing marks** señas particulares; **she escaped without a scratch on her body** salió sin un arañazo; **five years in prison have left their mark** cinco añosen la cárcel le han dejado huella; *(target)* blanco; **to be an easy mark** ser un blanco fácil

mark *(verb: stain, scar)* manchar; dejar una mancha en; **a marked man** un hombre fichado; **a marked woman** una mujer fichada

marked and severe functional limitation limitaciones funcionales severas y pronunciadas

market *(mercado)* mercado; lonja; **we put the house on the market for $300,000** pusimos la casa en venta en tres cien mil dólares; **a buyer's market** un mercado favorable al comprador; **a seller's market** un mercado favorable al vendedor; **they're in the market for a house** están buscando casa; **they're in the market for a car** están buscando coche

market value valor en el mercado

marriage *(noun: act)* casamiento; matrimonio; enlace; **to be related by marriage** ser parientes políticos; ser parientes por afinidad; **we're cousins by marriage** somos primos políticos

marriage ceremony ceremonia del matrimonio

marriage certificate acta de matrimonio; certificado de matrimonio

marriage counseling terapia de pareja

marriage counselor consejera matrimonial; consejero matrimonial

marriage guidance orientación matrimonial

marriage guidance counselor consejera matrimonial; consejero matrimonial

marriage licence certificado de matrimonio; partida de casamiento

marriage of convenience matrimonio de conveniencia para adquirir la nacionalidad

marriage settlement acuerdo matrimonial

marriage to a blood relative matrimonio consanguíneo

marriage to somebody casamiento con alguien; enlace con alguien

marriage vows votos matrimoniales

married *(adj)* casada; casado; **a married couple** un matrimonio; **the newly married couple** los recién casados; **he's married to his job** está casado con su trabajo; no vive más que para su trabajo; **her married name** su apellido de casada; **they are happily married** son muy felices en su matrimonio; **they have been married for two years** llevan dos años casados; hace dos años que se casaron; **to get married to somebody** casarse con alguien; **he's married to one of my cousins** está casado con una prima mía

married couple matrimonio; **the married couple** los cónyuges

married life vida matrimonial; vida conyugal

married name apellido de casada

marry *(verb: give or join in marriage)* casar; *(take in marriage)* casarse con; contraer matrimonio; **to get married** casarse con; **to get married to somebody** casarse con alguien

marshal *(noun: as title, police chief)* oficial de justicia; oficial de sala; jefa de policía; jefe de policía; *(fire chief)* jefa de bomberos; jefe de bomberos; *(law)* supervisor de los tribunales de un distrito judicial; supervisora de los tribunales de un distrito judicial

martial law ley marcial; **the country is under martial law** se ha impuesto la ley marcial en el país

masked *(adj: gunman)* enmascarada; enmascarado; *(terrorist)* encapuchada; encapuchado

masquerade *(noun: pretence)* mascarada; *(adj)* **to masquerade as** hacerse pasar por

mass *(adj)* de masas; colectiva; colectivo; en masa; **a mass escape** una huida en masa

mass grave fosa común

mass murder matanza

mass murderer autor de una matanza; autora de una matanza

mass transit transporte público

massacre *(noun: murder, slaughter)* matanza; carnicería; masacre; *(verb)* masacrar; matar; aniquilar

master sergeant sargento mayor

mastermind *(noun)* cerebro; *(verb)* planear y organizar; **he masterminded the robbery** él planeó y organizó el asalto; él fue el cerebro del asalto

match *(noun: for fire)* fósforo; cerilla; cerillo; **to strike a match** encender un fósforo; prender un fósforo; **to light a match** encender un fósforo; prender un fósforo; **to put a match to** prender el fuego a algo; **to set a match to** prender el fuego a algo; **a box of matches** una caja de fósforos; *(correspond to)* **does it match the description?** ¿se ajusta a la descripción?; ¿corresponde a la descripción?

matchbook *(noun)* librito de fósforos; librito de cerillos

matchbox *(noun)* caja de fósforos; caja de cerillos

mate *(noun)* compañera; compañero; *(both male and female)* colega

material *(adj: law, evidence)* material; sustancial; esencial; **to be material to something** ser esencial a algo

material *(noun: used in construction)* material; **building materials** materiales para la construcción

material damages daños materiales

material evidence *(law)* prueba esencial; prueba sustancial; **to be supported by material evidence** estar apoyada por prueba sustancial; estar apoyado por prueba esencial; **to be backed up by material evidence** estar apoyada por prueba esencial; estar apoyado por evidencia sustancial

material fact *(law)* hecho esencial; hechos influyentes; hecho pertinente

material participation participación material

material witness *(law)* testigo esencial

maternal *(adj: motherly)* maternal; *(on mother's side)* materna; materno; *(on grandfather's side)* materno; *(aunt)* por parte de madre

matter *(noun: question, affair)* asunto; cuestión; tema; **a matter of great importance** un asunto de gran importancia; **a matter of great interest** un asunto de gran interés; un tema de gran interés; **let's keep to the matter at hand** tratemos de ceñirnos al asunto que estamos tratando; **that's another matter** eso es otra cosa; **that's a different matter** eso es diferente; **this is a matter for the police** esto requiere la intervención de la policía; **it's a matter for her to decide** es ella quien tiene que decidir; **it's only a matter of time** sólo es cuestión de tiempo; **that's a matter of opinion** eso es discutible; **as a matter of principle** por principio; **it's no laughing matter** no es motivo de risa; **as matters stand** tal y como están las cosas; **to make matters worse** para colmo de males; **I can't see how that will help matters** yo no veo que eso vaya a ayudar; **in a matter of seconds** en cuestión de segundos; en cosa de segundos; **as a matter of fact** la verdad es que; en realidad; **for that matter** en realidad; **no matter what** pase lo que pase; **what's the matter?** ¿qué pasa?; **what's the matter with you?** ¿qué te pasa?; **what's the matter with Jane?** ¿qué le pasa a Jane?; **Is anything the matter with Alice?** ¿le pasa algo a Alice?; **it doesn't matter** no importa; da igual; **what matters most is that ...** lo más importante es que ...; **in the matter of** en cuanto a; en lo que se refiere a; **the matter is closed** el asunto está cerrado; **as a matter of course** automáticamente; **no matter what he says** diga lo que diga; **matter what they may say** digan lo que digan

matter of fact cuestión de hecho

matter of law cuestión de derecho

matter of record a constancia de las actas; cuestión de archivo

matter of urgency asunto urgente; **it's a matter of urgency** es un asunto urgente

matter which cannot be put off asunto impostergable; **the matter could not be put off** el asunto era impostergable

maturity *(noun: physical)* madurez; edad adulta; **to reach maturity** llegar a la madurez; *(of temperament, mentality)* madurez; *(financial note, debt)* vencimiento

maturity date fecha de vencimiento

maximum amount cantidad máxima

maximum reduction reducción máxima

maximum security prision prisión de máxima seguridad

May mayo *(see* **July** *for usage)*

may *(in phrases)* **it may be that ...** puede ser que + *subj*; **he may not be guilty** a lo mejor no es culpable; **they may well be related** puede que sean parientes; **may I see it?** ¿se puede verlo?; ¿me permite verlo?; **may I smoke?** ¿puedo fumar?; ¿me permite fumar?; **it may or may not be true** puede o no ser cierto; **he may not have seen us** puede ser que no nos haya visto; quizás no nos haya visto; tal vez no nos haya visto; **no matter what they may say** digan lo que digan; **as the case may be** según el caso; **we may therefore assume that ...** así, es de suponer que; **it may be an element in her decision** puede que haya sido un elemento que influyera en su decisión; **this may indeed be the case, but ...** quizás sea así, pero ...; **may that day never come** que ese día no llegue nunca; **come what may** pase lo que pase; **you may pay in cash or check** puede pagar en efectivo o con cheque

maybe *(adv)* quizá; quizás; tal vez; a lo mejor; **maybe I'll come later** tal vez venga luego; quizás venga luego; a lo mejor vengo luego; **maybe she didn't hear** a lo mejor no oyó; **maybe he'll come tomorrow** tal vez venga mañana; a lo mejor viene mañana; **maybe a little later** tal vez poco después

mayhem *(noun: law)* delito de mutilación

mayor *(noun)* alcalde; alcaldesa

meal *(noun)* comida

meals on wheels servicio de comidas a domicilio para ancianos

mealtime *(noun)* hora de comer

mean *(verb: in phrases)* **what does this word mean?** ¿qué significa esta palabra? ¿qué quiere decir esta palabra?; **that means trouble** eso quiere decir que va a haber problemas; **his children mean the world to him** sus hijos lo son todo para él; sus hijos son muy importantes para él; **what do you mean?** ¿qué quieres decir?; **that doesn't mean that ...** eso no quiere decir que ...; **do you mean to say that ...** ¿quieres decir que ...; **I know exactly what you mean** te entiendo perfectamente; **what do you mean you can't go?** ¿cómo que no puedes ir?; **he didn't mean any harm** no quiso hacer daño; **I'm sorry, I didn't mean to do that** perdón, lo hice sin querer; **he didn't mean to do that** lo hizo sin querer

means of protection recurso de amparo

means-tested public benefits beneficios públicos federales dependientes de los recursos económicos familiares

Medicaid *(drugs)* Seguro de Enfermedad; Medicaid: Government program to help low income people acquire healthcare -*(organismo y programa estatal de asistencia sanitaria a personas de bajos ingresos)*; ayuda médica

medical assistance asistencia médica

medical attention cuidado médico

medical card ficha médica

medical care asistencia médica

medical certificater certificado médico

medical coverage cobertura médica; protección médica

medical emergency emergencia médica

medical equipment equipo médico; accesorio médico

medical examination reconocimiento médico; examen médico

medical examiner médica forense; médico forense

medical history historial médico

medical improvement mejoramiento médico

medical insurance seguro médico; seguro de enfermedad

medical opinion opinión médica

medical reasons razones médicas, por razones de salud

medical report parte médico

medical sources fuentes médicas

medical tests exámenes médicos

medically determinable médicamente determinable

Medicare seguro médico del Estado. Government program asisting elderly people over sixty-five years of age acquire healthcare. - *(organismo y programa estatal de asistencia sanitaria a personas mayores de 65 años de edad)*

Medicare catastrophic coverage cobertura catastrófica de Medicare; protección catastrófica de Medicare

Medicare health insurance seguro de salud para los beneficiarios de Medicare

Medicare Office Oficina de Medicare

Medicare recipient receptor del seguro médico del Estado; receptora del seguro médico del Estado

Medicare secondary payer pagador secundario de Medicare; pagadora secundaria de Medicare

medication *(noun: substance)* medicamento; *(treatment)* tratamiento; *(drugs)* medicación; **he's under medication** está medicado; **she's under medication** está medicada

medicine *(noun: substance)* medicamento; medicina; remedio

medium *(adj: size)* mediana; mediano; **a person of medium built** persona de talla mediana; **a person of medium height** persona de estatura mediana

meet *(verb: encounter)* encontrarse con; tropezarse con; *(by arrangement)* reunirse con; **to arrange to meet somebody** citarse con alguien; **let's meet at 8** citémonos para las ocho; **until we meet again!** ¡hasta la vista!; **have we met?** ¿nos conocimos antes?; **pleased to meet you** encantada de conocerlo; encantado de conocerlo; encantada de conocerla; encantado de conocerla; **to meet by chance** encontrarse por casualidad; *(a requirement)* satisfacer, cumplir con

meet a test llenar los requisitos; cubrir los requisitos; reunir los requisitos; cumplir los requisitos

meet requirements reunir los requisitos; reunir las condiciones

meeting *(noun)* reunión; encuentro; cita

meeting place lugar de reunión; lugar de encuentro

memory lapse laguna; pérdida temporal de la memoria

menace *(noun)* amenaza; peligro; *(verb)* amenazar

menacing *(adj)* amenazador; amenazadora

mental anguish trauma mental

mental block bloqueo mental

mental capacity capacidad mental

mental cruelty crueldad mental; trato mental cruel

mental health salud mental

mental hospital hospital para enfermos mentales; manicomio

mental illness enfermedad mental

mental impairment impedimento mental

mental incapacity incapacidad mental

mental incompetence incompetencia mental

mental patient paciente psiquiátrica; paciente psiquiátrico

mental retardation retraso mental; retardación mental

mental state *(person)* estado mental

mental torture tortura psicológica

mentally disturbed trastornada; trastornado

mentally handicapped disminuida mental; disminuido mental

mentally ill enfermedad mental; **she is mentally ill** tiene una enfermedad mental

mention *(noun)* mención; *(verb)* mencionar; hablar de; **don't mention it!** ¡de nada!; ¡no hay de que!; **I will mention it to him** se lo diré; **I will mention it to her** se la diré; **he mentioned no names** no dijo los nombres; **I won't mention any names** no daré nombres; **to mention somebody in one's will** dejarle algo a alguien en el testamento; **your name was mentioned** se mencionó tu nombre; **please mention me to your parents** dales recuerdos a tus padres de mi parte; **it's worthy of mention** es digno de mención

merchant *(noun)* comerciante

merchant bank banco mercantil

mercy killing eutanasia; homicidio piadoso

merging traffic *(traffic sign)* convergencia del tránsito

mess *(noun: untideness, disorder)* desorden; revoltijo; **what a mess!** ¡qué desorden!; *(confused, troubled state)* **she's in such a mess, she has huge debts** está metida en un verdadero lío, tiene deudas enormes; **their marriage was a mess** su matrimonio andaba muy mal; **to get somebody out of a mess** sacar a alguien de un lío; sacar a alguien de un apuro; **she made a real mess of her life** se arruinó la vida

mess around *(adv: misbehave)* **she found out he'd been messing around** descubrió que había tenido líos; descubrió que había tenido enredos con otras; **he started messing around with drugs** empezó a meterse con drogas

mess with meterse con; **I wouldn't mess with her** yo no me metería con ella; **I wouldn't mess with him** yo no me metería con él; **I wouldn't mess with them** yo no me metería con ellos

message *(noun: communication)* mensaje; recado; **to leave a message** dejar un recado; **would you like to leave a message?** ¿quiere dejar algún recado?; ¿quiere dejar algún mensaje?; **could you give him a message?** ¿podría darle un recado?

messenger *(noun)* mensajera; mensajero

messy affair asunto turbio; **he was involved in a messy affair** estaba involucrado en un asunto turbio

messy divorce divorcio reñido y amargo; **theirs was a messy divorce** su divorcio fue muy reñido y amargo

metal detector detectedor de metales

metal worker metalúrgica; metalúrgico

method of payment forma de pago

Mexican *(adj & noun)* mexicana; mexicano

middle aged de mediana edad

middle-class *(adj)* de la clase media

middle class *(noun)* la clase media; **upper middle class** la clase media alta; **lower middle class** la clase media baja

middle ground terreno neutral

middle-income de ingresos medios

middle initial segunda inicial

middle management mandos intermedios; cuadros intermedios; gerencia media

middle name segundo nombre

midlife crisis crisis de los cuarenta

midwife *(noun)* partera; comadrona

might *(in phrases)* **might I make a suggestion?** ¿podría hacer una sugerencia?; **you might at least listen** al menos podrías escuchar; **I might have known ...** debería haber sabido ...; me podría haber imaginado ...; **she might be at home** pudiera ser que estuviera en casa; **somebody might have picked up by mistake** pudiera ser que alguien se lo hubiera llevado por equivocación; a lo mejor alguien se lo llevó por equivocación; **it might have been disasterous if the police hadn't shown up** podría haber sido catastrófico si no hubiera llegado la policía; **as you might imagine** como te podrás imaginar

migrant *(adj: work, labor, person)* migratoria; migratorio; itinerante

migrant worker *(person)* trabajador extranjero; trabajadora extranjera

migrate *(noun)* emigrar

migration *(noun)* migración; emigración

migratory *(adj)* migratoria; migratorio

military *(adj)* militar; **to do military service** hacer el servicio militar; prestar el servicio militar; hacer la mili

military discharge papers licencia honorable del servicio militar

military service servicio militar

mind-set *(noun)* modo de pensar

minimum sentence sentencia mínimasueldo mínimo

minimum wage salario mínimo; sueldo mínimo

minister *(noun)* ministera; ministro

minor *(law)* menor de edad

minor *(noun: education)* asignatura secundaria; *(verb)* **to minor in something** estudiar algo como asignatura secundaria

minor crime *(law)* delito de menor cuantía

minor damages daños menores

minor dispute *(law)* disputa menor

minor in possession of alcohol *(law)* tenencia de alcohol por un menor

minor offense *(law)* delito de menor cuantía

minority *(noun)* minoría; *(law)* minoría de edad; **to be in a minority** estar en la minoría; **to be in the minority** estar en la minoría; ser minoría; **you're in the minority of one** formas parte de una minoría de uno; **a small minority** una minoría pequeña; **a minority view** una punta de vista minoritaria

minors *(law)* menores de edad

minute *(noun: unit of time)* minuto; **seven minutes to eight** las ocho menos siete minutos; siete minutos para las ocho; **wait a minute, I'll be with you directly** espera un minuto, enseguida estoy contigo; un momento, enseguida estoy contigo; **I won't be a minute** es un minuto; **Could I see you for a minute?** ¿Puedo hablar contigo un momento?; **the minute that ...** en cuanto ...; **at that minute the phone rang** en ese momento sonó el teléfono; **tell me the minute he arrives** avísame en cuanto llegue; **every minute counts** no hay que perder tiempo; **it won't take five minutes** es cosa de pocos minutos

Miranda rights derechos según el fallo de Miranda; derechos de Miranda

misadventure *(noun)* desgracia; contratiempo; *(law)* **death by misadventure** muerte accidental

misappropriate *(verb)* malversar

misappropriate funds malversar fondos

misbehave *(verb)* portarse mal; comportarse mal

misbehavior *(verb)* mala conducta

miscarriage *(verb)* arborto; **to have a miscarriage** tener un aborto; sufrir un aborto; perder un niño

miscarriage of justice error judicial; fallo injusto; injusticia

miscarry *(verb)* arbortar; perder el niño

misconduct *(noun)* mala conducta; abuso de confianza; **professional misconduct** mala conducta en el ejercicio de la profesión; falta de ética profesional

misconstrue *(verb: meanings, words, motive)* mal interpretar

misdemeanor *(law)* delito menor; falta; fechoría

misfit *(noun)* inadeptada; inadeptado; **a social misfit** un adeptado social; una adeptada social; **he's a bit of a misfit here** no encaja en este ambiente

mishandle *(verb: deal with ineptly)* llevar mal; **the police mishandled the whole business** la policía no ha sabido llevar el asunto; *(treat roughly)* maltratar

missing person persona desaparecida

mislead *(law)* inducir a error; despistar; corromper; **I wouldn't want to mislead you** no quisiera inducirle a error; no me gustaría que se hiciera una idea equivocada

misleading *(adj)* engañosa; engañoso; **that could be misleading** eso podría inducir a error; eso podría ser malinterpretada; eso podría ser malinterpretado

mismanage *(verb)* administrar mal; llevar mal; manejar mal

mismanagement *(noun)* mala administración; manejo inadecuado; **the mismanagement of this case by the police is a scandal** lo mal que la policía ha llevado este caso es un escándalo; **their mismanagement of the situation is a scandal** la ineficacia con que han manejado la situación es un escándalo

miss *(shot)* perdida; *(in phrases)* **the shot just missed me** la bala me pasó rozando; **the bullet just missed him** la bala lo pasó rozando; **the bullet just missed his shoulder** la bala por poco le da en el hombro; **he narrowly missed being run over** por poco lo atropellan, faltó poco para que lo atropellaran; **you haven't missed much!** ¡no te has perdido mucho!; **I missed you by five minutes** si hubiera llegado cinco minutos antes te hubiera visto; **I missed what you said** no he oído lo que has dicho; **you don't miss much, do you?** no se te escapa nada ¿verdad?; **we missed each other** no nos vimos

missing perdida; perdido; desaparecida; desaparecido; *(in phrases)* **to be missing** faltar; **the missing papers haven't turned up yet** los papeles que faltaban no han aparecido todavía; **an important document was found to be missing** se descubrió que faltaba un importante documento; **to go missing** desaparecer; **to report missing** declarar como desaparecida; declarar como desaparecido; **to be missing** faltar; **how long has he been missing?** ¿cuánto hace que desapareció?

missing child *(boy)* niño desaparecido; *(girl)* niña desaparecida

missing children niños desaparecidos

missing items artículos que faltan

missing person desaparecida; desaparecido

missing persons personas desaparecidos; personas que están desaparecidas

mistake *(noun)* error; fallo; **a bad mistake** un error garrafal; **a serious mistake** un grave error; **a spelling mistake** una falta de ortografía; **there must be some mistake** debe de haber algún error; **by mistake** por error; por equivocación; **you're making a big mistake** estás cometiendo un grave error; **make no mistake about it** y que no quepa la menor duda; **we all make mistakes** todos cometemos errores; **sorry, my mistake** lo siento, es culpa mía; **my mistake!** ¡la culpa es mía!; ¡es culpa mía!; **to make a mistake** cometer un error

mistake of fact error de hecho

mistake of law error de derecho

mistaken identity identidad equivocada

mistrial *(law)* juicio nulo; juicio viciado de nulidad; juicio nulo por desacuerdo del jurado *(proceso declarado nulo por contener vicios de procedimiento; proceso en el cual el jurado no llega a un acuerdo)*

mistrial with prejudice *(law)* juicio nulo con prejuicio

mistrust *(noun)* desconfianza ; recelo; *(verb)* desconfiar de; recelar de

misunderstand *(verb)* entender mal; **don't misunderstand me** entiéndeme; no me malinterpretes

misunderstanding *(noun)* malentendido; diferencia; mal entendimiento; **they had a misunderstanding** tuvieron una diferencia

misunderstanding about something malentendido sobre algo

misuse uso indebido; mal uso; **the misuse of alcohol** el consumo abusivo de alcohol; *(funds)* malversar

misuse of benefits mal uso de beneficios; malversar los beneficios

mitigate *(noun)* aliviar; mitigar; atenuar la gravedad

mitigated sentence *(law)* pena atenuada

mitigating circumstances circunstancias atenuantes; circunstancias minorantes

mitigation *(noun)* mitigación; alivio; atenuante

mixed *(in phrases)* **to be a mixed blessing** tener su lado bueno y su lado malo; **to have mixed feelings about something** no tener muy claro algo; tener sus dudas acerca de algo; **the judge's proposals have had a mixed reception** las propuestas del juez han sido recibidas con reservas; **of mixed race** mestiza; mestizo

mobile home casa rodante; caravana fija; casa móvil; casa movible

modified formula fórmula modificada

molest *(verb: sexually)* agredir sexualmente de; abusar sexualmente de; *(harass)* importunar; molestar

molestation *(noun)* abusos deshonestos; *(harassment)* acoso

mom *(noun)* mamá

mom and pop familiar

moment *(noun)* momento; **a moment ago** hace un momento; **they should be arriving any moment** deberían llegar ahorita; deberían llegar de un momento a otro; **at the moment** en este momento; **at that moment** en ese momento; **at this moment in time** en este mismo momento; **for the moment** por el momento; por lo pronto; **he didn't hesitate for a moment** no vaciló ni un momento; **from that moment** desde entonces; desde ese momento; **tell me the moment he arrives** avísame en cuanto llegue

moments after the assault momentos después de la agresión

moments after the attack momentos después de la agresión

moments before the assault momentos antes de la agresión

moments before the attack momentos antes de la agresión

momma *(noun)* mamá

mommy *(noun)* mamá

Monday *(noun)* lunes; **I saw him last Monday** lo vi el lunes pasado; **we'll start on Monday** empezaremos el lunes; **I'll do it next Monday** lo haré el próximo lunes; **she will be away that Monday** ese lunes estará fuera; **every Monday** todos los lunes; **every second Monday** cada dos lunes; **the Monday after next** el lunes que viene no; el siguiente lunes; el otro lunes; **Monday morning** el lunes por la mañana; **Monday afternoon** el lunes por la tarde

money *(noun)* dinero; **how much money does he earn a month?** ¿cuánto gana por mes?; **to be short of money** andar mal de dinero

money back guarantee garantía de devolución del dinero

money laundering blanqueo de dinero; lavado de dinero

money matters asuntos financieros de dinero

money order giro postal; giro bancario

money troubles dificultades económicas

moneylender *(noun)* prestamista

monitoring device dispositivo de seguimiento; **to wear a monitoring device** llevar un dispositivo de seguimiento

month *(noun)* mes; **in the month of May** en el mes de mayo; **which day of the month is it?** ¿a cuántos estamos?; **at the end of the month** a fin de mes; a finales de mes; **every month** todos los meses; **it went on for months** duró meses y meses; **six months pregnant** embarazada de seis meses

month of election mes de elección

monthly benefit beneficio mensual; pago mensual

monthly cash payment cuota mensual al contado; cuota mensual en efectivo

monthly earnings test límite mensual de ganancias

monthly installments mensualidades; plazos mensuales; cuotas mensuales

monthly premium prima mensual

moral standards moral; **the decline in moral standards** la decadencia moral

moral turpitude vileza moral; conducta inmoral

moral values valores; **a set of moral values** una escala de morales

moratorium *(noun)* moratoria

more *(in phrases)* **I need more time** necesito más tiempo; **it'll take a few more days** llevará unos cuantos días más; **I have no more money** no me queda más dinero; **four more** cuatro más; **we can't afford more** no podemos pagar más; **is there any more?** ¿hay más?; **there isn't any more** ya no hay más; **a bit more?** ¿un poco más?; **a few more** algunos más; **a little more** un poco más; **many more** muchos más; **much more** mucho más; **there's no more left** no queda nada; **some more** más; **more than ever** más que nunca; **more than half** más de la mitad; **more than fifteen** más de quince; **not more than fifteen** no más de quince

morning *(noun: time of day)* mañana; **good morning!** ¡buenos días!; **in the morning** por la mañana; en la mañana; **tomorrow morning** mañana por la mañana; **early in the morning** a primera hora de la mañana; muy de mañana; **at six o'clock in the morning** a las seis de la mañana; **at three in the morning** a las tres de la madrugada; **the next morning** la mañana siguiente; **on Saturday morning** el sábado por la mañana; **tomorrow morning** mañana por la mañana; **yesterday morning** ayer por la mañana; **he hasn't been in all morning** no ha venido en toda la mañana; **every morning** todas las mañanas; cada mañana

morning-after pill píldora del día siguiente

morning sickness náuseas del embarazo

mortgage *(noun: charge)* hipoteca; **to take out a mortgage** obtener una hipoteca; **to pay off a mortgage** terminar de pagar una hipoteca; redimir una hipoteca; **to take out a mortgage on a house** hipotecar una casa; **we've paid off the mortgage on the house** hemos terminado de pagar la hipoteca de la casa; hemos terminado de pagar el préstamo de la casa; **we've taken out a second mortgage on the house** hemos rehipotecada la casa

mortgage arrears atrasos en el pago de la hipoteca

mortgage insurance seguro hipotecario

mortgage interest interés hipotecario

mortgage loan préstamo hipotecario

mortgage on the house *(noun: charge)* la hipoteca que pesa sobre la casa

mortgage payment pago de la hipoteca; plazo de la hipoteca

mortgage rate tipo de interés hipotecario

most people la mayoría de la gente

mother *(noun)* madre; mamá; **an expectant mother** una mujer embarazada; una futura madre; **an unmarried mother** una madre soltera

mother country patria

mother figure figura materna; imagen materna

mother-in-law *(noun)* suegra

mother-to-be *(noun)* futura madre

mother tongue lengua materna

motherhood *(noun)* maternidad

mother's first name nombre de pila de la madre

mother's last name apellido materno

mother's middle name segundo nombre de la madre

motion *(law)* pedimento; **deny a motion** denegar el pedimento; **grant a motion** dar lugar al pedimento

motion of extradition pedimento de extradición

motion for judgement of acquittal pedir un fallo absolutorio

motion for judgement notwithstanding the verdict pedimento no obstante el veredicto

motion for new trial petición de nuevo juicio

motion to continue pedimento de aplazamiento; pedimento de postergación

motion to dismiss pedimento de sobreseimiento

motion to quash pedimento de anulación

motion to set aside pedimento de dejar sin efecto un fallo

motion to sever pedimento de separación de procesos

motion to supress evidence pedimento de exclusión de pruebas

motion to vacate pedimento de invalidación

motive *(law)* motivo; móvil; razón

motor vehicle vehículo; auto; vehículo de motor; vehículo motorizado

Motor Vehicles Division División de Vehículos Motorizados

mourn *(noun: loss, tragedy)* llorar la muerte de; lamentar la muerte de; **she is still mourning his death** todavía llora su muerte; *(to be in mourning)* estar de luto; *(verb)* **to mourn for somebody** llorar a alguien; llorar la muerte de alguien

mouth *(anat)* boca

move *(law: to make an application to the court for a ruling)* pedir; presentar un pedimento; solicitar

move *(noun: movement)* movimiento; **one false move and I'll shoot** un movimiento en falso y disparo; **to watch somebody's every move** observar a alguien sin perder detalle; acechar a alguien cada movimiento; **what's the next move?** ¿qué hacemos ahora?; y ahora ¿qué?; **that was a bad move** fue una mala decisión; **to make a move** dar un paso; **it's up to him to make the first move** le toca a él dar el primer paso; **events moved rapidly** los acontecimientos se desarrollaron rápidamente; **things are moving at last** por fin se empiezan a mover las cosas; **he certainly knows how to get things moving** ése sí que sabe poner las cosas en marcha

move *(verb: change address)* mudarse de casa

movement *(noun)* movimiento; **the police questioned him about his movements** la policía le pidió informes sobre sus actividades

moving car coche en movimiento

moving truck camión en movimiento

moving vehicle vehículo en movimiento

mug *(noun: slang)* cara; rostro

mug shot fotografía para las fichas; foto de archivo policial

mugger *(noun)* atracador; atracadora

mugging *(noun: law, crime)* atracos; atraco callejero; **mugging is on the increase** está aumentando el número de atracos

multi-family unit grupo habitacional

murder *(law)* asesinato; homicidio calificado; **to commit murder** cometer un asesinato; **to be on trial for murder** ser procesada por asesino; ser procesado por asesino; **the murder of a policeman** el asesinato de un policía; **the murder weapon** el arma homicida; el arma del crimen

murder case caso de asesinato; caso de homicidio

murder inquiry investigación de un homicidio

murder of a policeman asesinato de un policía

murder trial proceso por asesinato; juicio por asesinato; **to be on trial for murder** ser procesada por asesino; ser procesado por asesino

murder weapon arma homicida; arma del crimen

mustache *(noun)* bigote; **to have a mustache** tener bigote; **to grow a mustache** dejarse crecer el bigote

mutilation *(noun)* mutilación

mutual *(adj)* mutua; mutuo; **the feeling is mutual** el sentimiento es mutuo; **by mutual agreement** de común acuerdo; **by mutual consent** de mutuo acuerdo, de común acuerdo

mutual insurance company mutua de seguros

mutually *(adj)* mutuamente; **these views are mutually exclusive** estas opiniones se excluyen mutuamente; **we arranged to meet at a mutually convenient time** acordamos vernos a una hora que nos viniera bien a los dos

my arm el brazo

my brother mi hermano

my grandparents mis abuelos

my leg la pierna

my sister mi hermana

N

nab *(verb: catch, person)* pescar; coger; agarrar

nail *(noun: of finger)* uña

name *(noun: of person)* nombre ; *(surname)* apellido; **what's your name?** ¿cómo te llamas? ¿cómo se llama?; **my name is John** me llamo John; *(on the phone)* **what name shall I say?** ¿de parte de quién?; **I know him by name only** lo conozco solamente de nombre; **a lawyer by the name of Johnson** un abogado llamado Johnson; **the victim was not mentioned by name** no se dio el nombre de la víctima; **the house is in her husband's name** la casa está a nombre de su marido; **open up, in the name of the law!** ¡abran en nombre de la ley!; **stop, in the name of the law!** ¡alto, en nombre de la ley!; **to call somebody names** insultar a alguien

name *(verb: identify, mention)* **my name is ...** me llamo ...; **her/his name is ...** se llama ...; **the police have named the suspect** la policía ha dado el nombre del sospechoso; **the victim has neen named as John Doe** la víctima ha sido identificada como John Doe; **have they named a date for the hearing?** ¿han fijado una fecha para la vista?; **she goes by the name of ...** se hace llamar ...; **a man named ...** un hombre llamado ..; **a woman named ...** una mujer llamada ...; **to have a bad name** tener mala fama; **to have a good name** tener buena fama

name and address nombre y dirección

name and last name of claimant nombre y apellido de la reclamante; nombre y apellido del reclamante

name-calling *(noun)* insultos

name of lawyer nombre de la abogada; nombre del abogado

name of victim nombre de la víctima

name of witness nombre del testigo

nanny *(noun)* niñera

narc *(noun)* agente de brigada de estupefacientes; estupa; camello

narcotic *(noun: drug)* estupefaciente; *(medicine)* narcótico; **to be on a narcotics charge** estar acusada de traficar con drogas; estar acusado de traficar con drogas; *(adj)* narcótica; narcótico

narcotics agent agente de narcóticos

narcotics squad brigada de estupefacientes

narcotics trafficking narcotráfico; tráfico de estupefacientes; tráfico de drogas

narcotics user toxicómana; toxicómano

narrow *(adj)* estrecha; estrecho; angosta; angosto; **to have a narrow escape** salvarse por los pelos; salvarse de milagro

Narrow Bridge *(traffic sign)* Puente Estrecho

narrow down reducir; limitar; descartar; **they've narrowed their investigation down to this area** han limitado su investigación a este área; **the police narrowed it down to only three suspects** la policía fue descartando sospechosos hasta quedar con sólo tres; **the list of suspects gradually narrowed down** la lista de sospechosos se fue reduciendo

nasty *(adj: repugnant, unpleasant, etc.)* desagradable; **I've got a nasty feeling that ...** tengo la horrible sensación de que ...; **he turned nasty** se puso agresivo; **she turned nasty** se puso agresiva; **a nasty temper** tener muy mal carácter; **he turns very nasty when he gets drunk** se pone de lo más desagradable cuando se emborracha; **the situation turned nasty** la cosa se puso fea

National Audit Office Tribunal de Cuentas

National Domestic Violence Hotline número nacional para denunciar la violencia doméstica

National Fraud Information Center Centro Nacional de Información de Fraude

National Immigration Law Center Centro Nacional de Leyes de Inmigración

National Institute for Literacy Instituto Nacional de Alfabetización

National Student Loan Data System (NSLDS) Sistema Nacional de Información de Préstamos para Estudiantes

nationality *(noun: citizenship)* nacionalidad; ciudadanía; **to have Mexican nationality** tener nacionalidad mexicana; tener ciudadanía mexicana; **what's your nationality?** ¿de qué nacionalidadf eres?; **what nationality are you?** ¿de qué nacionalidad eres?

native *(adj: of or by birth)* natal; materna; materno; nativa; nativo; **his native land is Mexico**; su patria natal es México; **her native country is Guatemala**; su tierra natal es Guatemala; **a native speaker of Spanish** un hablante nativo de español; una persona cuya lengua materna es el español; **she's not a native English speaker** el inglés no es su lengua materna

native *(noun: referring to place of birth)* oriunda de; oriundo de; **he is a native of Costa Rica** es oriundo de Costa Rica; **she speaks English like a native** habla inglés como una estadounidense; habla inglés como si fuera su lengua materna

native land patria

native language lengua materna

native speaker hablante nativa; hablante nativo

natural *(adj)* natural; **he died of natural causes** murió de muerte natural; **the rest of his natural life** el resto de sus días; **it's only natural that she should be upset** es natural que esté disgustada; **death from natural causes** muerte natural; muerte por causas naturales; **it is natural that ...** es natural que ...

natural born citizen ciudadana por nacimiento; ciudadano por nacimiento

natural causes causas naturales

natural childbirth parto natural

natural parent madre biológica; padre biológico

naturalization *(noun)* naturalización; nacionalización; **application for naturalization** solicitud de naturalización

naturalization certificate certificado de naturalización; acta de naturalización

naturalization papers carta de naturalización; carta de nacionalización; carta de ciudadanía

naturalize *(noun)* naturalizar; nacionalizar; **to become naturalized** naturalizarse

nature of deposition naturaleza de la deposición

near *(adj: in position)* cercana; cercano; *(in time)* cercana; cercano; próxima; próximo; *(closely related relative)* cercana; cercano; *(adv: & prep)* cerca; cerca de

necessary *(adj)* necesaria; necesario; **a good and necessary law** una ley buena y necesaria; **to be necessary** ser necesaria; ser necesario; **to be necessary to do something** ser necesario hacer algo; ser preciso hacer algo; **is it necessary for us to go?** ¿es necesario que vayamos?; ¿es preciso que vayamos?; **if necessary** si es necesario; si es preciso; **do whatever is necessary to find him** haz todo lo posible para encontrarlo; **to do what is necessary** hacer lo que hace falta; **is that really necessary?** ¿realmente es necesario eso?

neck *(anat)* cuello

need *(noun)* necesidad; *(verb)* necesitar; requerir; hacer falta; *(in phrases)* **there's no need to worry** no hay por qué preocuparse; **there's no need for you to go** no hace falta que vayas; no es preciso que vayas; **there's no need for that sort of language!** ¡no hay ninguna necesidad de usar ese vocabulario!; ¡no hace falta usar ese vocabulario!; **in times of need** en momentos de apuro; en momentos de necesidad; **there's no need for you to be present** no hay ninguna necesidad de que estés presente; no hace falta que estés presente; **I'll do it myself, if need be** si hace falta, lo haré yo mismo; si es necesario, lo haré yo mismo

need legal help necesitar ayuda legal

needy, the los necesitados

negligence *(noun: law)* negligencia; **through negligence** por negligencia; **to prove negligence** probar negligencia; **to establish negligence**

demostrar negligencia; **accident or negligence?** ¿accidente o negligencia?

negligence case *(law)* caso de delito culposo

negligent *(adj)* negligente; **to be negligent in doing something** pecar de negligencia al hacer algo; **the judge found that he had been negligent** el juez declaró que había sido negligente; **she was negligent about informing the authorities** faltó a su deber de informar a las autoridades

negligent arson *(law)* incendio culposo

negligent homicide *(law)* homicidio por negligencia

negligent use of a deadly weapon *(law)* uso negligente de armas mortíferas

negotiate *(verb)* negociar; **after months of negotiating** tras meses de negociaciones; **they will negotiate the terms of the agreement** negociarán los términos del acuerdo

negotiated settlement acuerdo negociado

negotiating table mesa negociadora

negotiation *(verb)* negociación; **to be in negotiation with somebody** estar negociando con alguien; **that will be a matter for negotiation** eso tendrá que ser discutido; **to enter into negotiations with somebody** entrar en negociaciones con alguien; **negotiations to secure their release are underway** se han iniciado negociaciones para lograr su liberación

negotiator *(noun)* negociador; negociadora

neighbor *(noun)* vecina; vecino

neighborhood *(noun)* barrio; **in the neighborhood** en los alrededores; por la zona; en la zona; **people in the neighborhood** la gente del barrio

neighborhood center centro de vecindario

neighborhood watch vigilancia de una calle o barrio a cargo de sus grupos habitantes; redes vecinales; red de vigilancia vecinal

neighboring *(adj)* vecina; vecino; cercana; cercano; de las proximidades; **the neighboring house** la casa vecina; la casa del al lado

neither *(conj)* ni; **neither ... nor** ni ... ni; **she neither knows nor cares!** ¡ni sabe ni le importa!; **neither good nor bad** ni bueno ni malo; **neither he nor I can go** ni él ni yo podemos ir; **he neither smokes nor drinks** ni fuma ni bebe

neither *(adj)* ninguna; ninguno; **neither proposal was accepted** no se aceptó ninguna de las propuestas; *(pron)* **neither of the guards saw him** ninguno de los guardías lo vio

nephew *(noun)* sobrino

nerd *(noun)* pazguata; pazguato; gansa; ganso

nervous breakdown crisis nerviosa

net earnings ganancia neta; ganancias netas *(may be used in the singular or plural)*

net earnings from self-employment ganancias netas de negocio propio; ganancias netas de trabajo por cuenta propia

net income ingreso neto; ingresos netos *(may be used in the singular or plural)*

net income from self employment ingreso neto de negocio propio; ingresos netos de negocio propio

net loss pérdida neta; pérdidas netas *(may be used in the singular or plural)*

network *(system)* red; *(of shops, TV)* cadena

networking *(with others)* creación de una red de conexiones; hacer contactos en el mundo de los negocios; **it's important to network** es importante hacer contactos en el mundo de los negocios

neurotic *(adj)* neurótica; neurótico; **to be neurotic about something** estar obsecionada con algo; estar obsecionado con algo

nevertheless *(adv)* sin embargo; no obstante; de todas maneras; **it is nevertheless true that ...** sin embargo es verdad que ...; no obstante es verdad que ...; **it's an unpleasant, but nevertheless necessary, task** es una tarea desgradable pero no obstante necesaria; **it may be a waste of time, but I'm going to try nevertheless** puede que sea una pérdida de tiempo pero de todas maneras lo voy a intentar; **I can't accept, but nevertheless I appreciate your offer** no puedo aceptar pero de todas maneras agradezco su oferta

new *(adj)* nueva; nuevo; **she is new to this country** lleva poco tiempo en este país; **he is new to the company** es nuevo en la compañía; **that's nothing new** eso no es nada nuevo; **to start a new life** empezar una nueva vida; **to start a new life as a single mother** empezar una nueva vida de madre soltera

new arrival *(baby)* recién nacida; recién nacido; *(foreigner)* recién llegada; recién llegado

new car coche nuevo

new paragraph punto aparte

new trial nuevo juicio; **prosecutors ask for new trial in Tyco corruption case** fiscales pedirán nuevo juicio en caso de corrupción en Tyco

New Year's Day día de Año Nuevo

New Year's Eve Noche Vieja

newborn *(baby)* recién nacida; recién nacido

newcomer *(adj)* recién llegada; recién llegado; **they are newcomers to the area** son nuevos en la zona; en la zona son unos recién llegados

newlyweds *(noun)* recién casados

news *(noun: fresh information)* información; noticia; **that's wonderful news!** ¡qué buena noticia!; **some sad news** una triste noticia; **is there any news about Juan?** ¿hay noticias de Juan?; **that's good news** es una buena noticia; *(colloquial)* **he's bad news** no trae más que problemas; **they wait for further news** quedan a la espera de más noticias; **we've had no news of him** no hemos tenido noticias de él; no hemos sabido nada de él; **how can we get news to him that ...?** ¿cómo podemos hacerle saber que ...?; **I have some good news** tengo buenas noticias; **I have some bad news** tengo malas noticias; **to break the news to somebody** comunicar una noticia a alguien; **I've got news for you!** ¡tengo una noticia que darte!; **news conference** rueda de prensa

newsletter *(noun)* bolitín informativo

newspaper *(noun)* periódico; diario

newspaper article artículo periodístico

next *(in phrases)* próxima; próximo; siguiente; **the week after next** la semana que viene; la semana próxima; **this time next week** la semana que viene a estas horas; **this time next year** el año que viene por estas fechas; **the next time you see him** la próxima vez que lo veas; **from one moment to the next** de un momento para otro; **from one day to the next** de un día para otro; **what did he do next?** ¿qué hizo después?; ¿qué hizo luego?; **when I next saw him** cuando lo volví a ver; **I next saw him in court** la siguiente vez que lo vi fue cuando compareció ante el tribunal; **what do we do next?** ¿y ahora qué hacemos?; **I'll see you next month** nos vemos el mes que viene; nos vemos próximo ; **the matter will be discussed at the next meeting** el asunto se tratará en la próxima reunión; **I'll ask him next time I see him** se lo preguntaré la próxima vez que lo vea; **the next few days will be very hectic** los próximos días van a ser muy agitados; **my client will have been here two months next Monday** el lunes que viene hará dos meses que mi cliente está aquí; **the hearing will continue next Monday** la vista se reanudará el próximo lunes; **you don't know what to expect from one day to another** no sabes qué va a pasar de un día para otro; **I'm as much against violence as the next person, but ...** estoy tan en contra de la violencia como cualquiera, pero ...; **the next best thing** la segunda posibilidad

next-door *(adj)* de al lado; **our next-door neighbors** nuestros vecinos de al lado

next door *(adv)* al lado; **who lives next door?** ¿quién vive al lado?; ¿quién vive en la casa de al lado?; **the people next door** los vecinos de al lado; **the boy next door** el chico de al lado; **the girl next door** la chica del al lado

next month el mes que viene; el mes próximo

next of kin parientes más cercanos

next Thursday el jueves siguiente

next year el año que viene; el año próximo

Nicaraguan *(adj)* nicaragüense

nickname *(noun)* apodo; sobrenombre; *(relating to personal characteristics)* mote

nickname *(verb)* apodar; dar el apodo de; **she is affectionately nicknamed Sunny** la llaman cariñosamente Sunny

niece *(noun)* sobrina

night *(noun)* noche; **Monday night** el lunes por la noche; **in the night** durante la noche; **all night long** toda la noche; **at night** por la noche; de noche; **nine o'clock at night** las nueve de la noche; **to stay up late at night** trasnochar; **good night!** ¡buenas noches!; **the night before last** anteanoche; **tomorrow night** mañana por la noche; **to work nights** trabajar de noche; **night school** escuela nocturna; **night shift** turno nocturno; turno de noche; **night watchman** vigilante nocturno

night-time *(noun)* noche; *(adj)* nocturna; nocturno

nightclub *(noun)* club nocturno; *(usually featuring dancing and cabaret)* sala de fiestas

nightmare *(noun)* pesadilla

nine *(adj)* nueve; **nine times out of ten** casi siempre; en el noventa por ciento de los casos; **nine times out of ten he's right** casi siempre tiene razón; **nine out of ten people agree** el noventa por ciento de la gente está de acuerdo; nueve de cada diez personas están de acuerdo

nineteen *(adj)* diecinueve

nineteenth *(adj)* decimonovena; decimonoveno

ninetieth *(adj)* nonagésima; nonagésimo

nine-to-five *(adj)* de nueve a cinco; **nine-to-five job** trabajo de nueve a cinco

ninety *(adj)* noventa

ninth *(adj)* novena; noveno

no *(in phrases)* no; **they have no children** no tienen hijos; **I am under no illusions** no me hago ilusiones; **there's no time for that now** no tenemos tiempo para eso ahora; **it's no trouble** no es ningún problema; no es ninguna molestia; **no experience is necessary for this job**; no es necesario tener experiencia para este trabajo; **no intelligent person would do that** ninguna persona inteligente haría eso; **I'm no expert, but ...** no soy ningún experto, pero ...; **please arrive no later than nine** por favor lleguen a las nueve a más tardar; por favor lleguen antes de las nueva; **I no longer work for them** ya no trabajo para ellos; no trabajo más para ellos; **don't take no for an answer** no te conformes con un no; **there's no denying it** es imposible negarlo; **he's no fool** no es tonto, ni mucho menos; no es ningún tonto; **he's no friend of mine** no es precisamente amigo mío; **there's no getting out of it** no hay posibilidad de evitarlo; **there's no pleasing him** es imposible tenerlo contento; **we'll be there in no time** llegamos en un dos por tres; no tardamos nada; **no one** nadie; **no one spoke** nadie habló; no habló nadie; **I won't take no for an answer** no acepto un no por respuesta

No Child Left Behind Act Ley para Que Ningún Niño Se Quede Atrás

no contest *(law)* no afirmo ni niego

no down payment sin anticipo

no-fault sin culpa; no hay falta; sin atribución de culpabilidad

no-fault agreement acuerdo de pago respectivo

no-fault auto insurance seguro automovilístico sin culpa

no-fault divorce divorcio sin culpa; divorcio en el que no se culpa a ninguno de los esposos

no-fault insurance seguro en el que no entra el factor de culpabilidad

no-good inútil; maldita; maldito

no law no hay ley; **there's no law against** no hay ley que lo prohíba

No Left Turn *(traffic sign)* Prohibido Doblar a la Izquierda

No Parking *(traffic sign)* No Estacione

No Passing Zone *(traffic sign)* Prohibido Pasar Otros Vehículos

No Right Turn *(traffic sign)* Prohibido Doblar a la Derecha

No Turn on Red *(traffic sign)* No Gire en Rojo

No U Turn *(traffic sign)* No gire en U

nobody *(in phrases)* nadie; **nobody spoke** nadie habló; no habló nadie; **nobody saw us** nadie nos vio; no nos vio nadie; **nobody must hear about this** que no se entere nadie de esto; **there was nobody there** no había nadie; **nobody has more right to it than she does** nadie tiene más derecho que ella

nominal *(adj)* nominal

nominal damages *(law)* resarcimiento nominal; resarcimiento no compensatorio

nominal value valor nominal

non-addictive *(adj)* que no crea dependencia

non-addictive pain pills analgésicos que no crean dependencia

non-addictive painkillers analgésicos que no crean dependencia; calmantes que no crean dependencia

non-aggression no agresión

non-aggression pact pacto de no agresión

non-alcoholic *(adj)* no alcohólica; no alcohólico

non-believer *(noun)* no creyente

non-belligerent no beligerante

non-Catholic *(adj & noun)* no católica; no católico

non-Christian *(adj & noun)* no cristiana; no cristiano

non-citizens *(noun)* no ciudadanos; extranjeros

non-committal *(adj)* evasiva; evasivo; que no compromete a nada; poco comprometida; poco comprometido; **he was very non-committal about it** no se definió al respecto

non-compliance *(noun)* incumplimiento

non-compliance with something incumplimiento de algo

non-covered work trabajo que no está cubierto por el Seguro Social

non-controversial *(adj)* no polémica; no polémico

non-detained juvenile offender delincuente juvenil que no está denenida; delincuente juvenil que no está denenido

non-discriminatory *(adj)* no discriminatoria; no discriminatorio

non-drinker no bebedor; no bebedora

none *(pronoun: not any; not one)* ninguna; ninguno; **none of us know her** ninguno de nosotros la conoce; **none of my suggestions were accepted** no aceptaron ninguna de mis sugerencias; **none of them** ninguno de ellos; **none of this is true** nada de esto es verdad; **"any news?" – "none!"** ¿alguna noticia? – ¡ninguna!; **we'll have none of that!** ¡basta ya!; **he would have none of it** no hubo forma de convencerlo

nonjury trial *(adj)* juicio sin jurado

nonpayment *(noun)* impago; **for nonpayment** por impago

nonpolitical *(adj)* apolítica; apolítico

nonprofit *(adj)* sin fines de lucro

nonprofit organization organización sin fines de lucro

non-renewable no renovable

nonresident *(noun & adj: of country)* no residente; transeúnte

nonreturnable *(adj: deposit)* no reembolsable; a fondo perdido

nonsense *(noun)* tonterías; estupideces; **to talk nonsense** decir tonterías; decir estupideces; **that's absolute nonsense** eso es una tontería; eso es una estupidez; **it's nonsense to claim it was an accident** es absurdo afirmar que fue un accidente; **what nonsense!** ¡qué tontería!; **it is nonsense to say that ...** es absurdo decir que ...; **I've never heard such nonsense!** ¡vaya una tontería!; **stop this nonsense!** ¡ya vale de tonterías!

nonskilled *(adj: worker)* no calificada; no calificado; *(work)* no especializada; no especializado

nonskilled worker trabajadora no calificada; trabajdor no calificado

nonsmoker *(noun)* no fumador; no fumadora; persona que no fuma; **for non-smokers** para no fumadores; **I'd prefer a non-smoker** preferiría un no fumador; preferiría una no fumadora

nontaxable *(adj)* no sujeta a impuestos; no sujeto a impuestos; exenta de impuestos; exento de impuestos

nonviolent *(adj)* no violenta; no violento; pacífica; pacífico

nonwhite *(adj)* de color; *(noun)* persona de color

nonwork day día no laborable

noon *(noun)* mediodía; **at noon** a mediodía; **until noon** hasta mediodíanope *(slang)* no

nor *(conj)* ni

nose *(anat)* nariz

not *(in phrases)* **why not?** ¿por qué no? **I hope not** espero que no; **I think not** creo que no; **not guilty** no culpable; **I asked them not to tell anyone** les pedí que no se lo dijeran a nadie; **he's not sure** no está seguro; **she's not sure** no está segura; **they are not sure** no están seguros; **he's not here** no está aquí; **it's too late, isn't it?** es demasiado tarde, ¿no?; **you owe me money, don't you?** me debes dinero, ¿verdad?; **he asked me not to do it** me pidió que no lo hiciera; **to tell somebody not to do something** decir a alguien que no haga algo; **I don't mind at all** no me importa en absoluto; **he's not at all selfish** no es nada egoísta; **not for anything in the world** por nada del mundo; **are you coming or not?** ¿vienes o no?

not guilty plea *(law)* declaración judicial de no culpabilidad

notary public notaria pública; notario público; escribana pública; escribano público

note *(noun: record, reminder, message)* **to make a note of something** anotar algo; apuntar algo; **she made a mental note of it** tomó nota de ello mentalmente; **to take notes** tomar apuntes; tomar notas; **to compare notes** cambiar impresiones; **just a quick note to tell you that ...** sólo una nota para decirte que ...; **keep a note of all your expenses** apunta todos tus gastos; **they will take note of what you say** tendrán en cuenta lo que digas; **worthy of note** digno de mención

nothing *(in phrases)* **nothing has changed** nada ha cambiado; **she said nothing to me** a mí no me dijo nada; **there's nothing to be afraid of** no tienes nada que temer; **it's nothing to be ashamed of** no hay por qué apenarse; no hay por qué avergonzarse; **nothing seems to bother her** nada parece preocuparla; **there is a case for doing nothing** hay razones para no hacer nada; **he felt nothing but contempt for them** no sentía más que desprecio por ellos; no sentía más que desdén por ellos; **I have nothing else to say** no tengo nada más que decir; **I've done nothing illegal** no he hecho nada ilegal; **there's nothing to indicate whether they approve or not** no hay nada que indique si les parece bien o no; **from their father they inherited nothing but debts** de su padre no heredaron más que deudas; **they lack for nothing** no les falta nada; **that's nothing new** eso no es nada nuevo; **she said nothing to me** no dijo nada más; **we achieved absolutely nothing** no logramos absolutamente nada; **there's nothing worse** no hay nada peor; **nothing but** solamente; **to have nothing to do with** no tener nada que ver con; **to say nothing of ...** sin mencionar ... ; **it's nothing like him** no se le parece en nada

notice *(noun)* notificación; letrero; aviso; **it has come to my notice that ...** ha llegado a mi conocimiento que; **it has been brought to my notice that ...** se me ha señalado que ...; **it was never brought to his notice** no se le dijo nada al respecto; **until further notice** hasta nuevo aviso; **to give somebody notice to do something** avisar a alguien que haga algo; **notice to vacate** aviso de desalojo; notificación de desalojo;

a week's notice una semana de antelación; to give somebody a week's notice avisar con una semana de antelación; despedir a alguien con una semana de preaviso; to give two months notice avisar con dos meses de antelación; without prior notice sin previo aviso; to give one's notice dimitir; renunciar; to hand in one's notice dimitir; renunciar; death notice nota necrológica; I didn't notice anything odd no noté nada raro; I didn't notice anything strange no noté nada extraño; I couldn't help noticing but ... no pude menos que notar que ...

notice of appeal aviso de apelación

notice of appearance *(provided by lawyer)* notificación de comparecencia

notice of application approval aviso de aprovación de solicitud

notice of new mailing address aviso de nueva dirección postal

notice of non-coverage aviso de cobertura negada; aviso de protección negada

notice of planned action aviso de acción proyectada

notice to appear *(subpoena)* citación

notify *(verb)* avisar; notificar; **the authorities must be notified** se debe dar parte a las autoridades; se debe informar a las autoridades; **to notify somebody of something** comunicar algo a alguien; notificar algo a alguien; **please notify us immediately of any change of address** les rogamos nos comunique de inmediato cualquier cambio de domicilio

notwithstanding *(prep)* a pesar de; pese a; no obstante

notwithstanding *(adv)* no obstante

notwithstanding *(conj)* a pesar de que

notwithstanding the fact that a pesar de que

November noviembre *(see* **July** *for usage)*

now *(adv: at this time)* ahora; en este momento **I feel better now** ahora me siento mejor; **the suspect is now leaving the building** ahora el sospechoso sale del edificio; en este momento el sospechoso sale del edificio; **you can come in now** ya puedes entrar; **they'll be here any minute now** en cualquier momento llegan; **now is the time to decide** este es el momento de decidir; **now's your chance** ésta es tu oportunidad; **he's talking to the client now** en este momento está hablando con el cliente; **right now** inmediatamente; ahora mismo; **what should I do now?** ¿ahora qué hago?; **what shall we do now?** ¿qué hacemos ahora?; **he's been living here for two years now** ya hace dos años que vive aquí; lleva dos años viviendo aquí; **it's too late now** ya es demasiado tarde; **can I go now?** ¿ya me puedo ir?; **they've been married now for five years** ya llevan cinquo años casados; hace cinquo años que se casaron; **it's some days now since I heard anything** hace varios días que no sé nada; **every now and again** de vez en cuando; **any moment now** de un momento a otro; **any day now** cualquier día de estos; **as of now** a partir de ahora; **before now** ya; antes; **you should have done that before now** ya tendrías que haber hecho eso; tendrías que haber hecho eso antes; **she should have arrived long before now** hace tiempo que tenía que haber llegado; **between now and next Friday** entre hoy y el viernes que viene; **they must be there by now** ya deben de haber llegado; **by now it is clear that ...** en este momento ya está claro que ...; **that will do for now** por ahora basta con eso; por el momento basta con eso; **just now** ahora mismo; en este momento; **they won't be long now** no tardarán en venir; al rato vienen; **from now on** a partir de ahora; de ahora en adelante; **now, as you all know ...** bueno, como todos saben ...; **now then, what's the problem?** ¡entonces a ver! ¿Cuál es el problema?; **now is your chance to talk to him** ésta es tu oportunidad de hablar con él; **now that you mention it** ahora que lo dices; **don't get me wrong, now** no me vayas a malinterpretar

nowadays hoy día; hoy en día; en la actualidad; actualmente

nowhere *(adv; be)* en ninguna parte; *(go)* a ninguna parte; **she was nowhere to be found** no se la encontraba por ninguna parte; no se la veía por ningún lado; **to get nowhere** no conseguir nada; no lograr nada; **you'll get nowhere with that attitude** con esa actitud no vas a conseguir nada; con esa actitud no vas a lograr nada; **we're getting nowhere fast** no estamos avanzando nada de nada; **to go nowhere** no conducir a nada; **he had nowhere to go** no tenía donde ir; **he had nowhere to hide** no tenía donde esconderse; **she had nowhere else to go** no tenía otro lugar a donde ir; **nowhere in California** en ninguna parte de California

no-win *(adj)* sin salida; imposible; **to be in a no-win situation** estar en una situación sin salida; estar en una situación imposible

nuclear family familia nuclear

nuisance *(law)* **a public nuisance** una alteración del orden público

nuisance *(noun)* fastidia; fastidio; pesada; pesado; **to be a nuisance** ser un fastidio; ser una fastidia; ser una lata; **what a nuisance!** ¡qué lata!; ¡qué pesadez!; **what a nuisance you are!** ¡eres un pesado!; ¡eres un latoso!; ¡eres una latosa!; **to make a nuisance of oneself** dar la lata; ponerse pesada; ponerse pesado; **stop being a nuisance!** ¡déjate de molestar!; déjate de dar la lata; **he's always making a nuisance of himself** siempre está dando la lata

nuisance call llamada anónima

nuisance caller llamante anónima; llamante anónimo

nullify *(noun)* anular; invalidar

number *(noun)* número; **license number** matrícula; **telephone number** número de teléfono; **wrong number** número equivocado; **identity number** número de identificación; **in a large number of cases** en un gran número de casos; **in a small number of cases** en unos pocos casos; en contados casos; **there are a number of reasons why you shouldn't go** hay una serie de razones por las que no deberías ir; **I've mentioned it a number of times** lo he mencionado varias veces; **on a number of occasions** en varias ocasiones; **we live at number 210** vivimos en el número 210; **my number is 414 3925** mi número de teléfono es el 414 3925; **it's my number one priority** es lo más importante para mí; **a number of people** varias personas; cantidad de gente

number holder nombre de la asegurada; nombre del asegurado

number of highway patrols will be increased aumentará el contingente de vigilancia en las carreteras

nurse *(noun)* enfermera; enfermero

nursing care cuidado de enfermería

nursing home hogar de ancianos; clínica de reposo; casa de reposo

nursing home comparison comparación de asilo de ancianos

O

oath *(noun)* juramento; **to break one's oath** romper su juramento; **to make an oath** jurar; hacer un juramento; **to take an oath** jurar; hacer un juramento; *(law)* **to take the oath** jurar; prestar juramento; **under oath** bajo juramento; **to place somebody under oath** tomarle juramento a alguien; juramentar a alguien

oath of a witness juramento de un testigo de decir verdad

oath of allegiance juramento de lealtad

obedience *(noun)* obediencia; **to show obedience to somebody** obedecer a alguien; **to show obedience to something** obedecer a algo

obedient *(adj)* obediente; **to be obedient to something** obedecer a algo; **to be obedient to somebody** obedecer a alguien

obey an order acatar una orden

obey the law acatar la ley; obedecer las leyes

object *(verb: express objection, oppose)* **to object to something** oponerse a algo; poner objeciones a algo; *(law)* **to object to a question** oponerse a una pregunta; objetar una pregunta; **I object!** ¡protesto!; **if you don't object** si no le molesta; si no le importa

objection *(law)* objeción; **objection!** ¡protesto! *(**overruled:** no hay lugar a la protesta; **sustained:** ha lugar a la protesta; **upheld:** ha lugar a la protesta; (argument against)* **that's a valid objection** es una objeción válida; **to make an objection** hacer una objeción; **to raise an objection** poner una objeción; **to voice an objection** expresar una objeción; **I have no objection to her** no tengo nada en contra de ella; **I have no objection to helping out** no tengo ningún inconveniente en ayudar; no tengo ningún reparo en ayudar; **are there any objections?** ¿alguna objeción?; ¿alguien en contra?; protesta?; oposición?; **what is your objection?** ¿qué objeción tienes?; **do you have any objection to my going?** ¿tienes algún inconveniente en que vaya yo?

obligate *(verb)* **to obligate somebody to +** *infin* obligar a alguien a + *infin*; **the agreement obligates us to do it** el acuerdo nos obliga a hacerlo; **to be obligated to +** *infin* estar obligada a + *infin*; estar obligado a + *infin*; **to feel obligated to** + *infin* sentirse obligada a + *infin*; sentirse obligado a + *infin*; **he felt obligated to look after his parents** se sentía obligado a cuidar de sus padres; **don't feel obligated** no te sientas obligado

obligation *(noun)* obligación; compromiso; **moral obligation** obligación moral; **legal obligation** obligación legal; **family obligations prevented me from attending** compromisos familiares me impidieron asistir; **professional obligations prevented me from attending** compromisos profesionales me impidieron asistir; **we have an obligation to help them** tenemos la obligación de ayudarlos; **without obligation** sin compromiso; **it is your obligation to see that ...** le cumple a usted comprobar que + *subj*; **to meet one's obligations** cumplir sus compromisos; **to fail one's obligations** no cumplir sus compromisos

oblige *(verb)* obligar; **to oblige somebody to do something** obligar a alguien a hacer algo; **you are not obliged to do it** no estás obligada a hacerlo; no estás obligado a hacerlo; **much obliged!** ¡muchísimas gracias!; ¡muy agradecida!; ¡muy agradecido!; **you're not obliged to attend** no estás obligada a asistir; no estás obligado a asistir

observation *(noun)* observación; **the police are keeping him under observation** la policía lo tiene vigilado

observe *(verb)* observar; ver; **police observed the suspect closely** la policía vigilaba de cerca a la sospechosa; la policía vigilaba de cerca al sospechoso; **he was observed entering the building** se le vio entrar el edificio; **he was observed leaving the building** se le vio salir del edificio

observe the law *(law)* respetar la ley; cumplir con la ley; obedecer la ley

obsessed with obsesionada con; obsesionado con; **he's obsessed with the idea** está obsesionado con la idea

obstruct *(verb)* obstruir; bloquear

obstruct justice obstruir la justicia

obstruction of justice obstrucción de la justicia; obstrucción de justicia; obstrucción a la justicia

obtain *(verb)* obtener; conseguir; lograr

obvious *(adj)* evidente; obvia; obvio; **his disappointment is obvious** su decepción es evidente; **it is perfectly obvious that she was lying** no cabía la menor duda de que estaba mintiendo; estaba clarísimo que mentía; **we've made a big mistake — that's obvious** hemos cometido un gran error — eso es obvio; **the obvious thing to do is ...** no cabe duda de que lo que hay que hacer es ...; **it's obvious the thieves got in through the window** está claro que los ladrones entraron por la ventana; **it's an obvious lie** es claramente mentira; es una burda mentira; **he isn't going to resign, that much is obvious** no va a dimitir, eso está claro; **he's the obvious man for the job** es la persona obvia para el puesto; **it's the obvious thing to do** está claro que es eso lo que hay que hacer; **it was obvious to everyone that it had been a mistake** todo el mundo se daba cuenta de que había sido un error

obviously *(adv)* obviamente; **he was obviously very angry** se notaba que estaba muy enfadado; **he was obviously not drunk** era evidente que no estaba borracho; **there'll obviously be an investigation** por supuesto se hará una investigación; **she's obviously lying** está claro que miente; es obvio que miente; **obviously, I am delighted** por supuesto, estoy encantada; por supuesto, estoy encantado

occasion *(noun)* ocasión; **on that occasion** en aquella ocasión; esa vez; **on the occasion referred to** en la ocasión que se indica; **on occasion** de vez en cuando; **on one occasion** una vez; **on the occasion of his retirement** con motivo de su jubilación; **to take the occasion to do something** aprovechar la oportunidad para hacer algo; **it was quite an occasion** fue todo un acontecimiento; **what's the occasion?** ¿qué se celebra?; **to rise to the occasion** ponerse a la altura de las circunstancias; **should the occasion arise** si se da el caso; **to have occasion to do something** tener ocasión de hacer algo; **on several occasions** en varias ocasiones; varias veces

occupancy *(noun: of building)* ocupación; *(tenancy)* inquilinato

occupant *(noun; of house, building)* ocupante; *(tenant)* inquilina; inquilino

occupation *(noun)* empleo; profesión; **what is your present occupation?** ¿cuál es su ocupación actual?; **what is his occupation?** ¿cuál es su profesión?

occupational *(noun: training)* profesional; ocupacional

occupational accident accidente laboral

occupational disease enfermedad profesional

occupational hazard riesgo laboral

occupational pension scheme plan de jubilación

occupational safety salubridad ocupacional

Occupational Safety and Health Administration Administración de Seguridad y Salubridad Ocupacional

occupational therapist terapeuta ocupacional

occupational therapy terapia ocupacional

occupational training formación profesional; formación ocupacional

occur *(verb; take place)* tener lugar; ocurrir; suceder; **if the opportunity occurs ...** si se presenta la oportunidad ...; **it occurs to me that ...** se me ocurre que ...

occurrence *(noun)* suceso; hecho; **it's an everyday occurrence** es cosa de todos los días; es un hecho cotidiano; **that is a common occurrence** eso sucede a menudo; **murders are an everday occurence here** aquí los asesinatos son cosa de todos los días; **a common occurence** un caso frecuente

o'clock *(telling time)* **it's four o'clock** son las cuatro; **it is seven o'clock** son las siete; **it is one o'clock** es la una; **at eight o'clock sharp** a las ocho en punto; **it is just after two o'clock** son las dos pasadas; son un poco más de las dos; **it is nearly eight o'clock** son casi las ocho; **it is**

just after one acaba de dar la una; **the five o'clock train** el tren de las cinco

October *(noun)* octubre *(see* **July** *for usage)*

odd *(noun)* rara; raro; extraña; extraño; curiosa; curioso; **the odd thing is that ...** lo raro es que ...; lo curioso es que; **how odd that ...** qué raro que ...; **it was odd of her not to say anything** fue raro que no dijera nada; **how odd!** ¡qué raro!; ¡qué curioso!; ¡qué extraño!; **he acted a bit odd when I told him** reaccionó de manera rara cuando se lo dije; se puso algo raro cuando se lo dije; **odd job** trabajillos; **he's done odd jobs for us** nos ha hecho algunos trabajillos; **he says some odd things** dice cosas muy raras

of *(in phrases)* **a friend of mine** un amigo mío; una amiga mía; **love of country** el amor a la patria; **there were four of them** eran cuatro; **all of them** todos ellos; **out of fear** por temor; **out of anger** de rabia; **of necessity** por necesidad; **a boy of eight** un niño de ocho años

of age de edad

of counsel persona empleada como abogada de un caso; persona empleada como abogado de un caso

of record registrado

off drugs quien ha dejado las drogas

off the record extraoficialmente; en confianza

offend *(verb: cause indignation, anger)* ofender; **I am sorry if I have offended you in any way** perdona si te he ofendido de alguna manera; **many people were offended by his remarks** mucha gente se sintió ofendida por este comentario; **don't be offended, but ...** no te vayas a ofender, pero ...; **to be offended** ofenderse

offender *(noun: against traffic regulations etc)* infractor; infractora; *(crime)* delincuente; **first offender** delincuente sin antecedentes penales; **previous offender** reincidente; **alleged offender** presunta delincuente; presunto delincuente; presunta infractora; presunto infractor; **repeat offender** delincuente habitual; delincuente reincidente

offense *(law, regulations)* acto antijurídico; acto punible; infracción; *(crime)* **criminal offense** delito; **to commit an offense** cometer una infracción; **a traffic offense** una infracción de tráfico

offense charged *(law)* infracción imputada; acto delictivo imputado

offer of proof ofrecimiento de la prueba

offers and negotiations settlement convenio de ofertas y negociaciones

office *(noun)* oficina; despacho; *(of lawyer)* bufete; despacho de abogado

office job trabajo de oficina

office hours horas de oficina

Office of Civil Rights División de Derechos Civiles

Office of Hearings and Appeals (OHA) Oficina de Audiencias y Apelaciones

officer of the law agente de la ley; **law enforcement officer** agente de la ley

officer of the court funcionaria de tribunales; funcionario de tribunales; **personnel officer** jefa de personal; jefe de personal

Office on Violence Against Women Oficina de Violencia contra la Mujer

official notice aviso oficial

official receiver *(law)* síndico de quiebras

official records registros oficiales

official statement comunicado oficial

offset *(verb)* compensar; *(noun)* ajuste; descuento; reducción

offspring *(noun)* hija; hijo; descendencia; *(children)* prole

often *(adv)* a menudo; con frecuencia; frecuentemente seguido; **I see her quie often** la veo a menudo; **how often do you see her?** ¿con qué frecuencia la ves? ¿cada cuánto la ves?; **do you come here often?** ¿vienes a menudo por aquí?; **how often?** ¿cuántas veces?

old *(of certain age)* **how old are you?** ¿cuántos años tienes? ¿qué edad tienes?; **he's 20 years old** tiene veinte años; **my older brother** mi hermano mayor; **my older sister** mi hermana mayor; **her/his older brother** su hermano mayor; **my two-year-old daughter** mi hija de dos años; **my five-year-old son** mi hijo de cinco años

old age edad avanzada; vejez; **to die of old age** morirse de vieja; morirse de viejo

old people's home asilo de ancianos

oldest *(adj)* el más viejo; la más vieja; el mayor; la mayor

on a yearly basis cada año; anual

on a first-name basis tutearse; tratarse de tú con alguien; **we've known each other long enough to be on a first-name basis** nos conocemos hace bastante tiempo como para tratarnos de tú

on Friday el viernes

on grounds of ill health por motivos de salud

on legal grounds por motivos legales; por razones legales

on medical grounds por razones de salud

on Monday el lunes

on or about aproximadamente

on Saturday el sábado

on Sunday el domingo

on the following day al día siguiente

on Thursday el jueves

on Tuesday el martes

on Wednesday el miércoles

on-the-job training cursos de capacitación en el trabajo

once or twice a year una o dos veces al año; una o dos veces por año

oncoming traffic tráfico que viene en sentido opuesto

One Car per Green *(traffic sign)* Un Vehículo Por Cada Luz Verde

one-half support la mitad del mantenimiento

one stop completa; completo; servicios integrados

One Way *(traffic sign)* Un Solo Sentido

ongoing benefits beneficios regulares

online en línea

only child hija única; hijo único

onset *(noun)* llegada; comienzo; *(of desease)* aparición

onset of disability fecha de comienzo de la incapacidad

onus of proof peso de la prueba; **the onus of proof lies with the prosecution** el peso de la prueba recae sobre el fiscal

open *(in phrases)* **to open the case for the presecution** hacer la primera presentación por parte de la acusación; **to open fire on somebody** abrir fuego contra alguien; **it is open to doubt whether ...** queda la duda sobre si ...; **it is open to question whether ...** es cuestionable que ...; **it's an open secret that ...** es un secreto a voces que ...

open court audiencia pública

open to challenge recusable

open up! police! ¡abran! ¡policía!

open verdict juicio en el que se determina el crimen sin designar el culpable

opening statement *(law)* exposición de apertura; exposición inicial del caso; declaración de apertura

operate *(in phrases)* **the law operates to our advantage** la ley nos favorece; **we have to operate within the laws of the country** tenemos que actuar de acuerdo a las leyes del país; **a gang of thieves is operating in this area** una banda de ladrones opera en la zona; **she operates a small business from home** lleva un pequeño negocio desde su casa

opinion *(law)* opinión; asesoría legal

opinion *(noun)* opinión; parecer; **what's your opinion?** ¿qué opinas?; **I haven't had time to form an opinion** no he tenido tiempo de formarme una opinión; **in my opinion** en mi opinión; a mi parecer; a mi juicio; **that's a matter of opinion** eso es discutible; **what's your opinion of him?** ¿qué opinas de él?; **there are differences of opinion as to what happened** hay discordancia de opiniones respecto a lo que pasó; **could you give us your professional opinion?** ¿nos puede dar su opinión como profesional?

opinion poll sondeo de opinión; encuesta de opinión

opinions differ hay differente opiniones al respecto

opportunity *(noun)* oportunidad; ocasión; **to seize the opportunity** aprovechar la oportunidad; aprovechar la ocasión; **at the earliest opportunity** en la primera oportunidad que se presente; cuanto antes; **to have the opportunity to do something** tener la oportunidad de hacer algo; **to miss one's opportunity** perder la oportunidad; **to take the opportunity to do something** aprovechar la oportunidad para hacer algo

opposing counsel abogada de la parte contraria; abogado de la parte contraria

opt *(noun)* optar; **to opt for something** optar por algo; decidirse por; **to opt to do something** optar por hacer algo; **she opted to try to plea bargain** optó por intentar llegar a un acuerdo con el fiscal; se decidió por intentar llegar a un acuerdo con el fiscal; **you just can't opt out of your responsibilities** no puedes desentenderte así como así de tus responsabilidades

option *(noun)* opción; **I have no option** no tengo más remedio; no tengo otro remedio; **what are my options?** ¿qué opciones tengo?; **she had no option but to leave** no tuvo más remedio que irse; **to have the option of doing something** tener la posibilidad de hacer algo; **to keep one's options open** no descartar ninguna posibilidad; **you have the option to keep your maiden name** tienes la opción de conservar tu nombre de soltera; **he was given the option of early retirement** le dieron la opción de anticipar su jubilación

option to buy opción de compra

optional method método opcional; método alternativo

optional state supplement suplemento opcional del estado

oral arguments *(law)* alegatos orales

oral evidence *(law)* prueba testimonial

orange *(adj & noun: color)* naranja; naranjo; anaranjada; anaranjado; *(fruit)* naranja

order *(law decree)* orden; **to issue an order** dictar una orden; evacuar una orden; **to carry out an order** cumplir una orden; **to obey an order** obedecer una orden; **disobey an order** desobedecer una orden; **his papers are in order** tiene los papeles en regla; **everything is in order** todo está en regla; **to put one's affairs in order** poner sus asuntos en orden; **in good order** en buen estado; en buenas condiciones

order *(verb)* disponer; **the judge ordered her release** el juez dispuso que fuera puesta en libertad

order that the text remain sealed mandar que el texto permanezca sellado

organized labor sindicalización; sindicación

orphan *(noun)* huérfana; huérfano; **to be orphaned** quedarse huérfana; quedarse huérfano; **she was orphaned at the age of two** quedó huérfana a los dos años; **hundreds of children were orphaned by the accident** el accidente dejó huérfanos a cientos de niños

orphanage *(noun)* orfanato; orfelinato; orfandad

other *(adj, adv & pronoun)* demás; **the others** las demás; los demás; las otras; los otros

out of court settlement resolución extrajudicial; transacción extrajudicial; arreglo extrajudicial

out of pocket un pago en efectivo; **to pay for something out of pocket** pagar algo de su propio bolsillo; **to pay for something out of one's own pocket** pagar algo de su propio bolsillo

out of work sin trabajo; **to be out of work** estar sin trabajo

outlaw *(verb)* prohibir; declarar ilegal; proscribir; declarar fuera de la ley

outpatient *(verb)* paciente externa; paciente externo; paciente ambulatoria; paciente ambulatorio

outpatient physical therapy services servicio de fisioterapia para paciente externa; servicio de fisioterapia para paciente externo, servicio de fisioterapia para paciente ambulatoria; servicio de fisioterapia para paciente ambulatorio

outrage *(noun)* atropello; **this is an outrage** esto es un atropello; **it's an outrage that ...** es un escándalo que ...

outside *(adj, adv & noun)* fuera; afuera; fuera de

outside the U.S. fuera de Estados Unidos

outsider *(person not belonging)* persona de afuera

over the limit *(liquor)* beber demasiado; tomar demasiado

over the telephone por teléfono

overcrowding *(noun: of prison)* hacinamiento; *(of classroom)* apiñamiento; *(of town)* sobrepoblación; superpoblación

overcrowding of prisoners hacinamiento de reclusos

overdraft *(noun)* sobregiro; giro en descubierto; **to have an overdraft** tener la cuenta en descubierto

overdose *(noun)* sobredosis; **to take an overdose** tomar una sobredosis

overdraft limit límite del descubierto

overdraw *(verb)* girar en descubierto; **your account is overdrawn** su cuenta tiene un saldo deudor; **I'm overdrawn** tengo un descubierto

overdrawn *(adj)* sobregirada; sobregirado

overdue *(adj: salary, wages)* atrasada; atrasado; *(bill)* vencido y no pagado; *(plane, train)* retrasado; con retraso; **the baby is two weeks overdue** el niño tenía que haber nacido hace quince días; **that change was long overdue** ese cambio tenía que haberse hecho hace tiempo

overpayment *(noun)* sobrepago; pago en exceso

overpayment recovery recuperación de sobrepago

overpayment refund reembolso de sobrepago

overpower *(verb)* dominar; derrotar; vencer

overrule *(law)* anular; invalidar; echazar

overruled *(law)* no hay lugar a la protesta

overt act *(law)* acto manifiesto

overtime *(extra work)* horas extra; sobretiempo; **to work overtime** hacer horas extra; trabajar sobretiempo

own judgement propio criterio; **use your own judgement** usa tu propio criterio

P

pacemaker *(noun)* marcapasos

package of benefits conjunto de beneficios

packed red blood cells glóbulos rojos concentrados

pact *(noun)* pacto; **to make a pact with somebody** hacer un pacto con alguien; **to make a pact not to do something** acordar no hacer algo; pactar no hacer algo; **suicide pact** pacto suicida

paddy-wagon *(noun)* furgón policial

paid *(adj)* pagada; pagado

paid member of the union liberada del sindicato; liberado del sindicato

pain *(noun)* dolor

painter *(noun)* pintor; pintora; *(decorator)* pintor de brocha gorda; pintora de brocha gorda; **portrait painter** retratista

pal *(noun: friend)* amiga; amigo; compinche; cuate; **we've been pals for ages** hace años que somos amigos; **your'e a pal!** ¡eso es amigo!; **they're great pals** son íntimos amigos

palimony *(noun: friend)* pensión alimenticia que se paga a un ex-concubino

palm of hand palma de la mano

palpitations *(noun)* palpitaciones

pamphlet *(noun: informative)* folleto; *(political)* panfleto; volante

pan out resultar; salir bien; **things didn't pan out as they'd hoped** las cosas no salieron como esperaban; las cosas no resultaron como esperaban

Panamanian *(noun & adj)* panameña; panameño

panel *(noun: law)* lista de personas de la cual se selecciona un jurado

panel of judges jurado; tribunal

panhandler *(noun)* mendiga; mendigo; pordiosera; pordiosero; limosnera; limosnero

panic-stricken aterrorizada; aterrorizado; presa del pánico; preso del pánico; sentirse acorralada; sentirse acorralado

papa *(noun)* papá

paper *(noun: newspaper)* diario; periódico; **I read it in the paper** lo leí en el diario; lo leí en el periódico; lo vi en el diario; **what did the paper say about it?** ¿qué salió en los diarios al respecto?

papers *(noun: documents)* documentos; papeles; **he had to hand over his identity papers** tuvo que entregar sus documentos de identidad; tuvo que entregar su documentación personal; **you have to carry your papers at all times** hay que llevar siempre los documentos encima; **your papers, please** la documentación, por favor

pappy *(noun)* papá; papi

paragraph párrafo; **new paragraph** punto aparte

Paraguayan *(noun & adj)* paraguaya; paraguayo

paralegal *relativo a los asistentes de los abogados*

parallel *(adj)* paralela; paralelo; análoga; análogo; **a case without parallel** un caso inaudito; un caso único; un caso insólito; **this is a parallel case to the last one** este caso es análogo al anterior

paralysis *(noun)* parálisis

paralyze *(adj)* paralizar; **she is paralyzed from the waist down** está paralizada de la cintura para abajo; es paralítica de la cintura para abajo; **the factory was paralyzed by the strike** la fábrica quedó paralizada por la huelga

paramedic *(noun)* paramédica; paramédico

paranoid *(adj)* paranoica; paranoico

paranoid schizophrenia esquizofrenia paranoide

paraplegic *(noun & adj)* parapléjica; parapléjico

pardon *(law)* indulto; **to grant somebody a pardon** indultar a alguien; **president refuses to pardon two condemned to death** presidente rechaza indultar dos condenados a muerte; *(verb)* **pardon me, but could you ...?** perdone la molestia, pero ¿podría usted ...?; disculpe la molestia, pero ¿podría usted ...?; **to pardon somebody something** perdonar algo a alguien

pardon *(noun: forgiveness)* perdón

parent *(noun: father)* padre; *(mother)* madre; **my parents** mis padres; **it has to be signed by a parent** tiene que firmarlo uno de los padres; **many of the children have only one parent** muchos de los niños provienen de hogares monoparentales; muchos de los niños provienen de familias monoparentales; **the responsibility of being a parent** la responsabilidad que conlleva el ser madre; la responsabilidad que conlleva el ser padre; la responsabilidad que conlleva el tener hijos

parent-teacher association asociación de padres de alumnos y profesores

parental *(adj)* de los padres

parental leave permiso por maternidad; permiso por paternidad

parental responsibility responsabilidad de los padres

parenthood *(noun)* paternidad; **the responsibilities of parenthood** las responsabilidades que conlleva el ser padre; las responsabilidades que conlleva el ser madre; **planned parenthood** planificación familiar

parenting *(noun)* crianza de los hijos; el ser padres; **parenting is a full-time occupation** el cuidar de los hijos es una labor de plena dedicación

parents *(noun)* padres

park *(in town)* parque; *(verb: car)* estacionar; aparcar; parquear; *(gear shift)* posición P; **were you in park?** ¿estaba el coche en la posición P?; ¿estaba el cambio de velocidades en la posición P?; **was the car in park?** ¿estaba el coche en la posición P?; ¿estaba el cambio de velocidades en la posición P?

parking brake freno de mano

parking garage parking; estacionamiento

parking lot estacionamiento; aparcamiento

parking meter parquímetro

parking ticket multa por aparcamiento; multa por estacionamiento indebido

parking violation infracción por aparcamiento; estacionamiento indebido

parole *(law)* libertad condicional; **to be on parole** estar en libertad condicional; **he was released on parole** fue dejado en libertad condicional; **to break one's parole** quebrantar las condiciones impuestas por la libertad condicional; *(verb)* dejar en libertad condicional

parole board *(law)* junta de la libertad condicional

parole revocation *(law)* revocación de la libertad condicional

parole violation *(law)* quebrantamiento de las normas de la libertad condicional

part *(in phrases)* **the worst part of it was that ...** lo peor de todo fue que ...; **the funny part of it is that ...** lo gracioso del asunto es que ...; **it was all part of the job** formaba parte del trabajo; **it went on for the best part of an hour** continuó durante casi una hora; **in part** en parte; **in large part** en gran parte; **to do one's part** poner de su parte; **for my part** por mi parte; por mi lado; **to take part in something** tomar parte en algo; participar en algo; **in foreign parts** en el extranjero; **she is not from these parts** no es de por aquí; **I want no part of this** no quiero tener nada que ver con esto; **they parted as friends** quedaron como amigos

part-time *(adv: worker, job, student)* trabajador a tiempo parcial; trabajadora a tiempo parcial; estudiante a tiempo parcial

part-time nursing care servicio de enfermería de tiempo parcial

partial adjudication adjudicación parcial

partial verdict *(law)* veredicto parcial

participating *(adj)* participando; participante

participating hospital hospital participante

parties to an action partes en un pleito

partner *(noun)* compañera; compañero; **partners in crime** cómplices; compinches

partnership *(noun)* sociedad; propiedad común; negocio común

pass away *(die)* fallecer

passbook *(noun* libreta de ahorros

passenger *(noun: in vehicle)* pasajero

passenger seat asiento de pasajero

passer-by *(noun)* transeúnte

passport *(noun)* pasaporte; **US passport holder** titular de pasaporte estadounidense; titular de pasaporte americano

passport control control de pasaportes

password *(noun)* contraseña

past *(in time)* **it's ten past six** son las seis y diez; **it's half past two** son las dos y media; **it's half past one** es la una y media; **it's a quarter past one** es la una y cuarto; **it was past eleven** eran las once pasadas; **it's long past after midnight** son mucho más de las doce; **he's past 40** tiene más de cuarenta años

past criminal record antecedentes penales previos

pat down *(verb)* cachear; palpar de armas

patent attorney abogada especialista en patentes; abogado especialista en patentes

patent law derecho de patentes

patent office oficina de patentes

paternal aunt tía paterna; tía por parte de padre

paternal grandmother abuela por parte de padre

paternity suit litigio por paternidad; juicio de filiación

paternity test prueba de investigación de la paternidad

patient *(noun)* paciente

Patriot Act Ley Patriota

patrol *(noun)* patrulla; **to be on patrol** estar de patrulla; **patrol car** coche patrulla; **patrol wagon** furgón policial; **they patrolled the streets at night** patrullaban las calles de noche

patrolman *(noun)* policía

patrolwoman *(noun)* mujer policía

pawn *(verb)* empeñar

pawnbroker *(noun)* prestamista

pawnshop *(noun)* casa de empeños; monte de empiedad

pay *(verb)* pagar; abonar

pay *(noun)* sueldo; salario; pago; *(in phrases)* **equal pay** igualdad de retribución para hombres y mujeres; **the pay is not very good** no pagan muy bien; **to pay somebody to do a job** pagar a alguien para que haga un trabajo; **to pay cash** pagar en efectivo; pagar al contado; **to get paid on Fridays** cobrar los viernes; **does your current account pay interest?** ¿le rinde intereses su cuenta corriente?; **to pay money into an account** depositar dinero en una cuenta; **to pay somebody a visit** ir a ver a alguien; **I'll pay** lo pago yo; **she paid for it with her life** le costó la vida; **they made him pay dearly for it** le hicieron pagarlo muy caro

pay-as-you-go-basis pago según se recibe

pay back reembolsar; devolver; restituir

pay child support pagar la manutención de un menor

pay increase aumento salarial; incremento salarial

pay rent pagar el alquiler; pagar el arrendamiento

pay settlement acuerdo salarial

pay slip *(noun)* nómina

del sueldo; recibo del sueldo

pay stub recibo de pago; talón de pago; talonario

pay the fine pagar la multa

pay to the order of pagar a la orden de

pay up *(verb)* saldar; liquidar

payable *(adj)* pagadera; pagadero; abonable; **to make a check payable to** extender un cheque a favor de

payable on demand pagadera a presentación; pagadero a presentación

paycheck cheque de la paga; cheque del sueldo

payday *(noun)* día de paga; día de cobro

payee *(noun)* beneficiaria; beneficiario

payer *(noun)* pagador; pagadora

payment *(noun: debt, money)* pago; **the first payment is due on Monday** el primer pago vence el lunes; el lunes hay que pagar la primera cuota; **they only accept cash payments** sólo aceptan pagos en efectivo; **I've made the first payment on the house** he pagado el primer plazo de la casa; **she made several payments into her account** hizo varios depósitos en su cuenta; **in payment for** en pago de; **payment by installments** pago a plazos; **down payment** depósito; enganche; **to make a payment** efectuar un pago; **to stop a payment** suspender los pagos

payment for the first six months pago de los primeros seis meses

payment in advance pago por adelantado

payment in cash pago al contado; pago en efectivo

payment in full pago total

payment in kind dación en pago

payment in terms condiciones de pago

payoff *(noun)* soborno; coima; mordida

payola *(noun)* soborno; coima; mordidas

payroll *(noun)* nómina; planilla de sueldos; **to be on the payroll** estar en planilla; **the company has a payroll of fifty** la empresa tiene cincuenta empleados en planilla

payroll tax *(noun)* impuesto sobre las remuneraciones

peace *(law)* paz; **to keep the peace** mantener el orden; **to disturb the peace** alterar el orden público

Peace Corps Cuerpos de Paz

Pedestrian Crossing Ahead *(traffic sign)* Cruce Peatonal Adelante

peer group grupo paritario

peer pressure la presión que ejercen los compañeros; la influencia que ejercen los compañeros

peer review organization organización de revisión de normas profesionales

Pell Grants Becas Pell

pelvic exam examen pélvico; examen ginecológico

penal code código penal

penal offense delito penal

penalize *(verb)* sancionar; penalizar; **heavily penalized offenses** delitos que son severamente castigados; **penalized by law** penado por la ley

penalty *(law: punishment)* pena; castigo; *(fine)* multa; **on penalty of death** bajo pena de muerte; **to pay the penalty** pagar las consecuencias

penalty deductions deducciones por multa; deducciones por penalidad

pending *(adj)* pendiente; **patent pending** patente en trámite; **to be pending** estar pendiente; **pending the arrival of ...** hasta que llegue ...; **he has been suspended pending further investigation** ha sido suspendido en espera de que continúe la investigación

penitentiary *(noun)* prisión; penitenciaria; presidio

penniless *(adj)* sin dinero; **to be penniless** no tener un céntimo; no tener un centavo; **I'm absolutely penniless** estoy sin un céntimo

pension *(noun)* pensión; **to retire on full pension** retirarse con toda la jubilación; **disability pension** pensión de invalidez; **retirement pension** retiro; pensión de jubilación; **to draw a pension** cobrar una pensión; cobrar una jubilición; **widow's pension** pensión de viudedad; pensión de viudez; **half pension** media pensión; **full pension** pensión completa

pension contributions aportaciones a la pensión

pension fund fondo de pensiones

pension plan plan de pensiones

People *(prosecuting agency)* parte acusadora; **the People rest** la parte acusadora ha concluido la presentación de pruebas

people *(noun)* gente; **what will people think?** ¿qué va a pensar la gente?; **the place was full of people** el local estaba lleno de gente; **old people** los ancianos; la gente mayor; **young people** los jóvenes; la gente joven; **people say that ...** dicen que ...; la gente dice que ...; **many people think that ...** mucha gente cree que ...; muchos creen que ...; **the people** el pueblo; **the will of the people** la voluntad popular; la voluntad del puebo; **local people** la gente del lugar; los lugareños; **the American people** los estadounidenses; los americanos; el pueblo estadounidense; el pueblo americano

people change their minds la gente cambia de opinión

people of color gente de color

people of different beliefs gente de distinta fe; gente de distintas creencias

people say that ... dicen que ...; se dice que ...

People's case *(prosecuting agency)* pruebas de la parte acusadora

people without identity papers indocumentados

peremptory challenge recusación sin causa

pepper spray rociador de pimiento

perform *(verb)* rendir; trabajar; desempeñar

period *(in phrases)* **a two year period** un período de dos años; **within a two month period** dentro de un plazo de dos meses; **for a period of three weeks** durante un período de tres semanas; **I said no, period** he dicho que no, y punto

period of benefits período de beneficios

periodic accounting rendición periódica de cuentas

periods of unemployment períodos de cesantía

perjure *(law)* **to perjure oneself** cometer perjurio; jurar en falso

perjure *(law)* perjurio

perjured evidence *(law)* falso testimonio

perjury *(law)* perjurio; falso testimonio; **to commit perjury** cometer perjurio; jurar en falso; perjurarse

permanent *(adj: address, job)* permanente; fija; fijo; estable; **on a permanent basis** de forma permanente

permanent address domicilio permanente

permanent exclusion exclusión permanente

permanent kidney failure insuficiencia renal permanente; fallo permanente del riñón

permanent legal resident residente permanente legal

permanent staff personal fijo

permanent work trabajo fijo

permission *(tax)* permiso; **to ask somebody's permission to do something;** pedir permiso a alguien para hacer algo; **by permission of** con permiso de; **to get permission from somebody to do something** obtener permiso de alguien para hacer algo; **to give permission for something** dar permiso para algo; **to give somebody permission to do something** dar permiso a alguien para hacer algo; **with your permission** con su permiso; **without permission** sin permiso; **you'll need written permission** necesitas un permiso escrito; **you have my permission** te doy permiso; **by permission of the author** con permiso del autor

permit *(noun)* permiso; licencia; **building permit** permiso de obras; **work permit** permiso de trabajo; **residence permit** permiso de residencia; **gun permit** licencia de armas

permit *(verb)* permitir; **to permit somebody to do something** permitir a alguien hacer algo; permitir que alguien haga algo; **if time permits** si hay tiempo suficiente

perpetrator *(noun)* autor; autora

perpetrator of a crime autor de un delito; autora de un delito

person *(noun)* persona; **she's a charming person** es una persona encantadora; **she's a mean persona** es una tacaña; **Sue's the person to ask** a quien hay que preguntarle es a Sue; **to have a weapon on one's person** ser portador de armas; ser portadora de armas; **to have a weapon concealed about one's person** llevar encima una arma oculta

person born in the United States persona nacida en Estados Unidos

person in contempt of court contumaz

person of sound judgement persona de buen criterio

person or persons unknown *(law)* persona o personas no identificadas; **juristic person** persona jurídica; **artificial person** persona jurídica

person who reports a crime denunciante

personal *(in phrases)* **I will give it my personal attention** me encargaré personalmente; **this is a personal matter** éste es un asunto privado; éste es un asunto personal; **I know from personal experience that ...** sé por experiencia personal que ...; **he was a personal friend** era un amigo íntimo; era un amigo personal; **to have a personal interest in something** tener un interés personal en algo; **to take a personal interest in** interesarse personalmente en; **my personal opinion is that ...** en mi opinión personal ...; **personal belongings** efectos personales; **his personal life** su vida personal; su vida privada; **a personal matter** un asunto personal; **for personal reasons** por razones personales

personal allowance *(tax)* monto que un individuo puede ganar sin pagar impuestos

personal assets bienes muebles

personal belongings efectos personales; objetos personales

Personal Earnings and Benefit Estimate Statement (PEBES) Declaración Personal de Ganancias y Cálculo de Beneficios

personal damages daños personales

personal effects efectos personales

personal expenses gastos personales

personal friend amiga íntima; amigo íntimo

personal grooming aseo personal

personal identification number número de identificación personal

personal injuries lesiones personales

personal interview entrevista personal

personal life vida personal

personal loan préstamo personal

personal opinion opinión personal

personal physician médica personal; médico personal

personal preference preferencia personal

personal reasons razones personales; motivos personales; **for personal reasons** por razones personales; por motivos personales

personal remarks comentarios insolentes

personality trait rasgo de la personalidad

personnel manager jefa de personal; jefe de personal

pertinent *(adj)* pertinente

pertinent facts hechos pertinentes

Peruvian *(noun & adj)* peruana; peruano

petition *(law)* demanda; solicitud; **a petition for divorce** una demanda de divorcio; **to file a petition** presentar una demanda; interponer una petición

petition for alien relative petición para familiar extranjero (see BCIS)

petition for divorce demanda de divorcio; petición de divorcio

petitioner *(law)* demandante

pet name apodo; sobrenombre

petty crime *(law)* delito menor

petty larceny *(law)* hurto

petty theft *(law)* hurto menor

petty thief *(law)* ladronzuela; ladronzuelo

pharmaceutical *(noun)* producto farmacéutico, fármaco

pharmacist *(noun)* farmacéutica; farmacéutico; boticaria; boticario

phone *(noun)* teléfono; **to be on the phone** estar hablando por teléfono; **there's someone on the phone for you** te llama alguien por teléfono; hay alguien al teléfono que quiere hablar **I can't talk about it over the phone** no puedo hablar de ello por teléfono

photo array rueda fotográfica de presos

physical addiction dependencia física

physical or mental impairment impedimento físico o mental

physical therapy fisioterapia

physical therapy and independent practice terapia física provista por práctica independiente

physical violence violencia física

physician médica; médico

piece of circumstantial evidence indicio

piece rate pago por pieza; pago a destajo

piece rate basis en base a destajo

piece work trabajo a destajo; trabajo por pieza

pileup accidente en cadena; choque múltiple; carambola

pimp *(noun)* proxeneta; cafiche; chulo de putas; *(verb)* **to pimp for somebody** ser el proxeneta de alguien

pistol *(noun)* pistola; revólver

pistol shot *(noun)* pistoletazo

pistol-whip *(verb)* **pistol-whip somebody** pegarle a alguien en la cara con una pistola

place *(noun)* lugar

place and date lugar y fecha

place of abode *(law)* domicilio; residencia

place of birth lugar de nacimiento

place of business lugar de trabajo; local

place of employment lugar de trabajo

place of payment lugar de pago

place of work lugar de trabajo

place the blame on echarle la culpa a; responsabilizar la culpa a

place under custody *(law)* poner bajo custodia; **to place somebody under custody** poner a alguien bajo custodia

plain *(in phrases)* **it is plain that ...** es evidente que ...; **it's just plain common sense** es de sentido común; **in plain language** en lenguaje claro; en lenguaje sencillo

plain clothes *(noun)* **in plain clothes** de civil; **a plain clothes policeman** un policía de civil

plaintiff *(law)* demandante; actor; actora

plaintiff's claim *(law)* reclamo del demandante

plaintiff's lawyer *(law)* abogado del demandante

plan *(verb & noun)* **to plan a robbery** planear un robo; **to draw up a plan** elaborar un proyecto; **to change one's plan** cambiar de proyecto; **to make plans** hacer proyectos; hacer planes

Plan for Achieving Self-Support (PASS) Plan de Ayuda a Sí Solo (PASS); Plan de Ayuda a Sí Propio

planned *(adj: crime, murder)* premeditada; premeditado

planned parenthood planificación familiar

planning laws ley de ordenación urbana; **they are in breach of the planning laws** están infringiendo la ley de ordenación urbana

plea *(noun: law)* alegación; alegato; confesión judicial de culpabilidad; declaración judicial de culpabilidad; **to enter a plea of not guilty** declararse inocente; **to enter a plea of guilty** declararse culpable; *(arrangement)* alegato; petición; ruego

plea agreement llegar a un acuerdo con el fiscal; acuerdo sobre la alegación; convenio de culpabilidad

plea bargain *(law)* convenio declaratorio

plea bargaining *acuerdo táctico entre fiscal y defensor para agilizar los trámites judiciales;* **we could try plea bargaining** podríamos intentar llegar a un acuerdo con el fiscal

plea of guilty *(law)* alegación de culpabilidad

plea hearing *(law)* declaración judicial de culpabilidad

plea of insanity *(law)* alegación de insania

plea of not guilty *(law)* alegación de inocencia

plea withdrawal *(law)* retiro de alegación

plead *(law)* declararse oficialmente; **to plead somebody's case** llevar el caso de alguien

plead a cause defender una causa

plead guilty declararse culpable

plead innocent *(law)* **he pleaded innocent of the whole affair** alega no saber nada del asunto; aduce no saber nada del asunto

plead not guilty to the charges declararse inocente de los cargos

plead self-defense alegar légitima defensa; alegar propia defensa

plead the case for the prosecution llevar la acusación

pleading *(law)* alegato

pleas during the sentencing *(law)* alegatos durante la sentencia

please notify us haga el favor de notificarnos; sírvase notificarnos, por favor avísenos

pneumonia *(noun)* pulmonía; neumonía

point *(in phrases)* **to point a gun at somebody** apuntar a alguien con un fusil; **at this point in time** en este momento; **at what point did you begin to suspect?** ¿en qué momento empezó a sospechar?; **at no point did they mention money** en ningún momento hablaron de dinero.; **from this point on** a partir de este momento; **from that point on ...** de allí en adelante ...; **to be on the point of doing something** estar a punto de hacer algo; **up to a point** hasta cierto punto; en cierta medida; **to be beside the point** no venir al caso; **do you get the point?** ¿entiendes lo que quiero decir?; **to miss the point** no comprender; **that's not the point** esto no viene al caso; no es eso; **to get to the point** ir al grano; **to get back to the point** volver al tema; **to keep to the point** no salirse del tema; **what's the point?** ¿para qué?; ¿a cuento de qué?; **to make the point that ...** hacer ver que ...; hacer comprender que ...; **to make a point of doing something** poner empeño en hacer algo; **on this point** sobre este punto; **on that point** en cuanto a eso; **I take your point** acepto lo que dices; **point taken!** ¡de acuerdo!; **point of reference** punto de referencia; **point of view** punto de vista

point-blank *(adj: question)* directa; directo; *(aim a gun)* a quemarropa

point of view punto de vista

point out señalar; **to point out something to somebody** señalar algo a alguien; **to point out somebody's mistakes** señalar los errores de alguien; **to point out that ...** señalar que; ...; **let me point out that ...** permítame observar que ...; permítame señalar que ...

poison *(noun)* veneno; *(verb)* envenenar

poison gas gas tóxico

poisoning *(noun)* venenamiento; **to die of poisoning** morir envenenada; morir envenenado

poisonous *(adj)* venenosa; venenoso; tóxica; tóxico; *(verb)* envenenar

police *(noun)* policía; **to join the police** meterse de policía; **to call the police** llamar a la policía; **to have a police record** estar fichada; estar fichado; **the riot police** la policía antidisturbios; **to be in the police** ser policía; **the police outnumbered the demonstrators** el número de policías superaba al de los manifestantes

police *(verb)* patrullar; **the demonstration was heavily policed** hubo una gran presencia policial en la manifestación

police action intervención policial

police brutality brutalidad policial

police car coche de policía

police chaplain capellán de la policía

police composite retrato hablado; retrato robot

police custody custodia policial

police deaths muertes policiales

police dog perro policía

police evidence pruebas aportadas por la policía

police headquarters jefatura de policía

police harassment acoso por parte de la policía

police informer informante de la policía

police inspector inspector de policía; inspectora de policía

police lineup rueda de sospechosos; rueda de reconocimiento; rueda de presos

police officer policía; agente de policía

police photographs fotografías de filiación

police protection protección policial

police raid redada policial; incursión policial

police records fichas

police regulations código de policía

police report informe policial; parte policial

police search registro policial

police sources fuentes policiales

police station comisaria

police station lockup depósito policial; calabazo policial

police swoop redada policial

police trap trampa policial

policeman's badge placa de policía

policing *(noun: keeping order)* mantenamiento del orden; **he criticized the policing of the strike** critíco la actuación policial durante la huelga

policy number número de póliza

policyholder *(noun)* asugurada; asegurado

poll of jury *(law)* preguntas al jurado; escrutar los votos del jurado

polling the jury encuestar al jurado

polygraph *(noun)* polígrafo; detector de mentiras

polygraph test prueba del polígrafo

ponytail *(noun)* cola de caballo; coleta; **to tie one's hair in a ponytail** hacerse una cola de caballo

pool of blood charco de sangre

pooled income ingreso combinado

poor *(A common translation of* **poor** *is* **pobre.** *Note that* **pobre** *generally follows any noun it modifies when* **poor** *means* **not rich** *and precedes* *it when* **poor** *means* **unfortunate)** **a poor family** una familia pobre; **a poor man** un pobre; **a poor woman** una pobre; **to have a poor opinion of somebody** tener un concepto poco favorable de alguien; **I had a poor education** la educación que recibí no fue muy buena; **the poor** los pobres; **to be in poor health** estar mal de salud

poor housing conditions viviendas inadecuadas

poor memory mala memoria

pop *(noun)* papá

popgun *(noun)* pistola de juguete

population *(noun)* población

portability *(noun: of pension, insurance)* transferibilidad

portable *(noun: of pension, insurance)* transferibilidad

porter *(noun: at airport)* maletera; maletero; moza; mozo; *(hospital)* camillera; camillero; *(hotel, apartment complex)* portera; portero

position *(noun)* posición; ubicación; **the policemen had taken up positions around the building** los policías se habían apostados alrededor del edificio; *(responsibility, job)* puesto; **a position of responsibility** un puesto de responsabilidad; **a position of trust** un puesto de confianza

position *(verb)* colocar; poner; **police had been positioned at both ends of the street** habían apostado policías a ambos extremos de la calle

positive *(adj)* positiva; positivo; segura; seguro; **on the positive side** en el lado positivo; **look on the positive side** mira lo positivo; mira el lado positivo; **there is no positive evidence** no hay pruebas concluyentes; no hay pruebas positivas; **she is positive of the date** está muy segura de la fecha; **she was positive about having seen him** estaba muy segura de haberlo visto; **I'm positive I've met him before** estoy segura de que lo conozco; estoy seguro de que lo conozco; **it's positive proof** es una prueba incontrovertible; **you don't sound very positive** no pareces estar muy segura; no pareces estar muy seguro; **there are some positive results at last** por fin hay unos resultados positivos; **the positives outweigh the negatives** los aspectos positivos tienen más peso que los negativos; **to test positive** dar positivo

positive cash flow flujo positivo de efectivo

positively *(adv)* **to act positively** tener una actitud positiva; **the body has been positively identified** se ha hecho una identificación definitiva del cadáver; **the body has not yet been positively identified** todavía no se ha hecho una identificación definitiva del cadáver; **most employees view the new system positively** la mayoría de los empleados han reaccionado favorablemente al nuevo sistema; la mayoría de los empleados ve el nuevo sistema con buenos ojos; **this is positively the last time I'm going to tell you** está sí que es la última vez que te lo digo; **this is positively your last chance** decididamente, ésta es tu última oportunidad

possession *(law)* tenencia *(see criminal and minor)*

possible *(in phrases)* **is Tuesday possible for you?** ¿le es posible el martes?; ¿le viene bien el martes?; **as soon as possible** cuanto antes; lo antes posible; **if at all possible** si es posible; a ser posible; **it's just possible he may still be there** existe una pequeña posibilidad de que siga allí; **there is no possible excuse for his behaviour** su comportamiento no tiene excusa que valga; **what possible motive could she have?** ¿qué motivo puede tener?; **get there by eight if possible** llega antes de las ocho, si es posible

possibly *(adv)* **if I possibly can** si me es posible; si puedo; **that can't possibly be true** eso no puede ser verdad

post bail *(verb)* pagar la fianza

post bond *(verb)* pagar la fianza

post office *(noun)* oficina de correo; estafeta de correos

post office box apartado postal; casilla postal; casilla de correos

post-trial motions pedimentos después de juicio

postage free libre de franqueo

posters *(noun)* carteles; afiches

posthumous *(adj)* póstuma; póstumo

postman *(noun)* cartera; cartero

potential police trap posible trampa policial

poverty *(noun)* pobreza; **to live in poverty** vivir en la pobreza; vivir en la miseria; **they live on the poverty line** tienen apenas el mínimo necesario para vivir; viven del salario mínimo

poverty level umbral de pobreza

poverty line umbral de pobreza; **to live below the poverty line** vivir en la indigencia; **to live above the poverty line** vivir por encima del umbral de pobreza

poverty stricken muy pobre; sumida en la pobreza; sumido en la pobreza

power of attorney poder legal; poder notarial

practice law ejercer de abogado

practioner *(noun)* profesional

precedent *(noun)* precedente; decisión judicial

precinct *(noun: area)* recinto; *(politics, of police)* distrito electoral; distrito policial

preferential *(adj)* preferente; preferencial

pregnancy *(noun)* embarazo; preñez; **full term pregnancy** embarazo a término; **she decided to terminate the pregnancy** decidió interrumpir el embarazo

pregnancy prevention for teens prevención del embarazo para jóvenes de ambos sexos

pregnancy test prueba del embarazo

pregnant *(adj)* embarazada; encinta; **to be six months pregnant** estar embarazada de seis meses; **Elaine was pregnant with their first son** Elaine estaba embarazada de su primer hijo; **she got pregnant** quedó embarazada; **she became pregnant** quedó embarazada; **he got her pregnant** la dejó embarazada; **she went to the doctor because she couldn't get pregnant** fue al médico porque no quedaba embarazada

pregnant with *(adj)* embarazada de; **I was pregnant with Colleen at the time** en esa época yo estaba embarazada de Colleen; estaba esperando a Colleen

prejudice prejuicio; *(law)* **without prejudice** sin detrimento de sus propios derechos; **there's a lot of racial prejudice** hay muchos prejuicios raciales; **to have a prejudice against somebody** estar predispuesto en contra de alguien

prejudiced *(adj)* parcial; interesada; interesado

prejudicial *(adj)* perjudicial; **it would be prejudicial to her career** sería perjudicial para su carrera; **this could be prejudicial to our interests** esto podría perjudicar nuestros intereses; esto podría ser perjudicial para nuestros intereses

preliminary hearing audiencia preliminar; vista preliminar

preliminary injunction against mandamiento judicial preliminar contra

preliminary proceedings primeras diligencias del sumario

premarital *(adj)* prematrimonial

premarital agreement capitulaciones prematrimoniales

premeditate *(verb)* premeditar

premeditation *(noun)* premeditación

premarital sex relaciones prematrimoniales

premises *(building, site)* local; **they've moved to new premises** se han mudado a un nuevo local; **they're moving to new premises** se trasladan de local; *(shop, restaurant, hotel)* establecimiento; **meals are cooked on the premises** las comidas se preparan en el establecimiento; **the police ordered everyone to leave the premisis** la policía ordenó el abandono del recinto

premiums *(adj)* primas

prepaid *(adj)* porte pagado; pagado por adelantado

preparation *(noun)* preparación; **to make preparations for something** hacer preparativos para algo

prepare *(verb)* preparar; **to prepare somebody for something** preparar a alguien para algo; **to prepare something for somebody** preparar algo a alguien; **to prepare for something** prepararse para algo; **to prepare to do something** prepararse para hacer algo

prepared *(adj)* preparada; preparado; **he is prepared for anything** está preparado para cualquier eventualidad; **we were prepared for it** íbamos preparados; **we were not prepared for this** esto no lo esperábamos, no contábamos con esto; **to be prepared to do something** estar dispuesta a hacer algo; estar dispuesto a hacer algo

prepayment *(noun)* pago anticipado; pago adelantado; pago por adelantado

pre-retirement previo a la jubilación; antes de la jubilación

pre-school *(adj: child)* preescolar; *(noun)* jardín de infancia; jardín de niños; jardín de infantes; escuela de párvulos

prescribe *(verb)* recetar

prescription *(noun)* receta; prescripción

prescription drug droga recetada

prescription drug coverage cobertura de drogas recetadas

present *(adj: at scene)* presente; **to be present** estar presente **he was present at the scene of the accident** presenció el accidente; **at the present time** en este momento; en la actualidad; **in the present case** en este caso; en el caso que nos ocupa

present evidence presentar pruebas

present the case for the defense presentar descargos; formular descargos

present time actualidad

presentation of evidence presentación de evidencia; presentación de pruebas

pre-sentence hearing *(law)* audiencia precondenatoria

pre-sentence investigation *(law)* investigación precondenatoria

pre-sentence investigation report *(law)* informe precondenatorio

pre-sentence report *(law)* informe precondenatoria

presiding judge juez que preside; juez del caso

press *(verb: put pressure on)* insistir; presionar; **I must press you on this point** debo insistirle sobre este punto; **when pressed, she admitted it** cuando la presionaron, lo admitió; **they're being pressed by creditors** los están acosando los creedores; **I didn't press the point** no insistí más; **they've been pressing for an inquiry** han estado presionando para que se haga una investigación

press charges against somebody presentar cargos en contra de alguien; formular cargos en contra de alguien; hacer acusaciones contra alguien

presume *(verb: assume)* suponer; **a defendant is presumed innocent until proven guilty** un acusado es inocente hasta que se demuestre lo contrario; **to presume somebody to be innocent** suponer que alguien es inocente; **to presume that ...** suponer que ...; **it may be presumed that ...** es de suponer que ...; **I presume you know why I'm asking** supongo que sabe por qué lo pregunto; me imagino que sabe por qué lo pregunto; **I assume so** supongo que sí; me imagino que sí; **missing, assumed dead** desaparecida; desaparecido; dada por muerta; dado por muerto

presumption of innocence *(law)* presunción de inocencia

presumptive disability incapacidad presunta

pre-trial conference *(law)* consulta previo al juicio; conferencia con antelación al juicio

pre-trial detention *(law)* prisión preventiva

pre-trial motion *(law)* pedimentos preliminares al juicio; mociones antes del juicio

pre-trial release *(law)* libertad provisional

prevalence *(noun: widespread occurence)* preponderancia; grado; **the increasing prevalence of divorce** el número cada vez mayor de divorcios; **the increasing prevalence of violent crime** el número cada vez mayor de delitos de violencia

previous address dirección anterior

previous residence residencia anterior

preventive detention prisión preventiva

prevention of child abuse and domestic violence prevención de maltrato a niños y la violencia doméstica

previous offender reincidente

price freeze una congelación de precios

priest *(clergyman)* clérigo; sacerdote; cura; padre

prima facie *(law)* suficiente a primera vista; **there is prima facie evidence** existen pronunciaciones de hecho; **to have a prima facie case** parecer tener razón a primera vista

prima facie evidence *(law)* prueba semiplena

primary doctor médica de primer contacto; médico de primer contacto

primary education enseñanza primaria

primary insurance amount (PIA) cantidad de seguro primario

principal *(law)* autor; autora

principal *(noun: of school)* director; directora; *(sum of money)* capital; principal

principle *(noun: basic fact, law)* principio; **on that principle** sobre esa base; **it goes against my principles** va contra mis principios; **to have high principles** tener principios nobles; **as a matter of principle** por principio; **it's a matter of principle** es cuestión de principios; **a man of principles** un hombre de principios; **a woman of principles** una mujer de principios

print *(noun)* letra imprenta; **please print your full name** escriba el nombre completo en letra imprenta

prior convictions condenas previas

prior to trial antes del juicio; antes del proceso

prior written notice aviso previo por escrito

priority *(noun)* prioridad

prison *(noun: jail)* cárcel; prisión; **she's in prison** está presa; está en la cárcel; **he's in in prison** está en la cárcel; está en prisión; **to be in prison for five years** pasar cinco años en la cárcel; pasar cinco años en la prisión; **to send somebody to prison** encarcelar a alguien; **to send somebody to prison for two years** condenar a alguien a dos años de prisión; **he was released from prison** fue puesto en libertad; fue excarcelado; **after 15 years of prison** después de 15 años de prisión; después de 15 años de cárcel; **high security prison** prisión de alta seguridad

prison cell celda

prison guard funcionaria; funcionario; guardia

prison guard held hostage funcionaria retenida; funcionario retenido

prison inmate rea; reo; presa; preso

prison officer carcelera; carcelero

prison population reclusos; población penitenciaria

prison sentence condena privativa de libertad; pena de prisión; pena privativa de libertad

prison staff personal penitenciario

prison term condena

prison life la vida de la cárcel

prisoner *(noun: in jail)* presa; preso; reclusa; recluso; *(person arrested)* detenida; detenido; *(person accused)* rea; reo; acusada; acusado

prisoner in contempt of court rea contumaz; reo contumaz

prisoner of war prisionera de guerra; prisionero de guerra; presa de guerra; preso de guerra

prisoner on the run presa fugada; preso fugado

Privacy Act Ley de Confidencialidad

Privacy Rights Clearinghouse Cámara de Compensación Privada

private and confidential privado y confidencial

private discussion discusión en privado; discusión a solas; discusión a puerta cerrada

private driveway entrada privada

private enterprise el sector privado

private hearing *(law)* vista a puerta cerrada

private insurance seguro privado

private insurer asegurador privado; aseguradora privado

private medical counselor consultante médico privado

privilege *(noun: special right)* fuero; privilegio; imunidad; *(law)* honor; privilegio; **I had the privilege of speaking to her in person** tuve el privilegio de hablar con ella en persona; tuve el honor de hablar con ella en persona; **it is my privilege to be able to introduce ...** tengo el honor de presentarles a ...; tengo el privilegio de presentarles a ...

privileged *(law: document)* confidencial

probable cause *(law)* motivo de procesamiento

probate court tribunal de sucesiones

probation *(law)* libertad condicional; **to be on probation** estar en libertad condicional; **to put somebody on probation** dejar a alguien en libertad condicional; poner a alguien en libertad condicional; poner a alguien en libertad provicional; **she's on probation** está cumpliendo su período de prueba

probation department departamento de probatoria

probation officer funcionario que vigila a las personas que están en libertad

probation report informe sobre la libertad condicional; informe de presentencia preparado por el oficial de libertad condicional

probation violation *(law)* quebrantamiento de las normas de condena condicional probatoria

probationary *(law)* de prueba

probationary period *(law)* período de libertad condicional de prueba

probationer *(law) persona en libertad condicional*

probe *(noun)* investigación; *(verb)* investigar; **police are probing into his business affairs** la policía está investigando sus actividades financieras

procedure *(noun: practice)* procedimiento; *(step)* trámite; **legal procedures** trámites legales; **the normal procedure is to ...** lo que se hace normalmente es ...; **the procedures to be followed in such cases** el procedimiento a seguir en tales casos

procedureal law derecho procesal

process *(noun)* proceso; procedimiento; trámite; *(verb)* tramitar; procesar; tratar

professional *(adj: not amature)* profesional; de carrera; **you ought to take professional advice** deberías asesorarte con un profesional; **the break-in was a professional job** los que entraron eran profesionales del robo; **a professional person** un profesional; **they are all professional people** todos son profesionales; **a health professional** un profesional de la medicina

professional advice consejo profesional; **you ought to take professional advice** deberías asesorarte con un profesional

professional charges honorarios

professional ethics ética profesional

professional experience experiencia profesional

professional fees honorarios

professional misconduct mala conducta en el ejercicio de la profesión; falta de ética profesional

professional person un profesional; una profesional

professional qualifications títulos profesionales

professional standing reputación profesional

proficiency *(noun)* competencia; habilidad; **level of proficiency** nivel de competencia

proficiency test prueba de aptitud; examen de aptitud

proficient *(adj)* hábil; experta; experto; **she was already proficient in English** tenía ya un gran dominio del inglés; dominaba ya el inglés; **she is fully proficient in Spanish** domina el español

profit *(noun)* ganancias; beneficios; lucro

progressive illness enfermedad progresiva

promise *(noun)* promesa; **to keep one's promise** cumplir con su promesa; **you are still bound by your promise** sigues estando obligado a cumplir con lo que prometiste; **they made good their promise** cumplieron con su promesa; *(verb)* prometer; **to promise somebody something** prometer algo a alguien; **they've been promised help** se les ha prometido ayuda

promissory note *(noun)* pagaré

pronounce *(law: sentence, judgement)* pronunciar; dictar; **to pronounce sentence** pronunciar un fallo; pronunciar una condena; **he was pronounced dead** se dictaminó que estaba muerto

proof *(noun: conclusive evidence)* evidencia; prueba; pruebas; comprobante; **do you have any proof of this?**; ¿tienes pruebas de esto?; **where's your proof?** ¿qué pruebas tienes?; **we have no proof of that** no tenemos pruebas de eso; **you'll need proof of identity** necesitará un documento de identidad; **it is proof that he is innocent** eso prueba su inocencia; **as proof of** como prueba de; en prueba de; **by way of proof** a modo de prueba; **bombproof** a pruebas de bomba

proof of citizenship prueba de ciudadanía

proof of identity prueba de identidad; **you'll need proof of identity** necesitará un documento de identidad

proof of insurance prueba de aseguramiento

proof of legal residence status prueba de estado legal de residencia

proof of payment comprobante de pago

proof of purchase comprobante de compra; **to obtain a refund you must produce proof of purchase** para cualquier devolución necesitará el comprobante de compra

proper authorities autoridad competente

property *(noun: possessions)* propiedad; bienes; **whose property is it?** ¿de quién es?; ¿a quién pertenece?; **she left her property to her daughter** dejó sus propiedades a su hija; dejó sus bienes a su hija; **it's my personal property** es mío; es de mi propiedad

property damage daño a la propiedad

property owner terrateniente; propietaria; propietario

property tax impuesto de propiedad; impuesto sobre bienes

property valuation tasación de la propiedad

prorate *(verb)* prorratear, dividir

prosecute *(law)* encausar; enjuiciar; procesar; **to prosecute somebody for something** procesar a alguien por algo; enjuiciar a alguien por algo; *(bring action)* iniciar procedimiento criminal; interponer una acción judicial; *(be prosecutor)* llevar la acusación; **Gonzales, prosecuting, said that ...** Gonzales, por la acusación, dijo que ...; **to prosecute somebody for theft** procesar a alguien por robo

prosecuting attorney *(law)* fiscal

prosecuting case *(law)* acusación

prosecution *(law: legal proceeding)* enjuiciamento; procesamiento; interposición de una acción judicial; *(court case)* proceso; juicio; **to bring a prosecution against somebody** entablar una acción judicial contra alguien; interponer una acción judicial contra alguien; **to start a prosecution against somebody** entablar juicio judicial contra alguien; entablar una acción judicial contra alguien; **counsel for the prosecution** fiscal

prosecution *(law: party who proceeds in a criminal case)* parte acusadora

prosecuting witness *(law)* testigo de cargo; testigo de la acusación

prosecutor *(law)* fiscal; acusador; acusadora; abogada de la acusación; abogado de la acusación; abogada por la parte querellante; abogado por la parte querellante; abogada por la acusación; abogado por la acusación

prosecutor in the case *(law)* fiscal del caso; acusador del caso; acusadora del caso

prospective payment pago eventual; pago potencial

prostate cancer cáncer de la próstata

protection *(law)* protección; **to be under somebody's protection** estar bajo la protección de alguien; estar amparado por alguien; **the policy offers protection against ...** la póliza protege contra ...

protection money *(law)* dinero que se paga al chantajista para que no cause daños en un negocio; dólares de protección a la semana

protection of the rights of *(law)* protección de los derechos de

protection racket *(law)* chantaje

protective custody *(law)* detención preventiva; custodia precautoria (detención de una persona para su propia protección)

prove *(law)* comprobar; verificar; **to prove somebody innocent** comprobar la inocencia de alguien

prove *(verb)* demostrar; probar; **they couldn't prove that she was lying** no pudieron demostrar que mentía; no pudieron probar que mentía; **to prove one's point** demostrar que uno tiene razón; demostrar que uno está en lo cierto; **can you prove where you were that night?** ¿tiene pruebas de dónde estaba usted aquella noche?; **to prove somebody right** demostrar que alguien tiene razón; **to prove somebody wrong** demostrar que alguien está equivocada; demostrar que alguien está equivocado; **can you prove it?** ¿lo puede probar?; **you can't prove anything against me** usted no tiene ninguna prueba en mi contra; usted no puede probar nada en mi contra; **to prove that ...** demostrar que ...; probar que ...

provide *(verb)* proporcionar; proveer; suministrar

provide services proveer servicios; suministrar servicios

provide treatment for drug addicts and alcoholics proveer tratamiento para adictos a drogas o alcohólicos

provider of physical and speech pathology proveedor de patología física y del habla

provider of services proveedor de servicios

provision of law estipulación legal; disposición legal

provision of special services prestaciones de servicios sociales

provisional coverage *(noun)* covertura provisional

proviso *(law)* condición; **with the proviso that ...** con la condición de que ...; **with the proviso that I'm paid in advance** con la condición de que me paguen por adelantado

proxy *(law: representative)* representante; apoderada; apoderado; **to stand proxy for somebody** representar a alguien; obrar con poder de alguien; **I gave him proxy to act on my behalf** le di poderes para que actuará en mi nombre; **to vote by proxy** votar por poder; **to get married by proxy** casarse por poder

psychiatrist *(noun)* siquiatra, psiquiatra

public assistance ayuda pública; asistencia pública

public assistance payments pagos de asistencia pública

public defender defensor de oficio; defensora de oficio; defensor de pobres; defensora de pobres

public disability benefits beneficios públicos de incapacidad; pagos públicos de incapacidad

public document escritura pública

public health sanidad pública

public office cargo público

public policy política pública

public prosecutor fiscal

public record registro civil

public restrooms sanitarios públicos

public safety seguridad ciudadana

public school escuela pública

Puerto Rican portorriqueña; portorriqueño; puertoprriqueña; puertoprriqueño

pull out of the area abandonar el área; **the police have started to pull out of the area** la policía ha comenzado a abandonar el área

pull the client away from separar al cliente de

pulmonary tuberculosis tuberculosis pulmonar

punish *(verb)* castigar; sancionar; **to punish somebody for something** castigar a alguien por algo; **to punish somebody for doing something** castigar a alguien por hacer algo

punishable *(adj)* punible; **a punishable offense** una infracción penada por la ley; una infracción sancionada por la ley; **a crime punishable by death** un delito castigado con la pena de muerte

punishment *(noun)* castigo; **to make the punishment fit the crime** determinar un castigo acorde con la gravedad del crimen

purchasing power capacidad adquisitiva; poder adquisitivo

purple *(adj & noun)* morada; morado; violeta; violeto; *(reddish)* púrpura; púrpuro

purpose *(noun)* motivo; propósito; intención; **for all practical purposes** a efectos prácticos; **for our purposes** para nuestros propósitos

purpose of visit motivo de la visita

pursue relentlessly acosar

pursue the matter further continuar con el tema; continuar con el asunto

pursuit *(noun)* caza; persecución; busca; búsqueda; **in pursuit of somebody** en busca de alguien; **with two policemen in hot pursuit** con dos policías pisándole los talones; **she set off in pursuit of the thief** salió en persecusión del ladrón; salió a la caza del ladrón

pusher *(noun: of drugs)* camello; traficante

put an end to the lawsuit poner término a la causa

put something to the test poner algo a prueba

put up a good case for presentar poderosos argumentos a favor de

putative marriage matrimonio supuesto

putting their lives at risk arriesgando sus vidas

putting their lives in danger arriesgando sus vidas

Q

quack *(noun)* curandera; curandero

quack doctor curandera; curandero

quadriplegic *(noun)* trapléjica; trapléjico

quagmire *(noun: situation)* atolladero

quaint *(adj)* curiosa; curioso; extraña; extraño

quaintly *(adj)* de forma extraña; rara; raro

qualification *(noun: diploma)* título; requisito; *(attribute)* calidad; excelente currículum; **what are his qualifications?** ¿qué títulos tiene?; **teaching qualifications** título de profesor; título de profesora; título de maestra; título de maestro; **the qualifications for the job are ...** los requisitos del puesto son ...; **his qualifications are very good** está muy bien calificado; *(elgibility)* derecho; **their qualification for financial assistance** su derecho a percibir ayuda económica

qualified *(adj: doctor, teacher, engineer)* titulada; titulado; **a shortage of qualified personnel** una escasez de personal calificado; **a qualified candidate** un candidato muy preparado; una candidata muy preparada; **to be qualified to** + *infin* estar capacitada para + *infin*; estar capacitado para + *infin*

Qualified Medicare Beneficiary (QMB) Beneficiario Calificado de Medicare

qualified designated entity entidad designada aprobada

qualified person persona calificada

qualify *(verb: make suitable, equip, entitle)* **his experience should qualify him for a better job** su experienca debería permitirle acceder a un puesto mejor; **their low income qualifies them for some benefits** sus bajos ingresos les dan derecho a recibir ciertas prestaciones; **it may qualify as a medical expense** puede que cuente como gastos médicos; **to qualify as disabled, he must ...** para ser declarado minusválido, tiene que ...; **she doesn't qualify for a grant** no tiene derecho a una beca; no puede optar a una beca; **that doesn't qualify him to speak on this** eso no le da derecho a hablar sobre esto; **some of her statements could be qualified as racist** algunos de sus comentarios se podrían calificar de racistas

quality *(degree of excellence)* calidad; **of poor quality** de calidad inferior; **of excellent quality** de primera calidad; **the quality of life** la calidad de vida; **of good quality** de buena calidad; **of high quality** de alta calidad; **one of his good qualities** una de sus buenas calidades; **I need to spend some quality time with my children** necesito pasar tiempo disfrutando con mis hijos; **to spend quality time studying** pasar tiempo estudiando en serio; **leadership qualities** dotes de mando; dotes de liderazgo

qualm *(noun: scruple)* escrúpelo; reparo; **to have no qualms about something** no tener ningún reparo en algo; no tener ningún escrúpelo en algo; **he had no qualms about throwing them out on the street** no tuvo ningún escrúpulo para echarlos a la calle

quandary *(noun: dilema)* dilema; **to be in a quandary** estar en un dilema; **he was in a quandary about whether to accept** estaba en un dilema sobre si aceptar o no; **this decision left them in a quandry** esta decisión les planteó un dilema

quarantine *(noun)* cuarentena; **to be in quarantine** estar en cuarentena; *(verb)* poner en cuarentena

quarrel *(noun: argument)* riña; pelea; disputa; **to have a quarrel with somebody** reñir con alguien; pelearse con alguien; **I have no quarrel with you** no tengo nada en contra de usted; no tengo queja de usted; *(verb: argue)* pelear; riñar; **he quarreled with his family over the inheritance** riñó con su familia por cuestiones de herencia; peleó con su familia por cuestiones de herencia; **they quarreled over money** riñeron por cuestión de dinero; **I can't quarrel with that** eso no lo discuto

quarters of coverage trimestres de cobertura; trimestres de protección; trimestres de créditos

quash *(verb: law, verdict, sentence)* anular; invalidar; *(revolt)* sofocar; aplastar; *(protest)* acallar; *(proposal)* rechazar

quell *(verb: revolt, riot, uprising)* sofocar; aplastar; *(crticism)* acallar; acabar con; *(fears)* disipar; acabar con; desechar

query *(noun: question)* pregunta; *(doubt)* duda; **if you have any queries, please do not hesitate to call** si tiene alguna pregunta, no dude en llamar

question *(noun: question)* interrogatorio; pregunta; cuestión; **to ask a question** hacer una pregunta; **the person in question** la persona en cuestión; **are there any questions?** ¿hay alguna pregunta?; **to ask somebody a question** hacer una pregunta a alguien; **ask yourself this question** hágase esta pregunta; **to obey orders without question** obedecer órdenes sin rechistar; **I asked you a question** te hice una pregunta; **a question of law** una cuestión de derecho; **there is no question about her talent** no hay duda de que tiene talento; **there's no question about it** no cabe duda

question *(verb: police)* interrogar; someter a una interrogación; preguntar; **were you questioned?** ¿te interrogaron? **were you questioned by the police?** ¿te sometió la policía a un interrogatorio?; **were you questioned at the police station?** ¿te interrogaron en la comisaria?; **his parents questioned him about where he had been all night** sus padres le preguntaron dónde había estado toda la noche; **at the time of the question** a la hora que nos interesa

questionable pay pago dudoso

questionable retirement retiro dudoso; jubilación dudosa

questionaire *(noun)* cuestionario

questioning *(noun: question, law)* interrogatorio; **he is wanted for questioning by the police** la policía requiere su presencia para someterlo a un interrogatorio;

questioning room sala de interrogatorio

quick *(in phrases)* **this is the quickest way to do it** ésta es la forma más rápida de hacerlo; **be quick!** ¡rápido!, ¡date prisa!, ¡apúrate!; **he was quick to point out that ...** señaló rápidamente que ... **to be quick to act** obrar con prontitud; **to be quick to anger** enfadarse con facilidad;

enojarse con facilidad; **to be quick to take offense** ofenderse por nada; **he made a quick recovery** se recuperó rápidamente; **to have a quick temper** tener un genio vivo; **can I have a quick word with you?** ¿puedo hablar un segundo contigo?; **I left as quick as I could** me fui lo más rápido que pude; **come as quick as you can** ven cuanto antes

quick-tempered de genio vivo; de mucho genio; irascible

quick-witted aguda; agudo; ingeniosa; ingenioso; perspicaz

quid pro quo compensación

quiet *(in phrases)* **you're very quiet today** hoy estás muy callada; hoy estás muy callado; **to keep quiet about something** no decir nada acerca de algo; **he managed to keep the whole thing quiet** consiguió que nadie se enterara del asunto; **business is quiet at this time of year** hay poco movimiento en esta época; **I'll have a quiet word with him** hablaré discretamente con él; **he gave them money to keep them quiet** les pagó para que se callaran; **I'd like a quiet word with you** me gustaría hablar contigo en privado; **I'd like you to keep it quiet** quiesiera que no dijeras nada

quite *(in phrases)* **that's not quite right** eso no es totalmente cierto; **she's not quite sure** no está del todo segura; **it's quite clear that ...** está clarísimo que ...; **that's quite enough for me** eso me basta a mí; **I quite understand** comprendo perfectamente; **I don''t quite understand it** no acabo de entenderlo; **quite frankly ...** para ser totalmente sincero ...; **he has not quite recovered yet** no se ha repuesto todavía del todo

quote *(noun: question)* **to quote my boss ...** para citar a mi jefe ...; como decía mi jefe...; **you can quote me** puedes decir que te lo he dicho yo; **don't quote me on that** no te lo puedo decir a ciencia cierta; **he is quoted as saying that ...** se le atribuye haber dicho que ...

R

rabbi *(noun)* rabina; rabino

race *(noun: anthropology)* raza; **the black race** la raza negra; **the white race** la raza blanca; **the human race** el género humano; **she is of mixed race** es mestiza; **he is of mixed race** es mestizo; *(of black and white)* es mulata; es mulato

racial discrimination discriminación racial

racial harassment hostilidad racial

racial pride orgullo de raza

racism *(noun)* racismo

racist *(noun)* racista

radiation therapy radioterapia; terapia de radiación

radiology *(noun)* radiología

rage *(noun: violent anger)* furia; cólera; **a fit of rage** un ataque de furia; **to be in a rage** estar furiosa; estar furioso; **to fly into a rage** ponerse hecho una furia

raid *(noun: across border)* incursión; *(on specific target)* asalto; *(by air)* ataque; *(by police)* redada; **a police raid** una redada policial; **a bank raid** un asalto a un banco; **the police raided the club** la policía hizo una redada en el club

Railroad Crossing *(traffic sign)* Cruce de Ferrocarril; Paso a Nivel

raise children criar niños

raise crops cultivar cosechas

raise objections *(law)* poner una objeción

ram *(verb: crash)* estrellar; **to ram into something** estrellararse contra algo; chocar contra algo; **he rammed his car into a tree** estrelló el coche contra un árbol

random bullet bala perdida; **a random bullet hit him on the side** una bala perdida lo alcanzó en el costado

ransack *(verb: house by police)* registrar de arriba abajo; **they ransacked the house for weapons** registraron la casa de arriba abajo buscando armas; *(by thieves)* saquear; **the place had been ransacked** el lugar había sido saqueado

ransom *(verb)* pagar un rescate por

ransom *(noun)* rescate; **to hold somebody for ransom** pedir un rescate por alguien

ransom demand petición de rescate; una nota exigiendo un rescate; una llamada exigiendo un rescate

rap sheet *(noun)* fichas policiales; antecedentes penales

rape *(noun)* violación; *(of a minor)* esturpo; **attempted rape** intento de violación; *(verb)* violar

rape shield law ley de protección a las víctimas de violación; leyes sobre violación que prohíben presentar como evidencia en un juicio la historia sexual de la víctima

rape trial proceso por violación

rape victim víctima de violación

rapist violador; violadora; **a convicted rapist** un violador convicto; una violadora convicta

rarely *(adv)* casi nunca; rara vez; pocas veces; raramente; **we rarely go out** rara vez salimos; pocas veces salimos; nunca salimos

rather *(in phrases)* **anything rather than that!**¡cualquier cosa menos eso!; **I'd rather not say** prefiero no decirlo; **it's rather a difficult task** es una tarea bastante difícil; **we're acquaintances rather than friends** somos conocidos, más que amigos

reach *(in phrases)* **beyond the reach of the law** fuera del alcance de la ley; **within reach of** al alcance de; **within my reach** a mi alcance; **within somebody's reach** al alcance de alguien; **within the reach of the**

average family al alcance de la familia media; **you can reach me at ...** puede ponerse en contacto conmigo a; **where can I reach you?** ¿dónde te puedo localizar? ¿dónde te puedo encontrar?; **to reach home** llegar a casa; **to reach a compromise** llegar a un compromiso

reach an agreement llegar a un acuerdo; **they reached an agreement** se pusieron de acuerdo

ready *(in phrases)* **to be ready** estar lista; estar listo; **I'll be ready in a minute** enseguida estoy lista; enseguida estoy listo; **your documents are ready and waiting** sus documentos están listos y a su disposición; **the lawyer is ready to see you** ya puede pasar a ver al abogado; **to be ready to** estar lista para; estar listo para; **are they ready to start** ¿están listos para empezar?; **to get ready** prepararse; **he is ready to do something** está listo para hacer algo; **she is ready for something** estar lista para algo; **ready for use** lista para usar; listo para usar; **ready when you are!** ¡cuando quieras!; **to be ready for anything** estar preparada para lo que sea; estar preparado para lo que sea; **ready cash** dinero en efectivo; **ready money** dinero en efectivo

real estate bienes raíces

real estate agency agencia de bienes raíces; agencia inmobiliaria

real estate agent agente de la propiedad inmobilaria; agente inmobilario

Real Estate Settlement Procedures Act (RESPA) Ley de Procedimientos de Liquidación de Bienes Raíces

release from custody dejar en libertad

realtor *(noun)* agente de la propiedad inmobilaria; agente inmobilario

rear *(noun)* parte trasera; parte de atrás; parte posterior

rear end choque trasero; colisión trasera; **he was involved in a rear end collision** estaba involucrado en un choque trasero; estaba involucrado en una colisión trasera

reason *(in phrases)* **we have reason to believe that ...** tenemos motivos para creer que ...; **he had every reason to be upset** estaba disgustado y con razón; **the reason for my going** la razón por la que me marcho; el motivo por el que me marcho; **for no reason** sin motivo; sin razón; **for personal reasons** por razones personales; por motivos personales; **for some reason** por la razón que sea; por el motivo que sea; **for this reason** por esta razón; por eso; **with good reason** con razón; **to listen to reason** atender a razones; **within reason** dentro de lo razonable; **it stands to reason** es lógico; **reasons for disagreement with the decision** razones por no estar de acuerdo con la decisión

reasonable razonable; **beyond reasonable doubt** sin que quede lugar a duda; **it must be proved beyond doubt** tiene que ser demostrado sin que quede lugar a duda; **it is reasonable to suppose that ...** es razonable suponer que ...; **reasonable grounds** motivos fundados; **within a reasonable time** dentro de un plazo de tiempo razonable; **be reasonable!** ¡sé razonable!

reasonable cause motivo fundado

reasonable charges cargos razonables

reasonable doubt duda razonable

rebellion *(noun)* sublevación

rebellious convicts convictas sublevadas; convictos sublevados

rebellious prisoners presas amotinadas; presos amotinados; presas sublevadas; presos sublevados

rebuttal *(noun)* refutación

recall *(noun: memory; remember)* memoria; *(verb)* recordar; **I have little recall of what happened** recuerdo muy vagamente lo que sucedió; **to have total recall** tener una memoria excelente; **I can still recall the day I met her** todavía recuerdo el día en que nos conocimos; **do you recall seeing this man before?** ¿recuerda haber visto antes a este hombre?; **I can't recall what he said** no puedo recordar lo que dijo; **I don't recall that we ever went there** no recuerdo que hayamos estado allí; **I can't quite recall whether ...** no recuerdo del todo si ...

receipt *(noun)* comprobante de pago; recibo; **to make out a receipt** extender un recibo

receiver *(law)* **official receiver** síndico de quiebras; **to call in the receiver** solicitar la suspensión de pagos; solicitar la cesación de pagos; entrar en liquidación

receivership *(law)* sindicatura; **to go into receivership** entrar en liquidación; **to be placed in receivership** ser declarado en suspensión

receiving stolen goods *(law)* tenencia de bienes hurtados

receiving stolen property *(law)* tenencia de bienes hurtados

recent *(adj)* reciente; última; último; **in the recent past** en los últimos tiempos; en un pasado reciente; **in recent years** en los últimos años; **a recent event** un suceso reciente

recently *(adj)* recientemente; hace poco; últimamente; **they've recently returned from abroad** han vuelto recientemente del extranjero; han vuelto del extranjero hace poco; **recently he's been much better** recientemente ha estado mejor; últimamente ha estado mucho mejor; **as recently as two days ago** hace apenas dos días; **I had never heard of him until recently** hasta hace poco ni siquiera había oído hablar de él

recess *(law)* **the court is in recess until tomorrow** el tribunal ha levantado la sesión hasta mañana

recipient reclamante, destinataria; destinatario

reckless *(adj: person)* temeraria; temerario

reckless driving conducción temeraria; imprudencia temeraria al conducir

reckless endangerment imprudencia temeraria; homicidio por imprudencia

reckless disregard indiferencia temeraria

reckless manslaughter homicidio por imprudencia

recollect *(verb: remember)* recordar; acordarse de; **I can recollect him vaguely** lo recuerdo vagamente; **I don't recollect seeing them there** no recuerdo haberlos visto allí; **as far as I can recollect** que yo recuerde

recollection recuerdo; **he has fond recollections of his childhood** tiene hermosos recuerdos de su infancia; **my recollection of the incident is quite different** según lo que yo recuerdo las cosas fueron muy distintas; **to the best of my recollection** si no me falla la memoria; **to the best of your recollection, he wasn't there?** ¿si la memoria no le falla, no estaba?

recommend *(verb)* recomendar; **would you recommend him for the job?** ¿lo recomendaría para el puesto?; **what do you recommend?** ×¿qué recomienda?; **it's not to be recommended** no es nada aconsejable; no es nada recomendable

recommendation *(law)* petición; **with a recommendation to serve 14 years** con una petición de catorce años de condena

recomputation *(noun)* volver a calcular

reconsideration reconsideración

reconstruct the crime reconstruir el delito; **they were able to reconstruct the crime** pudieron reconstruir el delito

reconstruction *(noun)* reconstrucción; reconstitución; **the police staged a reconstruction of the crime** la policía efectuó una reconstitución del delito

recontact contacto adicional

record *(noun)* documento; nota; apunte; registro; acta; historial; **let the record show that ...** que conste en acta que ...; **police records** fichas; **there is no record of it** no hay constancia de ello, no consta en ningún sitio; **for the record, I disagree** no estoy de acuerdo, que conste; **to keep a record of something** apuntar algo; tomar nota de algo; **it is a matter of public record that ...** hay constancia de que ...; **there is no similar example on record** no existe constancia de nada semejante; **the police had kept his name on record** la policía lo había fichado; **to be on record as saying that ...** haber declarado públicamente que ...; **to put something on record** hacer constar algo; dejar constancia de algo; **according to our records ...** según nuestros datos ...; **public records** archivos públicos; **he told me off the record** me lo dijo de forma confidencial; **set the record straight** que consten los hechos; **he has a clean record** no hay nada en su historial que le perjudique

record *(verb)* anotar; hacer constar; **it was recorded on his medical card** fue anotada en su ficha médica; quedó registrado en su ficha médica

record of a case *(law)* acta

recorded *(verb)* anotada; anotado registrada; registrado; grabada; grabado

recover recobrar; recuperar

recovery *(noun)* **recovery of long-standing debts** el cobro de deudas morosas; **sue for recovery of costs** *(law)* entablar juicio por daños y perjuicios

recoup recobrar; recuperar

recur recurrir; repetirse; presentarse de nuevo

recuse *(law)* recusar; inhibir; tachar

red *(noun & adj)* roja; rojo; colorada; colorado; **to have red hair** ser pelirroja; ser pelirrojo

red blood cells glóbulos rojos

red-haired *(adj)* pelirroja; pelirrojo

red-head *(adj)* pelirroja; pelirrojo

redneck (noun) **racist, usually poor and southern.** racista. sureño reaccionario de la clase baja rural; campesino blanco de los Estados del Sur

reduce reducir; disminuir

reduced benefits beneficios reducidos

reduced charge acusación de gravedad reducida

Reduced Speed Ahead *(traffic sign)* Reduzca la Velocidad Adelante

reentitlement readquirir derecho; recalificar; ser elegible de nuevo; tener derecho de nuevo

reentry permit permiso de reingreso

refer a dispute to arbitration remitir una disputa al arbitraje

refer for evaluation remitir a una evaluación; **refer somebody for evaluation** remitir a alguien a una evaluación

reference *(noun)* alusión; referencia; **I'll keep it for future reference** lo guardo por si hace falta consultarlo en el futuro; **I can't find any reference to him in the files** no encuentro nada que haga referencia a él en los archivos; **point of reference** punto de referencia; **can you provide references?** ¿puede facilitarnos referencias?

referral referencia; referida; referido

referral to an expert practitioner derivar a un profesional experto; derivar a una profesional experta

referred by referida por; referido por

reform reforma

reformatory *(noun)* reformatorio; *(for girls)* casa correccional; *(for young offenders)* institución

refrain from abstenerse de; **refrain from something** abstenerse de algo; **refrain from doing something** abstenerse de hacer algo

refuge *(noun)* refugio; albergue; amparo; **to seek refuge** buscar refugio; **to take refuge** ponerse al abrigo; refugiarse **to take refuge in something** refugiarse en algo

refugee *(noun)* refugiada; refugiado

refugee camp campamento para refugiados

refugee status estatus de refugiado; situación de rfugiado

refund form formulario de reembolso

refundable deposit depósito reembolsable

refusal *(noun: request, permission)* denegación; *(of offer)* rechazo; negativa; **a flat refusal** una negativa rotunda; **his refusal to cooperate with the police** su negativa a cooperar con la policía

refuse *(verb)* rechazar; no aceptar; rehusar

regain recuperar

regardless a pesar de; aunque; sin considerar; cueste lo que cueste; pase lo que pase

register *(noun)* lista; registro; censo; **the register of births, marriages and deaths** el registro civil; *(verb)* inscribir; matricularse; apuntarse

register of actions registro de acciones

register of births registros de nacimiento

registered letter carta certificada

registered name razón social

registered nurse enfermera titulada; enfermero titulado

registered sex offender delincuente sexual

registration *(noun)* inscripción; matrícula

registration fee cuota de inscripción; cuota de matrícula

regret *(noun)* pena; pesar; **my one regret is that I didn't see her before she died** lo único que siento es no haberla visto antes de que muriera; lo único que lamento es no haberla visto antes de que muriera; **I have no regrets** no me arrepiento de nada; **I say it with regret** lo digo con pesar; *(verb)* lamentar; arrepentarse; **we regret to inform you that ...** lamentamos tener que informarle que ...; **I regreted it as soon as I said it** me arrepentí en cuanto lo dije; **you'll regret this!** ¡te vas a arrepentir de esto!; **I regret not having kept in touch with them** lamento no haber mantenido el contacto con ellos; **it is to be regreted that ...** es lamentable que ...

regular services servicios regulares

regulation *(law)* regulación; reglamentación; reglamento

regulation *(noun: rule)* norma; regla; **safety regulations** normas de seguridad; **it's against the regulations** va contra las normas

rehabilitation *(verb: ex-prisoners, ex-addicts)* rehabilitar; reinsertar en la sociedad; *(disabled person)* rehabilitar

rehabilitation *(noun)* rehabilitación

rehabilitation expenses gastos de rehabilitación

reimburse *(verb)* reembolsar

reimbursement *(noun)* reembolso

reinstate *(verb)* reanudar; restablecer; reinstalar

reject *(law)* **the appeal was rejected** el recurso de apelación fue denegado; el recurso de apelación fue rechazado

reject *(verb)* rechazar; denegar; no aceptar; **to feel rejected** sentirse rechazada; sentirse rechazado

reject a contract rechazar un contrato

rejection *(noun)* rechazo; denegación; **to meet with rejection** ser rechazada; ser rechazado

relate *(verb: to bring into relation)* relatar; relacionar; relacionarse con; **to relate something to something** relacionar algo con algo; **to relate to** relacionarse con; tener que ver con; **he is unable to relate to other people** no es capaz de relacionarse con otras personas; **I can relate to that** yo eso lo entiendo; yo me identifico con eso; **relating to** relativo a; referente a; relacionado con

related *(adj)* relacionada; relacionado; *(of same family)* ser pariente; estar emparentada con; estar emparentado con; **to be related to** ser pariente de; **John and I are related** John y yo somos parientes; **this murder is not related to the other** este asesinato no está relacionado con el otro; **the two events are not related** los dos sucesos no guardan relación; **are you related to the prisoner?** ¿es usted pariente de la prisionera? ¿es usted pariente del prisionero?; **to be related to somebody by marriage** ser pariente político de alguien; **the two incidents are related** los dos incidentes están relacionados

related by marriage emparentada con, emparentado con; política; político, emparentada por afinidad; emparentado por afinidad; **be related to** ser pariente de; estar emparentada con; estar emparentado con

related charge delito conexo

related services servicios afines

related to relacionada con; relacionado con

relation *(noun: connection)* relación; *(relative)* pariente; **he's no relation of mine** no es pariente mío; no estamos emparentados; **what relation is she to you?** ¿qué parentesco tiene contigo?

relationship *(noun)* parentesco; relación; **to have a good relationship with somebody** llevarse bien con alguien; **we have a good working relationship** trabajamos bien juntos; tenemos una buena relación de trabajo

relative *(adj)* relativa; relativo; **it's all relative** todo es relativo; **he is a relative newcomer** es relativamente nuevo; **in relative terms** relativamente; **relative to** relativa a; relativo a; concerniente a

relative *(noun)* pariente familiar; pariente política; pariente político; **friends and relatives** amigos y familiares; **a close relative** un pariente cercano; una pariente cercana; **a distant relative** un pariente lejano; una pariente lejana

relavent evidence *(law)* prueba pertinente

release *(noun: prison, captivity)* liberación; puesta en libertad; **on his release from prison he ...** al salir de la cárcel ..

release *(verb: prisoner; hostage, captive)* poner en libertad; soltar; liberar; **to release somebody on bail** poner a alguien en libertad bajo fianza; **he was released on bail** lo pusieron en libertad bajo fianza; **she was released from jail** fue puesta en libertad; salió de la cárcel; fue excarcelada

release *(information)* divulgar; *(from hospital)* dar de alta

release on bail otorgarle a uno la libertad provisional bajo caución; otorgarle a uno la libertad provisional bajo fianza

release on one's own recognizance otorgarle a uno la libertad provisional bajo caución juratoria; libertad provisional bajo palabra

release to a third party otorgarle a uno la libertad provisional bajo caución personal

relevant *(adj)* pertinente; **that's not relevant to the case** eso no guarda relación con el caso

relevant authorities las autoridades competentes

relevant evidence *(law)* prueba pertinente

reliability *(noun)* confianza; **I doubt his reliability as a witness** como testigo no me inspira mucha confianza

reliable *(adj: information, source)* digna de confianza; digno de confianza; formal; fidedigna; fidedigno; solvente; **my memory is not too reliable these days** últimamente mi memoria no es muy de fiar; **she's very reliable** puedes confiar completamente en ella; es una persona muy formal; **I've always found him very reliable** siempre me ha parecido de mucha formalidad

reliable sources fuentes fidedignas

relief *(law: redress)* desagravio

relief *(in phrases)* **a sigh of relief** un suspiro de alivio; **a feeling of relief** una sensación de alivio; **that's a relief!** ¡qué alivio!; **to provide relief from something** aliviar algo; **to our great relief, she accepted** para gran alivio nuestro, aceptó; **it's a relief to get out of the office once in a while** es un alivio trabajar fuera de la oficina de vez en cuando; **disaster relief** auxilio a las víctimas de una catástrofe; **to be on relief** recibir prestaciones de la seguridad social

relocate *(verb)* mudarse; cambiarse

relocation allowance indemnización por desplazamiento

rely *(adj: trust, have confidence)* depender de algo; depender de alguien; contar con alguien; contar con algo; **to rely on something for something** depender de algo para algo; **to rely on somebody for something** depender de alguien para algo; **we are relying on you to do it** contamos con usted para hacerlo; **you can rely on him to be late** puedes tener por seguro que va a llegar tarde; **can I rely on you to behave?** ¿puedo confiar en que te vas a comportar?; **I wouldn't rely on him** yo no confiaría en él; yo no me fiaría de él; **can we rely on him to keep quiet** ¿podemos confiar en que no va a decir nada?; ¿podemos confiar en que no diga nada?; **never rely on him for help** nunca cuentes con que él te va a ayudar; **I was going to rely on you**

to lend me the money contaba con que tú me prestarías el dinero; **we are relying on you to do it** contamos con usted para hacerlo

remain *(noun)* **the right to remain silent** el derecho de quedarse callado; **the police must warn you that you have the right to remain silent and the right to see a lawyer** la policía tiene que decirle que usted tiene el derecho de quedarse callado y que tiene el derecho de hablar con un abogado

remain *(verbcontinue to be)* seguir; continuar; *(stay)* quedarse; permanecer; **they remained silent** permanecieron en silencio; guardararon silencio; **her condition remains critical** su estado sigue siendo crítico; su estado continúa en estado crítico; **these laws will remain in force** estas leyes continuarán en vigor; estas leyes permanecerán en vigor; **the best thing is to remain silent** lo mejor es quedarse callado; lo mejor es callarse; lo mejor es guardar silencio; **the crime remained unsolved** el delito no se llegó a resolver; el delito quedó sin resolver; **to remain seated** permanecer sentada; permanecer sentado; **please remain seated** por favor no se levanten; por favor permanezcan en sus asientos; **wait here until I call you** quedesé aquí hasta que lo llame; **how long do you intend to remain in the country?** ¿cuánto tiempo piensa quedarse en el país?; ¿cuánto tiempo piensa permanecer en el país?; **there are less than five minutes remaining** quedan menos de cinco minutos; **the fact remains that ...** el hecho es que ...; **what still remains to be done?** ¿qué falta hacer?¿qué queda por hacer?; **certain questions remain to be answered** hay ciertos puntos que hay que aclarar aún; **that remains to be seen** eso está por verse; **we remained there three weeks** nos quedamos allí tres semanas; **it will remain in my memory** se me quedará grabado en la memoria

remain silent quedarse callada; quedarse callado

remaining *(adj)* restante; que queda; que quedan; **the three remaining hostages** los tres rehenes restantes; los tres rehenes que quedan; **he is her only remaining relative** él es el único pariente que le queda; **the remaining prisoners** los otros presos; los demás presos

remand *(law)* **to be remanded on bail** quedar en libertad bajo fianza; **he was remanded in custody** se decretó su prisión preventiva; fue decretado su ingreso en prisión; *(to lower court)* **the case was remanded to a lower court** el caso fue remitido a un tribunal inferior

remark *(comment)* comentario; observación; **to make a remark** hacer un comentario; hacer una observación

remarriage *(instance)* nuevo casamiento; nuevo matrimonio; *(practice)* el volver a casarse

remarry *(verb)* volver a casarse

remedy *(law)* recurso; remedio; reparación

remember *(recall)* acordarse de; recordar; **don't you remember me?** ¿no te acuerdas de mí?; **he remembered me in his will** me dejó algo en su testamento; **she remembers the car coming towards her** se acuerda de cuando el coche se le vino encima; recuerda cuando el coche se le vino encima; **I can never remember phone numbers** tengo muy mala memoria para los números de teléfono; soy incapaz de recordar números de teléfono; **I remember seeing it** me acuerdo de haberlo visto; me acuerdo de que lo vi; **I seem to remember that ...** si mal no recuerdo ...; **remember that he carries a gun** recuerda que lleva una pistola; ten presente que lleva una pistola; **have you remembered your passport?** ¿te has acordado del pasaporte? ¿te has acordado de traer el pasaporte?; **I'll try to remember** intentaré acordarme; intentaré no olvidarme; **it is worth remembering that ...** vale la pena recordar que ...

remind *(verb)* recordarle a; hacerle recordar; **thank you for reminding me** gracias por recordármelo; **he needed no reminding** no hizo falta recordárselo; **don't remind me!** ¡no me hagas acordar!; **to remind somebody that ...** recordar a alguien que ...; **to remind somebody to do something** recordar a alguien que haga algo; **to remind somebody about something** recordar algo a alguien; **that reminds me!** ¡a propósito!; **she reminded him of his responsibilities** le recordó sus responsabilidades

remit *(law: transfer)* remitir; **to remit a case to the lower court** remitir un caso a un tribunal inferior; *(pardon, cancel)* reducir; **the judge remitted six months of his sentence** el juez le redujo la pena en seis meses; **three months of the sentence were remitted** se le redujo la pena en tres meses

remorse *(noun)* remordimiento; **without remorse** sin remordimientos; **to feel remorse** arrepentirse; **he was full of remorse** sentía un gran remordimiento; le remordía la conciencia; **the murderer was entirely without remorse** el asesino no sentía el menor remordimiento

removal of foreigners remoción de extranjeros

remuneration *(noun)* remuneración

renal failure insuficiencia renal; fallo del riñon

renal transplant trasplante del riñon

renewal commission comisión por renovación

rent *(noun)* alquiler; arrendamiento; arriendo; renta; **how much is their rent?** ¿cuánto pagan en alquiler?; ¿cuánto pagan en arrendamiento?; **we pay $900 in rent** pagamos novecientos dólares de alquiler; *(verb)* alquilar; rentar; arrendar; **to rent a house from somebody** alquilar una casa a alguien; arrendar una casa a alguien; rentar una casa a alguien; **to rent a house to somebody** alquilar una casa a alguien; arrendar una casa a alguien; rentar una casa a alguien; **to owe three months rent** deber tres meses de alquiler

rent contract acuerdo de alquiler; contrato de alquiler

rental income ingreso de rentas

renter arrendataria; arrendatario; inquilina; inquilino

renter's insurance seguro de alquiler

renting *(noun)* arrendamiento

renting an apartment alquilar un apartamento

repay *(money, loan)* devolver; reembolsar; **I have to repay him** tengo que devolverle el dinero; *(debt)* pagar; liquidar

repayment *(noun)* resarcimiento; recompensa; indemnización; *(act of repaying)* pago

repayment schedule plan de amortización

repeal *(law)* revocación; *(verb)* revocar

repeat offender delincuente habitual; delincuente reincidente

replace *(verb)* reemplazar

replacement rate porcentaje de reemplazo

reply *(noun)* respuesta; contestación; *(verb)* responder; contestar

report *(account)* informe; *(piece of news)* noticia *(in newspaper)* reportaje; crónica; **the latest reports indicate that ...** las últimas informaciones indican que ...; **medical report** parte médico

report *(to notify)* dar parte de; **to report something stolen** denunciar el robo de algo; dar parte del robo de algo; reportar el robo de algo; **to report somebody missing** dar parte de la desaparición de alguien

report of work activity informe de actividad de trabajo

report somebody missing dar parte de la desaparición de alguien

reporting events cobertura de acontecimientos, cobertura de eventos

repossess *(verb)* recuperar la posesión de

repossession *(noun)* recuperación de un artículo no pagado; recuperación de un inmueble no pagado

representative payee representante del beneficiaria; representante del beneficiario, tutor; tutora

representative of the law representante de la ley

reprieve *(noun)* indulto; conmutación; **to win a last-minute reprieve** ser indultado a última hora; **the building got a reprieve from being demolished** se retiró la orden de demoler el edificio; *(verb)* indultar; conmutar; **he refused to grant a reprieve** se negó a conmutar la pena; se negó a conceder el indulto

request *(noun)* solicitud; petición; pedido; **to make a request** hacer una petición; hacer una solicitud; hacer un pedido; presentar una petición; presentar una solicitud; presentar un pedido; **to refuse a request** denegar una solicitud; rechazar una solicitud; denegar una petición; rechazar una petición; **a request for help** una petición de socorro

request *(verb)* pedir; solicitar; **to request somebody to** + *infin* pedirle a alguien que + *subj*; **I requested them to leave** les pedí que se fueran; **to make a request for something** pedir algo; **a written request** una petición escrita

request for hearing petición de audiencia; petición de vista

request for reconsideration petición de reconsideración

Request for State Disability Insurance Claim Form Petición para formularios de Solicitud para Beneficios del Seguro Estatal de Incapacidad

request not timely filed petición fuera de tiempo

require *(verb)* requerir; necesitar; exigir; **the law requires that safety belts be worn** la ley exige el uso del cinturón de seguridad; **the law requires that you wear a helmet** la ley exige que lleve casco; **all I require now is your signature** todo lo que hace falta ahora es que usted firme; **to require somebody to do something** exigir que alguien haga algo; **as required by law** como exige la ley; según exige la ley

requirement *(noun)* requisito; necesidad; **to meet all the requirements for something** reunir todos los requisitos para algo; **it is one of the requirements of the contract** es una de las estipulaciones del contrato; **you must satisfy these requirements** debe llenar estos requisitos; debe satisfacer estos requisitos

resale *(noun)* retroventa; reventa; **not for resale** prohibida la venta; muestra gratis; **it has a low resale value** de segunda mano tiene poco valor; no se vende bien

resentencing *(verb)* nueva imposición de pena

Reserve Officer's Training Corps (ROTC) Cuerpo de Capacitación del Oficial de Reserva

reside *(verb)* residir; **to reside in** residir en

residence *(verb)* residencia; **to take up residence** fijar su residencia; establecerse; **after six months' residence** después de seis meses de permanencia

residence permit permiso de residencia

resident status estado legal de residente

Residential Care Facilities for the Elderly Asilos de Cuidado Residencial para Ancianos; Establecimientos de Vida Asistida

residents association asociación de vecinos

residual functional capacity capacidad funcional restante

Residual Functional Capacity Form Formulario de Capacidad Funcional Restante

resign *(from job, position)* dimitir; renunciar; presentar su dimisión; presentar su renuncia

resignation *(from job, position)* dimisión; renuncia; **to tender one's resignation** presentar su dimisión; presentar su denuncia

resisting arrest *(law)* resistencia a la autoridad

resolve *(law: dispute, charge, lawsuit)* dirimir; resolver; solucionar; **the case will be resolved without delay** la causa será dirimida sin demora

resort to force recurrir la fuerza

resource *(noun)* recurso; **human resources** recursos humanos; **valuable resource** valioso servicio; **the new center is a valuable resource for the community** el nuevo centro es un valioso recurso para la comunidad

resources for parents recursos para padres

respect *(verb: law)* respetar; acatar

respect *(noun)* respeto; consideración; **she has no respect for other people's feelings** no respeta los sentimientos de los demás; **out of respect for something** por respeto a algo; **out of respect for somebody** por respeto a alguien; **we have the greatest respect for him** le respetamos muchísimo; **show some respect!** ¡un poco de respeto!; **in other respects** por lo demás; **in some respects** en algunos aspectos; **in many respects** en muchos aspectos; **with respect to** en lo que respecta a; con respecto a; **in this respect** en cuanto a esto; en lo que a esto se refiere; **in all respects** desde todo punto de vista; en todo sentidorelevo de descanso al cuidador

respite care relevo de descanso a la cuidadora; relevo de descanso al cuidador

respondent *(law)* demandada; demandado; *(in an appeal)* apelada; apelado

responsibility *(noun)* responsabilidad; **that's her responsibility** eso es responsabilidad suya; **the child is my responsibility** el niño está bajo mi responsabilidad; **he's willing to take on more responsibility** está dispuesto a asumir más responsabilidades; **he denied all responsibility in the matter** negó toda responsabilidad en el asunto; **he has admitted responsibility for the tragedy** ha aceptado ser responsable de la tragedia; **the group which claimed responsibility for the attack** el grupo que reivindicó el atentado; **to have responsibility for something** ser responsable de algo

responsible *(adj)* responsable; **those responsible will be punished** se castigará a los responsables; **he is not responsible for his actions** no es responsable de sus actos; **who is responsible for this?** ¿quién es el responsable de esto?; **to hold somebody responsible for something** hacer a alguien responsable de algo, responsabilizar a alguien de algo; **she is responsible for forty children** tiene a su cargo cuarenta niños

rest a case terminar la presentación de pruebas; concluir la presentación de pruebas

rest home casa de reposo

restitution *(law)* restitución

restrain *(verb: prisoner)* contener

restraining order orden de interdicto; inhibitorio

restricted countries países restringidos

restricted function función restringida

restricted lane *(traffic sign)* carril restringido

resumption of payments reanudación de pagos

retain counsel contratar abogada; contratar abogado

retained counsel abogada contratada; abogado contratado

retainer fee *(law)* pago anticipado de honorarios de abogado

retarded *(adj)* retardada; retardado

retire *(verb)* jubilarse; retirarse

retired *(adj)* jubilada; jubilado; retirada; retirado

retired person pensionista

retirement *(law)* jubilación; retiro

Retirement Earnings Test límite anual de ganancias; **the Retirement Earnings Test has been eliminated for individuals between the ages of 65 and 69** el límite anual de ganancias ha sido eliminada para individuos entre los sesenta y cinco y los sesenta y nueve años

retirement insurance seguro de retiro; seguro de jubilación

retirement pension pensión de jubilación; pensión de retiro

retirement planner planificador de beneficios

retrial *(law)* nuevo juicio; revisión de la causa; nuevo proceso

retroactive *(law)* retroactiva; retroactivo

retroactivity *(noun)* retroactividad

return a verdict *(law)* declarar; emitir un veredicto; **the jury returned a verdict of guilty** el jurado emitió un veredicto de culpabilidad; el jurado lo declaró culpable

return an indictment *(law)* formular documento inculpatorio

reunite *(make united again, family, party)* volver a unir; *(be, come together again)* reencontrarse con; **she was reunited with him after many years** se reencontró con él después de muchos años

revaluation of assets revaluación de bienes

reversal *(noun)* revocación; **we appealed for a reversal of the decision** apelamos para que se revocara la decisión

reverse discrimination *giving unfair treatment to the group which traditionally is the group which gives unfair treatment to others.* discriminación dirigida a un grupo de ciudadanos con el objeto de remediar un patrón discriminatorio sufrido por otro grupo

review *(noun: book, film)* crítica; reseña; *(report, summary)* resumen; reseña; *(reconsideration)* revisión; **salary review** revisión salarial; **salary under review** el sueldo está en estudio; **his salary comes up for review next month** el mes que viene le toca la revisión salarial

review *(verb: situation, prospects)* examinar; estudiar; *(policy, case)* reconsiderar; reexaminar; reajustar

review of complaints revisión de quejas

revolt *(noun)* sublevación

rib *(anat)* costilla

right *(law)* derecho

right *(in phrases)* **you made the right choice** elegiste bien; **you made the right decision by not telling her** hiciste bien en no decírselo; **are you sure this is the right house?** ¿estás segura de que es la casa?;¿estás seguro de que es la casa? **to be right** tener razón; **you were right when you said that ...** tenías razón cuando decías que ...; **to do what is right** hacer lo correcto; actuar correctamente; **to do the right thing by somebody** portarse como es debido con alguien; **he's the right man for the job** es el hombre más indicado para el cargo; **I don't think he's the right sort of person for you** me parece que no es la persona que te conviene; **to get something right** acertar en algo; hacer algo bien; **are you sure you've got the right number?** ¿segura que es ése el número?; ¿seguro que es ése el número?

right not to talk to the police derecho de no hablar con la policía

right of appeal derecho de apelación

right of assembly derecho de reunión

right of asylum derecho de asilo

right of representation derecho de representación

right to a fair trial derecho a un juicio justo

right to a hearing derecho a una audiencia; derecho a una vista

right to a speedy trial derecho a un juicio sin demora

right to a trial derecho a un juicio

right to choose derecho a elegir

right to counsel derecho a tener un abogado; derecho a tener una abogada

right to freedom of expression derecho a la libertad de expresión

right to legal aid derecho a la asistencia letrada

right to legal assistance derecho a la asistencia letrada

right to privacy derecho a la intimidad

right to remain silent derecho a mantenerse callada; derecho a mantenerse callado; derecho de no decir nada

right to speak to a lawyer derecho a hablar con un abogado; derecho a hablar con una abogada

right to talk to a lawyer before talking to the police derecho de hablar con un abogado antes de hablar con la policía

right turn lane carril de viraje a la derecha

rightful owner derechohabiente

riot *(noun)* disturbio; desorden; motín; **there were riots in the streets** hubo disturbios callejeras; hubo desórdenes callejeras; *(verb)* causar disturbio; causar desórdenes; amotinarse

riot control agent agente de control de motines

risk *(noun)* riesgo; **the benefits outweigh the risks** los beneficios superan los riesgos; **the risks are too great** hay demasiados riesgos; **the risks involved are enormous** los riesgos que implica son enormes; **there's an element of risk in any investment** toda inversión implica un cierto riesgo; **at the risk of ...** a riesgo de ... + *infin*; **it's not worth the risk**

no merece la pena correr el riesgo; **a health risk** un peligro para la salud; **a security risk** un peligro para la seguridad; **at the risk of seeming stupid** a riesgo de parecer estúpido; **at one's own risk** por su cuenta y riesgo; bajo su propia responsabilidad; **I can't take the risk** no me puedo exponer a eso; no me puedo arriesgar a eso; no puedo correr ese riesgo; **that's a risk you'll have to take** ése es un riesgo que vas a tener que correr

risk of assessment evaluación del riesgo

risk of flight riesgo de fuga

road *(noun)* carretera; camino; **a dirt road** una camino sin pavimiento; **he shouldn't be on the road** no debería conducir; no debería manejar

road accident accidente de tránsito; accidente de tráfico; accidente de circulación

road sign señal de tráfico; señal vial; señal de tránsito

road signs, signals and bearings signos, señales y marcaciones de la calzada

roadblock *(noun)* control de carretera

roadhog *(noun)* loca de volante; loco de volante·

rob *(verb)* robar; robarle; asaltar; atracar; **I've been robbed!** ¡me han robado!; **to rob somebody of something** robar algo a alguien; **she was robbed of all her savings** le robaron todos los ahorros

robber *(noun)* ladrón; ladrona; atracador; atracadora; asaltante

robbery *(noun)* robo; asalto

robbery with violence robo con fuerza; robo con violencia; robo a mano armada

room *(noun)* cuarto; sala; **furnished room** cuarto amurblado

room and board alojamiento y comida; cuarto y comida

roominghouse casa de huéspedes; pensión

roommate *(noun)* compañera de cuarto; compañero de cuarto

root canal tratamiento de canal dental

rough *(verb: treatment)* brutal

rough up *(adj: treatment)* **to rough somebody up** dar una paliza a alguien

rowdy *(adj)* escandalosa; escandaloso

royalties *(noun)* regalías; derechos de autor; derechos de inventor; derechos de patente

rubber bullets pelotas de goma

rude *(adj)* grosera; grosero; descortés; **to be rude to somebody** ser grosera con alguien; ser grosero con alguien; **don't be so rude!** ¡no seas tan descortés!

rudely *(adv)* groseramente

rule *(law)* dictar fallo; fallar; **the court is expected to rule on the case this week** se espera que el tribunal falle esta semana; **the rule of law** el imperio de la ley

rule *(in phrases)* **as a general rule** por regla general; en general; normalmente; **to break the rules** infringir las reglas; infringir las normas; infringir el reglamento; **he makes it a rule to get up early** tiene por norma levantarse temprano; **to play by the rules** obedecer las reglas; obedecer las normas; **a rule of thumb** en general

rules of criminal procedure *(law)* ley de enjuiciamiento criminal

rules of evidence *(law)* normas que controlan el tipo de evidencia que puede ser admitida ante un tribunal

rules of law *(law)* imperio de la ley

ruling *(law)* auto; fallo; providencia; resolución; sentencia; **make a ruling that** fallar que; resolver que; **in today's ruling** en el fallo de hoy; **this ruling allows us to** este fallo nos permite

run a red light pasarse un semáforo en rojo

run a stop sign pasarse un señal de alto; pasarse un señal de parada; pasarse un señal de pare

run a traffic light pasarse un semáforo en rojo

run away *(prisoner)* huir; escaparse; fugarse; **to run away from one's responsibilities** evadir sus responsabilidades; **you can't run away from your responsibility** no puedes evadirte de tus responsabilidad; **she ran away from school** se escapó de la escuela

run away from home huir de casa; irse de casa

run into *(car, driver)* embestir; chocar con; **a truck ran into the car** el coche fue embestido por un camión; *(meet by chance)* encontrarse; toparse con; *(a problem, opposition)* toparse con; tropezar con

run over atropellar; **she was run over by a car** la atropelló un coche

rural health clinics clínicas rurales de salud

rural road camino vecinal

S

safe *(in phrases)* segura; seguro; **to feel safe** sentirse segura; sentirse seguro; **to be safe from** estar a salvo de; **to keep something safe** guardar algo en lugar seguro; **keep these documents safe** guarda estos documentos en un lugar seguro; **I'll keep it safe for you** yo te lo guardo; **the secret is safe with me** guardaré el secreto; **safe and sound** sano y salvo; **they were found safe and sound** los encontraron sanos y salvo; **it's not safe to go out after dark** es peligroso salir de noche; **to be a safe driver** conducir con prudencia; conducir con cuidado; **keep your alcohol consumption within safe limits** mantén tu consumo de alcohol dentro de los límites de seguridad; **just to be on the safe side** para mayor seguridad; por si acaso; **the safest thing is to ...** lo más seguro es + *infin*; **to be in safe hands** estar a salvo; estar en buenas manos; **safe journey!** ¡buen viaje!; **to play it safe** ir a lo seguro; no arriesgarse; **safe sex** sexo seguro; sexo sin riesgo; **you are not safe here** corres peligro aquí

safeguards to protect salvaguardias para garantizar

safety measure medida de seguridad

safety of food and medicines seguridad de alimentos y medicamentos

safety regulations normas de seguridad

safety standards condiciones de seguridad

salaried employment empleo asalariado

salary salario; sueldo; paga

sale *(noun)* venta

sales manager jefa de ventas; jefe de ventas

sales rep agente comercial

same *(in phrases)* misma; mismo; **they live at the same address** viven en la misma dirección; **don't make the same mistake again** no vuelvas a cometer el mismo error; **she's not the same person** ya no es la misma; **he's not the same person** ya no es el mismo; **this place won't be the same without you** esto no va a ser lo mismo sin ti; **he will never be the same again** nunca volverá a ser el mismo; **for the same reason** por la misma razón; **if it's all the same to you** si a ti te da igual; **one and the same person** la misma persona; **it comes to the same thing** viene a ser lo mismo; **at the same time** al mismo tiempo; a la vez; **no, but thanks all the same** no, pero de todas formas, gracias; **the same goes for you** eso también va por ti; **same here!** ¡yo también!; **she always comes out with the same excuses** siempre sale con las mismas excusas; **is he the same one you were telling me about?** ¿es el mismo de quien me hablabas?; **the same thing happened to me** a mí me pasó lo mismo; **it all amounts to the same thing** todo viene a ser lo mismo; **same time, same place** a la misma hora en el mismo sitio; **I feel the same way about you** siento lo mismo por ti; **the same** lo mismo; **the same goes for you** también va por ti; **at the same time** al mismo tiempo; **in the same way** de la misma manera

sample *(noun)* muestra; **a blood sample** una muestra de sangre; **a urine sample** una muestra de orina; **to take a sample** tomar una muestra; **we looked at a few sample cases** estudiamos algunos ejemplos; **we took a random sample** hicimos un muestreo aleatorio; **sample question** pregunta tipo

savings account cuenta de ahorros

savings bank caja de ahorros

savings deposit caja de ahorros

say *(in phrases)* decir; **to say good morning to somebody** decirle los buenos días a alguien; **I said yes** dije sí; **I said no** dije no; **he said yes to my proposal** aceptó mi propuesta; **he said no to my proposal** rechazó mi propuesta; **to say something to somebody** decirle algo a alguien; **what exactly did she say to you?** ¿qué te dijo exactamente?; **I can't say when they'll be back** no sé cuando volverán; **to have one's say** dar su opinión; **to have a say in the matter** tener voz y voto en al asunto; **to have no say in the matter** no tener ni voz ni voto en el asunto; **let him have his say!** ¡que hable él!; **let her have her say!** ¡que hable ella!; **shall we say Tuesday?** ¿quedamos en el martes?; **let's say for instance that ...** supongamos por ejemplo que; **that goes without saying** eso cae de su peso; **it goes without saying that ...** ni que decir tiene que ...; huelga decir que ...; **no sooner said than done** dicho y hecho; **would you really say so?** ¿lo crees de veras?; **there's no saying what he'll do** quién sabe lo que hará; **when all is said and done** al fin y al cabo; a fin de cuentas; **the rules say that ...** según las reglas ...; en las reglas pone ...; **my watch says three o'clock** mi reloj marca las tres; **I'd rather not say** prefiero no decirlo; **you were saying?** ¿qué decías?; **I have no say in the matter** no tengo ni voz ni voto en el asunto; **they want a say in the decision making** quieren participar en la toma de decisiones

scar *(on skin from cut, burn, operation)* cicatriz; *(from smallpox, vaccination)* marca; señal; **the scars left by an unhappy childhood** las cicatrices que deja una infancia infeliz; la marca que deja una infancia infeliz; **his face was badly scarred** tenía la cara cubierta de cicatrices

scarce *(adj & adv)* escasa; escaso; apenas

scene *(noun)* escenario; escena; **the scene of the crime** la escena del crimen; el lugar del crimen; el lugar del suceso; **the police were on the scene within minutes** la policía llegó al lugar de los hechos en pocos minutos; **the police were soon on the scene** la policía no tardó en acudir al lugar de los hechos; **at the scene of the crime** en el escenario del crimen; **to make a scene** hacer una escena; montar un número

scent *(trail)* rastro; pista; **the dogs soon picked up the scent** los perros pronto encontraron el rastro; **the police admitted that they had lost the scent** la policía admitió que habían perdido el rostro; la policía admitió que habían perdido la pista; **to pick up the scent** seguir la pista; **to lose the scent** perder la pista

scene of the crime la escena del crimen; el lugar del suceso

schedule *(verb)* programar; poner en una lista; establecer el horario de; fijar la hora de

schedule *(noun)* programa; calendario; **the day's schedule** el programa del día; el calendario del día; **we are falling behind schedule** nos estamos atrasando con respecto al programa; nos estamos atrasando con respecto al calendario; **the work is on schedule** llevamos el trabajo al día; **the work is ahead of schedule** llevamos el trabajo adelantado; **we finished ahead of schedule** terminamos antes del plazo establecido en el programa; **we are working on a very tight schedule** tenemos un programa de trabajo muy apretado; tenemos un calendario de trabajo muy apretado; **I was running one hour behind schedule** llevaba una hora de retraso con respecto a mi agenda; **as scheduled** según lo previsto; de acuerdo con lo previsto; **you are scheduled to speak for 20 minutes** según el programa hablarás durante veinte minutos; **at the scheduled time** a la hora prevista

schedule a deposition fijar la hora de una deposición

schedule in calculating child support lista para calcular los costos de la manutención de un menor

schedule of charges *(law)* pliego de cargos

schizophrenic *(adj)* esquizofrénica; esquizofrénico

scholarship *(noun: subsidy)* beca

school *(noun: subsidy)* escuela: **to go to school** ir a la escuela; ir al colegio; **he teaches school** es maestro; **children of school age** niños en edad escolar; **to miss school** faltar a la escuela **I missed school yesterday** ayer falté a la clase; ayer falté al colegio

school attendance asistencia escolar

School Crossing *(traffic sign)* Cruce Escolar

school culture cultura escolar

school district distrito escolar

school friend amiga del colegio; amigo del colegio

school record libro de escolaridad

school year año escolar

School Zone *(traffic sign)* Zona Escolar

scope of the law alcance de la ley

scratch *(noun: injury)* rasguño; arañazo; **it's just a scratch** no es más que un rasguño; **he escaped without a scratch** resultó ileso; salió sin un rasguño

scratch mark rasguño

seal the records sellar el expediente

sealed document pliego

sealed letter pliego

sealed orders órdenes secretas

sealed records expedientes sellados

search *(inspection of a place)* allanamiento; registro; registrar; **the police made a thorough search of the premises** la policía registró todo el local; **they made a search of the building** registraron el edificio

search *(in phrases)* **they searched the woods for the missing child** registraron el bosque en busca de la niña desaparecida; registraron el bosque en busca del niño desaparecido; **the search for the child continues** continúa la búsqueda de la niña; continúa la búsqueda del niño; **we went in search of a policeman** fuimos a buscar un policía; **in search of** en busca de; **rescuers searched through the rubble for survivors** los del equipo de rescate buscaron supervivientes entre los escombros; **to search one's memory** hacer memoria; **they are searching for a way to ...** están buscando la manera de ...; **they searched him for drugs** lo cachearon para ver si tenía drogas; **we searched everywhere** buscamos en todas partes

search and seizure registro e incautación

search party pelotón de búsqueda; pelotón de salvamento; partida de rescate

search warrant mandato judicial; orden de registro

seat *(noun: place to sit)* asiento; **please have a seat** tome asiento, por favor; **please take a seat** siéntese, por favor; **are there any seats left?** ¿quedan plazas?; **to take one's seat** sentarse; tomar asiento; **keep a seat for me** guárdame un lugar; guárdame un asiento; *(verb)* sentar; sentarse; **please be seated** tomen asiento, por favor; **to remain seated** permanecer sentada; permanecer sentado; permanecer sentados

seat belt cinturón de seguridad

second *(in phrases)* segunda; segundo; **second child** segundón; segundona; **her second husband** su segundo marido; **every second Tuesday** cada dos martes; **every second week** cada dos semanas; **give somebody a second chance** darle a alguien otra oportunidad; **for the second time** por segunda vez; **you won't get a second chance** no tendrás otra oportunidad; **to ask for a second opinion** pedir una segunda opinión; **on second thought** pensándolo bien; **on his second birthday** en su segundo cumpleaños; cuando cumpla dos años; **they have a second home in Santa Fe** tienen otra casa en Santa Fe; en Santa Fe tienen una segunda vivienda; **he arrives on May fourteenth**; llega el catorce de mayo; **he arrives on the fourteenth of May** llega el catorce de mayo; **just a second!** ¡un momento!; ¡momentito!; **in a split second** en un instante; en un abrir y cerrar de ojos

second cousin prima segunda; primo segundo

second degree murder homicidio en segundo grado; asesinato en segundo grado

second generation segunda generación

second house segunda vivienda

second language segundo idioma; segunda lengua

second mortgage segunda hipoteca

second name apellido

second opinion segunda opinión

second year of high school el segundo año de la escuela secundaria

secondary education enseñanza secundaria

secondary evidence evidencia secundaria; prueba secundaria

secondhand car coche de ocasión

secret service agent agente del servicio secreto

secure *(verb: obtain)* conseguir; obtener; **to secure somebody's release** conseguir la libertad de alguien; **a secured loan** un préstamo con garantía; **to be financially secure** tener seguridad económica; **secure in the knowledge that** segura de que; seguro de que; confiada de que; confiado de que; **with that evidence they were able to secure a conviction** con esas pruebas lograron que se la condenara; con esas pruebas lograron que se lo condenara; **negotiations to secure their release are underway** se han iniciado negociaciones para lograr su liberación

secure *(adj: safe)* segura; seguro; *(home, childhood, relationship)* estable

secured bail bond caución real

secured creditor acreedor garantizado; acreedora garantizada; acreedor asegurado; acreedora asegurada

secured loan préstamo con garantía

security *(noun)* seguridad; **financial security** seguridad económica; **a security lapse** una falla en el sistema de seguridad; un fallo en el sistema de seguridad; un descuido en el sistema de seguridad; **a security breach** una infracción de las normas de seguridad; **job security** seguridad profesional

security agreement contrato de garantía

security check control de seguridad

security deposit depósito de seguridad; depósito de garantía

security guard guarda jurada; guarda jurado

security risk riesgo para la seguridad

security system sistema de seguridad

sedan *(car)* sedán

see *(in phrases)* ver; **I can't see a thing!** ¡no veo nada!; **we haven't seen her for a while** hace un tiempo que no la vemos; **I didn't see her arrive** no la vi llegar; **we'll be sorry to see her go** nos va a dar pena que se vaya; **he saw the accident** prensenció el accidente; fue testigo del accidente; **as you can see** como ves; **see for yourself** compruébalo tú mismo; **I'll go and see** voy a ver; **I see nothing wrong in it** no le encuentro nada malo; **we'll see** ya veremos; vamos a ver; **I want to see you about ...** quiero hablar con usted acerca de ...; **what did he want to see you about?** ¿qué asunto quería discutir contigo?; **to see the doctor** ir a ver al médico; consultar al médico; **I see from your application form that ...** he leído en su solicitud que ...; **to go and see somebody** ir a ver a alguien; **we don't see much of them nowadays** ahora les vemos bastante poco; **see you on Sunday!** ¡hasta el domingo!; **see you tomorrow!** ¡hasta mañana!; **see you later!** ¡hasta luego!; **see you soon!** ¡hasta pronto!; **I see** ya entiendo; **this is how I see it** éste es mi modo de verlo; yo lo entiendo así; **I saw only too clearly that ...** percibí claramente que ...; **as far as I can see** por lo que yo veo; **the way I see it** a mi parecer; **we'll have to wait and see** habrá que esperar y ver; **that remains to be seen** eso está por verse; **see that you're there on time** no vayas a llegar tarde; **I'm seeing him on Friday** lo voy a ver el viernes; **when can I see you again?** ¿cuándo nos podemos volver a ver?; **I want to see the manager** quisiera ver al gerente; quisiera hablar con el gerente; **I went to see her about the loan** fui a hablar con ella por lo del préstamo

seeing-eye dog perro guía

seek *(verb)* buscar; pedir; solicitar; tratar de encontrar; **to seek the advice of a specialist** asesorarse con un especialista; consultar a un especialista

seek a preliminary injunction against solicitar un mandamiento judicial preliminar contra

seem *(in phrases)* parecer; **she seems friendly** parece simpática; **you don't seem very sure** no pareces muy segura; no pareces muy seguro; **you don't seem very happy** no pareces muy contenta; no pareces muy contento; **things aren't always what they seem** las apariencias engañan; **he seemed to be in difficulty** parecía tener dificultades; **what seems to be the trouble?** ¿qué pasa?; **I seem to have heard that before** me parece que ya me contaron eso antes; **that seems like a good idea** parece una buena idea; **it seems to me that ...** me parece que ...; **it seems to him that ...** le parece que ...; **how did he seem to you?** ¿qué te pareció?; **it now seems certain that ...** ahora parece seguro que ...

seizure *(law)* incautación; **the judge ordered the seizure of his assets** el juez ordenó la incautación de sus bienes; **to lift a seizure order** levantat un embargo

seizure *(medical)* convulsión

selection *(noun)* selección; elección

self-addressed *(adj)* con el nombre y la dirección del remitente; sobre con su nombre y dirección; **send a self-addressed envelope to** envíe un sobre con su nombre y dirección a

self-assured *(adj)* segura de sí misma; seguro de sí mismo

self-confident *(adj)* segura de sí misma; seguro de sí mismo; llena de confianza en sí misma; lleno de confianza en sí mismo

self-composed *(adj)* serena; sereno; compuesta; compuesto

self-defense *(law)* autodefensa; defensa propia; **she killed him in self-defense** lo mató en defensa propia; **to act in self-defense** obrar en defensa propia

self-dialysis *(noun)* autodiálisis

self-doubt duda de sí misma; duda de sí mismo

self-employment *(noun)* negocio propio; trabajo por cuenta propia; trabajo autónomo

self-employment earnings ganancias de negocio propio; ganancias de trabajo por cuenta propia

self-employment income ingresos de negocio propio; ingresos de trabajo por cuenta propia

self-employment tax return declaración de impuesto de negocio propio; declaración de trabajo por cuenta propia

self-esteem autoestima; amor propio

self-incrimination autoincriminación

semester *(noun)* semester

Senate *(noun)* Senado

send *(verb: letter, package, greetings)* enviar; mandar; **to send something by mail** mandar por correo; enviar por correo

senior citizen persona de la tercera edad; persona mayor; persona de edad avanzada

sentence *(law)* pena; condena; **concurrent sentence** pena simultánea; **he's serving a life sentence** está cumpliendo una condena a cadena perpetua; **the death sentence** la pena de muerte; **the court gave her a two year sentence** el tribunal la sentenció a dos años de prisión; el tribunal la condenó a dos años de prisión; el tribunal le impusó una pena de dos años de prisión; **to pass sentence on somebody** dictar sentencia contra alguien; pronunciar sentencia contra alguien; **she is under sentence of death** la han condenado a la pena de muerte; **they have been sentenced to death** los han condenado a la pena de muerte; los han sentenciado a muerte; **a long sentence** una larga condena; **the judge gave him a six-month sentence** el juez le condenó a seis meses de prisión; **lighter sentence** sentencia más ligera; **the sentences will run concurrently** las condenas se cumplirán al mismo tiempo

sentencing *(law)* imposición de la pena

sentencing guidelines *(law)* pautas de sentencia; pautas de condena

sentencing hearing *(law)* actos de sentencia

separate *(adj)* separada; separado; distinta; distinto; **after the divorce, they went their separate ways** después del divorcio cada uno se fue por su lado

separate check cheques individuales; cheques por separado

separated *(adj)* separada; separado; **he is separated from his wife** está separado de su mujer; **she is separated from her husband** está separada de su marido

September *(noun)* septiembre *(see* **July** *for usage)*

sequester *(law: in contempt case)* embargar; *(property in litigation)* secuestrar

sequestration *(law: in contempt case)* embargo; *(property in litigation)* secuestro

serial killer asesina en serie; asesino en serie

serial number número de serie

seriously injured sufrir heridas de carácter grave

seriously wounded herida de gravedad; herido de gravedad

serve a sentence *(law)* cumplir una pena

service charge cargos por servicio

service centers centros de atención

services covered by Medicaid servicios de Medicaid

services for the elderly servicios a los ancianos

set date for trial fijar fecha para juicio

set free puesta en libertad; puesto en libertad

set of moral values escala de morales

setback *(noun)* revés; contratiempo; **our defense has suffered a great setback** nuestra defensa ha sufrido un gran revés

settle *(law)* dirimir; resolver; solucionar; **to settle out of court** resolver una disputa extrajudicialmente; llegar a un acuerdo extrajudicial; **to settle a case out of court** llegar a un acuerdo sin recurrir al juicio; **to settle a claim out of court** llegar a un acuerdo sin recurrir al juicio; **the terms were settled by negotiations** se acordaron las condiciones mediante una negociación

settle *(in phrases)* **so that's settled then** así que ya está decidido; **the couple have settled their differences** la pareja ha resuelto sus diferencias

settle monetary disputes resolver conflictos monetarios

settlement finiquito; *(agreement)* acuerdo; convenio; **prompt settlement appreciated** se agradece la prontitud en el pago; **to reach a settlement** llegar a un acuerdo; llegar a un convenio; **legal settlement** acuerdo legal; **wage settlement** convenio laboral; acuerdo salarial

settlement out of court resolución extrajudicial; transacción extrajudicial

severance pay indemnización por despido; indemnización por cese; sueldo de despido; cesantía

severe condition condición grave; condición severa

severely disturbed child niña con graves trastornos emocionales; niño con graves trastornos emocionales

severely injured herida de gravedad; herido de gravedad; gravemente herida; gravemente herido

severity of impairments gravedad de impedimentos

sex *(sexual matters)* sexo; de sexo; *(gender)* sexo; **to have sex with somebody** tener relaciones con alguien; acostarse con alguien; **the opposite sex** sexo opuesto

sex crime delito sexual; crimen sexual

sex discrimination discriminación sexual

sexual abuse abuso deshonesto

sexual assault agresión sexual

sexual battery acceso carnal violento

sexual discrimination discriminación sexual

sexual harassment acoso sexual

sexual misconduct with a minor agresión sexual de un menor

sexually *(adv)* sexualmente; **they were sexually involved** tuvieron relaciones sexuales; **they were never sexually involved** nunca tuvieron relaciones sexuales

shackle *(prisoner)* grillete; **the accused had shackles on his ankles** el acusado llevaba grilletes en los tobillos

sham marriage matrimonio de conveniencia para adquirir la nacionalidad

shared custody custodia compartida

sharp instrument used as a weapon arma blanca; **for wounding someone with a sharp instrument** por causar heridas con un arma blanca

shell *(for artillery)* proyectil; obús; *(for small arms)* cartucho

shelter for battered women refugio para mujeres maltratadas

shelter for the homeless refugio para las personas sin hogar; refugio para las personas sin techo; refugio para las personas que viven en las calles

sheltered workshop taller de trabajo protegido

shield law *law preventing revelation of sensitive information.* ley que establece que los periodistas no están obligados a revelar fuentes de información

shirt *(man's)* camisa; *(woman's)* camisa; blusa; **blue shirt** camisa azul

shirtsleeve *(noun)* manga de camisa; **in shirtsleeves** en mangas de camisa

shoe *(noun)* zapato; **a pair of shoes** un par de zapatos

shoplifting *(noun)* hurto en establecimiento comercial; hurto en las tiendas; *(colloquial)* ratería en las tiendas

shoot *(verb: person)* balear; pegarle un tiro a; pegarle un balazo a; **they shot him three times in the leg** le pegaron tres tiros en las piernas; **I've been shot!** ¡me han herido!; **she was shot in the arm** recibió un balazo en el brazo; **they shot him dead** lo mataron a tiros; lo mataron de un tiro; **to shoot oneself** pegarse un tiro; **his car was hit by bullets in the attack** le balearon el auto en el atentado; **he was shot dead** murió baleado; **those who had been shot were taken to the hospital** las personas baleadas fueron llevadas al hospital; **several people have been shot** hay various baleados; **several people have received gunshot wounds** hay various baleados

shoot out *(verb)* tiros; balacera; **the terrorists shot it out with the police** los terroristas y la policía se emprendieron a tiros; **shoot out between police and robbers** balacera entre policías y asaltantes

shoot out *(noun)* tiroteo; balacera; abaleo

shooting *(noun)* disparos; tiros; tiroteo; balacera; asesinato

short *(adj: height)* corta; corto; baja; bajo; *(inadequate)* escasa; escaso

short description breve descripción; **give a short description of the crime** dé una breve descripción del delito

shoulder *(anat)* hombro

show up *(verb)* aparecer; llegar

shut off the electricity cortar la electricidad

shut off the gas cortar el gas

shut off the water cortar el agua

shut the electricity off cortar la electricidad

shut the gas off cortar el gas

shut the water off cortar el agua

shut up! ¡a callar!

shut your mouth! ¡cállate la boca!

sick leave ausencia por enfermedad; permiso por enfermedad; baja por enfermedad

sick pay pago por enfermedad

sickness benefit subsidio de enfermedad

side road *(traffic sign)* vía lateral

sidebar consulta en el estrado *(reunión del juez con los abogados de ambas partes a su banco y fuera del oído del jurado)*

sideswipe *(verb: car)* raspar al lado; rozar

sign *(noun)* señal; indicio; **all the signs are that ...** todo parece indicar que ...; **to show signs of ...** dar muestras de ...; *(verb)* firmar; **to sign one's name** firmar; **a signed copy** un ejemplar firmado

sign a contract firmar un contrato

sign here, please firme aquí, por favor

signatory firmante; signatoria; signatorio; **the signatories to the agreement** los firmantes del acuerdo; los signatorios del acuerdo

signature *(noun)* firma; **to put one's signature to a letter** firmar una carta

signed and dated firmada y fechada; firmado y fechado

significant and unanimous ruling trascendental y unánime decisión

signs, signals, and bearings on the road signos, señales, y marcaciones de la calzada

silent partner socia capitalista; socio capitalista

simply *(noun)* sencillamente; simplemente; solamente

simply fill in the form no tiene más que llenar el formulario

since *(conj: in time)* desde; desde que; *(introducing a reason)* ya que; *(from then till now)* desde entonces

sincere *(adj)* sincera; sincero

single *(woman)* soltera; *(man)* soltero

single father padre soltera

single mother madre soltera

sister *(noun)* hermana; **brothers and sisters** hermanos; **older sister** hermana mayor; **younger sister** hermana menor

sister-in-law *(noun)* cuñada

sit down siéntese

ski mask pasamontañas; verdugo

skilled nurse enfermera especializada; enfermero especializado

skilled nursing enfermería especializada

skilled nursing facility institución de enfermería especializada

skilled worker obrera calificada; obrero calificado; obrera especializada; obrero especializado

skin *(anat)* piel

slander *(noun)* calumnia; difamación; injuria; **to sue somebody for slander** querellarse contra alguien por injuria; *(when criminal act has been alleged)* demandar a alguien por calumnia; **to spread slander about somebody** levantar calumnias contra alguien; **he sued her for slander** se querelló contra ella por injuria

slander *(verb)* calumniar; difamar; deshonrar

slanderous *(adj)* calumniosa; calumnioso; difamatoria; difamatorio

slanderous allegation injuria

sliding door puerta corredera; puerta corrediza

Slippery Road *(traffic signs)* Vía Resbalosa

Slow Moving Vehicles *(traffic signs)* Vehículos Lentos

small business pequeña empresa; pequeño negocio

Small Business Administration Administración de Pequeña Empresa *(agencia gubernamental en Estados Unidos que asiste a la pequeña empresa con préstamos, garantías y asistencia técnica)*

small claims court corte con juridicción sobre cargos pequeños; tribunal que conoce de causas de mínima cuantía

small minority minoría pequeña

smuggle *(tobacco, drugs)* contrabandear; pasar de contrabando; hacer de contrabando

smuggler *(tobacco, drugs)* contrabandista; **drug smuggler** traficante de drogas

smuggling *(tobacco, drugs)* contrabando

smuggling ring banda de narcotráfico; red de contrabando

sniffing glue inhalación de pegamento

sniper *(noun)* francotirador; francotiradora

so many tantas; tantos

social *(adj)* social; **to feel social** estar sociable

social climber arribista; trepador; trepadora

social drinker persona que sólo bebe cuando está con gente

social engagement compromisos sociales

social issues problemática social

social life vida social

Social Security benefits beneficios del Seguro Social

Social Security contributions contribuciones al Seguro Social

Social Security number número del seguro social

Social Security office oficina de Seguro Social

Social Security Statement Declaración de Seguro Social

social services servicios sociales

social skills don de gentes

social worker trabajador social; trabajadora social

social worker who makes home visits visitador social; visitadora social

sodomy *(law)* sodomía

soft drugs drogas blandas

sole proprietor empresaria única; empresario único

sole proprietorhip propiedad de una sola persona

solution *(noun)* solución; **to think of a solution** pensar en una solución; **to find a solution** encontrar una solución

some *(in phrases)* **would you like some tea?** ¿quieres té?; **some boys were shouting at him** unos chicos le estaban gritando; **some people say that ...** algunos dicen que ...; algunas personas dicen que ...; hay gente que dice que ...; **in some ways he's right** en cierto modo, tiene razón; en cierto sentido, tiene razón; **some day** algún día; **some day next week** algún día de la semana que viene; **for some reason** por alguna razón; **there must be some solution** alguna solución tiene que haber; **some man was asking for you** un hombre estuvo preguntando por ti; **this will give you some idea of ...** esto te dará una idea de ...; **let's make it some other time** hagámoslo otro día; **I haven't seen him for some time** hace bastante tiempo que no lo veo; **some day soon** un día de éstos

something *(adv, pron & noun)* algo; **do you want something to drink?** ¿quieres algo de beber?; **may I ask you something?** ¿puedo preguntarte algo?; **something else** otra cosa

something has happened to her algo le ha pasado

something important algo importante; **I have something important to tell you** tengo algo importante que decirte

son-in-law *(noun)* yerno

sound judgement buen criterio; **a person of sound judgement** persona de buen criterio

source *(noun)* fuente; **police sources** fuentes policiales; **reliable sources** fuentes fidedignas

source of income fuente de ingresos

Spanish *(adj & noun)* español; española

Spanish-speaking de habla española

speak privately hablar a solas; hablar en privado

special agent agente especial

special-delivery letter carta urgente

special education educación especial

Special Veteran's Benefits (SVB) Beneficios Especiales de Veteranos

Specified Low Income Medicare Beneficiary (SLMB) Beneficiario de Medicare con Ingreso Bajo Especificado

speech defect defecto en el habla

speech impediment defecto del habla

speech therapy terapia del habla

speed *(verb)* conducir a exceso de velocidad

speeding *(noun)* exceso de velocidad; *(driving)* conducir a exceso de velocidad

speeding ticket multa por exceso de velocidad; **to get a speeding ticket** ser multado por exceso de velocidad

speed limit *(traffic sign)* límite de velocidad

speedy trial *(law)* juicio sin demora

spinal column columna vertebral; espina dorsal

spleen *(law)* bazo

split sentence *(law)* pena mixta

sports jacket chaqueta americana

spouse *(noun)* cónyuge; consorte

spring primavera; **in the spring** en primavera; en la primavera

St Valentine's Day día de los enamorados

stab *(verb)* apuñalar; auchillar; **he had been stabbed to death** había muerto apuñalado; había muerto acuchillado; **she was stabbed repeatedly in the chest** fue acuchillada repetidamente el el pecho; **he was stabbed as he came out of the bar** lo acuchillaron al salir del bar

stab *(noun)* puñalada; cuchillada; navajazo

staff *(noun)* personal; empleados

stalk *(verb: a person)* acechar; seguir los pasos de

stalking *(noun: a person)* acecho furtivo a una persona

stand *(witness box)* estrado; **to take the stand** subir al estrado; subir al tribunal de los testigos; *(law: remain unchanged, valid)* seguir vigente; seguir en vigor; **the law still stands in 20 states** la ley aún sigue vigente en veinte estados; *(attitude)* postura; posición

stand *(noun: position)* postura; posición; **what is your stand on this issue?** ¿cuál es su postura en cuanto a este problema?; ¿cuál es su posición en cuanto a este problema; *(hold position)* **where do you stand on this issue?** ¿cuál es su posición en cuanto a este problema?

stand trial *(law)* someterse a juicio

standard of proof *(law)* criterio probatorio; nivel de prueba que se requiere en un caso para probar un hecho

start criminal proceedings against somebody *(law)* iniciar proceso penal contra alguien; iniciar enjuiciamiento contra alguien

state *(verb)* declarar; manifestar

state *(political; nation)* estado; *(health)* condición

state *(adj)* del estado; estatal

State Attorney General fiscal general del estado

state guidelines *(adj)* pautas estatales; directrices estatales

State Child Health Insurance Program (CHIP) Programa Estatal para la Salud Infantil

State Department Departamento de Estado

state-of-the-art lo más moderno; al día; lo último

state police policía estatal

state police officer oficial de la policía estatal

state prison prisión estatal; **humiliating treatment of women state prisoners in the New Mexico state prison** trato degradante a las mujeres presas en la prisión estatal de Nuevo México

state supplement suplemento estatal; suplemento del estado

statement *(noun)* declaración; manifestación; **official statement** comunicado oficial

statement of account estado de cuenta; extracto de cuenta

statement of earnings declaración de ganancias

statement under oath declaración bajo juramento

state's evidence *(law)* prueba de cargo

state's witness *(law)* testigo de cargo

status conference *(law)* consulta ante el juez

status of estado de

statute *(law)* ley; **by statute** por ley

statute book *(law)* código de leyes

statute law *(law)* derecho escrito; derecho positivo

statute of limitations *(law)* ley de prescripción; estatuo de limitaciones

statutory rape estupro *(relaciones sexuales con un menor)*

stay *(law)* suspensión; aplazamiento

stay *(in specific place, position)* quedarse; permanecer; *(remain, not leave)* quedarse

stay in contact with quedarse en contacto con; permanecer en contacto con

stay of execution *(law)* suspensión del cumplimiento de la sentencia; suspensión de ejecución

stay of proceedings *(law)* suspensión de procedimientos

steady worker trabajador estable; trabajadora estable, trabajador regular; trabajadora regular

steal *(law)* hurtar; robar; **to steal something from somebody** robar algo a alguien; **he stole it from school** lo robó del colegio; **he was convicted of stealing** lo condenaron por robo

Steep Hill *(traffic sign)* Pendiente en Bajada

stepbrother *(noun)* hermanastro

stepchild *(noun)* hijastra; hijastro

stepchildren *(noun)* hijastros

stepdaughter *(noun)* hijastra

stepfather *(noun)* padrastro

stepgrandchildren *(noun)* nietos políticos

stepmother *(noun)* madrastra

stepsister *(noun)* hermanastra

stepson *(noun)* hijastro

stipulate *(verb: law)* disponer; estipular; **the law stipulates that ...** la ley dispone que ...

stolen property bienes hurtados

stomach *(noun)* estómago

STOP *(traffic sign)* Alto; Pare

stop *(verb: person)* detener; parar; **we were stopped by the police** nos paró la policía; *(bring to an end)* detener; parar; suspender; acabar con; poner fin a; **the trial was stopped** se suspendió el juicio

stop and frisk detener y registrar a una persona sospechosa de estar armada

stopped by a police officer detenido por un agente policial

stopped by the police parada por la policía; parado por la policía; **we were stopped by the police** nos paró la policía

stop sign señal de pare; señal de parada; señal de alto; disco pare

stranger *(noun)* desconocida; desconocido; **a total stranger** un perfecto desconocido; una perfecta desconocida

stray bullet bala perdida; **a stray bullet hit him on the side** una bala perdida lo alcanzó en el costado

street *(noun)* calle; **city street** calle de la ciudad; calle urbana; **grow up on the streets** criarse en la calle; **the whole street** todos los vecinos; **the whole street turned out to welcome him** todos los vecinos salieron a recibirlo

street brawl reyerta callejera

street fight reyerta callejera

street number número de calle

strike *(verb: hit a person)* pegarle a; golpear; dar; pegar; **he struck the child on the face** le pegó al niño en la cara; **who struck the first blow?** ¿quién dio el primer golpe?; **to strike somebody a blow** darle un golpe a alguien; golpear a alguien; **he struck me a blow on the head** me dio un golpe en la cabeza

strike *(noun: by workers)* huelga; paro; **to be on strike** estar en huelga; **to go on strike** declarar la huelga

strike from the record tachar de las actas

strikebreaker *(noun: by substitute workers)* rompehuelgas; esquirol

striker *(noun: worker)* huelguista

stroke *(noun)* derrame cerebral

strong weapon for the prosecution arma poderosa para la acusación

stubble *(noun)* barba

Student Aid Report (SAR) Informe de Ayuda Estudiantil

Student Financial Aid (SFA) Ayuda Económica para Estudiantes

student loans préstamos para estudiantes; préstamos a estudiantes

stutter *(noun)* tartamudeo; **to have a slight stutter** tartatamudear un poco; *(verb)* tartamudear; **to speak with a stutter** tartamudear

subcontract *(verb)* subcontratar; **to sub contract work to other firms** subcontratar trabajo a otras empresas

sublease *(verb)* subalquiler; subarrendar

subpoena *(law)* citación; *(verb)* citar; **to serve a subpoena on somebody** notificar a alguien una orden de comparecencia

subsequent claim reclamación subsiguiente

subsidy *(noun)* subsidio; subvención

substantial earning ganancia sustancial

substantial evidence pruebas de peso

substantial gainful activity (SGA) trabajo sustancial y lucrativo

substantial services servicios sustanciales

subversive activities actividades subversivas

sue *(law)* demandar

sue for recovery of costs *(verb: law)* entablar juicio por daños y perjuicios

sue somebody for damages demandar a alguien por daños y perjuicios; poner pleito a alguien por daños y perjuicios

sufficient evidence pruebas suficientes

sufficient grounds for motivo suficiente de

suicide pact pacto suicida

suit *(law)* demanda; juicio; pleito

suit *(clothing)* traje; vestido

summary conviction condena sumaria

summary of the case resumen de la causa

summation *(noun)* alegatos de clausura; alegatos finales

summer *(noun: season)* verano; **in the summer** en verano; en el verano

summon *(law)* citar; emplazar

summons *(noun)* citación; citatorio; requerimiento judicial; **to issue a summons** despachar una citación; despachar un citatorio; **to serve a summons on somebody** entregarle una citación a alguien; entregarle un citatorio a alguien; citar a alguien ante el juicio

supervised release *(law)* libertad supervisada

supper *(noun)* cena; comida; **to have supper** cenar; comer; **what's for supper?** ¿qué hay de cena?

suppertime *(noun)* hora de cenar; hora de comer

supplemental income ingreso suplementario

supplemental income security payment pago de seguridad de ingreso suplementario

Supplemental Security Income (SSI) Seguridad de Ingreso Suplementario

supplier *(noun)* proveedor; proveedora

supplier of portable X-ray services abastecedor de servicios de rayos-X portátiles; abastecedora de servicios de rayos-X portátiles

supply *(noun)* suministro; *(verb)* surtir; proveer; abastecer; suministrar

support *(noun)* soporte; apoyo; respaldo; *(verb)* sostener; mantener; sustentar; respaldar

support payment pago de manutención

supportive devices aparatos ortopédicos

supress evidence excluir prueba

supression hearing audiencia de exclusión de prueba

surgeon *(noun)* cirujana; cirujano

surgery *(noun)* cirugía

surgical dressings vendajes; vendas

surgical ward sala de cirugía

surplus *(noun)* superávit

survive *(verb)* sobrevivir

surviving *(adj)* que quedan vivos; supérstite; sobreviviente; superviviente; *(of living person)* **his surviving relatives** los parientes que aún le quedan vivos; *(of dead person)* los parientes que lo sobrevivieron

surviving spouse cónyuge sobreviviente

survivor *(noun)* sobreviviente; superviviente

survivor's claim reclamación de sobreviente

suspect *(verb: law)* sospechar de; **whom do they suspect?** ¿de quién sospechan?; **to suspect somebody of something** sospechar a alguien de algo; **to suspect somebody of a crime** sospechar a alguien de haber cometido un crimen; **I suspect him of the murder** sospecho que es el asesinato; **I suspect him of the robbery** sospecho que es el ladrón; **we suspect him of lying** sospechamos que miente; **arson is not suspected** no existen sospechas de que el incendio haya sido provocado; **the suspected murderer** el presunto asesino; la presunta asesina

suspect *(noun: law)* sospechosa; sospechoso

suspended sentence *(law)* pena suspendida; pena de prisión que no se cumple a menos que el delincuente reincida

suspense files archivo de sueldos sin dueño

suspicion *(noun)* sospecha; **everybody is under suspicion** todos son sospechosos; **their behavior aroused the suspicions of the police** su conducta despertó las sospechas de la policía

sustain an objection aceptar una objeción; admitir una objeción

sustained *(law)* ha lugar a la protesta

swear *(law)* jurar; prestar juramento

swear an affidavit hacer una declaración jurada

swearing in toma de juramento

swearword *(noun)* palabrota; mala palabra

sweatshirt sudadera; camiseta gruesa

sweatshop fábrica donde se explota a los trabajadores

sweatsuit equipo de deportes; chándal; buzo

sweetheart *(noun)* novia; novio; enamorada; enamorado

sweethearts *(noun)* enamorados

swelling *(noun)* hinchazón; inflamación

swing voter votante indeciso

sworn statement declaración jurada; affidávit

sworn testimony testimonio jurado; affidávit; *(to give sworn testimony out of court)* deponer

T

tackle *(verb: come to grips with)* abordar; enfrentar; tratar de resolver; **they will have to tackle these problems** tendrán que abordar estos problemas; tendrán que enfrentar estos problemas

tainted juror jurado inficionado

tainted jury jurado inficionado

take *(in phrases)* **he took the case to the Court of Appeals** llevó el caso al Tribunal de Apelación; **I'll take you in the car** te llevo en el coche; **let**

me take your coat** permíteme tu abrigo; **it took him by surprise** lo cogió desprevenido; lo pilló desprevenido; **he took me home in his car** me llevó a casa en su coche; **he took it badly** le afectó mucho; **take it from me!** ¡escucha lo que te digo!; **you can take it from me that ...** puedes tener la seguridad de que ...; **it took three policemen to hold him down** se necesitaron tres policías para sujetarlo; **it takes a lot of courage** exige gran valor; **that will take some explaining** a ver cómo explicas eso; **it takes an hour to get there** se tarda una hora en llegar; **it will only take me five minutes** sólo tardo cinco minutos; **the job will take a week** el trabajo llevará una semana; **it won't take long** no tardaré mucho tiempo; **it takes time** lleva tiempo; **I take it that ...** supongo que ...; me imagino que ...; **I took him for a doctor** lo tenía por médico; creí que era médico; **what do you take me for?** ¿por quién me has tomado?; **I don't quite know how to take that** no sé muy bien cómo tomarme eso; **take Colleen, she never complains** por ejemplo Colleen, ella nunca se queja; **what's your take on ...?** ¿qué piensas de ...?

take a confession tomar una confesión

take a picture sacar una fotografía; tomar una fotografía

take an oath jurar; prestar juramento

take off *(verb)* **they took her off to prison** se la llevaron a la cárcel; **she's taking the morning off work** se ha tomado la mañana libre

take out *(verb)* sacar; **he took out a gun** sacó una pistola; **he took out a knife from his pocket** sacó una navaja del bolsillo

take out insurance contratar un seguro; hacerse un seguro

take place *(verb)* tener lugar

take the Fifth acogerse a la Quinta Enmienda *(para no prestar testimonio)*

tamper with *(law)* sobornar

tampering with evidence *(law)* manipulación de evidencia

tangible evidence *(law)* prueba real

tax assessment tasación para impuesto

tax base base de impuesto

tax bracket banda impositiva

tax burden carga fiscal

tax evasion evasión fiscal; evasión de impuestos

tax exempt exento de impuestos; no gravable

tax forms formularios de impuestos

tax fraud fraude fiscal

tax free libre de impuestos

tax law derecho fiscal

tax liability responsabilidad contributiva; pasivo exigible en concepto de impuestos

tax lien gravamen de impuestos

tax payer contribuyente

tax penalty multa sobre impuestos

tax rate tasa de impuesto

tax refund reembolso de impuesto

tax relief desgravación de impuestos

tax return declaración de la renta; declaración de impuestos

tax shelter refugio fiscal; abrigo tributario

tax year ejercicio fiscal; año tributario

taxable income renta gravable; renta imponible

taxation *(noun)* tributación; imposición de impuestos

taxes *(noun)* contribuciones; impuestos

teaching qualifications título de profesor

technical school centro de capacitación; escuela vocacional; escuela técnica

technical skill destreza

teen fathers padres adolescentes

teen mothers madres adolescentes

teen parents padres adolescentes

teenager *(boy)* el adolescente; *(girl)* la adolescente

teeth *(anat)* dientes

telephone *(noun)* teléfono; **over the telephone** por teléfono

telephone book guía de teléfono

telephone directory guía de teléfono; directorio telefónico

telephone follow up recordatorio telefónico

telephone interview entrevista telefónica

telephone number número de teléfono

tell *(in phrases)* **to tell somebody the truth** decirle la verdad a alguien; **to tell somebody a lie** decirle una mentira a alguien; **as I was telling you** como te estaba diciendo; como iba diciendo; **I don't know how to tell you this but ...** no sé como decírtelo, pero ...; **I've been told that ...** me han dicho que ...; **he was told that ...** le dijeron que ...; **I'll tell him you are here** le diré que has llegado; **I'll tell him what happened** le diré que pasó; le contaré que pasó; **to tell somebody something** decir algo a alguien; **to tell somebody how** decir a alguien cómo; **to tell somebody that ...** decir a alguien que ...; **to tell a lie** mentir

teller cajera; cajero

Temporary Assistance for Needy Families (TANF) Ayuda Temporera Para Familias Necesitadas

temporary benefits beneficios temporeros

temporary custody guarda provisorio; **the child was in temporary custody with the maternal grandfather** el niño había quedado en guarda provisoria con el abuelo materno

temporary detention detención temporal

temporary disability incapacidad temporal

temporary disability benefits pagos por incapacidad temporal

temporary restraining order interdicto provisional; juicio de amparo temporal

temporary workers trabajadores temporales

tenancy *(noun)* inquilinato

tenant *(noun)* inquilina; inquilino; arrendataria; arrendatario

tenement *(noun)* vivienda

tenement house casa de vecinos; casa de vecindad

terminally ill en fase terminal; enferma terminal; enfermo terminal; estar desahuciada; estar desahuciada; enferma mortal; enfermo mortal

terminate *(discussion, relationship)* poner fin a; *(contract)* poner término a; *(employee)* despedir; cesar; **his employment will be terminated next month** causará baja el mes que viene; quedará cesante el mes que viene

termination *(noun)* rescisión

termination notice aviso de terminación

termination of employment baja; cese

termination of pregnancy interrupción del embarazo

terms *(law)* condiciones; **the terms of the contract** las condiciones del contrato; los términos del contrato; **the terms of the agreement** las condiciones del acuerdo

terms of sale *(law)* condiciones de venta

testify *(law)* prestar declaración; declarar; testificar; deponer; testimoniar; **to testify that ...** declarar que ...; testificar que ...; dar fe de algo

testimony *(law)* testimonio; expert testimony prueba pericial; **eye witness testimony** testimonio de testigo de vista; testimonio de testigo ocular; testimonio de testigo presencia

thank you gracias

thank you, very kind of you gracias, muy amable

that is es decir

that's why por eso; por ello; por esa razón

the accused el acusado; la acusada; las acusadas; los acusados

the best thing lo mejor

the best thing to do is to wait lo mejor es esperar

the cost of living el costo de la vida

the court is adjourned se levanta la sesión

the full weight of the law todo el peso de la ley

the homeless las personas sin hogar

the injured los accidentados; los heridos; **the injured were taken to the hospital** los accidentados fueron trasladados al hospital

the insured el asegurado; la asegurada; las aseguradas; los asegurados

the register of births, marriages and deaths el registro civil

The Patriot Act La Ley Patriota

the people below us los vecinos de abajo

the people downstairs los vecinos de abajo

the People rest *(law)* la parte acusadora ha concluido la presentación de pruebas

the police handling of the case la manera en que la policía llevó el caso

the truth, the whole truth and nothing but the truth la verdad, toda la verdad y nada más que la verdad

the undersigned el abajo firmante; la abajo firmante; las abajo firmantes; los abajo firmantes

theft *(law)* hurto; robo; **he was charged with theft** lo acusaron de robo; **there have been several cases of theft lately** últimamente ha habido varios robos; **theft is on the increase** el número de robos está aumentando

then *(in phrases)* **it was then that ...** fue entonces cuando ...; **since then** desde entonces; **from then on** desde entonces; a partir de entonces; **by then** para entonces; **just then** en ese mismo momento; **until then** hasta entonces; **then and there** en ese mismo momento; en aquel mismo momento; **every now and then** de vez en cuando; **what happened then?** ¿qué pasó luego?; **and then what?** y luego ¿qué?; **just then he came in** entró justo entonces; **I wasn't doing anything just then** justo en ese momento no estaba haciendo nada; **he wanted it done there and then** quería que lo hicieran en ese mismo momento; **and then again** por otra parte

therapy *(noun)* terapia; tratamiento

thigh *(anat)* muslo

third parties terceros

third-party action acción de una tercera parte

third party insurance seguro contra terceros

third party liability responsabilidad de tercera persona

this course of conduct este curso de comportamiento

those hurt los accidentados; **those hurt were taken to the hospital** los accidentados fueron trasladados al hospital

those injured los accidentados; **those injured were taken to the hospital** los accidentados fueron trasladados al hospital

threat *(noun)* amenaza; **death threat** amenaza de muerte; **they issued a death threat against him** lo amenazaron de muerte; **to make a threat against somebody** amenazar a alguien

threaten *(verb)* amenazar; **they threatened to kill him** lo amenazaron de muerte; **they threatened him with a knife** lo amenazaron con una navaja; **he threatened to call the police** nos amenazó con llamar a la policía; **are you threatening me?** ¿me estás amenazando?

threatening behavior *(law)* conducta amenazadora; conducta amenazante; conducta intimidatoria

throat *(anat)* garganta

through *(adv & prep)* mediante; a través de; por

through negligence por negligencia

ticket *(fine)* multa; *(for bus, train. plane)* boleto; billete; *(political, list of candidates)* lista

Ticket to Hire Boleto a Emplear

Ticket to Work Boleto a Trabajar

Ticket to Work and Work Incentives Improvement Act of 1999 Ley de Boleto a Trabajar y Mejoría de Incentivos de Trabajo de 1999

Ticket to Work and Self-Sufficiency Program Programa de Boleto a Trabajar y el Autosuficiencia

time served pena de prisión ya cumplida

time zone huso horario

timely *(adj)* a tiempo, oportuna; oportuno

timely report of earnings informe puntual de ganancias

T-Intersection Ahead *(traffic sign)* Intersección en "T" adelante

tips *(noun)* propinas

title *(law: right of ownership)* **title to something** derecho a algo; titularidad de algo; *(document)* título de propiedad

title deed título de propiedad

title search registro de título

to tell the truth a decir verdad

to your knowledge a sabiendas; a su entender

today *(adv)* hoy; **a week from today** dentro de una semana; de aquí a una semana; **what's the date today?** ¿a qué estamos hoy?; ¿qué fecha es hoy?; **what's today's date** ¿a qué estamos hoy?; ¿qué fecha es hoy?

today's date la fecha de hoy

toes *(anat)* dedos del pie

together *(adv)* junta; junto

together with junto a; junto con

toilet *(noun)* baño; servicio; **where is the toilet?** ¿dónde está el baño?

tolerance rule regla de tolerancia

toll free call llamada gratis; llamada libre de cargo

tort *(law)* agravio; **liability in tort** responsabilidad extracontractual

torts *(law)* daños y perjuicios

total income ingreso total

total payable total a pagar

town *(noun)* ciudad; *(smaller)* pueblo; población

trade name nombre comercial; *(of company)* razón social

trade secret secreto comercial

trade union sindicato; gremio

trademark razón social

traffic accident accidente de circulación; accidente de tráfico

traffic lights semáforo; **she ran a red light** se pasó un semáforo en rojo; **she went through a red light** se pasó un semáforo en rojo

traffic policeman policía de tráfico; agente de tráfico

Traffic Signal Ahead *(traffic sign)* Señal de Tránsito Adelante

traffic signs señales de tráfico

traffic violation infracción de tráfico; infracción de tránsito

trafficking in tráfico de

trafficking in illegal drugs tráfico de sustancias ilícitas

trafficking in stolen property tráfico de bienes hurtados

training *(noun)* capacitación; adiestramiento

training for self-dialysis entrenamiento de autodiálisis

trait *(noun)* rasgo; característica

transactional immunity inmunidad absoluta

transit visa visa de tránsito

transit without visa tránsito sin visado

travel *(verb: make a journey)* viajar; **when are you traveling?** ¿cuándo viajes?; *(move, go)* desplazarse

travel agency agencia de viajes

travel agent agente de viajes

treating physician médica de tratamiento; médico de tratamiento

treatment *(handling of person)* trato; *(medical)* tratamiento; **give somebody the treatment** dar una buena paliza a alguien

trespass *(law) entrar sin autorización en propiedad ajena*; **they were trespassing on my land** habían entrado en mi propiedad sin autorización; **no trespassing** prohibido el paso

trial *(noun: law, court hearing)* proceso; juicio; **criminal trial** causa criminal; **rape trial** proceso por violación; **murder trial** proceso por asesinato; **to be on trial for murder** ser procesada por asesino; ser procesado por asesino; **if the case goes to trial** si el caso va a juicio; **she was brought to trial** fue procesada; **to be on trial for murder** estar siendo procesado por asesinato; **he is on trial for the murder of a policeman** está siendo procesado por asesinato de un policía; **to stand trial** ser procesada; ser procesado; ser juzgada; ser juzgado; **she is awaiting trial** está a la espera de ser procesada; **fair trial** juicio imparcial; **to give somebody a fair trial** juzgar a alguien con imparcialidad

trial judge juez de tribunal

trial by judge juicio con juez

trial by jury juicio con jurado; juicio por jurado; proceso con jurado

trial court tribunal de primera instancia

trial date fecha del proceso

trial work period período probatorio de trabajo

trouble *(in phrases)* **he got into trouble with the police** se metió en un lío con la policía; **what's the trouble?** ¿cuál es el problema?; ¿qué pasa?; **the trouble is ...** el problema es ...; lo que pasa es ...; **that's just the trouble** ahí está; **engine trouble** problemas con el motor; **there'll be trouble if she finds out** se armará una buena si se entera; **he got into trouble for saying that** se mereció una bronca diciendo eso; **to get somebody into trouble** meter a alguien en un lío; meter a alguien en problemas; **to get out of trouble** salir del apuro; **she never gave us any trouble** nunca nos causó problemas; **I had no trouble finding the house** encontré la casa sin problemas; **we had trouble getting here in time** nos costó trabajo llegar aquí a tiempo; **to be in trouble** estar en un apuro; estar en un aprieto; **don't go looking for trouble** no busques problemas; no busques camorra; **to make trouble for somebody** crear un lío a alguien; **money troubles** dificultades económicas; **to take the trouble to do something** tomarse la molestia de hacer algo; **it's more trouble than it's worth** no vale la pena; **I'm sorry to trouble you** disculpe la molestia

trouble free sin problemas

trouble spot zona conflictiva

truancy *(noun)* ausentismo escolar

truant *(noun) alumno que falta a la clase sin autorización;* **to play truant** faltar a clase; hacer novillos; irse de pinta

truant *(verb)* faltar a clase

truce *(noun)* tregua

truck *(noun)* camión; troca

truck driver *(noun)* camionera; camionero

truck farmer *(noun)* horticultor; horticultora

trucker *(noun)* camionera; camionero

trucking *(noun)* transporte por carretera

true *(in phrases)* **it is true that ...** es verdad que ...; es cierto que ...; **is it true?** ¿es verdad?; **it can't be true!** ¡no me lo creo!; **it is true to say that ...** puede afirmarse que ...; **that's true** es cierto; es verdad; **give me your true opinion** dime de verdad lo que piensas

trust *(law)* fideicomiso; **to hold someting in trust for somebody** mantener algo en fideicomiso para alguien

trust *(in phrases)* **you've betrayed their trust** has traicionado la confianza que tenían puesta en ti; **to put one's trust in somebody** depositar su confianza en alguien; **to set up a trust** crear un fondo fiduciario; **trust me, I know what I'm doing** confía en mí, sé lo que estoy haciendo; **she is not to be trusted** ella no es de fiar; **I'd trust him with my life** pondría mi vida en sus manos; **you can't trust a word he says** es imposible creer ninguna palabra suya; no se puede uno fiar de nada de lo que dice

trust account cuenta de fideicomiso

trust fund fondo en fideicomisos; fondo de fideicomisos

truth *(noun)* verdad; **the truth, the whole truth and nothing but the truth** la verdad, toda la verdad y nada más que la verdad; **is there any truth in the story?** ¿hay algo de verdad en esa historia?; **I doubt the truth of ...** dudo la veracidad de ...; **the truth is that ...** la verdad es que ...; **there is some truth in this** hay una parte de verdad en esto; **there is no truth in the rumour that ...** no hay nada de verdad en el rumor de que ...; **in truth** en verdad; a la verdad; **to tell the truth** a decir verdad

truthful *(adj)* veraz; **I testify that the above statement is true** doy fe que la declaración más arriba es veraz

try *(law)* juzgar; conocer de; ver; **to try somebody for something** juzgar a alguien por algo; **to try a case** conocer de una causa; ver una demanda; **to try small cases** conocer de causas pequeñas

try *(noun)* intento; tentativa; **it's worth a try** vale la pena intentarlo; merece la pena intentarlo; **to give something a try** intentar algo; intentar hacer algo; *(verb)* intentar; probar; poner a prueba; **to try to do something** intentar hacer algo; tratar de hacer algo; **to try doing something** probar a hacer algo

tuition *(noun)* matrícula

turn state's evidence declarar como testigo de la acusación *(con el propósito de obtener una reducción de la propia pena)*

turn up dead aparecieron muertos; **the three turned up dead in their house** los tres aparecieron muertos en su domicilio

turned over to juvenile court entrgada al tribunal de menores; entregado al tribunal de menores

twin melliza; mellizo; gemela; gemelo; **identical twins** gemelos idénticos; *(colloquial)* cuates; **she had twins** tuvo gemelos

Two-way Traffic Ahead *(traffic sign)* Doble Vía Adelante

unable *(law)* **to be unable to do something** no poder hacer algo; ser incapaz de hacer algo; **she was unable to attend the hearing** no pudo asistir a la audiencia; **I'm afraid we're unable to help you** me temo que no podemos ayudarlo

unappealable judgement *(law)* sentencia definitiva; sentencia firme

unauthorized *(adj)* no autorizada; no autorizado; sin autorización

unavoidable circumstance ineludible circunstancia

unaware *(law)* **to be unaware that ...** ignorar que ...; **to be unaware of something** ignorar algo; **she seemed unaware of the fact that ...** parecía ignorar el hecho de que ..; no parecía ser consciente de que ...; **they were unaware of my presence** no sabían que yo estaba allí

unbelievable *(adj)* **it is unbelievable that ...** es increíble que + *subj*; **we had unbelievable luck** tuvimos una suerte increíble

Unborn Baby Law ley del niño que todavía no ha nacido; ley del nonato

uncertain *(adj)* **to be uncertain about something** no estar segura de algo; no estar seguro de algo; **I'm uncertain how to proceed** no sé muy bien cómo proceder; **for a moment he looked uncertain** por un momento pareció no estar seguro; **to be uncertain about something** no estar segura de algo; no estar seguro de algo; **she is uncertain about the future** no está segura sobre el futuro; **she is uncertain about what to do next** no está segura sobre de qué hacer ahora; **I am uncertain whether to accept** no estoy segura si aceptar; no estoy seguro si aceptar; **in no uncertain terms** sin dejar lugar a dudas; claramente; **we live in uncertain times** vivimos unos tiempos muy inestables

uncivil *(noun)* descortés; incivil

uncle *(noun)* tío

uncle by marriage tío político

uncollectable *(adj)* incobrable

uncover *(verb)* dejar al descubierto; descubrir; revelar

undecided voter votante indeciso

undeferrable *(adj)* impostergable

undeliverable *(adj)* imposible de entregar

undeniable *(adj)* innegable

under age menor de edad; **be under age** ser menor de edad

under age children hijos menores de edad

under age daughter hija menor de edad

under age son hijo menor de edad

under any circumstances bajo ninguna circunstancia

under existing legislation de acuerdo a la legislación vigente; conforme a la legislación vigente

under house arrest bajo arresto domiciliario

under oath bajo juramento

undercover policeman policía encubierto

undercover state trooper policía estatal encubierta; policía estatal encubierto

underpayment pago insuficiente; pago de menos

under police escort escoltada por la policía; escoltado por la policía

under pressure bajo presión; **to work under pressure** trabajar bajo presión; **they are under pressure to accept the offer** los están presionando para que acepten la oferta; **he confessed under pressure from the police** confesó presionado por la policía; **I've been under a lot of pressure recently** ultímamente he estado muy agobiada; ultímamente he estado muy agobiado; **he's under a lot of pressure** está bajo mucha presión; está sometido a mucha presión

under the protection of bajo el amparo de

under the influence of bajo la influencia de

undersigned judge infrascrito juez

understand *(in phrases)* **I can't understand it!** ¡no lo entiendo!; **that's what I can't understand** eso es lo que no logro entender; eso es lo que no logro comprender; **to make oneself understood** hacerse entender; **do I make myself understood?** ¿queda claro?; **I understand you have been absent** tengo entendido que usted ha estado ausente; **as I understand it, he's trying to set up a meeting** según tengo entendido está intentando convocar una reunión; **am I to understand that ...?** ¿debo entender que ...?; **he let it be understood that ...** dio a entender que ...; **nobody understands me** nadie me entiende

understanding *(in phrases)* **to reach an understanding** llegar a un entendimiento; **she was very understanding about it** fue muy comprensiva; **that's my understanding of the situation** esa es mi interpretación de la situación; así es como veo la situación; **thank you for your kindness and understanding** le agradezco su amabilidad y comprensión; **my understanding was that ...** tenía entendido que ...; según yo creía ...; **to come to an understanding with someone** llegar a un acuerdo con alguien; **on the understanding that ...** a condición de que + *subj*

unearned income ingreso no derivado del trabajo

unemployment benefits prestaciones por desempleo; seguro de desempleo; subsidio de desempleo

unemployment compensation prestaciones por desempleo; subsidio de desempleo; compensación por desempleo

unfair competition competencia desleal

unfair dismissal despido improcedente; despido injustificado

uninsured *(adj)* no asegurada; no asegurado

unintentional *(adj)* involuntaria; involuntario; no deliberada; no deliberado

unintentionally *(adv)* involuntariamente; sin querer

union *(noun)* sindicato

union bosses dirigentes sindicales

unions and employers sindicatos y la patronal; sindicatos y los empresarios

United States Estados Unidos

universal access to health care services acceso universal a servicios de salud

unknown suspect *(law)* sospechosa desconocida; sospechoso desconocido

unlawful *(adj)* ilegal; ilícita; ilícito

unlawful assembly reunión no autorizada

unlawful entry violación de domicilio

unlawful entry on property allanamiento de propiedad ajena

unlawful imprisonment privación ilegal de la libertad

unlawful killing cuasidelito de homicidio

unlawful possession of controlled substance tenencia ilícita de sustancias reguladas

unlawful possession of weapons tenencia ilícita de armas

unless *(conj)* a menos que + *subj*; a no ser que + *subj*

unmarked *(adj: without identification)* sin marcar

unmarked car coche particular *(utilizado por la policía)*; coche camuflado

unmarried *(adj)* soltera; soltero

unmarried mother una madre soltera

unmortgaged property *(adj)* propiedad libre de hipotecas

unposted earnings ganancias no acreditados; salarios no acreditados; ganancias no registrados

unpunished *(person)* **to go unpunished** quedar sin castigo; *(crime)* quedar impune; quedar sin castigo; quedar en la impunidad; **the crime went unpunished** el crimen ha quedado en la impunidad

unqualified *(adj)* inhábil; sin titulación; no calificada; no calificado

unsecured bail bond caución sin garantía real

unsuccessful work attempt intento de trabajo no exitoso; intento de trabajo sin exito

untenable *(adj)* insostenible; indefendible

until *(conj)* hasta que; **please wait until I arrive** por favor espera hasta que yo llegue; *(prep)* hasta; **until Monday** hasta el lunes; **until now** hasta ahora; **until tomorrow** hasta mañana

until further notice hasta nuevo aviso

up the street calle arriba

up-to-date al día; actualizada; actualizado

updating the records puesta al día de los archivos; **updating the records will take a long time** la puesta al día de los archivos va a llevar mucho tiempo

upheld *(law)* ha lugar a la protesta; **conviction upheld** convicción confirmada; **the sentence was upheld on appeal** la sentencia fue confirmada en la apelación

uphold *(law)* confirmar; **the court upheld that** el tribunal confirmó que

upper income groups grupos de altos ingresos

upper middle class la clase media alta

uprising *(noun)* sublevación

urine sample muestra de orina

U. S. Citizenship and Immigration Services (CIS) Cuidandnia y Servicio Inmigratorios de Estados Unidos

U.S. Customs Service Servicio de Aduanas de Estados Unidos

U.S. Highway *(traffic sign)* Autopista Nacional

U.S. passport holder titular de pasaporte estadounidense

use bad language decir palabrotas; **don't use bad language** no digas palabrotas

use drugs consumir drogas

use immunity inmunidad parcial

use force hacer uso de la fuerza

use of force empleo de la fuerza; uso de la fuerza

used car coche de ocasión

utilities *(noun)* servicios públicos (gas, electricidad, etc.)

V

vacate *(law)* invalidar; anular; rescindir

vacate the premises abandonar el recinto; abandono del recinto; **the police ordered everyone to vacate the premises** la policía ordenó el abandono del recinto

vacation pay pago de vacaciones

vaccination *(noun)* vacuna

vagrancy *(noun)* vagabundeo; vagancia

vagrant *(noun)* vagabunda; vagabundo

valid *(adj)* válida; válido; legítima; legítimo

validity *(noun)* validez

validly *(adj)* con legitimidad

valuable resource valioso servicio; **the new center is a valuable resource for the community** el nuevo centro es un valioso recurso para la cmunidad

van *(auto)* furgoneta; camioneta; vagoneta

vehicular homicide *(law)* homicidio culposo por el conductor de un vehículo; homicidio culposo por la conductora de un vehículo

vehicular manslaughter *(law)* homicidio culposo por el conductor de un vehículo; homicidio culposo por la conductora de un vehículo

verbal agreement acuerdo verbal

verdict *(law)* veredicto; **a verdict of guilty** verdicto de culpabilidad; **a verdict of not guilty** veredicto de inocencia; **to bring in a verdict** dar un veredicto; **return a verdict** emitir un veredicto; **to deliver a verdict** *(magistrate)* pronunciar sentencia; fallar; **they failed to reach a verdict** no llegaron a un acuerdo sobre el veredicto

verdict of not guilty fallo absolutorio

very pressing matter *(noun)* asunto impostergable; **the matter was very pressing** el asunto era impostergable

Veteran's Administration Administración de Veteranos

vicarious *(adj)* indirecta; indirecto

vicarious liability *(adj)* responsabilidad indirecta

vice *(noun)* vicio

vice police policía anti-vicio

vice squad policía anti-vicio

victims of crimes víctimas de delitos

victims of crimes whose health has been impaired víctimas de delitos que hayan sufrido menoscabo de su salud

VIN number el número del motor

violation *(of agreement, law, right)* violación; *(of promise)* incumplimiento; **human rights violation** violaciones de los derechos humanos; **a border violation** una infracción fronteriza; **a traffic violation** una infracción de tráfico; **to be in violation of something** contravenir algo

violate *(law)* violar; infringir; quebrantar; *(constitution, agreement, treaty)* violar; infringir; vulnerar; *(sanctions)* incumplir; desobedecer; *(contract)* no cumplir; incumplir; *(rights)* violar; vulnerar; *(privacy)* invadir

violence *(noun)* violencia; fuerza física; **crimes of violence** delitos violentos; **physical violence** violencia física; **use violence** hacer uso de la fuerza; hacer uso de la violencia; **he threatened me with violence** me amenazó con recurrir a la violencia; **a rise in levels of violence** una escalada de violencia; **robbery with violence** robo con fuerza; robo con violencia; robo a mano armada; **to do violence to somebody** agredir a alguien

violence against women violencia contra las mujeres

Violence Against Women Act Ley de Violencia Contra las Mujeres

violent violenta; violento; **to get violent** ponerse violenta; ponerse violento; **by violent means** por la fuerza; por la violencia

violent death muerte violenta; **he met a violent death** tuvo una muerte violenta

violent men hombres violentos

violent temper mal genio; genio terrible; **he has a violent temper** tiene muy mal genio; tiene un genio terrible

visa office oficina de visas

visitation rights derecho de visita

visiting hours horas de visita; horario de visitas

visitor's visa visa de visitante

vocation *(noun)* vocación

vocational evaluation evaluación vocacional

vocational guidance orientación profesional

vocational rehabilitation rehabilitación vocacional

vocational training formación profesional

void *(law: noun)* nulo; inválida; inválido; *(law: verb)* anular; invalidar

voluntary compliance *(law)* cumplimiento voluntario

voluntary manslaughter *(law)* homicidio culposo voluntario; homicidio con circunstancias atenuantes

voluntary medical insurance seguro médico voluntario

vouch *(verb)* **to vouch for somebody** responder por alguien; **to vouch for something** responder de algo

vote *(noun: ballot cast)* voto; sufragio; **to cast one's vote** emitir su voto; *(law)* votar

voter registration inscripción en el registro

voter registration application solicitud para inscribirse para votar

voucher *(cash substitute)* vale; cupón; *(receipt)* justificante; comprobante

vulnerability *(noun)* vulnerabilidad; **emotional vulnerability** vulnerabilidad emocional

vulnerable *(adj)* vulnerable

wage *(rate of pay)* sueldo; salario

wage agreement acuerdo salarial

wage attachment adjunto de sueldo

wage claim reinvindicación salarial; demanda de aumento salarial

wage earner asalariada; asalariado; trabajador asalariado; trabajadora asalariada

wage freeze congelación salarial

wage garnishment embargo de salario; embargo de sueldo

wage increase aumento salarial; aumento de sueldo

wage scale escala salarial

wage settlement convenio laboral; acuerdo salarial

wage worker asalariada; asalariado

wages *(noun)* sueldo; paga; **a decent wage** un sueldo decente; **she earns a good wage** gana bien; gana un buen sueldo

wages and self-employment income sueldo e ingresos de negocio propio

waiting around for 20 minutes una antesala de veinte minutos

waiting for trial en espera de juicio

waiting list lista de espera

waiting period período de espera

waiting room sala de espera

waive a right desistir de un derecho

waiver *(of rule)* no aplicación; exención; renuncia; *(of payment)* exoneración; *(of claim, right)* renuncia

waiver of immunity desistimiento del derecho de inmunidad; renuncia al derecho de inmunidad

waiver of appearance for arraignment renuncia de comparecencia ante el tribunal

waiver of responsibility exención de responsabilidad

waiver of right to appear renuncia voluntaria del derecho a presentarse

waiving a right desistimiento

wandering around the streets vagando por las calles; deambulando por las calles

wanted *(adj)* buscada por la policía; buscado por la policía; **he is wanted for murder** lo buscan por asesinato; **she is wanted for questioning** la buscan para interrogarla

wanted person persona buscada por la policía

ward of the court *(law)* bajo tutela judicial

warrant *(law)* mandamiento judicial; orden judicial; **a warrant was issued for his arrest** se expidió una orden de arresto en su contra; se expidió una orden de detención en su contra; **issue a warrant** expedir una orden

web address dirección de Internet

wedding *(noun: act)* boda

welfare *(noun)* prestaciones sociales; **to be on welfare** recibir prestaciones de la seguridad social

welfare worker asistente social; visitador social; visitadora social

weapon *(noun)* arma

wearing *(adj)* vestida de; vestido de

weigh *(verb)* pesar; **how much do you weigh?** ¿cuánto pesas?

weight of the evidence *(law)* peso de la evidencia; peso de la prueba

weighted benefits beneficios ajustados

Welfare Department Departamento de Bienestar Público

what *(pronoun)* qué; **what's that?** ¿qué es eso?; **what caused the accident?** ¿qué causó el accidente?

what's the date today? ¿a qué estamos hoy?; ¿qué fecha es hoy?

what's today's date ¿a qué estamos hoy?; ¿qué fecha es hoy?

where *(adv & conj)* dónde; adónde; **where are you from?** ¿de dónde eres?; **where is Albuquerque?** ¿dónde está Albuquerque?; ¿dónde queda Albuquerque?; **where are you going?** ¿adónde vas?

whereabouts ... ? *(adv)* ¿en qué parte ...?; **whereabouts in Albuquerque do you live?** ¿en qué parte de Albuquerque vives?

whereabouts *(noun)* paradero; **nobody knows his whereabouts** nadie sabe su paradero

whereabouts unknown paradero desconocido

white *(adj & noun)* blanca; blanco

white-collar *(worker, job)* no manual; de oficina

White House Casa Blanca

who *(pronoun)* quien; quienes

who are they? ¿quienes son?

who can ...? ¿quién puede ...?

who cares ...? ¿a quién le importa ...?

who did you go with? ¿con quiénes fuiste?

who does that car belong to? ¿de quién es ese coche?

who does this belong to? ¿a quién pertenece esto?; ¿de quién es esto?

who else knows? ¿quién más lo sabe?;

who is covered? ¿quiénes cuentan con protección?

who is responsible for this? ¿quién es el responsable de esto?

who is that? ¿quién es ése?

who is this Juan Torres, anyway? ¿y quién es el tal Juan Torres?

who lives next door? ¿quién vive al lado?; ¿quién vive en la casa de al lado?

who struck the first blow? ¿quién dio el primer golpe?

why *(noun)* por qué

widow's pension pensión de viudedad; pensión de viudez

willful *(noun)* intencional; premeditada; premeditado

willful misconduct mala conducta intencional

willful neglect descuido porfiado

will *(law)* testamento; **to make one's will** hacer su testamento; **last will and testament** última voluntad y testamento

win a case *(law)* ganar un pleito

win a lawsuit *(law)* ganar un pleito

win an action *(law)* ganar un pleito

win business from a competitor *(law)* quitarle clientes a la competencia; **they've won business from their competitors** le han quitado clientes a la competencia

windfall benefits beneficios inesperados

winter *(season)* invierno; **in the winter** en invierno; en el invierno

withdraw *(verb)* retirar

withdraw charges retirar acusaciones

withdraw the claim retirar la reclamación

withdrawn *(adj)* retraída; retraído; encerrada en sí misma; encerrado en sí mismo

withholding of evidence esconder evidencia; destruir evidencia; remover evidencia

without a doubt sin duda

without auto insurance sin seguro automovilístico

without fault sin culpa

without health insurance sin seguro de enfermedad

without paying rent sin pagar el alquiler; sin pagar el arrendamiento

without revealing your name sin revelar tu nombre

without your permission sin tu permiso

witness *(law)* testigo; **material witness** testigo esencial; **in witness hereof** en fe de todo ello; **I was a witness to the accident** yo fui testigo del accidente; yo presencié el accidente; **to be a witness to something** ser testigo de algo; **to call somebody as a witness** citar a alguien como testigo

witness *(evidence; testimony)* **eye witness** testigo ocular; **the accident was witnessed by two people** hay dos testigos del accidente; **to testify to something** atestiguar algo; ser prueba de algo; ser testimonio de algo; **to bear witness** *(in court of law)* atestiguar; testificar; **to give witness against somebody** atestiguar en contra de alguien; **to give witness for somebody** atestiguar a favor de alguien; **to witness a document** firmar un documento como testigo

witness for the defense testigo de defensa; testigo de descargo

witness for the prosecution testigo de cargo

witness interview interrogatorio del testigo

witness name nombre del testigo

witness stand estrado; **to take the witness stand** subir al estrado

witness with comprehension problems testigo con problemas de comprensión

woman *(noun)* mujer; **a woman friend of mine** una amiga mía; **he ran off with another woman** se fue con otra

woman lawyer abogada

woman with a past mujer con pasado

women have the right to invoke the fourteenth amendment of the Constitution mujeres tienen el derecho a invocar la catorceava enmienda de la Constitución

women's prison casa correccional

women's rights derechos de la mujer

women's shelters albergues para mujeres

work *(noun)* trabajo; **place of work** lugar de trabajo; **go to work** ir a trabajar; ir al trabajo; *(verb)* trabajar

work accident accidente laboral

work address dirección del trabajo

work claims of compensation reclamaciones de compensación laboral

work conditions condiciones de trabajo

work contract contrato de trabajo

work experience experiencia laboral

work incentives incentivos de trabajo

work place lugar de trabajo

work on actuar sobre; *(police)* tener pocas pistas; estar investigando

work on a "commission only" basis trabajar a porcentaje

work out a deal with llegar a un acuerdo con

work out a deal with the authorities llegar a un acuerdo con las autoridades

work outside the U.S. empleo fuera de Estados Unidos

work permit permiso de trabajo; **we cannot employ him without a work permit** no podemos contratarlo si no tiene permiso de trabajo

work schedule horario de trabajo

work study programs programas de trabajo-estudio

worker's compensation compensación legal por accidentes de trabajo

workforce *(noun)* fuerza laboral

workforce centers centros de fuerza laboral

working without a contract trabajando sin contrato

workmate *(noun)* compañera de trabajo; compañero de trabajo; colega de trabajo

workplace rights derechos en el trabajo

worksheet *(record of work)* hoja de trabajo; hoja de cálculos

worthless *(adj)* sin valor; sin ningún valor; **to be worthless** *(adj)* no tener ningún valor

worthwhile *(verb)* valer la pena

wound *(noun)* herida; **bullet wound** herida de bala; **chest wound** herida en el pecho; **head wound** herida en la cabeza

wound *(verb)* herir; **be wounded on the arm with a sharp instrument** resultar herido de arma blanca en el brazo; **he was wounded in the leg** lo hirieron en la pierna; **he was fatally wounded** fue herido de muerte

wound fatally herir de muerte; **he was fatally wounded** fue herido de muerte

wound seriously herir de gravedad

writing *(noun)* escritura

written agreement acuerdo escrito

written evidence constancia por escrito; evidencia por escrito

written request petición escrita

written request una petición escrita; **please file a written request** haga el favor de presentar una petición escrita

written statement declaración escrita

wrongdoer *(noun)* malhechor; malhechora

wrongful act acto que viola los derechos de una persona y que resulta en daños

wrongful arrest arresto ilegal

wrongful death action acción jurídica a consecuencia de una muerte

wrongful dismissal despido improcedente; despido injustificado

Wrong Way *(traffic sign)* Contravía

W-2 Form Comprobante de Retención de Salarios Formulario W-2

X

x *(letter)* x; **if you can't write, just make an X** si no sabe escribir, ponga una cruz

xenophobia *(noun)* xenofobia

X-ray machine aparato de rayos X

X-ray picture radiografía

Y

yard *(school, prison)* patio

yea *(adv)* sí

year *(noun)* año; **last year** el año pasado; **next year** el año que viene; el próximo año; **this time last year** el año pasado por estas fechas; **every year** todos los años; cada año; **once or twice a year** una o dos veces al año; una o dos veces por año

years ago hace muchos años

yearly *(adj)* anual; **on a yearly basis** cada año; anual

yellow *(adj & noun)* amarillo; amarillo

yellowish *(adj)* amarillenta; amarillento

yesterday *(adv)* ayer; **I spoke to him yesterday** hablé con él ayer; **the day before yesterday** anteayer

yesterday morning ayer por la mañana; ayer en la mañana

Yield *(traffic sign)* Cede el Paso

Y Intersection Ahead *(traffic sign)* Bifurcación en "Y" Adelante

young *(adj: early life)* joven; **I have a younger brother** tengo un hermano menor; **I have a younger sister** tengo una hermana menor; **I have younger brothers and sisters** tengo hermanos menores

your case tu caso

your family tu familia

your fault culpa tuya; **it wasn't your fault** no fue culpa tuya

your friends tus amigos

your request su petición; su pedido

your rights after arrest los derechos después de la detención

youth *(noun: person)* juventud

Youth Law Center Centro de leyes para menores

youthful offender *(noun: person)* delincuente joven

Z

zany chiflada; chiflado; loca; loco

zapatos *(noun)* shoes

zealot *(noun)* fanática; fanático

zero *(number)* cero; **you'll get zero help from him** no te va a ayudar para nada; **a policy of zero tolerance** una política de mano dura

zero in on *(target)* apuntarle directamente a; *(issue, problem)* centrarse en; concentrar la atención en

zip code código postal

zip gun *pistola de fabricación casera*

zoning *(noun)* zonificación

IDIOMS

A

a

a lack of la falta de, por falta de
A lack of affordable housing is one of the primary causes of homelessness.
La falta de vivienda asequible es una de las principales causas del número de personas sin techo.

Many families break up because of a lack of money.
Muchas familias se deshacen por falta de dinero.

a little while un ratito
I'll stay a little while longer.
Me quedaré un ratito más.

It'll still be a little while before he comes out.
Todavía tardará un ratito en salir.

a little while ago hace un ratito
He was here a little while ago.
Hace un ratito estaba aquí.

The jury reached a verdict a little while ago.
Hace un ratito el jurado llegó a un acuerdo sobre el veredicto.

a little while later al poco rato
A little while later the judge entered the room
Al poco rato el juez entró en la sala.

A little while later the judge was back.
Al poco rato el juez estaba de vuelta.

A little while later the jury returned.
Al poco rato el jurado regresó.

a long while ago hace mucho tiempo
He testified that it happened a long while ago.
Testificó que pasó hace mucho tiempo.

According to the witness, it happened a long while ago.
Según el testigo, pasó hace mucho tiempo.

a lot of mucho, un montón de
He has a lot of personal problems.
Tiene muchos problemas personales.

I have a lot of problems.

Me he metido en un montón de problemas.

I've seen a lot of her recently.
La he visto mucho últimamente.
She has a lot of alibis.
Tiene muchas coartadas.

That calls for a lot of patience.
Eso requiere mucha paciencia.

The defense doesn't have a lot of options.
La defensa no tiene un montón de opciones.

The defense was faced with a lot of circumstantial evidence.
La defensa se vio enfrentada con un montón de pruebas indirectas.

There is a lot of circumstantial evidence.
Hay un montón de pruebas indirectas.

They asked a lot of questions.
Hicieron muchas preguntas.

We were faced with a lot of problems.
Nos vimos enfrentados con un montón de problemas.

a while un tiempo, hace tiempo
He lived abroad for a while.
Vivió un tiempo en el extranjero.

I lived in Albuquerque for a while.
Viví un tiempo en Albuquerque.

It is a while since we had any news.
Hace tiempo que no tenemos noticia.

Wait a while.
Espera un tiempo.

a while ago hace un rato
He left a while ago.
Hace un rato que se fue.

They left a while ago.
Hace un rato que se fueron.

abandon
He abandoned her for another woman.
La abandonó por otra mujer.

His biological mother abandoned him.
Su madre biológica lo abandonó.

It is difficult to show that a property has been abandoned.
Es difícil demostrar que una propiedad ha sido abandonada.

She abandoned the baby at the entrance to the hospital.
Abandonó al bebé en la puerta del hospital.

The baby was found abandoned.
Encontraron al bebé abandonado.

abandoned property propiedad abandonada
The police were working until yesterday on the confirmation of the identity of an indigent, whose dead body was found on an abandoned property.
La policía trabajaba hasta ayer en la ratificación de la identidad de un indigente, cuyo cadáver fue hallado en una propiedad abandonada.

abandonment
Abandonment and the lack of parental care in homes is a big problem.
El abandono y la falta de atención paterna en los hogares es un gran problema.

abandonment of children abandono de los niños
Ill-treatment and abandonment of children are problems that are terribly too frequent in the world.
Los malos tratos y el abandono de los niños son problemas espantosamente frecuentes en el mundo.

Abandonment of children is when a parent leaves a child without enough care, supervision, support, or parental contact for an excessive period of time.
El abandono de los niños es cuando un padre deja a un niño sin suficiente cuidado, supervisión, respaldo o contacto con los padres por un período de tiempo excesivo.

abduct
A pedofile was found guilty of abducting six young girls.
Un pedófilo fue declarado culpable de secuestrar a seis muchachas.

Julie and Melissa were abducted in June of 2000 near the city of Albuquerque.
Julie y Melissa fueron secuestradas en junio de dos mil cerca de la ciudad de Albuquerque.

abduction
Do you think that the abduction and murder of your father has something to do with the secret accounts?
¿Cree que las cuentas secretas tienen algo que ver con el rapto y asesinato de su padre?

The crime of abduction carries a high penalty.
El delito de secuestro trae aparejada una pena grave.
The jury found him guilty of the abduction of six girls and the death of two of them.
El jurado lo declaró culpable del rapto de seis niñas y la muerte de dos de ellas.

abide

abide by acatar, atenerse a, respetar
He was willing to abide by the ruling.
Estaba dispuesto a acatar la sentencia.

He was willing to abide by the wishes of the court.
Estaba dispuesto a acatar la voluntad de la corte.

They did not abide by the terms of the agreement.
No respetaron los términos del acuerdo.

You'll have to abide by the rules.
Tendrás que atenerte a las reglas.

ability

He's a lawyer of great ability.
Es un abogado muy capaz.

She did it to the best of her ability.
Lo hizo lo mejor que pudo.

ability in aptitud para
She has shown that she has an ability in English.
Ha demostrado tener aptitud para el inglés.

ability to speak el habla
He lost the ability to speak in a car accident
Perdió el habla en un accidente de coche.

ability to walk movilidad
Due to the accident, her ability to walk is now severely impaired.
Debido al accidente, su movilidad se ha visto seriamente afectada.

able

I was able to identify the car from his description.
Pude identificar el coche gracias a su descripción.

My friend was able to provide an interpretation.
Mi amigo pudo hacer de intérprete.

They were able to reconstruct the crime.
Pudieron reconstruir el delito.

With that evidence they were able to secure a conviction.
Con esas pruebas lograron que se la condenara.

able to answer poder contestar
I think he is best able to answer that question.
Creo que él es quien mejor puede contestar a esa pregunta.

able to convince lograr convencer, poder convencer
He wasn't able to convince her.
No pudo convencerla.

He wasn't able to convince the jury of his innocence.
No logró convencer al jurado de su inocencia.

He wasn't able to convince them.
No logró convencerlos.

He wasn't able to convince them of his innocence.
No pudo convencerlos de su inocencia.

able to expose poder desenmascar
They were finally able to expose him.
Finalmente pudieron desenmascarlo.

able to go poder ir
Will you be able to go?
¿Podrás ir?

able to look after capaz de valerse, poder valerse
He proved able to look after himself.
Demostró que era capaz de valerse muy bien por sí mismo.

She proved able to look after herself.
Demostró que podía valerse muy bien por sí misma.

able to speak saber hablar
By then you'll be able to speak English fluently.
Para entonces vas a saber hablar inglés con fluidez

able to testify poder testificar
I think you'll be able to testify tomorrow.
Creo que mañana vas a poder testificar.

able to walk poder andar
He's not able to walk.
No puede andar.

Since he had the accident, he's not able walk.
Desde que sufrió el accidente, no puede andar.

ablest

The solution in this case is to reduce the staff and keep the ablest workers.
La solución en este caso es reducir el personal y quedarse con los trabajadores más capaces.

They are some of our ablest police officers.
Son algunos de nuestros policías más capaces.

abortion

Has she had any abortions?
¿Ha tenido abortos?

She had an abortion.
Se hizo un aborto.

illegal abortion aborto ilegal
He was arrested on suspicion of having carried out illegal abortions.
Fue detenido como presunto autor de prácticas abortivas ilegales.

Illegal abortions are carried out in unhealthy and unhygienic conditions, which make them twice as harmful.
El aborto ilegal se practica generalmente en condiciones insalubres y antihigiénicas, lo que lo hace doblemente perjudicial.

about

Don't feel guilty about that.
No te sientas culpable por eso.

Have you approached her about it?
¿Ya ha hablado con ella del asunto?

He is worried about his health.
Está preocupado por su salud.

He said nothing about that.
No dijo nada acerca de eso.

His parents questioned him about where he had been all night.
Sus padres le preguntaron dónde había estado toda la noche.

I can't talk about it over the phone.
No puedo hablar de ello por teléfono.

I'll call you in about three hours.
Te llamo en unas tres horas.

I would like a word with you about that.
Quisiera hablar con usted acerca de eso.

Nobody must hear about this.
Que no se entere nadie de esto.

Nothing was said about the matter.
No dijeron nada acerca del asunto.

She is uncertain about what to do next.
No está segura sobre de qué hacer ahora.
She was positive about having seen him.
Estaba muy segura de haberlo visto.

The police questioned him about his movements.
La policía le pidió informes sobre sus actividades.

The trial will begin in about four weeks.
El juicio empezará en unas cuatro semanas.

There's no point getting so angry about it.
No vale la pena enojarse tanto por eso.

They had an argument about money.
Tuvieron una discusión por una cuestión de dinero.

What did the paper say about it?
¿Qué salió en los diarios al respecto?

about her/his sobre su
I'll have a talk with him about his behavior.
Hablaré con él sobre su comportamiento.

We made inquiries about his past.
Hicimos averiguaciones sobre su pasado.

about my age más o menos mi edad
He's about my age.
Tiene más o menos mi edad.

about to a punto de
He is about to get married.
Está a punto de casarse.

I was just about to leave when he called.
Estaba a punto de salir cuando llamó.

The jury is about to start deliberating.
El jurado está a punto de empezar a deliberar.

We are about to take our first break during the trial.
Estamos a punto de hacer la primera pausa del juicio.
about forty alrededor de 40 años

She must be about forty.
Debe tener alrededor de cuarenta años.

above

He is above suspicion.
Está por encima de toda sospecha.

He is above that sort of thing.
Está muy por encima de esas cosas.
No one is above the law.
Nadie está por encima de la ley.

They are not above the law.
No están por encima de la ley.

above all sobre todo
Above all, let's keep calm.
Sobre todo, no perdamos la calma.

Divorce can be very complicated, above all if there are kids involved.
El divorcio puede ser complicado, sobre todo si hay hijos de por medio.

abroad al extranjero, en el extranjero
He has never been abroad.
Nunca ha viajado al extranjero.

He lived abroad for a while.
Vivió un tiempo en el extranjero.

She lives abroad.
Ella vive en el extranjero.

They often travel abroad.
Viajan mucho al extranjero.

absolutely

Are you absolutely sure?
¿Estás completamente seguro?

He is absolutely penniless.
Está sin un céntimo.

I trust her absolutely.
Tengo plena confianza en ella.

In my opinion, it is absolutely true.
En mi opinión, es la pura verdad.

It is absolutely true.
Es la pura verdad.

The jury is not absolutely convinced.
El jurado no está totalmente convencido.

We achieved absolutely nothing.
No logramos absolutamente nada.

absolve

He was absolved of guilt.
Fue absuelto de culpa.
Fue eximido de culpa.

She was absolved of all blame.
La absolvieron de toda culpa.

abstain

The judge should abstain from expressing an opinion.
El juez debe abstenerse de expresar una opinión.

abuse

He is accused of abusing his children.
Lo acusan de abusar de sus hijos.

He is accused of beating and sexually abusing six children between the ages of thirteen and fifteen.
Lo acusan de golpear y abusar sexualmente de seis chicos — de entre trece y quince años de edad.

Domestic violence is defined as abuse committed by an ex-husband, ex-wife, boyfriend or girlfriend.
La violencia doméstica se define como el abuso cometido por el esposo o ex-esposa, novio o novia.

Every year millions of children fall victim to sexual abuses.
Cada año, millones de niños caen víctimas de los abusos sexuales.

Pedophiles are adults, most of them males, that sexually abuse little boys and girls.
Los pedófilos son adultos, en su mayoría varones, que abusan sexualmente de niños y niñas.

The twelve jurors, who deliberated for three days, found him guilty of kidnapping and abusing six girls.
Los doce jurados, que deliberaron tres días, lo declararon culpable de secuestrar y maltratar a seis niñas.

They charged him with child abuse.
Lo acusaron de malos tratos a la infancia.

accept

That is accepted practice in this kind of case.
Es la práctica establecida en este tipo de casos.

acceptable

Would that be acceptable to you?
¿Eso le resultaría aceptable?

acceptable evidence prueba admisible
One can also conclude that if there is no other acceptable evidence then dismissal occurs.
También podría concluir que la desestimación procede de no existir ninguna otra prueba admisible.

accessible

Education must be accessible to all.
La educación deber ser asequible a todos.

He may be accessible to bribery.
Puede que se lo pueda sobornar.

Housing must be accessible to all.
La vivienda debe ser asequible a todos.

Public buildings should be more accessible to disabled visitors.
Se debería facilitar el acceso de los minusválidos a los edificios públicos.

She may be accessible to persuasion.
Puede que se la pueda convencer.

accessory

accessory to the murder of cómplice en la muerte de
His ex-wife, Michelle, was found guilty of belonging to a gang that abducted and locked up young girls, and of being the co-author of the imprisonment of six of them and an accessory to the murders of Julie and Melissa.
Su ex mujer, Michelle, fue hallada culpable de pertenecer a una banda que secuestraba y encerraba a niñas y de ser coautora de la reclusión de las seis chicas y cómplice en la muerte de Julie y Melissa.

The court gave the defendant twenty years in prison as an accessory to the murder of the agent.
El tribunal ha impuesto veinte años de prisión al acusado como cómplice en el asesinato del agente.

accident

After a traffic accident, don't leave the crash site.
Después de un accidente de tráfico, no abandone el lugar del accidente.

After the accident, get in touch with your insurance company.
Después del accidente, comuníquese con su compañía de seguro.

At the scene of the accident call 911.
En el lugar del accidente llame al 911.

Did the accident occur on the street?
¿Ocurrió el accidente en la calle?

Due to the accident, her ability to walk is now severely impaired.
Debido al accidente, su movilidad se ha visto seriamente afectada.

Have you ever had an accident?
¿Ha tenido alguna vez un accidente?

He was at the scene of the accident.
Presenció el accidente.

I am sorry, it was an accident.
Lo siento, lo hice sin querer.

I hope they haven't had a car accident.
Espero que no hayan tenido un accidente de coche.

She is to blame for the accident.
Ella tiene la culpa del accidente.

The accident was witnessed by two people.
Hay dos testigos del accidente.

The boy told the police that he witnessed the accident.
El chico le dijo a la policía que presenció el accidente.

The manager was held accountable for the accident.
Al director se le imputó la responsabilidad del accidente.

Was anybody else hurt in the accident?
¿Se lastimó alguien más en el accidente?

Was anybody else involved in the accident?
¿Se vio alguien más envuelto en el accidente?

accident insurance seguro de accidentes
He took out accident insurance.
Contrató un seguro de accidentes.
Se hizo un seguro de accidentes.

accident scene lugar del accidente

Did the police come to the accident scene?
¿Acudió la policía al lugar del accidente?

accompany

accompanied by acompañada de, acompañado de, junto a
He was accompanied by two bodyguards.
Iba acompañado de dos guardaespaldas.

Mr. Ortiz proclaimed his innocence in an emotional court appearance accompanied by his wife.
El señor Ortiz proclamó su inocencia en una emotiva comparecencia junto a su esposa.

The application must be accompanied by a medical certificate.
La solicitud ha debe ir acompañada de un certificado médico.

The application should be accompanied by a certificate.
La solicitud debe ir acompañada de un certificado.

according

according to según
According to American authorities, 80 people have died between January and May trying to cross the border.
Entre enero y mayo de este año, según las autoridades estadounidenses, han fallecido ochenta personas intentando cruzar la frontera.

According to eye witnesses, the car was stopped with its flashing lights on.
Según testigos presenciales, el coche se encontraba parado con los intermitentes puestos.

According to his lawyer, he has nothing to do with the case.
Según su abogado, no tiene nada que ver con el caso.

You get a different answer according to who you ask.
La respuesta es diferente según a quién le preguntes.

account

Her account is backed up by evidence.
Hay pruebas que confirman su versión.

account for dar cuenta de
He gave a good account of the accident.
Dio buena cuenta del accidente.

She gave a good account of what happened.
Dio buena cuenta de lo que pasó.

She met with the journalists to account for the situation.

Se reunió con los periodistas para dar cuenta de la situación.

The suspect was unable to account for his movements.
El sospechoso no fue capaz de dar cuenta de sus movimientos.

The suspect was unable to account for his movements at the time of the crime.
El sospechoso no fue capaz de dar cuenta de sus movimientos a la hora del crimen.
account of versión de
She gave me a very different account of the events.
Me dio una versión muy distinta de los hechos.

accuse
A 16 year old boy was accused of shooting his girlfriend.
Un muchacho de dieciseis años fue acusado de matar a balazos a su novia.

An 18 year old boy was accused of shooting his parents.
Un muchacho de 18 años fue acusado de matar a balazos a sus padres.

An 18 year old girl was accused of stealing some money from the cash register.
Una muchacha de dieciocho años fue acusada de robar dinero de la caja.

He is accused of abusing his children.
Lo acusan de abusar de sus hijos.

He is accused of beating and sexually abusing six children between the ages of 13 and 15.
Lo acusan de golpear y abusar sexualmente de seis chicos — de entre trece y quince años de edad.

He is accused of killing his neighbor.
Él es acusado de haber matado a su vecino.

He was accused of bribery and corruption.
Lo acusaron de soborno y corrupción.

He was accused of using a gun to rob a store.
Fue acusado de usar una pistola para robar una tienda.

His client is accused of double murder.
Su cliente está acusado de doble asesinato.

She is not guilty of the crime of which she is accused.
No es culpable del delito que se le imputa.

She was accused of criminal possession of a controlled

substance.
Fue acusada de tenencia ilícita de sustancias reguladas.

The district attorney's office accuses Peterson of murdering his wife Laci in their house in Modesto.
La fiscalía acusa a Peterson de asesinar a su esposa Laci en su casa de Modesto.

The man from Oaxaca was accused of first degree murder.
El oaxaqueño fue acusado de homicidio en primer grado.

The man was accused of battering his wife.
El hombre fue acusado de maltratar a su esposa.

The prison dismissed a guard who is accused of ill-treating prisoners.
La prisión destituyó a un funcionario acusado de vejar a presos.

They are accused of murder.
Se les acusa de asesinato.

They stand accused of robbing a bank.
Se les acusa de asaltar un banco.

They were accused of breaking and entering.
Los acusaron de allanamiento de morada.

They were accused of handling stolen goods.
Se les acusó de comerciar con objetos robados.

They were accused of racial discrimination.
Los acusaron de discriminación racial.

accused

the accused el acusado, la acusada
Does it match the discription of the accused?
¿Corresponde a la descripción del acusado?

During the hearing the accused remained silent.
Durante la audiencia el acusado permaneció silencioso.

The accused acknowledged that he knew the victim.
El acusado reconoció que conocía a la víctima.

The accused announced his decision to take the Fifth in order to avoid testifying on the bankruptcy of the company.
El acusado anunció su decisión de acogerse a la Quinta Enmienda para no prestar testimonio sobre la quiebra de la empresa.

The accused declared himself innocent through his lawyer.
El acusado hizo su declaración de inocencia a través de su abogado.

The accused denies having raped the young woman last summer.
El acusado niega haber violado a la joven el verano pasado.

The accused is innocent until proven guilty.
El acusado es inocente hasta que se le pruebe ser culpable.

The accused maintains that they had consensual sex.
El acusado argumenta que mantuvieron sexo consensuado.

The accused persisted in her denial.
La acusada se mantuvo en su negativa.

The accused took the Fifth.
El acusado se acogió a la Quinta Enmienda.

The accused was convicted of four misdemeanors related to tampering with evidence and attempting to cover up the incident.
El acusado fue condenado por cuatro delitos menores, relacionados con manipulación de evidencia y tratar de encubrir el incidente.

The accused was wearing shackles around his ankles.
El acusado llevaba grilletes en los tobillos.

The accused will conduct his own defense.
El acusado se hará cargo de su propia defensa.

The Code of Judicial Proceedings of Texas stipulates that the accused must be competent in order to stand trial.
El Código de Procedimientos Judiciales de Texas dispone que los acusados deben ser competentes para someterse a juicio.

The criminal system in the US is based on one essential principle: the accused is innocent until proven guilty.
El sistema criminal de Estados Unidos está basado en un principio esencial: el acusado es inocente hasta que se le pruebe ser culpable.

The family members of the accused stated that she is one month pregnant.
Los familiares de la acusada manifestaron que está embarazada de un mes.

The indictment was read out to the accused.
Se leyeron los cargos al acusado.

The judge refused the accused bail.
El juez le denegó la libertad bajo fianza al acusado.
The older sister of both said she never saw anything inappropriate between the brothers and the accused.
La hermana mayor de ambos dijo que nunca había pressenciado nada inapropiado entre los hermanos y el acusado.

The prosecution has the obligation to prove that the accused are guilty beyond a reasonable doubt.
La fiscalía tiene la obligación de probar que los acusados son culpables más allá de toda duda razonable.

The prosecutor added that none of the evidence that he studied was sufficient enough to charge the accused.
El fiscal agregó que ninguna de las pruebas que estudió eran suficientemente determinantes para imputar al acusado.

What can you say in defense of the accused?
¿Qué puede formular en descargo del acusado?

acknowledge, acknowledgement

The accused acknowledged that he knew the victim, but he reduced the relationship between them to a matter of neighborhood.
El acusado reconoció que conocía a la víctima pero redujo la relación entre ambos a una mera cuestión de vecindad.

The Child Welfare League of America has acknowledged the necessity of the Spanish speaking community to participate in the determination of policies concerning child welfare.
La Liga Norteamericana para el Bienestar del Niño ha reconocido la necesidad de que la comunidad de habla hispana participe en la determinación de políticas para el bienestar infantil.

I acknowledge that there is no evidence.
Reconozco que no existen pruebas.

Once they have paid what they owe you, file a form called Acknowledgment of Satisfaction of Judgment.
Una vez que haya pagado lo que le debe, presente un formulario llamado Reconocimiento de Pago del Fallo.

acknowledged fact hecho reconocido
It's an acknowledged fact that the judicial system has its shortcomings.
Es un hecho reconocido que el sistema judicial tiene sus defectos.

acquaint

acquainted with conocer a, al corriente de, al tanto de
I didn't know you were acquainted with the victim.
No sabía que conocías a la víctima.

Perhaps they are not acquainted with the facts.
Quizás ellos no estén al tanto de los hechos.

Perhaps you are not acquainted with the facts.
Quizás usted no esté al corriente de los hechos.

Perhaps you are not fully acquainted with the facts.
Quizás usted no esté totalmente al corriente de los hechos.

acquaintance
I am very glad to make your acquaintance.
Tengo mucho gusto en conocerle.

They are old acquaintances.
Se conocen desde hace tiempo.

acquit
All the others were acquitted.
Todos los demás feuron absueltos de toda culpa.

He asked the court to acquit his client on all counts.
Solicitó la total absolución de su cliente.

He doesn't stand a chance of being acquitted.
No tiene ninguna posibilidad de ser absuelto.

He was acquitted on appeal.
Su condena fue revocada en la apelación.

She was acquitted.
La absolvieron de toda culpa.

act
Acting on the information received, the police made two arrests.
Actuando sobre la base de información recibida, la policía realizó dos arrestos.

The lawyer acting for my family is named Johnson.
El abogado que actúa en nombre de mi familia se llama Johnson.

They were acting on the instructions of the chief of police.
Cumplían órdenes del jefe de policía.

We must act now.
Tenemos que tomar medidas inmediatamente.

act alone actuar sola, actuar solo
The charges show that the defendant acted alone.
Las acusaciones consideran que el procesado actuó solo.
The lawyer stated that the evidence indicates that his client acted alone and that he has no connections to terrorist groups.
El abogado declaró que las pruebas indican que su cliente actuó solo y no tiene conexiones con grupos terroristas.

act as hacer de
She will act as the interpreter of the court.

Hará de intérprete de la corte.

act as if hacer como si
He acted as if he didn't know anything about the case
Hizo como si no supiera nada del caso.

He acted as if nothing had happened.
Hizo como si no hubiera pasado nada.

act in actuar en
He acted in self-defense.
Actuó en defensa propia.

My client acted in self-defense.
Mi cliente actuó en legítima defensa.

They acted in self-defense.
Actuaron en defensa propia.

The accused maintains that he acted in self-defense.
El acusado mantiene que actuó en legítima defensa.

act of violence acto de violencia
It is clear that no act of violence will be tolerated against any workers, and measures will be taken against the perpetrators.
Está claro que no se tolerará ningún acto de violencia contra los trabajadores y se tomarán medidas contra los autores.

It is an incomprehensible and senseless act of violence.
Es un acto de violencia incomprensible y sin sentido.

These acts of violence will not go unpunished.
Estos actos de violencia no quedarán impunes.

act strangely actuar de una manera rara
When the police arrived on the scene of the crime, he was acting strangely.
Estaba actuando de una manera rara cuando la policía llegó al lugar del delito.

catch somebody in the act sorprender a alguien en el acto
The police caught the robber in the act.
La policía sorprendió al ladrón en el acto.

senseless act of violence acto de violencia sin sentido
Once again it has been innocent people killed by these gang members in an act of senseless violence.
Una vez más han sido inocentes los asesinados por estos pandilleros en un acto de violencia sin sentido.

actual

The judge cited actual cases.
El juez citó casos reales.

This is the actual spot where it happened.
Ocurrió aquí mismo.

Those were her actual words.
Ésas fueron sus palabras textuales.

actually

Actually, he would rather not take the stand.
La verdad es que prefiere no subir al estrado.

Actually, he would rather not talk.
La verdad es que prefiere no hablar.

Actually, she would rather not testify.
La verdad es que prefiere no testificar.

She is actually very bright.
En realidad es muy inteligente.

addicted

Are you addicted to crack?
¿Eres adicto al crack?

She is addicted to heroin.
Es adicta a la heroína.

The danger of becoming addicted to drugs is prevalent in the inner-cities.
El peligro de llegar a depender de drogas es muy corriente en los barrios de las zonas urbanas deprimidas.

address

How long have you been at this address?
¿Desde cuándo vives aquí?

I will inform my probation officer before changing address or work.
Le informaré a mi oficial de libertad condicional antes de cambiar de domicilio o empleo.

The judge addressed the jury.
El juez se dirigió al jurado.

The letter is addressed to you.
La carta está dirigida a usted.

The letter was addressed to your home address.

La carta estaba dirigida a tu domocilio particular.

The package is addressed to your name.
El paquete está dirigido a tu nombre.

They live at the same address.
Viven en la misma dirección.

We have not yet been informed of any change of address.
Todavía no se nos ha informado de ningún cambio de dirección.

What is her address?
¿Cuál es su dirección?

What is your address?
¿Cuál es su dirección?

Would you like the address?
¿Quiesiera la dirección?

adjourn
The court adjourned for lunch.
El tribunal levantó la sesión para ir a comer.

The court is adjourned.
Se levanta la sesión.

They court was adjourned at the request of the defense.
La sesión se levantó a instancias de la defensa.

admissible
admissible evidence prueba admisible
One can also conclude that if there is no other acceptable evidence, then dismissal occurs.
También podría concluir que la desestimación procede de no existir ninguna otra prueba admisible.

They met to discuss, among other things, the admissible proof of the trial.
Se reunieron para discutir, entre otras cosas, la prueba admisible en juicio.

admit
He admitted having lied.
Admitió que había mentido.
Reconoció que había mentido.

He has admitted his guilt.
Se ha reconocido culpable.

She has admitted her guilt on charges of fraud.
Se ha reconocido culpable de cargos por fraude.

The accused admitted his guilt during a court appearance.
El acusado reconoció su culpabilidad durante la comparecencia ante un juez.

The lawyer accused of defrauding his client has admitted his guilt during the trial.
El abogado acusado de estafar a su cliente ha reconocido su culpabilidad durante el juicio.

advance

advance payment pago por adelantado
They only accept advance payments.
Sólo aceptan pagos por adelantado.

in advance con antelación.
Let me know in advance.
Avísame con antelación.

advice

He gave me some good advice.
Me dio buenos consejos.

I would like some advice on these contracts.
Quisiera que me aconsejara sobre estos contratos.

I would like your advice.
Quisiera que me aconsejara.

It was a good piece of advice.
Fue un buen consejo

It was good advice.
Fue un buen consejo

She declined to give me some advice.
Se abstuvo de aconsejarme.

She gave me some good advice.
Me aconsejó bien.

advise

I advise against your going.
Aconsejo que no vayas.

I advise on immigration matters.
Aconsejo en los aspectos inmigratorios.

I need someone to advise me.

Necesito que alguien me aconseje.

What do you advise?
¿Qué me aconseja?

You've been badly advised.
Han sido mal aconsejados.
Has sido mal aconsejada.
Has sido mal aconsejado.

advisory
He did it in an advisory capacity.
Lo hizo en calidad de asesor.

affair
He doesn't want anything to do with the whole affair.
Se desentendió por completo del asunto.

He had an affair with her years ago.
Tuvo relaciones con ella hace muchos años.

He washed his hands of the whole affair.
Se desentendió por completo del asunto.

Police are probing into his business affairs.
La policía está investigando sus actividades financieras.

The affair destroyed their relationship.
El lío acabó con su relación.

They are having an affair.
Tienen relaciones.

afford
afford to hire poder contratar a; poder pagar por
Can you afford to hire a lawyer?
¿Puede contratar a un abogado?
¿Puede pagar por un abogado?

How much can you afford?
¿Cuánto puede gastar?

I can't afford to pay for it.
No tengo con qué pagarlo.
No puedo pagarlo.

I can't afford the time.
No tengo el tiempo.

In your position you can't afford to be outspoken.

En la posición en que está, no puede permitirse el lujo de decir lo que piensa.

If you cannot afford to hire a lawyer, one will be appointed.
Si usted no puede contratar a un abogado, uno le será nombrado.
Si usted no puede pagar por un abogado, uno le será nombrado.

This is an opportunity you cannot afford to miss.
Esta es una ocasión que no puede desperdiciar.

You can't afford to miss the opportunity to plea bargain.
No puede perderse la oportunidad de llegar a un acuerdo con el fiscal.

You can't afford to miss this opportunity.
No puede perderse esta oportunidad.

affordable

affordable housing ivienda asequible
A lack of affordable housing is one of the primary causes of homelessness.
La falta de vivienda asequible es una de las principales causas del número de personas sin techo.

Americans support the construction of more affordable housing, be it for sale or for rent, in their communities if the housing fits in with the zoning.
Los estadounidenses apoyan la construcción de más vivienda asequible, sea para venta o alquiler, en sus comunidades si la vivienda encaja con la zona.

The poor also deserve affordable housing.
Los pobres dignos de ayuda también merecen una vivienda asequible.

afraid

Don't be afraid.
No temas.

He was afraid that nobody would believe him.
Temía que nadie le creyera.
I'm afraid that won't be possible.
Temo que no va a ser posible.

Never be afraid to ask for help.
Si necesitas ayuda, no tengas miedo de pedirla.

She's afraid he might not testify.
Teme que no vaya a testificar.

She's afraid to testify.

Le da miedo testificar.

She was afraid of losing her job.
Temía perder su trabajo.

There's nothing to be afraid of.
No tienes nada que temer.

after
The police are after him.
La policía lo está buscando.
La policía está detrás de él.

after después de
After the accident get in touch with your insurance company.
Después del accidente comuníquese con su compañía de seguro.

after a few después de unos cuantos
Okay, I will see you after few days.
Bueno, te veo después de unos cuantos días.

Okay, I will see you after few hours.
Bueno, te veo después de unas cuantas horas.

Okay, I will see you after a few weeks.
Bueno, te veo después de unas cuantas semanas.

after all a fin de cuentas
After all, it's the result that counts.
A fin de cuentas, lo que importa es el resultado.

After all, you are the one who has to take the responsibility.
A fin de cuentas, el que carga con la responsabilidad eres tu.

after an hour después de una hora
Okay, I will see you after an hour.
Bueno, te veo poco después de una hora.

after years después de años
She was reunited with her children after years.
Se reencontró con sus hijos después de años.
after college al terminar la universidad
After college she got married.
Al terminar la universidad se casó.

After college she joined the army.
Al terminar la universidad se alistó en el ejército.

after days of tras días de
The jury reached a verdict after days of deliberating.
Tras días de deliberaciones el jurado llegó a un veredicto.

They reached an agreement after days of negotiating.
Tras días de negociaciones llegaron a un acuerdo.

after long tras largas, tras largos
After long deliberations the jury found him guilty.
Tras largas deliberaciones el jurado lo declaró culpable.

After long deliberations the jury found him not guilty.
Tras largas deliberaciones el jurado lo absolvió de toda culpa.

after many después de mucha , después de mucho
After much thought she decided not to accept the offer.
Después de mucho pensar decidió no aceptar la oferta.

He was reunited with his wife after many years.
Se reencontró con su esposa después de muchos años.

She was reunited with her children after many years.
Se reencontró con sus hijos después de muchos años.

after murdering tras asesinar
After murdering her, so alleges the prosecution, Peterson got rid of the dead body by dumping it from his small boat into the waters of the San Francisco Bay.
Tras asesinarla, alega la acusación, Peterson se deshizo del cadáver arrojándolo a las aguas de la bahía de San Francisco desde su pequeña embarcación.

after selling tras vender
The brothers were arrested after selling four kilos of cocaine to an undercover policeman.
Los hermanos fueron detenidos tras vender cuatro kilos de cocaína a un policía encubierto.

after the arrest después del arresto
After the arrest the initial appearance takes place.
Después del arresto ocurre la vista inicial.

after years después de años
She was reunited with her children after years of being apart.
Se reencontró con sus hijos después de años de estar separados.

again
I had to do it again.
Tuve que hacerlo de nuevo.

In May, he was arrested again for attacking one of his classmates.
En mayo, fue detenido otra vez por agredir a uno de sus compañeros de clase.

She had to take the stand again.
Tuvo que subir al estrado otra vez.

Two years later, he was arrested again accused of rape.
Dos años después, fue detenido otra vez acusado de violación.

against

He was against pleading guilty.
Estaba en contra de declararse culpable.

He was against taking the stand.
Estaba en contra de subir al estrado.

It's against the law.
Es ilegal.

It's against the law to import that type of article.
La importación de ese tipo de artículo es ilegal.

She has started legal proceedings against them.
Ha procedido judicialmente en contra de ellos.
Les ha entablado pleito.

They have spoken out against the verdict.
Se han manifestado en contra del veredicto.

What have you got against her?
¿Qué tiene usted contra ella?

What you did is against the law.
La ley lo prohíbe lo que hizo.
Lo que hizo es ilegal.

age

He has aged a lot.
Ha envejecido mucho.

She has aged a lot.
Ha envejecida mucho.

I have a daughter the same age as you.
Tengo una hija de tu misma edad.
The children's ages are three, four and six.
Los niños tienen, respectivamente, tres, cuatro y seis.

They are the same age.
Tienen la misma edad.

What age is she?
¿Qué edad tiene?
¿Cuántos años tiene?

What age was she when she died?
¿Qué edad tenía cuando murió?

¿Cuántos años tenía cuando murió?

at the age of a los ... años de edad
He left school at the age of 16.
Abandonó los estudios a los dieciseis años de edad.

She died at the age of 85.
Murió a los ochenta y cinco años de edad.

it has been ages since hace siglos que
It's been ages since I saw her.
Hace siglos que no la veo.

to be of age ser mayor de edad
I believe she is of age.
Creo que ella es mayor de edad.

to be under age ser menor de edad
I believe she is under age.
Creo que ella es menor de edad.

aggravate

aggravated battery robo con agravantes
Ramón Martínez Robles, who is mentally retarded, was accused of aggravated burglary.
Ramón Martínez Robles, quien padece de retraso mental, fue acusado de robo con agravantes.

ahead

They arrived ahead of schedule.
Llegaron antes de la hora.

We are ahead of time.
Vamos adelantados.

We finished ahead of schedule.
Terminamos antes del plazo establecido en el programa.

We are three months ahead of schedule.
Llevamos tres meses de adelanto sobre la fecha prevista.

You'll get there ahead of us.
Llegarás antes que nosotros.

aid

aided and abetted by instigado y secundado por
He was aided and abetted by his partner.
Fue instigado y secundado por su socio.

She was aided and abetted by her partner.
Fue instigada y secundada por su socio.

alive

The hopes of finding her alive are slight.
Las esperanzas de encontrarla con vida son escasas.

The hopes of finding him alive are slight.
Las esperanzas de encontrarlo con vida son remotas.

The hopes of finding them alive are slight.
Las esperanzas de encontrarlos con vida son remotas.

They find three missing women alive in Juarez.
Localizan con vida a tres mujeres desaparecidas en Ciudad Juárez.

all

All the best!
¡Buena suerte!

All the best!
¡Que le vaya bien!

Are you all right?
¿Está bien?

He disavowed all knowledge of the matter.
Negó tener conocimiento del asunto.

He is not at all selfish.
No es nada egoísta.

It is all right.
No se preocupe.

It is all right with me.
Lo que es por mí, no hay problema.
Yo, de acuerdo.

It was all part of the job.
Formaba parte del trabajo.

She disclaimed all knowledge of his whereabouts.
Negó conocer su paradero.

She is out till all hours.
Se queda fuera hasta muy tarde.

Yes, that's all right.
Sí, de acuerdo.

All of his possessions were confiscated.
Fue privado de sus bienes.

She had all her possessions confiscated.
Fue privada de sus bienes.

He was all covered in blood.
Estaba completamente cubierto de sangre.

all agreed estar todos acordes
They all agreed.
Están todos acordes.

We are all agreed.
Estamos todos acordes.

all along desde el primer momento, desde el principio
This is what I feared all along.
Esto es lo que estaba temiendo desde el primer momento.

This is what the defense feared all along.
Esto es lo que estaba temiendo la defensa desde el primer momento.

This is what we feared all along.
Esto es lo que estábamos temiendo desde el principio

all day long todo el día
I've been trying to get you all day long.
He estado intentando hablar contigo todo el día.

The jury deliberated all day long.
El jurado deliberó todo el día.

all in all resumiendo, en definitiva, en general
All in all, I think it was a good hearing.
Resumiendo, creo que fue una buena vista.

All in all, it was a good defense.
En definitiva fue una buena defensa.

All in all, things turned out quite well.
En general, las cosas salieron bastante bien.

We thought, all in all, it wasn't a bad idea.
Pensamos que, en general, no era una mala idea.

all kinds of toda suerte de
All kinds of people came.
Toda suerte de gente vino.

There were all kinds of remarks.
Hubo toda suerte de comentarios.

all the others todos los demás
All the others were acquitted.
Todos los demás feuron absueltos de toda culpa.

All the others were released on bail.
Todos los demás fueron puestos en libertad bajo fianza.

all the same a pesar de todo
All the same, I think you should enter a plea of not guilty.
A pesar de todo, creo que debe declararse inocente.

all week toda la semana
I've been trying to get you all week.
He estado intentando hablar contigo toda la semana.

The jury deliberated all week.
El jurado deliberó toda la semana.

beyond all doubt sin que quepa la menor duda
It has been proved beyond all doubt.
Se ha probado sin que quepa la menor duda.

beyond all doubt más allá de toda duda
The prosecution has the obligation to prove that the accused are guilty beyond all doubt.
La fiscalía tiene la obligación de probar que los acusados son culpables más allá de toda duda.

already

By nine o'clock the jury was already deliberating.
A las nueve el jurado ya estaba deliberando.

Have you two already met?
¿Ya se conocen?

He is here already.
Ya está aquí.

I already spoke with her.
Ya hablé con ella.

I already spoke with him.
Ya hablé con él.

I already spoke with them.
Ya hablé con ellos.

I've been here twice already.
Ya he estado aquí dos veces.

Is it that late already?
¿Ya es tan tarde?

It emerged from the testimony that he already knew.
Durante el testimonio se reveló que ya lo sabía.

It is already two o'clock and she hasn't called yet.
Ya son las dos y aún no ha llamado.

Meet with a probation officer immediately, if you have not already done so.
Encuéntrate de inmediato con un funcionario que vigila a las personas que están en libertad, si no lo has hecho todavía.

She told us little beyond what we already knew.
No nos dijo gran cosa fuera de lo que ya sabíamos.

We learned that she had already left.
Nos enteramos de que ya se había ido.

also

One can also conclude that if there is no other acceptable evidence then dismissal occurs.
También podría concluir que la desestimación procede de no existir ninguna otra prueba admisible.

The children are also victims of violence in the hands of other minors.
Los niños también son víctimas de la violencia a manos de otros menores.

The court clerk will also be present in the courtroom.
En la sala del tribunal también estará presente el secretario del juzgado.

The poor also deserve affordable housing.
Los pobres dignos de ayuda también merecen una vivienda asequible.

The primary doctor will also evaluate the need for additional laboratory tests.
El médico de primer contacto también evaluará la necesidad de pruebas adicionales de laboratorio.

The victims between the ages of 14 and 17 must also sign the application.
Las víctimas de entre 14 y 17 años de edad también deben firmar la solicitud.

They also discussed other matters.

Hablaron también de otros temas.

alter

He altered the official report.
Amañó el informe oficial.

That doesn't alter things much.
Eso no cambia mucho las cosas.

Then that alters things.
Entonces la cosa cambia.

although

He is very nervous, although you would never think so.
Es muy nervioso, aunque no lo parezca.

He said he wouldn't tell me even if he knew.
Me dijo que no me lo diría, aunque lo supiera.

He said he wouldn't testify even if he could.
Me dijo que no testificaría, aunque pudiera.

You must testify, even if you don't want to.
Debes testificar, aunque no quieras.

You must plead guilty, even if you don't want to.
Debe confesarse culpable, aunque no quiera.

always

He always has to impose his point of view.
Siempre tiene que imponer su punto de vista.

He's always late.
Siempre llega tarde.

It is no good giving her advice, in the end she always does what she wants.
Es inútil darle consejos, al fin y al cabo hace siempre lo que quiere.

The lawyer must always keep his client informed of all important matters that develop in the case.
El abogado debe mantener siempre informado a su cliente de todo asunto importante que surja en el caso.

She's always ready to help.
Siempre está dispuesta a ayudar.

Their kids are always in trouble.
Sus hijos siempre se meten en líos.

There's always the danger that he'll forget.
Siempre existe el peligro de que se le olvide.

We always get paid at the end of the month.
Siempre cobramos a fines de mes.

You are late, as always.
Llegas tarde, como siempre.

among

Tom was arrested last Friday along with six other persons, among them four women who on Thursday were released by the judge for lack of evidence, according to sources familiar with the case.
Tom fue detenido el viernes pasado con otras seis personas, entre ellas cuatro mujeres que el jueves fueron excarceladas por el juez por falta de pruebas, según fuentes del caso.

I count her among one of my best friends.
La cuento entre mis mejores amigas.

Murder with a firearm is the main cause of death among Hispanics.
El homicidio con armas de fuego es la causa principal de muertes entre hispanos.

Suicide among young adolescents of this country has seen a dramatic increase in recent years.
El suicidio entre los adolescentes de este país ha tenido un aumento dramático en los últimos años.

They quarreled among themselves.
Riñeron entre sí.

We are among friends.
Estamos entre amigos.

amount

A co-payment is a fixed amount of money that you pay to the provider, the medical center, the pharmacy, etc. when you receive certain benefits.
Un copago es una cantidad fija de dinero que usted paga al proveedor, al centro médico, a la farmacia, etc. cuando recibe determinados servicios.

Child support is the amount of money that the court orders one parent to pay the other each month for support of the children.
La manutención de los hijos es la cantidad de dinero que la corte ordena a un padre pagar al otro cada mes para mantener a los hijos.

No amount of arguing will change their minds.
Por más que discutamos no van a cambiar de opinión.

amount to ascender a, ser prácticamente, venir a ser lo mismo
Her silence amounted to an admission of guilt.
Su silencio era prácticamente una admisión de su culpabilidad.

It amounts to stealing.
Viene a ser lo mismo que robo.

It all amounts to the same thing.
Viene a ser lo mismo.

The legal expenses amounted to $10,000.
Los costos legales ascendieron a diez mil dólares.

and

and for the better ¡y para bien!
He's changed — and for the better!
Ha cambiado — ¡y para bien!

and while y de paso
And while I'm about it I'll talk to your father.
Y de paso hablaré con tu padre.

and with good cause y con razón.
She was furious, and with good cause.
Estaba furiosa, y con razón.

answer

He answered the question of his own accord.
Contestó la pregunta por propia voluntad.

He has an answer for everything.
Lo justfica todo.
Tiene una respuesta para todo.

He saw a woman answering to that description.
Vio una mujer que respondía a esa descripción.

I am sorry to force the issue, but I must have an answer today.
Siento tener que presionar, pero necesito la respuesta para hoy.

I can't get an answer out of her.
No consigo que ella me dé una respuesta.

I can't get an answer out of him.
No consigo que él me dé una contestación.

I think he is best able to answer that question.
Creo que él es quien mejor puede contestar a esa pregunta.

I will answer for him.
Yo respondo por él.

She took a long time to answer me.
Tardó mucho en contestarme.

She will have to answer for what she did.
Va a tener que dar cuentas de lo que hizo.

The lawyer has to answer your questions and return your calls within a reasonable time period.
El abogado tiene que contestar sus preguntas y devolverle sus llamadas de teléfono dentro de un plazo de tiempo razonable.

To testify in court means to answer questions under oath.
Prestar testimonio ante un tribunal significa responder a preguntas bajo juramento.

Violence is not the answer.
La violencia no es la solución.

What is your answer?
¿Cuál fue su contestación?

What was their answer?
¿Cuál fue su contestación?

You get a different answer according to who you ask.
La respuesta es diferente según a quién le preguntes.

anticipate

His defense is better than I anticipated.
Su defensa es mejor de lo que esperaba.

Her defense is worse than I anticipated.
Su defensa es peor de lo que esperaba.

I don't anticipate any problems.
No creo que vaya a haber ningún problema.

I don't anticipate making any major changes in your defense.
No tengo previsto hacer ningún cambio importante en su defensa.

The police do not anticipate violence.
La policía no prevé actos de violencia.

The trial was more difficult than I anticipated.
El juicio resultó más difícil de lo que esperaba.

We get along better than I anticipated.
Nos llevamos mejor de lo que esperaba.

any

A defendant does not have to present any evidence.
El acusado no tiene que presentar evidencia.

Do you feel any better now?
¿Se siente mejor?

Do you have any brothers and sisters?
¿Tiene hermanos?

Do you have any children?
¿Tiene hijos?

Has she had any abortions?
¿Ha tenido abortos?

It is a while since we had any news.
Hace tiempo que no tenemos noticia.

any one of cualquiera de
Any one of them could be the murderer.
Cualquiera de ellos podría ser el asesino.

any problem algún problema, ningún problema
I don't anticipate any problems.
No creo que vaya a haber ningún problema.

Let me know if there is any problem.
Avísame si hay algún problema.

any questions alguna pregunta
Are there any questions?
¿Hay alguna pregunta?

If you have any questions, please do not hesitate to call.
Si tiene alguna pregunta, no dude en llamar.

any truth algo de verdad
Is there any truth in what he says?
¿Hay algo de verdad en lo que dice?

Is there any truth to her story?
¿Hay algo de verdad en su historia?

Is there any truth to her testimony?
¿Hay algo de verdad en su testimonio?

any way you look at it a todas luces
Any way you look at it, he is the guilty party.
Él es, a todas luces, el culpable.

It is true any way you look at it.

A todas luces es cierto.

in any en cualquier
The judge can turn up at any moment.
El juez puede aparecer en cualquier momento.

The jury can reach a verdict at any moment.
El jurado puede llegar a un acuerdo sobre el veredicto en cualquier momento.

There's an element of risk in any operation.
En cualquier operación hay un componente de riesgo.

They should be arriving at any moment
Deberían llegar en cualquier momento.

anybody

anybody else alguien más, cualquier otra persona
Anybody else have this problem?
¿Alguien más tiene este problema?

Anybody else would have done the same.
Cualquier otra persona habría hecho lo mismo.

Anybody else would have gone to court.
Cualquier otra persona habría acudido a los tribunales.

Anybody else would have pleaded guilty.
Cualquier otra persona se habría confesado culpable.

Is there anybody else I can talk to?
¿Hay alguien más con quien pueda hablar?

Was anybody else hurt in the accident?
¿Se lastimó alguien más en el accidente?

Was anybody else involved in the accident?
¿Se vio alguien más involucrado en el accidente?

Was anybody else there?
¿Estaba alguien más allí.?

anything

anything else nada más
I can't think of anything else.
No se me ocurre nada más.

We can't do anything else.
No podemos hacer nada más.

anything urgent cualquier caso urgente

Anything urgent should be brought to my attention.
Se me debe informar inmediatamente de cualquier caso urgente.

anything you say cualquier osa que diga
Anything you say may be taken down and used in evidence against you.
Cualquier cosa que diga podría utilizarse como prueba en su contra.

appear
Everyone appears to be here.
Parece que ya está aquí todo el mundo.

He'll appear in court tomorrow without question.
Indiscutiblemente comparecerá mañana ante el juez.

The judge summoned him to appear as a witness.
El juez requirió su presencia como testigo.

She's appearing on a charge of murder.
Comparece acusada de asesinato.

This would appear to be what happened.
Parecería que esto fue lo que pasó.

appear before comparecer ante
He is due to appear before the court next week.
Debe comparecer ante los tribunales la semana próxima.

He won't have to appear before the court to answer the ten charges related to child abuse until September.
No tendrá que volver a comparecer ante los tribunales para responder de los diez cargos relacionados con abuso de menores hasta septiembre.

His brother was ordered to appear before a judge for fraud.
Su hermano fue conminado a comparecer ante la justicia por estafa.

The judge summoned him to appear as a witness.
El juez requirió su presencia como testigo.

appearance
Judging by appearances, they have a lot of money.
A juzgar por las apariencias, tienen mucho dinero.

The suspect proclaimed her innocence in an emotional court appearance accompanied by her children and husband.
La sospechosa proclamó su inocencia en una emotiva comparecencia junto a sus hijos y esposo.

initial appearance vista inicial
After the arrest the initial appearance takes place.

Después del arresto ocurre la vista inicial.

The initial appearance is the first introduction of the accused to the proper authorities.
La vista inicial es la primera presentación de un acusado ante la autoridad competente.

court appearance comparecencia, comparición
Appearance in a court is the act of presenting oneself before the court and submitting to its authority.
Comparecencia es el acto de presentarse ante un tribunal y someterse a su autoridad.

The accused admitted his guilt during a court appearance in federal district court in New York.
El acusado reconoció su culpabilidad durante la comparecencia ante un juez federal de Nueva York.

Your next court appearance is in a week.
Tu próxima comparecencia ante el juez es en una semana.

appeal

appeal against reclamar contra
She appealed against the fine.
Reclamó contra la multa.

appeal the sentence apelar la sentencia
If you are found guilty after a nonjury trial, you can appeal the sentence.
Si se le encuentra culpable después de un juicio sin jurado, usted puede apelar la sentencia.

appeal to apelar ante
He will appeal to the Supreme Court.
Apelará ante el Tribunal Supremo.

enter an appeal interponer un recurso de apelación
The defense lawyer entered an appeal with the appellate court.
El abogado defensor interpuso un recurso de apelación con el tribunal de segunda instancia.

file an appeal presentar una apelación
If you didn't go to court because you didn't get a copy of the plaintiff's claim, you have 30 days to file an appeal.
Si no fue a la corte porque no recibió la copia del reclamo del demandante, tiene treinta días para presentar una apelación.

grant an appeal conceder una apelación
What happens if the judge doesn't grant my appeal?
¿Qué pasa si el juez no me concede la apelación?

lose the appeal perder en la apelación, perder la apelación

After losing her appeal, she asked the US Supreme Court to review her case.
Después de perder en la apelación, ella pidió la revisión de su caso ante el Tribunal Supremo de los Estados Unidos.

on appeal en la apelación.
He was acquitted on appeal.
Su condena fue revocada en la apelación.

appellate

appellate court tribunal de apelación
An appellate court is a higher court which has the authority to review the decision of lower courts and administrative agencies.
Un tribunal de apelación es un tribunal que tiene la autoridad de revisar las resoluciones de otros tribunales con efecto suspensivo o devolutivo.

appellate court tribunal de segunda nstancia
The defense lawyer entered an appeal with the appellate court.
El abogado defensor interpuso un recurso de apelación con el tribunal de segunda instancia.

apply

Cross out what does not apply.
Táchese lo que no proceda.

The judge is applying the rules very strictly.
El juez está aplicando muy estrictamente las reglas.

This law should have never been applied to this case.
Esta ley no debería aplicarse nunca a este caso.

appoint

If he cannot afford to hire a lawyer, one will be appointed.
Si él no puede contratar a un abogado, uno le será nombrado.

If you cannot afford to hire a lawyer, one will be appointed free of charge.
Si usted no puede pagar por un abogado, uno le será nombrado gratis.

The judge appointed the date for the hearing.
El juez designó la fecha para la audiencia.

They appointed him to the case.
Lo nombraron al caso.

appointment

Do you have an appointment?
¿Tiene cita?.

He failed to turn up for the appointment.

No acudió a la cita.

Have you made an appointment with the probation officer?
¿Te has citado con el funcionario que vigila a las personas que están en libertad?

I have to make an appointment with my lawyer.
Tengo que concertar una cita con mi abogado.

I have an appointment at ten.
Tengo cita a las diez.

I have arranged an appointment for Tuesday.
He concertado cita para el martes.

I made an appointment for three.
Pedí cita para las tres.

Make an Appointment with the U.S. Citizenship and Immigration Services.
Haga una cita con la Oficina de Ciudadanía y Servicios de Inmigración de Estados Unidos.

apprehend

He was apprehended shortly after the attempted robbery.
Fue detenido poco después de la tentativa de robo.

The suspect was apprehended on Tuesday in possession of a false passport.
El sospechoso fue detenido el martes, en posesión de un pasaporte falso.

To apprehend means to take into custody an individual pursuant to a criminal charge.
Aprehender quiere decir privar de la libertad a una persona que se presume ha cometido un acto punible.

approach

All drivers must drive carefully and reduce their speed below the speed limit when approaching a railroad crossing.
Todos los conductores deben extremar la prudencia y reducir la velocidad por debajo de la máxima permitida al aproximarse a un paso a nivel.

He approached me with an idea to sell drugs.
Me abordó para hablarme de una idea para vender drogas.

It is important to maintain a profesional approach with your lawyer.
Es importante mantener una actitud profesional con su abogado.

She was approached by a man in the street.
Un hombre la abordó en la calle.

Two policemen approached him.
Se le acercaron dos policías.

Why don't we try a different approach?
¿Por qué no probamos de otra manera?

are

are you ...? ¿es usted ...?, ¿está usted ...?, ¿darse cuenta ...?, etc.
Are you a lawyer?
¿Es usted abogada?
¿Es usted abogado?

Are you a social worker?
¿Es usted trabajador social?
¿Es usted trabajadora social?

Are you all right?
¿Está bien?

Are you aware of what this means?
¿Te das cuenta de lo que esto significa?

Are you carrying any money?
¿Traes dinero?

Are you carrying any weapons?
¿Llevas armas?

Are you depressed?
¿Está usted deprimida?
¿Está usted deprimido?

Are you divorced?
¿Está usted divorciada?
¿Está usted divorciado?

Are you easily angered?
¿Se enoja con facilidad?

Are you implicated in this?
¿Andas metido en esto?

Are you OK?
¿Está usted bien?

Are you injured?
¿Está usted lastimada?
¿Está usted lastimado?

Are you ready to cooperate with the authorities?
¿Estás dispuesto a cooperar con las autoridades?

Are you related to the driver of the vehicle?
¿Eres pariente del conductor del coche?
¿Estás emparentado con el conductor del coche?

Are you related to the prisoner?
¿Es usted pariente del prisionero?
¿Estás emparentado con el prisionero?

Are you sick?
¿Está usted enferma?
¿Está usted enfermo?

Are you speaking to me?
¿Se dirige usted a mí?

Are you sure this is the right man?
¿Estás segura de que es el hombre?

Are you sure you have got the right number?
¿Seguro que es ése el número?

Are you the owner?
¿Es usted el dueño?
¿Es usted la dueña?

Are you the owner of the car?
¿Es usted la dueña del coche?

Are you threatening me?
¿Me estás amenazando?

Are you very angry at the way you have been treated?
¿Estás muy enfadada por cómo te han tratado?
¿Estás muy enojada por cómo te han tratado?

Are you very annoyed?
¿Estás muy enfadada?
¿Estás muy enojada?

argue

Don't argue and do as I say!
¡No me discutas y hazlo que te digo!

Don't argue with me!
¡No me discutas!

His parents were always arguing.
Sus padres estaban siempre discutiendo.
Sus padres estaban siempre peleándose.

I don't want to argue with you.
No quiero discutir con usted.

In the trial the defense argued that the death of Laci was accidental.
La defensa argumentó en el juicio que la muerte de Laci fue accidental.

It was a well argued case.
Fue un argumento bien expuesto.

No amount of arguing will change their minds.
Por más que discutamos no van a cambiar de opinión.

The lawyer argued provocation.
El abogado alegó provocación.

We're supposed to be settling things, not arguing.
Se trata de arreglar la situación, no de discutir.

argue against manifestarse en contra
He argued against doing it.
Se manifestó en contra de hacerlo.

argument

Arguments are a line of reasoning presented by the parties in order to support a position.
Alegatos son el razonamiento que las partes postulan ante el tribunal para sostener su pretensión.

arm

A marine was arrested for illegal possession of arms.
Un marino fue arrestado por tenencia ilegal de armas.

He is an arms dealer.
Es traficante de armas.
Her arms were black with bruises.
Tenía los brazos llenos de moretones.

The woman, held in the Albuquerque detention center, had cuts on her face, neck and arms which she attributed to a fight with another girl.
La mujer, detenida en el centro de detención de Albuquerque, tenía cortes en la cara, el cuello y los brazos que atribuyó a una pelea con otra muchacha.

She was shot in the arm.
Recibió un balazo en el brazo.

The witness stated that the defendant was not armed.
El testigo manifestó que el acusado no llevaba armas.

armed and dangerous armado y peligroso
The suspect should be considered armed and dangerous.
El sospechoso debe ser considerado armado y peligroso.

This individual should be considered armed and dangerous.
Este individuo debería considerarse armado y peligroso.

armed robbery robo a mano armada, atracado a mano armada
Armed robbery is the forcible taking of property from another person by the use or threatened use of a deadly or dangerous weapon, or by causing seriouis bodily injury.
Robo a mano armada es el poderamiento a la fuerza de bienes ajenos mediante el uso de armas mortíferas o peligrosas, o mediante la amenaza de usarlas o causándole lesiones
corporales graves a la víctima.

He is doing eight years for armed robbery.
Está cumpliendo ocho años por atracado a mano armada.

The government charges the defendant with armed robbery.
El gobierno formula cargos de robo a mano armada contra el acusado.

The number of violent crimes, which include murder, rapes and armed robbery, have decreased.
El número de crímenes violentos, que incluyen homicidios, violaciones y robo a mano armada, se han reducido.

to arm oneself with armarse con, armarse de
They armed themselves with clubs and knives.
Se armaron con porras y cuchillos.

around

around alrededor de
He is somewhere around.
Anda por ahí.
He must be somewhere around here.
Debe estar por aquí.

Is he around?
¿Está por aquí?

I will get around to it sometime.
Yo lo haré en algún momento.

She must be around forty.
Tendrá alrededor de cuarenta años.

The accused was wearing shackles around his ankles.
El acusado llevaba grilletes en los tobillos.

The courthouse is around the corner.

El juzgado está a la vuelta de la esquina.

The policemen had taken up positions around the building.
Los policías se habían apostados alrededor del edificio.

There is no one around.
Aquí no hay nadie.

They found him wandering around the streets.
Lo encontraron vagando por las calles.

around the middle of a mediados de
The trial will begin around the middle of the year.
El juicio empezará a mediados de año.

We get paid around the middle of the month.
Nos pagan a mediados de mes.

arraign
He was arraigned on Monday.
Compareció ante un tribunal el lunes.

The suspect will be arraigned tomorrow.
El sospechoso comparecerá ante el juez mañana.

To arraign is to inform a defendant in open court of the charges filed against him or her and to enter a plea of guilty or not guilty.
Celebrar la vista incoatoria es informarle al acusado de las acusaciones que se le imputan, con posterior recibimiento de su declaración culpable o no culpable.

arraignment
arraignment comparecencia ante el juez
The arraignment has been postponed until further notice.
La comparecencia ante el juez ha sido aplazada hasta nuevo aviso.

The arraignment is in a week.
La comparecencia ante el juez tiene lugar en una semana.

The arraignment is on Tuesday
La comparecencia ante el juez tiene lugar el martes.

The arraignment takes place tomorrow.
La comparecencia ante el juez tiene lugar mañana.

arrange
Everything is arranged.
Todo está arreglado.

I arranged to meet him a week from today.
Quedé en encontrarme con él de aquí a una semana.

I have arranged an appointment for Wednesday.
He concertado cita para el miércoles.

Is everything arranged?
¿Está todo arreglado?

It was arranged that we would meet before the beginning of the trial.
Quedamos en que nos encontraríamos antes del comienzo del juicio.

She had arranged to meet them for lunch.
Había quedado en encontrarse con ellos para comer.

We have arranged for you to see a lawyer.
Le hemos pedido cita con el abogado.
Le hemos pedido hora con el abogado.

arrest

A warrant was issued for his arrest.
Se expidió una orden de arresto en su contra.
Se expidió una orden de detención en su contra.

Acting on the information received, the police made two arrests.
Actuando sobre la base de información recibida, la policía realizó dos arrestos.

After the arrest the initial appearance takes place.
Después del arresto ocurre la vista inicial.

He is under arrest on a robbery charge.
Ha sido arrestado acusado de robo.
Ha sido detenido acusado de robo.

He was arrested hours later.
Fue arrestado horas más tarde.

He was heading for the office when he was arrested.
Se dirigía a la oficina cuando lo arrestaron.

The brothers were arrested after selling four kilos of cocaine to an undercover policeman.
Los hermanos fueron detenidos tras vender cuatro kilos de cocaína a un policía encubierto.

They were heading for the border when they were arrested.
Se dirigían hacia la frontera cuando los arrestaron.

We were heading for the airport when we were arrested.
Nos dirigíamos al aeropuerto cuando nos arrestaron.

You are under arrest.

Queda arrestada.
Queda arrestado.
Queda detenida.
Queda detenido.
Quedan arrestados.
Quedan detenidos.

arrest order pedido de detención
The arrest order was signed by a judge.
El pedido de detención fue firmado por un juez.

The judge issued an arrest order for Charles Taylor.
El juez emitió una orden de arresto contra Charles Taylor.

arrested for
He was arrested for being drunk and disorderly.
Lo detuvieron por embriaguez y alteración del orden público.

She was arrested for disorderly conduct.
La detuvieron por alteración del orden público.

The man was arrested for battering his pregnant wife.
El hombre fue detenido por maltratar a su esposa embarazada.

The police have arrested a man who violated his parole.
La policía ha detenido a un hombre que quebrantó las condiciones impuestas por la libertad condicional.
The police have arrested a 40 year old man for allegedly battering his wife who is pregnant.
La policía ha detenido a un hombre, de unos cuarenta años, como presunto autor de los malos tratos ocasionados a su esposa, que está embarazada.

arrested on detener bajo acusación de
He was arrested on a charge of murder.
Le detuvieron bajo acusación de asesinato.

arrested on detener como presunto autor
The doctor was arrested on suspicion of having carried out illegal abortions.
El médico fue detenido como presunto autor de prácticas abortivas ilegales.

under house arrest bajo arresto domiciliario
He is under house arrest.
Se encuentra bajo arresto domiciliario.

arrive
Everybody who arrives in the United States, with or without papers, has Constitutional rights.
Toda persona que llega a Estados Unidos, con o sin documentos, tiene derechos Constitucionales.

For all I know he hasn't arrived yet.
Que sepa yo todavía no ha llegado.

He arrived just in time.
Llegó justo a tiempo.

He arrived shortly after you left.
Llegó al poco rato de irte tú.

Please wait until I arrive.
Por favor espera hasta que yo llegue.

She arrived at the courthouse at three in the afternoon.
Llegó al juzgado a las tres de la tarde.

The documents arrived late at night.
Los papeles llegaron a altas horas de la noche.

arrive at llegar a
She arrived at her mother's house.
Llegó a casa de su madre.

The jury hasn't arrived at a verdict.
El jurado no ha llegado a un veredicto.

The woman arrived at work with two black eyes.
La mujer llegó a su empleo con los dos ojos morados.

They still haven't arrived at a decision.
Todavía no han llegado a una decisión.

arrive on llegar el
He arrives on the fourteenth of May.
Llega el catorce de mayo.

She should arrive on the seventh of January.
Debe llegar el siete de enero.

as

as a en calidad de, de + profession
As a permanent resident you may travel outside the United States.
En su calidad de residente permanente, usted puede viajar fuera de Estados Unidos.

She's got a job as a hairdresser.
Trabaja de peluquera.

as a general rule por lo general
As a general rule the courts don't permit it.
Por lo general los tribunales no lo permiten.

as a juror como miembro del jurado
As a juror you must decide if the person accused is guilty or not.
Como miembro del jurado, debe decidir si la persona acusada es o no culpable.

As a juror your duty is to be fair and impartial.
Como miembro del jurado es su deber ser justo e imparcial.

as a last resort a la desesperada, como último recurso
He made that decision as a last resort.
Tomó aquella decisión a la desesperada.

Abortion should only be considered as a last resort.
El aborto debe ser sólo considerado como un último recurso.

Force should only be used as a last resort.
La fuerza sólo debe ser usada como último recurso.

as a legal guardian como tutor legal
Upon being named as a legal guardian of the child, you have the responsibility of the daily care of the minor.
Al ser designado por la corte como tutor legal del niño, usted es responsable del cuidado diario del menor.

What should I do as a legal guardian?
¿Qué debo hacer como tutor legal?

as a member of como miembro de
He was identified as a member of the gang.
Se lo identificó como miembro de la banda.

as a minor como menor
It is still not known whether he'll be tried as a minor or an adult.
Todavía no sabe si será juzgado como menor o como adulto.

as a private individual a título personal
I am speaking as a private individual.
Hablo a título personal.

as a result of a raíz de
As a result of the article an inquiry was launched.
A raíz del artículo se inició una investigación.

as a single father de padre soltero
He started a new life as a single father.
Empezó una nueva vida de padre soltero.

as a single mother de madre soltera
She started a new life as a single mother.
Empezó una nueva vida de madre soltera.

as a warning de advertencia
This will act as a warning.
Esto servirá de advertencia.

as a witness como testigo
The defense called him as a witness.
La defensa lo citó como testigo.

They called his friend as a witness.
Llamaron a su amigo como testigo.

They called his girlfriend as a witness.
Llamaron a su novia como testigo.

The judge summoned him to appear as a witness.
El juez requirió su presencia como testigo.

as far as en cuanto a
As far as I'm concerned, he is a big disappointment to us.
En cuanto a mí, nos ha decepcionado mucho.

as far as I know que yo sepa
As far as I know, he is a big disappointment to us.
Que yo sepa, nos ha decepcionado mucho.

As far as I know, there were no fatalities.
Que yo sepa, no hubo muertos.

as I see it a mi ver
As I see it, his suggestion isn't worth anything.
A mi ver su sugerencia, no vale nada.

as soon as en cuanto
As soon as I heard it I left.
En cuanto lo supe me fui.

I'll come as soon as I can.
Vendré en cuanto pueda.

as well as al igual que, así como
His brother, as well as his sister, will attend the meeting.
Su hermano, al igual que su hermana, acudirá a la reunión.

His father as well as his mother, speaks English.
Su padre, así como su madre, habla inglés.

as you know como usted sabe
As you know, the medical insurance pays all the medical expenses.
Como usted sabe el seguro médico paga todos los gastos médicos.

ask

Ask him if he has seen her.
Pregúntale si la ha visto.

Ask the owner to sign it.
Pídale al dueño que lo firme.
Pídale a la dueña que lo firme.

Did you ask him his name?
¿Le preguntaste su nombre?

If you need anything, just ask.
Si quieres algo no tienes más que pedirlo.

ask a question hacer una pregunta
I asked you a question.
Te hice una pregunta.

ask about preguntar acerca de, preguntar por
Nobody at school can ask about the immigration status of the family.
Nadie en la escuela puede preguntar acerca de la situación de inmigración de la familia.

Did you ask him about the job?
¿Le has preguntado por el trabajo?

ask for a continuance pedir que el caso se posponga
Ask the judge for a continuance when you go to court.
Cuando vaya a la corte pídale al juez que posponga su caso.

ask for a referral to pedir derivarle a, pedir mandarle a
I asked for a referral to a specialist.
Pedí que me derivaran a un especialista.

She asked for a referral to a specialist.
Pidió que la mandaran a un especialista.

ask many questions hacer muchas preguntas
He asked many questions.
Hizo muchas preguntas.

They asked many questions.
Hicieron muchas preguntas.

ask the judge for pedirle al juez que
Ask the judge for a continuance when you go to court.
Cuando vaya a la corte pídale al juez que posponga su caso.

assault

Assault is the attempt or threat to cause physical injury with an apparent present ability to do so, or the act of causing physical injury.

Agresión es la tentativa o amenaza de causarle lesiones corporales a una persona con la habilidad aparente de hacerlo, o el acto de causar lesiones corporales.

Assault may be committed without actually touching or striking a person.
Se puede cometer agresión con contacto fisico o sin él.

assault with agresión con
Assault with a deadly weapon is the willful attempt or threat to cause serious physical injury with an apparent present ability to do so, with an instrument capable of causing death or serious bodily harm.
Agresión con arma mortífera o arma de fuego es la tentativa o amenaza intencional de causar lesiones corporales graves, con la habilidad aparente de hacerlo, con un instrumento capaz de causar la muerte o lesiones corporales.

assault with intent to agresión con ánimo de
Assault with intent to kill is the attempt to injure a person for the purpose of committing the above-named act.
Agresión con ánimo de matar es la tentativa de lesionar a una persona con el propósito de cometer el acto susodicho.
He was arrested on a charge of assault with intent to kill.
Le detuvieron bajo acusación de agresión con ánimo de matar.

He was arrested on a charge of assault with intent to commit rape.
Le detuvieron bajo acusación de agresión con ánimo de cometer el delito de violación.

assist
She assisted them in preparing the case.
Los ayudó a preparar el caso.

The man is assisting the police with their inquiries.
La policía está interrogando a un sospechoso.

The woman is assisting the police with their inquiries.
La policía está interrogando a una sospechosa.

assisted living vida asistida
The cost of an assisted living facility can fluctuate from less than $10,000 to much more than $100,000 a year.
El costo de las instituciones de vida asistida puede oscilar desde menos de diez mil dólares hasta mucho más de cien mil dólares al año.

assistance
Can I be of any assistance.
¿Puedo ayudarle?
¿Le puedo servir en algo?

May I be of assistance.
¿Puedo servirle en algo?

They came to her assistance.
Vinieron en su ayuda.

Your assistance in the case is greatly appreciated.
Se le agredece enormemente su colaboración en el caso.

assume

Let's assume they are right.
Supongamos que tienen razón.

Let's assume you are right.
Supongamos que usted tiene razón.

You are assuming a lot.
Supones demasiado.
Eso es mucho suponer.

at

at any en cualquier
He can turn up at any moment.
Puede aparecer en cualquier momento.

The jury can reach a verdict at any moment.
El jurado puede llegar a un veredicto en cualquier momento.

They should be arriving at any moment
Deberían llegar en cualquier momento.

at close range a quemarropa
He shot him at close range.
Lo disparó a quemarropa.

at first al principio, en un principio
At first, I accepted the verdict.
En un principio acepté el veredicto.

At first, I didn't like him, but I do now.
Al principio no me gustaba, pero ahora, sí.

I didn't recognize him at first.
Al principio no lo reconocí.

at hand próxima, próximo, disponer de, contar con
Don't worry, help is at hand.
No te preocupes, disponemos de ayuda.
No te preocupes, contamos con ayuda.

The day of the hearing was at hand.

El día de la audiencia estaba próximo.

at home en casa, en su casa
He's not at home.
No está en casa.

I feel at home here.
Aquí me siento en casa.

I'll be at home after four.
Estaré en casa después de las cuatro.

Make yourself at home.
Está en su casa.
Siéntese como en su casa.

Make yourselves at home.
Siéntensen como en su casa.

at large andar suelto, en general
The prisoner is at large.
El prisionero anda suelto.

It will benefit society at large.
Beneficiará a la sociedad en general.

It will benefit the country at large.
Beneficiará al país en general.

at least por lo menos, de al menos
At least 400 people without identity papers have been detained in raids in Southern California.
Por lo menos cuatrociento indocumentados han sido detenidos en redadas en el sur de California.

It is estimated that the trial will last at least three months.
Se estima que el juicio durará por lo menos tres meses.

It is expected that the interrogation will last at least several hours.
Se espera que el interrogatorio durará por lo menos varias horas.

It is expected that the trial will last at least six weeks.
Se espera que el juicio durará por lo menos seis semanas.

The trial will last at least half a year.
El juicio durará por lo menos medio año.

Without mortgage insurance, lenders usually require a down payment of at least 20 percent.
Sin seguro hipotecario, los prestamistas usualmente requieren un pago al contado de al menos un veinte por ciento.

at one time or another en algún momento
All these youngsters have, at one time or another, been in trouble with the police.
Todos estos chicos han tenido, en algún momento, problemas con la policía.

at present en la actualidad
It is unquestionable that at present there are many obstacles which immigrants must overcome in order to enter into the country.
Es indudable que en la actualidad son muchas las trabas que deben superar los inmigrantes para entrar en el país.

at the age of a los ... años de edad
He left school at the age of 20.
Abandonó los estudios a los ciento años de edad.

She died at the age of 30
Murió a los treinta años de edad

at the beginning of a principios de
They trial began at the beginning of May.
El juició comenzó a principios de mayo.

They got married at the beginning of the year.
Se casaron a principios de año.

at the end of a fines de
I'll be home at the end of May.
A fines de mayo volveré a mi casa.

We always get paid at the end of the month.
Siempre cobramos a fines de mes.

at the entrance to en la puerta de
The baby was found abandoned at the entrance to the hospital.
Encontraron al bebé abandonado en la puerta del hospital.

at the last moment a última hora, a último momento
At the last moment he changed his mind.
A último momento cambió de opinión.

At the last moment he thought better of it.
A última hora cambió de idea.

At the last moment we decided to plead self-defense.
A última hora decidimos alegar légitima defensa.

at the latest a más tardar
Be here by nine in the morning at the latest.
Venga a más tardar a las nueve de la mañana.

I'll call you on Monday, at the latest.
A más tardar, te llamaré el lunes.

We'll get together tomorrow, at the latest.
Nos vemos mañana, a más tardar.

at the moment en este momento
She's between jobs at the moment.
En este momento no está trabajando.

at the police station en la comisaria
They kept me at the police station for hours.
Me tuvieron horas en la comisaria.

Were you interrogated at the police station?
¿Te interrogaron en la comisaria?

at the request of a instancias de
The court was adjourned at the request of the defense.
La sesión se levantó a instancias de la defensa.

They called him to testify at the request of the prosecution.
Lo llamaron a testificar a instancias de la acusación.

at the scene en el lugar, presenciar
At the scene of the accident call 911 so that anyone with injuries can be taken to the hospital right away.
En el lugar del accidente llame al nueve-uno-uno para que lleven a cualquier persona con heridas o lesiones al hospital inmediatamente.

At the scene of an accident, exchange information with the other driver.
En el lugar del accidente intercambie información con el otro conductor.

He was at the scene of the accident.
Presenció el accidente.

at the time in a la hora que, a la hora de
Where were you at the time in question?
¿Dónde estabas a la hora que nos interesa?

The suspect was unable to account for his movements at the time of the crime.
El sospechoso no fue capaz de dar cuenta de sus movimientos a la hora del crimen.

attempt

Attempt is an overt act directed toward the commission of an offense, which is performed with the intent and ability to commit the offense.
Tentativa de delito es el acto que indica el comienzo de la

ejecución de un delito por el autor y que se realiza con el ánimo y la capacidad de consumar dicho delito.

attempted kidnapping intento de secuestro
The police are investigating two persons without papers on attempted kidnapping.
La policía investiga a dos indocumentados por intento de secuestro.

attempted murder
The woman was the victim of attempted murder in her house in Albuquerque and she remained in a coma for several weeks in the hospital.
La mujer fue víctima de una tentativa de asesinato en su domicilio de Albuquerque y permaneció varias semanas en estado de coma en el hospital.

attempted suicide intento de suicida
The methods of attempted suicide vary from those that are relatively non-violent to those that are violent.
El método de intento de suicidio varía, desde métodos relativamente no violentos hasta métodos violentos.

attempted rape tentativa de violación
The alleged kidnappers captured in Albuquerque have previous convictions for attempted rape.
Los presuntos secuestradores capturados en Albuquerque tienen antecedentes penales por tentativa de violación.

attempted robbery tentativa de robo
He was apprehended shortly after the attempted robbery.
Fue detenido poco después de la tentativa de robo.

attend
Every child has the right to attend a public school until he or she gets a high school diploma.
Cada niño tiene el derecho de asistir a una escuela pública hasta que el o ella obtenga un diploma de escuela secundaria.

He was unable to attend the meeting because he was ill.
No pudo asistir a la reunión por hallarse enfermo.

Her parents did not attend the hearing.
Sus padres no asistieron a la audiencia.

His brother, as well as his sister, will attend the meeting.
Su hermano, al igual que su hermana, acudirá a la reunión.

Immigrant students have the right to attend school no matter what their legal immigration status or that of their family is.
Los estudiantes inmigrantes tienen el derecho de asistir a la escuela sin importar su estado de inmigración legal o el de su familia.

The parents of the alleged victim attended the hearing.
Los padres de la supuesta víctima asistieron a la audiencia.

attorney
It is a court to be used by people without the aid of attorneys, to settle monetary disputes of $3000 or less.
Es un tribunal que se utiliza por gente sin la asistencia de un abogado para resolver conflictos monetarios que suman menos de 3.000 dólares.

Questions and objections made by the attorneys are not evidence.
Las preguntas y objeciones de los abogados no son evidencias.

Statements and arguments made by the attorneys are not evidence.
Las declaraciones y argumentos de los abogados no son evidencia.

The district attorney prepared a response to the papers.
El fiscal del distrito preparó una respuesta en cuanto a los documentos.

The district attorney's office accuses Peterson, who has pleaded innocense, of murdering his wife Laci in their house in Modesto.
La fiscalía acusa a Peterson, que se ha declarado inocente, de asesinar a su esposa Laci en su casa de Modesto.

The district attorney's office has had more than a year to prepare the case.
La fiscalía ha tenido más de un año para preparar el caso.

attorney-client privilege secreto profesional
The attorney-client privilege is a professional relationship between attorney and client which prevents the attorney from disclosing the content of communications with his or her client without the latters consent.
El secreto profesional es la reserva que obliga a un abogado a no divulgar las comunicaciones con su cliente en el ejercicio de sus actividades profesionales sin mediar autorización de su representado.

Attorney General Fiscal General, Procurador General, Fiscalía
The Attorney General is investigating several cases of fraude.
La Fiscalía está investigando varios casos de estafa.

The Attorney General is investigating the case.
El Procurador General está investigando el caso.

The Attorney General is the chief law officer of a state or country in charge of seeing to it that the law is complied with and prosecuting criminals for a crime.
El Fiscal General es el funcionario de mayor rango en un

estado o país encargado de hacer cumplir la ley y enjuiciar a alguien por un crimen.

authenticity
I bear witness to the authenticity of the document.
Doy fe de que el documento es auténtico.

auto stripping desmantelamiento de coche
Auto stripping is the removal, intentional destruction or defacing of any part of a vehicle without consent of the owner, or the removal, destruction or defacing of any part of an abandoned vehicle.
El desmantelamiento de vehículo se la sustracción, destrucción o desfiguración intencional de cualquier parte de un vehículo abandonado o en caso de no ser abandonado el vehículo, sin autorización del dueño.

They are bringing a charge of auto stripping against him.
Formulan cargos de desmantelamiento de coche contra él.

avail
You must avail yourself of all the legal resources.
Debe valerse de todos los recursos legales.

B

back
He's at the back of all this trouble.
Él está detrás de todo este lío.

He's not back yet.
Aún no está de vuelta.
Aún no ha vuelto.

His family backed him up during the trial.
Su familia lo apoyó durante el juicio.

We'll back him in his request.
Le apoyaremos en su petición.

bad
bad check cheque sin fondos
If someone writes you a bad check, you can sue for up to 4 times the amount of the check.
Si alguien le paga con un cheque sin fondos, puede hacerle una demanda por 4 veces el valor del cheque.

Send a bad check demand letter to the person who wrote the check by certified mail with return receipt requested.
Envíe una carta de demanda por cheque sin fondos a la persona que le

dio el cheque, por correo certificado con aviso de entrega.

bad choice mala elección
It was a bad choice.
Hicimos una mala elección.

My client made a bad choice.
Mi cliente hizo una mala elección.

bad crowd malas compañías
He's in with a really bad crowd.
Anda en muy malas compañías.

bad day mal día
I've had a bad day.
He tenido un mal día.

bad liar no saber mentir
He's a bad liar.
No sabe mentir.

bad moment mal momento
You've come at a bad moment.
Vienes en un mal momento.

badly
badly advised mal aconsejado
You've been badly advised.
Ha sido mal aconsejado.

badly hurt gravemente herida, gravemente herido
They were badly hurt.
Estaban gravementa heridos.

badly injured gravemente herida, gravemente herido
He was badly hurt.
Estaba gravementa herido.

badly scarred llena de cicatrices, lleno de cicatrices
His face was badly scarred.
Tenía la cara llena de cicatrices.

bail fianza judicial, caución
Bail is the money or property deposited with the court so that a person in custody can be released while awaiting disposition of his or her case.
Fianza judicial es el dinero o bienes que se depositan con el tribunal para la excarcelación de un acusado mientras dure el proceso penal.

bail bond contrato de fianza

A bail bond is a document which guarantees the appearance of the defendant in court.
Un contrato de fianza es un documento que garantiza el cumplimiento de las obligaciones del acusado a efectos de asegurar su comparecencia ante el tribunal.

A bail bond is signed by the person who is to be released and the individual providing the security and it indicates the amount of money or property deposited as a guarantee.
Un contrato de fianza es firmado por el fiador y el acusado, e indica la suma de dinero o los bienes que se depositan como garantía.

cash bail fianza en dinero efectivo
Cash bail is a sum of money which is deposited by the defendant or a representative with the court, and which is forfeited if the defendant does not comply with the requirements of the court.
Fianza en dinero efectivo es dinero que se deposita en el tribunal, y que se pierde si el acusado no cumple con las condiciones establecidas por la corte.

release on bail poner en libertad bajo fianza
He was released on bail.
Fue puesto en libertad bajo fianza.
Lo pusieron en libertad bajo fianza.

secured bail bond caución real
A secured bail bond is a bond for which money or property is deposited as security that is forfeited if the defendant fails to comply with the conditions set forth by the court.
Una caución real es la promesa de garantía por la cual se deposita una suma de dinero o bienes que se perderán si el acusado no cumple con las condiciones impuestas por el tribunal.

unsecured bail bond caución sin garantía real
An unsecured bail bond is a bail bond for which no money or property is deposited as security, and therefore nothing is forfeited if the defendant fails to appear in court.
Una caución sin garantía real es una promesa de garantía por la cual no se depositan bienes ni dinero como garantía y por lo tanto no se pierde nada si el acusado no comparece ante el tribunal.

battery
Battery is the intentional infliction of bodily injury upon another person or the act of effecting any offensive contact upon another person.
Lesiones es el acto de infligirle intencionalmente lesiones corporales a otra persona o de realizar cualquier contacto físico lesivo e indebido con ella.

be

be a question of tratarse de
It's a question of knowing what to do.

Se trata de saber lo que hay que hacer.

It's a question of money.
Se trata de dinero.

That is not the question.
No se trata de eso.

be about to estar a punto de
He is about to get married.
Está a punto de casarse.

He was about to plead guilty but he thought better of it.
Estaba a punto de confesarse culpable pero cambió de opinión.

The jury is about to reach a verdict.
El jurado está a punto de llegar a un veredicto.

The jury is about to start deliberating.
El jurado está a punto de empezar a deliberar.

We are about to take our first break during the trial.
Estamos a punto de hacer la primera pausa del juicio.

be at fault hacer mal, obrar mal, tener la culpa
He was at fault in not reporting the theft.
Obró mal al no denunciar el robo.

It's all your fault.
Tú tienes toda la culpa.

It's all your fault.
Usted tiene toda la culpa.

It's my brother's fault.
Mi hermano tiene la culpa.

My mother says it's my fault.
Mi madre dice que tengo la culpa.

They were at fault in not reporting the theft.
Hicieron mal al no denunciar el robo.

Whose fault is it?
¿Quién tiene la culpa?

be at hand estar próxima, estar próximo
The day of the hearing was at hand.
El día de la audiencia estaba próximo.

be at home estar en casa
I'll be at home after 4.

Estaré en casa después de las cuatro.

I was at home all day yesterday.
Ayer estuve en casa todo el día.

Will you be at home this afternoon?
¿Estará usted en casa esta tarde?

be aware of darse cuenta de, estar al tanto de
Are you aware of what this means?
¿Te das cuenta de lo que esto significa?

I am aware of my legal problems.
Estoy al tanto de mis problemas legales.

be aware of estar consciente de, ser consciente de
We are aware of what is happening.
Estamos conscientes de lo que ocurre.

be back estar de vuelta
I'll be back at four.
Estaré de vuelta a las cuatro.

She'll be back tomorrow.
Estará de vuelta mañana.

We'll be back in two hours.
Estaremos de vuelta en dos horas.

be bankrupt estar en bancarrota, estar en quiebra
He's on the verge of being bankrupt.
Está al borde de estar en bancarrota.

They are on the verge of being bankrupt.
Están al borde de estar en quiebra.

be better valer más
It's better to plea bargain.
Vale más llegar a un acuerdo con el fiscal.

It's better to plead guilty.
Vale más confesarse culpable.

It's better to wait.
Vale más esperar.

be better off estar mejor
You're better off divorced than unhappily married.
Estás mejor divorciado que en un matrimonio infeliz.

be between jobs no estar trabajando
She's between jobs at the moment.

En este momento no está trabajando.

be born nacer
He was born in Albuquerque.
Nació en Albuquerque.

She was born in 1964.
Nació en 1964.

When was she born?
¿Cuándo nació?

Where were you born?
¿Dónde naciste?

be crazy to estar loca si, estar loco si
You're crazy to believe what she tells you.
Estás loco si te crees lo que te cuenta.

be dangerous ser peligrosa, ser peligroso
The police believe him to be dangerous.
La policía cree que es peligroso.

be depressed estar deprimida, estar deprimido
Are you depressed?
¿Está usted deprimida?
¿Está usted deprimido?

How long have you been depressed?
¿Desde cuándo estás deprimido?

How long were you depressed?
¿Cuánto tiempo estuviste deprimido?

There are a number of reasons why you shouldn't be depressed.
Hay una serie de razones por las que no deberías estar deprimido.

What difference is there between being sad and being depressed?
¿Qué diferencia hay entre estar triste y estar deprimido?

be disabled estar incapacitada, estar incapacitado
Do you think you will be disabled for twelve months or more?
¿Cree usted que va a estar incapacitado por doce meses o más?

Inaddition to being disabled, your child must have a low income and scarce resources in order to be eligible.
Además de estar incapacitado, su niño debe tener ingresos bajos y recursos escasos para ser elegible.

be distressed estar angustiada, estar angustiado
When a young boy is distressed, the parents usually note some change in his behavior.
Cuando un muchacho está angustiado, los padres suelen notar algún cambio en su comportamiento.

be divorced estar divorciada, estar divorciado
Are you divorced?
¿Estás divorciada?
¿Estás divorciado?

Are you divorced?
¿Está usted divorciada?
¿Está usted divorciado?

His parents are divorced.
Sus padres están divorciados.

His sister is divorced.
Su hermana está divorciada.

How long have you been divorced?
¿Desde cuándo estás divorciado?

be free to ser dueña de, ser dueño de
Each one is free to get together with whom ever they want.
Cada uno es dueño de juntarse con quien quiera.

You are free to do as you see fit with your money.
Eres dueño de hacer lo que te parezca con tu dinero.

be heading for dirigirse a
He was heading for the office when he was arrested.
Se dirigía a la oficina cuando lo arrestaron.

They were heading for the border when they were arrested.
Se dirigían hacia la frontera cuando los arrestaron.

We were heading for the airport when we were arrested.
Nos dirigíamos al aeropuerto cuando nos arrestaron.

be held imputar
I cannot be held responsible.
No se me puede imputar la responsabilidad.

be home late llegar tarde a casa
I'll be home late today.
Hoy llegaré tarde a casa.

be in agreement estar de acuerdo
A contingent fee is when the lawyer is in agreement to not get paid unless you win the case.

Un honorario de contingencia es cuando el abogado está de acuerdo en que no le pagarán a no ser que usted gane el caso.

If you are in agreement with the contingency fee, your lawyer must explain to you how the fees are calculated and put the agreement in writing.
Si usted está de acuerdo con la tasa de contingencia, su abogado le debe explicar cómo calculan los honorarios y poner el acuerdo por escrito.

We're in agreement on that.
En eso estamos de acuerdo.

be in custody of bajo la custodia de
The child is in the custody of his grandparents.
El niño está bajo la custodia de sus abuelos.

be in default estar en mora
She is in default of her mortgage.
Está en mora en los pagos de la hipoteca.

be in force estar en vigencia, estar en vigor
The law is no longer in force.
La ley ya no está en vigencia.

The law is no longer in force.
La ley ya no está en vigor.

be in jail estar en la cárcel
He was in jail for ten years.
Estuvo en la cárcel diez años.

be in prison estar presa, estar preso, estar en prisión
He was in prison for ten years.
Estuvo preso diez años.

He is in prison for manslaughter.
Está en prisión por homicidio culposo involuntario.

He was in prison for ten years.
Estuvo en prisión diez años.

She was in prison for two years.
Estuvo presa dos años.

be in session estar reunida, estar reunido, estar en sesión
The court is now in session.
El tribunal está reunido.

The court is not in session.
El tribunal no está en sesión.

be in trouble tener problemas
All these youngsters have, at one time or another, been in trouble with the police.
Todos estos chicos han tenido, en algún momento, problemas con la policía.

be investigating investigar
The police are investigating to see if it's a matter of domestic violence or if both committed suicide.
La policía investiga si se trata de un caso de violencia doméstica o si ambos se suicidaron.

be killed in morir en
She was killed in a car crash.
Murió en un accidente de coche.

He was killed in a shooting.
Murió en un una balacera.

She was killed in a shooting.
Murió en un un tiroteo.

be left homeless quedar sin hogar, quedar sin techo
She was left homeless.
Quedó sin hogar.

Many families were left homeless.
Muchas familias quedaron sin techo.

be negligent faltar a su deber, ser negligente
She was negligent about informing the authorities.
Faltó a su deber de informar a las autoridades.

The judge found him to be negligent.
El juez declaró que había sido negligente.

be of no account no tener importancia
What he said is of no account
Lo que dijo no tiene importancia.

be off alcohol dejar el alcohol
Is he off alcohol now?
¿Ha dejado el alcohol?

be off drugs dejar las drogas
Is he off drugs now?
¿Ha dejado las drogas?

be on hand estar disponible, estar cerca
The police were on hand.
La policía estaba cerca.

She's never on hand when I need her.
Nunca está disponible cuando la necesito.

be on record declarar públicamente
She's on record saying that she is innocent of the charges.
Ha declarado públicamente que es inocente de los cargos.

be on the way to dirigirse a
He was on his way to the office when he was arrested.
Se dirigía a la oficina cuando lo arrestaron.

They were on their way to the border when they were arrested.
Se dirigían hacia la frontera cuando los arrestaron.

We were on our way to the airport when we were arrested.
Nos dirigíamos al aeropuerto cuando nos arrestaron.

be pregnant estar embarazada
She is three months pregnant
Está embarazada de tres meses.

The family members of the accused stated that she is one month pregnant.
Los familiares de la acusada manifestaron que está embarazada de un mes.

The police have arrested a 40 year old man for allegedly battering his wife who is pregnant.
La policía ha detenido a un hombre, de unos cuarenta años, como presunto autor de los malos tratos ocasionados a su esposa, que está embarazada.

What to do if your girlfriend is pregnant?
¿Qué hacer si su novia esté embarazada?

be prepared to estar dispuesta a, estar dispuesto a
You must be prepared to take risks.
Hay que estar dispuesto a arriesgarse.

You must be prepared to take risks.
Hay que estar dispuesto a correr riesgos.

You must be prepared to take the stand.
Hay que estar dispuesto a subir al estrado.

be related to estar emparentado con, ser pariente de
Are you related to the driver of the vehicle?
¿Eres pariente del conductor del coche?

Are you related to the prisoner?
¿Es usted pariente del prisionero?
¿Estás emparentado con el prisionero?

be related to estar relacionado con
This murder is not related to the other.
Este asesinato no está relacionado con el otro.

be reunited estar juntos de nuevo
Santos and Carla are reunited.
Santos y Carla están juntos de nuevo.

be sedated administrarle un sedante
She was heavily sedated.
Le habían administrado un fuerte sedante.

be short ser baja, ser bajo
She's short.
Es baja.

be tall medir, ser alta, ser alto
How tall are you?
¿Cuánto mides?

He's tall.
Es alto.

She's tall.
Es alta.

be to blame tener la culpa
He is to blame for everything.
Él tiene la culpa de todo.

She is not to blame for his death.
Ella no tiene la culpa de su muerte.

She is to blame for the accident.
Ella tiene la culpa del accidente.

Who's to blame?
¿Quién tiene la culpa?

be on trial for seguirle proceso por
She is on trial for theft.
Se le sigue proceso por robo.

be tried on seguirle proceso por
She is being tried on a charge of theft.
Se le sigue proceso por robo.

He is being tried on a charge of rape.
Se le sigue proceso por violación.

be trusted ser de fiar

He can't be trusted.
No es de fiar.

be under age ser menor de edad
She was under age when she committed the crime.
Era menor de edad cuando cometió el delito.

She was under age when she got married.
Era menor de edad cuando se casó.

beat
He beats his children.
Les pega a sus hijos.
Maltrata a sus hijos.

He beat her black and blue.
Le dio una tremenda paliza.

He was badly beaten.
Le habían dado una buena paliza.

She nearly beat the life out of him.
Casi lo mata a golpes.

We need more officers on the beat.
Deberíamos tener más agentes haciendo la ronda.

beat her up, beat him up darle una paliza
They beat him up.
Le dieron una paliza.

They stole his wallet and beat him up.
Le robaron la cartera y le dieron una paliza.

beat to death matar a golpes
He was beaten to death?
Lo mataron a golpes.

beat up dar una paliza a
They beat him up.
Le dieron una paliza.

He stole his wallet and beat him up.
Le robó la cartera y le dio una paliza.

If three or more persons come together to beat up another because of some difference among themselves, it is considered gang activity and is punishable by 1 to 5 years in prison.
Si tres o más personas se juntan para golpear a otra por alguna diferencia entre sí, se considera pandillerismo, que se castiga con uno a cinco años de prisión.

beat up on dar una paliza
They beat up on him.
Le dieron una paliza.

because

because of a causa de, por, por causa de
Has he ever hit you because of the drinking?
¿Le ha pegado a usted alguna vez a causa de la bebida?

Many families break up because of a lack of money.
Muchas familias se deshacen por falta de dinero.

I need to get a new Social Security number because of domestic violence. How must I proceed?
Necesito obtener un número de Seguro Social nuevo por causa de violencia doméstica. ¿Cómo debo proceder?

become

He became a citizen two months ago.
Llegó a ser ciudadano hace dos meses.

He became a lawyer two years ago.
Llegó a ser abogado hace dos años.

She became a lawyer two weeks ago.
Se hizo abogada hace dos semanas.

It has become less and less noticeable.
Se nota cada vez menos.

The consequences of his actions will become apparent in the long term.
Las consecuencias de sus actos se manifestarán a largo plazo.

The defendant became arrogant.
El acusado se volvió arrogante.

They became estranged.
Se separaron.

They are estranged now.
Ahora están separados.

This is becoming difficult.
Esto se está poniendo difícil.

What has become of her?
¿Qué ha sido de ella?

What has become of him?
¿Qué ha sido de él?

What is to become of the house if he dies?
¿Qué va a pasar con la casa si él muere?

Whatever became of Juan?
¿Qué fue de Juan?

become aware of darse cuenta de
When did you become aware that something was wrong?
¿Cuándo se dio cuenta de que pasaba algo?

become clear hacerse evidente, hacerse patente
It became clear that he was lying.
Se hizo evidente que estaba mintiendo.

It became clear that the witness was lying.
Se hizo patente que el testigo estaba mintiendo.

can become poder convertirse, hacerse
How can I become an American citizen?
¿Cómo puedo convertirme en ciudadano estadounidense?

How can I become a naturalized American citizen?
¿Cómo me convierto en ciudadano estadounidense naturalizado?

Later on permanent residents can become naturalized and become American citizens.
Los residentes permanentes pueden más tarde naturalizarse y hacerse ciudadanos estadounidenses.

Those who come into the United States as refugees or who are granted political asylum, can become permanent residents in one year.
Los que entran a Estados Unidos como refugiados o a quienes se les otorga asilo político, pueden convertirse en residentes permanentes en un año.

in order to become para convertirse en
In order to become immigrants, your parents wll have to go through a three stage process.
Para convertirse en inmigrantes, sus padres deberán pasar por un proceso de tres etapas.

before

before antes de, antes de que
Before you enter the US, it is essential that you know your rights.
Antes de que usted ingrese a Estados Unidos, es esencial que usted conozca sus derechos.

Some states require that under age girls get the consent of their parents before having an abortion.
Algunos estados requieren que las adolescentes obtengan el consentimiento de sus padres antes de hacerse un aborto.

before beginning antes de empezar
Before beginning the process of purchasing a house, make sure that you really want to buy a house.
Antes de empezar el proceso de compra de una casa, asegúrese de que usted quiere realmente comprar una casa.

before changing antes de cambiar de
I will inform my probation officer before changing address or work.
Le informaré a mi oficial de libertad condicional antes de cambiar de domicilio o empleo.

before going to antes de ir a
I will inform my probation officer before going to work.
Le informaré a mi oficial de libertad condicional antes de ir al trabajo.

before or during antes o durante
If you cannot afford to hire a lawyer, one will be appointed free of charge before or during questioning, if you wish.

Si usted no puede pagar por un abogado, uno le será nombrado gratis antes o durante cualquier interrogatorio, si usted lo desea.

before Roe antes de Roe
Abortions were illegal in almost every state before Roe, with the exception when the health of the woman was in danger.
Antes de Roe, el aborto era ilegal en casi todos los estados, salvo cuando la salud de la mujer estaba en peligro.

Before Roe, women usually resorted to illegal and unsafe abortions in order to end a pregnancy.
Antes de Roe, las mujeres solían recurrir a abortos ilegales e inseguros para poner fin a un embarazo.

before the court ante los tribunales
He is due to appear before the court next week.
Debe comparecer ante los tribunales la semana próxima.

before ... + time antes de ... + tiempo
I will be at home before three.
Estaré en casa antes de las tres.

I won't be back before two.
No estaré de vuelta antes de las dos.

The trial will begin before the end of the month.
El juicio empezará antes de fin de mes.

The trial will begin before the summer.
El juicio empezará antes del verano.

The trial will begin before the 7th of January and the sentence could

be known four days later.
El juicio empezará antes del siete de enero y la sentencia podría conocerse cuatro días más tarde

before your visit antes de su visita
Before your visit make sure you organize and put in order any file, records or material that you have in your possession which may be useful to better consider your case.
Antes de su visita, asegúrese de organizar y ordenar cualquier archivo, registro, o material que tenga en su poder que pueda ser útil para considerar mejor su caso.

begin

At what point did you begin to suspect?
¿En qué momento empezó a sospechar?

I don't know where to begin.
No sé por dónde comenzar.
No sé por dónde empezar.

Let's begin at the beginning.
Empecemos por el principio.

Where do you want to begin?
¿Por dónde quieres empezar?

begin talking empezar a hablar
He began talking to the police.
Empezó a hablar con la policía.

He began talking about his role in the crime.
Empezó a hablar sobre su papel en el delito.

He began talking about the murder.
Empezó a hablar sobre el asesinato.

begin to empezar a
The jury is about to begin to deliberate.
El jurado está a punto de empezar a deliberar.

beginning

Before beginning the process of purchasing a house, make sure that you really want to buy a house.
Antes de empezar el proceso de compra de una casa, asegúrese de que usted quiere realmente comprar una casa.

I'll start again from the beginning.
Volveré a empezar desde el principio.

The trial began at the beginning of May.
El juició comenzó a principios de mayo.

They got married at the beginning of the year.
Se casaron a principios de año.

behave

He doesn't usually behave so badly.
Normalmente no se porta tan mal.

behave in actuar de
He's behaving in a strange manner.
Actúa de manera rara.

She behaved in a suspicious manner.
Actuó de forma sospechosa.

behave rudely portarse groseramente
He behaved rudely with the police.
Se portó groseramente con la policía.

behind

What's behind all of this?
¿Qué hay detrás de todo esto?

His family is behind him.
Tiene el apoyo de su familia.

behind bars entre rejas, tras las rejas
He's been behind bars for four years.
Hace cuatro años que está tras las rejas.

More than two million Americans currently live behind bars and five million live on parole.
Más de dos millones de norteamericanos viven actualmente entre rejas y cinco millones viven en libertad condicional.

belief

It is my belief that he lied to us.
Creo que nos mintió.

It is our belief that he lied under oath.
Creemos que mintió bajo juramento.

believe

Children often believe that they are the cause of the conflict between their parents.
Los niños con frecuencia creen que son la causa del conflicto entre su padre y su madre.

Do you believe that the other driver was at fault for this accident?
¿Cree usted que el otro conductor tiene la culpa por este

accicente?

He was afraid that nobody would believe him.
Temía que nadie le creyera.

I don't believe a word she says.
No le creo ni una palabra.

I don't believe in corporal punishment.
No soy partidaria del castigo corporal.
No soy partidario del castigo corporal.

I don't believe she is capable of telling the truth.
No la creo capazde decir la verdad.

The police believe them to be dangerous.
La policía cree que son peligrosos.

It is believed that the fire had been started deliberately.
Se cree que el incendio fue provocado.
It is believed that there are more than three million American children whose parents are without identity papers.
Se cree que hay más de tres millones de niños estadounidenses con padres indocumentados.

You believe me, don't you?
Tú me crees, ¿verdad?

You're crazy to believe what she tells you.
Estás loco si te crees lo que te cuenta.

belong
Do you still feel you don't belong here?
¿Todavía no se siente en casa?

I feel I belong here.
Aquí me siento en casa.

I still feel I don't belong here.
Todavía no me siento en casa.

belong to pertenecer a, ser de
Does this knife belong to you?
¿Le pertrenece a usted este cuchillo?

It belongs to her.
Le pertenece a ella.

The house belonged to my grandmother.
La casa perteneció a mi abuela.

This money doesn't belong to us.

Este dinero no nos pertenece.

Who does that car belong to?
¿De quién es ese coche?

Who does this belong to?
¿A quién pertenece esto?
¿De quién es esto?

below
From the window they saw what happened below.
Desde la ventana veían lo que pasaba abajo.

below the speed limit velocidad por debajo de la máxima permitida
All drivers must reduce their speed below the speed limit when approaching a school
Todos los conductores deben extremar la prudencia y reducir la velocidad por debajo de la máxima permitida al aproximarse a una escuela.

below the legal age no tener la edad establecida por la ley
She was below the legal age.
No tenía la edad establecida por la ley.

bench
bench conference consulta en el estrado
A bench conference is a meeting between the attorneys and the judge at the judge's bench to discuss an issue in the case or an aspect of the proceeding.
La consulta en el estrado es una conversación entre los abogados y el juez para tratar una cuestión, ya sea legal o procesal.

A bench conference may or may not be part of the official record.
La consulta en el estrado puede o no constar en las actas.

beside
He was beside himself with anger.
Estaba fuera de sí con rabia.

That's beside the point.
Eso no tiene nada que ver con el asunto.
Eso no viene al caso.

besides
besides además de, aparte de
No one knows besides you.
Nadie lo sabe aparte de usted.

There are five other witnesses, besides you.
Además de ti, hay otros cinco testigos.

There are five other witnesses, besides your brother.
Aparte de tu hermano, hay otros cinco testigos.

best

All the best!
¡Buena suerte!

All the best!
¡Que le vaya bien!

At best she can appeal the fine.
Puede reclamar contra la multa en el mejor de los casos.

He did it with the best of intentions.
Lo hizo con la mejor intención del mundo.
Lo hizo con la mejor voluntad.

He's the best judge.
Es el mejor juez.

He testified for the best part of an hour.
Prestó declaración durante casi una hora.

I know what's best for you.
Yo sé qué es lo que más le conviene.

I think he is best able to answer that question.
Creo que él es quien mejor puede contestar a esa pregunta.

It went on for the best part of an hour.
Continuó durante casi una hora.

The best thing is to remain silent.
Lo mejor es quedarse callado.
Lo mejor es guardar silencio.

The best thing to do is to wait.
Lo mejor es esperar.

They are some of our best lawyers.
Ellos son algunos de nuestros abogados más capaces.

To the best of your recollection, he wasn't there?
¿Si la memoria no le falla, no estaba?

Your best bet is to stay here.
Lo mejor que puede hacer es quedarse aquí.

better

At the last moment he thought better of it.
A última hora cambió de idea.

Do whatever you think is best.
Haz lo que mejor te parezca.

Do you feel any better now?
¿Se siente mejor?

He was about to plead guilty but he thought better of it.
Estaba a punto de confesarse culpable pero cambió de opinión.

He was all the better for it.
Le hizo mucho bien.

He has changed — and for the better!
Ha cambiado — ¡y para bien!

He is much better.
Está mucho mejor.

I have got an even better idea.
Tengo una idea aún mejor.

In my opinion it's better to plead guilty.
A mi entender es mejor declararse culpable.

In the long run it will be better to not call him to the stand.
A la larga será mejor no llamarlo al estrado.

In the long run it will be better to plea bargain.
A la larga será mejor llegar a un acuerdo con el fiscal.

It's better to plea bargain.
Vale más llegar a un acuerdo con el fiscal.

It's better to plead guilty.
Vale más confesarse culpable.

It is a change for the better
Es una mejora.

It is better to wait.
Vale más esperar.

No one was better liked than he was.
Nadie era tan querido como él.

The trial took a turn for the better.
El juicio dio un giro positivo.

They get along better than they used to.
Se llevan mejor que antes.

They're far better off without him.
Están mucho mejor sin él.

We get along better than we used to.
Nos llevamos mejor que antes.

Things took a turn for the better.
Las cosas dieron un giro positivo.

We'd better go.
Mejor que nos vámonos.

You'd better do exactly as I say.
Más te vale hacer exactamente lo que yo te diga.

You'd better not complain!
¡Más te vale no quejarte!

be better off estar mejor
You're better off divorced than unhappily married.
Estás mejor divorciado que en un matrimonio infeliz.

better liked than tan querida como, tan querido como
No one was better liked than she was.
Nadie era tan querido como ella

No one was better liked than he was.
Nadie era tan querido como él.

better than mejor de lo que, mejor que
This is better than I anticipated.
Esto es mejor de lo que esperaba.

We get along better than we used to.
Nos llevamos mejor que antes.

better working conditions mejores condiciones de trabajo
The unions are demanding better working conditions.
Los sindicatos reclaman mejores condiciones de trabajo.

beyond
His honesty is beyond all question.
Su honradez está fuera de toda duda.

His integrity is beyond question.
Su integridad está fuera de duda.

She told us little beyond what we already knew.
No nos dijo gran cosa fuera de lo que ya sabíamos.

They are living beyond their income.
Gastan más de lo que ganan.

The meeting won't last much beyond an hour.
La reunión no durará mucho más de una hora.

The trial won't last much beyond one month.
El juicio no durará mucho más de una mes.

beyond a reasonable doubt fuera de toda duda razonable
Beyond a reasonable doubt is the degree of certainty required by the judge or jury to find a criminal defendant guilty.
Fuera de toda duda razonable es el nivel de certeza que precisa el juez o jurado al examinar y valorar las pruebas para juzgar culpable al acusado.

beyond a reasonable doubt más allá de toda duda razonable
The prosecution has the obligation to prove that the accused are guilty beyond a reasonable doubt.
La fiscalía tiene la obligación de probar que los acusados son culpables más allá de toda duda razonable.

beyond a reasonable doubt sin que quepa duda razonable
It is in the courts where guilt beyond a reasonable is to be determined.
Es en los tribunales donde se tiene que determinar la culpabilidad sin que quepa duda razonable.

The presumption of innocense must be upheld from the moment in which the person becomes the accused until it is shown beyond a reasonable that he is guilty.
Se debe respetar la presunción de inocencia desde el momento en que la persona se convierte en acusado hasta que se demuestra su culpabilidad sin que quepa duda razonable.

beyond all doubt sin que quepa la menor duda
It has been proven beyond all doubt.
Se ha probado sin que quepa la menor duda.

His guilt has been proven beyond all doubt.
Su culpabilidad se ha probado sin que quepa la menor duda.

bilingual

Her children are in a bilingual program.
Sus hijos están en un programa bilingüe.

In its short history, the United States has received more bilingual people than any other country in the world.
En su corta historia, Estados Unidos han recibido a más gente bilingüe que cualquier otro país en el mundo.

bill

bill of particulars exposición revelatoria
Bill of particulars is the additional information in which the prosecu-

tor specifies the nature, character, place and time of a crime that is alleged in a charging document.
La exposición revelatoria es la información adicional en la cual el fiscal detalla los pormenores de los hechos acaecidos de la presunta infracción.

biological

biological father padre biológico
An American judge granted the biological father custody of the twin girls adopted on the Internet.
Un juez de Estados Unidos otorgó al padre biológico la custodia de las gemelas adoptadas en Internet.

He is the biological father.
Es el padre biológico.

She spent many years of her life looking for her biological father.
Pasó muchos años de su vida buscando a su padre biológico.

biological mother madre biológica
His biological mother abandoned him.
Su madre biológica lo abandonó.

She is the biological mother.
Es la madre biológica.

She spent many years of her life looking for her biological mother.
Pasó muchos años de su vida buscando a su madre biológica.

black
He beat her black and blue.
Le dio una tremenda paliza.

black eye ojo morado
He gave her a black eye.
Le puso un ojo morado.

The woman arrived at work with two black eyes.
La mujer llegó a su empleo con los dos ojos morados.

black with bruises lleno/a de moretones, lleno/a de cardenales
Her arms were black with bruises.
Tenía los brazos llenos de moretones.
Tenía los brazos llenos de cardenales.

Her face and her body are black with bruises.
Su rostro y su cuerpo están llenos de moretones.

blackmail
Le hacen chantaje.
He is being blackmailed.

He has just been accused of conspiracy to commit blackmail.
Acaba de ser acusado de conspiración para chantajear.

The man, of Panama, is currently serving a 40 year prison sentence in a Miami federal jail, accused of blackmail, drug traficking and money laundering.
El hombre, de Panamá, está cumpliendo una condena a 40 años de prisión en una cárcel federal de Miami, acusado de chantaje, tráfico de drogas y lavado de dinero.

blame

Don't lay the blame on me.
No me eches la culpa.

He is in part to blame.
En parte tiene la culpa.

He laid the blame on his girlfriend.
Le echó la culpa a su novia.

He laid the blame on us for the accident.
Nos echó la culpa del accidente.

She is not to blame for his death.
Ella no tiene la culpa de su muerte.

She is to blame for the accident.
Ella tiene la culpa del accidente.

The blame for what happened lies entirely with them.
La culpa de lo que pasó la tienen sólo ellos.

Who's to blame?
¿Quién tiene la culpa?

You have only yourself to blame.
La culpa la tienes tú.

blind

He has been blind since birth.
Es ciego de nacimiento.

He went blind five years ago.
Hace cinco años se quedó ciego.

She is blind.
Está ciega.

She was blinded in the accident.
Perdió la vista en un accidente.
Se quedó ciega en un accidente.

She was born blind.
Es ciega de nacimiento.

blind date
She went on a blind date with him two months ago.
Tuvo una cita a ciegas con él hace dos meses.

They met on a blind date .
Se conocieron en una cita a ciegas.

blindly
Don't rush blindly into important decisions like that.
No tomes decisiones importantes así, a ciegas.

He went into that business blindly.
Se metió en ese negocio a ciegas.

blood
He was all covered in blood.
Estaba completamente cubierto de sangre.

There was bad blood between them after their argument.
Quedaron resentidos a raíz de la discusión.

blood evidence evidencia de sangre
The blood evidence pointed directly to her.
La evidencia de sangre apuntó directamente hacia ella.

blood spatter evidence evidencia de sangre de salpicadura
Blood spatter evidence was found on the wall.
Evidencia de sangre de salpicadura se encontró en la pared.
spattered with blood salpicada de sangre, salpicado de sangre
The wall was spattered with blood.
La pared estaba salpicada de sangre.

book
The man, a resident of Albuquerque, was booked and remains detained for violating his parole.
El hombre, un residente de Albuquerque, fue fichado y permanece detenido por violar su libertad condicional.

To book means to enter a persson's name, the offense for which he or she was arrested and other pertinent information in the police files.
Fichar quiere decir anotar en los registros de la policía el nombre del detenido, los detalles de la infracción y otra información pertinente.

throw the book at castigar duramente, castigar con todo rigor
The judge threw the book at him.
El juez lo castigó con todo rigor.

The judge threw the book at her.
El juez la castigó duramente.

booking

booking ficha policial
Booking is the process by which law enforeement officials record an arrest, which icludes identificatíon of the individual, reason for the arrest and time and place of the arrest.
La ficha policial es el trámite mediante el cual los agentes de la policía anotan los hechos y las circunstancias relativas a una detención y los datos personales del presunto infractor.

border

A person who crosses the borders through Mexico or Canada without due inspection or documentation, has entered the United States illegally.
Una persona que cruce las fronteras por México o por Canadá sin la debida inspección o documentación, ha entrado de manera ilegal a Estados Unidos.

It is estimated that every year more than 300 thousand Mexicans try to cross the border with the United States illegally.
Se estima que cada año, más de 300 mil mexicanos intentan cruzar de manera ilegal la frontera con Estados Unidos.

The control of our common border is also a question of security.
El control de nuestra frontera común es también una cuestión de seguridad.

The suspects were on their way to the border when they were arrested.
Los sospechosos se dirigían hacia la frontera cuando los arrestaron.

border patrol patrulla fronteriza
Many of the Mexicans who were repatriated this week were arrested in raids carried out by the American border patrol.
Muchos de los mexicanos repatriados esta semana fueron arrestados en redadas efectuadas por la patrulla fronteriza de Estados Unidos.

borrow

How much can I borrow?
¿Cuánto puedo pedir prestado?

She asked if she could borrow my car.
Me pidió el coche prestado.

borrow money pedir dinero prestado
He had to borrow some money
Tuvo que pedir dinero prestado.

borrow up to pedir prestado hasta
You can borrow up to $10.000.
Usted puede pedir prestado hasta 10.000 dólares.

both
Shared custody entails benefits both for the minor as well as for the parents.
La custodia compartida conlleva beneficios tanto para el menor como para la relación entre los padres.

The authorities think that both committed the robbery in the House where Juana María worked as a maid.
Consideran las autoridades que ambos cometieron el robo en la casa donde Juana María trabajaba como empleada doméstica.

The jury is to consider both direct and circumstantial evidence.
El jurado debe considerar tanto la prueba testifical directa como la circunstancial.

The law permits the jury to give equal weight to both direct and circumstantial evidence.
La ley permite que el jurado le dé igual peso tanto a la prueba testifical directa como a la prueba circunstancial.

The police is investigating to see if it's a matter of domestic violence or if both committed suicide.
La policía investiga si se trata de un caso de violencia doméstica o si ambos se suicidaron.
They both committed errors.
Ambos cometieron errores.

both parents ambos padres
Children who live in shared custody arrangements usually feel loved by both parents.
Los niños que viven en arreglos de custodia compartida suelen sentirse amados por ambos padres.

both parties ambas partes
Both parties have agreed to come to the negotiating table.
Ambas partes han aceptado sentarse a la mesa de negociaciones.

both sides ambas partes
Both sides reached an agreement.
Hubo acuerdo entre ambas partes.

bounce
He gave me a bounced check.
Me dio un cheque sin fondos.

boy
A boy of 14 told the police that he witnessed the accident.
Un chico de 14 años le dijo a la policía que presenció el

accidente.

A boy of 16 was arrested.
Un chico de 16 años fue arrestado.

A 15 year old boy was accused of shooting a California Highway Patrol.
Un muchacho de 15 años fue acusado de matar a balazos a un oficial de la Patrulla de Caminos de California (CHP).

The boys were arrested at school.
Los chicos fueron arrestados en la escuela.

boyfriend
Do you have a boyfriend.
¿Tienes novio?

Domestic violence is defined as abuse committed by an ex-husband, ex-wife, boyfriend or girlfriend.
La violencia doméstica se define como el abuso cometido por el esposo o ex-esposo, novio o novia.

Is he your live-in- boyfriend.
¿Es tu compañero?

She's got boyfriend problems.
Tiene problemas de amores.
She lives with her boyfriend.
Vive con su novio.

brake
brake lights luces de freno
Were your brake lights working?
¿Funcionaban las luces de freno?

break, breaking
We are about to take our first break during the trial.
Estamos a punto de hacer la primera pausa del juicio.

break-in entrar a robar, entrar ladrones
They had a break-in next door.
Entraron a robar en la casa de al lado.

They had a break-in next door.
Entraron ladrones en la casa de al lado.

break into entrar a robar, entrar ladrones, echar manos de
Our house was broken into.
Nos entraron a robar.
Nos entraron ladrones.

They had to break into their savings.
Tuvieron que echar manos de sus ahorros.

Was your house broken into?
¿Les entraron a robar?
¿Les entraron ladrones?

break one's word faltarle la palabra a uno
He broke his word.
Faltó a su palabra.

They accuse me of breaking my word.
Me acusan de haber faltado a mi palabra.

break off romper, terminar
They broke off their marriage two months ago.
Hace dos meses terminaron su matrimonio.

They broke off their relationship last week.
Rompieron su relación la semana pasada.

break up deshacerse, fracasar, separarse
Their marriage broke up.
Se separaron.
Su matrimonio fracasó.

Many families break up because of a lack of resources.
Muchas familias se deshacen por falta de recursos.

break the law violar la ley
Due to the fact that the seller broke the law by not giving you the form, you have some additional time.
Debido a que el vendedor violó la ley al no darle el formulario, usted tiene tiempo adicional.

If your son is involved in a juvenile case, it means that he is being accused of breaking the law.
Si su hijo está involucrado en un caso de delincuencia juvenil, quiere decir que lo están acusando de violar la ley.

breaking and entering allanamiento de morada
He was accused of breaking and entering.
Lo acusaron de allanamiento de vivienda.

The suspect was arrested during a breaking and entering early in the morning yesterday.
El sospechoso fue detenido durante un allanamiento de vivienda en las primeras horas de la mañana de ayer.

They were accused of breaking and entering.
Los acusaron de allanamiento de morada.

breaking up of separación de, fracaso de
He felt responsible for breaking up their marriage.
Se sentía responsable del fracaso de su matrimonio.
Se sentía responsable de su separación de su matrimonio.

make a break with cortar con, romper con
He made a break with his past.
Cortó con su pasado.
Rompió con su pasado.

breathalyzer
He failed the breathalyzer test.
No pasó la prueba del alcohol.

He passed the breathalyzer test.
Pasó la prueba del alcohol.

bribe
Once the trial against him began, his attempts to murder his accusor and to bribe the jury failed.
Una vez iniciado el proceso en su contra, fracasaron sus intentos para asesinar a su acusador y sobornar a los jurados.

take a bribe dejarse sobornar
The mayor took a bribe.
El alcalde se dejó sobornar.

accept a bribe aceptar un soborno
The police willl investigate to see if Ríos accepted a bribe.
La policía investigará si Ríos aceptó un soborno.

bribery
He was accused of bribery and corruption.
Lo acusaron de soborno y corrupción.

His lawyers deny all implications in the crime of bribery.
Sus abogados niegan toda implicación en los delitos de soborno.

bring
Bring any evidence or witnesses you need to prove your case.
Traiga pruebas o testigos para probar su caso.

Bring your passport with you.
Traiga consigo el pasaporte.

For example, bring a letter from a doctor or a hospital bill.
Por ejemplo, traiga una carta de un médico o una factura del hospital.

How do I bring my parents to live in the US?
¿Cómo puedo traer a mis padres a vivir en Estados Unidos?

They had to bring in the police.
Tuvieron que hacer intervenir a la policía.

What is the easiest way for me to bring my parents and brothers and sisters to the US?
¿Cuál es la forma más fácil de traer a mis padres y hermanos a Estados Unidos?

bring a charge of formular cargos de
They are bringing a charge of auto stripping against him.
Formulan cargos de desmantelamiento de coche contra él.

They are bringing a charge of theft against him.
Formulan cargos de robo contra él.

bring a lawsuit demandar
I brought a lawsuit against him for damages.
Lo demandé por daños y perjuicios.

You have to bring a lawsuit against him for damages.
Tienes que demandarlo por daños y perjuicios.

bring before the authorities consignar por
The judge considered that the elements to try the alleged kidnappers were missing due to the fact that the prosecutor brought them before the authorities for disorderly conduct.
El juez consideró que no existían elementos para procesar a los presuntos secuestradores debido a que los fiscales sólo los consignó por alteración del orden público.

The police stated that the youth arrested was brought before the authorities for theft and not for gang activity.
La policía precisó que el joven detenido se le consignó por robo, no por pandillerismo.

bring in a verdict dar un veredicto
The jury deliberated for a while then it brought in its final verdict.
El jurado deliberó por un rato y luego dio su veredicto final.

bring in for questioning ser sometida/o a un interrogatorio
He was brought in for questioning for four hours without any results.
Fue sometido a un interrogatorio por 4 horas sin resultado alguno.

The police brought him in for questioning.
La policía lo sometió a un interrogatorio.

bring proof of traer un comprobante de
Bring proof of why you couldn't go to your first hearing.
Traiga un comprobante de por qué no pudo ir a la primera audiencia.

bring together unir a
A tragedy like this can bring a family together.
Una tragedia así puede unir a una familia.

bring trouble traer problemas
It brought us nothing but trouble.
No nos trajo más que problemas.

bring under control hacerse dueña de, hacerse dueño de
The police brought the situation under control.
La policía se hizo dueña de la situación.

He brought his drug problem under control.
Se hizo dueño de sus problemas con las drogas.

brush

brush up on repasar
He is brushing up on his English.
Está repasando su inglés.

brush with the law roce con la ley, roce con la policía
He had a brush with the law in Mexico.
Tuvo un roce con la policía en México.

My client had a small brush with the law three years ago.
Mi cliente tuvo un pequeño roce con la ley hace tres años.

slight brush with the law pequeño encontronazo con la ley
He had a slight brush with the law six months ago.
Tuvo un pequeño encontronazo con la ley hace seis meses.

build

build a new life empezar de nuevo
He tried to build a new life in the United States.
Intentó empezar de nuevo en Estados Unidos.

build up irse acumulando, ir camino de
His resentment had built up.
Había ido acumulando rencor.

I think he's building up to a nervous breakdown.
Creo que va camino de una crisis nerviosa.

Their debts had built up.
Sus deudas se habían ido acumulando.

heavy build fornida, fornido
The suspect is a man of medium height and heavy build.

El sospechoso es un hombre fornido de estatura mediana.

building
The policemen had taken up positions around the building.
Los policías se habían apostados alrededor del edificio.

bundle
She's a bundle of nerves.
Es un manojo de nervios.

burden
Don't burden me with your troubles.
No me vengas con tus problemas.

I've been burdened with all of the responsibility.
Me han cargado con toda la responsabilidad.

burden of proof carga de la prueba
The burden of proof lies with the prosecution.
El fiscal lleva la carga de la prueba.

It has been claimed that the burden of proof is nothing more than the necessity to win in the courtroom.
Se ha sostenido que la carga de la prueba no es otra cosa que la necesidad de probar para vencer en la sala de la corte..

burglar
The police arrested a burglar linked to the death of a policeman in Albuquerque.
La policía detuvo a un ladrón vinculado a la muerte de un policía en Albuquerque.

burglar alarm
A burglar alarm may act as a deterrent to thieves
Una alarma antirrobo puede servir para disuadir a los ladrones.

burglary
There have been several burglaries in the area.
Ha habido varios robos en la vecindad.

aggravated burglary
A Dallas grand jury accused Diaz of abduction and aggravated burglary of a woman in Carrollton on the 5th of June.
El gran jurado de Dallas acusó a Díaz por el secuestro y robo con agravante de una mujer en Carrollton el día 5 de junio

business
I will make it my business to tell him.
Yo me encargaré de decírselo.

It's no business of mine.
Yo no tengo nada que ver con eso.
No es cosa mía.

You had no business doing that.
No tenías derecho a hacerlo.

business affairs
Police are probing into his business affairs.
La policía está investigando sus actividades financieras.

by

Her account is backed up by evidence.
Hay pruebas que confirman su versión.

by a tainted jury por un jurado inficionado
The verdict was delivered by a tainted jury.
La sentencia fue pronunciada por un jurado inficionado.

El acusado fue ajusticiado por el Estado de Utah a resultas de la sentencia pronunciada por un jurado inficionado, hay pruebas de que existía "predisposición racial" de parte de sus miembros.

by car en coche
They went by car.
Fueron en coche.

by cooperating with mediante su cooperación con
It is very common for a prisoner accused of a crime to save himself from being punished by cooperating with the authorities.
Es muy corriente que un reo acusado de un delito se salve de ser castigado mediante su cooperación con la autoridad.

by her own admission ella misma admitía
She was, by her own admission, a poor mother.
Ella misma admitía que no era una buena madre.

by his partner por su socia, por su socio
He was aided and abetted by his partner.
Fue instigado y secundado por su socia.

by inheritance por sucesión
She acquired the property by inheritance.
Adquirió la propiedad por sucesión.

by the end of para fin de
It'll be ready by the end of the week.
Estará listo para el fin de semana.

by the police la policía, por la policía
He was hotly pursued by the police.
La policía le siguió muy de cerca.

The thieves were caught by the police.
Los ladrones fueron capturados por la policía.
La policía capturó a los ladrones.

Were you interrogated by the police?
¿Te sometió la policía a un unterrogatorio?

by the way a propósito
By the way, there's a letter for you.
A propósito, tienes una carta.

by then para entonces
By then you'll be able to speak English fluently.
Para entonces vas a hablar inglés con fluidez.
Para entonces vas a saber hablar inglés con fluidez.

by this time next de hoy en
We'll know the verdict by this time next month.
De hoy en un mes sabremos el veredicto.

We'll know the verdict by this time next week.
De hoy en una semana sabremos el veredicto.

by next week dentro de una semana
Can you finish it by next week?
¿Puedes terminarlo dentro de una semana?

by tomorrow para mañana
Can you finish it by tomorrow?
¿Puedes terminarlo para mañana?

by + time a la, a las
By nine o'clock the jury was already deliberating.
A las nueve el jurado ya estaba deliberando.

We must be in court by ten.
Debemos estar ante el tribunal a las diez.

C

call
Call me any time.
Llámame cuando quieras.

Call me if anything goes wrong.
Llámame si algo sale mal.

Call me if there are any changes.
Llámame si hay algún cambio.

Call me if there is any trouble.

Llámame si hay algún problema.

Did you call them?
¿Hizo usted la llamnada?

I had a call from him just before I left.
Justo antes de salir recibí una llamada suya.

If you have any questions, please do not hesitate to call.
Si tiene alguna pregunta, no dude en llamar.

I'll call you first thing in the morning.
Te llamaré a primera hora de la mañana.

I'll call you in a little while, I'm busy right now.
Dentro de un ratito te llamo, que ahora estoy ocupado.

I'll call you on Monday, at the latest.
A más tardar, te llamaré el lunes.

In the long run it will be better to not call him to the stand.
A la larga será mejor no llamarlo al estrado.

Let's try to call once more.
Tratemos de llamar una vez más.

Who can we call in an emergency?
¿A quién llamamos en caso de emergencia?

Try to call her before 2 p.m.
Trata de llamarla antes de las 2.

When the judge calls your name, go to the front of the court room.
Cuando el juez lo llame, vaya al frente de la sala de la corte.

call as a witness citar como testigo, llamar como testigo
The defense called him as a witness.
La defensa lo citó como testigo.

They called his brother as a witness.
Citaron a su hermano como testigo.

They called his sister as a witness.
Llamaron a su hermana como testigo.

call into question poner en duda
They called his character into question.
Pusieron en duda su carácter.

They called his credibility into question.
Pusieron en duda su credibilidad.

call off suspender
She is going to call off the wedding.
Va a suspender la boda.

The trial against Roberto Gúzman and 5 other gang members was called off for the second time this Friday..
El juicio contra Roberto Guzmán y otros 5 pandilleros fue suspendido por segunda vez este viernes.

call one's attention to llamarle la atención sobre
He called our attention to the mistake.
Nos llamó la atención sobre el error.

call 911 llamar al 911
At the scene of the accident call 911 so that anyone with injuries can be taken to the hospital right away.
En el lugar del accidente llame al 911 para que lleven a cualquier persona con heridas o lesiones al hospital
inmediatamente.

He was the one who called 911, but there was nothing that could be done.
Él fue quien llamó al 911 para pedir ayuda, pero no hubo nada que hacer.

can

A lawyer can file a divorce lawsuit for you in court.
Un abogado puede presentar una demanda de divorcio en la corte.

A lawyer can represent you in court.
Un abogado puede representarle a usted en la corte.

Can I have your name?
¿Me dice su nombre?

Can I have your address?
¿Me dice su dirección?

Can you afford to hire a lawyer?
¿Puede contratar a un abogado?

Can you come to the office?
¿Puedes venir a la oficina?

Can you remember her name?
¿Te acuerdas de cómo se llama?

Can you speak English?
¿Sabes hablar inglés?

He will do all he can to help you.
Hará todo lo posible por ayudarte.

He's a man who can't tell the truth.
Es un hombre que no puede decir la verdad.

I can't get an answer out of him.
No consigo que él me dé una contestación.

I can't think of anything else.
No se me ocurre nada más.

If you fail to comply with any of these conditions, you can be taken back to jail.
Si no logras cumplir con cualquier de estas condiciones, te pueden encarcelar de nuevo.

I'll come as soon as I can.
Vendré en cuanto pueda.

I'll tell you all I can.
Te diré todo lo que pueda.

Is there anybody else I can talk to?
¿Hay alguien más con quien pueda hablar?

Nobody at school can ask about the immigration status of the family.
Nadie en la escuela puede preguntar acerca de la situación de inmigración de la familia.

She couldn't answer the question.
No pudo contestar la pregunta

Tell me all you can.
Dime todo lo que pueda.

The jury can reach a verdict at any moment.
El jurado puede llegar a un acuerdo sobre el veredicto en cualquier momento.

We can't do anything else.
No podemos hacer nada más.
You can't blame her.
No puedes echarle la culpa.

can become poder convertirse en
Those who come into the United States as refugees or who are granted political asylum, can become permanent residents in one year.
Los que entran a Estados Unidos como refugiados o a quienes se les otorga asilo político, pueden convertirse en residentes permanentes en

un año.

can help poder ayudar
There are many things with which a lawyer can help you.
Hay muchas cosas con las que un abogado puede ayudarle.

can produce poder crear
Esta droga puede crear dependencia.
This drug can produce addiction.

cancel
He cancelled the appointment at the last moment.
A último momento canceló la cita.

If you want a new hearing, you must ask the judge to cancel, or "vacate", the judgement.
Si quiere una nueva audiencia, tiene que pedirle al juez que cancele, o "invalide", el fallo.

cancel a default judgement anular un fallo por falta de comparecencia
Do you know how to cancel a default judgement?
¿Sabes cómo cancelar un fallo por falta de comparecencia?

cancel a judgement anular un fallo
When can I cancel a judgement?
¿Cuándo puedo anular un fallo?

You have only 30 days to cancel your judgement after the court mails it to you.
Sólo tiene 30 días para cancelar el fallo desde el momento en que la corte se lo envió por correo.

capable
I don't believe she's capable of that.
No la creo capaz de eso.

I don't think I'm capable of doing it.
No me creo capaz de hacerlo.

car
A car pulled up in front of the house.
El auto paró enfrente de la casa.
A girl of 18 was accused of stealing a car.
Una muchacha de 18 años fue acusada de robar un coche.

A truck ran into the car.
El coche fue embestido por un camión.

According to eye witnesses, the car was stopped with its flashing lights on.

Según testigos presenciales, el coche se encontraba parado con los intermitentes puestos.

Do you have a car?
¿Tienes coche?

He has a blue car.
Tiene un coche azul.

He lost control of the car.
Perdió el control del coche.

He was hit by a car.
Le pilló un coche.

He went by car.
Fue en coche.

How do you know the driver of the car?
¿Cómo conoces al conductor del coche?
The car was hit by a truck.
El coche fue embestido por un camión.

They went by car.
Fueron en coche.

Was your car moving at the time of the accident?
¿Estaba su coche en movimiento en el momento del accidente?

Were you knocked down by a car?
¿Le atropelló un coche?

Who does that car belong to?
¿De quién es ese coche?

car accident accidente de coche
I hope they haven't had a car accident.
Espero que no hayan tenido un accidente de coche.

car chase persecución en coche
The shooting took place after a car chase on the highway.
El tiroteo se produjo tras una persecución en coche por la carretera.
The police arrested four juvenile delincuents after a car chase.
La policía detuvo a cuatro delincuentes juveniles tras una persecución en coche.

car crash accidente de coche
She was killed in a car crash.
Murió en un accidente de coche.

They were killed in a car crash.
Murieron en un accidente de coche.

car insurance seguro de auto
Do you have car insurance.
Tiene seguro de auto.

You'll need some proof of car insurance.
Ncesitará algún documento que acredite su seguro de auto.

drive a car conducir un coche, manejar un auto
Each state has different laws for driving a car.
Cada estado tiene diferentes leyes para conducir coches.

make of the car marca del coche
What is the make of the car?
¿Cuál es la marca del coche?

owner of the car dueña del coche, dueño del coche
She is the owner of the car used in the bank robbery.
Es la dueña del coche usado en el asalto al banco.
Are you the owner of the car?
¿Es usted la dueña del coche?
¿Es usted el dueño del coche?

care
He could care less what people say.
Le importa un bledo lo que diga la gente.

I don't care what you think.
No me importa tu opinión.

I could care less what people say.
Me importa un bledo lo que diga la gente.

He doesn't care what you think.
No le importa tu opinión.

She cares deeply about social issues.
Se preocupa muchísimo por la problemática social.

without due care and attention sin la debida precaución
He was convicted of driving without due care and attention.
Fue declarado culpable de conducir sin la debida precaución.

catch
I'll catch you later!
¡Nos vemos!

We won't get caught like that again.
No volveremos a caer en esta trampa.

You've caught me at a bad moment.
Me has pillado en un mal momento.

catch in the act pillar con las manos en la masa
They caught him in the act.
Le pillaron con las manos en la masa.

catch off guard agarrar desprevenida, agarrar desprevenido
The question from the prosecution caught him off guard.
La pregunta de la acusación lo agarró desprevenido.

They caught us off guard.
Nos agarraron desprevenidos.

cause
His death was due to natural causes.
Su muerte se debió a causas naturales.

Her refusal to testify caused us problems.
Su negativa a testificar nos causó más problemas.
What caused his death?
¿Qué causó su muerte?

What caused the accident?
¿Qué causó el accidente?

You have cause to be worried.
Usted tiene motivo para estar preocupado.

cause for complaint motivo de queja, motivo de preocupación
The immigrant problem is the main cause for complaint in California.
Los problemas de los inmigrantes es el principal motivo de queja en California.

They have no cause for complaint.
No tienen motivo de queja.

cause for concern motivo de preocupación
The fact that this happened should not be cause for concern.
Este hecho no debe ser motivo de preocupación.

cause for concern motivos para preocuparse
There's good cause for concern.
Existen motivos para preocuparse.

cause for concern razones para preocuparse
There is good cause for concern.
Existen razones para preocuparse.

cause of causa de
Children often believe that they are the cause of the conflict between their parents.
Los niños con frecuencia creen que son la causa del conflicto entre su padre y su madre.

The cause of death is unknown.
Se desconoce la causa de la muerte.

cause unease causar inquietud
The incident caused great unease.
El incidente causó gran inquietud.

caused by ocasionada por, ocasionado por
Flood insurance covers losses caused by water that enters your home after a severe storm, abnormal tides, sudden flooding and similar situations.
El seguro contra inundaciones cubre pérdidas ocasionadas por agua que entre a su hogar después de una tormenta severa, mareas anormales, inundaciones repentinas y similares situaciones.

Remember that the standard homeowner's policies do not cover damages caused by two natural disasters: flooding and eartquakes.
Recuerde que las pólizas estándares de seguro de propietario de vivienda no cubren daños ocasionados por dos desastres naturales: inundación y terremoto.

causing concern causando preocupación
His drinking is causing concern.
Lo mucho que bebe está causando preocupación.

main cause of causa principal de
Murder with a firearm is the main cause of death among Hispanics.
El homicidio con armas de fuego es la causa principal de muertes entre hispanos.

no cause of concern no haber por qué preocuparse
There's no cause for concern.
No hay por qué preocuparse.

certain
Be certain to tell her.
No dejes de decírselo.
No te olvides de decírselo.

Certain questions remain to be answered.
Hay ciertos puntos que hay que aclarar aún.

I'll make certain that he understands.
Me aseguraré de que entienda.

certain conditions ciertas condiciones
There are certain conditions which the court has placed upon you.
Hay ciertas condiciones que la corte te ha puesto.

for certain a ciencia cierta, con seguridad

I can't say for certain.
No puedo decirlo con seguridad.
No puedo decirlo a ciencia cierta.

We don't know for certain what caused the accident.
No sabemos a ciencia cierta lo que causó el accidente.
No sabemos con seguridad lo que causó el accidente.

that's for certain de eso no hay duda, eso es seguro
He's up to something, that's for certain.
Trama algo, de eso no hay duda.
Trama algo, eso es seguro.

chance

He doesn't stand a chance of being acquitted.
No tiene ninguna posibilidad de ser absuelto.

He has very little chance of winning the case.
Tiene muy pocas posibilidades de ganar el caso.

I don't want to take a chance.
No quiero aventurarme.

It was pure chance that they met.
Se encontraron de pura casualidad.

That's a chance we'll have to take.
Es un riesgo que tendremos que correr.

The defendant doesn't want to take a chance.
El acusado no quiere aventurarse.

The thief took a chance on not being recognized.
El ladrón se arriesgó confiando en que no lo iban a reconocer.

They have a good chance of success in the case.
Tienen bastantes posibilidades de éxito en el caso.

change

Call me if there are any changes.
Llámame si hay algún cambio.

Have you changed address?
¿Has cambiado de dirección?

He's changed — and for the better!
Ha cambiado — ¡y para bien!

Let's change the subject.
Cambiemos de tema.

change in one's behavior cambio en su comportamiento

When a young boy is distressed, the parents usually note some change in his behavior.
Cuando un muchacho está angustiado, los padres suelen notar algún cambio en su comportamiento.

change jobs cambiar de trabajo
I've changed jobs.
He cambiado de trabajo.

Have you changed jobs?
¿Has cambiado de trabajo?

How many times have you changed jobs?
¿Cuántas veces has cambiado de trabajo?

change of address cambio de dirección
We've not yet been informed of any change of address.
Todavía no se nos ha informado de ningún cambio de dirección.

change one's mind cambiar de opinión
At the last moment he changed his mind.
A último momento cambió de opinión.

He thought of pleading guilty, but he changed his mind.
Había pensado declararse culpado, pero cambió de opinión.

People change their minds all the time.
La gente cambia de opinión.

change one's name cambiarse el apellido
She changed her name from Romero to Torres.
Se cambió el apellido de Romero a Torres.

When did she change her name?
¿Cuándo se cambió el apellido?

charge
He denied the charge.
Negó la acusación.

He was cleared of all charges.
Lo absolvieron de todos los cargos.

She dropped the charges against her husband.
Retiró la acusación contra su marido.

She's on record saying that she is innocent of the charges.
Ha declarado públicamente que es inocente de los cargos.

That's my understanding of the charges.
Esa es mi interpretación de las acusacioness.

Esa es mi interpretación de los cargos.

The charges carry with them sentences of up to 10 years in prison.
Los cargos conllevan penas de hasta 10 años de cárcel.

The charges show that the defendant acted alone.
Las acusaciones consideran que el procesado actuó solo.

The charges were dropped.
Retiraron los cargos.

The charges were withdrawn owing to lack of evidence.
Retiraron la acusación por falta de pruebas.

The defendant has pleaded not guilty to the charges.
La acusada se ha declarada inocente de los cargos.

The police cleared him of all charges.
La policía lo absolvió de todos los cargos.

We are convinced that they are innocent of the charges brought against them.
Estamos convencidos de que son inocentes de los cargos que se les imputan.

What are the charges?
¿De qué se le acusa?

What is the charge against me?
¿Cuál es el cargo que se me hace?

a charge of bajo acusación de, formular cargos de
She was arrested on a charge of murder.
La detuvieron bajo acusación de asesinato.

They are bringing a charge of theft against him.
Formulan cargos de robo contra él.

charge with acusar de, formular cargos de
He is charged with a number of shootings a month ago.
Se le acusa de ser responsable de varias balaceras hace un mes.

He was charged with murder.
Fue acusado de asesinato.

The government charges the defendant with armed robbery.
El gobierno formula cargos de robo a mano armada contra el acusado.

Were you charged with murder?
¿Fue acusado de asesinato?

Were you charged with stealing?
¿Fue acusado de robar?

What are you charged with?
¿De qué se le acusa?

on a charge of acusada de, acusado de, proceso por
He is being tried on a charge of rape.
Se le sigue proceso por violación.

He is under arrest on a charge of robbery.
Ha sido arrestado acusado de robo.

She is appearing on a charge of murder.
Comparece acusada de asesinato.

She is being tried on a charge of theft.
Se le sigue proceso por robo.

chase

They all joined in the chase for the thief.
Todos tomaron parte en la caza del ladrón.

They were both chasing the same woman.
Ambos andaban detrás de la misma mujer.

car chase persecución en coche
Several eye witnesses said that the shooting took place after a car chase on the highway.
Varios testigos presenciales relataron que el tiroteo se produjo tras una persecución en coche por la carretera.

The police arrested four juvenile delincuents after a car chase.
La policía detuvo a cuatro delincuentes juveniles tras una persecución en coche.

chase a car perseguir un coche
The police were chasing a car with three men in it.
La policía perseguía un coche con tres hombres.

chase after ir tras, salir tras
We chased after the thief.
Fuimos tras el ladrón.
Salimostras el ladrón.

check

He gave me a bounced check.
Me dio un cheque rechazado.

Remember to check the instructions carefully.

Recuerde que debe revisar cuidadosamente las instrucciones.

The check bounced.
El cheque fue rechazado.

The drawer of a bounced check will be fined.
El librador de un cheque rechazado será sancionado con una multa.

We're going to check it out.
Vamos a averiguarlo.
Will you send me a check in the morning?
¿Me mandas un cheque mañana por la mañana?

If someone writes you a bad check, you can sue for up to 4 times the amount of the check.
Si alguien le paga con un cheque sin fondos, puede hacerle una demanda por 4 veces el valor del cheque.

child, children

A large percentage of the missing children run away from home on their own.
Un gran porcentaje de los niños desaparecidos huyen de casa por propia voluntad.

Do you have any children?
¿Tiene hijos?

He is accused of abusing his children.
Lo acusan de abusar de sus hijos.

He is accused of beating and sexually abusing six children.
Lo acusan de golpear y abusar sexualmente de seis chicos.

Her children are in a bilingual program.
Sus hijos están en un programa bilingüe.

She was reunited with her children after many years.
Se reencontró con sus hijos después de muchos años.

The child is in the custody of his grandparents.
El niño está bajo la custodia de sus abuelos.

The child was found abandoned.
Encontraron al niño abandonado.

child abuse abuso de menores, abuso de niños
He *won't have to appear before the court to answer the ten charges related to child abuse until September.*
No tendrá que volver a comparecer ante los tribunales para responder de los diez cargos relacionados con abuso de menores hasta septiembre.

They charged him with child abuse.
Lo acusaron de malos tratos a la infancia.

child support manutención de los hijos
Child support is the amount of money that the court orders one parent to pay the other each month for support of the children.
La manutención de los hijos es la cantidad de dinero que la corte ordena a un padre pagar al otro cada mes para mantener a los hijos.
child welfare bienestar infantil
Child welfare investigators determined that there was no basis to blame M.J. of having sexually abused the child that is now accusing him of said crime.
Investigadores de bienestar infantil determinaron que no había bases para culpar a M. J. de haber abusado sexualmente del niño que ahora le acusa del mismo delito.

If a child is in danger or has been injured or hurt in his home, the child welfare agency offers services to guarantee the child's safety.
Si un niño está en peligro o ha sido lastimado en su hogar, la agencia de bienestar infantil presta servicios para garantizar su seguridad.

The child welfare system was created to help and insure that every child have the opportunity to live in a safe and protected home environment.
El sistema de bienestar infantil fue creado para ayudar a que cada niño viva en un hogar seguro y protegido.

The main function of the child welfare system is to take care of the safety, the continuance and welfare of children.
La función principal del sistema de bienestar infantil es velar por la seguridad, permanencia y bienestar de los niños.

children who los niños que
Children who live in shared custody arrangements usually feel loved by both parents.
Los niños que viven en arreglos de custodia compartida suelen sentirse amados por ambos padres.

children under niños menores de
In Nicaragua, 35 percent of the children under the age of 15 don't live with their parents.
En Nicaragua, el 35 por ciento de los niños menores de 15 años no viven con sus padres.

childhood
He had an emotionally deprived childhood.
Tuvo una infancia con grandes carencias afectivas.
Tuvo una niñez con grandes carencias afectivas.

He underwent psychiatric treatments in his childhood.
Fue sometido a tratamientos psiquiátricos en su niñez.

childhood friends amigos de la infancia
He has fond recollections of his childhood friends.
Tiene hermosos recuerdos de sus amigos de la infancia.

He kept in touch with his childhood friends.
Se mantuvo en contacto con sus amigos de la infancia.

choice
He had no choice but to leave.
No tuvo más alternativa que marcharse.
No tuvo más remedio que marcharse.

She had no choice but to go.
No tuvo más remedio que ir.

The choice is yours.
Usted elige.

You had a free choice.
Le dejaron elegir.

choose
He chose to appear in court.
Optó por comparecer ante el tribunal.

She chose a jury trial.
Se decantó por un juicio por jurado.

She chose a nonjury trial.
Se decantó por un juicio sin jurado.

circumstantial
Evidence may be direct or circumstantial.
La evidencia puede ser prueba testifical directa o prueba circunstancial.

circumstantial evidence pruebas indirectas, prueba circunstancial
Circumstantial evidence is indirect evidence, that is, it is proof of one or more facts from which one can find another fact.
Evidencia circunstancial es aquella prueba que es indirecta, es decir, es prueba de uno o dos hechos de los cuales se puede deducir otro hecho.

The defense was faced with a lot of circumstantial evidence.
La defensa se vio enfrentada con un montón de pruebas indirectas.

The jury is to consider both direct and circumstantial evidence.
El jurado debe considerar tanto la prueba testifical directa como la circunstancial.

The law permits the jury to give equal weight to both direct and cir-

cumstantial evidence.
La ley permite que el jurado le dé igual peso tanto a la prueba testifical directa como a la prueba circunstancial.

There is a lot of circumstantial evidence.
Hay un montón de pruebas indirectas.

claim

He filed a claim against the company.
Presentó una demanda contra la empresa.

He's going to claim compensation.
Va a reclamar una indemnización.

His claim for disability allowance was rejected.
Rechazaron su solicitud de una prestación por invalidez.

It's nonsense to claim it was an accident.
Es absurdo afirmar que fue un accidente.

My claim for a disability allowance was rejected.
Rechazaron mi solicitud de una prestación por invalidez.

The company paid his claim for compensation in full.
La compañía pagó la totalidad de la suma que reclamó como indemnización.

clampdown

There has been a clampdown on illegal immigrants.
Se han tomado medidas drásticas contra los inmigrantes ilegales.

There has been clampdown on loans.
Se ha restringido severamente la concesión de créditos.

clear

Do I make myself clear?
¿Está claro?
¿Me explico?

Is that clear?
¿Está claro?

It is a clear case of murder.
Es un caso evidente de homicidio.

It is not entirely clear to me why it's necessary.
No me queda muy claro por qué es necesario.

They lack clear guidelines on this matter
Carecen de directices en esta materia.

Carecen de pautas en esta materia.

clear and convincing evidence prueba clara y contundente
The defense presented clear and convincing evidence.
La defensa presentó prueba clara y contundente.

clear of absolver de
He was cleared of all charges.
Lo absolvieron de todos los cargos.

He was cleared of murder.
Fue absuelto de asesinato.

The police cleared him of all charges.
La policía lo absolvió de todos los cargos.

clear of danger fuera de peligro
We must be clear of danger by now.
Ya debemos estar fuera de peligro.

clear of debts libre de deudas
He's clear of debts.
Está libre de deudas.
clear one's name limpiar su nombre

She is determined to clear her name.
Está decidida a limpiar su nombre.

clear the area evacuar la zona
The police cleared the area.
La policía evacuó la zona.

clear that with obtener autorización de
You'll have to clear that with Tom.
Tendrás que obtener autorización de Tom.

clear that with obtener el visto bueno de
You'll have to clear that with Tom.
Tendrás que obtener el visto bueno de Tom.

close, closely
It is a very close family.
Es una familia muy unida.

That file has been closed for years.
Ese caso se cerró hace ya muchos años.

The matter is closed.
El asunto está cerrado.

The police observed the suspect closely.
La policía vigilaba de cerca a la sospechosa.

They are close friends.
Son amigos íntimos.
Son muy amigos.

They have always been very close.
Siempre han sido muy unidos.

They were close collaborators.
Mantenían una estrecha colaboración.

close the file archivar el expediente
The file for corruption against him was closed for lack of evidence.
Por falta de pruebas, el expediente por corrupción contra él fue archivado.

close tie vínculo cercano
The young mother wants to establish a close tie with her young child.
La joven madre quiere establecer un vínculo cercano con su pequeña hija.

closing

closing costs costos de cierre
Remember that the closing costs are additional costs added to your initial payment.
Recuerde que los costos de cierre son adicionales a su pago inicial.

come

Come in! it's open!
¡Entra! Está abierto!

How come they don't know?
¿Cómo es que no saben?

How come you didn't know?
¿Cómo es que no sabías?

How did you come by that scar?
¿Cómo te hiciste esa cicatriz?

Such documents are hard to come by.
Esos documentos son difíciles de conseguir.

There's no guaranty that he'll come back.
No hay ninguna garantía de que vaya a volver.

When does it come up for discussion?
¿Cuándo se va a discutir?

Cuándo se va a tratar?
Where do you come from?
¿De dónde eres?

come at venir encima
She was coming at me with a knife.
Se me venía encima con un cuchillo.

come down in favor of fallar en favor de, fallar a favor de
The court came down in his favor.
La corte falló a su favor.

come from venir de
Where do you come from?
¿De dónde vienes?

Where has he come from?
¿De dónde ha venido?

come out salir
Come out with your hands in the air.
Salgan con los brazos en alto.

come to acudir a
Did the police come to the accident scene?
¿Acudió la policía al lugar del accidente?

come to the table sentarse a la mesa
Both parties have agreed to come to the negotiating table.
Ambas partes han aceptado sentarse a la mesa de negociaciones.

come to think of it ahora que lo pienso
Come to think of it, I have one at home.
Ahora que lo pienso, tengo uno en casa.

come up acercarse, discutirse, tratarse
Two policemen came up to him.
Se le acercaron dos policías.

When does it come up for discussion?
¿Cuándo se va a discutir?
Cuándo se va a tratar?

commit, committed
He committed adultery.
Cometió adulterio.

She committed adultery.
Cometió adulterio.

commit a crime cometer un crimen
You can tell your lawyer if you have committed a crime in the past and he cannot tell the court nor anyone else.
Usted puede decirle al abogado si usted cometió un crimen en el pasado y él no se lo puede decir a la corte o a nadie.

committed to dedicada a, dedicado a
He is committed to change.
Está dedicado a buscar el cambio.

He is committed to telling the truth.
Está dedicado a decir la verdad.

common
He was treated like a common criminal.
Le trataron como a un vulgar delincuente.

It is very common for a prisoner accused of a crime to save himself from being punished by cooperating with the authorities.
Es muy corriente que un reo acusado de un delito se salve de ser castigado mediante su cooperación con la autoridad.

Violence against wome is very common.
La violencia contra las mujeres es muy común.

communication
communication with comunicación con, contacto con
It is important to be in communication with your lawyer.
Es importante estar en contacto con su abogado.

The lawyer's communication with his client about important phases that he deals with must be direct and effective and not through a third party.
La comunicación con el cliente sobre fases importantes de los asuntos que atiende el abogado debe ser directa y efectiva, y no a través de terceras personas.

compare
compared to en comparación con
Health insurance may be too expensive compared to how much money you make.
Los seguros médicos pueden ser demasiado caros en comparación con lo que usted gana.

compensate
compensate for indemnizar por
They offered me $50,000 to compensate for the damage.
Me ofrecieron 50.000 dólares para compensarme por los daños.
Me ofrecieron 50.000 dólares para resarcirme de los daños.
Me ofrecieron 50.000 dólares de indemnización por los daños.

We had to compensate him for the damage.
Tuvimos que indemnizarlo por los daños.

compensation
in compensation for de indemnización, en compensación por
I received $20,000 in compensation for the damage.
Me dieron 20.000 dólares de indemnización.
Me dieron 20.000 dólares en compensación por los daños.

complain
He complained of being roughly treated by the police.
Se quejó de ser maltratado por la policía.

Take Colleen, she never complains.
Por ejemplo Colleen, ella nunca se queja.

You'd better not complain!
¡Más te vale no quejarte!

complain about quejarse de
They complained about police brutality.
Se quejaron de la dureza de la represión policial.

They complained about the severe overcrowding in our prisons.
Se quejaron del hacinamiento en nuestras cárceles.

complain of quejarse de
He complained of being roughly treated by the police.
Se quejó de ser maltratado por la policía.

The women complain of being accosted in the street.
Las mujeres se quejan de ser importunadas en la calle.

complaint
His lawyer filed the complaint.
Su abogado presentó la queja.
Su abogado presentó el reclamo.

They have no cause for complaint.
No tienen motivo de queja.

They have no grounds for complaint.
No tienen motivo de queja.

This is an outrage, I will make an official complaint.
Esto es un atropello, me quejaré a las autoridades.

Who can lodge a complaint against a lawyer?
¿Quién puede presentar una queja contra un abogado?

Before you file a complaint talk to the repair shop service manager.
Antes de presentar la queja hable con el gerente de servicio técnico del taller de reparaciones.

complete, completely

Complete and sign.
Llenar y firmar.

Complete as appropiate.
Rellenar lo que corresponda.

He is completely honest.
Es honrado a carta cabal.

I completely forgot.
Me olvidé completamente.
Me olvidé por completo.
Me olvidé totalmente.

It is completely and utterly untrue.
Es completa y absolutamente falso.

It is imperative that the work be completed by Friday.
Es imprescindible que el trabajo esté listo para el viernes.

It was completely out of character for him.
No era nada típico de él.

My mind was a complete blank.
Me quedé totalmente en blanco.

The defense was a complete failure.
La defensa fue un fracaso total.

The whole story was a complete fake.
Toda la historia era puro cuento.

This story is a complete fabrication.
Esto es pura mentira.

We completely failed to convince them.
No logramos convencerlos en absoluto.

comply

comply by atenerse a
You'll have to comply by the rules.
Tendrás que atenerte a las reglas.
Tendrás que atenerte a las normas.

comply with acatar, atenerse a, cumplir, respetar
If you fail to comply with any of these conditions, you can be taken

back to jail.
Si no logras cumplir con cualquier de estas condiciones, te pueden encarcelar de nuevo.

It is an infraction to not comply with traffic light signals.
Es una infracción no respetar la luz roja del semáforo.

She refused to comply with the order.
Se negó a acatar la orden.

You'll have to comply with the court order.
Tendrás que atenerte al mandamiento judicial.

You'll have to comply with the rules of the court.
Tendrás que acatar las reglas del tribunal.

comprehensive
comprehensive insurance seguro a todo riesgo
He took out comprehensive insurance.
Contrató un seguro a todo riesgo.
Se hizo un seguro a todo riesgo.

concern, concerning
His drinking is causing concern.
Lo mucho que bebe está causando preocupación.

It is best for all concerned.
Es lo mejor para todas las partes interesadas.

It's no concern of yours.
No es asunto tuyo.
Please contact the department concerned.
Póngase en contacto con la sección correspondiente.

There's no cause for concern.
No hay por qué preocuparse.

What concern is it of yours?
¿Qué tiene que ver contigo?

as far as ... concerned en cuanto a ...
As far as I'm concerned, he is a big disappointment to us.
En cuanto a mí, nos ha decepcionado mucho.

cause for concern motivo de preocupación
His health is giving cause for concern.
Su salud está dando motivo de preocupación.

The fact that this happened should not be cause for concern.
Este hecho no debe ser motivo de preocupación.

cause for concern motivos para preocuparse
There's good cause for concern.
Existen motivos para preocuparse.

concerning acerca de
He said nothing concerning that.
No dijo nada acerca de eso.

I'd like a word with you concerning the trial.
Quiesiera hablar con usted acerca del proceso.

Nothing was said concerning the matter.
No dijeron nada acerca del asunto.

grounds for concern motivos de preocupación
There are no grounds for concern.
No hay motivos de preocupación.

condemn

He was condemned to a life of poverty.
Estaba condenado a vivir en la miseria.

Such conduct is to be condemned.
Tal conducta es censurable.

condemn to death condenar a muerte
He was condemned to death.
Fue condenado a muerte.
Lo condenaron a muerte.

They have been condemned to death.
Los han condenado a la pena de muerte.

They have implemented safeguards to protect rhe rights of those condemned to death.
Han implementado salvaguardias para garantizar la protección de los derechos de los condenados a la pena de muerte.

condemnation

The judge expressed his condemnation of the attack.
El juez manifestó su condena del atentado.

condition

Her condition remains critical.
Su estado continúa siendo crítico.

If you fail to comply with any of these conditions, you can be taken back to jail.
Si no logras cumplir con estas condiciones, te pueden encarcelar de

nuevo.

She's in critical condition.
Se encuentra en estado crítico.

There are certain conditions which the court has placed upon you.
Hay ciertas condiciones que la corte requiere de usted.

confess

He confessed to five murders and one rape.
Confesó haber cometido cinco asesinatos y una violación.

He confessed under pressure from the police.
Confesó presionado por la policía.

She confessed to the murder.
Confesó haber cometido el asesinato.
Se confesó culpable del asesinato.

The general expectation is that he'll confess his guilt.
Se espera que reconocerá su cupabilidad.

The Miranda Rights warn you that you incriminate yourself if you confess to a crime at the time of your arrest or during the police interrogation.
Los derechos de Miranda previene que usted se incrimine por sí mismo si confiesa un crimen a tiempo de su arresto o durante el interrogatorio policial.

confession

Do you have a confession to make?
¿Tienes que confesar?
¿Tienes que hacernos una confesión?

I have a confession to make.
Tengo que confesar.
Tengo que hacerte una confesión.

confide

He confided his troubles to me.
Me confió sus problemas.

He confided to me that he had committed the murder.
Él me dijo en confianza que había cometido el asesinato.

He doesn't have anyone to confide in.
No tiene a nadie a quien confiarse.
She confided to me that she was planning to escape.
Ella me confió que pensaba huir.

She confided to me that she was scared.

Ella me confió que estaba asustada.

You can confide in me.
Puedes confiarte a mí.

confidence
He doesn't have enough confidence in himself.
No tiene suficiente confianza en sí mismo.

I have every confidence in her as a witness.
Tengo entera confianza en ella como testigo.

You can give your lawyer information in confidence.
Usted puede darle a su abogado información en confianza.

confidential
Every case involving guardiansip has a public and a confidential record.
Cada caso de tutela tiene un expediente público y otro confidencial.

The confidential record contains documents with personal information on the ward, such as the report by the court's investigator.
El expediente confidencial contiene documentos con información personal sobre el pupilo, como por ejemplo el informe del investigador de la corte.

The court investigator turns over to the judge a confidential report of his investigation.
El investigador de la corte le entrega al juez un informe confidencial de su investigación.

Your lawyer can advise on the documents that are to be filed in the confidential record.
Su abogado lo puede asesorar sobre los documentos que se deben archivar en el expediente confidencial.

confine
He was confined to bed for several months.
Tuvo que guardar cama varios meses.

Please confine yourself to the facts.
Por favor, limítese a los hechos.

The fire was confined to the basement.
El incendio se localizó en el sótano.
confinement
He has been in solitary confinement for three months.
Está incomunicado hace tres meses.

He is in solitary confinement.
Está incomunicado.

confiscate

A computer was confiscated.
Una computadora fue decomisada.

All his possessions were confiscated.
Fue privado de sus bienes.

More than 4 tons of cocaine have been confiscated in the first six months of the year.
En los primeros 6 meses del año se han decomisado más de 4 toneladas de cocaína.

She had all her possessions confiscated.
Fue privada de sus bienes.

They sell confiscated goods.
Venden artículos de decomiso.

confiscation

His car was seized under the controversial ordinance which allows the confiscation of vehicles.
Su auto fue decomisado bajo la polémica ordenanza, la cual permite el decomiso de vehículos.

Immigrants complain about the confiscation of cars for driving without a license.
Los inmigrantes se quejan del decomiso de autos por manejar sin licencia de conducir.

conflict, conflicting

Children often believe that they are the cause of the conflict between their parents.
Los niños con frecuencia creen que son la causa del conflicto entre su padre y su madre.

She was torn by conflicting emotions.
Se debatía en un mar de emociones contradictorias.

That conflicts with what he told me.
Eso contradice lo que me dijo.

The conflicts are ethnic in origin.
Los conflictos son de origen racial.

To date no conflicting evidence has been presented.
Hasta la fecha no ha presentado ninguna prueba contradictoria.

Our interests conflict.
Nuestros intereses están en conflicto.

confrontation

A Mexican dies in a confrontation with the police.
Un mexicano muere en un enfrentamiento con la Policía.

A policeman was shot in a confrontation with burglars.
Un policía fue baleado en un enfrentamiento con ladrones.

A wounded policeman, a civilian dead and another person arrested was the result of a confrontation provoked by three men.
Un policía herido, un civil fallecido y otra persona detenida fue el resultado de un enfrentamiento provocado por tres hombres.

In the confrontation, one of them pulled out a weapon and shot and a policeman fell.
En el enfrentamiento, uno de ellos sacó un arma y disparó y el policía se cayó.

connect, connected

An alleged hired assassin is connected to the murder of a 25 year old woman.
Un supuesto sicario está relacionado con asesinato de una mujer de 25 años de edad.

The murder is connected to a network of drug traffickers in Albuquerque.
El asesinato está relacionado con una red de tráficantes de drogas en Albuquerque.

connection

She disavowed any connection with the gang.
Negó tener ninguna relación con la pandilla.

She is wanted in connection with the killing.
Se la busca en conexión con el asesinato.
Se la busca en relación con el asesinato.

conscience

My conscience is clear!
¡Yo tengo la conciencia tranquila!

She has a guilty conscience.
No tiene la conciencia tranquila.
Tiene mala conciencia.

consensual

consensual sex sexo consensuado
The accused maintains that they had consensual sex.
El acusado argumenta que mantuvieron sexo consensuado.

consider, considered

The unknown suspect should be considered armed and

dangerous.
El sospechoso desconocido debe ser considerado armado y peligroso.

We are considering all the aspects of the plea bargain.
Estamos estudiando todos los aspectos del acuerdo con el fiscal.

We are considering the matter.
Estamos estudiando el asunto.

We are considering various ways of presenting the defense.
Estamos barajando varias ideas acerca de la forma de presentar la defensa.

consider both considerar tanto ... como
The jury is to consider both direct and circumstantial evidence.
El jurado debe considerar tanto la prueba testifical directa como la circunstancial.

consideration
His age is an important consideration.
Su edad es un factor importante.

under consideration estar estudiando
The matter is under consideration.
La cuestión se está estudiando.

constitutional
constitutional rights derechos constitucionales
Everybody who arrives in the United States, with or without papers, has constitutional rights.
Toda persona que llega a Estados Unidos, con o sin documentos, tiene derechos constitucionales.

It is a crime in that it violates constitutional rights.
Es un delito por cuanto vulnera los derechos constitucionales.

contain
The government charges the defendant with armed robbery contained in the indictment.
El gobierno formula cargos contenidos en la acusación de robo a mano armada contra el acusado.

contemplate
Do you contemplate any difficulties?
¿Prevé alguna dificultad?
¿Prevé que vaya a haber dificultades?

He felt so desperate that he even contemplated suicide.
Desesperado, llegó a pensar en el suicidio.

contempt

He felt nothing but contempt for them.
No sentía más que desdén por ellos.
No sentía más que desprecio por ellos.

contempt of court
He was in contempt of court.
Había cometido desacato al tribunal.

If you don't appear before the court, you can be subject to an immediate arrest order and be punished for contempt of court.
Si no comparece ante el tribunal, puede estar sujeto a que se ordene su arresto de inmediato y a ser castigada por desacato al tribunal.

contingent

contingent fee honorario de contingencia
A contingent fee is when the lawyer is in agreement to not get paid unless you win the case.
Un honorario de contingencia es cuando el abogado está de acuerdo en que no le pagarán a no ser que usted gane el caso.

contractor

Can I sue a contractor for not having a license?
¿Puedo demandar a un contratista por no tener licencia?

In general, contractors that fix your home must have a license from the State.
En general, los contratistas que hacen mejoras a la vivienda tienen que tener una licencia del estado.

To find out if your contractor is licensed, call the Contractors State License Board.
Para saber si un contratista tiene licencia, llame a la Junta Estatal de Licenciamiento de Contratistas.

convict, convicted

He is a convicted murderer.
Es un asesino convicto.

He is a convicted rapist.
Es un violador convicto.

There is enough evidence to convict him.
Hay pruebas suficientes para condenarlo.

They are looking for an escaped convict.
Están buscando a un preso que se ha fugado de la cárcel.

convicted of condenada por, condenado por
He was convicted of drunk driving.
Fue condenado por conducir en estado de embriaguez.

He was convicted of stealing.
Lo condenaron por robo.

The accused was convicted of four misdemeanors related to tampering with evidence and attempting to cover up the incident.
El acusado fue condenado por cuatro delitos menores, relacionados con manipulación de evidencia y tratar de encubrir el incidente.

convicted on declarada culpable de, declarado culpable de
She was convicted on eight charges of espionage.
Fue declarada culpable de ocho acusaciones de espionaje.

conviction
He has two previous convictions for theft.
Tiene dos condenas previas por robo.

There were 12 convictions for theft
Hubo 12 condenas por robo.

He spoke without much conviction.
Habló sin mucha convicción.

With that evidence they were able to secure a conviction.
Con esas pruebas lograron que se la condenara.

convince, convinced
His testimony doesn't convince me.
Su testimonio no me convence.

He failed to convince them of his innocence.
No logró convencerlos de su inocencia.

He wasn't able to convince the jury.
No pudo convencer al jurado.

How can we convince them to change their minds.
¿Cómo podemos convencerlos para que cambien de opinión?

It's not worth trying to convince him.
No vale la pena intentar convencerlo.

The jury is not absolutely convinced.
El jurado no está totalmente convencido.

We are convinced that they are innocent of the charges brought against them.
Estamos convencidos de que son inocentes de los cargos que se les imputan.

cooperate

Are you ready to cooperate with the authorities?
¿Estás dispuesto a cooperar con las autoridades?

He refused to cooperate with the police.
Se negó a cooperar con la policía.

He was offered immunity from prosecution provided that he cooperated.
Le ofrecieron no seguirle proceso si cooperaba.

could

He was the only one that could give them information about his son.
Era el único que podía darles razón de su hijo.

Her lawyer can use private investigators to gather evidence that could prove her innocence.
Su abogado puede usar investigadores privados para juntar la evidencia que podría comprobar su inocencia.

She came to see me whenever she could.
Siempre que podía, venía a verme.

That could be the case, but we have no evidence.
Pudiera ser, pero no tenemos pruebas.

The jury could not reach a verdict on the charge of reckless manslaughter.
El jurado no pudo llegar a un acuerdo sobre el cargo de homicidio por imprudencia.

We could try to plea bargain.
Podríamos intentar llegar a un acuerdo con el fiscal.

could be podría ser, se le puede
Any one of them could be the murderer.
Cualquiera de ellos podría ser el asesino.

If he is convicted of sexual assault he could be sentenced to four years of prison.
De ser convicto por asalto sexual, podría ser sentenciado a cuatro años de cárcel.

The trial will begin before the 5th of June and the sentence could be known four days later.
El juicio empezará antes del 5 de junio y la sentencia podría conocerse cuatro días más tarde.

There are several cases in which your son or daughter could be asked to testify in a court.

Existen varios casos en los que se le puede pedir a su hijo o hija que preste testimonio en un tribunal.

could get podría recibir
If they find him guilty he could get up to 20 years in prison.
Si lo encuentran culpable podría recibir una condena de hasta 20 años de cárcel.

could not reach no pudo llegar a
The jury said it could not reach a verdict on the charge of reckless manslaughter.
El jurado dijo que no pudo llegar a un acuerdo sobre el cargo de homicidio por imprudencia.

count
He was found guilty on all counts.
Fue declarado culpable de todos los cargos.

You're wrong on both counts.
Estás equivocado en los dos aspectos.

count as contarse como
Does that count as income?
¿Eso se cuenta como ingreso?

count on contar con
I'm counting on your help.
Cuento con su ayuda.

You can count on my support.
Puede contar con mi apoyo.
Puede contar con mi respaldo.

court
A default judgement is when the court decides you owe money even though you didn't go to court.
Un fallo por falta de comparecencia es cuando la corte decide que debe dinero aunque no haya ido a la corte.

A lawyer can file a divorce lawsuit for you in court.
Un abogado puede presentar una demanda de divorcio en la corte.

A lawyer can represent you in court.
Un abogado puede representarle a usted en la corte.

As a general rule the courts don't permit it.
Por lo general los tribunales no lo permiten.

Ask the judge for a continuance when you go to court.
Cuando vaya a la corte pídale al juez que posponga su caso.

Child support is the amount of money that the court orders one par-

ent to pay the other each month for support of the children.
La manutención de los hijos es la cantidad de dinero que la corte ordena a un padre pagar al otro cada mes para mantener a los hijos.

Do you know when you are supposed to go to court next?
¿Sabe cuándo debe acudir a los tribunales la próxima vez?

He asked the court to acquit his client on all counts.
Solicitó la total absolución de su cliente.

He failed to meet the court's standard.
No logró reunir los criterios del tribunal.

He is due to appear before the court next week.
Debe comparecer ante los tribunales la semana próxima.

He is willing to abide by the wishes of the court.
Está dispuesto a acatar la voluntad de la corte.

He was willing to abide by the court's ruling.
Estaba dispuesto a acatar la sentencia de la corte.

He will appeal to the Supreme Court.
Apelará ante el Tribunal Supremo.

The court adjourned for lunch.
El tribunal levantó la sesión para ir a comer.

The court gave the defendant 20 years in prison as an accessory to the murder of the agent.
El tribunal ha impuesto 20 años de prisión al acusado como cómplice en el asesinato del agente.

The court is adjourned.
Se levanta la sesión.

The court is now in session.
El tribunal está reunido.
El tribunal está en sesión.

The court was adjourned at the request of the defense.
La sesión se levantó a instancias de la defensa.

The Arizona courts have to inform immigrants — legal and ones without papers — about the consequenses of their migratory status in case they plead guilty of some crime.
Los tribunales de Arizona tienen que informar a los inmigrantes — residentes legales e indocumentados— sobre las consecuencias en su estatus migratorio en caso de declararse culpables de algún delito.

The court clerk, who administers the oath to witnesses, will also be

present in the courtroom.
En la sala del tribunal también estará presente el secretario del juzgado, quien les toma el juramento a los testigos.

The court does not collect the money for you.
La corte no cobra el dinero en su nombre.

There are certain conditions which the court has placed upon you.
Hay ciertas condiciones que la corte requiere de usted.

We must be in court by nine.
Debemos estar ante el tribunal a las nueve.

You can tell your lawyer if you have committed a crime in the past and he cannot tell the court nor anyone else.
Usted puede decirle al abogado si usted cometió un crimen en el pasado y él no se lo puede decir a la corte o a nadie.

You have been released from custody by the court.
La corte te ha dejado en libertad.

You have only 30 days to cancel your judgement after the court mails it to you.
Sólo tiene 30 días para cancelar el fallo desde el momento en que la corte se lo envió por correo.

When the judge calls your name, go to the front of the court room.
Cuando el juez lo llame, vaya al frente de la sala de la corte.

appear before comparecer ante
People can be summoned to appear before the court as a witness, either in a civil or criminal case.
Personas pueden ser citadas para que comparezca ante el Tribunal como testigo, sea el caso civil o criminal.
He is due to appear before the court next week.
Debe comparecer ante los tribunales la semana próxima.

If you didn't appear before the court because you didn't get a copy of the plaintiff's claim, you have 180 days to file your appeal.
Si no apareció ante la corte porque no recibió la copia del reclamo del demandante, tiene 180 días para presentar su apelación.

The accused won't have to appear before the court to answer the ten charges related to child abuse until September.
El acusado no tendrá que volver a comparecer ante los tribunales para responder de los diez cargos relacionados con abuso de menores hasta septiembre.

appellate court tribunal de segunda instancia
The defense lawyer entered an appeal with the appellate court.
El abogado defensor interpuso un recurso de apelación con el tribunal de segunda instancia.

contempt of court desacato al tribunal
He was in contempt of court.
Había cometido desacato al tribunal.

If you don't appear before the court, you can be subject to an immediate arrest order and be punished for contempt of court.
Si no comparece ante el tribunal, puede estar sujeto a que se ordene su arresto de inmediato y a ser castigada por desacato al Tribunal.

court appearance comparecencia, comparición
Appearance in a court is the act of presenting oneself before the court and submitting to its authority.
Comparecencia es el acto de presentarse ante un tribunal y someterse a su autoridad.

The accused proclaimed his innocence in an emotional court appearance accompanied by his wife.
El acusado proclamó su inocencia en una emotiva comparecencia junto a su esposa.

in court ante un tribunal
A lawyer can file a lawsuit for you in court.
Un abogado puede presentar una demanda ante un tribunal.
The person who makes a false statement in court will be punished with a prison sentence of up to five years.
La persona que formulara un testimonio falso ante un tribunal será castigado con pena privativa de libertad de hasta cinco años.

We must be in court by nine.
Debemos estar ante el tribunal a las nueve.

testify in court prestar testimonio ante un tribunal
There are several cases in which your son or daughter could be asked to testify in a court.
Existen varios casos en los que se le puede pedir a su hijo o hija que preste testimonio ante un tribunal.

Three persons have volunteered to testify in court in the Ríos case.
Tres personas han ofrecido prestar testimonio ante el tribunal en el caso Ríos.

To testify in court means to answer questions under oath.
Prestar testimonio ante un tribunal significa responder a preguntas bajo juramento.

the court is in recess el tribunal ha levantado la sesión
The court is in recess until next week.
El tribunal ha levantado la sesión hasta la semana que viene.

The court is in recess until this afternoon.

El tribunal ha levantado la sesión hasta esta tarde.

The court is in recess until tomorrow.
El tribunal ha levantado la sesión hasta mañana.

The court is in recess until two o'clock.
El tribunal ha levantado la sesión hasta las dos.

first court date primera fecha de corte
Your first court date is next Monday.
Tu primera fecha de corte es el próximo lunes.

could
Could I have a word with you?
¿Podría hablar contigo un momento?

You could have told me!
¡Podías habérmelo dicho!

You could try telephoning his office.
¿Por qué no le llamas a su despacho?

cover, covered
I want to know which expenses Medicare covers.
Quiero saber qué gastos cubre Medicare.

cover against cubrir contra
This policy covers you against all risks.
Esta póliza lo cubre contra todo tipo de riesgos.
cover damages cubrir daños
Homeowner's insurance covers damages to the structure of the home as well as to the possessions.
El seguro de propietario de vivienda cubre daños a la estructura del hogar al igual que a las pertenencias.

Remember that the standard homeowner's policies do not cover damages caused by two natural disasters: flooding and eartquakes.
Recuerde que las pólizas estándares de seguro de propietario de vivienda no cubren daños ocasionados por dos desastres naturales: inundación y terremoto.

cover for de tapadera, de pantalla
The bar served as a cover for illegal activities.
El bar servía de pantalla para negocios ilegales.
El bar servía de tapadera para negocios ilegales.

cover losses cubrir pérdidas
Flood insurance covers losses caused by water that enters your home after a severe storm, abnormal tides, sudden flooding and similar situations.
El seguro contra inundaciones cubre pérdidas ocasionadas por agua que entre a su hogar después de una tormenta severa, mareas anor-

males, inundaciones repentinas u similares situaciones.

cover up encubrir
The accused was convicted of four misdemeanors related to tampering with evidence.
El acusado fue condenado por cuatro delitos menores, relacionados con manipulación de evidencia.

covered by cubierta por, cubierto por
A witness said that he saw three men with their faces covered by ski masks.
Un testigo dijo que vio a tres hombres con el rostro cubierto por pasamontañas.

The services covered by Medicare include the cost of a semiprivate room, medicines and food.
Los servicios cubiertos por Medicare incluyen el costo de un cuarto semiprivado, medicinas y comida.

covered in cubierta de, cubierto de
He was all covered in blood.
Estaba completamente cubierto de sangre.

coverage
He doesn't have medical coverage.
No tiene cobertura médica.
No tiene protección médica.
The policy provides third party coverage.
La póliza cubre contra terceros.

crack
She is addicted to crack.
Es adicta al crack.

crack down on tomar medidas energéticas contra
The police cracked down on the gangs.
La policía tomó medidas energéticas contra las pandillas.

They cracked down on the drug dealers.
Tomaron medidas energéticas contra los narcotraficantes.

crash
We were in a crash.
Chocamos.
Tuvimos un accidente.

car crash accidente de coche
She was killed in a car crash.
Murió en un accidente de coche.
Se mató en un accidente de coche.

crash site lugar del accidente
After a traffic accident, don't leave the crash site.
Después de un accidente de tráfico, no abandone el lugar del accidente.

crime
Crimes of this nature carry a high penalty.
Este tipo de delito trae aparejada una pena grave.

Don't you know that what you have done is a crime?
¿Acaso no sabes que lo que has hecho es un delito?
He began talking about his role in the crime.
Empezó a hablar sobre su papel en el delito.

Hispanics who are victims of a violent crime are more likely than any other racial or ethnic group of being a victim of offenders who carry a weapon.
Las personas hispanas que son víctimas del crimen violento tienen más posibilidad que cualquier otro grupo racial o étnico de ser víctimas por ofensores que cargan un arma.

It is a crime punishable by death.
Es un delito castigado con la pena de muerte.

She was under age when she committed the crime.
Era menor de edad cuando cometió el delito.

The crime of abduction carries a high penalty.
El delito de secuestro trae aparejada una pena grave.

The Attorney General is the chief law officer of a state or country in charge of seeing to it that the law is complied with and prosecuting criminals for a crime.
El Fiscal General es el funcionario de mayor rango en un estado o país encargado de hacer cumplir la ley y enjuiciar a alguien por un crimen.

The number of violent crimes, which include murder, rapes and armed robbery, decreased by 14 percent.
El número de crímenes violentos, que incluyen homicidios, violaciones y robo a mano armada, se redujeron en un 14 por ciento.

The suspect was unable to account for his movements at the time of the crime.
El sospechoso no fue capaz de dar cuenta de sus movimientos a la hora del crimen.

This crime is punishable by three months in prison.
Este delito es castigado con la pena de tres meses de prisión.

criminal

Basically, there are two kinds of cases: criminal and civil.
Básicamente hay dos tipos de casos: penales y civil.

He was treated like a common criminal.
Le trataron como a un vulgar delincuente.

The criminal system in the US is based on one essential principle: the accused is innocent until proven guilty.
El sistema criminal de Estados Unidos está basado en un principio esencial: el acusado es inocente hasta que se le pruebe ser culpable.

criminal case caso penal, causa penal
A criminal case takes place when a person is accused of committing a crime.
Un caso penal resulta cuando una persona es acusada de haber cometido un crimen.

This is a criminal case brought by the United States government.
Esta es una causa penal presentada por el gobierno de Estados Unidos.

criminal possession tenencia ilícita, tenencia ilegal
A marine was arrested for illegal possession of a weapon.
Un marino fue arrestado por tenencia ilegal de armas.

He is on trial for criminal possession of a dangerous weapon.
Es procesado por tenencia ilícita de armas peligrosas.

He was arrested for criminal possession of a controlled substance.
Lo detuvieron por tenencia ilícita de sustancias reguladas.

He was arrested for criminal possession of a dangerous weapon.
Lo detuvieron por tenencia ilícita de armas peligrosas.

He was arrested for criminal possession of stolen property.
Lo detuvieron por tenencia ilícita de bienes hurtados.

critical

Her condition remains critical.
Su estado continúa siendo crítico.
Su estado sigue siendo crítico.

critical condition estado crítico
She's in critical condition.
Se encuentra en estado crítico.

cross

cross off tachar

Cross these off the list.
Tacha éstas de la lista.

They crossed him off the list of potential jurors.
Lo tacharon de la lista de jurados potenciales.

cross out tachar
Cross out what does not apply.
Táchese que no proceda.

crucial
You failed to mention the crucial point.
No has mencionado el punto crucial.

currently
currently en la actualidad
Currently, women have the right to choose.
En la actualidad, las mujeres tienen el derecho de elegir.

cut
He cut his finger.
Se cortó el dedo.

He cut his finger on a piece of glass
Se cortó el dedo con un cristal.

He took a cut in salary.
Aceptó un sueldo más bajo.

He had a cut on his chin from shaving.
Se había hecho un corte en la barbilla al afeitarse.

He was treated for minor cuts and bruises.
Recibió asistencia médica por heridas y hematomas.

cuts on her face cortes en la cara
Josefina S., held in the Albuquerque *detention center, had cuts on her face, neck and arms which she attributed to a fight with another girl.*
Josefina S., detenida en el centro de detención de Albuquerque, tenía cortes en la cara, el cuello y los brazos que atribuyó a una pelea con otra muchacha.

D

damage
If a tenant damages the property, the landlord can deduct the cost of fixing it from the security deposit.

Si un inquilino causa daños a la propiedad, el propietario puede deducir el costo del arreglo del depósito de seguridad.

A security deposit is any money a landlord takes from a tenant in case the property is damaged.
Un depósito de seguridad es cualquier dinero que el propietario toma del inquilino por si llega a causar daños a la propiedad.

I brought a lawsuit against him for damages.
Lo demandé por daños y perjuicios.

You have to bring a lawsuit against him for damages.
Tienes que demandarlo por daños y perjuicios.

Remember that the standard homeowner's policies do not cover damages caused by two natural disasters: flooding and eartquakes.
Recuerde que las pólizas estándares de seguro de propietario de vivienda no cubren daños ocasionados por dos desastres naturales: inundación y terremoto.

They offered me $50,000 to compensate for the damage.
Me ofrecieron 50.000 dólares para compensarme por los daños.
Me ofrecieron 50.000 dólares para resarcirme de los daños.
Me ofrecieron 50.000 dólares de indemnización por los daños.

We had to compensate him for the damage.
Tuvimos que indemnizarlo por los daños.

Damage was estimated at somewhere near $2.000.
Los daños se calcularon en cerca de 2.000 dólares.

date

In order to get a new arraignment (first court date), call the magistrate's office at 441-3754.
Para obtener una nueva fecha para la lectura de acusación (la primera fecha de corte), llame a la oficina del Magistrado al 441-3754.

She keeps up to date.
Se mantiene al día.

Show up in court for any and all court dates, and you must be there on time.
Aparezcas para todas las fechas de corte y tienes que llegar a tiempo.

The application must be signed and dated by the applicant.
La solicitud debe ser firmada y fechada por el solicitante.

The clerk will give you a date for your hearing.
El secretario le dará una fecha para su audiencia.

We got to the bottom of the problem before the first court date.
Llegamos al fondo del problema antes de la primera fecha de corte.

What's the date today?
¿Qué fecha es hoy?

Your court date is on Monday.
Tu fecha de corte es el lunes.

Your first court date is next Monday.
Tu primera fecha de corte es el próximo lunes.

earlier date fecha más cercana
An earlier date would be preferable.
Una fecha más cercana sería preferible.

deal
A good deal depends on what she testifies tomorrow.
Mucho depende de lo que testifique mañana.

He got a very good deal from the prosecutor.
Llegó a un buen arreglo con el fiscal.

It's a deal!
¡Trato hecho!
The disabled deserve a better deal.
Los minusválidos merecen algo mejor.
Los minusválidos merecen un mejor trato.

deal in comerciar en, dedicarse a, operar en
He deals in stolen goods.
Se dedica al tráfico de bienes hurtados.

They deal in drugs.
Comercian en el tráfico de drogas.

deal with abordar, ocuparse de, resolver, saber qué hacer
I don't know how to deal with this problem.
No sé qué hacer con este problema.

The judge dealt fairly with him.
El juez fue justo con él.
El juez lo trató con justicia.

The judge dealt with her severely.
El juez fue severo con ella.

The problem must be dealt with now.
Hay que ocuparse del problema ahora mismo.

The problem must be dealt with now.
Hay que resolver el problema ahora mismo.

The lawyer's communication with her client about important phases

that she deals with must be direct and effective and not through a third party.
La comunicación con el cliente sobre fases importantes de los asuntos que atiende la abogada debe ser directa y efectiva, y no a través de terceras personas.

They will have to deal with these problems.
Tendrán que abordar estos problemas.

work out a deal with llegar a un acuerdo con
He worked out a deal with the prosecutor.
Llegaron a un acuerdo con el fiscal.

dealer
He's a dealer in stolen cars.
Es reducidor de autos.

He's a dealer in stolen goods.
Es reducidor.

He's a well-known arms dealer.
Es un conocido traficante de armas.

He's a well-known drug dealer.
Es un conocido traficante de drogas.

He's charged with being a dealer in stolen cars.
Se le imputa de ser reducidor de autos.

dealings
I've never had dealings with her?.
Nunca he tratado con ella.

Have you ever had dealings with her?.
¿Has tratado alguna vez con ella?

He has a reputation for honest dealings.
Tiene fama de honradez en los negocios.

My dealings with him are purely professional.
Sólo trató con él por razones de negocio.

The company has a reputation for shady dealings.
La empresa tiene fama de hacer negocios turbios.

death
He bled to death.
Murió desangrado.

He was beaten to death?
Lo mataron a golpes.

He was stabbed to death?
Lo mataron a puñaladas.

His death was due to natural causes.
Su muerte se debió a causas naturales.

I was very distressed to hear about his death.
La noticia de su muerte me dejó muy consternada.

In the trial the defense argued that the death of Laci was accidental.
La defensa argumentó en el juicio que la muerte de Laci fue accidental.

It is a crime punishable by death.
Es un delito castigado con la pena de muerte.

She is not to blame for his death.
Ella no tiene la culpa de su muerte.

Murder with a firearm is the main cause of death among Hispanics.
El homicidio con armas de fuego es la causa principal de muertes entre hispanos.

She bled to death?
Ella murió desangrada.
Murió desangrada.

She is still mourning his death.
Todavía llora su muerte.

The cause of death is unknown.
Se desconoce la causa de la muerte.

The death of a spouse can be a devastating experience.
La muerte de un cónyuge puede ser una experiencia devastadora.

The jury foud him guilty of the abduction of six girls and the death of two of them.
El jurado lo declaró culpable del rapto de seis niñas y la muerte de dos de ellas.

The likely outcome is the death penalty.
El resultado más probable es la pena de muerte.

They have been sentenced to death.
Los han condenado a la pena de muerte.

They have implemented safeguards to protect rhe rights of those condemned to death.
Han implementado salvaguardias para garantizar la protección de los derechos de los condenados a la pena de muerte.

They issued a death threat against him.
Lo amenazaron de muerte.

What caused his death?
¿Qué causó su muerte?

death blow
He dealt him a death blow.
Le atestó un golpe mortal.
Le dio un golpe mortal.

He delivered her a death blow.
Le atestó un golpe mortal.
Le dio un golpe mortal.

debt
Their debts had built up.
Sus deudas se habían ido acumulando.

He's clear of debts.
Está libre de deudas.

decide, decided
A default judgement is when the court decides you owe money even though you didn't go to court.
Un fallo por falta de comparecencia es cuando la corte decide que debe dinero aunque no haya ido a la corte.

After much thought she decided not to accept the offer.
Después de mucho pensar decidió no aceptar la oferta.

As a juror you must decide if the person accused is guilty or not.
Como miembro del jurado, debe decidir si la persona acusada es o no culpable.

At the last moment we decided to plead self-defense.
A última hora decidimos alegar légitima defensa.

Have you decided anything yet?
¿Ya has decidido?
¿Ya has resuelto algo?

In a jury trial the members of the jury listen to the evidence and decide the result of the case.
En un juicio por jurado, los miembros del jurado oyen las pruebas y deciden el resultado.

Parents who separate have to decide how they will share the responsibilities of raising the children.
Los padres que se separan tienen que decidir cómo compartirán sus responsabilidades de crianza de los niños.

The prosecutor decided not to charge the defandant of corruption for lack of evidence.
El fiscal decidió no imputar al acusado de corrupción por falta de pruebas.

You must decide what to do.
Usted debe decidir qué hacer.
Usted tiene que decidir qué va a hacer.

declare
He declared his innocence in an emotional court appearance.
Proclamó su inocencia en una emotiva comparecencia.

The accused declared himself innocent in court.
El acusado hizo su declaración de inocencia en la corte.

The car was declared a total wreck.
El coche fue declarado un siniestro total.

default
by default en rebeldía de, por incomparecencia de
He won his case by default.
Ganó el caso por incomparecencia de su adversario
Ganó su caso en rebeldía del demandante

default judgement fallo por falta de comparecencia
A default judgement is when the court decides you owe money even though you didn't go to court.
Un fallo por falta de comparecencia es cuando la corte decide que debe dinero aunque no haya ido a la corte.

What is a default judgement?
¿Qué es un fallo por falta de comparecencia?

in default en mora en
She is in default of her mortgage.
Está en mora en los pagos de la hipoteca.

defend
A lawyer defends the legal rights of the accused.
Un abogado defiende los derechos legales de la acusada.
Un abogado defiende los derechos legales del acusado.

He said nothing to defend himself.
No dijo nada en su defensa.

No dijo para defenderse.

Jones was defending and Ríos prusecuting.
Jones actuaba por la defensa y Ríos por la acusación.

She hired a lawyer to defend her.
Contrató a un abogado para que la defendiera.

She is the right person for defending him in the trial.
Ella es la abogada apropiada para defenderlo en el juicio.

She was quick to defend him.
Salió rápidamente a defenderlo.

defend against defender de
He defended her against the acusations.
La defendió de las acusaciones.

He defended us against the muggers.
Nos defendió de los atracadores.

defend oneself conducir su propia defensa
The accused, who is defending himself, has waited for two years to present his version of the facts.
El acusado, quien conduce su propia defensa, ha esperado durante dos años para tener la oportunidad de presentar su versión de los hechos.

defendant

A defendant does not have to present any evidence.
El acusado no tiene que presentar evidencia.

A defendant has the right to remain silent.
El acusado tiene el derecho de quedarse callado.

A defendant never has to prove his innocence.
El acusado no tiene que probar su inocencia.

The charges show that the defendant acted alone.
Las acusaciones consideran que el procesado actuó solo.

The court gave the defendant 20 years in prison as an accessory to the murder of the agent.
El tribunal ha impuesto 20 años de prisión al acusado como cómplice en el asesinato del agente.

The defendant has pleaded not guilty to the charges.
La acusada se ha declarada inocente de los cargos.

The defendant has pleaded not guilty to the charges and is presumed innocent until proved guilty beyond a reasonable doubt.

La acusada se ha declarada inocente de los cargos y es inocente hasta que se demuestre lo contrario.

The government charges the defendant with armed robbery.
El gobierno formula cargos de robo a mano armada contra el acusado.

The indictment is the description of the charges made by the government against the defendant; it is not evidence of anything.
La acusación es la descripción de los cargos presentados por el gobierno contra el defendant, no es ninguna evidencia.

The witness stated that defendant was not armed.
El testigo manifestó que el acusado no llevaba armas.

Two of the survivors were found in the basement of the house. of the defendant.
Dos de las supervivientes fueron encontradas en el sótano de la casa del acusado.

defense

All in all, it was a good defense.
En definitiva fue una buena defensa.

His defense is on firm ground.
Su defensa está en lo firme.

I don't anticipate making any major changes in your defense.
No tengo previsto hacer ningún cambio importante en su defensa.

Ignorance of the law is no defense.
La ignorancia de la ley no exime de su cumplimiento.

In the trial the defense argued that the death of Laci was accidental.
La defensa argumentó en el juicio que la muerte de Laci fue accidental.

Much to my disappointment, our defense fell through.
Para mi gran desilusión, nos falló nuestra defensa.

Several people wll testify in his defense.
Varias personas testificarán en su descargo.

The accused will conduct his own defense.
El acusado se hará cargo de su propia defensa.

The court was adjourned at the request of the defense.
La sesión se levantó a instancias de la defensa.

The defense argued that the death of C. B. was accidental.
La defensa argumentó en el juicio que la muerte de C. B. fue accidental.

The defense called him as a witness.
La defensa lo citó como testigo.

The defense doesn't have a lot of options.
La defensa no tiene un montón de opciones.

The defense doesn't have to prove the innocence of the accused beyond a reasonable doubt, it's sufficient for doubt to exist.
La defensa no tiene que probar la inocencia del acusado más allá de toda duda razonable, basta que exista la duda.

The defense was faced with a lot of circumstantial evidence.
La defensa se vio enfrentada con un montón de pruebas indirectas.

We are considering various ways of presenting the defense.
Estamos barajando varias ideas acerca de la forma de presentar la defensa.

What can you say in defense of the accused?
¿Qué puede formular en descargo del acusado?

defense lawyer abogado defensor
The defense lawyer entered an appeal with the appellate court.
El abogado defensor interpuso un recurso de apelación con el tribunal de segunda instancia.

The defense lawyers have asked the judge to order a co-worker of the alleged victim DNA tests.
Los abogados defensores han pedido al juez que ordene a un compañero de trabajo de la presunta víctima que entregue pruebas de ADN.

defer

I defer to you.
Me someto a su opinión.

In this I defer to you.
A este respecto me someto a su opinión.

I defer to your experience.
Defiero a se experiencia.

She deferred making a decision.
Aplazó la decisión.
Postergó la decisión.

deferred inspection inspección diferida

If you return in three years it is possible that they will give you a deferred inspection in order to enter.

Si regresa en 3 años es posible que le hagan una inspección diferida para ingresar.

A deferred inspection is given to a foreigner who the inspection authority clearly does not consider admissable.

La inspección diferida se otorga a un extranjero que el funcionario de inspección no considera claramente admisible.

degree

It is a matter of degree.

Depende de hasta que punto.

Es cuestión de grados.

An instruction jury prosecuted the defendant for the crime of first degree murder.

Un jurado de instrucción encausó al acusado grado por un delito de asesinato en primer grado.

If they are convicted, the jury has the option of charging them wth first degree murder with a sentence of 25 years in prison to life imprisonment.

Si son convictos, el jurado tiene la opción de culparlos de asesinato en primer grado, con una pena de 25 años de cárcel a cadena perpetua.

The prosecutor asked the jury to find Michael Jones guilty of first degree murder.

El fiscal solicitó al jurado que declare culpables de homicidio en primer grado a Michael Jones.

The gang member was found guilty of second degree murder of a 14 year old minor in Albuquerque.

El pandillero fue encontrado culpable de homicidio en segundo grado de una menor de 14 años en Albuquerque.

delay

Call me if you are delayed for any reason.

Llámame si te retrasas por alguna razón

The beginning of the trial was delayed by 24 hours.

El comienzo del juicio se retrasó 24 horas.

There is no point delaying any longer.

No tiene sentido esperar más tiempo.

They delayed signing the contract.?

Retrasaron la firma del contrato.

Demoraron la firma del contrato.

This delayed the start of the trial.

Esto retrazó el comienzo del juicio.
Este demoró el comienzo del juicio.

What delayed you?
¿Por qué has tardado tanto?

What is the delay?
¿Qué estamos esperando?

deliberate, deliberated

Apparently the jury is still deliberating.
Al parecer el jurado todavía está deliberando.

By nine o'clock the jury was already deliberating.
A las nueve el jurado ya estaba deliberando.

The jury deliberated all day long.
El jurado deliberó todo el día.

The jury is about to start deliberating.
El jurado está a punto de empezar a deliberar.

The jury spent three hours deliberating.
El jurado deliberó tres horas.

The 12 jurors, who deliberated for 3 days, found him guilty of kidnapping and abusing six girls.
Los 12 jurados, que deliberaron tres días, lo declararon culpable de secuestrar y maltratar a seis niñas.

deliberated for deliberó
The jury deliberated for five hours during two days to reach this verdict.
El jurado deliberó cinco horas durante dos días para llegar a este veredicto.

deliberation

After long deliberations the jury found him guilty.
Tras largas deliberaciones el jurado lo declaró culpable.

After long deliberations the jury found him not guilty.
Tras largas deliberaciones el jurado lo absolvió de toda culpa.

The jury deliberation just went on and on.
La deliberación del jurado se alargó interminablemente.

The jury deliberations will take place before the 30th of April.
Las deliberaciones del jurado tendrán lugar antes del 30 de abril.

deny

He denied that other people had been present.
Negó que hubiera habido alguien más presente.

He denies being involved in the robbery.
Niega estar involucrado en el robo.
He denies having said it.
Niega haberlo dicho.

The accused denies having raped the young woman last summer.
El acusado niega haber violado a la joven el verano pasado.

She denied the existence of the document under oath.
Negó la existencia del documento bajo juramento.
She denied under oath that the document existed.
Negó la existencia del documento bajo juramento.

The five denied participation in the events of which are attributed to them.
Los cinco negaron su participación en los hechos que se les imputan.

There is no denying it.
No se puede negar.

They deny any involvement in the crime.
Niegan estar implicados en el delito.

depend, depending

A good deal depends on what she testifies tomorrow.
Mucho depende de lo que testifique mañana.

He depends on her for everything.
Depende de ella para todo.

I'll be there, you can depend on it.
Estaré allí, cuenta con ello.
Estaré allí, tenlo por seguro.

She depends on him for her livlihood.
Depende de él para su sustento.

Some people just can't be depended on.
No se puede confiar en ciertas personas.
No se puede contar con ciertas personas.

You can't depend on him to tell the truth.
No puedes estar seguro de que va a decir la verdad.

You can depend on it!
Tenlo por seguro!

You can depend on her support.

Puedes contar con su apoyo.
Puedes contar con su respaldo.

You can depend on me!
¡Cuenta conmigo!

depending on contar con, dependiendo de
We are depending on you to testify.
Contamos con usted para testificar.

You will be able to buy a house depending on your income and on your debts.
Usted podrá comprar una casa o no dependiendo de sus ingresos y sus deudas.

deportation
Foreigners who receive a deportation order from an immigration judge are not expelled immediately from the United States.
Los extranjeros que reciben una orden de deportación por parte de un juez de inmigración no son expulsados inmediatamente de Estados Unidos.

How can I straighten out my deportation?
¿Cómo se puede arreglar una deportación?

I am married to an American citizen, but there is a pending deportation order on me. What should I do?
Estoy casado con una ciudadana estadounidense, pero tengo pendiente una orden de deportación ¿Qué debo hacer?

deprive, deprived
He had an emotionally deprived childhood.
Tuvo una niñez con grandes carencias afectivas.

He was deprived of his freedom.
Se vio privado de su libertad.

description
The indictment is the description of the charges made by the government against the defendant; it is not evidence of anything.
La acusación es la descripción de los cargos presentados por el gobierno contra el defendant, no es ninguna evidencia.

The police was able to identify the car from his description.
La policía pudo identificar el coche gracias a su descripción.

despite
despite a pesar de

He appeared in court despite his illness.
Compareció ante el tribunal a pesar de estar enfermo.
Compareció ante el tribunal a pesar de su enfermedad.

despite all of a pesar de todas, a pesar de todos
Despite all of the other challenges that we face in the country, affordable housing is the third most important.
A pesar de todos los otros retos que enfrentamos en el país, la vivienda asequible es la tercera más importante.

despite everything a pesar de todo
They stayed friends despite everything.
Siguieron siendo amigos a pesar de todo.

destroy

destroy the lives of destruir las vidas
Drugs are destroying the lives of many people.
La droga está destruyendo muchas vidas.

The affair destroyed their relationship.
El lío acabó con su relación.

detention

A judge ordered the detention of a man accused of assault and battery and a death threat against a minor girl.
Una jueza ordenó el arresto de un hombre acusado de agresión con lesiones y amenaza de muerte a una joven.

He spent three weeks in detention.
Estuvo detenido tres semanas.

The teacher gave him detention.
El profesor lo dejó castigado después de la clase.

detention center centro de detención
Forty five young prisoners, all considered highly dangerous, escaped from a detention center of Albuquerque.
Cuarenta y cinco jóvenes reclusos, todos considerados altamente peligrosos, escaparon de un centro de detención juvenil de Albuquerque.

They can be held up to five days while they await their transfer to a detention center for minors.
Pueden estar detenidos hasta cinco días mientras esperan su traslado a un centro de detención de menores.

did ...? (often not translated)
Did any of the police officers talk to you?
¿Habló algún agente de policía con usted?

Did any fire department personnel or emergency medical personnel come to the scene of the accident?
¿Acudieron al lugar del accidente bomberos o personal de los servi-

cios de emergencia?

Did he hurt himself?
¿Se hizo daño?

Did she hurt herself?
¿Se hizo daño?

Did the accident occur in an alleyway?
¿Ocurrió el accidente en un callejón sin salida?

Did the accident occur on the street?
¿Ocurrió el accidente en la calle?

Did the police come to the accident scene?
¿Acudió la policía al lugar del accidente?

Did they abide by the terms of the contract?
¿Respetaron los términos del contrato?

Did you call them?
¿Hizo usted la llamnada?

Did you get the number?
¿Tomaste nota del número?

Did you have a green arrow?
¿Estaba la flecha en verde?

disclaim

He disclaimed all responsibility for the accident.
Negó toda responsabilidad en el accidente.

He disclaimed ownership of the knife.
Negó que el cuchillo fuera suyo.

She disclaimed all knowledge of his whereabouts.
Negó conocer su paradero.

do, did, does, doing, done

And do you know what she did?
¿Y sabes lo que hizo?

Are you done complaining?
¿Has terminado de quejarte?

Can I do anything to help?
¿Puedo ayudar en algo?

Do as you're told!
¡Haz lo que se te dice!

Do something!
¡Haz algo!

Do you know what she did?
¿Sabes lo que hizo?

Does it match the discription?
¿Se ajusta a la descripción?

Does it match the discription of the accused?
¿Corresponde a la descripción del acusado?
He's doing eight years for armed robbery.
Está cumpliendo ocho años por atraco a mano armada.

His rudeness did little to improve the situation.
Su groseria no contribuyó a mejorar las cosas, que digamos.

How are you doing?
¿Qué tal andas?
¿Qué tal estás?
¿Qué tal te va?

How do you do?
¿Cómo estás?

She'd do better to keep quiet.
Sería mejor que se callara.

The other car was doing 100 miles per hour.
El otro coche iba a 100 millas por hora.

They can do you for possession.
Te pueden agarrar por posesión.
Te pueden coger por posesión.

They have done nothing wrong.
No han hecho nada mal.
No han obrado nada mal.

Well done!
¡Muy bien!

What can I do for you?
¿En qué le puedo servir?

What do you do?
¿A qué se dedica?
¿Usted qué hace?

What do you do for a living?
¿En qué trabajas?

What does your father do for a living?
¿En qué trabaja tu padre?

What does your mother do for a living?
¿En qué trabaja tu madre?

What is she doing about getting a job?
¿Qué está haciendo para conseguir trabajo?

You did the right thing.
Hiciste lo correcto.
You did well to tell me.
Hiciste bien en decírmelo.

do not cover no cubren
Remember that the standard homeowner's policies do not cover damages caused by two natural disasters: flooding and eartquakes.
Recuerde que las pólizas estándares de seguro de propietario de vivienda no cubren daños ocasionados por dos desastres naturales: inundación y terremoto.

do not have carecer de
More than half a million Hispanics that reside in the South of Florida do not have medical insurance.
Más de medio millón de hispanos que residen en el sur del estado de Florida carece de seguro médico.

do you believe that ...? ¿cree usted que...?
Do you believe that the other driver was at fault for this accident?
¿Cree usted que el otro conductor tiene la culpa por este accicente?

Do you believe that you were at fault for this accident?
¿Cree usted que tenía la culpa por este accicente?

do you certify ...? ¿certifica usted...?
Do you certify under penalty of perjury that the foregoing is true and correct?
¿Certifica usted bajo la pena de perjurio que lo anterior es verdadero y correcto?

do you have ... tienes ...?
Do you have a car?
¿Tienes coche?

Do you have a question?
¿Tienes una pregunta?

Do you have any brothers and sisters?
¿Tienes hermanos?

Do you have any children?
¿Tienes hijos?

do you know ... sabe ...?
Do you know how to read and write?
¿Sabe como leer y escribir?

Do you know how to speak English?
¿Sabe hablar inglés?

Do you know what this is about?
¿Sabe de qué se trata esto?

Do you know when you are supposed to go to court next?
¿Sabe cuándo debe acudir a los tribunales la próxima vez?

Do you know who called them?
¿Sabe quién hizo la llamada?

do you remember ...? ¿se acuerda ...?
Do you remember how many police officers were there?
¿Se acuerda cuántos agentes de policía estuvieron presente?

do you think ...? ¿cree usted ...?
Do you think you will be disabled for twelve months or more?
¿Cree usted que va a estar incapacitado por doce meses o más?

do you understand entiende usted
Do you understand each of the rights just explained to you?
¿Entiende usted cada uno de los derechos que le acabamos de explicar?

do whatever haz lo que
Do whatever is necessary.
Haz lo que es necesario.

Do whatever you think is best.
Haz lo que mejor te parezca.

Do whatever you want.
Haz lo que quieras.

doctor
He went to the doctor's.
Fue al médico.

Which doctor are you under?
¿Qué doctor le atiende?
¿Qué doctora le atiende?
¿Qué médica le atiende?
¿Qué médico le atiende?

Who is your family doctor?
¿Quién es su médico de cabecera?

doctor the report amañar el informe
He doctored the official report.
Amañó el informe oficial.

domestic

domestic partner
Public employees will have medical insurance for their domestic partners.
Empleados públicos tendrán acceso a seguro médico para sus compañeros domésticos.

Three fourths of all women killed are murdered by their husbands, ex-husbands or domestic partners.
Tres cuartas partes de todas las mujeres asesinadas son asesinadas por sus esposos, ex-exposos o compañeros domésticos.

domestic violence violencia doméstica, violencia en el hogar
Domestic violence is defined as abuse committed by an ex-husband, ex-wife, boyfriend or girlfriend.
La violencia doméstica se define como el abuso cometido por el esposo o ex-esposo, novio o novia.

Domestic violence entails a series of elements of control and and abuse of power on the part of the assailant.
La violencia doméstica conlleva una serie de elementos de control y abuso de poder por parte del agresor.

Domestic violence is the kind of violence that women suffer from most frequently.
La violencia en el hogar es la forma de violencia que con más frecuencia padecen las mujeres.

I need to get a new Social Security number because of domestic violence. How must I proceed?
Necesito obtener un número de Seguro Social nuevo por causa de violencia en el hogar. ¿Cómo debo proceder?

don't

don't drink and si bebes, si tomas
Don't drink and drive.
Si bebes, no conduzcas.
Don't drink and drive.
Si bebes, no manejes.

Don't drink and drive.
Si tomas, no conduzcas.

Don't drink and drive.
Si tomas, no manejes.

don't hesitate to no dejar de, no dudar en
If you have any problems, please don't hesitate to ask.
Si tiene algún problema, no deje de preguntar.

If you have any questions, please don't hesitate to ask.
Si tiene alguna duda, no deje de preguntar.

If you have any questions, please don't hesitate to call.
Si tiene alguna pregunta, no dude en llamar.

If I thought he was wrong, I wouldn't hesitate to say.
Si creyera que está equivocado, no dudaría en decirlo.

don't you? ¿verdad?
You believe me, don't you?
Tú me crees, ¿verdad?

don't you know that ...? ¿acaso no sabes que ...?
Don't you know that what you have done is a crime?
¿Acaso no sabes que lo que has hecho es un delito?

don't you remember ...? ¿no te acuerdas de ...?
Don't you remember Elena?
¿No te acuerdas de Elena?

doubt
I have no doubt that it is true.
No me cabe duda de que es verdad.

No doubt he will testify.
Seguro que testifique.

The matter is still in some doubt.
El caso sigue siendo dudoso.

The defendant has pleaded not guilty to the charges and is presumed innocent until proved guilty beyond a reasonable doubt.
La acusada se ha declarada inocente de los cargos y es inocente hasta que se demuestre lo contrario.

The defense doesn't have to prove the innocence of the accused beyond a reasonable doubt, it's sufficient for doubt to exist.
La defensa no tiene que probar la inocencia del acusado más allá de toda duda razonable, basta que exista la duda.

The prosecution has the obligation to prove that the accused are guilty beyond a reasonable doubt.

La Fiscalía tiene la obligación de probar que los acusados son culpables más allá de toda duda razonable.

The result is still in doubt.
Aún se desconoce el resultado.

There is some doubt about it.
Sobre esto existen dudas.

We've every reason to doubt her testimony.
Tenemos razones de sobra para dudar de su declaración.
Tenemos razones de sobra para dudar de su testimonio.

We've every reason to doubt her word.
Tenemos razones de sobra para dudar de su palabra.

doubt that dudar que
I doubt that he will get here on time.
Dudo que llegue a tiempo.

I never doubted that he was innocent.
Nunca dudé que fuera inocente.

doubt whether dudar que
I doubt whether it is worth it.
Dudo que valga la pena.

down

Anything you say may be taken down and used in evidence against you.
Cualquier casa que diga podría utilizarse como prueba en su contra.

down payment desembolso inicial, pago al contado
Private Mortgage Insurance is required when the down payment is less than 20% of the value of the house.
El Seguro Privado de la Hipoteca se requiere cuando el desembolso inicial es menor que un 20% del valor de una casa.

Without mortgage insurance, lenders usually require a down payment of at least 20 percent.
Sin seguro hipotecario, los prestamistas usualmente requieren un pago al contado de al menos un 20 por ciento.

draw

He was drawn into the argument.
Pronto se vio envuelto en la discusión.

draw a gun sacar la pistola
When he saw he was cornered he drew his gun.
Cuando se vio acorralado sacó la pistola.

drink

His problems drove him to drink.
Sus problemas lo llevaron al alcohol.

It was drink that killed him.
La bebida acabó con él.
drink a lot tomar mucho
Does he continue to drink a lot?
¿Sigue tomando mucho?

She drinks a lot?
¿Toma mucho?

drinking and driving beber alcohol y conducir
Drinking and driving is prohibited and strictly enforced in all of the states.
Beber alcohol y conducir un automóvil está prohibido y estrictamente reforzado en todos los estados.

drinking problem la problema es la bebida
She has a drinking problem.
Su problema es la bebida.

drive

drive conducir, llevar en coche, ser, tener
He drives a taxi.
Es taxista.

He drives a truck.
Es camionero.

He drove me to the airport.
Me llevó en coche al aeropuerto.

She drives a Ford.
Tiene un Ford.

She drove me home.
Me llevó en coche a casa.

She was driving without due care and attention.
¿Conducía en forma imprudente y sin prestar la debida atención.
Were you driving on the highway?
¿Conducías por la carretera?

drive someone to drink llevar a alguien al alcohol
His problems drove him to drink.
Sus problemas lo llevaron al alcohol.

drive too fast conducir demasiado rápido
He was driving too fast.
Conducía demasiado rápido.

drive under conducir bajo
It's an infraction to drive under the influence of alcohol.
Es una infracción conducir bajo la influencia del alcohol.

Driving under the influence of drugs or alcohol can could mean a prison sentence.
Conducir bajo los efectos de drogas o alcohol puede suponer una pena de prisión.

driver

driver's license carné, permiso de conducción
He had his driver's license taken away.
Lo castigó con la privación del carné.
Lo castigó con la privación del permiso de conducción.

drop

Let the matter drop.
Déjalo ya, no insistas.

drop out of school abandonar los estudios
She dropped out of school a year ago.
Abandonó los estudios hace un año.

drop out of sight desaparecer, perderse de vista
She dropped out of sight a month ago.
Desapareció hace un mes.
Se perdió de vista hace un mes.

drop the charges retirar la acusación, retirar los cargos
She dropped the charges against her husband.
Retiró la acusación contra su esposo.
Retiró los cargos contra su marido.

The charges were dropped.
Retiraron la acusación.
Retiraron los cargos.

drop the charges retractar la querella
He dropped the charges against his wife.
Retractó la querella contra su esposa.

drop the subject cambiar de tema
Let's drop the subject.
Cambiemos de tema.

They dropped the subject.
Cambiaron de tema.

drunk

He was drunk.
Estaba borracho.

He was drunk and disorderly.
Estaba en estado de embriaguez y alternando el orden público.

She was dead drunk.
Estaba completamente borracha.

drunk driving conducir en estado de embriaguez
It was his second drunk driving offense.
Era la segunda vez que lo detenían por conducir borracho.

He was convicted of drunk driving.
Fue condenado por conducir en estado de embriaguez.

due

due on vencer el
It's due on the 30th.
El plazo vence el día 30.

The first payment is due on Monday.
El primer plazo vence el lunes.

due to debida a, debido a, deber, deberse a
Due to the accident, her ability to walk is now severely impaired.
Debido al accidente, su movilidad se ha visto seriamente afectada.

He explained that his lateness was due to a breakdown.
Explicó que su tardanza se debió a una avería.

He is due to appear before the court next week.
Debe comparecer ante los tribunales la semana próxima.

His death was due to natural causes.
Su muerte se debió a causas naturales.

in due course a su debido tiempo
We will discuss that in due course.
Eso ya lo discutiremos a su debido tiempo.

We'll let you know in due course
Le avisaremos a su debido tiempo.

rent is due hay que pagar el alquiler, se paga el alquilar
Rent is due on Monday?
Hay que pagar el alquiler el lunes.
El alquiler se paga el lunes.

When is the rent due?

¿Cuándo hay que pagar el alquiler?
¿Cuándo se paga el alquiler?

with all due respect con el debido respeto
With all due respect, I think you are making a mistake.
Con el debido respeto, creo que se equivoca.
without due imprudente, sin la debida, sin el debido
A person who crosses the borders through Mexico or Canada without due inspection or documentation, has entered the United States illegally.
Una persona que cruce las fronteras por México o por Canadá sin la debida inspección o documentación, ha entrado de manera ilegal a Estados Unidos.

She was driving without due care and attention.
¿Conducía en forma imprudente y sin prestar la debida atención.

during
The jury deliberated for five hours during two days to reach this verdict.
El jurado deliberó cinco horas durante dos días para llegar a este veredicto.

The suspect was arrested during a breaking and entering.
El sospechoso fue detenido durante un allanamiento de vivienda.

during questioning durante cualquier interrogatorio
If you cannot afford to hire a lawyer, one will be appointed free of charge before or during questioning, if you wish.
Si usted no puede pagar por un abogado, uno le será nombrado gratis antes o durante cualquier interrogatorio, si usted lo desea.

during the hearing durante la audiencia, durante la vista
During the hearing the accused remained silent.
Durante la audiencia el acusado permaneció silencioso.
Durante la vista el acusado permaneció silencioso.

E

each
Child support is the amount of money that the court orders one parent to pay the other each month for support of the children.
La manutención de los hijos es la cantidad de dinero que la corte ordena a un padre pagar al otro cada mes para mantener a los hijos.

Do you understand each of the rights just explained to you?
¿Entiende usted cada uno de los derechos que le acabamos de explicar?
Each state has different laws for driving a car.

Cada estado tiene diferentes leyes para conducir automóviles.

Each year thousands of people without identity papers are deported.
Cada año miles de indocumentados son deportados.

The number of separations and divorces increase each year in the United States.
Cada año aumentan los casos de separación y divorcio en Estados Unidos.

each case cada caso
Each case will be judged on its individual merits.
Cada caso se juzgará según sus propios méritos.

each of them mutuamente, uno por uno
Each of them blamed the other.
Se echaron la culpa mutuamente.

He questioned each of them in turn.
Les preguntó uno por uno.

each one cada uno
Each one is free to get together with whom ever they want.
Cada uno es dueño de juntarse con quien quiera.

In addition, each one of them was found guilty of armed robbery.
Además, cada uno de ellos fue hallado culpable de robo a mano armada.

each other mutuamente, uno al otro
They are always criticizing each other.
Siempre se están criticando el uno al otro.

They give each other advice.
Se consejan.

each other (not translated)
They hate each other.
Se odian.

They looked at each other.
Se miraron.

They love each other.
Se quieren.

They missed each other at the airport.
No se vieron en el aeropuerto.

They write to each other.
Se escriben.

We have known each other long enough to be on a first-name basis.
Nos conocemos hace bastante tiempo como para tratarnos de tú.

We missed each other at the airport.
No nos vimos en el aeropuerto.

each side cada lado
First, each side may make an opening statement.
Primero, cada lado puede prestar una declaración de apertura.

to each other (not translatable)
They are not speaking to each other.
No se hablan.

to see each other salir juntos, verse
They've been seeing each other for two months.
Hace dos meses que salen juntos.

They are not seeing to each other.
No salen juntos.

Upon returning from my trip we'll see each other.
A la vuelta de mi viaje nos veremos.

with each other (not translatable)
They have had a fight with each other.
Se han peleado.

early, earlier
earlier date fecha más cercana
An earlier date would be preferable.
Una fecha más cercana sería preferible.

He is in his early twenties.
Tiene poco más de veinte años.

He was given the option of early retirement.
Le dieron la opción de anticipar su jubilación.

He was released earlier than expected.
Lo pusieron en libertad antes de lo esperado.

Your are early!
¡Llegaste temprano!

electric
electric shock descarga eléctrica
He got an electric shock.
Recibió una descarga eléctrica.

element

There's an element of risk in any operation.
En cualquier operación hay un componente de riesgo.

Domestic violence entails a series of elements of control and and abuse of power on the part of the assailant.
La violencia doméstica conlleva una serie de elementos de control y abuso de poder por parte del agresor.

It may be an element in her decision.
Puede que haya sido un elemento que influyera en su decisión.

We have the elements for an agreement.
Tenemos las bases de un acuerdo.

They have the elements for a solution.
Tienen las bases de una solución.

The government must prove the elements of the crime to make its case.
El gobierno tiene que establecer con certeza los elementos del delito para probar el caso.
El gobierno tiene que establecer con certeza los elementos del delito para ganar el caso.

element of truth algo de verdad
There's an element of truth in what he says.
Hay algo de verdad en lo que dice.

eligible

eligible for cumplir con, tener derecho a, reunir ... para
He is now legally eligible for U.S. citizenship.
Ahora cumple con los requisitos legales para solicitar la ciudadanía americana.
Ahora tiene el derecho a solicitar la ciudadanía estadounidense.
Ahora reúne los requisitos legales para solicitar la ciudadanía estadounidense.

She is eligible for a grant.
Tiene derecho a solicitar una beca.

The family is eligible for Medicare.
La familia tiene derecho a solicitar Medicare.

You are now legally eligible for U.S. citizenship.
Usted ahora cumple con los requisitos legales para solicitar la ciudadanía estadounidense.

eligible for elegible para para
He is eligible for an immigrant visa.
Es elegible para recibir una visa de inmigración.

They are eligible to submit their citizenship applications.
Son elegibles para someter sus solicitudes de ciudadanía.

embezzle
He is accused of embezzling public funds.
Lo acusan de malversar fondos públicos.

embezzlement
for embezzlement por desfalco, por malversación
Prosecutor investigates mayor of Albuquerque for embezzlement and embezzlement of funds.
Fiscalía investiga por malversación y peculado al alcalde de Albuquerque.

The authorities arrest a treasurer of a parent-teacher association for embezzlement
Las autoridades detienen por desfalco a tesorero de una asociación de padres de alumnos y profesores.

emergency
Did any fire department personnel or emergency medical personnel come to the scene of the accident?
¿Acudieron al lugar del accidente bomberos o personal de los servicios de emergencia?

Who can we call in an emergency?
¿A quién llamamos en caso de emergencia?

emergency brake freno de emergencia
Was your emergency brake on?
¿Dejó puesto el freno de emergencia?

end
end a pregnancy poner fin a un embarazo
Before Roe, women usually resorted to illegal and unsafe abortions in order to end a pregnancy.
Antes de Roe, las mujeres solían recurrir a abortos ilegales e inseguros para poner fin a un embarazo.

extradition
The US government will ask for his extradition so that he may be tried in Virginia.
El Gobierno estadounidense pedirá su extradición para que sea juzgado en Virginia.

extradition order solicitud de extradición
The application for an extradition order has been refused.
La solicitud de extradición ha sido denegada.

The application for an extradition order has been turned down.
La solicitud de extradición ha sido denegada.
extradition papers documentos de extradición

The hearing paved the way so that Ríos can sign the extradition papers.
La audiencia allanó el camino para que Ríos firme los documentos de su extradición.

motion of extradition pedimento de extradición
The motion of extradition of Flores hasn't arrived in Mexico because it is still on the negotiating table.
Los pedimentos de extradición de Flores no han llegado a México porque sigue pendiendo sobre la mesa de negociación.

F

face

faced with verse enfrentada con, verse enfrentado con
The defense was faced with a lot of circumstantial evidence.
La defensa se vio enfrentada con un montón de pruebas indirectas.

false

false imprisonment privación ilegal de la libertad
The brothers face charges of false imprisonment.
Los hermanos enfrentan acusaciones por el delito de privación ilegal de la libertad.

false police report falso informe policial, falso parte policial
He was arrested on charges of filing a false police report.
Fue detenido por presentar un falso informe policial.
Fue detenido por presentar un falso parte policial.

fault

Tell the judge how you were affected by what the other person did, and why it is their fault.
Dígale al juez cómo lo afectó lo que la otra persona hizo, y por qué es culpa de la otra persona.

He was at fault in not reporting the theft.
Obró mal al no denunciar el robo.

It's all your fault.
Tú tienes toda la culpa.

Whose fault is it?
¿Quién tiene la culpa?

Do you believe that the other driver is at fault for this accident?
¿Cree usted que el otro conductor tiene la culpa por este accicente?

Also explain why it is not your fault.
También explique por qué no es culpa de usted.

file

A lawyer can file a divorce lawsuit for you in court.
Un abogado puede presentar una demanda de divorcio en la corte.

A lawyer can file a sexual harassment lawsuit for you in court.
Un abogado puede presentar una demanda de acoso sexual en la corte.

He was arrested on charges of filing a false police report.
Fue detenido por presentar un falso parte policial.

The file for corruption against him was closed for lack of evidence.
Por falta de pruebas, el expediente por corrupción contra él fue archivado.

Your file has been transferred to another department.
Han traslado su expediente a otro departamento.

If you want to sue the person who is suing you, file and serve a form called a Defendant's Claim and Order to Plaintiff.
Si quiere demandar a la persona que lo está demandando, presente y entregue un formulario llamado Reclamo del Demandado y Orden al Demandante.

Before you file a complaint talk to the repair shop service manager.
Antes de presentar la queja hable con el gerente de servicio técnico del taller de reparaciones.

fine

fine for aplicarle una multa por, poner una multa por
I got a fine for speeding.
Me pusieron una multa por exceso de velocidad.

She was fined for speeding.
Le aplicaron una multa por exceso de velocidad.

fine for multar por
She was fined for jaywalking.
La multaron por cruzar la calzada con riesgo de provocar un accidente.

first

first degree murder asesinato en primer grado
An instruction jury prosecuted the eighth grade student for the crime of first degree murder.
Un jurado de instrucción encausó al estudiante de octavo grado por un delito de asesinato en primer grado.

If they are convicted, the jury has the option of charging them wth first degree murder with a sentence of 25 years in prison to life imprisonment.
Si son convictos, el jurado tiene la opción de culparlos de asesinato en primer grado, con una pena de 25 años de cárcel a cadena perpetua.

first degree murder homicidio en primer grado
The prosecutor asked the jury to find Michael Jones, José Ramos y Jason Cazares, all 24 years old, guilty of first degree murder.
El fiscal solicitó al jurado que declare culpables de homicidio en primer grado a Michael Jones, José Ramos y Jason Cazares, todos de 24 años.

first hearing
Bring proof of why you couldn't go to your first hearing.
Traiga un comprobante de por qué no pudo ir a la primera audiencia.

for

for a while un buen rato
He didn't come back for a while.
No regresó hasta pasado un buen rato.

for quite a while bastante rato
He's been talking for quite a while with the police.
Lleva bastante rato hablando con la policía.

G

girl
A girl of 18 was accused of stealing a car.
Una muchacha de 18 años fue acusada de robar un coche.

She has three girls.
Tiene tres chicas.

She is a very good girl.
Es una chica muy buena.

They have two boys and a girl.
Tienen dos chicos y una chica.

girlfriend
Do you have a girlfriend.
¿Tienes novia?

Is she your girlfriend?
¿Es tu novia?

Domestic violence is defined as abuse committed by an

ex-husband, ex-wife, boyfriend or girlfriend.
La violencia doméstica se define como el abuso cometido por el esposo o ex-esposo, novio o novia.

Is she your live-in- girlfriend.
¿Es tu compañera?

He's got girlfriend problems.
Tiene problemas de amores.

He lives with his girlfriend.
Vive con su novia.

go

go out tener novia, tener novio
Are you going out with anybody?
¿Tienes novia?
¿Tienes novio?

guardianship

Every case involving guardiansip has a public and a confidential record.
Cada caso de tutela tiene un expediente público y otro confidencial.

guilty

Don't feel guilty about that.
No te sientas culpable por eso.

She entered a plea of not guilty.
Se declraró inocente.

They are equally guilty.
Son igualmente culpables.

find guilty of encontrar culpable de
All legal or undocumented immigrants that are found guilty of some felony face immediate deportation.
Todos los inmigrantes legales o indocumentados que sean encontrados culpables de algún delito mayor enfrentan deportación inmediata.

find not guilty of declarar inocente, absolver
She was found not guilty.
La declararon inocente.
La absolvieron de toda culpa.

guilty or not inocente o culpable
How do you plead? — guilty or not?
¿Se confesa inocente o culpable?
have a guilty conscience no tener la conciencia tranquila
She has a guilty conscience.
No tiene la conciencia tranquila.

plead guilty confesarse culpable
I get the impression that he wants to plead guilty.
Me da la impresión de que quiere confesarse culpable.

until proven guilty hasta que se pruebe la culpabilidad
A defendant is presumed innocent until proven guilty.
Un acusado es inocente hasta que se pruebe la culpabilidad.

verdict of guilty veredicto de culpabilidad, declarar culpable
The jury returned a verdict of guilty.
El jurado emitió un veredicto de culpabilidad.
El jurado lo declaró culpable.

H

have

have nothing to do with no tener nada que ver con
According to his lawyer, he had nothing to do with the kidnapping.
Según su abogado, no tuvo nada que ver con el secuestro.

According to his lawyer, he has nothing to do with the case.
Según su abogado, no tiene nada que ver con el caso.

hearing

hearing audiencia, instrucción de cargos, vista
Have they set a date for the hearing?
¿Han fijado una fecha para la vista?

The hearing takes place after three and a half years of thorough investigations by federal authorities.
La instrucción de cargos se produce tras dos años y medio de investigaciones minuciosas por las autoridades federales.

The hearing will continue Monday.
La vista se reanudará el próximo lunes.

The judge may ask you to try to settle your case before the hearing takes place.
El juez puede pedirle que trate de llegar a un acuerdo en su caso antes de tener la audiencia.

heavy

heavy drinker tener el vicio de la bebida
He's a heavy drinker.
Tiene el vicio de la bebida.

here

be here estar aquí

I am here on an H-1B temporary professional worker's status. I would like to take computer science classes as a part-time student. Can I do that without violating my H-1b status?
Estoy aquí con estatus H-1B para trabajadores profesionales temporales. Quisiera tomar clases de ciencias de la computación a tiempo parcial. ¿Puedo hacerlo sin violar mi estatus H-1B?

homeowner
Being a home owner is a big investment.
Ser propietario de una casa es una gran inversión.
Ser dueño de una casa es una gran inversión.

how
How do I bring my parents to live in the US?
¿Cómo puedo traer a mis padres a vivir en Estados Unidos?

How do I obtain a work permit?
¿Cómo puedo obtener un permiso de trabajo?

I

identify
identify as identificar como
He was identified as the robber.
Fue identificado como el autor del atraco.

in
get in touch with comunicarse con
After the accident get in touch with your insurance company.
Después del accidente comuníquese con su compañía de seguro.

in a week en una semana
The arraignment is in a week.
La comparecencia ante el juez tiene lugar en una semana.

in court en la corte
A lawyer can file a divorce lawsuit for you in court.
Un abogado puede presentar una demanda de divorcio en la corte.

A lawyer can represent you in court.
Un abogado puede representarle a usted en la corte.

in order to para
It is unquestionable that at present there are many obstacles which immigrants must overcome in order to enter into the country.
Es indudable que en la actualidad son muchas las trabas que deben superar los inmigrantes para entrar en el país.
in self-defense en defensa propia, en legítima defensa
He acted in self-defense.
Actuó en defensa propia.

She killed him in self-defense.
Lo mató en defensa propia.

They acted in self-defense.
Actuaron en legítima defensa.

The accused maintains that he killed him in self-defense.
El acusado mantiene que lo mató en defensa propia.

My client acted in self-defense.
Mi cliente actuó en legítima defensa.

in the morning de la mañana, en la mañana
Be here by nine in the morning at the latest.
Venga a más tardar a las nueve de la mañana.

use in evidence against utilizarse como prueba en ... contra
Anything you say may be taken down and used in evidence against you.
Cualquier casa que diga podría utilizarse como prueba en su contra.

inside
He went inside the house.
Entró en la casa.

Please step inside.
Pase.

Wait for me inside.
¿Espérame dentro.

Were the doors locked from the inside?
¿Estaban las puertas cerradas con llave por dentro?

an inside job alguien de la empresa está implicado, desde dentro
The police think the robbery was an inside job.
La policía cree que es un crimen organizado desde dentro.
La policía cree que alguien de la empresa está implicado.

institution
She was frightened of ending up in an institution.
Temía terminar en un manicomio.
Temía terminar en un asilo.

They committed him to an institution for the criminally insane.
Lo internaron en una institución penitenciaria para delincuentes psicóticos.

institutionalize
A man with psychiatric problems was arrested and institutionalized in a mentaql hospital in Albuquerque.

Un hombre con problemas síquicos fue detenido e internado en un hospital psiquiátrico de Albuquerque.

involve

The policeman involved in beating thought that the man was armed.
El policía involucrado en golpiza pensaba que el hombre tenía arma.

J

judge

Tell the judge how you were affected by what the other person did, and why it is their fault.
Dígale al juez cómo lo afectó lo que la otra persona hizo, y por qué es culpa de la otra persona.

He was ordered to appear before a judge for fraud.
Fue conminado a comparecer ante la justicia por estafa.

A little while later the judge entered the room
Al poco rato el juez entró en la sala.

A little while later the judge was back.
Al poco rato el juez estaba de vuelta.

The judge should abstain from expressing an opinion.
El juez debe abstenerse de expresar una opinión.

The judge refused the accused bail.
El juez le denegó la libertad bajo fianza al acusado.

The judge addressed the jury.
El juez se dirigió al jurado.

The judge summoned him to appear as a witness.
El juez requirió su presencia como testigo.

When the judge calls your name, go to the front of the court room.
Cuando el juez lo llame, vaya al frente de la sala de la corte.

The judge may ask you to try to settle your case before the hearing takes place.
El juez puede pedirle que trate de llegar a un acuerdo en su caso antes de tener la audiencia.

judicial

It's an acknowledged fact that the judicial system has its shortcomings.
Es un hecho reconocido que el sistema judicial tiene sus defectos.

The Code of Judicial Proceedings of Texas stipulates that the accused must be competent in order to stand trial.
El Código de Procedimientos Judiciales de Texas dispone que los acusados deben ser competentes para someterse a juicio.

juror

The 12 jurors, who deliberated for 3 days, found him guilty of murder
Los 12 jurados, que deliberaron tres días, lo declararon culpable de asesinato.

jury

The jury reached a verdict a little while ago.
Hace un ratito el jurado llegó a un acuerdo sobre el veredicto.

A little while later the jury returned.
Al poco rato el jurado regresó.

The jury foud him guilty of the abduction.
El jurado lo declaró culpable del rapto.

He wasn't able to convince the jury of his innocence.
No logró convencer al jurado de su inocencia.

The jury is about to start deliberating.
El jurado está a punto de empezar a deliberar.

The jury is not absolutely convinced.
El jurado no está totalmente convencido.

The judge addressed the jury.
El juez se dirigió al jurado.
The jury reached a verdict after days of deliberating.
Tras días de deliberaciones el jurado llegó a un veredicto.

The jury deliberated all day long.
El jurado deliberó todo el día.

just

I was just about to leave when he called.
Estaba a punto de salir cuando llamó.

He arrived just in time.
Llegó justo a tiempo.

If you need anything, just ask.
Si quieres algo no tienes más que pedirlo.

He has just been accused of conspiracy to commit blackmail.
Acaba de ser acusado de conspiración para chantajear.

I had a call from him just before I left.
Justo antes de salir recibí una llamada suya.

Some people just can't be depended on.
No se puede confiar en ciertas personas.
No se puede contar con ciertas personas.

Do you understand each of the rights just explained to you?
¿Entiende usted cada uno de los derechos que le acabamos de explicar?

K

kick

to kick someone darle un puntapié a alguien
The policeman tried to bring the suspect under control by kicking and striking him 11 times with a metal flashlight.
El policía intentó dominar al sospechoso, dándole de puntapiés y golpeándolo 11 veces con una linterna metálica.

kid

Don't kid yourself.
No te engañes.

He is a good kid.
Es un buen muchacho.

She is a good kid.
Es una buena muchacha.

Their kids are always in trouble.
Sus hijos siempre se meten en líos.

They have two kids.
Tienen dos hijos.

kid brother hemano menor
I have a kid brother.
Tengo un hemano menor.

kid sister hemana menor
She has a kid sister.
Ella tiene una hemana menor.

knife

They armed themselves with clubs and knives.
Se armaron con porras y cuchillos.

Does this knife belong to you?

¿Le pertrenece a usted este cuchillo?

They were coming at me with a knife.
Se me venían encima con un cuchillo.

He disclaimed ownership of the knife.
Negó que el cuchillo fuera suyo.

knock

He was knocked to the ground by the police.
La policía lo tiró al suelo.
La policía lo tumbó al suelo.

Did someone knock at the door?
¿Tocó alguien a la puerta?
¿Llamó alguien a la puerta?

Did the police knock at the door?
¿Tocó la policía a la puerta?
¿Llamó la policía a la puerta?

Were you knocked down by a car?
¿Le atropelló un coche?

Let's knock off for lunch.
Vamos a parar para comer.

knocking

The police went in without knocking.
La policía entró sin tocar.
La policía entró sin llamar.

know

What do you know about the crime?
¿Usted, qué sabe del crimen?

I didn't know you were acquainted with the victim.
No sabía que conocías a la víctima.

He acted as if he didn't know anything about the case
Hizo como si no supiera nada del caso.

Let me know in advance.
Avísame con antelación.

Let me know if there is any problem.
Avísame si hay algún problema.

It is still not known whether he'll be tried as a minor or an adult.
Todavía no sabe si será juzgado como menor o como adulto.

It's a question of knowing what to do.
Se trata de saber lo que hay que hacer.

Before you enter the US, it is essential that you know your rights.
Antes de que usted ingrese a Estados Unidos, es esencial que usted conozca sus derechos.

The trial will begin before the 7th of January and the sentence could be known four days later.
El juicio empezará antes del 7 de enero y la sentencia podría conocerse cuatro días más tarde

I don't know where to begin.
No sé por dónde comenzar.
No sé por dónde empezar.

No one knows besides you.
Nadie lo sabe aparte de usted.

We'll know the verdict by this time next month.
De hoy en un mes sabremos el veredicto.

We'll know the verdict by this time next week.
De hoy en una semana sabremos el veredicto.

Do you know how to cancel a default judgement?
¿Sabes cómo cancelar un fallo por falta de comparecencia?

How do you know the driver of the car?
¿Cómo conoces al conductor del coche?

He doesn't know for certain what caused the accident.
No sabe a ciencia cierta lo que causó el accidente.
No sabe con seguridad lo que causó el accidente.

How come they don't know?
¿Cómo es que no saben?

How come you didn't know?
¿Cómo es que no sabías?

Do you know when you are supposed to go to court next?
¿Sabe cuándo debe acudir a los tribunales la próxima vez?

knowledge
She disclaimed all knowledge of his whereabouts.
Negó conocer su paradero.

lack

A lack of affordable housing is one of the primary causes of homelessness.
La falta de vivienda asequible es una de las principales causas del número de personas sin techo.

Abandonment and the lack of parental care in homes is a big problem.
El abandono y la falta de atención paterna en los hogares es un gran problema.

He was released for lack of evidence.
Fue dejado en libertad por falta de pruebas.

Many families break up because of a lack of money.
Muchas familias se deshacen por falta de dinero.

The charges were withdrawn owing to lack of evidence.
Retiraron la acusación por falta de pruebas.

The file for corruption against him was closed for lack of evidence.
Por falta de pruebas, el expediente por corrupción contra él fue archivado.

The lack of direct evidence is a major problem for the prosecution.
La falta de prueba testifical directa es un gran problema para la acusación.

We lack the resources.
Nos faltan los recursos para hacerlo.

We lack the time to do it.
Nos falta el tiempo para hacerlo.

landlord

The landlord is allowed to deduct the cost of cleaning if necessary to put the unit back to the same level of cleanliness it was in at the time the property was leased.
El propietario puede deducir del depósito el costo de limpiar la unidad si fuera necesario para que tenga el mismo nivel de limpieza que tenía cuando la propiedad se alquiló.

You can ask the landlord to look at the apartment before you move out.
Usted puede pedirle al propietario que mire su apartamento antes de mudarse.

After you move out, a landlord has 3 weeks to return the security deposit or send a list of how much each of the damages cost.
Después de mudarse, el propietario tiene 3 semanas para devolverle el depósito de seguridad o enviarle una lista de lo que costó reparar cada uno de los daños.

large

A large percentage of the missing children run away from home on their own.
Un gran porcentaje de los niños desaparecidos huyen de casa por propia voluntad.

A large percentage of the population doesn't speak English.
Un gran porcentaje de la población no habla inglés.

He is a large man.
Es un hombre corpulento.

It will benefit the country at large.
Beneficiará al país en general.

It will benefit society at large.
Beneficiará a la sociedad en general.

The prisoner is at large.
El prisionero anda suelto.

last

The accused denies having raped the young woman last summer.
El acusado niega haber violado a la joven el verano pasado.

Tom was arrested last Friday.
Tom fue detenido el viernes pasado.

He made that decision as a last resort.
Tomó aquella decisión a la desesperada.

Abortion should only be considered as a last resort.
El aborto debe ser sólo considerado como un último recurso.

Force should only be used as a last resort.
La fuerza sólo debe ser usada como último recurso.

It is estimated that the trial will last at least three months.
Se estima que el juicio durará por lo menos tres meses.
It is expected that the trial will last at least six weeks.
Se espera que el juicio durará por lo menos seis semanas.

At the last moment he changed his mind.
A último momento cambió de opinión.

At the last moment he thought better of it.
A última hora cambió de idea.

At the last moment we decided to plead self-defense.
A última hora decidimos alegar légitima defensa.

The meeting won't last much beyond an hour.
La reunión no durará mucho más de una hora.

The trial won't last much beyond one month.
El juicio no durará mucho más de una mes.

They broke off their relationship last week.
Rompieron su relación la semana pasada.

He cancelled the appointment at the last moment.
A último momento canceló la cita.

Some last minute problems have emerged.
Han surgido impedimentos de última hora.

lawyer

You can also talk to a small claims legal advisor or a lawyer before court.
También puede hablar con un asesor legal de reclamos menores o con un abogado antes de ir a la corte.

A lawyer can file a divorce lawsuit for you in court.
Un abogado puede presentar una demanda de divorcio en la corte.

A lawyer can represent you in court.
Un abogado puede representarle a usted en la corte.

A lawyer can write your will.
Un abogado puede escribir su testamento.

Can you afford to hire a lawyer?
¿Puede contratar a un abogado?
¿Puede pagar por un abogado?

Do I need the services of a lawyer?
¿Necesito los servicios de un abogado?

For most minor accidentes one doesn't need a lawyer.
Para la mayoría de accidentes pequeños, no se necesita abogado.
He is a lawyer?
Es abogado.

If you cannot afford to hire a lawyer, one will be appointed free of charge.
Si usted no puede contratar a un abogado, uno le será nombrado gratis.

She hired a lawyer to defend her.
Contrató a un abogado para que la defendiera.

They are some of our best lawyers.
Ellos son algunos de nuestros abogados más capaces.

leave
He leaves a wife and a child.
Le sobreviven su viuda y un hijo.
Deja mujer y un hijo.

He will soon be able to leave the hospital.
Pronto podrá abandonar el hospital.

leave alone dejar solo
It is best to leave her alone.
Es mejor dejarla sola.

It is best to leave him alone.
Es mejor dejarlo solo.

leave home irse de casa
He left home when he was 18.
Se fue de casa a los 18 años.

leave school dejar los estudios
He left school when he was 16.
Dejó los estudios a los 16 años.

He left school a year ago.
Abandonó los estudios hace un año.

legal
You can also talk to a small claims legal advisor or a lawyer before court.
También puede hablar con un asesor legal de reclamos menores o con un abogado antes de ir a la corte.

M

mainline
Does he mainline?
¿Se inyecta?

mainroad
The accident took place on the mainroad.
El accidente de coche ocurrió en la carretera principal.

majority verdict

It was a majority verdict.
Fue un veredicto por mayoría.

A majority verdict was reached by 9 against 3.
Se llegó al veredicto por mayoría de 9 contra 3.

make

Make the check out to P. Jones
Haga el cheque pagadero a P. Jones.
Haga el cheque pagadero a favor de P. Jones.
Extienda el cheque a la orden de P. Jones.
Extienda el cheque a nombre de P. Jones.

Make the check payable to Acme Inc.
Extienda el cheque a nombre de Acme Inc.

May I make a suggestion?
¿Puedo hacer una sugerencia?
¿Puedo sugerir algo?

Don't make life dificult for yourself.
No se complique la vida.

Make yourselves comfortable.
Póngasen cómodos.

Make yourself at home.
Está en su casa.

Did you make it a rule to never drink more than three glasses of wine?
¿Tenía usted por norma no beber nunca más de tres vasos de vino?

If nine o'clock is too early, make it later.
Si las nueve es muy temprano, podemos reunirnos más tarde.
Si las nueve es muy temprano, podemos encontrarnos más tarde.

You can't just make believe it never happened.
No puede pretender que no sucedió.
No puede hacer como si no hubiera sucedido.
We'll have to make do with the witnesses that we have.
Tendremos que arreglárnoslas con los testigos que tenemos.

How much did you make on the deal?
¿Cuánto sacó con el trato?
¿Cuánto ganó con el trato?

He made for the door, but the police stopped him.
Se dirigió hacia la puerta, pero la policía lo detuvo.

No amount of money can make up for losing a limb.

La pérdida de un miembro no se puede compensar con dinero.

What make is the car?
¿De qué marca es el coche?

making
Her problems are of her own making.
Ella se crea sus propios problemas.

They are involved in problems not of their own making.
Están metios en problemas de los que no son responsables.

malice
He did it without malice.
Lo hizo sin mala intención.

There was absence of malice
No hubo dolo.

man
He is a large man.
Es un hombre corpulento.

He is a man who can't tell the truth.
Es un hombre que no puede decir la verdad.

She left her husband for another man.
Dejó a su marido por otro hombre.

The man died instantly.
El hombre falleció en el acto.

The man was accused of battering his wife.
El hombre fue acusado de maltratar a su esposa.

The man was released on bail.
El hombre fue puesto en libertad bajo fianza.

The police are investigating an Albuquerque man for embezzlement.
La policía investiga por desfalco a un hombre de Albuquerque.

The police have arrested a man who violated his parole.
La policía ha detenido a un hombre que quebrantó las condiciones impuestas por la libertad condicional.

The police have arrested a 40 year old man for allegedly battering his wife who is pregnant.
La policía ha detenido a un hombre, de unos 40 años, como presunto

autor de los malos tratos ocasionados a su esposa, que está embarazada.

The police were chasing a car with three men in it.
La policía perseguía un coche con tres hombres.

manage

He seems unable to manage his life.
Parece incapaz de organizar su vida.

Was the situation more than you could manage?
¿No pudo usted con la situación?

She can't manage the stairs due to the car accident.
No puede subir la escalera debido al accidente de coche.

If you can't manage $500, give what you can afford.
Si no puedes dar 500 dólares, da lo que puedas.

Have you managed to find out her address?
¿Ha logrado averiguar su dirección?
¿Ha podido averiguar su dirección?

They have to manage on $900 a month.
Tienen que arreglarse con 900 dólares al mes.
Tienen que arreglárselas con 900 dólares al mes.

He managed to flee the country.
Logró huir del país.

manslaughter

He is in prison for manslaughter.
Está en prisión por homicidio culposo involuntario.

The jury could not reach a verdict on the charge of reckless manslaughter.
El jurado no pudo llegar a un acuerdo sobre el cargo de homicidio por imprudencia.

The district attorney charges three drug dealers of manslaughter.
El fiscal del distrito acusa a tres camellos del homicidio culposo.

many

Answer as many of the questions as you can.
Conteste todas las preguntas que pueda.

He's had one too many.
Ha tomado uno de más.

Many cases still remain unsolved.
Falta aún solucionar muchos casos.

married

They have been married for two years.
Llevan dos años casados.
Hace dos años que se casaron.

They are happily married.
Son muy felices en su matrimonio.

Did you get married in church?
¿Se casaron por la iglesia?

mastermind

He masterminded the robbery.
Él fue el cerebro del asalto
Él organizó el asalto.

match

Does it match the description?
¿Se ajusta a la descripción?
¿Corresponde a la descripción?

matter

This is a matter for the police.
Esto requiere la intervención de la policía.

Let's try and keep to the matter at hand.
Tratemos de ceñirnos al asunto que estamos tratando.
Tratemos de ceñirnos al tema que estamos tratando.

That's another matter.
Eso es otra cosa.
Eso es diferente.

What's the matter?
¿Qué pasa?

Is anything the matter with Alice?
¿Le pasa algo a Alice?

may

He may not be guilty.
A lo mejor no es culpable.

May I see it?
¿Se puede verlo?
¿Me permite verlo?

It may or may not be true.
Puede o no ser cierto.

mean

What does this word mean?
¿Qué significa esta palabra?
¿Qué quiere decir esta palabra?

What do you mean?
¿Qué quieres decir?

He didn't mean any harm.
No quiso hacer daño.
No lo hizo por mal.

I've been meaning to talk to you.
Hace tiempo que quiero hablar con usted.

medical

medical insurance seguro médico
Public employees will have medical insurance for their domestic partners.
Empleados públicos tendrán acceso a seguro médico para sus compañeros domésticos.

The application must be accompanied by a medical certificate.
La solicitud ha de ir acompañada de un certificado médico.

As you know the medical insurance pays all the medical expenses.
Como usted sabe el seguro médico paga todos los gastos médicos.

A co-payment is a fixed amount of money that you pay to the provider, the medical center, the pharmacy, etc. when you receive certain benefits.
Un copago es una cantidad fija de dinero que usted paga al proveedor, al centro médico, a la farmacia, etc. cuando recibe determinados servicios.

He doesn't have medical coverage.
No tiene cobertura médica.
No tiene protección médica.

Did any fire department personnel or emergency medical personnel come to the scene of the accident?
¿Acudieron al lugar del accidente bomberos o personal de los servicios de emergencia?

More than half a million Hispanics that reside in the south of Florida do not have medical insurance.
Más de medio millón de hispanos que residen en el sur del estado de

Florida carece de seguro médico.

medium

The suspect is a man of medium height and heavy build.
El sospechoso es un hombre fornido de estatura mediana.

meet

He first met her three years ago
La conoció hace tres años.

She first met him at a party.
Lo conoció en una fiesta.

Let's meet at eight.
Citémonos para las ocho.

Pleased to meet you.
Encantado de conocerlo.

merely

It's merely a formality.
Es simplemente una formalidad.
Es solamente una formalidad.
Es sólo una formalidad.
No es más que una formalidad.

mess

She's in such a mess, she has huge debts.
Está metida en un verdadero lío, tiene deudas enormes.

Their marriage was in a mess.
Su matrimonio andaba muy mal.

He started messing around with drugs.
Empezó a meterse con drogas.

message

Would you like to leave a message?
¿Quiere dejar algún recado?
Could you give him a message?
Podría darle un recado?

minor

The children are also victims of violence in the hands of other minors.
Los niños también son víctimas de la violencia a manos de otros menores.

Upon being named as a legal guardian of the child, you have the responsibility of the daily care of the minor.
Al ser designado por la corte como tutor legal del niño, usted es

responsable del cuidado diario del menor.

It is still not known whether he'll be tried as a minor or an adult.
Todavía no sabe si será juzgado como menor o como adulto.

Shared custody entails benefits both for the minor as well as for the parents.
La custodia compartida conlleva beneficios tanto para el menor como para la relación entre los padres.

He was treated for minor cuts and bruises.
Recibió asistencia médica por heridas y hematomas.

They can be held up to five days while they await their transfer to a detention center for minors.
Pueden estar detenidos hasta cinco días mientras esperan su traslado a un centro de detención de menores.

For most minor accidents one doesn't need a lawyer.
Para la mayoría de accidentes pequeños, no se necesita abogado.

Miranda Rights

The Miranda Rights warn you that you incriminate yourself if you confess to a crime at the time of your arrest or during the police interrogation.
Los derechos de Miranda previene que usted se incrimine por sí mismo si confiesa un crimen a tiempo de su arresto o durante el interrogatorio policial.

miscarriage

The defendant, sentenced to thirty years in prision, described it as a misscarriage of justice
El acusado, condenado a treinta años, calificó el fallo de injusto y alegó.

misdemeanor

The accused was convicted of four misdemeanors related to tampering with evidence.
El acusado fue condenado por cuatro delitos menores, relacionados con manipulación de evidencia.

miss, missing

The bullet just missed him.
La bala lo pasó rosando.

The bullet just missed his shoulder.
La bala por poco le da en el hombro.

He narrowly missed being run over.
Por poco lo atropellan.
Faltó poco para que lo atropellaran.

missing children niños desaparecidos
A large percentage of the missing children run away from home on their own.
Un gran porcentaje de los niños desaparecidos huyen de casa por propia voluntad.

go missing desaparecer
The 27 year old expectant mother went missing two weeks ago.
La mujer encinta de veintisiete años desapareció hace dos semanas.

report missing dar parte de la desaparición
The husband reported his wife missing.
El esposo dio parte de la desaparición de su esposa.

more
Public buildings should be more accessible to disabled visitors.
Se debería facilitar el acceso de los minusválidos a los edificios públicos.

The trial was more complicated than I anticipated.
El juicio resultó más complicado de lo que esperaba.

The district attorney's office has had more than a year to prepare the case.
La fiscalía ha tenido más de un año para preparar el caso.

Do you think you will be disabled for twelve months or more?
¿Cree usted que va a estar incapacitado por doce meses o más?

We need more officers on the beat.
Deberíamos tener más agentes haciendo la ronda.

More than two million Americans currently live behind bars and five million live on parole.
Más de dos millones de norteamericanos viven actualmente entre rejas y cinco millones viven en libertad condicional.

Did you make it a rule to never drink more than three glasses of wine?
¿Tenía usted por norma no beber nunca más de tres vasos de vino?

I need more time.
Necesito más tiempo.

The deliberations will take a few more days.
Las deliberaciones llevarán unos cuantos días más.

morning
Where were you on the morning of August 16th?
¿Dónde estaba usted la mañana del dieceseis de agosto?

Be here by nine in the morning at the latest.
Venga a más tardar a las nueve de la mañana.

I'll call you on Monday morning, at the latest.
A más tardar, te llamaré el lunes. por la mañana

The suspect was arrested during a breaking and entering early yesterday morning.
El sospechoso fue detenido durante un allanamiento de vivienda en las primeras horas de la mañana de ayer.

I'll call you first thing in the morning.
Te llamaré a primera hora de la mañana.

movement

The police questioned him about his movements.
La policía le pidió informes sobre sus actividades.

The suspect was unable to account for his movements.
El sospechoso no fue capaz de dar cuenta de sus movimientos.

The suspect was unable to account for his movements at the time of the crime.
El sospechoso no fue capaz de dar cuenta de sus movimientos a la hora del crimen.

mug, muggers, mugging

He defended us against the muggers.
Nos defendió de los atracadores.

Muggimg is on the increase in the inner cities.
Está aumentando el número de atracos in las zonas urbanas deprimidas.

murder

The court gave the defendant twenty years in prison as an accessory to the murder of the agent.
El tribunal ha impuesto veinte años de prisión al acusado como cómplice en el asesinato del agente.

His client is accused of double murder.
Su cliente está acusado de doble asesinato.

The man from Oaxaca was accused of first degree murder.
El oaxaqueño fue acusado de homicidio en primer grado.

They are accused of murder.
Se les acusa de asesinato.

Murder with a firearm is the main cause of death among Hispanics.
El homicidio con armas de fuego es la causa principal de muertes

entre hispanos.

She's appearing on a charge of murder.
Comparece acusada de asesinato.

The number of violent crimes, which include murder, rape and armed robbery have decreased.
El número de crímenes violentos, que incluyen homicidios, violaciones y robo a mano armada, se han reducido

The woman was the victim of attempted murder in her house in Albuquerque and she remained in a coma for several weeks in the hospital.
La mujer fue víctima de una tentativa de asesinato en su domicilio de Albuquerque y permaneció varias semanas en estado de coma en el hospital.

He began talking about the murder.
Empezó a hablar sobre el asesinato.

Were you charged with murder?
¿Fue acusado de asesinato?

She confessed to the murder.
Confesó haber cometido el asesinato.
Se confesó culpable del asesinato.

murder inquiry investigación de un homicidio
The murder investigation has been ongoing for several minths.
Se está llevando a cabo la investigación del homicidio desde hace meses.

murder weapon arma homicida
They never found the murder weapon.
No hallaron el arma el arma homicida.

N

nag
He was nagged by doubts.
Lo acosaban las dudas.

Her conscience nagged her.
Le remordía la conciencia.

name
What's your name?
¿Cómo se llama?
¿Cuál es su nombre?

The victim was not mentioned by name.
No se dio el nombre de la víctima.

The victim has been naned as John Brown.
La víctima ha sido identificado como John Brown.

The police have named the suspect.
La policía ha dado el nombre del sospechoso.

Have they named a date for the hearing?
¿Han fijado una fecha para la vista?

They have named a date for the hearing.
Ya han fijado una fecha para la vista.

narrow

The accident narrowed the road to two lanes.
El accidente dejó la carretera reducida a dos carriles.

They've narrowed their investigation down to this area.
Han limitado su investigación a este área.

The police narrowed it down to three suspects.
La policía fue descartando sospechosos hasta quedar con sólo tres.

The list of suspects gradually narrowed down.
La lista de sospechosos se fue reduciendo.

near

Damage was estimated at somewhere near $10.000.
Los daños se calcularon en cerca de diez mil dólares.

I'd say he's nearer forty than fifty.
Yo diría que está más cerca de los cuarenta que de los cincuenta.

We are no nearer to an agreement with the prosecution.
Seguimos sin llegar a un acuerdo con el fiscal.

nearly

It was nearly midnight when it happened.
Era casi medianoche cuando ocurrió.

The cross examination wasn't nearly as difficult as I'd expected.
La contrainterrogación no fue ni con mucho tan difícil como esperaba.
Las repreguntas no fueron ni con mucho tan difícil como esperaba.

negligent

The judge found that he had been negligent.
El juez declaró que había sido negligente.

She was negligent in informing the authorities.
Faltó a su deber de informar a las autoridades.

negotiate, negotiating

Tell the service manager if you are willing to negotiate.
Dígale al gerente de servicio técnico si está dispuesto a negociar.

Both parties have agreed to come to the negotiating table.
Ambas partes han aceptado sentarse a la mesa de negociaciones.

negotiation

They reached an agreement after days of negotiating.
Tras días de negociaciones llegaron a un acuerdo.

nervous breakdown

I think he's building up to a nervous breakdown.
Creo que va camino de una crisis nerviosa.

She suffered a nervous breakdown.
Sufrió una crisis nerviosa.

new

His daughters requested the new trial.
El nuevo juicio fue pedido por sus hijas.

Martha Stewart's lawyers presented a request for a new trial.
Los abogados de Martha Stewart presentaron a la corte una petición de nuevo juicio.

night

It was eleven o'clock at night when it happened.
Eran las once de la noche cuando ocurrió.

His parents questioned him about where he had been all night.
Sus padres le preguntaron dónde había estado toda la noche.

The documents arrived late at night.
Los papeles llegaron a altas horas de la noche.

He works at night.
Trabaja por la noche.
Trabaja de noche.

no

They have no children.
No tienen hijos.

No two fingerprints are exactly alike.
No hay dos huellas digitales exactamente iguales.

It's no trouble.

No es ningún problema.
No es ninguna molestia.

Please arrive no later than nine o'clock.
Por favor lleguen a las nueve a más tardar.
Por favor lleguen antes de las nueve.

No fewer than twenty witnesses are expected.
Se espera nada menos que a unos veinte testigos.

nobody

There was nobody there when it happened.
No había nadie cuando ocurrió.

Nobody saw us.
Nadie nos.
No nos vio nadie.

notice

He was indignant about the way in which he was dismissed without notice.
Lo indignó que lo despidieron sin previo aviso.

The arraignment has been postponed until further notice.
La comparecencia ante el juez ha sido aplazada hasta nuevo aviso.

We didn't get adequate notice.
No se nos avisó con la suficiente anticipación.

O

oath

Explain to your son or daughter that an oath is a simple promise to tell the truth.
Explíquele a su hijo o hija que un juramento es una simple promesa de decir la verdad.

It is suggested that Clark lied under oath.
Sugieren que Clarke mintió bajo juramento

She administered the oath to the witness.
Le tomó juramento a la testigo.

The court clerk, who administers the oath to witnesses, will also be present in the courtroom.
En la sala del tribunal también estará presente el secretario del juzgado, quien les toma el juramento a los testigos.

under oath bajo juramento

She denied the existence of the document under oath.
Negó la existencia del documento bajo juramento.

She denied under oath that the document existed.
Negó la existencia del documento bajo juramento.

Keep in mind that you are under oath.
Tenga en cuenta que usted está bajo juramento.

To testify in court means to answer questions under oath.
Prestar testimonio en el tribunal significa responder a preguntas bajo juramento.

object

She felt she was being treated as a sex object.
Sintió que se la trataba como a una mujer objeto.
Sintió que se la trataba como un mero objeto sexual.

He was the object of a smear campaign.
Fue objeto de una campaña de difamación.

There is no object in continuing.
No tiene sentido continuar.
No tiene objeto continuar.

The defense objected to the presence of cameras.
La defensa puso objeciones a la presencia de cámaras.

We object strongly to your accusations!
¡No podemos dejar pasar sus acusacionas sin protestar enérgicamente!

The lawyer objected to the question.
El abogado se opuso a la pregunta.
El abogado objetó la pregunta.

objection

The lawyer raised an objection.
El abogado protestó.

Objection!
¡Protesto!

obligation

There is no obligation to buy.
No hay obligación de comprar.

overrule

Overruled.
No ha lugar a la protesta.

obvious

My client made a big mistake, that's obvious.
Mi cliente ha cometido un gran error, eso está claro.
Mi cliente ha cometido un gran error, es obvio.

My client made a big mistake, that much is obvious.
Mi cliente ha cometido un gran error, eso está claro.
Mi cliente ha cometido un gran error, es obvio.

If there is a connection, it's not at all obvious to me.
Si es que hay alguna relación, yo no la veo nada clara.

It was perfectly obvious that the witness was lying.
No cabía la menor duda de que el testigo estaba mintiendo.
Estaba clarísimo que el testigo mentía.

It's obvious the thieves got in through the window.
Está claro que los ladrones entraron por la ventana.

She's the obvious candidate for the job.
Es la candidata indiscutible para el puesto.
Es la candidata obvia para el puesto.

obviously

She's obviously lying.
Está claro que miente.
Se ve a las claras que miente.
Es obvio que miente.

The two crimes are obviously not related.
Es evidente que los dos delitos no tienen relación.
Es obvio que los dos delitos no tienen relación.

There will obviously be an investigation.
Por supuesto se hará una investigación.

Obviously, she's upset: she just lost her job.
No es extraño que esté disgustada: acaba de quedarse sin trabajo.

occurrence

Murders are an everday occurrence here.
Aquí los asesinatos son cosas de todos los días.

Breaking and entering is an everday occurrence here.
Aquí el llanamiento de morada es cosas de todos los días.

Rapes are an everday occurrence here.
Aquí las violaciones son cosas de todos los días.

There were two separate occurrences.

Hubo dos casos independientes.

owe

If the other person owes you money, try to get them to pay you.
Si la otra persona le debe dinero, trate de cobrarlo.

Once they have paid what they owe you, file a form called

Acknowledgment of Satisfaction of Judgment.
Una vez que haya pagado lo que le debe, presente un formulario llamado Reconocimiento de Pago del Fallo.

If you owe money, pay the court or the other person.
Si usted debe dinero, páguele a la corte o a la otra persona.

P

passport

Bring your passport with you.
Traiga consigo el pasaporte.

This passport is a fake.
Este pasaporte es falso.

Have you remembered your passport?
¿Te has acordado del pasaporte?
¿Te has acordado de traer el pasaporte?

plaintiff

As the plaintiff, you can't appeal the judge's decision on your claim.
Si usted es el demandante, no podrá apelar el fallo del juez sobre su reclamo.

If you didn't go to court because you didn't get a copy of the plaintiff's claim, you have thirty days to file an appeal.
Si no fue a la corte porque no recibió la copia del reclamo del demandante, tiene treinta días para presentar una apelación.

If you want to sue the person who is suing you, file and serve a form called a Defendant's Claim and Order to Plaintiff.
Si quiere demandar a la persona que lo está demandando, presente y entregue un formulario llamado Reclamo del Demandado y Orden al Demandante.

police

Did the police question you about your movements?
¿Le pidió la policía informes sobre sus actividades?

Did the police stage a reconstruction of the crime?
¿Efectuó la policía una reconstitución del delito?

He criticized the conduct of the police.
Criticó la actuación de la policía.

He confessed under pressure from the police.
Confesó presionado por la policía.

He got into trouble with the police.
Se metió en un lío con la policía.

He is wanted for questioning by the police.
La policía requiere su presencia para someterlo a un interrogatorio.

He was stopped by a police officer.
Fue detenido por un agente policial.

His behavior aroused the suspicions of the police.
Su conducta despertó la sospecha de la policía.

It might have been disasterous if the police hadn't shown up.
Podría haber sido catastrófico si no hubiera llegado la policía.

Open up! Police!
¡Abran! ¡Policía!

Somebody informed the police.
Alguien informó a la policía.
Alguien le pasó el dato a la policía.

The mismanagement of this case by the police is a scandal.
Lo mal que la policía ha llevado este caso es un escándalo.

The police are after him.
La policía le está buscando.

The police are bound to prosecute in such cases.
La policía está obligada a remitir tales casos a la justicia.

The police are investigating several cases of fraude.
La policía está investigando varios casos de estafa.

The police are keeping him under observation.
La policía lo tiene vigilado.

The police are looking for the murderer.
La policía está buscando al asesino.

The police are looking for your brother.
La policía está buscando a tu hermano.

The police are making inquiries into the murder.

La policía está investigando el asesinato.

The police believe him to be dangerous.
La policía cree que es peligroso.

The police fired on the demonstrators.
La policía disparó sobre los manifestantes.

The police had kept his name on record.
La policía lo había fichado.

The police have a lead.
La policía tiene una pista.

The police have named the suspect.
La policía ha dado el nombre de la sospechosa.
La policía ha dado el nombre del sospechoso.

The police have named the suspects.
La policía ha dado los nombres de los sospechosos.

The police made a thorough search of the premises.
La policía registró todo el local.

The police managed to capture one of the abductors.
La policía logró capturar a uno de los plagiarios.
La policía logró capturar a uno de los raptores.
La policía logró capturar a uno de los secuestradores.

The police managed to capture one of the kidnappers.
La policía logró capturar a uno de los plagiarios.
La policía logró capturar a uno de los raptores.
La policía logró capturar a uno de los secuestradores.

The police mishandled the whole business.
La policía no ha sabido llevar el asunto.

The police must warn you that you have the right to remain silent and the right to see a lawyer.
La policía tiene que decirle que usted tiene el derecho de quedarse callado y que tiene el derecho de consultar con un abogado.

The police narrowed it down to only three suspects.
La policía fue descartando sospechosos hasta quedar con sólo tres.

The police questioned him about his movements.
La policía le pidió informes sobre sus actividades.

The police raided the club.
La policía hizo una redada en el club.

The police raided the house.

La policía hizo una redada en la casa.

The police think the robbery was an inside job.
La policía cree que alguien de la casa está implicado en el robo.
La policía cree que alguien de la empresa está implicado en el robo.

The police went in to break up the demonstration.
La policía intervino para dispersar a los manifestantes.

The police were on hand.
La policía estaba cerca.

The police were on the scene within minutes.
La policía llegó al lugar de los hechos en pocos minutos.

The police were out in force.
Había una gran presencia policial.

Their behavior aroused the suspicions of the police.
Su conducta despertó la sospecha de la policía.

They denounced him to the police as a thief.
Lo denunciaron a la policía por ladrón.

They had to bring in the police.
Tuvieron que hacer intervenir a la policía.

This is a matter for the police.
Esto requiere la intervención de la policía.

Were the police on hand?
¿Etaba la policía cerca?

We were stopped by the police.
Nos paró la policía.

Were you questioned by the police?
¿Te sometió la policía a un unterrogatorio?

Were you stopped by the police?
¿La paró la policía?
¿Lo paró la policía?
¿Los paró la policía?

Who informed the police?
¿Quién informó a la policía?
¿Quién le pasó el dato a la policía?

You have the right not to talk to the police.
Usted tiene el derecho de no hablar con la policía.

You have the right to talk to a lawyer before talking to the police.

Usted tiene el derecho de consultar con un abogado antes de hablar con la policía.

police brutality dureza de la represión policial
They complained about police brutality.
Se quejaron de la dureza de la represión policial.

police record antecedentes penales, antecedentes delictivos
Police sources told The Albuquerque Journal that Ríos had a police record, including two sentences for armed robbery and weapons related charges.
Fuentes policiales dijeron al diario The Albuquerque Journal que Ríos tenía antecedentes delictivos, incluyendo dos
condenas por robo a mano armada y cargos relacionados con armas.

police station en la comisaria
She is being held at the police station for questioning.
Está detenida en la comisaria para ser interrogada.

They kept me at the police station for hours.
Me tuvieron horas en la comisaria.

Were you interrogated at the police station?
¿Te interrogaron en la comisaria?

to be under police custody estar detenida, estar detenido
He is under police custody.
Está detenido.

possession
The arrested him on a charge of weapons possession and he was in prison for two months.
Lo aprehendieron bajo el cargo de posesión de armas y estuvo en prisión por espacio de doce meses.

previous
previous convictions condenas previas, antecedentes penales
He had several previous convictions for theft.
Tenía varias condenas previas por robo.

He has previous convictions for aggravated assault.
Tiene antecedentes penales por agresión mayor.

It was established that the driver of the car has previous convictions for the crime of car theft.
Se estableció que el conductor del automóvil cuenta con antecedentes penales por el delito de robo de vehículo.

The suspect has two previous convictions on similar crimes.
El sospechoso cuenta con dos antecedentes penales por delitos similares.

The suspect has four previous convictions for theft and one for murder.
El sospechoso tiene cuatro antecedentes penales por robo y uno por homicidio.

The three alleged kidnappers captured in Albuquerque have previous convictions for attempted rape.
Los tres presuntos secuestradores capturados en Albuquerque tienen antecedentes penales por tentativa de violación.

primary

primary doctor médico de primer contacto
Your primary doctor can help you choose a primary health services provider.
Tu médico de primer contacto puede ayudarte a escoger un proveedor primario de servicios de salud.

problem

Abandonment and the lack of parental care in homes is a big problem.
El abandono y la falta de atención paterna en los hogares es un gran problema.

Anybody else have this problem?
¿Alguien más tiene este problema?

He has a girlfriend problems.
Él tiene problemas de amores.

His problems drove him to drink.
Sus problemas lo llevaron al alcohol.

I am aware of my legal problems.
Estoy al tanto de mis problemas legales.

I don't know how to deal with this problem.
No sé qué hacer con este problema.

Now then, let's get this problem cleared up.
Ahora bien, hay que aclarar este problema.

She has a drinking problem.
Su problema es la bebida.

She has boyfriend problems.
Ella tiene problemas de amores.

Some last minute problems have emerged.
Han surgido impedimentos de última hora.

The lack of direct evidence is a major problem for the prosecution.

La falta de prueba testifical directa es un gran problema para la acusación.

The problem must be dealt with now.
Hay que ocuparse del problema ahora mismo.
Hay que resolver el problema ahora mismo.

They will have to deal with these problems.
Tendrán que abordar estos problemas.

Violence against women in the United States is a serious social and public health problem.
En Estados Unidos, la violencia contra las mujeres constituye un grave problema social y de salud pública.

We have a problem on our hands.
Tenemos un problema en nuestras manos.

What is the problem?
¿Cuál es el problema?

You have a problem.
Usted tiene un problema.

any problem algún problema
Call me if there is any problem.
Llámame si hay algún problema.

I don't anticipate any problems.
No creo que vaya a haber ningún problema.

If you have any problems, please don't hesitate to ask.
Si tiene algún problema, no deje de llamar.

Let me know if there is any problem.
Avísame si hay algún problema.

problem with problema con
All these youngsters have, at one time or another, had problems with the police.
Todos estos chicos han tenido, en algún momento, problemas con la policía.

Has he ever had any problems with the police?
¿Ha tenido alguna vez un problema con la policía?

The problem with drugs is that they're addictive.
El problema con las drogas es que crean hábitos.

a lot of problems muchos problemas, un montón de problemas
He has a lot of problems.
Tiene muchos problemas.

I have a lot of problems.
Me he metido en un montón de problemas.

We were faced with a lot of problems.
Nos vimos enfrentados con un montón de problemas.
Decida cuáles son sus puntos principales y lleve pruebas.

proof

Decide what your main points are and bring proof.
Decida cuáles son sus puntos principales y lleve pruebas.

What kind of proof should I bring?
¿Qué tipo de pruebas debo llevar?

property

If a tenant damages the property, the landlord can deduct the cost of fixing it from the security deposit.
Si un inquilino causa daños a la propiedad, el propietario puede deducir el costo del arreglo del depósito de seguridad.

Q

question

A suspect is being questioned by police.
La policía está interrogando a un sospechoso.

Are there any questions?
¿Hay alguna pregunta?

Do you have a question?
¿Tienes una pregunta?

He answered the question of his own accord.
Contestó la pregunta por propia voluntad.

I asked you a question.
Te hice una pregunta.

I think he is best able to answer that question.
Creo que él es quien mejor puede contestar a esa pregunta.

If you have any questions, please do not hesitate to call.
Si tiene alguna pregunta, no dude en llamar.

The question from the prosecution caught him off guard.
La pregunta de la acusación lo agarró desprevenido.

They questioned him about his past.

Le hicieron preguntas acerca de su pasado.
Le preguntaron acerca de su pasado.

This raises the question of her suitability.
Esto plantea la cuestión de si es la persona adecuada.

Where were you at the time in question?
¿Dónde estabas a la hora que nos interesa?

ask questions hacer preguntas
He asked many questions.
Hizo muchas preguntas.

They asked many questions.
Hicieron muchas preguntas.

be a question of tratarse de
It's a question of knowing what to do.
Se trata de saber lo que hay que hacer.

It's a question of money.
Se trata de dinero.

That is not the question.
No se trata de eso.

The lawyer has to answer your questions and return your calls within a reasonable time period.
El abogado tiene que contestar sus preguntas y devolverle sus llamadas de teléfono dentro de un plazo de tiempo razonable.

They bombarded me with questions regarding his whereabouts.
Me acosaron con preguntas sobre su paradero.

The question took him by surprise.
La pregunta lo agarró desprevenido.

To testify in court means to answer questions under oath.
Prestar testimonio en el tribunal significa responder a preguntas bajo juramento.

beyond question fuera de duda, fuera de toda duda
Her integrity is beyond question.
Su integridad está fuera de duda.

His honesty is beyond all question.
Su honradez está fuera de toda duda.

be out of the question no haber que pensar en
To plead quilty is out of the question.
No hay que pensar en confesarte culpable.

A plea bargain is out of the question.
No hay que pensar en intentar llegar a un acuerdo con el fiscal.

call into question poner en duda
The defense called his character into question.
La defensa puso en duda su carácter.

They called his credibility into question.
Pusieron en duda su credibilidad.

further questions alguna otra pregunta, más preguntas
Have you any further questions?
¿Tiene más preguntas?
¿Tiene otra pregunta?

They had no further questions.
No tenían más preguntas.
No tenían otra pregunta.

question about pedir informes sobre, preguntar acerca de
The police questioned him about his movements.
La policía le pidió informes sobre sus actividades.
La policía le preguntó acerca de sus actividades.

They questioned him about his past.
Le preguntaron acerca de su pasado.

questions and objections preguntas y objeciones
Questions and objections made by the attorneys is not evidence.
Las preguntas y objeciones de los abogados no son evidencias.

without question indiscutiblemente, sin duda
He'll appear in court tomorrow without question.
Sin duda comparecerá mañana ante el juez.

She'll be there tomorrow without question.
Indiscutiblemente estará mañana allí.

to have several questions tener varias preguntas
I'm glad you came today, because I have several questions.
Me alegro de que haya venido hoy porque tengo varias preguntas.

R

raid
The police raided the club.
La policía hizo una redada en el club.

The police raided the house.
La policía hizo una redada en la casa.

At least four hundred people without identity papers have been detained in raids in Southern California.
Por lo menos cuatro cientos indocumentados han sido detenidos en redadas en el sur de California.

Many of the Mexicans who were repatriated this week were arrested in raids carried out by the American border patrol.
Muchos de los mexicanos repatriados esta semana fueron arrestados en redadas efectuadas por la patrulla fronteriza de Estados Unidos.

raise

There is a point I would like to raise.
Hay un asunto que quisiera mencionar.
Hay un asunto que quisiera plantear.

There are a couple of matters I want to raise with you.
Hay un par de asuntos que quisiera plantearle.
Hay un par de asuntos que quisiera tratar con usted.

Where were you raised?
¿Dónde creció usted?
¿Dónde se crió usted?

I was raised in New Mexico.
Crecí en Nuevo México.
Me crié en Nuevo México.

rally

The whole family rallied to the support of the defendant.
Toda la familia se unió en apoyo del acusado.

They all rallied around him.
Todos acudieron a ofrecerle apoyo.

All the neighbors rallied around to help her.
Todos los vecinos se juntaron para ayudarla.

release

Miller was released from prison in February and has a past police record which dates back to 2000 that includes car theft and armed robbery, according to the records.
Miller salió de prisión en febrero y tiene antecedentes delictivos que datan de dos mil y que incluyen robo de automóvil y robo a mano armada, según los archivos.

refuse

The application for an extradition order has been refused.

La solicitud de extradición ha sido denegada.

report, reporting

He altered the official report.
Amañó el informe oficial.

He was at fault in not reporting the theft.
Obró mal al no denunciar el robo.

They did not report the theft.
No denunciaron el robo.

The confidential record contains documents with personal information on the ward, such as the report by the court's investigator.
El expediente confidencial contiene documentos con información personal sobre el pupilo, como por ejemplo el informe del investigador de la corte.

The court investigator turns over to the judge a confidential report of his investigation.
El investigador de la corte le entrega al juez un informe confidencial de su investigación.

He was arrested on charges of filing a false police report.
Fue detenido por presentar un falso informe policial.
Fue detenido por presentar un falso parte policial.

report missing

The husband reported his wife missing.
El esposo dio parte de la desaparición de su esposa.

right, rights

A defendant has the right to remain silent.
El acusado tiene el derecho de quedarse callado.

Before you enter the US, it is essential that you know your rights.
Antes de que usted ingrese a Estados Unidos, es esencial que usted conozca sus derechos.

Do you understand each of the rights just explained to you?
¿Entiende usted cada uno de los derechos que le acabamos de explicar?

The police must warn you that you have the right to remain silent and the right to see a lawyer.
La policía tiene que decirle que usted tiene el derecho de quedarse callado y que tiene el derecho de hablar con un abogado.

Are you all right?
¿Está bien?

It is all right.
No se preocupe.

It is all right with me.
Lo que es por mí, no hay problema.
Yo, de acuerdo.

Are you sure this is the right man?
¿Estás segura de que es el hombre?

Are you sure you have got the right number?
¿Seguro que es ése el número?

Everybody who arrives in the United States, with or without papers, has Constitutional rights.
Toda persona que llega a Estados Unidos, con o sin documentos, tiene derechos Constitucionales.

Let's assume they are right.
Supongamos que tienen razón.

Let's assume you are right.
Supongamos que usted tiene razón.

There is no right of appeal against the judgement.
El fallo es inapelable.

There is no right of appeal against the rulimg.
El fallo es inapelable.

At the scene of the accident, call 911 so that anyone with injuries can be taken to the hospital right away.
En el lugar del accidente llame al 911 para que lleven a cualquier persona con heridas o lesiones al hospital inmediatamente.

Every child has the right to attend a public school until he or she gets a high school diploma.
Cada niño tiene el derecho de asistir a una escuela pública hasta que el o ella obtenga un diploma de escuela secundaria.

Immigrant students have the right to attend school no matter what their legal immigration status or that of their family is.
Los estudiantes inmigrantes tienen el derecho de asistir a la escuela sin importar su estado de inmigración legal o el de su familia.

I'll call you in a little while, I'm busy right now.
Dentro de un ratito te llamo, que ahora estoy ocupado.

They have implemented safeguards to protect rhe rights of those condemned to death.
Han implementado salvaguardias para garantizar la protección de los derechos de los condenados a la pena de muerte.

Currently, women have the right to choose.
En la actualidad, las mujeres tienen el derecho de elegir.

A lawyer defends the legal rights of the accused.
Un abogado defiende los derechos legales de la acusada.
Un abogado defiende los derechos legales del acusado.

She is the right person for defending him in the trial.
Ella es la abogada apropiada para defenderlo en el juicio.

You did the right thing.
Hiciste lo correcto.

S

say
Plan what you are going to say in court.
Piense en lo que va a decir en la court.

Try to think of what the other person might say in court and how you will answer.

Trate de pensar en lo que la otra persona puede decir en la court y cómo le va a contestar.

Say what happened, in the order it happened.
Diga lo que pasó, en el orden en que pasó.

A subpoena can also say that someone has to bring certain papers to court at your hearing.
Una orden de comparecencia también dice que determinada persona tiene que traer ciertos documentos a su audiencia.

search
search operation operativo de búsqueda
The police organized a search operation for the suspect.
La Policía organizó un operativo de búsqueda del sospechoso.

second
second degree murder asesinato en segundo grado
The gang member was found guilty of second degree murder of a fourteen year old minor in Albuquerque.
El pandillero fue encontrado culpable de asesinato en segundo grado de una menor de catorce años en Albuquerque.

second degree murder homicidio en segundo grado
The gang member was found guilty of second degree murder of a fourteen year old minor.

El pandillero fue encontrado culpable de homicidio en segundo grado de una menor de catorce años.

security

A security deposit is any money a landlord takes from a tenant in case the property is damaged.

Un depósito de seguridad es cualquier dinero que el propietario toma del inquilino por si llega a causar daños a la propiedad.

If you rent a place without furniture, the security deposit can't be more than two months' rent.

Si alquila un lugar sin muebles, el depósito de seguridad no puede ser mayor de dos meses de alquiler.

settlement

Tell the service manager what you think is a fair settlement.

Propóngale al gerente de servicio técnico un acuerdo que usted considere justo.

shared custody

Shared custody entails benefits both for the minor as well as for the parents.

La custodia compartida conlleva beneficios tanto para el menor como para la relación entre los padres.

Children who live in shared custody arrangements usually feel loved by both parents.

Los niños que viven en arreglos de custodia compartida suelen sentirse amados por ambos padres.

small

small claims court

Learn about how small claims court works.

Aprenda cómo funciona la corte de reclamos menores.

Aprenda cómo funciona la corte con juridicción sobre cargos pequeños.

You can also talk to a small claims court legal advisor or a lawyer before court.

También puede hablar con un asesor legal de reclamos menores o con un abogado antes de ir a la corte de reclamos menores.

small claims cases

Small claims cases usually only last ten to fifteen minutes. So you have to be prepared to tell your story.

Los casos de reclamos menores en general duran sólo diez a quince minutos, de manera que tiene que estar preparado para contar su versión de la historia.

small claims hearing

Go to the courthouse and watch a small claims hearing.

Vaya a la corte y vea una audiencia de reclamos menores.
Vaya a la corte y vea una audiencia de juridicción sobre cargos pequeños.

sober

Were you perfectly sober?
¿Estaba perfectamente sobrio?
¿Estaba perfectamente despejado?

spatter

spattered with blood salpicada de sangre, salpicado de sangre
The wall was spattered with blood.
La pared estaba salpicada de sangre.

specific

Give some specific examples.
Dé ejemplos concretos.

Let's get down to the specifics.
Pasemos a los detalles.

speeding

He was returning home from work when the police stopped him for speeding.
Regresaba a su hogar de su trabajo cuando la policía lo paró por exceso de velocidad.

statement

make a statement prestar declaración
He made a statement to the judge.
Prestó declaración ante el juez.

study

study part-time estudiar a tiempo parcial
You can study part time while you have an H-1B status.
Puede estudiar a tiempo parcial mientras tenga estatus H-1B.

subpoena

What is a subpoena?
¿Qué es una orden de comparecencia?
¿Qué es una orden decitación?

A subpoena is a court order that says that your witness has to come to court.
Una orden de comparecencia es una orden de la corte que dice que su testigo tiene que ir a la corte.

A subpoena can also say that someone has to bring certain papers to court at your hearing.
Una orden de comparecencia también dice que determinada persona tiene que traer ciertos documentos a su audiencia.

If you need papers that you don't have, you can fill out a subpoena form.
Si necesita documentos que no tiene, puede llenar un formulario de citación.

Do I need to subpoena someone?
¿Tengo que pedir una orden de comparecencia?

You need to subpoena a witness if your witness won't come to court.
Tiene que pedir una orden de comparecencia si su testigo no quiere venir a la corte.

You need to subpoena someone if they won't give you the documents you need to prove your case.
Tiene que pedir una orden de comparecencia si alguien se niega a darle los documentos que necesita para probar su caso.

You can get your subpoena from the small claims court clerk.
Puede obtener el formulario de orden de comparecencia del secretario de la corte de reclamos menores.

sue

Talk to the person or business that is suing you and try to work things out before going to court.r
Hable con la persona o empresa que lo está demandando y trate de llegar a un arreglo antes de ir a la corte.

Figure out if you're being sued in the wrong court.
Averigue si lo están demandando en la corte equivocada.

If you want to sue the person who is suing you, file and serve a form called a Defendant's Claim and Order to Plaintiff (Small Claims).
Si quiere demandar a la persona que lo está demandando, presente y entregue un formulario llamado Reclamo del demandado y Orden al demandante (Reclamos menores)

If you are suing the other person, you will talk first.
Si usted es el que presenta la demanda, hablará primero.

If someone writes you a bad check, you can sue for up to four times the amount of the check.
Si alguien le paga con un cheque sin fondos, puede hacerle una demanda por cuatro veces el valor del cheque.

support

Bring any papers and documents that support your story.
Lleve todos los papeles y documentos que respalden su historia.

Child support is the amount of money that the court orders one parent to pay the other each month for support of the children.
La manutención de los hijos es la cantidad de dinero que la corte

ordena a un padre pagar al otro cada mes para mantener a los hijos.

You can count on my support.
Puede contar con mi apoyo.
Puede contar con mi respaldo.

You can depend on her support.
Puedes contar con su apoyo.
Puedes contar con su respaldo.

suspect

The suspect was unable to account for his movements.
El sospechoso no fue capaz de dar cuenta de sus movimientos.

The suspects were unable to account for their movements at the time of the crime.
Los sospechosos no fuerron capaces de dar cuenta de sus movimientos a la hora del crimen.

The suspect proclaimed her innocence in an emotional court appearance accompanied by her children and husband.
La sospechosa proclamó su inocencia en una emotiva comparecencia junto a sus hijos y esposo.

The suspect was apprehended on Tuesday in possession of a false passport.
El sospechoso fue detenido el martes, en posesión de un pasaporte falso.

The suspect should be considered armed and dangerous.
El sospechoso debe ser considerado armado y peligroso.

The suspect will be arraigned tomorrow.
El sospechoso comparecerá ante el juez mañana.

At what point did you begin to suspect?
¿En qué momento empezó a sospechar?

The suspects were on their way to the border when they were arrested.
Los sospechosos se dirigían hacia la frontera cuando los arrestaron.

The suspect was arrested during a breaking and entering early in the morning yesterday.
El sospechoso fue detenido durante un allanamiento de vivienda en las primeras horas de la mañana de ayer.

The suspect is a man of medium height and heavy build.
El sospechoso es un hombre fornido de estatura mediana.

The police observed the suspect closely.
La policía vigilaba de cerca a la sospechosa.

The police have named the suspect.
La policía ha dado el nombre de la sospechosa.
La policía ha dado el nombre del sospechoso.

The police narrowed it down to only three suspects.
La policía fue descartando sospechosos hasta quedar con sólo tres.

Arson is not suspected.
No existen sospechas de que el incendio haya sido provocado.

suspicion

He was arrested on suspicion of having carried out illegal abortions.
Fue detenido como presunto autor de prácticas abortivas ilegales.

He is above suspicion.
Está por encima de toda sospecha.

His behavior aroused the suspicions of the police.
Su conducta despertó la sospecha de la policía.

They are being held on suspicion.
Los han detenido como sospechosos.

T

take

He took the case to the Court of Appeal.
Llevó el caso al Tribunal de Apelación.

Her job often takes her to Houston.
Va a Houston con frecuencia a Houston por motivo de trabajo.

He took the knife from her.
Le quitó el cuchillo.

We are about to take our first break during the trial.
Estamos a punto de hacer la primera pausa del juicio.

The accused announced his decision to take the Fifth in order to avoid testifying on the bankruptcy of the company.
El acusado anunció su decisión de acogerse a la Quinta Enmienda para no prestar testimonio sobre la quiebra de la empresa.

Actually, he would rather not take the stand.
La verdad es que prefiere no subir al estrado.

After the arrest the initial appearance takes place.

Después del arresto ocurre la vista inicial.

She had to take the stand again.
Tuvo que subir al estrado otra vez.

Anything you say may be taken down and used in evidence against you.
Cualquier cosa que diga podría utilizarse como prueba en su contra.

The arraignment takes place tomorrow.
La comparecencia ante el juez tiene lugar mañana.

To apprehend means to take into custody an individual pursuant to a criminal charge.
Aprehender quiere decir privar de la libertad a una persona que se presume ha cometido un acto punible.

The mayor took a bribe.
El alcalde se dejó sobornar.

If you fail to comply with any of these conditions, you can be taken back to jail.
Si no logras cumplir con cualquier de estas condiciones, te pueden encarcelar de nuevo.

A criminal case takes place when a person is accused of committing a crime.
Un caso penal resulta cuando una persona es acusada de haber cometido un crimen.

A security deposit is any money a landlord takes from a tenant in case the property is damaged.
Un depósito de seguridad es cualquier dinero que el propietario toma del inquilino por si llega a causar daños a la propiedad.

He had his driver's license taken away.
Lo castigó con la privación del carné.
Lo castigó con la privación del permiso de conducción.

The judge may ask you to try to settle your case before the hearing takes place.
El juez puede pedirle que trate de llegar a un acuerdo en su caso antes de tener la audiencia.

The deliberations will take a few more days.
Las deliberaciones llevarán unos cuantos días más.

talk

You can also talk to a small claims legal advisor or a lawyer before court.
También puede hablar con un asesor legal de reclamos menores o con

un abogado antes de ir a la corte.

tell

Tell the judge how you were affected by what the other person did, and why it is their fault.
Dígale al juez cómo lo afectó lo que la otra persona hizo, y por qué es culpa de la otra persona.

tenant

If a tenant damages the property, the landlord can deduct the cost of fixing it from the security deposit.
Si un inquilino causa daños a la propiedad, el propietario puede deducir el costo del arreglo del depósito de seguridad.

trespass

They were trespassing on my land.
Habían entrado en mi propiedad sin autorización.

trial

She is on trial for theft.
Se le sigue proceso por robo.

She was brought to trial.
Fue procesada.

The trial will begin around the middle of the year.
El juicio empezará a mediados de año.

The trial will begin in about four weeks.
El juicio empezará en unas cuatro semanas.

The Code of Judicial Proceedings of Texas stipulates that the accused must be competent in order to stand trial.
El Código de Procedimientos Judiciales de Texas dispone que los acusados deben ser competentes para someterse a juicio.

They met to discuss, among other things, the admissible proof of the trial.
Se reunieron para discutir, entre otras cosas, la prueba admisible en juicio.

If you are found guilty after a nonjury trial, you can appeal the sentence.
Si se le encuentra culpable después de un juicio sin jurado, usted puede apelar la sentencia.

In the trial the defense argued that the death of Laci was accidental.
La defensa argumentó en el juicio que la muerte de Laci fue accidental.

He is on trial for murder.
Se le sigue proceso por asesinato.

She chose a jury trial.
Se decantó por un juicio por jurado.

She chose a nonjury trial.
Se decantó por un juicio sin jurado.

turn

turn down denegar
The application for an extradition order has been turned down.
La solicitud de extradición ha sido denegada.

U

unhealthy

unhealthy conditions condiciones insalubres
Illegal abortions are carried out in unhealthy and unhygienic conditions, which make them twice as harmful.
El aborto ilegal se practica generalmente en condiciones insalubres y antihigiénicas, lo que lo hace doblemente perjudicial.

They work in unhealthy conditions.
Trabajan en condiciones insalubres.

unexpected

unexpected pregnancy embarazo inesperado
Do you feel alone and distressed faced with an unexpected pregnancy?
¿Te sientes sola y angustiada ante un embarazo inesperado?

unpaid

You can sue for unpaid wages if you weren't paid for work you did.
Puede hacer una demanda por sueldo no pagado si no le pagaron por un trabajo que hizo.

unwanted

unwanted pregnancy embarazo no deseado
Do you feel alone and distressed faced with an unwanted pregnancy?
¿Te sientes sola y angustiada ante un embarazo no deseado?

upset, upsetting

Be careful not to upset the witness.
Procure no disgustar al testigo.

He had every reason to be upset.
Estaba disgustado y con razón.

It's only natural that she should be upset.
Es natural que esté disgustada.

The separation was upsetting for thr child.
La separación afectó mucho al niño.
La separación perturbó mucho al niño.

The whole incident was very upsetting for me.
Todo el incidente me afectó mucho.
Todo el incidente me disgustó mucho.

There is no point in upsetting your parents, don't tell them about the accident.
Para qué disguatar a tus padres, no les cuentes lo del accidente.

V

vacate
He had to vacate the premises.
Tuvo que desocupar el local.
Tuvo que desalojar el local.

vague
There is a vague likeness between them.
Existe un ligero parecido entre ellos.
Existe un ligero parecido entre ellas.

There was vague talk about a plea bargain.
Se habló vagamente de un acuerdo con el fiscal.

I haven't the vaguest idea.
No tengo la más mínima idea.
No tengo la más vaga idea.

vaguely
I know him vaguely.
Lo conozco vagamente.

He looks vaguely like his brother.
Tiene un ligero parecido con su hermano.
Tiene un ligero parecido a su hermano.

valid
That's a very valid point.
Ése es un comentario muy pertinente.

value
Don't place too much value on what he says.

No le des mucha importancia a lo que diga.

The information may be of value to the police.
La información puede resultarle valiosa a la policía.

vanish
All his savings have vanished into nothing.
Sus ahorros han desaparecido sin rostros.

He's just vanished into thin air.
Se ha esfumado.
Ha desaparecido sin dejar rostro.

vary
Opinions on the subject vary.
Hay diversas opiniones al respecto.

Emotions varied enormously.
Las emociones fueron muy variadas.

Reactions varied enormously.
Las reacciones fueron muy variadas.
Las reacciones fueron muy diversas.

vehicle
Are you related to the driver of the vehicle?
¿Eres pariente del conductor del coche?
¿Estás emparentado con el conductor del coche?

Auto stripping is the removal, intentional destruction or defacing of any part of a vehicle without consent of the owner, or the removal, destruction or defacing of any part of an abandoned vehicle.
El desmantelamiento de vehículo se la sustracción, destrucción o desfiguración intencional de cualquier parte de un vehículo abandonado o en caso de no ser abandonado el vehículo, sin autorización del dueño.

His car was seized under the controversial ordinance which allows for the confiscation of vehicles.
Su auto fue decomisado bajo la polémica ordenanza, la cual permite el decomiso de vehículos.

verdict
We'll know the verdict by this time next week.
De hoy en una semana sabremos el veredicto.

The jury reached a verdict a little while ago.
Hace un ratito el jurado llegó a un acuerdo sobre el veredicto.

The jury reached a verdict after days of deliberating.
Tras días de deliberaciones el jurado llegó a un veredicto.

The jury can reach a verdict at any moment.
El jurado puede llegar a un acuerdo sobre el veredicto en cualquier momento.

The jury hasn't arrived at a verdict.
El jurado no ha llegado a un veredicto.

At first, I accepted the verdict.
En un principio acepté el veredicto.

The jury deliberated for a while then it brought in its final verdict.
El jurado deliberó por un rato y luego dio su veredicto final.

The verdict was delivered by a tainted jury.
La sentencia fue pronunciada por un jurado inficionado.

The jury could not reach a verdict on the charge of reckless manslaughter.
El jurado no pudo llegar a un acuerdo sobre el cargo de homicidio por imprudencia.

The jury returned a verdict of guilty.
El jurado emitió un veredicto de culpabilidad.
El jurado lo declaró culpable.

It was a majority verdict.
Fue un veredicto por mayoría.

verify
Her suspicions were verified when she found the letter.
Confirmó sus sospechas al encontrar la carta.

version
What's your version of the events?
¿Cuál es su versión de los hechos?

There are several versions of what happened.
Hay varias versiones de lo que pasó.

very
She was very upset.
Estaba muy disgustada.

He is a very special friend.
Es un amigo muy querido.

She is a very special friend.
Es una amiga muy querido.

W

wait

He kept me waiting.
Me hizo esperar.

I've been waiting all this while.
Hace tanto rato que estoy esperando.

It's better to wait.
Vale más esperar.

Please wait until I arrive.
Por favor espera hasta que yo llegue.

The best thing to do is to wait.
Lo mejor es esperar.

They are waiting for further news.
Quedan a la espera de más noticias.

Wait a minute, I'll be with you directly.
Espera un minuto, enseguida estoy contigo.

Wait a while.
Espera un rato.

Wait here until I call you.
Quedesé aquí hasta que lo llame.

Would you like me to wait?
¿Quiere que espere?

Your documents are ready and waiting.
Sus documentos están listos y a su disposición.
Sus papeles están listos y a su disposición.

wait and see esperar a ver
We must wait and see what she is going to do.
Tenemos que esperar a ver lo que hace.

We must wait and see what she is going to say on the stand.
Tenemos que esperar a ver lo que dice en el estrado.

We'll have to wait and see.
Habrá que esperar y ver.

week

After you move out, a landlord has three weeks to return the

security deposit or send a list of how much each of the damages cost.
Después de mudarse, el propietario tiene tres semanas para devolverle el depósito de seguridad o enviarle una lista de lo que costó reparar cada uno de los daños.

The trial will begin in about four weeks.
El juicio empezará en unas cuatro semanas.

Okay, I will see you after a few weeks.
Bueno, te veo después de unas cuantas semanas.

I've been trying to get you all week.
He estado intentando hablar contigo toda la semana.

The jury deliberated all week.
El jurado deliberó toda la semana.

He is due to appear before the court next week.
Debe comparecer ante los tribunales la semana próxima.

Your next court appearance is in a week.
Tu próxima comparecencia ante el juez es en una semana.

The arraignment is in a week.
La comparecencia ante el juez tiene lugar en una semana.

I arranged to meet him a week from today.
Quedé en encontrarme con él de aquí a una semana.

It is expected that the trial will last at least six weeks.
Se espera que el juicio durará por lo menos seis semanas.

They broke off their relationship last week.
Rompieron su relación la semana pasada.

We'll know the verdict by this time next week.
De hoy en una semana sabremos el veredicto.

He spent three weeks in detention.
Estuvo detenido tres semanas.

went

went missing *desapareció*
The twenty seven year old expectant mother went missing two weeks ago.
La mujer encinta de veintisiete años desapareció hace dos semanas.

who

Who is that?
¿Quién es?

Who are they?
¿Quiénes son?

with

He is charged with a number of shootings a month ago.
Se le acusa de ser responsable de varias balaceras hace un mes.

I would like a word with you about that.
Quisiera hablar con usted acerca de eso.

I'll have a talk with him about his behavior.
Hablaré con él sobre su comportamiento.

with a lot of con un montón de
The defense was faced with a lot of circumstantial evidence.
La defensa se vio enfrentada con un montón de pruebas indirectas.

without

without due care and attention sin la debida precaución
He was convicted of driving without due care and attention.
Fue declarado culpable de conducir sin la debida precaución.

witness

You'll need to know the name of the witness that you want to come to court.
Tiene que saber el nombre del testigo que quiere citar a la corte.

He is a witness for the defense.
Es testigo de la defensa.
Es testigo del descargo.

He is a witness for the prosecution.
Es testigo de cargo.

He was a witness to the incident.
Fue testigo del incidente.
Presenció el incidente.

The accident was witnessed by two people.
Hay dos testigos del accidente.

There were no witnesses.
No hubo testigos.

They called him as a witness.
Lo citaron como testigo.

You will need a witness for your signature.
Necesitas a alguien que atestigue tu firma.

Witnesses who are not friends or relatives may be more

effective in proving your case.
Los testigos que no son amigos ni parientes pueden ser mejores para probar su caso.

Y

year

How much do you earn in a year?
¿Cuánto ganas al año?
¿Cuánto gana usted al año?

The court gave the defendant twenty years in prison as an accessory to the murder of the agent.
El tribunal ha impuesto veinte años de prisión al acusado como cómplice en el asesinato del agente.

A sixteen year old boy was accused of shooting his girlfriend.
Un muchacho de dieciseis años fue acusado de matar a balazos a su novia.

An eighteen year old boy was accused of shooting his parents.
Un muchacho de dieciocho años fue acusado de matar a balazos a sus padres.

An eighteen year old girl was accused of stealing some money from the cash register.
Una muchacha de dieciocho años fue acusada de robar dinero de la caja.

He had an affair with her years ago.
Tuvo relaciones con ella hace muchos años.

She was reunited with her children after years.
Se reencontró con sus hijos después de años.

Two years later he was arrested again accused of rape.
Dos años después fue detenido otra vez acusado de violación.

He is doing eight years for armed robbery.
Está cumpliendo ocho años por atracado a mano armada.

The trial will begin around the middle of the year.
El juicio empezará a mediados de año.

The trial will last at least half a year.
El juicio durará por lo menos medio año.

They got married at the beginning of the year.
Se casaron a principios de año.

They got married at the beginning of the year.
Se casaron a principios de año.

The district attorney's office has had more than a year to

prepare the case.
La fiscalía ha tenido más de un año para preparar el caso.

He was in jail for ten years.
Estuvo en la cárcel diez años.

Those who come into the United States as refugees or who are granted political asylum, can become permanent residents in one year.
Los que entran a Estados Unidos como refugiados o a quienes se les otorga asilo político, pueden convertirse en residentes permanentes en un año.

He went blind five years ago.
Hace cinco años se quedó ciego.

My client had a small brush with the law three years ago.
Mi cliente tuvo un pequeño roce con la ley hace tres años.

yell

He yelled at them to stop.
Les gritó que se detuvieran.

She yelled for help.
Pidió ayuda a gritos.

yesterday

I spoke to him yesterday.
Ayer hablé con él.

They left yesterday.
Se fueron ayer.

The police were working until yesterday on the confirmation of the identity of an indigent, whose dead body was found on an abandoned property.
La policía trabajaba hasta ayer en la ratificación de la identidad de un indigente, cuyo cadáver fue hallado en una propiedad abandonada.

I was at home all day yesterday.
Ayer estuve en casa todo el día.

The suspect was arrested during a breaking and entering early in the morning yesterday.
El sospechoso fue detenido durante un allanamiento de vivienda en las primeras horas de la mañana de ayer.

yet

As yet, wev'e had no reply.
Aún no hemos recibido respuesta.
Todavía no hemos recibido respuesta.
Hasta ahora no hemos recibido respuesta.

Has he decided yet?

¿Ya se ha decidido?
¿Ya se decidió?

Did she decide yet?
¿Ya se ha decidido?
¿Ya se decidió?

The story becomes yet more complicated.
El cuento se complica aún más.
El cuento se complica todavía más.

We found yet another witness to the accident.
Encontramos otro testigo del accidente más.

yield

The investigation yielded no new evidence.
La investigación no aportó nuevas pruebas.

She yielded to their threats.
Cedió a sus amenazas.
Cedió ante sus amenazas.

you

You'll have to abide by the rules.
Tendrás que atenerte a las reglas.

Will you be able to go?
¿Podrás ir?

I think you'll be able to testify tomorrow.
Creo que mañana vas a poder testificar.

Have you approached her about it?
¿Ya ha hablado con ella del asunto?

I'll call you in about three hours.
Te llamo en unas tres horas.

Are you absolutely sure?
¿Estás completamente seguro?

Would that be acceptable to you?
¿Eso le resultaría aceptable?

Have you ever had an accident?
¿Ha tenido alguna vez un accidente?

Once they have paid what they owe you, file a form called Acknowledgment of Satisfaction of Judgment.
Una vez que haya pagado lo que le debe, presente un formulario llamado Reconocimiento de Pago del Fallo.

How long have you been at this address?
¿Desde cuándo vives aquí?

young

A pedophile was found guilty of abducting six young girls.
Un pedóphilo fue declarado culpable de secuestrar a seis muchachas.

He denies having raped the young woman last summer.
Él niega haber violado a la joven el verano pasado.

Is Patricia your youngest?
¿Es Patricia la menor?
¿Es Patricia la más pequeña?

your

After the accident get in touch with your insurance company.
Después del accidente comuníquese con su compañía de seguro.

I am very glad to make your acquaintance.
Tengo mucho gusto en conocerle.

The letter was addressed to your home address.
La carta estaba dirigida a tu domocilio particular.

The package is addressed to your name.
El paquete está dirigido a tu nombre.

What is your address?
¿Cuál es su dirección?

The lawyer has to answer your questions and return your calls within a reasonable time period.
El abogado tiene que contestar sus preguntas y devolverle sus llamadas de teléfono dentro de un plazo de tiempo razonable.

Your next court appearance is in a week.
Tu próxima comparecencia ante el juez es en una semana.

Your assistance in the case is greatly appreciated.
Se le agredece enormemente su colaboración en el caso.

It's all your fault.
Tú tienes toda la culpa.

It's all your fault.
Usted tiene toda la culpa.

If you are in agreement with the contingency fee, your lawyer must explain to you how the fees are calculated and put the agreement in writing.
Si usted está de acuerdo con la tasa de contingencia, su abogado le debe explicar cómo calculan los honorarios y poner el acuerdo por escrito.

In order to become immigrants, your parents wll have to go through a three stage process.
Para convertirse en inmigrantes, sus padres deberán pasar por un proceso de tres etapas.

Before you enter the US, it is essential that you know your rights.
Antes de que usted ingrese a Estados Unidos, es esencial que usted conozca sus derechos.

yours
Is this yours?
¿Esto es tuyo?
¿Esto es suyo?

Is he a friend of yours?
¿Es amigo tuyo?
¿Es amigo suyo?

yourself
Make yourself at home.
Está en su casa.
Siéntese como en su casa.

You must avail yourself of all the legal resources.
Debe valerse de todos los recursos legales.

Were you by yourself?
¿Estabas solo?
¿Estabas sola?

youth
The police stated that the youth arrested was brought before the authorities for theft and not for gang activity.
La policía precisó que el joven detenido se le consignó por robo, no por pandillerismo.

Z

zero
His chances of winning are zero.
No tiene ninguna posibilidad de ganar.
Sus posibilidades de ganar son nulas.

Visibility was down to zero.
La visibilidad era nula.

zip
The morning zipped by.
La mañana pasó volando.

What is your zip code?
¿Cuál es su código postal?

CRIMINAL MATTERS

Law Office Intake For Criminal Matters:

WARNING!

IT NEEDS TO BE EMPHASIZED that the questions below are designed to determine whether there are basic issues which the client needs to speak with a criminal defense lawyer about in much greater detail. The questions below are only sufficient for, and are designed for the purpose of, helping the practitioner determine whether a deeper interrogation of the client and/or witnesses may be necessary in order to defend the legal rights of the accused. These questions are not sufficient in and of themselves to determine whether a crime was in-fact committed, whether a valid legal defense exists, or whether liability attaches. They are sufficient to determine whether or not further questioning or referral to an expert practitioner is required. The topic of **homicide** is left out in its entirety, owing to the fact that it ought not be handled, under any circumstance, by any practitioner who is not fluent in the language of the defendant, or who does not have a competent interpreter on hand at all times.

Criminal

Often times a potential criminal client will come to a lawyer with a spouse and other family members. Although this is nice on some level (it helps the client relax a bit and stay a bit more focused), there are legal and practical issues to consider. Before you begin the actual intake interview and asking substantive questions about the matter(s) the client is there to discuss, you will need to pull the client away from his/her spouse and/or family and have a private discussion with him/her. A diplomatic way to present this to the spouse is as follows:

1. Antes de empezar, voy a tener que hablar con ______________ un momento en privado.	1. Before I can begin, I will need to speak to ______________ privately for a moment.
2. Hay unas cuestiones legales que son muy importantes. Eso me obliga ha hablar con él/ella al principio en privado.	2. There are a couple of very important technical legal issues which I am only allowed to talk with him about at first.
3. Después de nuestras conversaciones iniciales, usted puede entrar mientras continuemos la dicusión.	3. It is possible that after we talk, you will be able to come into the room while we discuss matters further.
4. Tengo que hacer esto. De este modo puedo darle a ______________ la mejor representación legal posible.	4. I have to do it this way in order to be certain that I am giving ______________ the best representation I possibly can.

It is very important to say this to the spouse for a pair of reasons. First, from a practical standpoint, the client may not be inclined to fully and openly discuss a case in front of a spouse. You can serve as the interference person who interjects the legal necessity of a private meeting, thereby relieving the client of the pressure of having to ask a loved one to wait outside. The second, and equally important reason for this step is to be able to privately advise the client about the attonicy/client privilege.

Critical Admonition(s) to the client regarding attorney/client privilege

The following statement should be made to the client, with no one other than the attorney present. Although staff, other attorneys and paralegals may be covered by the privilege, many people from Spanish speaking cultures have an extremely difficult time trusting authority figures when it comes to private legal matters. A good rule of thumb is, the fewer people in the room, the better.

Criminal

1. Cada vez que viene a mi bufete, todo lo que discutimos es totalmente confidencial.

1. Any time that you come to my office, everything that you and I talk about is completely confidential.

2. Eso quiere decir que nadie, ni su familia, ni la policía, ni los tribunales pueden recibir información acerca de nuestras conversaciones sin su permiso.

2. That means that nobody, not your family, not the police, not the courts, can get any information about anything that you and I discuss, without your permission.

3. No me pueden obligar a discutir nuestras conversaciones con terceros. Además, yo nunca discutiré su caso fuera de este bufete con otros sin su permiso.

3. I cannot be made to tell anybody about our conversations, and I will never discuss your case outside of this office with anybody without your permission.

4. Esto se denomina secreto profesional entre abogado y cliente en el sistema judicial estadounudense.

4. The U.S. Legal system calls this the Attorney-Client privilege.

5. Esta norma existe para permitir que un cliente le explique a su abogado todo detalle acerca de su caso. No importa si usted cree que es ilegal o que es muy vergonzoso.

5. This rule exists in order to allow you to tell me every single detail about your case, no matter how illegal you may think it is, and no matter how embarrassing it may be.

6. Si usted me da cuenta de todo lo que sabe acerca de su caso, entonces le puedo dar el mejor consejo posible.

6. If you tell me everything that you know I can give you the best help I am capable of.

7. Si no me revela toda la verdad, puedo hacer o decir algo que resulte perjudicial para su caso debido a que no sé la verdad.

7. If you hold back part of the truth, I may end up doing things that turn out to be harmful to your case, just because I don't know the truth.

8. Le voy a hacer preguntas. Usted deber responder sinceramente y dar respuestas completas. Todo lo que usted me dice es confidencial, a menos que usted diga lo contrario.

8. *Please know that you can and must answer the questions that I am going to ask completely and truthfully. Everything you tell me will stay here in this office, unless you say otherwise.*

9. El derecho a la protección legal que le otorga el secreto profesional entre abogado y cliente se puede perder. Tenemos que proteger este derecho y no hacer nada que lo ponga en peligro.

9. *The legal protection you get from the attorney-client privilege can be lost, so we must be very careful to protect it and to not do anything that might cause it to disappear.*

10. Se puede perder si discutimos su caso en la presencia de terceros.

10. *The main way that it can be lost is if you and I discuss your case in front of a third party.*

11. Por ejemplo, si usted me dice que robó un coche, ese secreto sería protegido bajo la norma y no quedaría al descubierto.

11. *For example, if you were to tell me that you stole a car, your secret would be absolutely protected and safe with me.*

13. Si me dijera usted lo mismo en presencia de un amigo, un juez puede ordenar que el amigo comparezca ante el tribunal y revele lo que usted dijo, es decir, que usted robó un coche.

13. *If you told me the same thing, but your best friend was in the room at the time, a judge could order your friend to come to court and tell everyone that you admitted to stealing a car.*

Optional Parts

1. El mismo tipo de privilegio existe entre un matrimonio.

1. *The same sort of privilege of secrecy exists between married people.*

2. *Uno puede y debe hablar con su cónyuge y ser franco con él/ella.*

2. *Your are supposed to talk to your spouse and be honest with him/her.*

3. *Según la ley, la importancia de un matrimonio feliz tiene más peso que cualquier otra consideración, incluso lo que uno discute con su cónyuge.*

3. *The law says that the importance of a good marriage outweighs the need to know what you may have told your spouse.*

4. *Por esta razón, algunos abogados permiten que el conyúge asista las reuniones.*

4. *Because of this, some lawyers tell their clients that it is okay to have the spouse in the room while we meet.*

5. *Hay dos maneras en que uno puede contemplar la situación.*

5. *There are two ways of looking at the situation.*

6. *En primer lugar, tener una buena relación con la cónyuge es muy importante.*

En primer lugar, tener una buena relación con el cónyuge es muy importante.

6. *The first way to see it is that it is indeed very important to have a good relationship with your spouse.*

7. *No dejar al cónyuge participar en las conversaciones acerca del caso puede causar sospechas. No sabe si usted ha sido franco con él. (male)*

No dejar a la cónyuge participar en las conversaciones acerca del caso puede causar sospechas. No sabe si usted ha sido franco con ella. (female)

7. *Keeping your spouse out of the room when we talk about your case could make him/her suspicious about what you are telling me, or, whether or not you have been telling him/her the truth.*

8. En segundo lugar, algunos cónyuges no pueden mantener la información en secreto.

8. *The other way of looking at it is that some spouses have a hard time keeping a secret.*

9. Si su cónyuge está en el cuarto cuando usted me dice que robó un coche, y ella se lo repite a otra persona, esto puede perjudicar su caso seriamente.

   Si su cónyuge está en el cuarto cuando usted me dice que robó un coche, y él se lo repite a otra persona, esto puede perjudicar su caso seriamente.

   9. If your spouse were in the room when you told me that you stole a car, and then he/she were to let it slip to a friend that you confessed, it could seriously hurt your case.

10. Puede ser que podamos o no controlar el daño.

    10. We may or may not be able to control the damage.

11. El mejor modo de mantener los secretos privados es limitar el número de personas que sepan de ellos.

    11. The best way to keep secret matters private is to strictly limit the number of people who know them.

12. Basándose en todo lo que le he dicho, es usted quien debe decidir si su cónyuge puede estar presente durante nuestras conversaciones acerca de su caso.

    12. Based upon all of the things I just told you, you alone must decide whether or not you want your spouse in the room when we talk about your case.

Sub-Options

1. Yo recomiendo que no permita a otros participar en nuestras conversaciones, aparte de los miembros de mi personal. A ellos se les garantiza la misma protección del secreto profesional entre abogado y cliente.

   1. I recommend that you do not allow anybody into the room when we talk, other than members of my staff who share the same attorney client privilege.

2. Su caso es demasiado serio, las consecuencias pueden ser muy severas, y éste es el camino más seguro a seguir.

   2. Your case is much too serious, the consequences are too severe, and this is simply the safest course of action.

3. Quizá usted querrá decirle a su cónyuge que le aconsejé que no permita a nadie asistir a nuestras reuniones, no solamente a ella.

   3. You may want to tell your spouse that I advised you to keep everyone out, not just her.

   Quizá usted querrá decirle a su cónyuge que le aconsejé que no permita a nadie asistir a nuestras reuniones, no solamente a él.

   You may want to tell your spouse that I advised you to keep everyone out, not just him.

5. Echándome la culpa puede ayudar a paliar la tensión a la que está sometida ella debido a la la situación.

   5. Putting the blame on me helps to ease any tension she might feel over the situation.

   Echándome la culpa puede ayudar a paliar la tensión a la que está sometido él debido a la la situación.

   Putting the blame on me helps to ease any tension he might feel over the situation.

6. Se le dejo a usted la elección de decidir si quiere que su cónjuge asista nuestras reuniones o no.

   6. I leave it up to you to decide whether or not you want your spouse in the room when we talk.

7. No suele ser problema que asistan a la reunión.

   7. It is usually not a problem to allow them into the room.

THE INTERVIEW QUESTIONS

The most critical parts of the initial intake interview are (1) to determine which legal issues, if any, are relevant, (2) acquiring factual information from the client and (3) determining what the client's expectation of your representation are. In criminal matters, it is often times assumed that the client wants to be acquitted of whatever crime he/she is charged with. On occasion, the client actually seeks counsel to prevent charges from ever being filed, to get help with an addiction or psychological compulsion which may lead to illegal behavior, or to determine a course of action which is legal (i.e., "My neighbor shot my dog. Can I shoot his?").

FOR THE PURPOSES OF THIS BOOK, the client's expectations are critical. Initial intake questions are supposed to be used solely to determine whether the client even needs a lawyer. If the client expects you to fully understand and resolve their issues for them, the situation may become sticky.

1. Lo que un abogado puede hacer para usted depende de una evaluación para ver si usted ha violado la ley o no.

1. What a lawyer can do for you depends upon an evaluation of whether or not you have broken the law.

2. Si usted ha violado la ley, quizá un abogado pueda ayudarle a que no lo acusen de un crimen.

2. If you have broken the law, a lawyer may be able to help you avoid being charged.

3. Si usted ha violado la ley, quizá un abogado pueda ayudarle a que lo acusen solamente por los crímenes que usted de hecho ha cometido.

3. If you have broken the law, a lawyer may be able to help you make sure that you are only charged for what you actually did which was illegal.

4. Si usted ha violado la ley, quizá un abogado pueda ayudarle a llegar a un acuerdo con el fiscal a conseguir una sentencia más ligera, que le acusen de menos cargos o a una combinación de ambos.

4. If you have broken the law, a lawyer may be able to help you work out a deal with the authorities for a lighter sentence, fewer charges, or a combination of both.

6. Si usted no violó la ley, o si la policía no lo han acusado debido a que no poseen suficiente datos como para acusarlo, un abogado puede ayudarle a prevenir que la policía lo busque.

6. *If you did not break the law, or if the police have not charged you yet because they have not gathered enough information against you to charge you, a lawyer can help you to void giving them any help in coming after you.*

7. Un abogado puede ayudarle a prevenir cualquier trampa policial.

7. *A lawyer can help you avoid any potential police traps.*

DETERMINING LEGAL ISSUES

MUST BE SAID BEFORE THE QUESTIONING BEGINS:

1. Favor de contestar lo que le voy a preguntar de manera sencilla y honesta.

1. *Please answer the questions I am about to ask you simply and honestly.*

2. Por favor, no me diga lo que usted hizo ni lo que usted piensa que hizo.

2. *Please do not tell me about what you did, or what you think you did, wrong.*

3. A menudo uno hace algo que se le aparece ilegal, o uno tiene remordimientos de conciencia, pero que son perfectamente legal.

3. *Often times people do things that they think are illegal or that they feel guilty about, which turn out to have been perfectly legal.*

4. Por ello y por el momento, usted debe contestarme de manera sencilla y honesta. ¿Entiende?

4. *That's why, for right now, I need you to simply and honestly answer my questions. Do you understand?*

Optional

1. Como usted pueda haber notado, no domino el español.

1. *As you may have noticed, I am not fluent with Spanish.*

2. Voy a tratar de ayudarle con la asistencia de este libro.

2. *I am going to attempt to help you with the aid of this book.*

3. FAVOR DE contestar lo más sencillo y honestamante como posible.

3. *PLEASE keep all of your answers as simple and honest as possible.*

4. Basado en sus respuestas, podré determinar si usted necesita representación legal o no, cuáles son los problemas legales que usted enfrenta, y las consecuencias posibles de cualquier problema legal que yo halle.

4. *Based upon the answers you will give me to the questions I am about to ask, I should be able to determine whether or not you even need legal representation, what sorts of legal problems you may be having, and the possible consequences of any legal problems I find.*

Basic Questions

1. ¿De qué delito lo acusaron?

1. *What crime were you charged with?*

2. ¿Por qué cree que lo puedan arrestar o lo puedan acusar de un delito.

2. *Why do you think you might get arrested or be charged with a crime?*

3. ¿Quiere interrogarle la policía acerca de un crimen que otra persona cometió?

3. *Do the police want to ask you questions about a crime that they think somebody else committed?*

4. ¿Quiere interrogarle la policía acerca de una persona que busca?

3. *Do the police want to ask you questions about a person they are looking for?*

5. ¿Trata la policía de conseguir de usted información acerca de una persona que busca por un delito?

5. *Are the police trying to get you to tell them where a wanted person is?*

Intent

1. A veces uno hsce algo sin intención de hacerlo, en tal caso puede resultar que la persona no cometió un delito.

1. Sometimes if you do something but it was unintentional, you may not have committed an actual crime.

2. Por ejemplo, si una persona le ofrece dinero a una prostituta, pero su intención fue pagarle para que limpiara su coche, entonces la persona no es culpable de cometer un delito. Por ello, es muy importante que yo entienda su intención a la hora que el acontecimiento ocurrió.

2. For instance, if a person offers a prostitute money but it was his intent to pay her to wash his car, he is not guilty of a crime. So you can see how important it is that I understand what your intentions were at the time the incident occurred.

3. ¿Fue su intención de hacer lo que la policía lo acusa de hacer?

3. Was it your intention to do the thing that the police accused you of?

4. ¿Intentó usted un resultado diferente?

4. Did you intend a different result?

5. ¿Entendió usted del todo lo que sucedía?

5. Did you have any idea at all as to what was happening?

6. ¿Sólo trataba usted de espantar a la víctima?

6. Were you merely trying to frighten the victim ?

7. ¿Fue lo que ocurrió un accidente?

7. Was the incident merely an accident?

8. ¿Entendió usted que actuaba de forma que pudiera hacerle daño a alguien?

8. Did you realize that you were acting in a manner that was likely to harm someone?

Criminal

Stop/Frisk/Search/Seizure

1. ¿Intentó explicarle al agente de policía que usted no habla/entiende inglés?

1. Did you try to explain to the officer that you do not speak English?

2. ¿Intentó explicarle al policía que usted no habla/entiende inglés muy bien?

2. Did you try to explain to the officer that you do not speak/understand English very well?

3. ¿Habló el policía español?

3. Did the officer speak Spanish?

4. ¿Entendió usted todo lo que el policía dijo?

4. Did you understand everything that the officer said

5. ¿Lo detuvieron mientras conducía un coche?

5. Did you get stopped while you were driving a car?

6. ¿A quién le pertenece el coche que usted conducía?

6. Whose car were you driving?

7. ¿Le preguntó el policía si usted había tomado?

7. Did the officer ask you if you had been drinking?

8. ¿Dijo el policía que podía oler algo (alcohol/tobaco)?

8. Did the officer say that he could smell anything (alcohol/smoke)?

9. ¿Le dijo el policía por qué lo paró o qué pensaba que usted hizo mal?

9. Did the officer tell you why he stopped you, or what he thought you did wrong?

10. ¿Le pidió el policía que se bajara del coche?

10. Did the officer ask you to get out of the car?

11. ¿Le preguntó el policía si pudiera registrar su coche?

11. Did the officer ask you if he could search your car?

12. ¿Registró el policía el coche?

12. Did the officer search the car?

13. ¿Se llevó el agente de policía algo del coche?	13. *Did the officer remove anything from the car?*
14. ¿Lo detuvo el policía en un lugar público?	14. *Did a police officer stop you while you were in a public place?*
15. ¿Qué hacía usted cuando el policía se le acercó?	15. *What were you doing when the officer approached you?*
16. ¿Le pidió el policía hacer un cacheo?	16. *Did the officer ask you if he could search you?*
17. ¿Cómo vestía el policía?	17. *How was the officer dressed?*
18. ¿Le mostró una placa de policía o algún tipo de identificación?	18. *Did he show you a badge or identification?*
19. ¿Le explicó el policía por qué lo paró?	19. *Did the officer tell you why he stopped you?*
20. ¿Vino un policía a su domicilio?	20. *Did a police officer come to your home?*
21. ¿Tocó el policía a la puerta?	21. *Did the officer knock on the door?*
22. ¿Esperó el policía hasta que usted abriera la puerta?	22. *Did the police officer wait for you to answer the door?*
23. ¿Le pegó el policía una patada a la puerta?	23. *Did the police officer kick your door open?*
24. ¿Dijo el policía que tenía un orden de registro emitido por la corte?	24. *Did the police officer say that he had a warrant from the court?*
25. ¿Le explicó el policía por qué estaba allí?	25. *Did the police officer say why he was there?*

26. ¿Estaba el policía allí en busca de usted?

26. *Was the officer there for you?*

27. ¿Estaba el policía allí en busca de otro miembro de su familia?

27. *Was the police officer there for another member of your household?*

28. ¿Lo cacheó el policía?

28. *Did the officer pat your clothing down and search you?*

29. ¿Le dijo usted al policía que estaba bien que lo cacheara a usted?

29. *Did you tell the officer that it was okay to search you?*

30. ¿Le quitó algo el policía de su persona o le sacó algo de su bolsillo?

30. *Did the officer take anything away from you or out of your pockets?*

31. ¿Halló el policía cualquier arma, cuchillos o pistolas que usted portaba?

31. *Did the police officer find any weapons, knives or guns on your person?*

32. ¿Halló el policía cualquier droga que usted tenía en su posesión?

32. *Did the police officer find any drugs on you?*

33. ¿Le quitó el policía dinero?

33. *Did the police officer take any money away from you?*

34. ¿Le pidió un policía si pudiera registras su domicilio?

34. *Did an officer ask you if he could search your home?*

35. ¿Qué tenía puesto el policía que le pidió registrar el domicilio?

35. *How was the officer who asked to search dressed?*

36. ¿Cuándo el policía le pidió registrar el domicilio, dónde estaban las manos del policía?

36. *When the officer asked if he could search your home, where were his hands?*

37. ¿Cuándo el policía le pidió registrar el domicilio, dónde estaba su pistola?

37. *When the officer asked if he could search your home, where was his gun?*

38. ¿Cuándo el agente de policía le pidió registrar el domicilio, se hallaban otros agentes cercanos?	*38. When the officer asked if he could search your home, were there other police officers nearby?*
39. ¿Cuántos agentes?	*38. How many officers?*
40. ¿Qué tenían puestos?	*40. How were they dressed?*
41. ¿Dónde estaban las manos de los agentes?	*41. Where were their hands?*
42. ¿Dónde estaban sus pistolas?	*42. Where were their guns?*
43. ¿Cuándo el policía le pidió registrar el domicilio, ¿había perros policías cercanos?	*43. When the officer asked if he could search your home, were there any police dogs nearby?*
44. ¿Dijo el policía que tenía un orden de registro para su domicilio?	*44. Did the officer claim to have a warrant to search your home?*
45. ¿Le mostró el policía un orden de registro?	*45. Did the officer show you a warrant?*
46. ¿Lo detuvieron?	*46. Were you detained?*
47. ¿Lo hicieron sentarse en un sólo lugar?	*47. Were you made to sit in one place?*
48. ¿Fue usted vigilado por un agente o un perro policía mientras esperaba?	*48. Were you guarded by a person or a dog while you waited?*
49. ¿Le dijeron 'espere aquí'?	*49. Were you told to'Wait here'?*
50. ¿Le dijeron que no podía irse hasta que el policía acabara el registro?	*50. Were you told that you are not free to leave until the officer is done?*
51. ¿Lo esposaron?	*51. Were you placed in handcuffs?*

52. ¿Le parecía que usted pudiera irse siempre que usted quisiera?	*52. Did you feel as if you were free to leave whenever you wanted to?*
53. ¿Lo detuvieron?	*53. Were you arrested?*
54. ¿Le dijo el policía que estaba arrestado, lo esposó a usted y lo llevó a la cárcel?	*54. Did the officer tell you that you were under arrest, handcuff you and take you to jail?*
55. ¿Le parecía que usted estaba arrestado?	*55. Did you feel like you were under arrest?*
56. ¿Lo llevaron a la cárcel?	*56. Were you taken to jail at all?*
57. ¿Ha pagado la fianza?	*57. Have you posted any bail?*
58. ¿Tiene los documentos que la policía le dio?	*58. Do you have any of the your papers the police officers gave you?*
59. ¿Tiene los documentos que la corte le dio?	*59. Do you have any of the papers the Court gave you?*
60. ¿Ha consultado con cualquier otro abogado?	*60. Have you spoken with any other lawyers?*

Miranda Warning Issues

1. ¿Le hizo preguntas el agente de policía?	*1. Did the officer ask you any questions?*
2. ¿Antes de hacerle cualquier pregunta a usted, le explicó el agente de policía que usted tiene el derecho de no decir nada a la policía?	*2. Before he asked you any questions, did the officer tell you that you had the right to not say a single word to the police?*
3. ¿Antes de hacerle cualquier pregunta, le explicó el policía que cualquiera cosa que usted le diga a la policía se usara para declararlo a usted culpable de un delito.	*3. Before he asked you any questions, did the officer tell you that anything that you tell the police will be used to try to convict you of a crime?*

4. ¿Antes de hacerle cualquier pregunta a usted, le explicó el agente de policía que usted tiene el derecho de consultar con un abogado?

4. Before he asked you any questions, did the officer tell you that you were allowed to talk to a lawyer?

5. ¿Antes de hacerle cualquier pregunta a usted, le explicó el agente de policía que si usted no puede contratar a un abogado, uno le será nombrado gratis, incluso antes de ser interrogado?

5. Before he asked you any questions, did the officer tell you that if you can't afford to hire a lawyer, you can get one, before you are questioned, free of charge ?

6. ¿En cualquier momento, quiso usted consultar con un abogado?

6. At any point, did you want to talk to a lawyer?

7. Dijo usted expresamente que quería consultar con un abogado.

7. Did you specifically say that you wanted to speak to a lawyer?

8. Dijo usted o hizo cualquier cosa que le indicara a la policía que usted quería consultar a un abogado?

8. Did you say or do anything that you thought would indicate to the police that you wanted to talk to a lawyer?

Acquiring Basic Factual Information

1. ¿Estaba usted solo cuándo la policía habló con usted?

1. Were you alone at the time the police talked to you?

2. ¿Estaba usted solo cuándo la policía lo arrestó?

2. Were you alone at the time the police arrested you?

3. ¿Quién más estaba con usted?

3. Who else was with you?

4. ¿Cuál es su relación con esa persona? ¿ Es un amigo? ¿Es un miembro de la familia?

4. What is your relationship to that person? Friend? Family member?

5. ¿Fue alguien más arrestado junto con usted?

5. Was anybody else arrested along with you?

6. ¿Estaba el agente de policía allí solo?

6. Was the officer alone?

7. ¿Había otros agentes de policía?

7. Were there other officers present?

8. ¿Había civiles con los agentes de policía?

8. Were there civilians with the officer(s)?

9. ¿Había un perro policía?

9. Was there a police dog?

10. ¿Había reporteros de televisión o reporteros gráficos?

10. Were there any television reporters or photographers?

11. ¿Se dio cuenta de que otras personas estaban allí mirando?

11. Did you notice any people standing around watching?

12. ¿Le dijo usted algo a la policía?

12. Did you tell the police anything?

13. ¿Le explicó usted a la policía su versión de lo que pasó?

13. Did you tell the police your version of what happened?

14. A veces, lo que uno le dice a la policía al principio y lo que uno le dice más tarde, no es lo mismo. Esto no es necesariamente algo equivacado ni malo. Lo importante es que usted me diga, lo mejor que usted pueda recordarse, exactamente lo que usted le dijo a la policía.

14. Sometimes what you tell the police at the time you first deal with them and what you say later are different. This is not necessarily wrong or bad. What is very important is that you tell me, as best as you can remember, exactly what you told the police.

15. ¿Estaba usted tomando al tiempo que el delito, del cual usted fue arrestado, ocurrió?

15. When the crime that you were arrested for happened, had you been drinking?

16. ¿Qué estaba tomando?

16. What had you been drinking?

17. ¿Cuántas bebidas había tomado?

17. How many drinks did you have?

18. ¿Al tiempo que el delito ocurrió, del cual usted fue arrestado, había tomado usted drogas, legales o ilegales? Esto incluye fumando marihuana.

18. When the crime that you were arrested for happened, had you been taking any drugs, either legal or illegal? This includes smoking marijuana.

Specific Criminal Activity Issues

1. ¿Dice la policía que usted usó un arma?

1. Do the police say that you used a weapon ?

2. ¿Dice la policía que usted usó una pistola?

2. Do the police say that you used a gun ?

3. ¿Dice la policía que usted trató de hacer algo ilegal?

3. Do the police say that you tried to do something illegal?

4. ¿Dice la policía que usted dejó de hacer algo ilegal o que ellos lo capturaron antes de que pudiera hacer algo ilegal? ¿Intentó usted hacer las cosas que la policía dice que usted intentaba hacer?

4. Do the police say that you either stopped before you actually did something illegal, or that they caught you before you were able to do something illegal? Did you intend to do the thing that the police say you were trying to do?

Conspiracy

1. ¿Dice la policía que usted intentó cometer un delito junto con otras personas, o con la ayuda de otras personas?

1. Do the police say that you tried to commit a crime along with, or with the help of other people?

2. ¿Dice la policía que usted fue un cómplice en vez de ser un jugador principal en un delito?

2. Do the police say that you were a helper, rather than a main player in a crime?

3. ¿Llegó usted a algún acuerdo con la otra persona?

3. Did you make some kind of an agreement with the other person?

4. ¿Intentó usted llegar a un acuerdo con él/ella/ellos?

4. Did you intend to make an agreement with him/her/them?

5. ¿Acordaron hacer la cosa por la cual lo arrestaron?

5. Was the agreement to do the thing that you were arrested for?

Accessory

1. ¿Dice la policía que usted ayudó en un delito por ayudarles a planear el delito?

1. Do the police say that you helped someone else commit a crime by helping them to plan the crime?

2. ¿Dice la policía que usted ayudó en un delito por darles asistencia en la comisión de un delito, como herramientas o armas?

2. Do the police say that you helped someone else commit a crime by giving them something to aid in the commission of the crime, like tools or weapons?

3. ¿Dice la policía que usted participó en un delito por ayudarles a fugarse o esconderse?

3. Do the police say that you helped someone else commit a crime by helping them to get away or hide afterwards?

4. ¿Sabía usted que la persona a quien usted ayudaba, había cometido un delito? ¿Se había escapado?

4. Did you know that the person you were helping had committed a crime? Had escaped?

5. ¿Inentó usted ayudarles a escapar, a esconderse o a evitar ser capturados?

5. Was it your intention to help them escape, hide or avoid being captured?

Theft

1. ¿Cree la policía que usted se llevó algo que le pertenece a otra persona?

1. Do the police think that you took something that belongs to someone else?

. ¿Qué es lo que dicen que usted se llevó.

2. What do they say you took?

3. ¿A quién le pertenecía lo que la policía dice que se llevó? — *3. Who do they say you took it from?*

4. ¿Fue esta persona su empleador? — *4. Was this person your employer?*

5. ¿Cuánto vale el artículo que dicen que usted se llevó? — *5. How much is the item that they say you took worth?*

6. ¿Se llevó usted el artículo? — *6. Did you take the item?*

7. ¿Cree que el artículo le pertenece a usted? — *7. Do you believe that the item is yours?*

8. ¿Pensó que la supuesta víctima le debía dinero/el artículo llavado? — *8. Did you think that the alleged victim owed you money/the item?*

9. ¿Intentó quedarse con el artículo? — *9. Did you intend to keep it?*

10. ¿Intentó venderlo? — *10. Did you intend to sell it?*

11. ¿Intentó devolver el artículo al dueño? ¿Cuándo? — *11. Did you intend to return the item to the owner? When?*

Destruction of Property / Malicious Mischief

1. ¿Dice la policía que usted dañó/destruyó algo? — *1. Do the police say that you damaged/destroyed something?*

2. ¿Qué era? — *2. What was that thing?*

3. ¿Qué daño le causó? — *3. What sort of damage was done to it?*

4. ¿Pertenecía el artículo dañado/destruido a usted? — *4. Was the damaged/destroyed item yours?*

Possession

1. ¿Lo acusó la policía de tenencia ilícita de drogas? ¿Qué clase? ¿Qué cantidad?

   1. Do the police say that you were in possession of drugs? What type? How much?

2. ¿Dijo la policía si piensa que usted las vendía o no?

   2. Did they say whether or not they think you were selling?

3. ¿Lo acusó la policía de tenencia de alcohol? ¿Cuántos años tiene?

   3. Do the police say that you were in possession of alcohol? How old are you?

4. ¿Lo acusan de tomar alcohol en un coche?

   4. Do they say that you were drinking in a car?

5. ¿Lo acusó la policía de tenencia de bienes hurtados?

   5. Do the police say that you were in possession of stolen property?

6. ¿Indicaron si piensan que usted lo robó o no?

   6. Did they indicate whether or not they think you stole it?

7. ¿Le preguntaron de dónde usted los consiguió?

   7. Did they ask where you got it?

8. ¿Le pertenecía a ustel el artículo?

   8. Was the item yours?

9. ¿Dónde lo consiguió? ¿Cuándo?

   9. Where did you get it? When?

10. ¿Puede demostrar que le pertenece a usted? (recibos, testigo que puede decir que usted lo compró, testigo que puede decir que se lo vendió a usted)

    10. Can you prove it's yours? (receipts, witness who says you bought it, witness who sold it to you)

11. ¿Lo acusó la policía de tenencia de documentos de identificación ilegales?	*11. Do the police say that you were in possession of illegal identification documents.*
12. ¿Qué clase de documento era?	*12. What kind of document was it?*
13. ¿Dónde lo consiguió?	*13. Where did you get it?*
14. ¿Se dio cuenta de que era falso?	*14. Were you aware that it was fake?*
15. ¿Lo acusó la policía de tenencia de moneda falsificada?	*15. Do the police say that you were in possession of counterfeit currency?*
16. ¿Había tenido usted tenencia de los billetes que la policía dice son falsos?	*16. Had you been in possession of the bills that they say are fake?*
17. ¿Dónde los consiguió?	*17. Where did you get them?*
18. ¿Cuándo los adquirió?	*18. When did you acquire them?*
19. ¿Sabía usted que eran falsos?	*19. Did you know that they were counterfeit?*
20. ¿Lo llevaba consigo o estaba en el coche con usted?	*20. Did you actually have it on your person, or was it in the car with you?*
21. ¿Lo llevaba consigo o estaba en su casa?	*21. Did you actually have it on your person, or was it in your home?*
22. ¿Lo llevaba consigo o estaba en un edificio que usted alquilaba?	*22. Did you actually have it on your person, or was it in any type of building you rented?*

Trespass/Burglary

1. ¿Lo acusa la policía de encontrarse en un lugar donde no debía estar?

1. Do the police say that you were some place where you should not have been?

2. ¿Dónde se encontraba usted?

2. Where were you?

3. ¿Era un negocio?

3. Was this a business?

4. ¿Estaba abierto?

4. Was it opened for business?

5. ¿Era un domicilio?

5. Was this a home?

6. ¿A quién le pertenecía el domicilio?

6. Who did the home belong to?

7. ¿Estaba alguien en casa?

7. Was there anybody home at the time?

8. ¿Le parecía que usted tenía el derecho de estar en ese lugar?

8. Did you feel that you had the right to be in that place?

9. ¿Le pidieron que se fuera? ¿Cuándo? ¿De parte de quién?

9. Were you asked to leave? When? By whom?

10. ¿Ya le habían advertido que no fuera a ese lugar? ¿Cuándo? ¿De parte de quién?

10. Had you been warned not to go there, or not to return there before? When? By whom?

11. ¿Había señales indicando que no entrara o señales de PROHIBIDO EL PASO?

11. Were there signs telling you not to enter, or NO TRESPASSING signs?

12. ¿Se dio cuenta de dónde estaba?

12. Did you realize where you were?

13. ¿Lo acusa la policía de hacer algo malo o illegal mientras usted estaba allí?

13. Do the police say that you did anything wrong or illegal while you were there?

14. ¿Lo acusan de robar algo?	*14. Do they say that you stole something?*
15. ¿Lo acusan de lastimar a alguien o de amenazar a lastimar a alguien?	*15. Do they say that you hurt someone, or threatened to hurt someone?*
16. Lo acusan de planear hacer algo malo mientras usted estaba allí?	*16. Do the police say that you were planning to do something bad while you were there?*

Driving While Intoxicated

1. ¿Había consumido bebidas alcohólicas?	*1. Had you been drinking?*
2. ¿Qué estaba tomando?	*2. What were you drinking?*
3. ¿Estaba tomando a solas?	*3. Were you drinking alone?*
4. ¿Dónde estaba tomando?	*4. Where were you drinking?*
5. ¿Cuántas bebidas había consumido?	*5. How many drinks had you consumed?*
6. ¿Cuánto tiempo hacía antes de que el policía lo detuvo que tomó su última bebida?	*6. How long before the officer stopped you was your last drink?*
7. ¿Conducía?	*7. Did you drive a car?*
8. ¿Estaba dormido en el coche?	*8. Were you asleep in the car?*
9. ¿Estaba estacionado el coche con el motor en marcha?	*9. Was the engine running?*
10. ¿Estuvo involucrado en un accidente?	*10. Were you involved in an accident?*
11. ¿Resultó alguien herido?	*11. Was anybody hurt?*

12. ¿Tuvo usted que tomar la prueba de alcohol?

12. *Did the police officers make you blow into a machine?*

13. ¿Se acuerda cuál fue el resultado?

13. *Do you remember what number came up on the machine?*

14. ¿Le sacó sangre la policía, o lo hizo un médico?

14. *Did the police officers take blood from you, or have a doctor do so?*

Solicitation/Prostitution

1. ¿Lo acusaron de tratar de solicitar los servicios de una prostituta?

1. *Do the police say that you tried to hire a prostitute?*

2. ¿Pretendía una agente de policía ser una prostituta?

2. *Was there a police officer pretending to be a prostitute?*

3. ¿Discutieron la clase de relaciones sexuales que iban a tener por el dinero?

3. *Did either of you talk about what kind of sex he/she would perform for the money?*

4. ¿Lo acusaron de contratar los servicios de una prostituta?

4. *Do the police say that you were engaged in prostitution?*

5. ¿Lo pillaron teniendo relaciones sexuales con alguien?

5. *Did they catch you having sex with someone?*

6. ¿Lo pillaron acceptando dinero de alguien?

6. *Did they catch you accepting money from someone?*

7. ¿Prentendió un agente de policía ser un cliente?

7. *Did they have a police officer pretend to be a customer?*

Assault/Domestic Violence

1. ¿Lo acusaron de amenazar a alguien?

   1. Do the police say that you threatened to hurt someone?

2. ¿Lo acusaron de amenazar a alguien por teléfono?

   2. Do they say that you threatened someone over the telephone?

3. ¿Lo acusaron de amenazarlos en persona?

   3. Do they say that you threatened them in person?

4. ¿Lo acusaron de blandir un arma?

   3. Do they say that you showed a weapon of any kind?

5. ¿En cuanto a la acusación, pretendió usted espantar a la víctima?

   5. As for the accusation, did you intend to scare the victim?

6. ¿Lo acusan de lastimar a alguien?

   6. Do the police say that you actually hurt someone?

7. Según la policîa, ¿cómo lo lastimó usted?

   7. How do they say you hurt him?

   Según la policîa, ¿cómo la lastimó usted?

   How do they say you hurt her?

8. ¿Afirma la policía que la persona que usted lastimó o trató de lastimar es un agente de policía?

   8. Do they claim that the person you hurt or tried to hurt is a police officer?

9. ¿Al tiempo del acontecimiento, se dio cuenta de que la persona era un agente de policía?

   9. Did you realize that the person was a police officer at the time?

10. ¿Qué llevaba puesto él?

    10. What was he wearing?

11. ¿Qué llevaba puesto ella?

    11. What was she wearing?

12. ¿Se identificó él/ella como agente de policía?

    12. Did he/she identify himself/herself to you as an officer?

13. Según la policía, ¿usted pilló a alguien con su coche?

13. Do the police say that you hit someone with your car?

14. Según la policía, ¿usted trató de pillar a alguien con su coche?

14. Do the police say that you tried to hit someone with your car?

15. Según la policía, ¿usted abandonó el lugar del accidente?

15. Do the police say that you left the scene of the accident?

16. Según la policía, ¿usted estaba borracho al tiempo que se alega que usted pilló a alguien con el coche?

16. Do the police say that you were intoxicated at the time you are alleged to have hit someone?

17. ¿Sabe si la víctima está viva o muerta?

17. Do you know whether the victim is alive or dead?

18. ¿Está viva la víctima?

18. Is the victim alive?

19. ¿Está muerta la víctima?

19. Is the victim dead?

Kidnapping / Custodial Interference

1. Según la policía, ¿usted forzó a alguien acompañarlo a otro lugar?

1. Do the police say that you forced someone to go with you somewhere?

2. Según la policía, ¿usted forzó a alguien quedarse con usted contra su voluntad?

2. Do the police say that you forced someone to stay with you against their will?

3. Según la policía, ¿usted uso un arma para forzar a una persona acompañarle?

3. Do the police say that you used a weapon to make the person come with you?

4. Es usted el padre/la madre de la víctima?

4. Are you the father/mother of the victim?

5. ¿Está usted divorciado de la madre de la víctima?

5. Are you divorced from the child's mother?

6. ¿Está usted divorciada del padre de la víctima?

6. Are you divorced from the child's father?

7. ¿A quién le otorgaron la custodia física del niño?

¿A quién le otorgaron la custodia física de la niña?

7. Who was granted physical custody of the child?

8. ¿Cree usted que, para poder proteger a la víctima, usted tuvo que llevarlo consigo?

8. Do you believe that, in order to protect the victim, you had to take him with you?

¿Cree usted que, para poder proteger a la víctima, usted tuvo que llevarla consigo?

Do you believe that, in order to protect the victim, you had to take her with you?

Sex Offenses/Rape Assault

1. ¿Tuvo relaciones sexuales con la supuesta víctima?

1. Did you have sex with the alleged victim?

2. ¿Tuvo cualquier tipo de contacto sexual con la supuesta víctima?

2. Did you have any kind of sexual contact with the alleged victim?

3. ¿Tocó los senos de la víctima?

3. Did you touch her breasts?

4. ¿Tocó el área genital de la víctima?

4. Did you touch his/her genital area?

5. ¿Tocó las nalgas de la víctima?

5. Did you touch his/her buttocks?

6. ¿Ocasionó usted que algún instrumento, tal como un vibrador, un palo, un vegetable o cualquier cosa lo/la tocó?

6. Did you cause any sort of instrument, like a vibrator, a stick, a vegetable or anything at all to touch him/her?

7. ¿Estaba él/ella consciente al momento del acontecimiento?

7. Was he/she conscious at the time?

8. ¿Estaba él borracho?

8. Was he drunk?

¿Estaba ella borracha?

Was she drunk?

9. ¿Estaba intoxicado con drogas?

9. Was he high?

¿Estaba intoxicada con drogas?

Was she high?

10. ¿Ocurrió el contacto sexual con la supuesta víctima en la parte exterior de la ropa?

10. Was the sexual contact with the alleged victim on the outside of the clothing?

11. ¿Ocurrió el contacto sexual con la supuesta víctima en la parte interior de la ropa?

11. Was the sexual contact with the alleged victim underneath the clothing?

12. ¿Ambos?

12. Both?

13. ¿Afirmó ella que usted podía tener relaciones sexuales con ella?

13. Did she say that it was okay to have sex with her?

14. ¿Dijo que usted podía tener relaciones sexuales con él?

14. Did he say that it was OK to have sex with him?

15. ¿Hizo algo usted que provocó a la supuesta víctima tocar partes de su cuerpo? Esto incluye tocar cualquier parte del cuerpo de la supuesta víctima, incluso el cabello, los pies y la boca.

15. Did you do anything to cause the alleged victim to touch parts of your body? This includes any part of the alleged victims body, including hair, feet and mouth.

16. ¿Hizo algo usted que provocó a la supuesta víctima tocar sus genitales? ¿Sus nalgas?

16. Did you do anything to cause the alleged victim to touch your genitals? Your buttocks?

Sexual Abuse of a Minor

1. ¿Cuántos años tenía la supuesta víctima al tiempo que esto supuestamente occurrió?

   1. How old was the alleged victim at the time this is supposed to have occurred?

2. ¿Era la supuesta víctima un pariente?

   2. Was the alleged victim a relative?

3. ¿Cómo está emparentada la víctima con usted?

   3. How is he/she related to you ?

4. ¿Estaba viviendo la supuesta víctima con usted?

   4. Was the alleged victim Living in your home?

5. ¿Era la supuesta víctima hijo/a de un compañero de cuarto? ¿De habitación?

   5. Was the alleged victim the child of a roommate? Of a housemate?

   ¿Era la supuesta víctima hijo/a de una compañera de cuarto? ¿De habitación?

   ¿Era la supuesta víctima hijo/a de una novia? De un novio?

   Was the alleged victim the child of a girlfriend? Of a boyfriend?

Victim's Relation to Client

1. Según la policía, ¿quién es la víctma?

   1. Who do the police say the victim is?

2. ¿Conoce usted a la víctima?

   2. Do you know the victim?

3. ¿Desde cuándo lo conoce?

   3. How long have you known him?

   ¿Desde cuándo la conoce?

   How long have you known her?

4. ¿Es la víctima un pariente? Un amigo? Una amiga?

   4. Is the victim a relative? A friend?

5. ¿Estás casada con él?	*5. Are you married to him?*
¿Estás casado con ella?	*Are you married to her?*
6. ¿Has estado casada con él?	*6. Were you ever married to him?*
¿Has estado casado con ella?	*Were you ever married to her?*
7. ¿Cuándo se divorciaron?	*7. When did you divorce?*
8. ¿Vive él/ella con usted?	*8. Does he/she live with you?*
9. ¿Eran novios? ¿Por cuánto tiempo?	*9. Were you boyfriend and girlfriend? For how long?*
10. ¿Cuándo se separaron?	*10. When did you split up?*
11. ¿Ha vivido él/ella con usted? ¿Por cuánto tiempo? ¿Dónde? ¿Cuándo?	*11. Has he/she ever lived with you? For how long? Where? When?*

Client/Victim Past Problems

1. ¿Aparte de esta más reciente ocasión, ha llamado la víctima a la policía? ¿En qué fecha?	*1. Aside from on this most recent occasion, has the victim ever called the police to complain about you? On which dates?*
2. ¿Qué le dijo él/ella a la policía que usted le hizo a él/ella en esa ocasión?	*2. What did he/she tell the police that you did to him/her on that occasion?*

Client's Present Legal Status

1. ¿Ha sido arrestado por un delito?	*1. Have you ever been arrested for a crime?*
2. ¿Le han retirado la acusación alguna vez?	*2. Have you ever had the case against you dropped?*
3. ¿Ha sido procesado y absuelto de toda culpa?	*3. Have you ever gone to trial and been found not guilty?*

4. ¿Ha sido declarado culpable de un delito, en este estado o en cualquier otro? ¿Cuántas veces?

4. *Have you ever been convicted of a crime, either in this state or any other? How many times?*

5. Le voy a preguntar acerca de cada condena previa por separado.

5. *I will ask you about each prior conviction separately.*

6. ¿Fue la primera/segunda/-tercera/cuarta/quinta condena un delito menor?

6. *Was the first/second/third-/fourth/fifth conviction a misdemeanor?*

¿Fue la primera/segunda/-tercera/cuarta/quinta condena un delito mayor?

Was the first/second/third-/fourth/fifth conviction a felony ?

7. ¿Por qué lo condenaron?

¿Por qué la condenaron?

7. *What was the conviction for?*

8. ¿Cuándo fue declarado culpable?

8. *When were you convicted?*

9. ¿En la actualidad, está en libertad condicional por este delito?

9. *Are you currently on parole for this offense?*

En la actualidad, está usted cumpliendo su período de prueba por este delito?

Are you currently on probation for this offense?

10. ¿Cuándo terminó su situación de libertad condicional?

10. *When did your parole status end?*

¿Cuándo terminó su situación de período de prueba?

When did your probation status end?

11. ¿Cómo se llama su más reciente funcionario que vigila a las personas que están en libertad?

11. *Who was your most recent parole officer?*

12. ¿En qué cuidad tenía él/ella su base?

12. *In what city was he/she based?*

Restraining Orders

1. ¿Ha solicitado la víctima una orden de interdicto contra usted en el pasado?	*1. Has the victim ever had a restraining order against you in the past?*
2. ¿Había solicitado la víctima una orden de interdicto contra usted al tiempo que él/ella dice que este delito ocurrió?	*2. Did the victim have a restraining order against you at the time he/she says this crime occurred?*
3. ¿Fue por violencia doméstica, agresión o abuso del cónyuge?	*3. Was it for domestic violence, assault or spousal abuse?*
4. ¿Cuándo obtuvo él/ella esa orden?	*4. When did he/she obtain that order?*
5. ¿Dónde se obtuvo esa orden?	*5. Where was that order obtained?*
6. ¿Cuándo él/ella acudió a la corte para obtener esa orden, lo/la acompañó usted?	*6. When he/she went to court to get that order, did you go too?*
7. ¿Cuándo se dio cuenta por primera vez que existía una orden de interdicto contra usted?	*7. When did you first become aware that there was a restraining order against you?*
8. ¿Quién lo/la notificó acerca de la orden de interdicto?	*8. Who served the restraining order on you?*
9. ¿Lo/la notificó la policía o un juez?	*8. Was it the police or a judge?*
10. ¿Tiene una copia de la orden?	*10. Do you have a copy of that order?*

Citizenship

1. ¿Es usted ciudadano estadounidense?

   ¿Es usted ciudadana estadounidense?

   1. Are you a US Citizen?

2. ¿Cuándo entró usted en Estados Unidos?

   2. When did you enter the U.S.?

3. ¿Tiene por qué cree que la policía sabe que usted está aquí ilegalmente?

   3. Do you have any reason to believe that the police know that you are here illegally?

4. ¿Está usted aquí en una visa? ¿Qué clase?

   4. Are you here on a visa? What kind?

5. ¿Tiene usted un permiso de residencia y trabajo?

   5. Do you have a green card?

Defense/Mitigators

1. ¿Una coartada es una excusa dada para indicar que al momento de la comisión de un delito, el sospechoso estaba en otro lugar. ¿Tiene usted una coartada?

   1. An alibi is a defense argued by a defendant claiming to have been elsewhere when the alleged crime was committed. Do you have an alibi?

2. ¿Posee usted documentos, como fotografías o recibos que apoya su historia?

   2. Do you have any documents, like photographs or receipts that back up your story?

3. ¿Hay testigos que pueden jurar en la corte que usted estaba con ellos al momento que se alega que usted cometió este delito?

   3. Do you have any witnesses who will swear in court that you were with them at the time you were supposed to have been committing this crime?

4. A veces el tribunal puede justificar el hecho que una persona ha violado la ley si existe un buen motivo. Por ejemplo, si le han acusado por conducir en estado de embriaguez, y usted en realidad conducía en estado de embriaguez, el trinunal podría permitirlo si usted llevaba a un amigo a la sala de emergencias del hospital. ¿Es esto algo semejante a lo que ocurrió con usted?

4. Sometimes the courts will excuse you from having broken the law if you have a very good reason. For instance, if you were charged with drunk driving, and you really were driving while drunk, it might still be allowed if you were rushing a friend to the hospital in an emergency. Does this sound like what happened with you?

Duress

1. ¿Hizo usted lo que le han acusado de hacer porque alguien lo/la amenazó?

1. Did you do what you are charged with because someone else threatened you?

2. ¿Hizo usted lo que le han acusado de hacer porque alguien amenazó a otra persona con hacerle daño o con la muerte si usted no lo hizo?

2. Did you do what you are charged with because someone else threatened another person with harm or death if you didn't do it?

3. ¿A quién le amenazaron con hacerle daño o a matar?

3. Who was the person that they threatened to harm or kill?

Self Defense/Defense of Others/Defense of Property

1. ¿Estaba la persona que usted lastimó en su propiedad al tiempo que usted usó fuerza contra esa persona?

1. Was the person you injured on your property at the time that you used force against them?

2. ¿Intentaba él/ella entrar en su casa?

2. Was he/she trying to enter your home?

3. ¿Ya estaba él/ella dentro de su casa?

3. Was he/she already in your home?

4. ¿Cuándo esto ocurrió, le parecía que usted u otra persona sería lastimada si usted no actuaba de inmediato?

4. At the time this happened, did you feel that if you failed to act immediately, either you or someone else would have been seriously hurt?

5.¿Cuándo esto ocurrió, le parecía que su propiedad sería seriamente dañada o destruida si usted no actuaba de inmediato?

5. At the time this happened, did you feel that if you failed to act immediately that property would have been seriously damaged or destroyed?

6. ¿Cuándo esto ocurrió, se defendía usted de un ataque?

6. Were you defending yourself from an attack at the time this occurred?

7. ¿Cuándo esto ocurrió, defendía usted a otra persona de un ataque?

7. Were you defending someone else from an attack at the time this occurred?

8. ¿A quién defendía?

8. Who were you defending?

Entrapment

1. El término legal "incitación por agentes de la ley a la comisión de un delito" tiene un sentido específico. Es un acto por el cual un agente de policía o un funcionario público induce a una persona a cometer un delito que de otra forma la persona no hubiera cometido?

1. The legal term "entrapment" has a very specific meaning. It means that, the police or somebody helping the police enticed you to do something which you would not have otherwise done.

2. Por ejemplo, el hecho de que una agente de policía se disfrazaba de prostituta no quiere decir que es una incitación por agentes de la ley a la comisión de un delito, especialmente si usted intentaba contratarla por sexo.

2. For example, the mere fact that a police officer was dressed up as a hooker is not entrapment, especially if you were trying to hire her for sexual purposes.

3. Pero si usted no intentaba contratar a una prostituta por sexo y una agente de policía disfrazada como una lo fastidió y fastidió hasta tal punto que usted acordó pagarle, eso sí podría ser incitación por agentes de la ley a la comisión de un delito. ¿A sabiendas de esto, le parece a usted fue incitado a la comisión de un delito?

3. But, if you had no intention of hiring a prostitute, and a police officer dressed as one bugged you and bugged you until you finally broke down and agreed to give her money, that may amount to entrapment. Knowing all of this, do you feel that you may have been entrapped?

Consent

1. ¿Le dio a usted la víctima su consentimiento para tener relaciones sexuales con él/ella?

1. Did the victim give you consent to have sex with him/her?

2. ¿Le dio a usted la víctima su consentimiento para llevar al niño consigo?

2. Did the victim give you consent to take the child with you?

3. ¿Le dio a usted la víctima su consentimiento para llevarlo/a consigo?

3. Did the victim give you consent to take him/her with you?

4. ¿Le dio a usted la víctima su consentimiento para detenerlo/a en un solo lugar, no dejarlo/a irse?

4. Did the victim give you consent to keep him/her in one place, or from leaving?

5. ¿Le dio a usted la víctima su consentimiento para llevarse consigo lo que la policía afirma que usted robó?

5. Did the victim give you consent to take whatever the police say you stole?

6. ¿Le dio a usted la víctima su consentimiento para hacer lo que le acusan de hacer?

5. Did the victim give you consent to do the thing that you are accused of?

Statute of Limitations

1. ¿Cuánto tiempo hace que ocurrió el delito, del cual se le acusa?

1. How long ago was the crime you are charged with committed?

2. ¿Cuánto tiempo hace que ocurrió el delito, del cual usted cree que le pudieran acusar?

2. How long ago was the crime that you think you may be charged with committed?

Insanity/Diminished Capacity

1. ¿Le parece a usted que en el momento de los hechos estaba en pleno uso de sus facultades?

1. Do you feel that you were in your right mind at the time you did this?

2. ¿Estaba usted enfurecido con la víctima?

2. Were you enraged at the victim?

Intoxication

1. ¿Estaba usted en estado de intemperancia y efecto de drogas en el momento cuándo esto ocurrió?

1. Were you intoxicate by drugs or alcohol at the time this occurred?

2. ¿Tomó el alcohol/la droga voluntariamente?

2. Did you take the drugs/alcohol yourself?

3. ¿Le puso alguien el alcohol o las drogos en la comida o bebida?

3. Did someone slip them into your food or drink?

4. ¿Estaba tomando droga recetada al tiempo de lo ocurrido?

4. Were you taking prescription medication at the time?

5. ¿Lo forzó alguien que tomara alcohol o drogas?

5. Did someone force you to drink or take drugs?

6. ¿Cuántos años tenía usted al tiempo que esto ocurrió?

6. How old were you at the time this occurred?

7. ¿Cuántos años tenía el niño al tiempo que esto ocurrió?

¿Cuántos años tenía la niña al tiempo que esto ocurrió?

7. How old was the child at the time this occurred?

Some Standard Responses/Admonitions/Advice

1. Usted va a necesitar la ayuda de un abogado con el asunto.

1. You will definitely need to have an attorney help you with this.

2. Probablemente le convendría contratar a un abogado?

2. You may wish to hire an attorney.

3. En este momento, no creo que usted necesita el servicio de un abogado?

3. At this time, I don't think that you need a lawyer.

Severity of the Situation

1. Le han acusado de un delito serio. Se llama delito mayor. Un delito mayor puede ser castigado con una pena de prisión mínima de al menos un año y una máxima de cinco a veinte años.

1. The matter with which you are charged is very serious. It is what is called a Felony. A felony is a crime that can get you a jail sentence of at least one year, and at a maximum five/ten/twenty years.

2. Además, delitos mayores generalmente son penalizados con una multa de hasta cincuenta/cien mil dólares.

2. *Also, felonies generally carry fines of up to fifty-thousand/one-hundred thousand dollars.*

3. Un delito menor es un crimen que puede ser castigado con una pena de prisión máxima de un año. Además, delitos menores generalmente son penalizados con una multa de hasta dos mil quinientos/cinco mil dólares.

3. *A misdemeanor is a crime with a maximum jail sentence of one year. Also, misdemeanors generally carry fines of up to Twenty-five hundred/five thousand dollars.*

3. Parece que la policía cree que usted ha cometido un delito mayor/menor.

3. *It appears that the police think that you have committed the crime of felony/misdemeanor.*

4. Yo creo que eventualmente lo van acusar de cometer un delito mayor/menor.

4. *I believe that you will eventually be charged with a felony/misdemeanor.*

5. No me parece que hay probabilidades de que le vayan acusar de un delito.

5. *I do not feel that it is likely that you will be charged with anything.*

6. No considero que usted ha cometido un delito.

6. *I do not believe that you have committed any crime.*

Referral

1. Quisiera mandarlo a consultar a un/a colega mío/mía que solamente trata de estos asuntos. ¿Está bien con usted?

1. *I would like to send you to see a colleague of mine who limits his/her practice to just this kind of matter. Is that okay with you?*

2. Creo que usted reúne los requisitos para que un abogado le será nombrado gratis.

2. *I believe that you may be qualified to have an attorney appointed to represent you at public expense.*

Advice: Dealing with the Police

1. Si la policía quiere hacerle más preguntas o si quiere interrogarlo en la comisaria, debe negárselo con buenos modelos y llamarme.

1. If the police come to ask you more questions or ask you to come to their station, you should definitely refuse them politely, and call me.

2. Si la policía quiere hacerle más preguntas o si quiere interrogarlo en la comisaria, dígale que no va a contestar ninguna pregunta sin la presencia de un abogado.

2. If the police come to ask you more questions or ask you to come to their station, tell them that you will not answer any questions without a lawyer.

3. No dé, bajo ninguna circunstancia, su consentimiento para que la policía lo cachee.

3. Do not, under any circumstance, consent to allow the police to search your person.

4. No dé, bajo ninguna circunstancia, su consentimiento para que la policía registre su domicilio, autos o cualquier cosa.

4. Do not, under any circumstance, consent to allow the police to search your home, vehicles or anything.

5. No dé, bajo ninguna circunstancia, su consentimiento para que la policía le saque sangre, se lleve muestras de su cabello, saliva o cualquier otra cosa.

5. Do not, under any circumstance, give your permission for the police or their agents to take your blood, your hair, saliva or anything else.

6. No le diga nada a la policía, bajo ninguna circunstancia, antes de consultar a un abogado.

6. Do not, under any circumstance, say anything to the police before contacting a lawyer.

7. Si tienen una orden, lo van a hacer de todos modos.

7. If they have a warrant, they will do it anyway.

8. Aunque no tengan una orden, es posible que intenten hacerlo con o sin su permiso.

8. Even if they do not have a warrant, they may try to do so with or without your permission.

9. No se resista a la autoridad si intenta detenerlo/a.

9. Do not resist the police if they try to take you into custody

10. No se resista a la autoridad si intenta tomar muestras de saliva, sangre o cualquier otra cosa.

10. Do not resist the police if they try to take specimens of saliva, blood or anything else.

11. No se resista a la autoridad si intenta cachearlo a usted, registrar su domicilio o auto sin su consentimiento.

11. Do not resist the police if they try to search you, your home or your car without your consent.

12. Recuerde que usted tiene el derecho de quedarse callado.

12. Remember that you have the right to remain silent.

13. No diga nada del todo hasta que se asesore con un abogado.

13. Keep quiet at all times, until a lawyer is with you to give you advice.

Talking To Others

1. En este momento es mejor si usted discute su caso solamente con un abogado.

1. At this point it is best if you only discuss your case with lawyers.

2. Nunca, bajo nunguna circunstancia, discute cualquier aspecto de su caso con otras personas a menos que su abogado esté con usted y le dé permiso a hablar con ellos.

2. Do not, under any circumstances, ever discuss any aspect of your case with anybody outside of your lawyer's office unless he or she is with you and he or she gives you permission to talk.

3. Si usted habla con otras personas acerca de este caso sin primero consultar a su abogado, casi cualquier pesona que habló con usted puede ser obligada a acudir al tribunal y repetir lo que usted le dijo, aunque usted no lo desee.

3. If you say anything about this case to anybody without first discussing whether or not you should with your lawyer, almost any of the persons you talk to can be made to come to court and repeat what you say, whether you want them to or not.

4. Usted es libre de discutir su caso con su sacerdote, rabino o ministro. Ellos no son obligados a revelar lo que usted les dijo.

4. You are free to discuss your case with your priest, rabbi or minister. They cannot be forced to tell anyone what you said to them.

5. En este estado su cónyuge no puede ser obligado/a a testificar en su contra a menos que usted le dé permiso. A esto se le llama privilegio conyugal, y le pertenece a usted, no a su esposo/a. Si usted dice que él/ella no debe hablar, entonces él/ella no lo puede hacer.

5. In this state, your spouse cannot be forced to come to court and testify against you unless you give permission. This is called the spousal immunity privilege, and it belongs to you, not your wife/husband. If you say that he/she cannot talk, then he/she cannot.

6. En este estado su cónyuge puede ser obligado/a a testificar en su contra, con o sin su permiso. Recomiendo no discutir aspectos de este caso con su cónyuge.

6. In this state, your spouse can be forced to come to court and testify against you, whether or not you give permission. I recommend that you do not speak about any aspect of this case with your spouse.

7. Usted puede ser acusado en el tribunal federal. En ese sistema de tribunal, la decisión de testificar en su contra le pertenece a su cónyuge y no a usted. Si, en cualquier momento, su cónyuge se enoja con usted, él/ella puede decir todo lo que sabe. Si él/ella no sabe nada, no hay nada que decir.

7. You may be charged in Federal Court. In that court system, the decision as to whether or not to testify against you belongs to your spouse, not you. If, at any point your spouse becomes angry at you, he/she may tell everything he/she knows. If he/she knows nothing, then there will be nothing to tell.

Release from Custody

1. Usted está aquí y no en la cárcel porque usted fue excarcelado/a por la corte.

1. The reason that you are here and not in jail right now is that you have been released from custody by the court.

2. Le otorgaron la libertad provisional bajo caución juratoria. Esto quiere decir que usted no tuvo que pagar la fianza.

2. You were released on your own recognizance. This means that you did not have to post any bail.

3. Le otorgaron la libertad provisional bajo caución juratoria. Esto quiere decir que a la corte le parece que lo que usted hizo no es muy serio.

3. You were released on your own recognizance.This means that the court feels that what you are accused of doing is not very serious.

4. Le otorgaron la libertad provisional bajo caución juratoria. Esto quiere decir que usted no es una persona peligrosa.

4. You were released on your own recognizance.This means that you are not a dangerous person.

5. Le otorgaron la libertad provisional bajo caución juratoria. Esto quiere decir que usted es una persona que probablemente no va a fugarse.

5. You were released on your own recognizance.This means that you are not a person who is likely to run away.

6. Le otorgaron la libertad provisional bajo caución juratoria. Esto quiere decir que usted probablemente acudirá a todas las fechas de corte.

6. You were released on your own recognizance.This means that you will probably show up for all of your court dates.

7. Le otorgaron la libertad provisional bajo caución juratoria. Esto quiere decir que el caso contra usted podría ser muy débil.

7. You were released on your own recognizance.This means that he case against you may be very weak.

4. Le otorgaron la libertad provisional bajo caución juratoria. Esto quiere decir que sus antecedentes penales previos son inexistentes o no demasiado terribles.	*4. You were released on your own recognizance.This means that your past criminal record is either non-existent or not too bad.*
5. Existen varias cosas que la corte le han puesto como condiciones. Si usted no cumple con cualquier aspecto de las condiciones, lo pueden encarcelar de nuevo.	*5. There are certain conditions which the court has placed upon you. If you fail to comply with any of these conditions, you can be taken back to jail.*
6. Usted tiene que permanecer en contacto con el/la fiador/a personal.	*6. You must stay in contact with your third-party custodian.*
7. Usted tiene que permanecer dentro de los límites del domicilio al que fue devuelto.	*7. You must stay within the confines of the home you were released to.*
8. Usted tiene que obedecer todas las leyes. Si lo paran por cruzar la calzada con riesgo de provocar un accidente, lo pueden encarcelar de nuevo.	*8. You must obey all laws. If you get stopped for jay-walking, they could throw you back into jail.*
9. Tiene que acudir al tribunal para todas las fechas de corte y tiene que llegar a tiempo. Sugiero que siempre llegue temprano.	*9. You must show up in court for any and all court dates, and you must be there on time. I suggest that you always get there early.*
10. Tiene que citarse de inmediato con el funcionario que vigila a las personas que están en libertad, si no lo ha hecho.	*10. You must meet with a probation officer immediately, if you have not already done so.*
11. Tiene que llevar puesto la pulsera de seguimiento electrónica.	*11. You must wear the electronic monitoring bracelet.*

12. Usted tiene que instalar un dispositivo de llave del arranque interlock en su coche.

12. You must install an ignition interlock device on your car.

13. Usted tiene que presentarse inmediatamente en un programa de ayuda para alcohólicos en rehabilitación.

13. You must report to a drug and alcohol rehabilitation program immediately.

14. Usted tiene que permanecer en contacto con su abogado.

14. You must stay in touch with your lawyer.

15. Debe evitar todo contacto con la/las supuesta/s víctima/s.

15. You must not have any contact with the alleged victim/victims.

16. Esto incluye los hijos de la víctima, aunque también sean sus hijos.

16. This includes the victim's kids, even if they are also your children.

17. Usted no debe llamarlos por teléfono ni aceptar sus llamadas telefónicas.

17. You must not call them on the phone or accept calls from them.

18. Usted no debe visitarlos en su casa, aunque también sea la casa suya y aunque ellos digan que usted puede visitarlos.

18. You must not visit them at their home, even if it is also your home, and even if they say it is okay.

19. Usted no debe enviarles cartas ni tarjetas postales.

19. You must not send them letters or postcards.

20. Terceros no pueden enviarles mensajes por su parte.

20. You must not have a third party send them a message for you.

21. Usted no debe tomar bebidas alcohólicas.

21. You must not consume any alcohol.

22. Usted no debe conducir.

22. You must not operate a motor vehicle.

23. Usted no debe tomar drogas ilegales.

23. You must not take any illegal drugs.

Violation of Release Terms

1. Si lo encarcelan de nuevo por violar las condiciones de su puesta en libertad, la persona que pagó la fianza probablemente perderá ese dinero.

1. If you are taken back to jail for violating the conditions of your release, whoever posted bail for you will probably lose that money .

2. Probablemente tendrá que permanecer en la cárcel hasta que el asunto se resuelva. Eso quiere decir que si el caso va a juicio en tres meses a partir de ahora, usted va a tener que pasar ese tiempo en la cárcel.

2. You will probably have to stay in jail until this matter is completely resolved. That means that if you go on trial three months from now, you will spend that entire three months locked up.

3. Si lo encarcelan de nuevo por violar las condiciones de su puesta en libertad, puede empeorar su caso.

3. If you are taken back to jail for violating the conditions of your release, it can make getting you out of this first mess even harder.

Fundamental Constitutional Rights as a Defendant

1. Bajo la Constitución de Estados Unidos y de este estado, el/la acusado/a tiene ciertos derechos. La corte debe suponer que usted es inocente y obrar en consecuencia.

1. Under the United States Constitution and the Constitution of this State, as an accused person, you have certain rights.You are presumed by the courts to be innocent and are to be treated accordingly.

2. El gobierno tiene que probar, fuera de toda duda razonable, que un delito fue cometido y que usted fue la persona que lo cometió.

2. The government has to prove, beyond a reasonable doubt, that a crime was committed and that you are the person who committed it.

3 Usted tiene el derecho de juicio con jurado o juicio con juez.

3. You have the right to trial by jury or trial by judge.

4. Usted tiene el derecho de decidir quien será miembro del jurado. Usted tiene el derecho de excluir algunas personas del jurado porque usted no quiere que sean miembros.

4. You have the right to have a say in who sits on the jury. You have the right to exclude some people from the jury just because you don't want them on it.

5. Usted tiene el derecho de ser representado por un abogado todo el tiempo.

5. You have the right to have a lawyer represent you at all times.

6. Usted tiene el derecho de que su abogado les haga preguntas a los testigos de la acusación.

6. You have the right to have your lawyer ask questions of any witness that the government tries to use against you

7. Usted tiene el derecho de examinar todas las pruebas presentadas en su contra antes de ir a juicio.

7. You have the right to examine any and all evidence presented to the court against you in advance of going to court.

Opinion

1. Es mi opinión, basado en lo que usted me ha dicho y en lo que yo he observado, que lo van a declarar culpable del cargo.

1. It is my opinion that, based upon everything that you have told me and everything I have seen, that you are probably going to be convicted of this charge.

2. Es mi opinión, basado en lo que usted me ha dicho y en lo que yo he observado, que usted puede ganar este caso.

2. It is my opinion that, based upon everything that you have told me and everything I have seen, that you have a chance at beating this charge.

3. No creo que el gobierno puede probar todos los elementos del delito que le acusan de cometer.

3. I do not believe that the government can prove all of the elements of the crime you are charged with.

4. Es mi opinión, basado en lo que usted me ha dicho y en lo que yo he observado, que usted es la persona que cometió el delito.

4. *It is my opinion that, based upon everything that you have told me and everything I have seen, that you are the one who committed the crime.*

5. Creo que podemos convencer a un juez/jurado que existe duda razonable que un delito fuera cometido.

5. *I think that we can convince a judge/jury that there is a reasonable doubt as to whether a crime was actually committed.*

6. Creo que podemos convencer a un juez/jurado que existe duda razonable en cuanto a la persona que cometió el delito.

6. *I think that we can convince a judge/jury that there is a reasonable doubt as to who committed the crime.*

7. Creo que podemos convencer a un juez/jurado que existe duda razonable en cuanto a la validez de la denuncia contra usted.

7. *I think that we can convince a judge/jury that there is a reasonable doubt as to the validityof the victim's complaint against you.*

8. Según todo lo que usted me ha dicho, no sé si puede ser declarado culpable o no.

8. *From everything you have told me, I cannot tell whether you might or might not be convicted.*

Retain / Referral / Conflict

1. Para poder darle consejos y opiniones más detallados, usted necesitará contratarme para representarlo en la corte. Esto me permitirá coseguir los informes policiales, documentos, fotografías, grabaciones y cualquier otras pruebas que la acusación tiene en su contra. Entonces puedo hacer más indagaciones y darle mis consejos.

1. *In order to be able to give you more detailed advice and opinion, I will need to be hired to represent you. This will enable me to get ahold of all of the police reports, documents, photos, recordings and any other evidence the government has against you. Then I can investigate further and tell you what I think.*

2. Para asegurar sus drechos de defenderse en la corte, le voy a dar cl nombre de otro abogado que habla español y que es abogado de defensa penal.

2. *In order to make sure that your rights are being fully defended, I am going to give you the name of another attorney who speaks Spanish (and) who practices a lot of criminal defense law.*

3. Lamentablemente, no puedo discutir este asunto con usted más a fondo. Por razones que no puedo discutir con nadie, tengo que mandarlo a otro abogado.

3 *Unfortunately I am unable to discuss this matter with you any further. For reasons which I am unable to discuss with anybody, I have to refer you to another attorney.*

TORTS

Plaintiffs in vehicular accidents, civil assault and civil battery cases only

Notes to endusers! This section is not intended as a comprehensive treatment of the subject. Rather, it is designed to allow the legal professional to gin out legal issues through a dialogue with the client, and to offer competent advice. Furthermore, this is not a legal outline. Nothing in this section should be deemed as a substitute for your own professional, competent legal knowledge. Several parts of this section contain majority and minority rules, which means that you the legal professional must make a determination as to which phrase(s) need to be selected.

Notes to lawyers: how to use this section

You should familiarize yourself with the organization of this section. It is organized so as to allow you to skip from section to section depending upon the answers which are given at any particular point. Knowing in advance when to skip ahead and where to skip ahead to will make the process much faster, seamless and productive.

Attorney/client privilege admonitions

Often times a potential **tort/personal injury** client will come to a lawyer with a spouse or other family members. Although this is nice on some level (it helps the client relax a bit and stay a bit more focused), there are legal and practical issucs to consider.

Before you begin the actual intake interview and asking substantive questions about the matter(s) the client is there to discuss, you will need to pull the client away from his/her spouse and/or family and have a private discussion with him/her. A diplomatic way to present this to the spouse is as follows on the next page:

1. Antes de empezar, voy a tener que hablar con ________________ un momento en privado.	*1. Before I begin, I will have to speak to ________________ privately for a moment.*
2. Hay unas cuestiones legales que son muy importantes. Eso me obliga ha hablar con él/ella al principio en privado.	*2. There are a some important legal issues which I am only allowed to talk with him about at first.*
3. Después de nuestras conversaciones iniciales, usted puede entrar mientras continuemos la dicusión.	*3. It is possible that after we talk, you will be able to come into the room while we discuss matters further.*
4. Tengo que hacer esto. De este modo puedo darle a ________________ la mejor representación legal posible.	*4. Please understand that I always have to do it this way in order to be certain that I am giving ________________ the best legal representation I possibly can.*

It is very important to say this to the spouse for a couple of reasons. First, from a practical standpoint, the client may not be inclined to fully and openly discuss a case in front of a spouse. You can serve as the interference person who interjects the legal necessity of a private meeting, thereby relieving the client of the pressure of having to ask a loved one to wait outside. The second, and equally important reason for this step is to be able to privately advise the client about the attorney-client privilege.

Critical Admonition(s) to the client regarding attorney/client privilege

The following statement should be made to the client, with no one other than the attorney present. Although staff, other attorneys and paralegals may be covered by the privilege, many people from Spanish speaking cultures have an extremely difficult time trusting authority figures when it comes to private legal matters. A good rule of thumb is, the fewer people in the room the better.

1. Usted vino a discutir un asunto civil. Sin embargo, a veces cuestiones de responsabilidades criminales pueden surgir.

1. It is important to know that, even though you are here to discuss a civil matter with me, sometimes issues of criminal liability may arise.

2. Por ejemplo, si usted estuviera envuelto en un accidente de coche mientras conducía en estado de embriaguez, tuviera que explicarle cómo afectaría su caso por lesiones además de explicarle sus derechos como posible acusado en un proceso criminal.

2. For example, if you were involved in a car crash in which you were driving while intoxicated, I would have to tell you about both how that would affect your injury case and your rights as a potential criminal defendant.

3. Cada vez que usted viene a mi bufete, todo lo que discutimos es totalmente confidencial.

3. Any time that you come to my office, everything that you and I talk about is completely confidential.

4. Eso quiere decir que nadie, ni su familia, ni la policía, ni los tribunales pueden recibir información acerca de nuestras conversaciones sin su permiso.

4. That means that nobody, not your family, not the police, not the courts, can get any information about anything that you and I discuss, without your permission.

5. No me pueden obligar a discutir nuestras conversaciones con terceros. Además, yo nunca discutiré su caso fuera de este bufete con otros sin su permiso.

5. I cannot be made to tell anybody about our conversations, and I will never discuss your case outside of this office with anybody without your permission.

6. Esto se denomina secreto profesional entre abogado y cliente en el sistema judicial estadounudense.

6. The U.S. Legal system calls this the Attorney-Client privilege.

7. Esta norma existe para permitir que un cliente le explique a su abogado todo detalle acerca de su caso. No importa si usted cree que es ilegal o que es muy vergonzoso.

7. *This rule exists in order to allow you to tell me every single detail about your case, no matter how illegal you may think it is, and no matter how embarrassing it may be.*

8. Si usted me da cuenta de todo lo que sabe acerca de su caso, entonces le puedo dar el mejor consejo posible.

8. *If you tell me everything that you know I can give you the best help I am capable of.*

9. Si no me revela toda la verdad, puedo hacer o decir algo que resulte perjudicial para su caso debido a que no sé la verdad en su totalidad.

9. *If you hold back part of the truth, I may end up doing things that turn out to be harmful to your case, just because I don't know the entire truth.*

10. Le voy a hacer preguntas. Usted deber responder sinceramente y dar respuestas completas.

10. *Please know that you can and must answer the questions that I am going to ask completely and truthfully.*

11. El derecho a la protección legal que le otorga el secreto profesional entre abogado y cliente se puede perder. Tenemos que proteger este derecho y no hacer nada que lo ponga en peligro.

11. *The legal protection you get from the attorney-client privilege can be lost, so we must be very careful to protect it and to not do anything that might cause it to disappear.*

12. Se puede perder si discutimos su caso en la presencia de terceros.

12. *The main way that it can be lost is if you and I discuss your case in front of a third party.*

13. Por ejemplo, si usted me dice que sufrió un accidente de coche mientras estaba borracho, ese secreto sería protegido bajo la norma y no quedaría al descubierto conmigo.

13. For example, if you were to tell me that you crashed a car while you were drunk, your secret would be absolutely protected and safe with me.

14. Si me dijera usted lo mismo en presencia de un amigo, un juez puede ordenar que el amigo comparezca ante el tribunal y revele lo que usted dijo.

14 If you told me the same thing, but your best friend was in the room at the time, a judge may be able order your friend to come to court and tell everyone that you admitted to all of that.

Optional Parts

1. El mismo tipo de privilegio existe entre un matrimonio.

1. The same sort of privilege of secrecy exists between married people.

2. Uno puede hablar con su cónyuge y ser franco con él/ella.

2. You are supposed to talk to your spouse and be honest with him/her.

3. Según la ley, la importancia de un matrimonio feliz tiene más peso que cualquier otra consideración, incluso lo que uno discute con su cónyuge.

3. The law says that the importance of a good marriage outweighs the need to know what you may have told your spouse.

4. Por esta razón, algunos abogad0s permiten que el conyúge asista las reuniones.

Por esta razón, algunos abogados permiten que la conyúge asista las reuniones.

4. Because of this, some lawyers tell their clients that it is okay to have the spouse in the room while we meet.

5. Hay dos maneras en que uno puede contemplar la situación.

5. There are two ways of looking at the situation.

6. En primer lugar, tener una buena relación con el cónyuge es muy importante.

En primer lugar, tener una buena relación con la cónyuge es muy importante.

6. The first way to see it is that it is indeed very important to have a good relationship with your spouse.

7. No dejar al cónyuge participar en las conversaciones acerca del caso puede causar sospechas. No sabe si usted ha sido franco con él.

No dejar a la cónyuge participar en las conversaciones acerca del caso puede causar sospechas. No sabe si usted ha sido franco con ella.

7. Keeping your spouse out of the room when we talk about your case could make him/her suspicious about what you are telling me, or, whether or not you have been telling him/her the truth.

8. En segundo lugar, algunos cónyuges no pueden mantener la información en secreto.

8. The other way of looking at it is that some spouses have a hard time keeping a secret.

9. Si su cónyuge está en el cuarto cuando usted me dice que estaba borracho cuando sufrió el accidente de coche, y ella se lo repite a otra persona, esto puede perjudicar su caso seriamente.

Si su cónyuge está en el cuarto cuando usted me dice que estaba borracha cuando sufrió el accidente de coche, y él se lo repite a otra persona, esto puede perjudicar su caso seriamente.

9. If your spouse were in the room when you told me that you were drunk when you wrecked a car, and then he/she were to let it slip to a friend that you confessed, it could seriously hurt your case.

10. Puede ser que podamos o no controlar el daño.

10. We may or may not be able to control the damage.

11. El mejor modo de mantener los secretos privados es limitar el número de personas que sepan de ellos.

11. The best way to keep secret matters private is to strictly limit the number of people who know them.

12. Basándose en todo lo que le he dicho, es usted quien debe decidir si su cónyuge puede estar presente durante nuestras conversaciones acerca de su caso.

12. Based upon all of the things I just told you, you alone must decide whether or not you want your spouse in the room when we talk about your case.

13. Yo recomiendo que no permita a otros participar en nuestras conversaciones, aparte de los miembros de mi personal. A ellos se les garantiza la misma protección del secreto profesional entre abogado y cliente.

13. I recommend that you do not allow anybody into the room when we talk, other than members of my staff who share the same attorney client privilege.

14. Su caso es demasiado serio, las consecuencias pueden ser muy severas, y éste es el camino más seguro a seguir.

14. Your case is much too serious, the consequences are too severe, and this is simply the safest course of action.

15. Quizá usted querrá decirle a su cónyuge que le aconsejé que no permita a nadie asistir a nuestras reuniones, no solamente a ella.

15. You may want to tell your spouse that I advised you to keep everyone out, not just her.

Quizá usted querrá decirle a su cónyuge que le aconsejé que no permita a nadie asistir a nuestras reuniones, no solamente a él.

You may want to tell your spouse that I advised you to keep everyone out, not just him.

16. Dígale que le aconsejé que no discutiera este caso con nadie, ni con ella.

    Dígale que le aconsejé que no discutiera este caso con nadie, ni con él.

16. *You may want to tell your spouse that I advised you to keep everyone out, not just her.*

    You may want to tell your spouse that I advised you to keep everyone out, not just him.

17. Echándome la culpa puede ayudar a paliar la tensión a la que está sometida debido a la la situación.

    Echándome la culpa puede ayudar a paliar la tensión a la que está sometido debido a la la situación.

17. *Putting the blame on me helps to ease any tension she might feel over the situation.*

    Putting the blame on me helps to ease any tension he might feel over the situation.

18. Le dejo a usted la elección de decidir si quiere que su cónjuge asista nuestras reuniones o no.

18. *I leave it up to you to decide whether or not you want your spouse in the room when we talk.*

Preliminary Questions for Persons Injured in Vehicular Accidents

1. ¿Se lastimó en un accidente de coche?

   ¿Resultó herido en el accidente de coche?

1. *Were you injured in a car accident?*

2. ¿Conducía usted

2. *Were you the driver?*

3. ¿Quién conducía el coche en el que usted viajaba?

3. *Who was driving the car you were in?*

4. Está usted emparentado con el conductor del coche en el que vijaba?

4. *Are you related to the driver of the vehicle you were in?*

6. ¿Era usted el pasajero?

6. Were you the passenger?

7. ¿Cómo conoce usted al conductor del coche en el que usted viajaba?

7. How do you know the driver of the car you were in?

8. ¿Le pilló otro coche mientras ...
   caminaba?
   andaba en bicicleta?
   viajaba en motocicleta?
   viajaba en autobús?
   viajaba en taxi?
   viajaba en una ambulancia?

8. Were you hit by another car while ...
   walking?
   bicycling?
   riding a motorcycle?
   riding a bus?
   riding a taxi cab?
   riding in an ambulance?

9. ¿Cuándo sucedió el accidente?

9. When did the accident occur?

10. Dónde sucedió el accidente?
   Sucedió en este estado?
   Sucedió en el condado de ______________?
   Sucedió en la ciudad de ______________.

10. Where did the accident occur?
   Was it in this state?
   Was it in the county of ______________?
   Was it in the city of ______________?

11. ¿Sucedió el accidente ...
   en un estacionamiento?
   en una calle de la ciudad?
   en la carretera?
   en una entrada privada?

11. Did this accident occur ...
   in a parking lot?
   on a city street?
   on the highway?
   in a private driveway?

12. ¿Se lastimó alguien más en el accidente?

12. Was anybody else hurt in the accident?

13. ¿Viajaban ellos en el auto con usted?

13. Were they riding in the car with you?

14. ¿Cuántas otras personas se lastimaron, aun cuando levemente?

14. How many other people were injured, even slightly?

General Liability Questions for Persons Injured in Vehicular Accidents

1. ¿Le pilló una persona que... conducía?	1. *Were you hit by person... in a car?*
que conducía un coche de compañía?	*driving a car for a company?*
un vehículo perteneciente al gobierno?	*a government vehicle?*
2. ¿Era un camión o coche perteneciente a la ciudad?	2. *Was it a city truck or car?*
3. ¿Era un vehículo perteneciente al estado?	3. *Was it a state vehicle?*
4. ¿Oyó o vio algo que le dio a entender que el otro conductor involucrado en el accidente utilizaba el coche para uso comercial, como para transporte?	4. *Did you hear or see anything that leads you to believe that the person you were in the accident with was driving their vehicle for work purpose, such as making a delivery?*
5. ¿Le pilló un vehículo perteneciente a la ciudad?	5. *Were you hit by a city vehicle?*
6. ¿Tenía el vehículo que le pilló un letrero o logotipo en el lado?	6. *Were you hit by a vehicle with a sign or logo on the side?*
7. ¿Era un taxi? ¿Un autobús? ¿Una limusina?	7. *Was it a taxicab? A bus? A limousine?*
8. ¿Era un camión de transporte, como un camión con remolque o un camión de carga?	8. *Was it a comercial transport truck, like a semi, or a large cargo truck?*
9. ¿Es el dueño del vehículo el otro conductor envuelto en el accidente con usted?	9. *Was the person you were in the accident with the owner of the vehicle he was driving?*

Factual Issues

1. ¿Estaba su coche en movimiento en el momento del accidente?
   1. Was your car moving at the time of the accident?

2. ¿Conducía usted en la calle?
   2. Were you driving on the road?

3. ¿En qué calle??
   3. Which road?

4. ¿Sabe cómo se llama la calle traviesa cercana?
   4. Do you know which cross-street you were near?

5. ¿Era la calle recta o curvada?
   5. Was the street straight or was it curved?

6. ¿Conducía usted dentro del carril?
   6. Were you in your lane?

7. ¿Conducía usted en la carretera? ¿En cuál?
   7. Were you on the highway? Which one?

8. ¿Salía de la carretera en ese momento?
   8. Were you getting off the highway at the time?

9. ¿Entraba en la carretera en ese momento?
   9. Were you getting on the highway at the time?

10. ¿Tomaba usted una curva?
    10. Were you turning a corner?

11. ¿Estaba usted en un cruce de cuatro direcciones?
    11. Were you at a four-way intersection?

12. ¿Giraba a la izquierda o a la derecha?
    12. Were you turning left or right?

13. ¿Cruzaba tráfico que venía en sentido opuesto?
    13. Were you turning across oncoming traffic?

14. ¿Venía el coche envuelto en el accidente justo hacia usted o de lado?
    14. Was the car you collided with coming from straight ahead or from the side?

15. ¿Había semáforo? ¿Estaba la flecha en verde?

15. Were there traffic lights? Did you have a green arrow?

16. ¿Estaba su coche en un estacionamiento?

16. Were you in a parking lot?

17. ¿Salía usted de un lugar de estacionamiento?

17. Were you pulling out of a parking spot?

18. ¿Salía la otra parte de un lugar de estacionamiento?

18. Was the other party pulling out of a parking lot?

19. ¿Caminaba usted a su coche?

19. Were you going to your car?

20. ¿Estaba su coche detenido?

20. Were you stopped?

21. ¿Estaba usted parado en un semáforo en rojo o en una señal de alto?

21. Were you at a light or a stop sign?

22. ¿Tenía el coche estacionado?

22. Were you parked?

23. ¿Estaba el coche engranado o en punto muerto?

¿Estaba el coche engranado o en la posición "P"?

23. Was your car in gear or was it in park?

24. ¿Dejó puesto el freno de emergencia?

24. Was your emergency brake on?

25. ¿Funcionaba bien el coche?

25. Was your car working properly?

26. ¿Funcionaba la señal de dirección?

26. Was your turn signal working?

27. ¿Funcionaban las luces de freno?

27. Did your brake lights work?

Fault

1. ¿Cree que usted tiene la culpa por este accidente?

1. Do you believe you were at fault for this accident?

2. ¿Cree que el otro conductor tiene la culpa?

   ¿Cree que la otra conductora tiene la culpa?

2. Do you believe that the other driver was at fault?

3. ¿Se pasó una señal en alto?

3. Did you run a stop sign?

4. ¿Se pasó un semáforo en rojo?

4. Did you run a red light?

5. ¿Se pasaron una señal en alto o un semáforo en rojo?

5. Did they run a stop sign or a stop light?

6. ¿Se pasaron un semáforo en rojo?

6. Did they run a red light?

7. ¿Cruzaron el carril central al chocar contra su coche?

7. Did they cross over the center line and hit you?

Evidentiary Questions For Vehicular Accidents

1. ¿Acudió la policía al lugar del accidente?

1. Did the police come to the scene of the accident?

2. ¿Se acuerda cuántos policías se encontraban allí? ¿Cuántos?

2. Do you remember how many police officers were there? How many?

3. ¿Habló algún agente de policía con usted?

3. Did any of the police officers talk to you?

4. ¿Lo arrestaron por causa del accidente?

4. Were you arrested because of the accident?

5. ¿Lo multaron por causa del accidente?

5. Were you given a citation because of the accident?

6. ¿Trajo la multa consigo?

6. Do you have the citation with you?

7. ¿Sabe por qué lo multaron?

7. Do you know what the citation was for?

8. ¿Sabe cuándo debe acudir a los tribunales la próxima vez? ¿Cuándo?

8. Do you know when you are supposed to go to court next? When?

9. ¿Acudieron al lugar del accidente bomberos o personal de los servicios de emergencia?

9. Did any fire department personnel or emergency medical personnel come to the scene of the accident?

10. ¿Sabe quién hizo la llamada?

10. Do you know who called them?

11. ¿Hizo la llamada alguien con quien usted viajaba?

11. Did someone you were riding with call them?

12. ¿Habló con usted algún agente del servicio de emergencia?

12. Did any of the emergency service people talk to you?

13. ¿Le hizo preguntas algún agente del servicio de emergencia?

13. Did any of the emergency service people ask you any questions?

14. ¿Le hizo preguntas acerca del accidente algún agente del servicio de emergencia?

14. Did any of the emergency service people ask you about the accident?

15. ¿Le administró tratamiento médico algún personal del servicio de emergencia?

15. Did any of the emergency service people give you medical treatment?

16. ¿Le sacó sangre algún personal del servicio de emergencia?

16. Did any of the emergency service people take any blood from you?

17. ¿Le entablillaron o le enseyaron una pierna o brazo?

17. Did you have any splints or casts applied?

18. ¿Entabló usted conversación con ellos acerca del accidente sin que ellos le hicieran preguntas acerca del mismo?

18. Did you talk to them about the accident without being asked questions?

19. ¿Lo trasladaron a un hospital o a un consultorio médico?	19. *Did they transport you to a hospital or to a doctor?*
20. ¿Cuál hospital?	20. *Which hospital?*
21. ¿Cuál consultorio médico?	21. *Which doctor?*
22. ¿Ha visitado al médico?	22. *Have you been to see a doctor?*
23. ¿Cuánto tiempo después del accidente visitó al médico por primera vez?	23. *How long was it after the accident that you first saw a doctor?*
24. ¿Estaba consciente cuando visitó al médico?	24. *Were you conscious at the time you went to the doctor?*
25. ¿Pidió que le trasladaran al hospital en el lugar del accidente?	25. *Did you ask to be taken to the hospital at the scene of the accident?*
26. ¿Se despertó en el hospital?	26. *Did you wake up at the hospital?*
27. ¿Le atendió un médico?	27. *Did the doctor perform medical services on you?*
28. ¿Le suturaron una herida?	28. *Did you receive stitches?*
29. ¿Le sacaron una radiografía?	29. *Were you X-rayed?*
30. ¿Lo sometieron a una intervención quirúrgica?	30. *Was any surgery performed?*
31. ¿Lo sometieron a una intervención quirúrgica para .... soldar los huesos? controlar el sangramien-interno?	31. *Was it to ......* *set bones?* *stop internal bleeding?*

32. ¿Le administró medicamento el médico?
    ¿Eran píldoras?
    ¿Le pusieron una inyección?

32. Were you given any drugs by the doctor?
    Were they pills?
    By injection?

33. ¿Le adsministró calmantes o sedantes inmediatamente después del accidente ...
    un médico?
    el personal de servicio de emergencia?

33. Were you given any pain killers, tranquilizers or sedatives immediately after the accident, by...............
    a doctor
    emergency medical personnel?

34. Después de su tratamiento, ¿le recetaron medicina?

34. Was any medicine prescribed for you to pick up at a pharmacy after you were treated?

35. ¿Tiene la receta consigo, y si no, recuerda lo que era?

35. Do you have it with you or do you recall what it was?

36. Mientras estaba en el lugar del accidente......
    ¿intercambió información, tal como permisos de conducción, nombres, apellido y dirrecciones, con la otra parte?
    ¿consiguió la información del seguro de la otra parte?

36. While you were at the scene of the accident, ...
    did you exchange personal information, such as driver's licenses, names, last names and addresses, with the other party?
    did you get insurance information from the other party?

37. Informó la otra parte que tenía cobertura de seguro de auto? ¿Tiene la información consigo? ¿Me la puede dar lo antes posible?

37. Did the other party say that they had car insurance coverage? Do you have that information with you? Can you get that information to me very soon?

38. ¿Contaba usted con cobertura de seguro de auto en el momento del accidente?

38. Did you have car insurance coverage at the time of the accident?

39. ¿Se lo informó a la otra parte?

39. Did you tell the other party?

40. ¿Se puso en contacto con su compañía de seguros? ¿Cuándo?

40 .Did you contact your insurance company? When did you do that?

41. ¿Sabe el nombre y número de teléfono de la persona con quien usted habló?

41. Do you know the name and phone number of the person you spoke with?

42. ¿Ha discutido los acontecimientos del caso con alguna otra persona?

42. Have you duscussed this case with anyone?

43. ¿Con su cónyuge?

43. With your spouse?

44. ¿Con otro abogado?

44. With another lawyer?

45. ¿Con un amigo?

45. With a friend?

46. ¿Con otros familiares?

46. With other family members?

Assault And Battery Questions

1. ¿Intentó tocar a otra persona?	1. *Did you attempt to touch another person?*
2. ¿Tocó a otra persona?	2. *Did you touch another person?*
3. ¿Le tocó alguien a usted?	3. *Did someone touch you?*
4. ¿Quién le tocó?	4. *Who was it?*
5. ¿Con qué le tocó él?	5. *What did he touch you with?*
6. ¿Con qué le tocó ella?	6. *What did she touch you with?*
7. ¿Le dolió eso?	7. *Did that hurt?*
8. ¿Había sangre?	8. *Was there any blood?*
9. ¿Cuántas veces le tocó él?	9. *How many times did he touch you?*
10. ¿Cuántas veces le tocó ella?	10. *How many times did she touch you?*
11. ¿Les dio usted un puñetazo?	11. *Did you throw a punch at them?*
12. ¿Le dio un puñetazo ...... en el estómago? en la cara? en la nariz?	12. *Did you punch him ......* *in the stomach?* *in the face?* *on the nose?*
13. ¿Se dieron puñetazos?	13. *Did you trade punches?*
14. ¿Los empujó?	14. *Did you shove them?*
15. ¿Los empujó contra la pared?	15. *Did you shove them against the wall?*

17. ¿Los agarró.	17. *Did you grab them?*
18. ¿Lo agarró del brazo?	18. *Did you grab him by the arm?*
19. ¿La agarró del brazo?	19. *Did you grab her by the arm?*
20. ¿Le agarraron del brazo?	20. *Did they grab you by the arm?*
21. ¿Tocó usted parte de la persona?	21. *Did you touch part of them?*
22. ¿Intentó agarrarles la ropa?	22. *Did you grab at their clothing?*
23. ¿Le hizo caer algo de la mano?	23. *Did you knock something out of his hand*
24. ¿Le tocó a usted otra persona?	24. *Did another person touch you?*
25. ¿Alguien le dio un puñetazo o le empujó?	25. *Did someone punch or shove you?*
26. ¿Le agarraron?	26. *Did they grab at you?*
27. ¿Le rozaron ligeramente?	27. *Did they touch part of you?*
28. ¿Le hicieron caer algo de la mano?	28. *Did they knock something out of your hand?*
29. ¿Se sintió agredido/a?	29. *Did you see the attack coming?*
30. ¿Fue atacado/a?	30. *Were you under attack?*
31. ¿Se dejó expuesto/a a un ataque?	31. *Did you leave yourself open to attack?*

32. ¿Se les venía encima por adelante, por el lado o por detrás?

32. *Did you come at them from the front, the side or the back?*

33. ¿Se le venían encima por adelante, por el lado o por detrás?

33. *Did they come at you from the front, the side or the back?*

34. ¿Se le venía encima con un cuchillo?

34. *Did she come at you with a knife?*

35. ¿Hizo usted contacto físico con ellos?

35. *Did you make contact with them?*

36. ¿Los tocó usted suave o duramente?

36. *Did you touch them softly or hard?*

37. ¿Le tocaron a usted suave o duramente?

37. *Did they touch you softly or hard?*

38. ¿Cuántas veces le pegaron a usted?

38. *How many times did they hit you?*

39. ¿Cuántas veces les pegó usted?

39. *How many times did you hit them?*

General Advice: Distinguishing Assault from Battery

1. En derecho civil, los términos "asalto" y "agresión" quieren decir dos cosas distintas.

1. *In civil law, "assault" and "battery" mean two different things.*

2. Para asaltar a alguien, la persona tiene que tener miedo de ser dañada.

2. *To assault someone, you have to put them in fear of being harmed.*

3. Para cometer agresión uno tiene que tocar a la persona de algún modo.

3. *To commit battery, a person has to touch them in some way.*

The Plaintiff Must Prove The Following

1. ¿Hubo un acto volitivo por parte del acusado?

   1. Was there a volitional act by the defandant?

2. ¿Ocasionó ese acto contacto físico con el demandante?

   2. Did that act bring about contact with the plaintiff?

3. ¿Le resultó el contacto perjudicial al demandante o lo insultó?

   3. Was the contact harmful or offensive to the plaintiff?

4. ¿Hubo intención por parte del acusado de ocasionar ese contacto?

   ¿Hubo intención por parte de la acusada de ocasionar ese contacto?

   4. Was there intent on the part of the defendant to bring about that contact.

5. ¿Fueron las actuaciones del acusado de hecho la causa del contacto?

   ¿Fueron las actuaciones de la acusada de hecho la causa del contacto?

   5. Were the defendants actions in fact the cause of the contact?

Details of Specific Elements

1. "Acto volitivo" quiere decir que la persona actuaba por propia voluntad.

   1. "Volition act" means that the person was acting with a degree of will of their own.

2. Si sus actuaciones están fuera de su control, entonces no puede ser lesiones.

   2. If their actions are out of their control, then it can't be battery.

3. Si un epiléptico sufre un ataque y le pega, esas actuaciones no son voluntarias y no se considera como agresión con lesiones.

   3. If an epileptic has a seizure and smacks you, those actions are not voluntary, and are not battery.

4. El contacto con el demandante incluye ...
   la ropa del demandante.
   cosas que el demandante lleva consigo.

4. Contact with the plaintiff includes ...
   the plaintiff's clothing.
   things that a plaintiff is carrying.

5. Le toca a un juez o a un jurado decidir si el contacto resultó perjudicial o insultante.

5. It is up to a judge or a jury to decide if the contact was harmful or offensive.

6. Tendrán que decidir si una persona común y razonable considerara el contacto perjudicial e insultante.

6. They will have to decide whether an ordinary reasonable person would consider the contact harmful or offensive.

7. Contacto de menor importancia, como una persona en un ascensor lleno de gente que se da contra usted, no se considerara como suficiente contacto para constituir lesiones.

7. Incidental contact, such as a person in a crowded elevator bumping up against you, would not be sufficient contact to constitute battery.

Prima Facie Case

1. ¿Hubo un acto volitivo por parte del acusado?

1. Was there a volitional act by the defendant?

2. Creó el acto temor en el demandante de un contacto inmediato, perjudicial e insultante.

2. Did the act create an apprehensiuon in the plaintiff of a harmful or offensive contact to their person?

3. ¿Fue razonable el temor que el demandante sintió?

3. Was the apprehension that the plaintiff axperienced reasonable?

4. ¿Hubo intención por parte del acusado de ocasionar ese temor?

4. Was there intent on the part of the defendant to bring that apprehension or fear about?

5. ¿Fueron las actuaciones del acusado de hecho la causa del temor?

5. Were the defendant's actions in fact the cause of the apprehension.

Details of Specific Elements

1. "Acto volitivo" quiere decir que la persona actuaba por propia voluntad.

1. "Volition act" means that the person was acting with a degree of will of their own.

2. Si sus actuaciones estaban fuera de su control, eso no constituye un acto de asalto.

2. If their actions were out of their control, then it can't be assault

3. Si un epiléptico sufre un ataque y se agita, sus actuaciones no son voluntarias y no se consideran como un asalto.

3. If an epileptic has a seizure and flails about, those actions are not voluntary, and cannot be assault.

4. La víctima de un asalto no necesita sentir miedo. Por ejemplo, una persona que ve un puñetazo viniéndole encima puede esperar que el puñetazo le dé en la cara. Sin embargo, si no le tiene miedo al agresor porque es pequeño y débil, esa actuación todavía constituye un asalto.

4. The victim of an assault does not need to experience fear. For example, a person can see a punch coming to their face and expect that they are going to get touched, but not be afraid of the small, weak person throwing the punch. It is still assault.

5. La víctima tiene que ser consciente del contacto inminente. Si recibe un golpe en la parte de atrás de la cabeza y no lo ve viniéndole encima, no constituye un asalto.

5. The victim has to be aware of the impending contact. If they get hit in the back of the head and never see the blow coming, it is not an assault.

6. Palabras solas no son suficiente para constituir una agrsión.

6. Words alone are not sufficient to constitute an assault.

7. La persona que amenaza tiene que hacer un gesto declarado.

7. The person making the threat has to make some form of overt gesture.

8. Apuntando una pistola siempre es suficiente	*8. Pointing a weapon is always sufficient.*
9. Amenazar a una persona con "hay que darle una lección" y luego dar un paso hacia la persona amenazada, es suficiente.	*9. Threatening to "teach you a lesson" and then stepping toward the threatened person is sufficient.*
10. Amenazas que vienen acompañadas de un tipo de actuación son suficiente como para considerarse un asalto.	*10. Threats which come wth conditions are also sufficient if they are accompanied by some form of act.*
11. Alguien se le acerca y le amenaza con el puño: "Si animas al equipo contrincante una vez más, te voy a dar un puñetazo." Este acto se considera como un asalto, tanto si usted animó al equipo contrincante o no.	*11. A person approaches you and holds up a fist and says, "if you cheer for the other team one more time, I'll punch you". This is considered an assault whether you cheer or not.*
12. La víctima tiene que estar convencida de que, en el momento del asalto, el asaltante tenía la capacidad de cumplir con la amenaza.	*12. A victim has had to have a reasonable belief, at the time of the assault, that the person assaulting them had the ability to do whatever they were threatening.*
13. Por ejemplo, si una persona le apunta con una pistola de juguete, es razonable que usted piense que se encuentra en peligro. Esto constituye un asalto.	*13. For example, if a person with one of those real-looking toy guns points it at you, it is reasonable for you to think that you are in danger, and that is enough.*
14. Una víctima de asalto tiene que enfrentar un temor de contacto inmediato. La amenaza de daño en el futuro no es suficiente.	*14. A victim of an assault has to have been placed in apprehension of immediate contact. The threat of harm at some future time is insufficient.*

15. Ser amenazado por una persona que se encuentra demasiado lejos como para cumplir con la amenaza, no constituye un asalto. Sin embargo, la amenaza puede dar lugar a otras causas de demandas.

15. The threat of harm made by someone who is to far away to actually harm you does not count, although it may give rise to other causes of action.

16. Le toca a un juez o a un jurado decidir si el contacto que usted temó resultó perjudicial o insultante.

16. Whether the contact you apprehended was harmful or offensive is a matter for the judge or jury to decide.

17. Tendrán que decidir si una persona común y razonable considerara el contacto perjudicial e insultante.

17. They will have to decide whether a reasonable person would consider the contact harmful or offensive.

Intent

1. Para conseguir que un jurado llegue a un veredicto contra el acusado, el demandante tiene que probar intención por parte del acusado.

1. In order to get a jury verdict against a defendant, a plaintiff has to prove intent on the part of the defendant.

2. Una intención específica es cuando el acusado intentó ocasionar el resultado real del que se le acusa.

2. Specific intent means that the defendant intended to bring about the actual result for which he is charged.

3. Una intención generalizada es cuando el acusado supo, con considerable certeza, que sus actuaciones ocasionarían el resultado del que se le acusa.

3. General intent means that the defendant knew, with substantial certainty, that his actions would result in the outcome he is charged with.

4. Sin reparar en el nivel de intención que el demandante tiene que probar, no tiene que probar que el acusado intentó ocasionar alguna lesión o algún daño real. Lo importante es que el acusado intentó actuar en el modo en que lo hizo.

4. Regardless of the level of intent a plaintiff has to prove, he does not have to prove that the defendant intended to cause any sort of injury or actual damage. What is important is that the defendant intended to act in the way that he did.

1. En casos civiles de asalto y agresión existe una norma denominada "intención transferida".

1. In civil assault and battery there is a rule called the transferred intent doctrine.

2. Un ejemplo demuestra mejor la aplicación de la norma. Digamos, Anthony intenta tirar una pelota a Rodrigo para asustarlo. Sin embargo, la pelota le pasó a Rodrigo, pero alcanzó a Christina en el ojo y dañó el ojo. Anthony puede ser acusado de agresión contra Christina. Anthony intentó cometer un asalto y esa intención malograda se transfirió al daño causada a Christina. Según la ley, el acto no puede ser un accidente.

2. This rule is best illustrated by example. If Anthony is trying to throw a ball at Rodrigo in order to scare him, but he misses and hits Christina in the head and puts her eye out, Anthony is guilty of a civil battery against Christina. Anthony intended to commit a civil assault, and that bad intent transferred to the damage cause to Christina. The law does not regard this as an accident in the least.

Defenses: Consent and Self-Defense

1. No puede existir ni caso de asalto ni de agresión si la persona que los cometió lo hizo con permiso.

1. There cannot be an assault or a battery if the person who committed the act had permission to do so.

2. Existen varias maneras de dar el consentimiento.

2. Consent can be given in a number of ways.

3. Consentimiento implicado-aparente — Si una persona razonable concluiera que las circunstancias significaban consentimiento, luego el consimiento es implicado. Por ejemplo, si voy a un bar y participo en un combate de lucha libre, no puedo reclamar que el otro luchador me asaltó o me agredió porque mis acciones de competir en la lucha significan consentimiento por mi parte.

3. Implied-Apparent Consent — If a reasonable person would conclude that the circumstances amounted to consent, then it is implied. For example, if I go to a bar and I enter a wrestling contest, I cannot claim that the other wrestler assaulted or battered me, as my actions of getting into the ring are essentially consent.

4. Implicado por la Ley — A veces la ley fundamentalmente le da a los ciudadanos permiso de cometer asalto y agresión. Esto casi siempre ocurre en situaciones de emergencias. Por ejemplo, un agente de rescate puede sacarlo de un accidente de coche y administrarle tratamiento médico si usted está sin sentido.

5. Una persona no puede consentir en un acto que es ilegal.

6. Una persona sí puede consentir en un acto que es ilegal.

7. Si una persona puede consentir en dejar a otra persona cometer un acto ilegal contra él o no, depende de varios factores.

8. *Si un acto ilegal en el que una persona ha copnsentido se prohibió para proteger a un cierto grupo o clase al que la víctima pertenece o no. Esto ocurre conmúnmente cuando una menor de edad consiente en tener relaciones sexuales. Los miembros de esta clase de menores de edad no están aurorizadas a dar su consentimiento. Si lo intenta, el consimiento es inválido.*

4. *Implied By Law — Sometimes the law essentially gives people permission to commit assault and battery. This is almost always in an emergency situation. For example, an emergency rescue officer has to be able to grab you and pull you out of a car crash, and then apply medical treatment if you are unconscious.*

5. *A person cannot consent to an action which is illegal.*

6. *A person can consent to an action which is illegal.*

7. *Whether or not a person may legally consent to allowing another person to do something illegal to them depends upon several factors.*

8. *Whether or not the illegal act being consented to was made illegal in order to protect a certain group or class to which the victim belongs. This is most commonly seen where an underage woman consents to sexual relations. The members of this class of underage women cannot give consent: if she tries, it is invalid.*

9. Si el acto al que consiente una persona viene a ser ana alteración del orden público o no. Por ejemplo, si dos personas borrachas que se encuentran en un aparcamiento de un bar consienten en pelearse, el consentimiento no es válido porque viene a ser una alteración del orden público.

9. Whether or not the action being consented to amounts to a disturbance of the peace. For example, if two drunks in the parking lot of a bar consent to fight each other, that is probably not valid consent, as it breaches the peace.

10. No tener la capacidad — Para que una persona pueda consentir en hacer algo legalmente, tiene que poseer lo que según la ley se denomina "la capacidad para dar su consentimiento". Si una persona no tiene la capacidad para consentir en algo, aunque den su consentimiento, el consentimiento no es válido.

10. Lack of capacity — In order for a person to be able to legally give consent, they must have what the law calls, "the capacity to consent". If a person lacks the capacity to consent, even if they give it, the consent is not valid.

11. Una person puede ser demasiado joven como para dar su consentimiento. En esta jurisdicción, una persona tiene que tener al menos ______ años de edad como parta consentir en participar en la mayoría de los casos de contacto físico.

11. A person can be too young to consent. In this jurisdiction, a person must be at least ______ years old in order to legally consent to most physical contact.

12. Una persona puede encontrarse en estado de embriaguez e irresponsabilidad. Si una persona está demasiado borracha o está intoxicada con drogas como para entender lo que ocurre, cada intento de consentimiento es inválido según la ley.

12. A person can be too drunk to consent. If a person is too drunk or high to understand what they are doing, the law says that any attempt to consent is void.

13. Una persona retardada, lesionada o considerada incapaz de rendir decisiones competentes no puede dar su consentimiento.

13. A person who is mentally retarded, injured, or otherwise rendered unable to make competent decisions can't give consent.

14. Abusar del consentimiento dado: Si una persona abusa del consentimiento dado, esa persona puede ser responsabilizada de asalto o agresión. Por ejemplo, si usted le dio a un tatuador el permiso de tatuar un tatuaje pequeño en su hombro y ella le tatua un dragón grande en la espalda, ese acto abusa de su consentimiento significamente y se puede considerar como una agresión.

14. Exceeding consent granted: If a person goes significantly beyond the consent which was granted, then the person taking the action is liable for the assault and or battery. For example, if you gave a tattoo artist permission to do a small tattoo of a heart on your shoulder blade and she puts a big dragon on your back, that exceeded your consent in a significant way, and is thus battery.

Self-Defense

1. Si una persona tiene motivos razonables de creer que está a punto de ser asaltada, o está siendo asaltada, entonces esa persona tiene el derecho de usar una cantidad razonable de fuerza para defenderse de que otros le causen daño.

1. If a person has reasonable grounds to believe that he is about to be attacked, or is being attacked, then that person has the right to use a reasonable amount of force to protect himself from harm.

2. Para alegar propia defensa, una persona solo tiene que tener una creencia razonable acerca de lo que el asaltante hace.

2. In order to use a claim of self defense, a person only has to have a reasonable belief about what the attacking party is doing.

3. Si la creencia es razonable o no le toca a un jurado o a un juez decidir.

3. Whether or not the belief is reasonable is a matter for the jury or judge to decide.

4. Si la creencia es razonable, no importa si la creencia resultó correcta o no: un error sobre el peligro que se considera razonable es suficiente a los ojos de la ley.

4. If the belief is reasonable, it does not matter whether or not it was correct: a mistake about the danger which is reasonable is enough.

5. Fuerza excesiva: una persona que se defiende de un asalto solo puede hacer uso de la fuerza hasta tal punto que sea necesaria para prevenir cualquier daño que enfrenta.

5. Excessive force: a person defending himself may only use as much force as is reasonably necessary to prevent whatever harm he faces.

6. Esto quiere decir que una persona no puede hacer uso de la fuerza letal a menos que tenga la creencia razonable que él mismo la enfrenta.

6. This means that a person cannot use deadly force unless he reasonably believes that he is facing it from the other party.

7. Si uno hace uso excesivo de la fuerza letal, el privilegio de la defensa propia se puede perder.

7. If excessive force is used, then the self defense privilege may disappear.

8. Le toca a un juez o a un jurado decidir si la cantidad de fueza usada fue razonable y necesaria o no.

8. Whether the amount of force used in self-defense was reasonable and necessary is a matter for the jury or judge to decide.

9. La persona que instiga un pleito o quien crea una situación peligrosa, por lo general no puede alegar defensa propia. Una excepción existe, y esa excepción gira en torno al término "fuerza letal".

9. The person who starts a fight, or who creates the dangerous situation cannot generally claim self defense. An exception exists, and it revolves around the term, "deadly force".

10. La "fuerza letal" es la cantidad de fuerza que probablemente puede resultar en serio daño corporal o en la muerte de otra persona.

10. "Deadly force" is an amount of force which is likely to result in serious bodily harm or death to another person.

11. Si la persona que inicialmente instigó la situación peligrosa estaba usando fuerza no letal, y la víctima responde con fuerza letal, entonces el instigador puede alegar defensa propia en cuanto ...
    a) usa fuerza no letal.

    b) usa cualquier fuerza que sea necesaria para defenderse, incluso el uso de fuerza letal.

11. If the person who creates the danger initially was using non-deadly force, and the victim responds by using deadly force, then the initial aggressor may claim self defense by ...
    a) the use of non-deadly force.

    b) the use of any amount of force necessary, even deadly force.

12. El deber de batirse en retirada: Una persona (tiene/no tiene) que optar por batirse en retirada antes de poder alrgar defensa propia.

12. Duty to retreat: A person who may claim self defense (does/does) not have to retreat before they can defend themselves.

13. Para poder recurrir a la fuerza letal como un medio para defenderse, la persona tiene que hacer el esfuerzo de batirse en retirada antes de usar la fuerza letal.

13. In order to use deadly force as self defense, a person has to try to retreat before they use the deadly force.

14. Esta regla solo se aplica se la persona puede batirse en retirada sin peligro alguno.

14. This rule only applies if the retreat can be done safely.

15. Represalias: una vez que la persona que se defiende ha logrado anular el peligro, tiene que terminar el uso de fuerza.

15. Retaliation: once a person defending himself has neutralized the danger, he has to stop using force.

16. El uso continuo e indebido de la fuerza después de que la amenaza se ha anulado puede considerarse como el uso excesivo de la fuerza o como represalia por el asalto.

16. The continued use of force after the threat has been neutralized may be found to be excessive, or *retaliatory.*

17. La defensa de terceros: una persona solo puede usar la fuerza para defender a terceros cuando la otra persona hubiera podido usar la fuerza para defenderse a sí misma.

17. *Defense of third parties: a person can only use force to defend another person when that other person would have been able to use force to defend themselves.*

18. Una persona puede usar la fuerza para defender a terceros cuando dicha persona está casi segura de que la otra persona tenía el derecho de usar la fuerza para defenderse a sí misma.

18. *A person can use force to defend another person when the person defending the other person reasonably believes that the other person had the right to use force to defend themselves.*

19. Al defender a otra persona, uno tiene el derecho a usar tanta fuerza como la otra persona hubiera podido usar para defenderse a sí misma.

19. *In defending another person, you are entitled to use as much force as the person you are defending could have used to defend themselves.*

Negligence

1. Negligencia: por lo general, cuando una persona lastima a otra persona y no hay por qué pensar que lo hizo a propósito, la causa de demanda se refiere como caso de delito culposo.

1. *Negligence: generally speaking, when someone injures someone else and there is no reason to believe that they did so on purpose, the cause of action is referred to as a negligence case.*

2. En la jurisprudencia, el término "negligrencia" tiene un significado muy especial. Por lo general, quiere decir que todo el mundo tiene una obligación o deber general de actuar en una manera razonable y prudente en presencia de otros.

2. *In law, the word "negligence" has a very special meaning. Typically it means that everyone has a general obligation or duty to act in a reasonable and prudent manner around their fellow citizen.*

3. Lo que se considera "razonable y prudente" depende de las circunstancias.

3. *What is "reasonable and prudent" depends upon the circumstances.*

4. En cualquier situación específica, como cuando una persona conduce un coche, este deber es específico en cuanto a esa circunstancia. El conductor tiene el deber de conducir el coche en una manera que es razonable y prudente bajo las circunstancias que existen en ese momento.

4. In any specific situation, such as when a person is driving a car, this duty becomes specific to that circumstance. A driver has a duty to drive their car in a manner which is reasonable and prudent under the circumstances which exist at that moment.

5. Normalmente, esto quiere decir que, aparte de conducir según la ley, el conductor también tiene que...

   star despierto.

   no ser afectado por drogas recetadas o por drogas que se pueden comprar sin receta.

   mantener el coche en buenas condiciones.

5. Usually this means that, aside from obeying the law, a driver must also ...

   not be too sleepy.

   not be impaired by prescription or over the counter drugs.

   keep their car working in a safe manner.

6. Esto significa que el conductor tiene que hacer caso al ámbito en el que maneja el coche.

6. This means that a driver has to operate their car with their full attention to the surrounding environment.

7. Si está lloviendo o nevando, o si la carretera está en malas condiciones, es el deber del conductor de reducir la velocidad por debajo del límite de velocidad.

7. If it is raining or snowing, or the road conditions are bad, a duty to slow down below the speed limit may arise.

8. Si el conductor entra en una zona escolar o hospitalaria, debe reducir la velocidad aunque no haya ningún señal.

8. If a driver enters a school zone or a hospital zone, they may have a duty to slow down, even if there are no signs posted.

9. También significa que el conductor que se deja distraer por pasajeros, por el radio o por teléfonos celulares puede poner en peligro a otros.

9. This also means that a driver who is unreasonably distracted by passengers, the radio, cell phones or other things may be breaching their duty of care to others.

10. Por lo general, el deber de actuar con prudencia al conducir se aplica a la protección de situaciones y de gente que se pueden prever.

10. Typically, your duty to act reasonably applies for the protection of reasonably foreseeable people.

11. Se reconoce que a veces ocurren accidentes imprevistos, es decir, los cuales no se preven y por tanto, no pertenecen bajo la definición de negligencia en cuanto a la ley.

11. The law recognizes that sometimes freak accidents occur, and they are unforeseeable, and thus not covered under the definition of negligence.

12. Sin embargo, si una parte lastimada fue previsible o no, y si la circunstancias de un accidente fueron previsibles o no, le toca a un juez o a un jurado decidir.

12. However, whether or not a particular injured party was foreseeable, and whether or not the circumstances of an accident were foreseeable are matters for juries or judges to decide.

13. En esta competencia hay que seguir la regla que establece que si una persona lastimada se hallaba dentro de una zona de peligro previsible, entonces existe la responsabilidad de la tercera persona por el daño que se le causó a la persona lastimada.

13. In this jurisdiction, we follow the rule that says, that if the person who was injured was within a reasonably foreseeable "zone of danger", then there should be liability for the injury to them.

14. Si una parte lastimada puede demostrar que la persona que le causó el daño tenía el deber de cuidado hacia otros, entonces ese deber también puede extenderse a esa persona.

14. If one injured party can prove that the person who caused their injury owed a duty of care to anybody, then the duty should extend to them as well.

15. Este llamado "deber de actuar razonable" significa que una persona tiene que actuar, en lo mínimo, como una persona de inteligencia y capacidad mental medias hubiera actuado si esa persona hubiera tenido las mismas características que el malhechor.

15. This "duty to act reasonably" means that a person has to act, at a minimum, as a person of average intelligence and mental ability would if that person had the same physical characteristics of the wrongdoer.

16. Si un deber a otros existe o no, y en qué radica ese deber, depende en gran medida de las circunstancias del caso particular.

16. Whether or not a duty to others exists, and what that duty is, depends greatly upon the circumstances of the individual case.

17. Por lo general, los tribunales examinan las relaciones entre ambas partes.

17. Typically, the courts look at the relationships between the parties.

18. Si no existen relaciones particulares, como cuando dos extranjeros están envueltos en un accidente de coche, los tribunales examinan otros factores.

18. If there are no particular relationships, such as when two strangers get into a car accident, then the courts look at other factors.

19. Los tribunales miran a ver si alguna ley fue violada. Si el daño que resultó es del tipo que la ley debe prevenir, entonces esa ley puede establecer el deber que la persona culpable tenía.

19. The courts look to see if any law was broken. If the kind of harm that occurred is the type that the violated law was designed to prevent, then that law may establish what the duty was.

20. La cosa habla por sí misma: Presunción controvertible con prueba en contrario. En algunas circunstancias, la ley establece que el demandado fue negligente, si aquello que ocasionó el daño estaba bajo el control absoluto del demandado, y que el suceso o accidente era uno que de ordinario no ocurre a menos que haya habido negligencia. Por ejemplo, si un conductor se estrella contra otro coche por detrás a una velocidad muy alta, los tribunales pueden determinar que el conductor había sido negligente.

20. *Res Ipsa Loquitur: In some circumstances, where the person who caused the harm is the person who was in sole control of the instrumentality that caused the harm, and the kind of accident which occurred is the type which ordinarily does not occur in the absence of negligence, the mere fact that the harm occurred may give rise to an inference that they acted negligently. For example, if a person driving a car plows into another car from behind at a high rate of speed, a court may find that the driver had to have been negligent.*

21. Seleccionada forma especial de comportamiento normalmente requerida de una persona ante una situación específica.

21. *Selected Special Standards of Care.*

22. Transportadores comunes son personas que reciben pago para transportan personas de un lugar a otro, como taxistas y conductores de autobús. Los transportadores comunes tienen un deber especial de conducir en forma prudente y prestar la debida atención.

22. *Common carriers are people who get paid to transport you from place to place, such as cab drivers and bus drivers. Common carriers have a special duty to act with extra care.*

23. Los tribunales distinguen entre "pasajeros que pagan por viajar en un automóvil" y "una persona que es un pasajero en un automóvil que no es el conductor".

23. *The courts distinguish between automobile "passengers" and "guests". A "guest" is just someone to whom you are giving a ride to, whereas a "passenger" is someone who bestows some economic benefit upon you for the ride.*

24. Ejemplos de pasajeros son aquellas personas que le dan a usted dinero con regularidad para pagar por el gas o por costos asociados con el acuerdo entre varias personas que se trasladan juntas al lugar de trabajo etc. utilizando por turnos el coche de cada una. Alguien que le ofrece dinero para contribuir con el gas no es considerado un pasajero.

24. Examples of passengers are people who give you money regularly for gas and other expenses in a carpool. Someone who simply offers you gas money does not count.

25. Regla de derecho consuetudinario: una persona tiene la obligación hacia la persona que es un pasajero en su automóvil de conducir el coche con prudencia y aconsejarlo de cualquier defectos que el automóvil tenga.

25. Common law rule: a person has a duty to their guests to operate their car with reasonable care, and to warn their guests of dangers or defects that their car has.

26. Por lo general, un pasajero invitado a viajar en un coche sin pago tiene el derecho de entablar juicio contra el conductor en caso de un accidente. Sin embargo, en algunos estados existen leyes que no permiten tal demanda a menos que descuido porfiado esté involucrado en el caso. A veces, la prohibición se aplica solamente a los pasajeros que son familiares cercanos del conductor.

26. Generally, a passenger who has been invited to ride in a vehicle without any charge or expected payment has the right to bring suit against a negligent driver in the event of an accident. However, some states have laws that prohibit such a suit unless willful or wanton negligence is involved. The prohibition sometimes applies only to passengers who are close relatives of the driver.

Immigration

Note to the practioner: This outline is not intended as legal advice. It is merely a set of statements and questions which allows the user to apply their knowledge of the law in the way they see fit. If anything in this outline conflicts with what you believe to be the law, you should always go with your owns understanding.

This outline addresses the most common immigration issues that a Spanish-speaking individual is likely to encounter. Issues such as Asylum, refugee status, illegal work and hiring etc. are left to a more comprehensive treatment elsewhere.

Immigration

1. Presencia en Estados Unidos.	1. *Presence in the United States.*
2. ¿Posee un pasaporte de otro país?	2. *Do you have a passport from another country?*
3. ¿Posee alguna visa que le permite estadía en este país?	3. *Do you have any visas which allow you to be in this country?*
4. Que usted sepa, ¿entró usted legalmente en Estados Unidos?	4. *To the best of your knowledge, did you enter the United States legally?*
5. Que usted sepa, ¿presentó algún formulario con las autoridades inmigratorias estadounidenses?	5. *To the best of your knowledge, did you file any forms with the US Immigration Authorities?*
6. Que usted sepa, ¿presentó algún formulario con la Patrulla Fronteriza estadounidense?	6. *To the best of your knowledge, did you file any forms with the U.S. Border Patrol?*
7. Que usted sepa, ¿presentó algún formulario con alguna autoridad estadounidense?	7. *To the best of your knowledge, did you file any forms with any U.S. Authority?*
8. ¿Cuánto hace que vive en Estados Unidos??	8. *How long have you been in the United States?*
9. ¿Ha tenido una relación amorosa con alguien desde que vive en Estados Unidos?	9. *Have you been romantically involved with anyone since you entered the United States?*
¿Ha tenido un enredo con alguien desde que vive en Estados Unidos?	
10. ¿Todavía tiene una relación con esa persona?	10. *Are you still involved with them?*
11. ¿Cuándo se conocieron?	11. *When did you meet them?*

11. ¿Se ha casado con ella? ¿Se ha casada con él?
11. *Have you married them?*

12. ¿Es la persona **ciudadano** estadounudense?
¿Es la persona **ciudadana** estadounudense?
12. *Is that person a United States Citizen?*

13. ¿Vive aquí legal o ilegalmente?
13. *Are they here legally or illegally?*

14. ¿Existen fotos de la boda o de la recepción de la boda?
14. *Do you have wedding pictures or reception pictures?*

15. ¿Han ustedes conjuntos abierto una cuenta bancaria conjunta?
15. *Have you and this person opened a joint checking account?*

16. ¿Han ustedes conjuntos arrendado una vivienda bajo ambos nombres?
16. *Have you and this person taken out a lease on a residence together, under both names?*

17. ¿Han ustedes conjuntos hecho una compra de auto o vivienda?
17. *Have you and this person purchased a car or home together?*

18. ¿Existen recibos de servicio público bajo ambos nombres?
18. *Are there utility bills in both of your names?*

19. ¿Ha hecho una declaración de la renta conjunta con su cónyuge?
¿Ha hecho una declaración de impuestos conjunta con su cónyuge?
19. *Have you filed a joint tax return with your spouse?*

20. ¿Tienen algunas pólizas de seguros conjuntas?	*20. Do you have any insurance policies together?*
21. ¿Tienen alguna cuenta de tarjeta de crédit conjunta?	*21. Do you have any joint credit card accounts?*
22. ¿Existen recibos algunos que vienen a ambos nombres con la misma dirección?	*22. Do you have bills of any kind which are addressed to the two of you at the same address?*
23. Ha estado empleado desde que llegó a Estados Unidos? Ha estado empleada desde que llegó a Estados Unidos?	*23. Have you been employed at all since you entered the U.S.?*
24. ¿Trabaja actualmente?	*24. Are you presently employed?*
25. ¿Quién es su empleador?	*25. By whom?*
26. ¿Dónde? ¿Aquí en (nombre de la ciudad)?	*26. Where? Here in (city name)?*
27. ¿Cuántos meses hace que trabaja allí?	*27. For how many months?*
28. ¿A qué se dedica usted?	*28. What do you do?*
29. ¿Cuántos puestos de trabajo ha tenido?	*29. How many jobs have you had?*
30. ¿Cuál es la fecha de su primer empleo en Estados Unidos?	*27. When did you first begin working in the U.S.?*
31. ¿A qué se ha dedicado en sus puestos de trabajo?	*28. What did you do at your various jobs?*

Special Circumstances

1. ¿Tiene familiares en este país?

1. Do you have family in this Country?

2. ¿Sabe usted si algún o algunos de sus familiares tienen la ciudadanía estadounidense?

2. Do you know whether or not any of your family members in this country are U.S. Citizens?

3. ¿Cuál es su parentesco con ellos?

3. What is your relation to them?

4. ¿Son ...
   sus padres?
   sus hermanos?
   sus abuelos?
   sus hijos?

4. Are they ...
   parents?
   brothers or sisters?
   grandparents?
   children?

4. ¿Dónde viven?

4. Where do they live?

5. ¿Está dispuesto a cambiar de domocilio a fin de vivir cerca de ellos?

   ¿Está dispuesta a cambiar de domocilio a fin de vivir cerca de ellos?

   ¿Están dispuestos a cambiar de domocilio a fin de vivir cerca de ellos?

5. Would you be willing to move to be near them?

6. Ahora le voy a preguntar acerca de su empleo, habilidad y destreza.

6. Now I am going to ask you about your employment and skills.

7. Cuál es su nivel de educación más alto que ha logrado?

7. What is the highest level of education you have obtained?

8. ¿Se ha licenciado/a?

8. Do you have any college degrees?

9. ¿En qué se ha licenciado/a?

9. In what field?

10. ¿Ha tenido experencia laboral previa en su campo de estudios?	*10. Do you have practical experience using your education?*
11. ¿Tiene **entrenamiento** de empleo especial o habilidades esapeciales? ¿Tiene **adiestramiento** de empleo especial o habilidades esapeciales?	*11. Do you have any special job training or skills?*
12. ¿Hay algún negocio que está dispuesto a financiar su estadio en este país?	*12. Do you know of a business which is willing to sponsor you in this country for employment?*
13. Esto quiere decir que tienen que emplearlo. Esto quiere decir que tienen que emplearla. Esto quiere decir que tienen que emplearlos.	*13. This means that they have to hire you.*
14. Esto quiere decir que tienen que estar dispuestos a demostrar que usted tiene la destreza que necesitan.	*14. This means that they have to be willing to say that you have a skill that they need.*
15. Esto quiere decir que tienen que jurar que no pueden encontrar a otra persona que pueda hacer el trabajo.	*15. This means that they have to swear that they cannot find anybody else to do the job.*
16. Esto quiere decir que le pueden pagar el salario.	*16. This means that they have to be able to pay you.*

In U.S. On Business

1. Vino a este país con el propósito de hacer negocio?	*1. Did you come to this country for business purposes?*
2. ¿Trabaja para una empresa estadounidense o para un país extranjero?	*2. Are you doing business for a U.S. company, or a foreign country?*
3. ¿Vive usted en el extranjero?	*3. Do you have a residence abroad?*
4. ¿Cuenta usted con los recursos para financiar su estadía en este país?	*4. Do you have the ability to support yourself financially for the entire time you are in this country?*
5. ¿Desea usted permanecer en este país después de terminar su negocio?	*5. Do you wish to stay in this country once the business dealings are concluded?*

Students

1. ¿Piensa usted asistir a la universidad en este país? ¿Cuándo piensa en empezar a estudiar?	*1. Are you planning on going to college in this country? When do you plan to start?*
2. ¿Asiste usted a la universidad en este país?	*2. Are you going to college in this country?*
3. ¿Cuál universidad? ¿Cuándo empezó?	*3. Which school? When did you start?*
4. ¿Ha hecho el Examen de Inglés como Lengua Extranjera (TOEFL)?	*4. Have you taken the Test of English as a Foreign Language (TOEFL)?*
5. ¿Cuenta usted con los recursos para financiar sus estudios sin tener que trabajar?	*5. Do you have adequate resources to support yourself, so that you do not have to take an outside job?*

6. ¿Tendría que trabajar más de 20 horas la semana para ganarse la vida?

6. Would you need to work more than 20 hours a week in order to survive?

7. ¿Existe alguna circunstancia que requiera que usted trabaje durante sus estudios?

7. Do you have any special circumstances which might require you to get a job while going to school?

8. ¿Tiene cónyuge?

8. Do you have a spouse?

9. ¿Tiene hijos?
¿Tiene niños?

9. Do you have children?

Visa Denial Factors

1. Se considera que usted está en Estados Unidos ilegalmente si usted ha violado su situación de inmigrante.

1. You are considered to be in the U.S. illegally if you have violated your immigrant status.

2. Se considera que usted está en Estados Unidos ilegalmente si usted entró en el país sin la autorización del INS.

2. You are considered to be in the U.S. illegally if you have entered the country without INS authorization.

3. Se considera que usted está en Estados Unidos ilegalmente si usted entró en el país de manera fraudulenta, tal como impartir falsa información al INS.

3. You are considered to be in the U.S. illegally if you have entered the U.S. by fraudulent means, such as by giving the INS false information.

4. Se considera que usted está en Estados Unidos ilegalmente si usted ha permanecido en el país más tiempo de lo que su visa le permite.

4. You are considered to be in the U.S. illegally if you have stayed in the country longer than your visa allows.

2. ¿Ha vivido en este país ilegalmente?

2. Have you been in this country illegally?

3. ¿Ha sido más de un año?

3. Has it been for more than a year?

4. ¿Ha sido más de 180 días?

4. Has it been for more than 180 days?

5. ¿Ha sido **detenido** por algún delito?

¿Ha sido **detenida** por algún delito?

5. Have you been arrested for any crimes?

6. ¿Por cuál delito?

6. What crime was it?

7. ¿Fue **condenado** por alguna acusación?

¿Fue **condenada** por alguna acusación?

7. Were you convicted of any charge?

Patriot Act Rules

1. ¿Es usted representante de alguna organización?

1. Are you a representative of any organizations?

2. ¿De cuál? ¿De cuáles?

2. Which one? Which ones?

3. ¿Ha recaudado dinero para alguna organización?

3. Have you ever raised funds for any organization?

4. ¿Para cuál? ¿Para cuáles?

4. For which one? For which ones?

5. ¿Ha reclutado alguna vez miembros para alguna organización?

5. Have you ever recruited members for an organization?

6. ¿Ha sido alguna vez asociacdo con alguna organización que el gobierno estadounidense considere ser una organización terrorista?

6. Have you ever been associated with any organization which the U.S. Government might consider to be a Terrorist Organization?

Advice

1. Hay varias maneras en que uno puede entrar a Estados Unidos legalmente .

1. There are many ways to gain legal access to the U.S.

2. Una de las maneras es contraer matrimonio con un ciudadano estadounidense.

   Una de las maneras es contraer matrimonio con una ciudadana estadounidense.

2. One way is to marry a United States Citizen.

3. Esto le permite llegar a ser ciudadano estadounidense rápidamente.

   Esto le permite llegar a ser ciudadana estadounidense rápidamente.

3. This allows you to become a U.S. Citizen quickly.

4. Una de las maneras es comprometerse con un ciudadano estadounidense.

   Una de las maneras es comprometerse con una ciudadana estadounidense.

4. One way is to become engaged to a U.S. citizen.

5. Esto le permite solicitar una visa especial a través de una petición K-1.

5. This allows you to apply for a special visa through a K-1 petition.

6. Una de las maneras es entrar a Estados Unidos con visa de trabajo.

6. One way is to enter the U.S. on a work visa.

7. Una de las maneras es entrar a Estados Unidos con visa de estudios.

7. One way is to enter the U.S. on a student visa.

8. Un niño que nace en Estados Unidos es un ciudadono estadounidense, sin excepción.

8. Any child born in the U.S. is a U.S. citizen, without exception.

9. Después del nacimiento de un hijo en Estados Unidos, usted puede solicitar una visa de familia.

9. *You may apply for a family visa after the child is born.*

10. Es importante hacerlo de inmediato.

10. *It is important to follow up on this immediately.*

11. Si usted llega a ser ciudadano estadounidense, todos sus hijos menores también llegan a ser ciudadanos.

11. *If you become a U.S. Citizen, all of your minor children become U.S. Citizens as well.*

12. Usted debe hacer una declaración de impuestos si la Dirección General Impositiva lo requiere.

12. *If you are required to do so by the IRS, you must file a U.S. tax return.*

13. Yo recomiendo hacer una declaración de impuestos federal y estatal cada año, sin excepción.

13. *I recommend filing a Federal and State return every year, whether or not you believe you need to.*

14. Si usted deja de hacerlo y llega a ser elegible para obtener la ciudadanía en una fecha posterior, se lo pueden denegar.

14. *If you fail to do so, and you eventually become eligible for full citizenship, you may be denied.*

Misconceptions

1. El hecho de que actualmente está en Estados Unidos ilegalmente no debe impedirle solicitar una visa, un permiso de residencia y trabajo u otra situación jurídica.

1. *Just because you are now in the United States illegally, that does not preclude you from being able to apply for a visa, a green card, or other legal status.*

2. Es un problema si usted permanece en Estados Uni-- dos ilegalmente por mucho tiempo.

2. *It becomes a problem only if you stay in the U.S. illegally for too long.*

3. Usted debe resolver este problema lo más pronto posible.

3. *You should remedy this problem immediately.*

4. Delitos menores cometidos durante una estadía en Estados Unidos bajo una visa válida no es impedimiento para recibir la ciudadanía.

4. Minor criminal infractions do not stand as a bar to being admitted as a U.S. citizen, if you committed the infraction while legally in the U.S. on a valid visa.

5. Delitos tales como conducir en estado de embriaguez, infracciones de tráfico y delitos menores casi nunca afectan el proceso de inmigración.

5. Crimes like DUI, DWI, traffic citations and petty misdemeanors rarely affect the immigration process.

6. Usted puede entrar a este país con hijos menores bajo una petición de visa de familia aunque no esté casado.

6. You can come to this country under a family visa petition with minor children, even if you are not married.

7. Necesitará documentos que usted es padre o madre de los hijos.

7. You may be required to show proof that the children are yours.

8. Necesitará demostrar que usted tiene custodia legal de los hijos.

8. You may also have to show that you have legal custody of the children.

9. No es necesario poder hablar y escribir inglés para recibir la residencia permanente.

9. You do not have to be able to speak or write English in order to gain permanent residency status.

Non-immigrant

1. La visa "K" no-inmigrante permite a una persona entrar a Estados Unidos temporalmente para cumplir con varios propósitos limitados.

1. The non-immigrant visa allows a person to temporarily enter the United States for a variety of limited purposes.

2. Las visas de turista se otorgan para vacaciones, para visitas familiares, para asistir bodas o funerales, etc.

2. *Tourist visas are issued for such things as vacationing, visiting family, attending weddings, funerals and graduations and those sorts of events.*

3. Una visa de estudinte se le otorga a un estudiante que va a asistir a una escuela superior acreditada y reconocida por el INS.

3. *Student Visas are issued to students attending accredited higher educational institutions which are recognized by the INS.*

4. La persona debe estar capacitada para asistir a la universitad escogida en Estados Unidos.

4. *You must qualify to enter the university or college you wish to attend.*

5. Derberá demostrar que cuenta con los recursos para financiar sus estudios sin tener que trabajar.

5. *You will have to be able to prove that you have adequate resources to support yourself in the U.S. without working while you go to school.*

6. Usted podrá conseguir un trabajo de medio tiempo bajo una visa F-1 a través de la universidad.

6. *You may be able to get part –time work under an F-1 visa through the school.*

7. Hay también visas especiales de no inmigrantes disponibles para hombres de negocios, cónyuges, hijos de estudiantes y para aquellos comprometidos con un ciudadano estadounidense.

7. *There are also special non-immigrant visas available for business people, spouses and children of students, and for those engaged to U.S. citizens.*

Green Card

1. Un permiso de residencia y trabajo es una visa de inmigrante o visa de residencia permanente.

1. A green card is an Immigrant Visa or a Permanent Residency Visa.

2. Con un permiso de residencia y trabajo usted puede vivir y trabajar en Estados Unidos legalmente.

2. With a green card you can live and work legally in the U.S.

3. El permiso de residencia y trabajo le otorga muchos derechos y privilegios, incluyendo el derecho de traer a sus familiares legalmente a Estados Unidos.

3. The green card affords you many rights and privileges, including the right to bring family members into the U.S. legally.

4. Con el permiso de residencia y trabajo usted aprovecha de muchos de los derechos que los ciudadanos estadounidenses tienen, pero usted no tiene el derecho de votar.

4. You have many rights that U.S. citizens have once you receive your Green Card, but you cannot vote until you obtain citizenship.

Ways to Get a Green Card

1. Lotería: Éste es el modo más difícil de obtener un permiso de trabajo y residencia. Usted tiene que solictar el permiso de trabajo y residencia y esperar que escojan su nombre al azar. Sólo se escoge un número limitado de nombres (cincuenta mil). Solamente solicitantes procedentes de países que han inmigrado menos de cincuenta mil personas en los últimos cinco años pueden solicitar el permiso.

1. Lottery: This is the hardest way to get a Green Card. You have to apply for the card and then hope that your name is drawn at random. Only a limited number of names are drawn (fifty-five thousand). Only people who come from countries which have had fewer than fifty-thousand immigrants to the U.S. over the last five years may apply.

2. Permiso de trabajo y residencia basado en la familia: Si usted tiene parientes cercanos que son ciudadanos estadounidenses o residentes permanentes, usted puede solicitar este permiso.

2. *Family-based green card: If you have an immediate family member who is a U.S. Citizen or Permanent Resident, you can apply for one of these.*

3. Parientes cercanos incluyen, pero no son limitados a los hijos adultos solteros de un ciudadano estadounidense, hijos de residentes permanentes, los hermanos de ciudadanos estadounidenses que tengan más de 21 años de edad, los cónyuges e hijos de residentes permanentes, un hijo menor soltero de un ciudadano estadounidense, el padre o la madre de un ciudadano estadounidense, el cónyuge o la cónyuge de un ciudadano estadounidense, ya sea muerto o vivo.

3. *An immediate family member includes, but is not limited to adult unmarried children of a U.S. Citizen, children of permanent residents, siblings of U.S. Citizens over 21 years of age, spouses and children of permanent residents, an unmarried minor child of a U.S. Citizen, the parent of a U.S. citizen, or the spouse of a U.S. Citizen, whether dead or alive.*

4. Uno de estos familiares debe estar dispuesto a financiar la estadía del inmigrante en Estados Unidos.

4. *One of these family members must be willing to sponsor the potential immigrant's presence in the U.S.*

5. Esto quiere decir que tienen que presentar una solicitud con el INS.

5. *This means that they must file the paperwork with the INS.*

Marriage

1. Si una inmigrante se casa con un ciudadano estadounidense, recibe automáticamente el permiso de residencia y trabajo.

   Si un inmigrante se casa con una ciudadana estadounidense, recibe automáticamente el permiso de residencia y trabajo.

   1. If an immigrant marries an American Citizen, they are automatically granted a Green Card.

2. Si una persona se casa sólo con el propósito de obtener una visa, no obtendrá el permiso de residencia y trabajo.

   2. If you marry solely for the purpose of obtaining the Visa, then you will not get the green card.

3. El INS investigará su matrimonio para verificar si es legítimo o no.

   3. The INS will investigate whether or not your marriage is legitimate.

4. Usted debe estar preparado para demostrar que su matrimonio es legítimo.

   4. You should be prepared to justify your marriage as legitimate.

5. Usted debe tener sus cartas amorosas listas para presentarlas al INS.

   5. You should have love letters ready.

5. Reúna cuentas conjuntas, documentos legales u otros papeles que demuestren que mantienen una relación seria.

   6. Gather together joint bills, legal documents, credit card statements, contracts or other documents which show that you are in a serious relationship.

GENERAL ADVICE

Visas de empleo temporal: Este tipo de visa constituye una autorización para trabajar por un período determinado en Estados Unidos. En la mayor parte de los casos las visas de empleo temporal se emiten sobre la base de una oferta formal de trabajo validada por el Departamento de Empleos y las autoridades del Servicio de Inmigración. Las visas más comunes que permiten trabajar de manera temporal en Estados Unidos son las clasificadas con las letras H, L, E, O, P y R.

Temporary employment visas: *You can obtain a Work Visa by getting an American company or employer to sponsor you. The company has to obtain a certification from the INS stating that there are no American workers available to do the job which you are going to do. You then have to file a form with the INS along with the employer's form, and the INS will decide. The most common visas are those classified with the letters H, L, E. O, P and R.*

Indigencia: Si le aparece al INS que usted va a necesitar recibir ayuda estatal para sobrevivir en Estados Unidos, le pueden denegar la visa.

Indigency: *If it appears to the INS that you will require public assistance in order to survive in the U.S., you may be denied a visa.*

Vínculos con terroristas: Si usted está vinculado con una organización terrorista o cualquiera organización que mantenga vínculos con ellos, le pueden denegar la visa.

Terrorists links: *If you are in any way linked to a terrorist organization or any organization which raises funds or supports them, you may be denied a visa.*

Delitos: Si usted ha estado involucrado en delitos de fraude o involucrado con drogas illegales, le pueden denegar la visa.

Criminal acts: *If you have been involved in any crime which involves fraud, moral turpitude or illegal drugs, you may be denied a visa.*

EVIDENCE

NOTE TO END USERS: The explanations and examples contained herein are generalized and simplified. They cover the general topic of evidence from the perspective of general legal principles as have evolved over time. None of what is contained herein is to be substituted for what the user knows to be specifically applicable law: your state's policies and law may differ from the general rules laid out herein. As near as possible, the authors have attempted to stay as close to explanations which cover the Federal Rules and/or the majority rule, however many of the topics contained herein have been truncated, owing primarily to the purpose and format of this publication. **For example,** the parol evidence rule is truncated to cover the most common applications most professionals will face, and foundation issues are disregarded almost entirely. This section allows legal professionals to explain basic legal concepts generally, and clearly, without confusing the issues.

This section is designed to allow legal professionals to communicate key evidentiary concepts to Spanish speaking people. Evidentiary rules can be truly frustrating to the lay person. They may have information which they feel is vital to their case which a trained legal practitioner will determine to be legally irrelevant, immaterial or incompetent. This section will allow the practitioner to explain these concepts clearly, concisely and with a minimum of effort.

Evidence

1. Las pruebas son todo lo que se presenta ante un tribunal. El fin es probar alguna parte de su caso o de desmentir algún aspecto del caso de la otra parte.

1. Evidence is anything that is introduced into the courts to prove some part of your case, or to disprove some aspect of the other side's case.

2. Las pruebas pueden ser prueba testifical directa o prueba circunstancial. Ambos tipos de pruebas se admiten y ambos son muy valiosos.

2. Evidence can either be direct or it can be circumstantial. Both kinds are allowed, and both are very valuable.

3. La prueba testifical directa está directamente relacionada con el caso. Por ejemplo, si la policía para a una persona como sospechosa por manejar estando borracha, una botella de cerveza que está abierta junto a la persona es prueba testifical directa de ese crimen.

3. Direct evidence connects directly to the case. For example, if an individual person is stopped on suspicion of drunk driving, an open beer bottle on the seat next to him is direct evidence of that crime.

4. La prueba circunstancial no está directamente relacionada con el caso. En su lugar, la prueba obliga al juez o al jurado a deducir (inferir) algo. Por ejemplo, si un hombre encapuchado de negro asalta un banco con un revólver de seis tiros y luego la policía halla un revólver de seis tiros, una bolsa llena de dinero y una máscara negra dentro del coche de Bill, esto sí es prueba circunstancial de que Bill asaltó el banco: sin embargo, no significa necesariamente que ésta es la pistola o el mismo estilo de máscara, pero las circunstancias hacen que esto se está poniendo feo para Bill.

4. Circumstantial evidence does not directly connect to the case. Instead, the evidence requires the judge or jury to infer something. For, example, if a person wearing a black mask robs a bank using a six-shooter pistol, and then the police find a six shooter pistol, a bag of cash and a black mask in Bill's car, that's circumstantial evidence that he robbed the bank: it's not necessarily the right kind of gun, or the right style of mask, but the circumstances would make him look pretty bad.

Dése cuenta que aunque la prueba de la máscara, la pistola y el dinero en efectivo no son pruebas concluyente s(Bill podría ser narcotraficante o hombre de negocios que lleva una pistola para protegerse), un jurado lo puede condenar a prisión basándose en las pruebas.

Notice from this example that even though the evidence of the mask and gun and cash are not conclusive (Bill could be a drug dealer, or a businessman with a gun for protection) a jury could still send him to jail based on this evidence.

5. A veces las pruebas pueden ser un artículo físico como una pistola o un documento. Otras veces las pruebas pueden ser una prueba testimonial.

5. Sometimes evidence is a physical item, like a gun or a document, other times evidence is testimonial.

6. Las pruebas testimoniales son las palabras habladas de un testigo ante un tribunal. Hay varios tipos de pruebas testimoniales. Una persona que posee conocimiento de primera mano puede ser obligada a comparecer ante un tribunal y decir lo que sabe acerca del asunto o lo que ha presenciado. Una persona contratada para investigar asuntos pueder ser obligada a comparecer para decir lo que presenció, oyó o encontró. Éstos pueden ser un agente de policía, un investigador privado o cualquier otra persona que reúne información. Peritos pueden comparecer ante un tribunal para decir como ellos interpretan cierta información. Por ejemplo: un forense puede ser obligado a comparecer para dar su opinión profesional de cómo una persona llegó a ser herida en un accidente o si la herida fue el resultado de un crimen. Peritos científicos pueden

6. Testimonial evidence is the spoken words of a witness in court. It can come in a number of forms. A person who has first-hand knowledge of the situation can be made to come to court and tell what he or she knows or saw. A person who was hired to do investigations of matters can be brought in to tell what he saw, heard or found. This could be a police officer, private investigator, or anyone else who collects information. Experts can be brought in to tell the court about how they interpret certain pieces of information. For example: A forensics expert can be brought in to tell the court about how he believes a person became injured in an accident, or if injured as the result of a crime. Scientific experts can be brought in to tell the court about how an accident

comparecer y decir como un accidente ocurrió o explicar si los trabajos de otros peritos presentan serias deficiencias. Un perito en evaluación puede comparecer para presentar su valoración y decir cuánto un artículo vale. Expertos en sus campos especilizados, pueden testificar con respecto al estado de ánimo de la persona y decir si la persona estaba legalmente responsable por sus acciones al tiempo que las cometió. Distintos peritos son de distintas opiniones y por ello el jurado o el juez tiene la responsabilidad de decidir a quienes les otorga la mayor credibilidad.

occurred, or about how poorly a particular incident was tested by other experts. An expert in valuation can be brought in to testify as to his assessment as to what a particular item is actually worth. Psychological experts can testify as to whether or not a person was legally responsible for their actions at the time they committed it. Different experts can give different opinions, and so it is up to the jury or judge to determine which one to give the most belief to.

7. Prueba limitada: Una prueba determinada puede ser admitida sólo para un propósito específico y ninguna otra se puede admitir contra una persona específica. Un ejemplo es una condena previa. Si Tom es procesado por agresión por haber dado una paliza a un sacabullas, prueba del hecho de que fue condenado previamente porque le dio una paliza a su esposa en el pasado, esto no puede ser admitido para demostrar que él hizo lo que se le acusa en este caso. Si Tom sube al estrado y testifica, la condena previa por la paliza que le dio a su esposa puede ser admitida para demostrar que Tom carece de credibilidad. El juez instruirá al jurado que sólo consideren la condena previa para ese propósito, pero es probable que lo miren como una persona mala y violenta.

7. Limited purpose evidence: Sometimes a particular piece of evidence can only be admitted for a specific purpose and no other, or it can only be admitted against a particular person. One example is a prior conviction. If Tom is on trial for battery for beating up a bouncer, evidence of the fact that he was convicted of beating his wife in the past cannot be admitted to show that he did what he is charged with in this case. If Thomas takes the stand and testifies, the wife beating conviction may be allowed into court to show that Thomas lacks credibility. The judge will tell the jury to only consider the prior conviction for that purpose, but in reality, they are probably going to look at him as a bad, violent man too.

General Evidentiary Rules

1. **Todas las pruebas deben ser relevante:** A fin de admitir un dato ante el tribunal, el dato debe ser relevante. Típicamente, esto quiere decir que debe ser importante y probatorio.

*1. **All evidence must be relevant:** In order for a piece of information to be admitted into court, it must be relevant. Typically this means that it must be both material and probative.*

2. **Materialidad:** Una prueba se considera como importante al caso si se la ofrece al tribunal para probar una cuestión legal en el caso.

*2. **Materiality:** A piece of evidence is considered to be material to the case if it is being offered to the court to prove a legal issue in the case.*

Primer ejemplo: En un pleito por la guarda de niños, el deber legal del tribunal es servir a los mejores intereses de los hijos. Esto quiere decir que la prueba del uso ilegal de drogas por parte de uno o ambos padres es probablemente importante, ya que tiende a demostrar que el niño se encuentra en un ámbito peligroso cuando está en la presencia de ese padre.

***Example 1:** In a court battle for the custody of children, the court's legal duty is to decide what is in the best interest of the children. This means that evidence of one or both parent's illegal drug use is probably material, as it tends to show that the child is in an unsafe condition when around that parent.*

Segundo ejemplo: Si usted chocó el coche de un amigo contra un coche de otra persona, no importa si la matrícula del vehículo de la otra persona ya había vencido o no. El estado legal de la matrícula es irrelevante en cuanto a la cuestión si manejaba o no, o si el accidente se debió a una imprudencia temeraria al conducir.

***Example 2:** If you were in a car accident with another person's car, it does not matter at all whether or not that person had an expired vehicle registration. The status of their registration is immaterial to the question of whether or not they were driving and doing so in a negligent manner.*

3. Probidad: Para que un tribunal considere una prueba, de alguna manera la prueba tiene que hacer una aportación para probar el hecho esencial o para desmentirlo. Un hecho esencial es un hecho que está relacionado con el caso. Es decir, el hecho establece quién estaba involucrado, cuándo ocurrió, qué pasó, dónde ocurrió o cómo ocurrió.

__3. Probity:__ In order for a court to consider a piece of evidence, it must somehow contribute toward either proving a material fact, or toward disproving one. A material fact is a fact which relates to the case, either in that it establishes who was involved, when something happened, what happened, where it occurred or how it happened.

Ejemplo: Si usted sufrió un accidente de coche causado por un hombre llamado Tomás, prueba del hecho de que Tomás había recibido una citación en el pasado por imprudencia temeraria al conducir es importante. Esto demuestra que no siempre conduce con prudencia. Sin embargo, no es relevante en este caso ya que no tiene nada que ver con la pregunta si conducía con prudencia o no al tiempo del accidente. **Pero** si Tomás comparece ante el juez y jura que no puede tener la culpa porque siempre conduce con prudencia, entonces la citación previa se hace relevante ya que tiende a demostrar que se equivocó o mintió al manifestar que siempre conduce con prudencia.

__Example:__ If you were in a car accident caused by a man named Thomas, evidence of the fact that Thomas has been issued a citation in the past for reckless driving is material in that it shows that Thomas is not always a careful driver. However, it is not relevant to this case because it has nothing to do with whether or not he was being careful at the time he hit you. __But__, if Thomas comes to court and swears that he could not be at fault because he is always careful, the prior citation is suddenly relevant, as it tends to show that he was incorrect or lying when he claimed to always be careful.

4. **Competencia:** A veces, aunque una prueba es importante y relevante, hay reglamentos que no permiten al tribunal admitirla. Las reglas se desarrollaron durante muchas décadas, y en algunos casos durante siglos, principalmente para asegurar que aquellas pruebas que son más dañinas que útiles se prohibieran.

4. ***Competence:*** *Sometimes, even though a piece of evidence is material and relevant, there are rules which will not allow the court to admit it. These rules evolved over many decades, and in some cases centuries, primarily to assure that evidence which is more harmful than it is helpful be kept out.*

Primer ejemplo: Prueba de referencia—Por varias razones, no se le permite a una persona comparecer ante el juez y hablar acerca de lo que oyó , leyó u observó fuera de la sala de la corte. Pero si otra persona lo dijo, podemos obligarla a comparecer ante un tribunal y testificar. Esto nos permite obtener la información de ella misma e interrogarla acerca de lo que dijo que escuchó.

Example 1: Hearsay—*For a number of reasons, a person is not allowed to come into court and repeat statements which he heard, read or otherwise observed outside the courtroom. If someone else said it, we have a way to force them to come to court and say it themselves. This allows us to get it straight from them, and to ask them questions about what they say they heard.*

Segundo ejemplo: Rapeshield — Muchos Estados han adoptado reglamentos que estipulan que la conducta sexual pasada de una víctima de violación no se puede admitir como prueba. La opinión es que, aunque la víctima sea muy promiscua, e incluso una prostituta, eso no tiene nada que ver con la cuestión si fue victimizada en una ocasión específica o no.

Example 2: Rapeshield—*Many states have adopted rules which provide that the past sexual conduct of a rape victim cannot be admitted into evidence. The idea is that, even if the victim is very promiscuous, or even a prostitute, that has nothing to do with whether or not she was victimized on a specific occasion.*

5. Prueba testimonial del carácter de una persona: La prueba testimonial del carácter de una persona es, en realidad, un ataque contra un individuo. Trata de mostrar que, debido a un rasgo, la persona probablemente actuó en un manera de acuerdo con ese rasgo en una ocasión específica. Esto puede ser distorsionado para que el juez o el jurado le tomen antipatía en vez de mostrar que un crimen fue cometido. Si todo el mundo de una aldea me odia, me pueden condenar injustamente si el sherif decidió que me quiere encarcelar sin motivo alguno. Lo que él pudiera hacer es arreglar que todo el mundo comparezca y digan por qué me odian. Aunque no violé la ley, un jurado me podría tener aversión. Por esta razón, el jurado todavía me puede condenar. Por ello, hay muchas restricciones en cuanto al uso de la prueba testimonial del carácter de una persona.

5. Character evidence: *Character evidence is really an attack on an individual as a person. It attempts to show that, because of some character trait, the person probably acted in a manner consistent with their character in a particular instance. This could be twisted in order to make a judge or jury dislike someone rather than to show that some critical act, like a crime, occurred. If everyone in a small town hates me, I could be railroaded if the Sheriff decided that he wanted to lock me up for no good reason. All he would have to do is have everyone in town come to court to talk about why they hate me. Even though I did nothing wrong, a jury could dislike me. For this reason, the jury could still send me to jail. This is why there are strict limits on the use of character evidence.*

6. **Acusado de un delito:** Actos malos — Prueba de otros malos actos o delitos no puede presentarse como prueba para demostrar que un acusado tiene una predisposición a cometer delitos.

*6.**Criminal defendant:*** *Bad acts —Evidence of other bad acts or crimes cannot be introduced into evidence to show that an accused person has a predisposition to commit crimes.*

7. Prueba de actos malos o delitos previos pueden ser admisible para demostrar ciertas cosas. Por ejemplo, pueden ser utilizadas para probar motivos, preparación, conocimiento, intención, identidad o que no hubo intención por parte del acusado.

7. Evidence of prior bad acts or crimes may be admissible to show certain things. For example, they may be used to prove motive, preparation, knowledge, intent, identity, or absence of mistake on the part of a defendant.

8. El fiscal no puede intentar demostrar la mala reputación de una persona con el fin de intentar probar que es probable que habría cometido un delito.

8. A prosecutor may not try to show an accused person's bad character in order to try to prove that he is likely to have committed a crime.

9. Un acusado puede presentar prueba de su buena reputación con el fin de probar que no cometió un delito. Puede citar a personas que lo conocen como testigos de su buena reputación y de rasgos que pudieran ser importante en el caso. Esto puede conllevar a dificultades. Una vez el acusado ha introducido la cuestión de reputación en el caso, el fiscal puede refutar esa prueba y eso puede conducir a resultados no deseados.

9. A person accused of a crime may offer evidence of their good character in order to try to prove that he did not commit a crime. He may call witnesses who know him to be a good person to testify about character traits which might be important in the case. This could lead to problems. Once an accused person injects the issue of their character into the case, the prosecutor is allowed to rebut that evidence, and that might lead to some undesirable results.

10. Un acusado puede decidir testificar en su propia defensa. Si lo hace, eso deja constancia de su credibilidad pero no de su reputación.

10. A criminal defendant can choose to testify in his own defense. If he does, that puts his credibility, but not his character, into issue.

11. **Presunta víctima:** En la mayoría de las causas penales, el acusado puede presentar prueba acerca de la reputación de la presunta víctima con el fin de demostrar que actuó en manera de acuerdo con ese rasgo. Esto suele utilizarse en casos de propia defensa. El acusado intenta demostrar que la persona que asaltó o mató era una persona violenta al tiempo que el acusado le hizo daño o la mató. Una excepción a esta regla prohíbe la presentación de la mayoría de las pruebas testimoniales del carácter en cuanto a la presunta víctima en los casos de agresión sexual.

*11. **Alleged victim:** The defendant in most types of criminal cases may introduce evidence about the character of the alleged victim in order to show that they acted in a manner consistent with that character trait. This is usually used in self defense cases. An accused person tries to show that the person they assaulted or killed was a violent person. For this reason they acted violently at the time the defendant hurt or killed them. An exception to this rule prohibits the introduction of most character evidence about the alleged victim in sexual assault cases.*

12. **Rasgo:** En general, la prueba acerca del rasgo del litigante no puede ser presentada con el fin de demostrar que actuaron conforme a ese rasgo.

*12. **Character:** Generally speaking, evidence of a litigant's character traits cannot be introduced in order to show that they acted in conformity with that trait.*

13.**Excepciones /Distinciones:** Si el rasgo de una persona es la cuestión real en el caso, entonces las pruebas acerca de su rasgo no sólo son admisibles, sino de importancia fundamental. Hay una regla distinta que se aplica a la llamada prueba de la "costumbre". Si una persona tiene la costumbre de comportarse en una manera específica, pruebas de esa costumbre pueden ser presentadas para demostrar que es probable que actúe de esa manera en un caso específico.

*13. **Exceptions/Distinctions:** If the character of a person is the actual issue in the case, then evidence about their character is not only admissible, it is critical. There is a distinctly different rule for what is called "habit" evidence. If a person has a habit of acting in a particular way, evidence of that habit can be admitted in order to show that they probably acted in that manner in a specific case.*

Exemplo: Tomás tiene la costumbre de siempre pasarse los señales de tráfico en los caminos vecinales por la noche. Pruebas de esa costumbre se pueden presentar para demostrar que en una noche específica, tal como cuando atropelló a alguien en un cruce rural con señal de tráfico, es probable que se hubiera pasado el señal de tráfico.

***Example:** Thomas has a habit of always running stop signs on rural roads at night. Evidence of that habit can be introduced to show that on a specific night, such as when he ran over someone at a rural intersection with a stop sign, he probably ran the stop sign.*

14. **Interés por la política pública:** A veces la ley no permite una importante y relevante prueba. Esto ocurre cuando existe un motivo social de suma importancia. Esto suele significar que los tribunales tratan de proteger a la sociedad en general primero que al individuo.

*14. **Public policy concerns:** The law will sometimes exclude an important, relevant piece of evidence. It does this when there is some highly important social reason for doing so. Usually this means that the courts try to protect the public at large first.*

. **Primer ejemplo:** Ofertas y Negociaciones de un Acuerdo — Si choqué mi coche contra él de otra persona, nunca inentaría llegar a un acuerdo justamente y sin demora si mi ofertas y negociaciones feuran admitidas como pruebas para demostrar mi culpabilidad. Por lo tanto. no se admiten como prueba.

***Example 1:** Offers and Negotiations of Settlement — If I crashed my car into someone else's, I would never try to settle the case quickly and fairly if my negotiations and offers to settle were allowed into evidence to show that I was at fault. Therefore, they are not allowed into evidence.*

. **Segundo ejemplo:** Medidas de recuperación posteriores y pagos médicos — Digamos que presento una demanda contra el dueño de mi casa debido a que el pasamanos de la escalera se cayó cuando bajaba, lo

***Example 2:** Subsequent remedial measures and medical payments — Let's say that I am suing my landlord because the hand rail on the stairs came out of the wall as I was going down them, causing me to*

que causó que me cayera y rompiera la pierna. Si el dueño de mi casa reparó de inmediato el pasamanos y luego ofreció pagar la factura del hospital, yo no puedo introducir esos hechos ante un juez para demostrar que él es culpaple. Según la ley, es más importante reparar el peligro en vez de utilizar los hechos como pruebas y que la oferta de pagar la factura del hospital puede ser un favor de amabilidad.

fall and break my leg. If the landlord came over right away and fixed he hand rail and then offered to pay my medical bills, I could not bring those facts up in order to show that he was at fault. The law says that it is more important to get the danger fixed right away than it is to use that evidence, and that the offer to pay may just be out of kindness.

Tercer ejemplo: Declaración judicial de culpabilidad retirada: Las negociaciones para llegar a un acuerdo en un asunto criminal no se admiten como pruebas en un caso. Esto incluye una declaración judicial de culpabilidad o una declaración de ni afirmo ni niego retiradas. Si no fuera así, nadie entraría en negociaciones por miedo a que sus declaraciones se utilizen en su contra.

Example 3: *Withdrawn guilty pleas: Negotiations to settle a criminal matter are not admissible. This includes a guilty plea or a no contest plea which is later withdrawn. Were this not so, nobody would enter into negotiations for fear of having their good-faith concessions used against them.*

15. **Poder de libre discreción que posee una corte de excluir cualquier prueba pertinente:** Un juez de tribunal tiene gran criterio en decidir si una prueba pertinente tiene peso. Aunque una prueba pertinente sea importante, el juez de tribunal puede excluirla si:

- provoca confusión en cuanto a los asuntos reales del caso.
- provoca prejuicio injusto a unas de las partes.

15. ***Judicial discretion to exclude relevant evidence:*** *A trial judge has a great deal of discretion in deciding whether or not a piece of evidence is relevant. Even if a piece of evidence is relevant on its face, a trial judge may exclude it because it:*

- *causes confusion of the real issues of the case.*
- *causes unfair prejudice on one of the parties.*

tiende a engañar al jurado.
es repetitivo de algo ya admitido.
causa una sorpresa injusta a una de las partes.

tends to mislead the jury.
is repetitive of something already admitted.
causes unfair surprise to one of the parties.

Note to endusers: unfair surprise is a minority view.

16. **Prueba no-testimonial:** Muchas de las pruebas que se presentan a un tribunal se entregan a un juez o a un jurado para ser interpretadas. Éstas pruebas se llaman pruebas "reales". Suelen ser artículos como una pistola, un contrato, una fotografía de un accidente, una miniatura de un edificio, un gráfico o un objeto o documento que se exhibe en un juicio como prueba. El abogado puede discutir la importancia de cada prueba "real", pero en última instanca, la persona o personas que deciden el caso pueden interpretarlas a su modo y manera.

*16. **Non-testimonial evidence:** Many kinds of evidence which are presented to the court are simply handed to the judge or jury for them to interpret as they see fit. These pieces of evidence are called, "real" evidence. Usually they are items, like a gun, or a contract, a photograph of an accident, a model of a building or a chart or exhibit prepared for trial. Your lawyer can argue about the meaning of any piece of real evidence, but ultimately, whoever is deciding the case gets to interpret it in their own way.*

17. **Autentificación** A menudo acude un testigo al tribunal para testificar que tomó una foto, o que reconoce un documento en particular. A este proceso se le llama "autentificación". Si un artículo no puede ser corroborado, se puede retirar como prueba a petición de una de las partes.

*17. **Authentication** Often times a witness will come to court in order to testify that he took a photograph, or that he recognizes a particular document. This process is called "authentication". If an item cannot be authenticated, it can be excluded from evidence upon request.*

18. **Aviso judicial:** Existen algunos hechos que son muy comúnmente conocidos o que se han comprobados muchísimas veces o que se pueden comprobar fácilmente con examinar recursos competentes que un juez puede aceptarlos como pruebas sin que se presenten formalmente. A esto se le llama "aviso judicial"

Algunos ejemplos de hechos que se pueden avisar judicialmente son:

si una determinada carretera atraviesa una determinada ciudad con hacer referencia a un mapa.

la fecha de un día determinado con hacer referencia a un calendario.

19. **Documentos** pertinentes como fichas, fotografías, contratos y testamentos, suelen ser admitidos como pruebas sin problemas algunas.

Pueden existir cuestiones técnicas acerca de cada documento, tales como si es un documento auténtico, si la firma es real, pero estos detalles no suelen causar problemas.

Cada tipo de documento tiene que satisfacer los requisitos de relevancia, competencia y materialidad para ser admitidos.

18. ***Judicial notice:*** *There are some facts which are either so commonly known, have been proved to be true so many times already or are so easy to prove by examining competent resources, that a judge can simply accept them into evidence without any formal evidence being presented. This is called, "judicial notice".*

Some examples of facts which may be judicially noticed are:

whether or not a particular highway runs through a given city, by reference to a map.

which day of the week a certain date fell , by referring to a calendar.

19. ***Documents:*** *Relevant documents, such as police reports, photographs, contracts and wills, are usually admitted into evidence without much trouble.*

There may be some technical issues about each document, such as whether or not it is an authentic document, or whether a signature is real, but usually those details are not huge issues.

Every kind of document has to meet the requirements of relevance, competence and materiality in order to be admitted.

Regla sobre pruebas verbales: Doctrina legal que dice que cuando las personas hacen sus acuerdos por escrito, el sentido y los términos de esos acuerdos no pueden contradecirse por medio de previos acuerdos verbales a no ser que haya habido un error o un fraude.

Parol evidence rule: *If there is a written agreement between parties, that written agreement is presumed to be the agreement between the parties and is considered to be the only evidence as to what the agreement is.*

Mejor prueba: Principio que requiere que se presente la prueba más confiable y disponible. Si el original está disponible, una copia no es suficiente.

Best evidence: *Principal that requires that the most reliable and available evidence be presented. If the original is available, a copy will not do.*

Esto incluye pero no se limita a contratos, fotografías, testamentos, grabaciones y cartas.

This includes but is not limited to contracts, wills, photographs, tape recordings and letters.

Aplicabilidad: Testimonio de testigo — La regla sobre pruebas verbales se aplica a situaciones en las que un testigo quiere testificar acerca de lo que leyó o vio en un documento. Su testimonio no es tan confiable como el documento propio. Debido a que la memoria a veces es mala o corrupta, el documento es preferible.

Applicability: *Witness testimony — The parol evidence rule applies very tightly in a situation where a witness wants to testify about what he read or saw in a document. Their testimony is essentially a "less trustworthy copy" of the document itself. Because memories are sometimes bad or corrupt, the document is preferred.*

Witnesses

1. **Testimonio: Competencia** Se presume que cada testigo que sube al estrado es un testigo hábil. Pero esto se puede poner en duda y un abogado interrogará a un testigo para averiguar si es un testigo inhábil.

*1. **Testimony: Competence** Every witness who takes the stand in court is presumed to be competent. This presumption can be attacked though, and a lawyer will question a witness about one or all of the different aspects of being a trustworthy, competent witness.*

2. Reglas Federales: Bajo las reglas federales y de este estado, todos los testigos deben tener conocimientos personales acerca de lo que van a testificar. Esto quiere decir que no pueden testificar acerca de las cosas que no han observado personalmente.	***2. Federal Rules:*** *Under the Federal Rules and the rules of this state, all witnesses must have some personal knowledge of what they are testifying about. This means that they can't testify about things they did not personally observe.*
3. Bajo las reglas federales y de este estado, todos los testigos deben poder recordar, al momemto de testificar, las cosas que ellos mismos observaron. También deben jurar que van a decir la verdad ante el tribunal. Si mienten ante el tribunal, pueden ser encarcelados.	*3. Under the Federal Rules and the rules of this state, all witnesses must be able to recall, at the time they testify, the things that they observed. They must also swear to tell the truth before the court. If they lie in court, they could go to jail.*
4. Si un menor de edad debe testificar, tanto los abogados como el tribunal quieren estar seguros que el niño entiende la diferencia entre la verdad y la mentira, y que el niño entiende que él tiene que decir la verdad.	*4. If a child is asked to testify, all of the lawyers and the court want to be sure that the child understands the difference between the truth and a lie, and that the child knows that he has to tell only the truth.*
5. Un testigo que tiene mala vista puede ser declarado no apto para testificar acerca de lo que vio si, por ejemplo, estaba lejos del acontecimiento y no tenía los anteojos puestos.	*5. A witness who has very bad eyesight could be disqualified from testifying about what she saw if, for example, she was far away from the event and was not wearing her glasses.*
6. Algunas personas que padecen de enfermedades que afectan la memoria, como ancianos que están un poco chochas, podrían ser un testigo inhábil.	*6. Some people who have diseases which affect their memory, like very old, senile people, may not be competent to testify.*

7. Una persona debe poder comunicar convincentemente su testimonio con la corte. Esto no suele ser un problema ya que la corte permite varias maneras de obtener testimomios. Estos incluyen el testimonio a través de intérpretes, traductores y por escrito.

7. A person must be able to effectively communicate their testimony to the court. This is usually not a problem, as courts allow many different ways of acquiring testimony, such as through translators, interpreters, or in writing.

8. Opiniones: Los tribunales intentan restringir las pruebas a los hechos y excluir opiniones. A veces las opiniones de personas que no son expertos se admiten si las opiniones son imprescindibles para mejor entender algo importante acerca del caso.

8. Opinions: *The courts try to limit evidence to facts, and to exclude opinions. Sometimes the opinions of non-experts are allowed, if they are necessary to a better understanding of something important to the case, or are otherwise very helpful.*

La opiñión de un laico debe basarse en la percepción propia del mismo acerca de lo que va a testificar. Por ejemplo, un testigo puede testificar acerca de la velocidad de un auto, si el testigo personalmente observó al auto en movimiento. Un laico no suele poder testificar acerca de la velocidad de un auto basado en la examinación de las marcas de un patinazo, porque no es experto en tal asuntos.

The opinion of a lay person has to be based upon that witness's own perception of whatever they are testifying about. For example, a witness can give her own opinion as to how fast someone was driving if the witness actually saw the driving. A lay person usually would not be allowed to testify as to how fast a car was going based upon an examination of skid marks, because they are not an expert in such matters.

Las clases de opiniones que un laico puede expresar ante un tribunal abarcan observaciones que son muy comunes. Pueden ser observaciones acerca de la velocidad de un auto, si una persona parecía estar borracha o no, y si una persona estaba enojada o triste.

The kinds of opinions that lay-witnesses are allowed to give cover many common observations. These can be observations of the speed of cars, whether or not a person appeared drunk or not, and whether a person was angry or sad.

9. Expertos: Los peritos pueden opinar acerca de asuntos que tienen que ver con temas científicas o técnicas.

9. Experts: *Experts are allowed to offer their opinion about matters such as scientific or technical subjects.*

Una persona debe hacerse un nombre de reconocido prestigio antes de poder testificar ante un tribunal.

A person must be established as an expert to the satisfaction of the court before being allowed to give their testimony.

La opinión de un perito puede ser desafiada. La mejor manera de poner en duda la opinión de un perito es conseguir la opinión opuesta de otro perito. El abogado también puede formular preguntas de libros de texto o de artículos científicos que demuestran las opiniones de otros peritos que no están de acuerdo con las opiniones de él o de ella.

An expert's opinion can be challenged. The best ways to do this are either through having a different expert give a different opinion, or by asking technical questions from textbooks or scientific articles that show that there are other, better experts who disagree with him or her.

10. Interrogando a los testigos: En última instancia, el juez es la persona que decide si cualquiera de las preguntas formuladas ante el tribunal se pueden preguntar.

10. Questioning witnesses: *Ultimately, the Judge is in charge of deciding whether any particular questions are going to be allowed to be asked.*

El juez puede interrumpir o poner fin a un interrogatorio si el juez piensa que las preguntas contribuyen a perder el tiempo, a acosar al testigo con preguntas insignificantes, o si las preguntas están formuladas de manera mala.

The judge may interrupt or stop a lawyer from asking certain questions if the judge feels that the questions are wasting time, harassing a witness or are so poorly worded that they just aren't getting at anything helpful to the proceedings.

Objections

11. A menudo, cuando el abogado grita "**PROTESTO!**" ante el juez, intenta poner fin a que algo se presente como prueba. Cuando el abogado protesta acerca del testimomonio del testigo, esto quiere decir que el abogado le pregunta al juez que determine si la pregunta de otro abogado es incorrecta.

*11. Often times if a lawyer says, "***OBJECTION!***", in court, he is trying to stop something from coming into evidence. When he says this in regards to the testimony of a witness, this usually means that the judge is being asked to determine if a question asked by a different lawyer is improper.*

Típicamente, el juez no dejará que los abogados formulen preguntas que:

sean demasiado incómodas para el testigo.

soliciten del testigo la misma información una y otra vez o soliciten la información que otro testigo ya ha presentado.

requiera que el testigo conteste acerca de lo que no se le permite contestar. Por ejemplo, un abogado no puede preguntarle a un testigo que testifique acerca de los pensamientos de otra persona.

Typically, the judge will not allow lawyers to ask questions which:

are unduly harassing or embarrassing to the witness.

ask the witness for essentially the same information over and over, or for information which another witness has already given.

would require the witness to give an answer that he isn't permitted to give. For example, a lawyer cannot ask a witness to testify as to what someone else was thinking.

Questioning / Statements

1. **Pregunta sugerente:** Una pregunta sugerente es la pregunta que le sugiere al testigo cómo debe contestar.

*1. **Leading question:** A leading question is a question that a lawyer asks a witness that suggests to the witness what the answer should be, or at least what answer the lawyer wants to hear.*

2. **Refrescarle la memoria a un testigo:** Por lo general, un testigo no puede preparar su testimonio con antelación, apuntarlo y luego acudir ante el tribunal y leerlo. Los testigos tienen que testificar de memoria. A veces el testigo puede recordar un acontecimiento, pero los detalles están un poco confuso. En tal caso, el testigo puede refrescar la memoria con hacer anotaciones, pero no se le permite que lea en voz alta las anotaciones.

*2. **Memory refreshing via writing:** Generally speaking, a witness can't prepare testimony in advance, write it down, and then come to court and read it. Witnesses have to testify from memory. Sometimes a witness can remember an event, but the details are just fuzzy enough that they need help to recall them. In that case, they can jog their mind for details by using notes. They can't just read the notes though.*

3. **Repregunta:** Cada parte de una demanda tiene el derecho de interrogar a los testigos que la otra parte introduce. A esto se le llama "repregunta" o "contrainterrogación".

*3. **Cross examintion:** Every party to any legal action has an absolute right to ask questions of the witnesses that the other side calls to testify. This is called "cross examination"*

4. **Impugnar al testigo:** Impugnar al testigo quiere decir que el abogado puede demostrar que un testigo carece de credibilidad y no es confiable. Por eso, el tribunal debe hacer caso omiso de su testimonio.

*4. **Impeaching the witness:** Impeaching the witness means that a lawyer gets to show that the witness is not credible or reliable, and therefore that their testimony should be ignored or given very little consideration.*

5. **Manifestaciones anteriores inconsistentes:** Manifestaciones anteriores inconsistentes son declaraciones hechas por un testigo fuera de la corte que contradicen a su testimonio en corte, y que pueden usarse solamente para desacreditar a su testimonio.

*5. **Prior inconsistent statements:** A lawyer can show that a witness said things in the past which contradict what he is saying in court. This can be used only to discredit his or her testimony in court.*

6. **Condenas previas:** El abogado puede demostrar que el testigo tiene condenas previas que la corte considera importante como para determinar la credibilidad del testigo.

*6. **Prior convictions:** A lawyer can show that a witness has prior criminal convictions which the courts feel are important in determining the credibility of the witness.*

7. **Testimonio de referencia o de oídos:** El testimonio de referencia es el testimonio en el que se manifiesta la verdad de aquello que llegó a conocimiento del testigo a través de lo dicho por otra persona fuera de la sala de la corte.

*7. **Hearsay testimony:** Hearsay testimony is a statement made in court which repeats a statement made outside of court and is being made in court for the purpose of proving the truth of whatever was stated outside of court.*

CONTRACTS

HOW TO USE THIS SECTION

Please familiarize yourself with the contents of this section before you attempt to utilize it. The question, format and organization are designed to allow you to ask both general and specific questions from a combination of sections in order to get at the legal issues involved. It is incumbent upon the practitioner to make themselves competent in the use of this format before attempting to render legal counsel thereupon.

IT NEEDS TO BE EMPHASIZED that the questions below are designed to determine whether there are basic issues which the client needs to speak with a civil attorney about in much greater detail. They are not intended to be sufficient for most commercial contract issues (U.C.C.). The questions below are only sufficient for, and are designed exclusively for the purpose of, helping the practitioner determine whether a deeper interrogation of the client and/or witnesses may be necessary in order to defend the specific legal rights of the client. These questions may not be sufficient in and of themselves to determine whether a prima facie case has been met, whether a complete and valid legal defense exists, or whether liability attaches to any party. They are sufficient only to determine whether or not further questioning or referral to an expert practitioner is required, i.e. issue spotting.

Nothing in this text should be construed in any way to be a substantive legal opinion. This book is a language aid only. It is up to the practitioner to apply his or her legal expertise to the information gathered, and to not rely in any way upon this material as legal advice, research or otherwise. The absence of certain questions or of particular options is a reflection of the limitation of this format. It is up to the practitioner to recognize when issues specific to the individual case or jurisdiction are missing and to deal with it aa manner deemed competent by your bar association.

Please note that section headings are primarily used to indicate that there are supplemental questions or statements thereunder which may be helpful for the purpose of that heading. They do not indicate that a complete set of questions for that subject are contained therein.

If such a detailed questioning is determined to be necessary, the client will need to be referred to a Spanish speaking practitioner, or will need to be interviewed with the assistance of a competent legal translator.

Contracts Generally

1. Un contrato es un conjunto de promesas hechas entre dos personas o una persona y un negocio.

1. A contract is a set of promises between two people, or a person and a business.

2. Si una persona no cumple con lo estipulado en el contrato, lay ley ofrece varias maneras de hacer que las partes cumplan con él.

2. If a person fails to live up to his or her side of the deal, the law offers different ways of making them follow through.

3. Contratos pueden ser escritos, verbales o parte escritos y parte verbales.

3. Contracts can be written, they can be verbal, or they can be part written and part verbal.

4. A veces un contrato es implícito. Un contrato implícito es un acuerdo que, según los tribunales, existe si dos personas actúan de modo que está concorde con un acuerdo existente, aunque ninguna de las partes lo tenga por escrito o lo ha dicho verbalmente.

4. Sometimes a contract is implied. An implied contract is an agreement that courts say exist if two people act in a way that is consistent with an agreement existing, even if you never say or write down anything.

NOTE TO PRACTITIONERS: The statement below is a meld of quasi-contract and implied contract doctrine.

1. He aquí un ejemplo de un contrato implícito: un hombre conduciendo un camión con el letrero "Fred's Paint Service" para delante de su casa y se baja.

1. Here is an example of an implied contract: a guy pulls up in front of your house with a truck that says, "Fred's Paint Service", and the guy gets out of his truck.

2. Usted está sentado en el porche y lo observa mientras baja la escalera y su pistola pulverizadora para pintar y comienza a pintar su casa.

2. You sit on the porch and watch him while he gets out his ladder and paint sprayer, sets his stuff up, and paints your home.

3. Al cabo del día le pide a usted dinero.

3. At the end of the day, he comes to you for money.

4. Probablemente tendrá que pagarle.

4. You probably are going to have to pay him.

5. Según la ley, usted actuó como si quisiera que el hombre pintara su casa y que intentaba pagarle porque usted no dijo nada ni le dijo que terminara. No sería justo permitir que usted logre del trabajo y de la pintura sin pagar.

5. The law says that you acted like you wanted him to paint and that you intended to pay him because you never asked questions or stopped him. It just wouldn't be fair to allow you to get all of that paint and work for free.

6. A veces cuando usted se pone de acuerdo con otra persona acerca de ciertas cosas y forman un contrato, existen condiciones que ninguna parte declara pero que son insinuados o incluidos por la ley.

6. Sometimes when you agree to things with another person and form a contract, there are terms and conditions that neither one of you state, yet are either implied or are inserted by the law.

7. Esto ocurre a menudo porque los tribunales han intentado asegurar que los contratos sean tan justos como posible. Esto asegura que personas con poder no puedan aprovecharse de personas con poco o sin poder.

7. This happens most often because the courts have tried to make contracts as fair as possible. This keeps powerful people from taking advantage of people with little or no power.

8. Un buen ejemplo de esto es lo que sucede cuando usted firma un contrato de seguro de auto. Los abogados de la compañía de seguros escriben el contrato. Usted tiene muy poco o nada que ver con lo que se incluye en el contrato.

8. A good example of this is what happens when you sign an insurance contract for your car. The insurance company lawyers write the contract. You have little or no say in what the contract says.

9. La compañía puede incluir muchas cosas que les aprovecha a ellos y no a usted. Pero porque usted DEBE firmar un contrato de seguro de coche para poder conducir legalmente, ellos tienen la ventaja.

9. The company gets to put in all sorts of things that help them and hurt you. Because you MUST sign an insurance contract in order to legally drive, they sort of have you at a disadvantage.

10. Por esta razón la ley insinúa varias condiciones en ese contrato, aunque casi nunca estén escritas.

10. Because of this the law implies several conditions on that contract, even though they rarely if ever appear on paper.

11. Según la ley, por ejemplo, cuando existen partes de un contrato que tienen más de un sentido, el tribunal interpretará el contrato de manera que le ayude a usted.

11. For instance, the law says that any time there are parts of an insurance contract that can be read more than one way, the courts will interpret them to mean whatever helps you the most.

12. Existen muchos ejemplos como este, y si es necesario, hagaré preguntas que traten de apuntar sobre los ejemplos.

12. There are many such examples, and if necessary, I will ask questions that will try to zero in on them.

Preliminary questions: the first questions are for conflict checking as well as factual information

1. ¿Es la otra parte una persona o un negocio?

1. Is the other party a person or a business?

2. ¿Quién es?

2. Who is it?

3. ¿Trabajaba él/ella desde su domicilio o desde una oficina o tienda?

3. Was he/she operating out of a house, an office or a storefront?

4. ¿Sabe cuál es su dirección?

4. Do you know their address?

5. ¿Se trata el contrato en cuestión de seguro?

5. Does the contract which you are here about concern insurance?

6 ¿Se trata de la venta o compra de algún vehículo?

6. Does it concern the sale or purchase of any kind of vehicle?

7. ¿Se trata de bienes raíces?

7. Does it concern real estate?

8. ¿De propiedad?

8. Land?

9. ¿De una casa?

9. Home?

10. ¿De arrendar o alquiler?

10. Lease or rental?

11. ¿De una venta o compra?

11. Sale or purchase?

12. ¿De empleo?

12. Employment?

13. ¿Hubo más de dos partes involucradas en este contrato.

13. Did this contract involve more than two parties?

Third Parties and Documentation

1. ¿Existía un acuerdo entre dos otras partes que le permitiera a usted beneficiar de su acuerdo?

1. Was there an agreement between two other people which would have allowed you to gain something from their agreement?

2. Lo que usted sepa, ¿intentaron específicamente las dos otras partes que usted beneficiara del acuerdo que ellos firmaron?

2. To your knowledge, did the other parties specifically intend for you to benefit from their deal?

3. ¿Sólo resultó que usted beneficiara de ese acuerdo?

3. Did it just happen to be that you would get some benefit from their deal?

4. ¿Había otra persona que tenía el derecho de recibir algo bajo un contrato por separado, y luego usted de alguna manera obtuvo el derecho de recibirlo de ellos?

4. Was someone else entitled to receive something under a separate agreement, and then you somehow acquired the right to receive it from them?

5. ¿Tenía usted alguna obligación bajo un contrato que usted luego le pidió a otra persona que se lo arreglara?

5. Did you have some kind of an obligation under a contract which you tried to get someone else to take care of for you?

6. ¿Acordó la persona que firmó el contrat con usted dejar a esa persona cumplir con su obligación del contrato?

6. Did the person you owed the obligation to agree to let this other person take over for you?

7. ¿Existe un contrato por escrito?

7. Is there a written contract?

8. ¿Le envió la otra parte cartas, faxes o notas?

8. Did the other party send you any letters, faxes or notes?

9. ¿Tiene usted mensajes de voz, correos electrónicos o cualquier memos provenientes de la otra parte.

9. Do you have any voice mail, email or answering machine memos from the other party?

10. ¿Existen notas que usted o la otra parte apuntaron acerca de este asunto?

10. Are there any notes that you or the other party wrote about this?

11. ¿Fueron escritas al momento que usted consideraba esto o después?

11. Were they written at the time you were contemplating this, or after?

12. ¿Les observó otra persona a usted y a la otra parte discutir o apuntar esta transacción?

12. Did anybody actually see you and the other party discuss/write down this transaction?

13. ¿Sabe cómo ponerse en contacto con la persona?

13. Do you know how to contact this person?

14. ¿Le proveyó con algo de beneficio usted a esta otra parte?

14. Did you provide something of benefit to this other party?

15. ¿Le prestó usted servicios a la otra parte?

15. Did you render services to the other party?

16. ¿Utilizó usted artículos y materiales para el beneficio de la otra parte?

16. Did you use supplies for their benefit?

17. ¿Ofreció usted sus srvicios?

17. Did you volunteer to do this?

18. ¿Le pidió a usted la otra parte que lo hiciera?

18. Did the other party ask you to do it?

19. ¿Cree usted que la otra parte entendió que usted lo hacía y que usted esperaba recibir pago por sus esfuerzos o al menos por los artículos y materiales?

19. Do you believe that the other party understood that you were doing it and that you were expecting to get paid for your efforts and/or supplies?

20. Lo que usted sepa, ¿ha cumplido la otra parte con todo o casi con todo lo que supuestamente tenía que hacer bajo el contrato?

20. To the best of your knowledge, has the other party done most or all of what they were supposed to do under this contract?

Basic Contract Formation Questions

1. Los contratos requieren que usted y la otra parte "mutuamente dieron su consentimiento" al acuerdo.

1. Contracts require that you and the other party "mutually assented" to the agreement.

2. Esto quiere decir que tenemos que asegurarnos que ustedes ambos se pusieron de acuerdo acerca de las mismas cosas.

2. This is means that we need to make sure the two of you were agreeing to the same things.

3. ¿Cree usted que todas las partes del contrato pensaban que que se habían puesto de acuerdo acerca de las mismas cosas?

3. Do you believe that all of the parties to the contract thought they were agreeing to the same thing?

4. ¿Entendió usted mal el contenido del contrato?

4. Did you misunderstand what the agreement was for?

5. ¿Entendió usted mal lo que tenía que cumplir según el contrato?

5. Did you misunderstand what you were going to have to do under the agreement?

6. ¿Entendió usted mal qué era lo que usted debía recibir?

6. Did you misunderstand what you were supposed to receive?

Language Barrier

1. ¿Habló español la otra parte? — *1. Did the other party speak Spanish?*

2. ¿Hablaron español bien o no muy bien? — *2. Did they speak Spanish well or poorly?*

3. ¿Estuvo un intérprete presente? — *3. Was there an interpreter present?*

Offer

1. ¿Prometió la otra parte darle algo a usted? — *1. Did the other party promise to give you something?*

2. ¿Le prometió dinero? ¿Cuánto? ¿Qué le prometió? — *2. Was it money? How much? What was it?*

3. ¿Cuándo debían cumplir con la promesa? — *3. When were they supposed to follow through?*

4. ¿Cuándo debían hacer algo para usted? — *4. When were they supposed to do something for you?*

5. ¿Creía usted que iba a recibir algo específico? — *5. Did you think that you were getting a specific item?*

6. ¿Creía usted que iba a recibir un servicio específico? — *6. Did you think that you were getting a specific service?*

7. ¿Afirmó categóricamente la otra parte que usted iba a recibir exactamente eso? — *7. Did the other party say explicitly to you that you would get exactly that?*

8. ¿Ofreció usted vender un artículo específico? ¿Cuál? — *8. Did you offer to sell a specific item? What?*

9. ¿Ofreció usted vender un servicio específico? ¿Cuál? — *9. Did you offer to sell a specific service? What?*

10. ¿Le dijo usted a la otra parte que usted iba a hacer eso exactamente? — *10. Did you explicitly tell the other party that you would give exactly that?*

11. ¿A quién le hizo la oferta la otra parte?	*11. Who did the other party make the offer to?*
12. ¿A usted?	*12. Was it to you?*
13. ¿A su cónyuge?	*13. Your spouse?*
14. ¿A su hijo/a?	*14. Your child?*
15 A alguien que vive con usted?	*15. Someone living with you?*
16. ¿Cómo presentaron la oferta?	*16. How was this offer made?*
17. ¿Llegó por correo?	*17. Did it come in the mail?*
18. ¿Se hizo por teléfono?	*18. Was it made over the phone?*
19. ¿Se hizo cara a cara?	*19. Was it made face to face?*
20. ¿Ocurrió en una oficina, tienda o afuera?	*20. Were you in an office, in a store, or outside?*
21. ¿Llamó alguien a la puerta de su casa?	*21. Did someone come to your door?*
22. ¿Le dio usted algo a la otra parte con el fin de que le hicieran una oferta a usted?	*22. Did you give the other party anything in order to get him to make the offer?*
23. ¿Qué regaló usted?	*23. What did you give?*
24. ¿Intentó usted/la otra parte retirar la oferta?	*24. Did you/the other party try to take back the offer?*
25. ¿Se vendió el artículo o se le regaló a otra persona?	*25. Did the item get sold or given to someone else?*
26. ¿Se destruyó el artíclo?	*26. Was the item destroyed?*
27. ¿Cómo se enteró de esto?	*27. How did you find out about this?*

28.¿Indicó alguna vez usted que no estaba dispuesto a aceptar la oferta?

28. Did you ever indicate that you were not willing to accept the offer?

29. ¿Le indicó a usted alguna vez la otra parte que no estaban dispuesto a aceptar su oferta?

29. Did the other party ever indicate that they were not willing to acept your offer?

30. ¿Le hizo usted una contra oferta a él/ella, tal como, "Es demasiado alto, qué tal este precio"?

30. Did you make a counter-offer to him/her, such as, "That's too high, so how about this price."?

31. ¿Cuánto tiempo pasó entre el momento en el que se hizo la oferta y el momento en el que se aceptó?

31. How long was it between the time the offer was made and when it was accepted?

Acceptance

1. Una oferta sólo se puede aceptar por la persona a quien se le hizo la oferta.

1. An offer can only be accepted by the person to whom it was made.

2. ¿Le dijo usted expresamente a la otra parte que usted aceptó la oferta?

2. Did you expressly tell the other party that you accepted the offer?

3. ¿Le dijo la otra parte expresamente a usted que aceptaron la oferta?

3. Did the other party expressly tell you that they accepted the offer?

4. ¿Se aceptó la oferta en persona?

4. Was the offer accepted face to face?

5. ¿Se aceptó la oferta por teléfono?

5. Was the offer accepted over the phone?

6. ¿Se aceptó la oferta por correo?

6. Was the offer accepted by mail?

7. ¿Se aceptó la oferta por escrito?

7. Was the offer accepted in writing?

8. ¿Tiene usted una copia?	*8. Do you have a copy of that?*
9. ¿Firmó usted in contrato por escrito?	*9. Did you sign a written contract?*
10. ¿Firmaron ellos un contrato por escrito?	*10. Did they sign a written contract?*
11. ¿Se aceptó la oferta tal y como se hizo, o intentó una de las partes cambiar las condiciones del acuerdo?	*11. Was the offer accepted exactly as it was made, or did one of you try to modify the terms of the deal?*
12. ¿Se propusieron condiciones adicionales?	*12. Were additional conditions proposed?*
13. ¿Intentó usted o la otra parte eliminar algunas de las cosas en el contrato?	*13. Did either of you try to eliminate some of the things that they wanted?*
14. ¿Pidió usted o la otra parte una clarificación de alguna parte del acuerdo?	*14. Did either of you ask for clarification of some part of the deal?*
15. ¿Compró usted materiales o artículos de oficina?	*15. Did you purchase supplies?*
16. ¿Le dio usted empleo a otras personas?	*16. Did you hire helpers?*

Consideration

1. ¿Qué prometió regalar o hacer para la otra parte para asegurar que el acuerdo se cumpliera? ¿Dinero?	1. *What did you promise to give or do for the other party in order to make the deal? Money?*
2. ¿Cosas o artículos de algún tipo?	2. *Some kind of property?*
3. ¿Rendir alguna tarea?	3. *Perform some act or do some task?*
4. No cumplir con algo que usted pudiera hacer?	4. *Not to do something which you could have done?*
5. ¿Qué le prometió regalar o hacer para usted la otra parte?	5. *What did the other party promise to give to you or do for you?"*
6. ¿Fue una promesa de regalarle algo a usted?	6. *Was this a promise to give a gift to you?*
7. ¿Le debía usted algo a ellos?	7. *Did you already owe something to them?*
8. ¿Prometió usted cumplir con el deber?	8. *Did you promise to follow through on what you already owed?*
9. ¿Prometió usted hacer más de lo que ya se le requería?	9. *Did you promise to do more than you already were supposed to?*
10. ¿Ya le debían ellos algo a usted?	10. *Did they already owe something to you?*
11. ¿Prometieron hacer lo que ya supuestamente debían hacer?	11. *Did they promise to do the thing they were already supposed to do?*

12. ¿Prometieron hacer más de lo que ya debían hacer?

12. Did they promise to do more than they already owed?

Promissory Estoppel

1. ¿Hizo usted algo, regaló algo o tomó alguna acción debido a que usted creyó que ellos habían llegado a un acuerdo?

1. Did you do anything, give anything, or take any action because you believed that they agreed to a deal?

2. ¿Hicieron ellos algo, regalaron algo o tomaron una acción debido a que pensaron que usted había llegado a un acuerdo?

2. Did they do anything, give anything, or take any action because they believed that you agreed to a deal?

Failure of Assent

1. ¿Cree usted que hubo un malentendimiento acerca de lo que las partes iban a aprovechar del acuerdo?

1. Do you believe that there was a misunderstanding about what one of you was getting out of the deal?

2. ¿Hubo un malentendimiento acerca del precio?

2. Was there a misunderstanding about the price?

3. ¿Hubo un malentendimiento acerca de la cantidad de los pagos?

3. Was there a misunderstanding about how much the payments would be?

4. ¿Hubo un malentendimiento acerca del número de pagos?

4. Was there a misunderstanding about how many payments there would be?

5. ¿Hubo un malentendimiento acerca de quién era la otra parte?

5. Was there a misunderstanding about who the other party was?

6. ¿Se equivaron ustedes ambos?

6. Were both of you mistaken?

7. ¿Se equivocó usted?

7. Were you mistaken?

8. ¿Se equivocaron ellos?

8. Were they mistaken?

9. ¿Sabía usted que la otra parte estaba equivocada?

9. Were you aware that the other party was mistaken?

Ambiguity and Fraud

1. ¿Existía alguna ambigüedad en el acuerdo?

1. Was there some ambiguity in the agreement?

2. ¿Cuándo se dio cuenta de la ambigüedad?

2. When did you become aware of this ambiguity?

3. ¿Cree usted que la otra parte sabía que existía alguna ambigüedad?

3. Do you believe that the other party knew of it?

4. ¿Cree usted que la otra parte mintió o tergiversó algunos aspectos del contrato?

4. Do you believe that the other party lied about or misrepresented some aspect of the contract?

Construction, Interpretation and Enforcement

1. Un juez interpretará el contrato de modo que sea válido y que conforme a la ley.

1. A judge will construe this agreement in a way that makes it a valid and enforceable contract.

2. Los jueces intentan entender los contratos según los significados corrientes de las palabras contenidas, a menos que usted o la otra parte les demuestren que ambas partes intentaron algo diferente y distinto.

2. Judges try to read contracts based upon the plain, ordinary meaning of any words it contains, unless you or the other party can demonstrate that all parties to the agreement intended something different.

3. A veces existen palabras con significados especiales, tal como existen entre la gente que construye casas.

3. Sometimes there are words that have a special meaning between two people, such as between two people who build houses.

4. El juez intentará interpretar el acuerdo en cuanto determinará los significados e intenciones reales de todas las partes cuando el acuerdo se firmó.

4. The judge will try to interpret your agreement by determining what the real, true intentions of all of the parties were at the time they made the deal.

5. El juez o la jueza hará todo lo posible para interpretar las condiciones del contrato de tal modo que no cambiará el intento o propósito general del contrato.

5. The judge will go out of his or her way to construe all of the terms in a way that does not change the overall purpose or intent of the agreement.

6. Las condiciones específicas se interpretarán en el contexto de la totalidad del contrato.

6. Specific terms of a contract are going to be construed within the context of the entire contract.

7. Es decir, una cláusula que contradice el contexto o propósito general del acuerdo, será interpretado de tal modo que quedará concorde con el propósito general.

7. In other words, a clause that contradicts the overall purpose of the agreement will usually be interpreted in a way that makes it consistent with that overall purpose.

8. Si existen dos o más partes específicas del contrato que parecen estar en conflicto, los tribunales suelen examinar el contrato en su totalidad.

8. If there are two or more specific parts of a contract that seem to be in conflict with each other, the courts tend to examine the entire agreement.

9. Las partes del contrato que se imprimieron por adelantado tienen menos peso con los tribunales.

9. Parts of the contract which are printed in advance usually have the least weight with the court.

10. Las adiciones a máquina o las escritas a mano tienen más peso con los tribunales debido a que muestran la intención específica de las partes y no lo que los abogados han preparado por adelantado.

10. Type-written or hand-written additions to the contract carry more weight with the court, as they show the specific intent of the parties, and not just what some lawyers printed up in a form.

11. Tales provisiones del contrato suelen considerarse válidos y aplicables por la ley

11. These types of provisions are usually held to be the valid, enforceable terms of the deal.

Parol Evidence

1. Por lo general, si existe un contrato escrito u oral, y ese contrato debió contener el contrato final en su totalidad, las pruebas externas de lo que se discutió o se puso por escrito antes de o al tiempo que se firmó el contrato, no pueden presentarse en la corte para añadirlas o para cambiar las condiciones del contrato.

1. Ordinarily, if there is a written or oral contract and that agreement was supposed to fully contain the final agreement, outside evidence of things that were discussed or written prior to or at the time of the making of the agreement cannot be brought into court to add to the terms of the contract or to vary them.

2. Esta norma NO impide que se presenten pruebas que usted no intentó firmar el contrato o que lo engañaron a usted.

2. This rule does NOT preclude bringing in evidence to show that you never intended to form a contract, or that you were defrauded or tricked.

3. Estas normas son muy complicadas y detalladas. Para poder determinar los efectos de esta norma en nuestra jurisdicción, sería necesario que usted me contrate o que contrate a otro abogado para investigar a fondo su caso y averiguar los asuntos.

3. This set of rules is very complicated and very detailed. In order to really determine the effect of this rule in our jurisdiction, it would be necessary for you to either hire me, or to hire another attorney to thoroughly investigate your case and research the issue.

Promises and Conditions

1. Los tribunales separan los contratos en partes. Una distinción clave en cualquier contrato es entre lo que se llama *condiciones y promesas*. La distinción es muy importante.

1. Courts break contracts into parts. A key distinction in any contract is between what we call conditions and promises. The distinction is very important.

2. Una promisa no es nada más que lo que ambas partes del acuerdo aprovechan. Usted acepta hacer algo o abstenerse de hacer algo a cambio de que la otra parte haga algo o igualmente se abstenga de hacer algo.

2. A promise is really what you and the other parties to a contract get out of the deal. You are agreeing to do something, or to refrain from doing something, in exchange for the other party doing something or refraining from doing something.

3. Una condición es distinta a una promesa. Condiciones son incidentes que ocurren o no ocurren. Cuando ocurren o no ocurren, las condiciones crean, destruyen o alteran las obligaciones que una persona tiene bajo el contratro.

3. A condition is different from a promise. Conditions are events that either happen or fail to happen. When they do or don't happen, they create, destroy or modify someone's obligations under a contract.

Enforcement: Client Has Been Harmed

1. ¿Desea usted que se le obligue a la otra parte que cumpla con las condiciones del contrato?

1. Do you want the other party to be forced to live up to their end of the contract?

2. Por lo general, los tribunales no obligarán a una persona a hacer exactamente lo que prometieron hacer.

2. Usually the courts will not force a person to do precisely what they promised to do.

3. Por lo general, los tribunales no obligarán a una persona repartir el artículo exacto que prometieron venderle.

3. Usually the courts will not force a person to deliver the exact thing that they promised to sell you.

4. ¿Desea usted que se le obligue a la otra parte aceptar la devolución de lo que le vendieron y que le devuelvan el dinero?

4. Do you want the other party to be forced to take back what they sold you and give you your money back?

5. ¿Desea usted que se le obligue a la otra parte que le paguen a usted lo que le deben?

5. Do you want the other party to be forced to pay you what is owed to you?

Client Has Caused Harm

1. ¿Desea la otra parte obligarle a usted que cumpla con las condiciones del acuerdo?

1. Does the other party want to force you to live up to the terms of the agreement?

2. ¿Desea la otra parte la devolución de lo que le dieron a usted bajo el acuerdo?

2. Does he other party want to get back whatever he gave you under the agreement?

3. ¿Desea la otra parte devolverle el asunto del contrato

3. Does he other party want to give back the subject matter of the contract?

4. ¿Desea la devolución de su dinero?

4. Does he want his money back?

Breach: Material Breach

1. ¿No cumplió la otra parte con darle lo que le prometió?

1. Did the other party fail to give you what you were promised?

2. ¿Le dieron otra cosa?

2. Did they give you the wrong thing?

3. ¿Le dieron lo que le prometieron, pero no funciona bien?

3. Did they give you the right thing, but it doesn't work properly?

4. ¿No cumplió con la promesa la otra parte?

4. Did the other party fail to do what they promised to do?

5. ¿Cumplió usted con todo lo que debía hacer?

5. Did you do everything that you were suposed to do?

6. ¿Le han indicado a usted la otra parte que ellos creen que han cumplido con la totalidad del acuerdo?

6. Has the other party indicated to you in any way, that they think that they have nothing left to do under the contract?

Prospective/ Anticipatory Breach, Repudiation & Frustration

1. ¿Le informaron a usted la otra parte que no intentaban cumplir con las condiciones del acuerdo?

1. Did the other party inform you that they were not going to live up to the contract?

2. Es posible que podríamos demandar lo que se llaman "seguros adicionales". Los seguros adicionales son promesas adicionales que ellos pueden y que tienen que cumplir.

2. We may be able to demand what are called further assurances from them. Further assurances are just additional promises that they can and will follow through.

3. Podemos ayudarle terminar el acuerdo cordialmente.

3. We can help you end the agreement amicably.

4. Podemos tratar sus palabras como un rechazo total del contrato y podemos demandarlos de inmediato.

4. We can treat his/her words as a total repudiation of the contract and sue immediately.

5. Usted podría suspender la parte de su cumplimiento del contrato hasta que vencé la fecha de cumplimiento.

5. You could suspend your performance of your side of the contract until he goes past the due date to perform.

6. ¿Ocurrió algo que le hace pensar que la otra parte no va a cumplir con las condiciones del acuerdo?

6 Did something happen which leads you to believe that the other party won't be living up to their side of the deal?

7. ¿Murió la persona?

7 Did they die?

8. ¿Se fueron a la bancarrota?

8 Did they go bankrupt?

9. ¿Se destruyó el propósito del contrato?

9. *Was the thing that you made the contract about destroyed?*

Conclusions

1. Creo que existe un caso por su parte. Para poder investigar a fondo los detalles del caso y darle a usted una opinión legal completa, recomiendo que contrate a un abogado.

1. *I believe that you may have a case. In order to fully investigate the details of this matter and give a complete legal opinion, I recommend that you retain an attorney.*

2. Es mi opinión que no hay nada más que puedo hacer para ayudarle.

2. *I do not think that there is anything further that I can do for you.*

3. El caso parece ser demasido complicado para mí, dado la limitada habilidad de comunicarme con usted.

3. *The case appears to be far too complex for me to sort out, given my limited ability to communicate with you.*

4. Parece que el contrato es válido y su deber de cumplir con las condiciones son válidas.

4. *You appear to be in a valid contract and your duty to perform seems to be valid.*

5. Usted va a tener que cumplir con todas las condiciones del contrato.

5. *You are going to have to do all of the things that the contract requires of you.*

Special contract issues: was there a contract?

1. Creo que usted probablemente formó un contrato con la otra parte.

1. *I believe that you probably formed a contract with the other party.*

2. Creo que usted probablemente intentó formar un contrato, pero debido a varios motivos legales, no se puede hacer respetar.

2. *I believe that you may have tried to form a contract, but that, for various legal reasons, it is not enforceable.*

3. Creo que es inválido porque va en contra de la política pública ya que fue una transacción ilegal.	*3. I think that it is void because it was against public policy as it was for an illegal transaction.*
4. Parece existir la posibilidad de que algunas partes del contrato no se pueden hacer respetar.	*4. There appears to be the possibility that some parts of the contract cannot be enforced against you.*
5. Algunas partes del contrato no se pueden hacer respetar.	*5. Some parts of the contract are unenforceable.*
6. Para que un contrato exista, algunas cosas básicas tienen que ocurrir.	*6. In order for there to be a contract, some basic things have to happen.*
7. Una persona tiene que hacer una oferta válida.	*7. Somebody must make a valid offer.*
8. Creo que se hizo una oferta.	*8. I think that an offer was made.*
9. No se hizo una oferta válida.	*9. No valid offer was made.*
10. Usted hizo la oferta.	*10. The offer was made by you.*
11. Ellos hicieron la oferta.	*11. The offer was made by them.*
12. Esa oferta probablemente ya venció.	*12. That offer probably expired.*
13. Rechazaron esa oferta.	*13. That offer was rejected.*
14. Esa oferta se retiró.	*14. That offer was retracted.*

The opposite party must accept the offer

1. Es mi opinión que usted aceptó la oferta.

1. I think that you accepted the offer.

2. Es mi opinión que la otra parte aceptó la oferta.

2. I think that the other party accepted the offer.

Something of Value has to have been Exchanged between the parties

1. En este caso, se intercambio dinero por efectos personales.

1. In this case, money was exchanged for personal property.

2. En este caso, se intercambio propiedad por propiedad.

2. In this case, property was exchanged for property.

3. En este caso, se intercambio dinero por una promesa de cumplir con algo de valor.

3. In this case, money was exchanged for a promise to do something of value.

4. En este caso, se prometió dinero en cambio de una promesa de hacer algo en el futuro.

4.In this case, money was promised in exchange for a promise to do something.

No Valid Legal Defenses Can Exist

1. Creo que para usted no existe ninguna defensa legal válida.

1. I do not believe that you have any valid legal defenses.

2. Creo que para la otra no existe ninguna defensa legal válida.

2. I do not believe that the other party has any valid legal defenses.

3. Es probable que usted tenga una defensa válida en cuanto al contrato. De ser así, es probable que usted no tenga que cumplir con la obligación.

3. You may have a valid defense to the contract. If so, you may be able to avoid having to perform it.

5. Es probable que la otra parte tenga una defensa válida y no tenga que complir con las condiciones del contrato.

5. The other party may have a valid defense, and may be able to avoid honoring the agreement because of it.

6. Este contrato puede "ser anulado" por los tribunales. Esto quiere decir que los tribunales lo pueden anular, si usted lo desea.

6. This contract may be what is called "voidable" by the courts. This means that you may be able to have it declared null and void, if that is what you want to do.

No Contract was Formed

1. Es mi opinión que no existe un contrato con la otra parte.

1. I don't think that you ever technically formed a contract with the other party.

2. Es probable que los tribunales determinen que no existe un consentimiento mutuo porque las partes del contrato no se pusieron de acuerdo con las mismas cosas.

2. It is likely that a court will determine that there was no mutual assent, because the parties to the agreement were not agreeing to the same essential things.

3. Es probable que los tribunales determinen que nunca existía una oferta válida.

3. It is likely that a court will determine that there never was a valid offer made.

4. Es probable que los tribunales determinen que la oferta nunca se aceptó debidamente.

4. It is likely that a court will determine that the offer was never properly accepted.

5. Es probable que los tribunales determinen que no existe ninguna causa porque lo que se ofreció no constituye una causa.

5. It is likely that a court will determine that there was no real consideration given because what was offered doesn't constitute consideration.

6. El contrato no tiene ningún valor.

6. The contract is worthless.

7. El contrato es ilegal.

7. The contract is is illegal.

Statute of Frauds

1. Existe una ley llamada "ley de fraudes" o "ley contra fraudes".

1. There is a law called the Statute of Frauds.

2. Según la ley de fraudes, se requiere que algunos tipos de contratos estén escritos y firmados para poder ser válidos.

2. According to the Statute of Frauds, some types of contracts must be made in writing.

3. Su acuerdo parece ser el tipo de contratro describido abajo.

3. Your agreement appears to have been the following type of contract described below.

4. Una promesa de pagar las deudas de otra persona.

4. A promise to pay the debts of another person.

5. Una promesa por parte del administrador de la suseción de una persona difunta de pagar las deudas del difunto.

5. A promise by the administrator of a deceased person's estate to pay any debts owed by the deceased.

6. Una promesa de regalar algo de valor a otra persona con el fin de asegurar que acepten casarse con usted o con otra persona.

6. A promise to give something of value to a person in order to get them to agree to get married to you or to another person.

7. Un acuerdo que no se purde cumplir en menos de un año.

7. An agreement which can't be completed in under one year.

8. Un acuerdo para vender mercancías que tienen un valor de más de 500 dólares.

8. A contract for the sale of goods over $500.00 in value.

9. Debido a esto, creo que su situación pertenece bajo esta norma.

9. Because of this, I believe your situation might fall under this rule.

10. Debido a que no es un contrato por escrito, no es válido.

10. Because the contract was not in writing, it is not valid.

11. Pueden existir otras maneras de enforzar el cumplimiento del acuerdo.

11. There may be other ways to enforce the agreement.

Unconscionability

1. Creo que este contrato contiene condiciones que los tribunales podrían encontrar como excesivamente opresivos.

1. I believe that this agreement contains provisions which a court would probably find to be unconscionable.

2. Esto quiere decir que el contrato contiene condiciones que son demasiado injustas con respeto a una parte o que existen condiciones no aparentes que ponen la mayor parte del peso de la responsabilidad sobre usted y muy poco o ningún peso sobre la otra parte.

2. This means that the contract has terms or conditions in it which are either grossly unfair to one party, or that there are hidden terms which put too much of the burden of the contract on you, and little or none on the other party.

3. En este caso, creo que usted debe contratar a un abogado para investigar a fondo lo de abajo.

3. In this case, I think you should hire an attorney in order to thoroughly determine the following.

4. ¿Existen condiciones injustas que tratan de cargar la mayor parte de la responsabilidad a usted?

4. Are there unfair terms which shifted too much risk to you?

5. ¿Existe una renuncia de garantía injusta hecha por la otra parte?

5. Is there an unfair disclaimer of warranty by the other party?

6. ¿Existen condiciones monetarias que son demasiado injustas?

6. *Are there financial terms which are grossly unfair?*

7. ¿Es este el tipo de contrato que le obligó a usted a consentir a condiciones que usted no quería aceptar, pero tuvo que hacerlo debido a la manera en que se escribió el acuerdo.

7. *Is this the kind contract which forced you into terms that you probably didn't want to accept but had to because of how it was written.*

8. Creo que usted puede obligar a la otra parte cumplir con las condiciones del acuerdo, o que usted puede escaparse del acuerdo y no ser obligado a cumplir con las condiciones, lo que usted desea.

8. *I believe that you probably can enforce the contract against the other party, or that you can walk away from the deal and not be made to perform your part of it, whichever you want.*

9. Esto quiere decir que el acuerdo es anudable.

9. *This means that the contract is voidable.*

Remedies: Damages

1. Usted puede demandar a la otra parte por violación de contrato.

1. *You could file a lawsuit against the other party for breach of contract.*

2. La otra parte puede demandarle a usted por violación de contrato.

2. *The other party may file a lawsuit aginst you for breach of contract.*

3. La otra parte ya le ha demandado a usted por violación de contrato.

3. *The other party has already filed a lawsuit against you for breach of contract.*

4. Usted podría pedirle al tribunal que le adjudique resarcimiento de daños y perjuicios. Esto quiere decir, en caso que usted gane, que usted puede recuperar dinero para poder ser compensado.

4. *You would be able to ask the court to award you compensatory damages. This means that, if you win, you could recover money to compensate you.*

5. Ellos podrían pedirle a los tribunales que les adjudiquen resarcimiento de daños y perjuicios. Esto quiere decir, en caso que ganen, que ellos pueden recuperar dinero para poder ser compensados.

5. They would be able to ask the court to award them compensatory damages. This means that, if they win, they could recover money to compensate them.

Reliance Damages

1. Usted puede pedirle a los tribunales que le adjudiquen resarcimiento de daños y perjuicios por "el acto de creer en esa representación". Estos tipos de resarcimiento de daños y perjuicios se adjudican cuando una parte actúa de acuerdo con esa creencia del acuerdo.

1. You can ask the court to award you reliance damages. These types of damages are awarded in cases where you gave them something of value in reliance upon their promise to give you something of value.

2. Ellos pueden pedirle a los tribunales que les adjudiquen resarcimiento de daños y perjuicios por "el acto de creer en esa representación". Estos tipos de resarcimiento de daños y perjuicios se adjudican cuando una parte actúa de acuerdo con esa creencia del acuerdo.

2. They would be able to ask the court to award them reliance damages. These types of damages are awarded in cases where they gave you something of value in reliance upon your promise to give them something of value.

Restitution Damages

1. Usted puede pedirle a los tribunales que le adjudiquen daños de restitución. Estos tipos de daños se adjudican en casos en los que usted le ha conferido algún beneficio a la otra parte, y sería injusto que la otra parte recibiera los beneficios gratis.

1. You can ask the court to award you restitution damages. These types of damages are awarded in cases where you have bestowed some benefit upon them, and it would be unfair for them to get that benefit for free.

2. Ellos pueden pedirle a los tribunales que les adjudiquen daños de restitución. Estos tipos de daños se adjudican en casos en los que ellos le han conferido algún beneficio a usted, y sería injusto que usted recibiera los beneficios gratis.

2. They can ask the court to award them restitution damages. These types of damages are awarded in cases where they have bestowed some benefit upon you, and it would be unfair for you to get that benefit for free.

Punitive Damages and Quasi Contracts

1. Usted puede pedirle a los tribunales que castiguen a la otra parte y que adjudiquen daños punitivos. Estos daños son muy raros en casos que involucran contratos y muy difícil de conseguir.

1. You might be able to request that the courts punish the other party by awarding punitive damages. These damages are very rare in contract cases, and very hard to get.

2. Ellos pueden pedirle a los tribunales que lo castiguen a usted y que adjudiquen daños punitivos. Estos daños son muy raros en casos que involucran contratos y muy difícil de conseguir.

2. They might be able to request that the courts punish you by awarding punitive damages. These damages are very rare in contract cases, and very hard to get.

3. Le pidieron a los tribunales que le castiguen a usted y que adjudiquen daños punitivos. Estos daños son muy raros en casos que involucran contratos y muy difícil de conseguir.

3. They are requesting that the courts punish you by awarding punitive damages. These damages are very rare in contract cases, and very hard to get.

4. La ley ha creado una norma llamada cuasicontrato. Es una obligación creada no por un acuerdo, sino por ley.

4. The law has created a rule called quasi-contract. This is an obligation created by law in absence of an agreement.

Specific Performance

1. Desafortunadamente, la ley en raras ocasiones permite lo que se llama cumplimiento específicos.

1. Unfortunately, the law rarely allows what is called specific performance.

2. El cumplimiento específico es cuando un juez ordena a una persona que entregue un artículo específico.

2. Specific performance is when a judge orders someone to deliver a specific item.

3. Por ejemplo, si usted firma un contrato de compra con un comerciante de autos, uno generalmente no puede obligar al comerciante que le entregue un auto específico. Solamente está obligado a entregar un auto del mismo año, misma marca, mismo diseño y color que uno pidió.

3. For instance, if you sign a contract to buy a car from a dealership, you usually can't force the dealer to give you the exact car you want. All he has to do is deliver to you the same year, make, model and color that you agreed upon.

4. Si el artículo que usted compró es muy especial, entonces es posible que haya una manera de obligar a la otra parte que entregue ese artículo específico.

4. If the item you purchased was very special, then there might be a way to force the other party to deliver the specific item.

5. Si usted acordó comprar un específico Chevrolet Bel Aire de 1956 de un coleccionista, o si acordó comprar una propiedad, entonces la otra parte sería obligada a entregarle ese artículo específico.

5. If you agreed to buy a specific 1956 Chevrolet Bel Aire from a collector, or if you agreed to buy a piece of real estate, then the other party could probably be forced to deliver that specific item to you.

6. Creo que usted puede exponer los argumentos para obligar a la otra parte cumplir con las condiciones específicamente.

6. I think that you can make a strong case for forcing the other party to perform their duties specifically.

7. En cuanto a este caso, no creo que usted puede obligar un cumplimiento específico.

7. *I do not believe that you can force specific performance in this matter.*

8. Usted probablemente será limitado a la recuperación de dinero y nada más.

8. *You are probably going to be limited to the recovery of money damages only.*

Specific Case Types: Employment

1. La mayoría de los contratos de empleo en este estado se llaman "Empleo a Voluntad".

1. *Most employment contracts in this state are called, "Employment at Will".*

2. Es un término legal que quiere decir que tanto usted como el empleador son libres de terminar su relación cuando ustedes quieran y por cualquiera razón.

2. *This is a legal term meaning that both you and the employer are free to end your relationship at any time and for almost any reason.*

3. Usted tendrá que consultar con un abogado que se dedica específicamente con casos de contratos de empleo.

3. *You will need to see an attorney who works specifically on employment contract cases.*

4. Creo que es posible que usted haya sido perjudicado y que usted puede tener un fundamento legal y material de una demanda contra su antiguo empleador.

4. *I believe that you may have been harmed, and that you may have a cause of action against your former employer.*

5. Creo que una situación de "a voluntad" existía y que su empleador era libre de terminar la relación.

5. *I believe that an at-will situation existed, and that your employer was free to legally end the relationship.*

6. Puede existir una cuestión sobre si su empleador lo despidió por razones no permitidas, tal como su raza o sexo.

6. There may be an issue as to whether or not your employer fired you for a reason which is not allowed, such as your race or your gender.

7. Creo que pudiera haber existido un contrato válido entre usted y su empleador.

7. I believe that there may have been a valid employment contract between you and your employer.

8. Puede servirle mejor ponerse en contacto con el Departamento de Trabajo Estatal de inmediato e informarles de su situación. Ellos tienen un systema eficaz para resolver asuntos de este tipo.

8.It may best serve your interests to contact the State Department of Labor immediately and inform them of your situation. They have an effective system for dealing with this type of matter.

9. Casos que involucran heridas conseguidas en el trabajo suelen no ser casos legales que tienen que ver con contratos. Existe una ley completamente separada que se llama "indemnización por accidentes laborales" que cubre estos tipos de casos. Le puedo mandar a un abogado que se dedica a estos tipos de casos.

9. Cases that involve on-the-job injuries are usually not contract types of legal matters. There is an entirely separate kind of law called Worker's Compensation law which covers these types of cases. I can refer you to a lawyer who handles these types of cases regularly.

Vehicles

1. Debido a los asuntos de seguridad y a las cantidades de dinero involucradas, la venta de automóviles suelen ser reguladas por el gobierno. Ellos se ven obligados a proteger a los consumidores.

1. Because of the safety issues and the amounts of money usually involved, the sale of motor vehicles tends to be regulated to some degree by the government. They see fit to protect consumers in many ways.

2. En nuestro estado tenemos una ley que se conoce con el nombre de "Ley del Limón" (ley de protección contra daños ocultos).

2. In our state, we have what is known as a "lemon law".

3. Esta ley prohíbe que un vendedor de un auto o un concesionario autorizado le venda un auto defectivo.

3. This law prevents car sellers or dealers from selling you a car which is defective from the start.

4. En este caso, es mi opinión que los tribunales encontrarían que la persona que le vendió este auto violó la ley del limón.

4. In this case, I believe that a court would likely find that the person who sold you this car violated the lemon law.

5. Desafortunadamente, la ley del limón no le aplica a la persona que le vendió el auto.

5. Unfortunately, the person who sold you the car is not the kind of seller to whom this law applies.

Assignmen, Assumption

1. Creo que una asunción de contrato válida tuvo lugar.

1. I believe that a valid assumption of a contract occurred.

2. No creo que una asunción de contrato válida tuvo lugar.

2. I do not believe that a valid assumption of a contract occurred.

3. Creo que un acto válido de transferir el contrato tuvo lugar.

3. I believe that a valid assignment of the contract occurred.

4. No creo que un acto válido de transferir el contrato tuvo lugar.

4. I do not believe that a valid assignment of the contract occurred.

5. Creo que un acto válido de la transferencia de derecho bajo el contrato tuvo lugar.

5. I believe that a valid assignment of a right under the contract occurred.

6. No creo que un acto válido de la transferencia de derecho bajo el contrato tuvo lugar.

6. *I do not believe that a valid assignment of a right under the contract occurred.*

7. Creo que un acto válido de la transferencia de obligación bajo el contrato tuvo lugar.

7. *I believe that a valid assumption of an obligation under a contract occurred.*

8. No creo que un acto válido de la transferencia de obligación bajo el contrato tuvo lugar.

8. *I do not believe that a valid assumption of an obligation under a contract occurred.*

What You Can Do For Them

1. Para poder determinar los detalles de este asunto a fondo, usted necesaría contratarme para poder representarlo en el futuro.

1. *In order to properly and completely determine the details of this matter, I would need to be retained to represent you further.*

2. A veces la otra parte evitará problemas si recibe una carta escrita por un abogado que representa sus intereses.

2. *Sometimes the other party will make the situation right if they receive a letter from a lawyer on your behalf.*

3. En tal carta, el abogado le explica a la otra parte que ellos son de alguna manera responsables a usted de conformidad con el contrato.

3. *In such a letter, the lawyer tells the other party that they are liable in some way to you pursuant to the contract.*

4. Se les cominicará lo que usted desee y se les dirá que ellos tienen que resolver el asunto, de lo contrario usted los demandará.

4. *They are told what you want, and that they need to resolve matters to your satisfaction or else you will sue them.*

5. Con la carta incluiría un formulario que ellos pueden firmar y que explica que se resolvió el asunto y que ellos están de acuerdo.

5. *I would include a form with the letter for them to sign which says that the matter is resolved, and that they no longer want any legal trouble with you.*

6. Ellos lo pueden firmar e incluir la cantidad de dinero que usted acepte para resolver el asunto.

6. *They can sign it and include whatever money you will accept to make this matter go away.*

6. Se les puede devolver lo que ellos le entregaron a usted y ellos le pueden devolver el dinero a usted o devolver cualquier artículo que usted les entregó.

6. *They can take back what they gave you and refund your money or give back what you gave to them.*

7. Ellos pueden aceptar que el asunto se termine en ese momento.

7. *They can agree to let the whole thing end right there.*

Referral and Retention

1. Creo que usted necesita consultar con un abogado que hable español mejor que yo y que se dedica con este tipo de caso de contrato.

1. *I believe that you need to talk with an attorney who Speaks Spanish better than I do and works primarily on this type of contract case.*

2. ¿Quisiera usted que le de el nombre y número de teléfono de tal abogado?

2. *Would you like me to provide you with the name and number of such an attorney?*

3. ¿Si usted consulta con otro abogado, debe informarle que usted consultó conmigo acerca del asunto.

3. *If you do speak to another attorney about this matter, you should tell them that you have talked to me about it.*

4. Ellos me pueden llamar por teléfono acerca del asunto y acerca de lo que discutimos.

4 *You may have them call me if they need to discuss what we talked about.*

5. Típicamente, yo cobro (100/150/200/250/300) de dólares por hora por este tipo de caso.

5. *Typically I charge (100/150/200/250/300) per hour to handle this sort of matter.*

6. Estimo que podré resolver este caso en (1,2,3,4,5) horas.

6. *I estimate that it will take me (1,2,3,4,5) hours to take care of this.*

7. Estimo que me llevará más de 5 horas para resolver el caso. ¿Quisiera usted contratarme para que yo resuelve el asunto para usted?

7. *I estimate that it will take me more than five hours to take care of this. Would you like to hire me to do this for you?*

Spanish Grammar At A Glance

PRONUNCIATION

- The Spanish vowel consists of one short, crisp sound that basically never changes in pronunciation.

- The Spanish **a** is pronounced like the *a* of the English word father. casa *(house)* parte *(part)* vamos *(let's go)* mañana *(tomorrow)*

- The Spanish **e** is pronounced like the *e* in the word met. **Do not** pronounce a Spanish *e* as the *a* in may. (mesa is pronounced meh-sa — not **may**-sa).
  mesa *(table)* me *(me)* este *(this)* tela *(cloth)*

- The Spanish **i** is pronounced like the *e* in the English word *me*.
  Fino *(fine)* libro *(book)* sí *(yes)* chico *(little)*

- The Spanish **o** is pronounced like the *o* in the English note.
  mucho *(much)* todo *(all)* corte *(court)*

- The Spanish **u** is pronounced like the English *oo* in b**oo**t.
  puro *(pure)* tú *(you)* uno *(one)*

- The Spanish **qu** is pronounced like the English *k* or '*hard c*' in the words **k**ettle or candy.
  Que *(that)* queso *(cheese)*

- The Spanish **ñ** is pronounced like the *ni* in English o**ni**on.
  año *(year)* niño *(boy)* niña *(girl)*

- The Spanish **h** is always silent. 'Hacienda' is pronounced 'Ah-see-en-da.'
  hermano *(brother)* hambre *(hunger)* hasta *(until)*

- The Spanish **ll** is pronounced like the English *y* in **y**es. The word **llamar** *(to be named)* is pronounced 'ya-mar.'
  calle *(street)* ella *(her)* milla *(mile)*

- The Spanish **g** has two pronunciations. The most common is like the English *g* in **g**et.
  gato *(cat)* grito *(scream)* golfo *(gulf)*

- The Spanish **g** is also pronounced like the English *h* in **h**e.
  gente *(people)* gira *(tour)* gitano *(gypsy)*

- The Spanish **j** is pronounced similar to the English *h* in **h**oe. Junta *(meeting)* is pronounced 'hun-ta.'
  jornada *(working day)* jabón *(soap)* jalar *(to pull)*

Spanish Grammar At A Glance

NOUNS AND ARTICLES

Spanish nouns have a gender: either **masculine** or **feminine**. Nouns that specifically refer to males (*father, brother, man* etc.) are masculine. Nouns that refer to females (*mother, sister, woman* etc.) are feminine. The same is true for animals. For all other nouns, it is necessary to learn the gender of the noun.

1. Nouns ending in -o are usually masculine. Thus:

el tío	the uncle
el niño	the boy
el gato	the cat
el centro	the center

2. Nouns ending in -a are usually feminine. Thus:

la tía	the aunt
la niña	the girl
la hermana	the sister
la puerta	the door

3. Nouns have **definite** and **indefinite** articles; both have four forms. The definite articles are: **el, la, los, las.**

el niño	the boy
la niña	the girl
los niños	the boys
las niñas	the girls

The indefinite articles are: **un, una, unos, unas.**

un libro	a book
una casa	a house
unos libros	some books
unas casas	some houses

4. **Un,** *(a, one)* is used before a masculine noun; **una,** *(a, one)*, is used before a feminine noun. **Unos,** *some,* is used before a masculine plural noun; **unas,** *some,* is used before a feminine plural noun.

5. To form the plural of nouns ending in -o or -a, an -s is added. Note that the plural of **el** is **los,** and the plural of **la** is **las.**

el hermano	los hermanos
el cuarto	los cuartos
la hermana	las hermanas
la casa	las casas

Add -es to nouns ending in a consonant.

la lección	las lecciones
el profesor	los profesores
el mineral	los minerales

6. All nouns ending in **-dad, -tad, -tud, -ción, -umbre, -sión** are feminine.

la ciudad	the city
la universidad	the university
la dificultad	the difficulty
la actitud	the attitude
la nación	the nation
la cumbre	the summit
la transfusión	the transfusion

THE DEFINITE ARTICLE

In Spanish the definite article must be used in certain situations:

1. The definite article is used with general or abstract nouns.
   La leche es buena para la salud.
   Milk is good for you.
   El azúcar es dulce.
   Sugar is sweet.
   El amor es una cosa divina.
   Love is a divine thing.

2. Use the definite article before titles when talking about a person.
   El doctor Rodríguez es dentista.
   Doctor Rodriguez is a dentist.
   La señora López es abogada.
   Mrs. Lopez is a lawyer.

3. Use the definite article with parts of the body or with clothing.
   Charlotte tiene los ojos verdes.
   Charlotte has green eyes.
   Juan tiene el pelo negro.
   John has black hair.
   María se puso la chaqueta.
   Mary put on her coat.

4. Use the definite article before the name of a language.
   El francés es un idioma muy bonito.
   French is a beautiful language.
   El inglés es la lengua de Estados Unidos.
   English is the language of the United States.

5. Use the definite article with the days of the week when it means on a certain day.
   Vamos de compras el lunes.
   We are going shopping on Monday.
   No estudio los domingos.
   I do not study on Sundays.

6. Omit the definite article in direct discourse.
   "Buenos días, profesor López?".
   " Good morning, professor Lopez."
   "¿Cómo está usted, señorita García"?
   " How are you, Miss Garcia?"

7. Do not use the definite article before a language if the language is used immediately after **hablar** or after **en** or **de.**
   El señor López no habla inglés.
   Mr. Lopez does not speak English.
   El libro está escrito en español.
   The book is written in Spanish.
   Hablo inglés.
   I speak English.

8. Do not use the definite article before an unmodified noun denoting occupation, rank or nationality.
   Es estadounidense.
   She is an American.
   Es médico.
   He is a doctor.
   Es abogada.
   She is a lawyer.

Spanish Grammar At A Glance

CONTRACTED ARTICLES

The masculine definite article **el** is contracted when it appears with the prepositions **a** or **de**. Note that such a contraction does not exist with the feminine article **la** nor with the plural article **los** or **las**.

1. The preposition **de** contracts with the article **el** to form **del** (of, from the).
   ¿Dónde está el libro del alumno.
   Where is the student's book?
   La mayoría del grupo está aquí.
   The majority of the group is here.
   El diccionario es del profesor, ¿no?
   The dictionary is the teacher's, isn't it?

2. The preposition **a** (to) contracts with the article **el** to form **al** (to the).
   Vamos al cine.
   We are going to the movies.
   María va al mercado.
   Mary is going to the market.

3. No other forms of articles contract with **de** or **a**.
   Juan y Carlos van a la escuela.
   Juan and Carlos go to school.
   La madre de los niños está aquí.
   The children's mother is here.
   Van a las montañas.
   They are going to the mountains.

THE NEUTER ARTICLE "LO"

The neuter article **lo** is used before a masculine singular adjective. It is also used before a past participle or a possessive to express their value in an abstract sense. In addition, it forms abstract nouns.

1. Here are a few adjectives which may be combined with **lo**.

lo bello	**the beautiful**
lo bueno	**the good**
lo difícil	**what is difficult**
lo justo	**that which is just**
lo mejor	**the best**
lo necesario	**the necessary**
lo útil	**what is useful**

   Es lo mejor que tenemos.
   It is the best that we have.
   Quiero lo justo.
   I want what is just.

2. Here are a few past participles used together with **lo**.

lo inesperado	**the unexpected**
lo ocurrido	**what happened**

3. Possesives such as **mío** and **suyo** can be used together with **lo**.

lo mío	**what is mine**
lo suyo	**what is yours**
Defiendo lo mío.	**I defend what is mine.**

ADJECTIVES

In Spanish, adjectives agree in gender and number with the nouns or pronouns they modify.

1. Most adjectives in Spanish end in **-o** and have four forms. The forms are **-o, -os, -a, -as**. To form the plural of an adjective ending in **-o**, add an **-s**.
   el carro moderno
   the modern car
   los carros modernos
   the modern cars
   la casa moderna
   the modern house
   las casas modernas
   the modern houses

2. Adjectives that end in **-e** do not change the **-e** ending in the feminine. To form the plural, add an **-s**.
   el carro grande
   the large car
   los carros grandes
   the large cars
   la casa grande
   the large house
   las casas grandes
   the large houses

3. Adjectives that end with a consonant do not change for feminine nouns, either. To form the plural, add **-es**.

el auto azul	**the blue car**
la casa azul	**the blue house**
los autos azules	**the blue cars**
las casas azules	**the blue houses**
la niña bella	**the pretty girl**
las niñas bellas	**the pretty girls**

SHORT FORMS OF ADJECTIVES

Some adjectives have a shortened form before masculine singular nouns; they drop the **-o**. These adjectives are:

bueno	**good**
un buen hombre	**a good man**
malo	**bad**
un mal niño	**a bad child**
primero	**first**
el primer niño	**the first child**
tercero	**third**
el tercer niño	**the third child**
alguno	**some**
algún* día	**some day**
ninguno	**no one**
ningún* hombre	**no man**

***algún** and **ningún** carry a written accent in this shortened form. The adjective **grande** has a shortened form in both the masculine and the feminine. However, it means *famous* or *great* instead of *big* or *large*.

un gran hombre	**a great man**
una gran mujer	**a great woman**

Spanish Grammar At A Glance

COMPARATIVE ADJECTIVES
To form the comparative of adjectives in Spanish, the construction **más...que** is used. This is equivalent to the comparative in English **more ... than.**

Juan es más alto que Carlos.
John is taller than Carl.
Tengo más dinero que él.
I have more money than he (has).

When a comparative is followed by a number, use **más de** instead of **más ... que.**

Tengo más de veinte dólares.
I have more than twenty dollars.

When the sentence is negative, **más que** and not **más de** is used with numbers.

No tengo más que diez dólares.
I have no more than ten dollars.

SUPERLATIVE ADJECTIVES
Form the superlative by using the word **más** and the appropriate article.

1. Superlatives are followed by the preposition **de** (**más de**). The article goes before the person or thing being compared.

   Nueva York es la ciudad más grande de EE UU.
   New York is the largest city in the US.
   Ana es la niña más alta de la clase.
   Ana is the tallest girl in the class.
   Juan y Carlos son los más altos del grupo.
   John and Carl are the tallest of the group.

2. The adjectives **bueno, malo, grande,** and **pequeño** have irregular forms in the comparative and the superlative. Note that each irregular form ends with the letters "or."

bueno	mejor
malo	peor
grande	mayor
pequeño	menor

3. The four irregular adjectives noted above take no articles in the comparative. Use a definite article to form the superlative.
   Este auto es mejor que el otro.
   This car is better than the other one.
   Este auto es el mejor de todos.
   This car is the best of all.

POSSESSIVE ADJECTIVES
Possesive adjectives are used to denote ownership or possession. They are placed before nouns and agree in number and in gender with the thing possessed, and not with the possessor.

mi profesor
mis profesores
tu profesor
tus profesores
su profesor
sus profesores
nuestro profesor
nuestros profesores
nuestra profesora
nuestras profesoras

1. Because **su** and **sus** can have several meanings, the definite article may be used with the following forms:

de usted	de ustedes
de él	de ellos
de ella	de ellas

   Es el libro de él.
   It's his book.
   Es la casa de ellos.
   It's their house.

2. The possessive adjective **nuestro** (our) has four forms: **nuestro, nuestros, nuestra** and **nuestras.**
   Es nuestro coche.
   It's our car.
   Son nuestros coches.
   They are our cars.
   Es nuestra casa.
   It's our house.
   Son nuestras casas.
   They are our houses.

DEMONSTRATIVE ADJECTIVES
Demonstrative adjectives agree in gender and number with the noun or pronoun they modify.

1. The demonstrative adjective **este** (this) has four forms:
   Este libro es interesante.
   This book is interesting.
   Estos libros son interesantes.
   These books are interesting.
   Esta casa es bonita.
   This house is pretty.
   Estas casas son bonitas.
   These houses are pretty.

2. In Spanish there are two ways to express the demonstrative adjective *that*. One of them is **ese**. It is used when the object is near to the person spoken to, but not to the speaker. **Ese** has four forms.
   Ese niño es español.
   That child (boy) is Spanish.
   Esa niña es española.
   That child (girl) is Spanish.
   Esos niños son españoles.
   Those children (boys) are Spanish.
   Esas niñas son españolas.
   Those children (girls) are Spanish.

3. **Aquel** is used when the object is far from both the speaker and the person spoken to. **Aquel** also has four forms.
   Aquel señor es médico.
   That man is a doctor.
   Aquella señora es abogada.
   That woman is a lawyer.
   Aquellos señores son chilenos.
   Those men are Chilean.
   Aquellas señoras son españolas.
   Those women are Spanish.

PERSONAL PRONOUNS

Spanish Grammar At A Glance

A personal pronoun can be used as either the subject or object of a verb. Personal pronouns may also be the object of a preposition, or a reflexive pronoun object. Since the verb ending in Spanish indicates the subject, it is most common to eliminate the subject pronoun. This is particularly true with **yo, tú, nosotros,** and **nosotras.**

1. The subject pronouns in Spanish are:

SINGULAR	PLURAL
yo **I**	nosotros/as **we**
tú **you**	ustedes **you**
usted **you**	ustedes **you**
él **he**	ellos **they**
ella **she**	ellas **they**

NOTE:* In Latin America **vosotros/as has been replaced by the pronoun **ustedes. Vosotros/as** is used mainly in Spain.

2. Direct object pronouns receive the action of the verb. The direct object pronouns in Spanish are:

SINGULAR	PLURAL
me **me**	nos **us**
te **you**	los **you, them**
lo **you, him**	las **you, them**
la **you, her, it**	lo **it**

Jean me ve.
Jean sees me.
Juan te ve.
John sees you.
Rosa lo ve.
Rosa sees you.
Yo lo veo.
I see him.
Juan la ve.
John sees her.
Tomás nos ve.
Thomas sees us.
Sofía los ve.
Sofia sees them.
Ana lee el libro.
Ana reads the book.
Ana lo lee.
Ana reads it.

3. The indirect object pronoun denotes the person *to, for, or from whom* any thing is given, told, sent, etc.

SINGULAR	PLURAL
me **to me**	nos **to us**
te **to you**	les **to you**
le **to you**	les **to them**
le **to him, to her**	

Juan me mandó dinero.
John sent me some money.
Ella te compró un regalo.
She bought you a gift.
Yo le hablo en inglés.
I speak to him (to her) in English.
Pablo nos habla.
Paul is talking to us.
Ella les habla.
She is talking to them.

4. When using both direct and indirect object pronouns in the same sentence, the indirect object pronoun always comes first.
¿Cuándo me pagas el dinero? Te lo pago mañana.
When are you paying me the money? I'll pay (it to) you tomorrow.

5. When the main verb is an infinitive, attach both object pronouns to the end of the infinitive. The indirect object comes before the direct object.
José quiere mandármelo por correo.
Joe wants to send it to me by mail.

6. If the main verb is **poder, saber,** or **querer,** the two object pronouns may be placed in front of the verb.

María me lo quiere comprar.
Mary wants to buy it for me.

REFLEXIVE PRONOUNS

A reflexive verb is one whose subject and object are the same. The subject acts upon itself. A reflexive verb is indicated by the pronoun se attached to the infinitive.

1. The singular reflexive pronouns are:

me	**myself; to (for) myself**
te	**yourself; to (for) yourself**
se	**himself; to (for) himself** **herself; to (for) herself** **yourself; to (for) yourself** **itself; to (for) itself** **themselves; to (for) themselves**

Yo me visto.
I dress myself.
Tú te vistes.
You dress yourself.
Él se viste.
He dresses himself.
Ella se viste.
She dresses herself.

2. The plural reflexive pronouns are:

nos	**ourselves; to (for) ourselves**
se	**yourselves; to (for) yourselves**

Nos vestimos.
We dress ourselves.
Se visten.
They dress themselves.

*In order to make these sentences negative, place no in front of the reflexive pronoun.
No se levanten todavía. **Don't get up yet.**

PRONOUNS AS OBJECTS OF A PREPOSITION

Some prepositions require a pronoun, called a prepositonal pronoun.

mí **me**	nosotros/as **us**
ti **you**	ustedes **you**
usted **you**	usted **you**
él **him**	ellos **them**
ella **her**	ellas **them**
ello **it**	sí **yourself, himself, herself**

sí (plural) yourselves, themselves

Esos libros son para mí.
Those books are for me.
Las flores son para ti.
The flowers are for you.
Hablamos de él.
We're talking about him.
Su padre insistió en ello.
Her father insisted on it.

NOTE: The preposition con combines with mí, ti, and sí to form the words conmigo, *with me*, contigo *with you*, and consigo *with yourself, with himself, with herself, with yourselves, with themselves.*

Charlotte va conmigo.
Charlotte is going with me.
Iré contigo.
I'll go with you.
No voy contigo.
I'm not going with you.
Voy con ellos.
I'm going with them.

RELATIVE PRONOUNS

A relative pronoun refers to something previously mentioned in the sentence. It may serve as the subject or object of a verb, or as the object of a preposition. Que and quien are the relatives most commonly used.

1. The relative pronoun que can be used to replace either a person or a thing, and can function as either the subject or object of the clause.
   La muchacha que habla con Juan es mi hermana.
   The girl who is talking to John is my sister.
   El libro que está en la mesa es mío.
   The book that is on the table is mine.
   La casa en que viven es grande.
   The house in which they live is large.

2. The relative pronoun quien (quienes), *who/whom*, can replace the pronoun que.
   Hablé con Ana, quien es su tía.
   I spoke with Ana, who is his aunt.
   El señor Molina, quien es profesor, conoce a mi padre.
   Mr. Molina, who is a teacher, knows my father.

3. Quien and quienes, when used with a preposition, means *whom.*
   El médico, a quien llamamos, vino enseguida.
   The doctor, whom we called, came right away.
   Los amigos, a quienes espero, no han llegado.
   The friends, whom I am waiting for, have not arrived.

4. Lo que, *what* or *that which*, is used as a neuter relative pronoun when referring to an abstract or general idea.
   Lo que necesita es más dinero.
   What he needs is more money.
   Lo que él pide es imposible.
   What he asks is impossible.

5. Lo cual is used in supplementary clauses when the antecedent is a clause, phrase or an idea.
   María estudia todos los días, lo cual es bueno.
   Mary studies every day, which is good.
   Ella se negó a recibirme, lo cual lamento mucho.
   She refused to see me, which I regret.

6. El cual, la cual, los cuales, las cuales, *who, that, who, which, the one/s which, the one/s who*, may be used in place of que, to clarify number and gender.

   Los libros, los cuales están sobre la mesa, son míos.
   The books, which are on the table, are mine.

VERBS

Verbs are classified according to their infinitive ending: -ar, -er, or -ir. The three classes are called the first, second, and third conjugation.

THE PRESENT TENSE

1. The FIRST CONJUGATION is the -ar conjugation. To form the present tense, replace the -ar ending with -o, -as, -a, -amos, -an.

NOTE: In Spain, vosotros(as) is the plural form of tú and is used when addressing two or more relatives, intimate friends, small children, or animals. In the south of Spain and in Latin America, vosotros has been replaced by ustedes. We will omit the vosotros form in these conjugations.

yo hablo	I speak
tú hablas	you speak
él habla	he speaks
ella habla	she speaks
usted habla	you speak
nosotros/as hablamos	we speak
ustedes hablan	you speak
ellos hablan	they speak
ellas hablan	they speak

Yo hablo español.	I speak Spanish.
Tú hablas inglés.	You speak English.
Ella habla árabe.	She speaks Arabic.

Nosotros hablamos español.
We speak Spanish.
¿Hablan ustedes inglés?
Do you speak English?
Ellos hablan alemán.
They speak German.

**NOTE:* Omit subject pronouns except when needed for clarity and emphasis.

Hablo español. I speak Spanish.
Hablan inglés. They speak English.

COMMON 1ST CONJUGATION VERBS

buscar	to look for
cambiar	to change
gastar	to spend
hablar	to talk
cantar	to sing
invitar	to invite
enseñar	to teach
lavar	to wash
esperar	to wait
pagar	to pay
estudiar	to study
viajar	to travel

2. The SECOND CONJUGATION is referred to as the -er conjugation. The personal endings -o, -es, -e, -emos, -en are added to the stem.
yo como I eat
tú comes you eat
él come he eats
ella come she eats
usted come you eat
nosotros/as comemos we eat
ustedes comen you eat
ellos comen they eat
ellas comen they eat

Nosotros comemos carne.
We eat meat.
¿Comen ustedes carne?
Do you eat meat?

COMMON 2ND CONJUGATION VERBS
aprender to learn
esconder to hide
beber to drink
leer to read
comer to eat
meter to insert
correr to run
vender to sell

3. The THIRD CONJUGATION is referred to as the -ir conjugation. The personal endings for the -ir verbs are -o, -es, -e,
-imos, -en. Note that most of the personal endings are the same for both the -er and -ir verbs.
yo vivo I live
tú vives you live
él vive he lives
ella vive she lives
usted vive you live
nosotros/as vivimos we live
ustedes viven you live
ellos viven they live
ellas viven they live

Yo vivo en Tejas.
I live in Texas.
¿Dónde vives tú?
Where do you live?
Nosotros vivimos en México.
We live in Mexico.

COMMON 3RD CONJUGATION VERBS
abrir to open
admitir to admit
asistir to attend
cubrir to cover
subir to go up
sufrir to suffer
vivir to live

THE IMPERFECT
There are two past tenses in Spanish. One is the imperfect and the other is the preterite. Their uses vary. The imperfect tense is used for events that *used* to happen or *repeated* or habitual events in the past. The translation of the imperfect into English depends on the context.

1. In order to form the imperfect tense of regular -ar verbs, drop the infinitive ending -ar and add the following endings: -aba, -abas, -aba, -ábamos, -aban.

hablaba — I used to speak; talk / I was speaking; talking / I spoke; talked

hablaba	hablábamos
hablabas	
hablaba	hablaban

María hablaba de su viaje.
Mary was talking about her trip
Mary used to talk about her trip.
Mary talked about her trip.

Yo nadaba cada verano.
I used to swim every summer.
I swam every summer.

Ella cenaba en aquel restaurante todos los viernes.
She used to eat dinner in that restaurant every Friday.
She ate dinner in that restaurant every Friday.

Tú cantabas muy bien.
You used to sing very well.
You sang very well.

2. The imperfect tense of regular -er and -ir verbs is the same. To form the imperfect tense, drop the infinitive ending and add the following to the stem: -ía, ías, -ía, -íamos, -ían.

comía — I was eating / I used to eat / I ate / I was living

vivía	{ I used to live I lived

comía	comíamos
comías	
comía	comían
vivía	vivíamos
vivías	
vivía	vivían

Comíamos en ese restaurante.
We used to eat in that restaurant.
Yo leía mucho cuando era niño.
I used to read a lot when I was young.
Ustedes vivían en Madrid.
You used to live in Madrid.

THE PRETERITE
The **preterite** is the past tense used to express an action completed at a definite time in the past. The English auxiliary **did** is always understood.

1. The preterite of the regular **-ar** verbs is formed by dropping the infinitive ending and adding the following endings: **-é, -aste, -ó, -amos, -aron.**

hablé	hablamos
hablaste	
habló	hablaron

Tú hablaste con él ayer.
You spoke with him yesterday.
El halló el dinero la semana pasada.
He found the money last week.
Ellos compraron una casa pequeña.
They bought a small house.

2. The preterite of regular **-er** and **-ir** verbs is formed by dropping the infinitive ending and adding the following personal endings: -í, -iste, -ió, -imos, -ieron.

comí	comimos
comiste	
comió	comieron
viví	vivimos
viviste	
vivió	vivieron

Viví en España tres años.
I lived in Spain for three years.
Ellos comieron aquí ayer.
They ate here yesterday.
Recibió la carta esta tarde.
He received the letter this afternoon.
Carlos no asistió ayer a la clase.
Carlos didn't attend class yesterday.

THE FUTURE
The future tense in Spanish has only one set of endings for all three conjugations.

1. Add the following endings to the infinitive: -é, -ás, -á, -emos, -án.

hablaré	hablaremos
hablarás	
hablará	hablarán
comeré	comeremos
comerás	
comerá	comerán
viviré	viviremos
vivirás	
vivirá	vivirán

Hablaré con él mañana.
I'll speak with him tomorrow.
Comerán a las seis. **They will eat at six.**
Ana escribirá la carta.
Ana will write the letter.

2. In spoken Spanish, the future is often formed by using **ir a** + infinitive. This is equivalent to the English "going to."

Voy a trabajar allí.
I'm going to work there.
Vamos a comer en casa.
We are going to eat at home.

THE CONDITIONAL
The conditional tense expresses an idea dependent on a condition which is either expressed or understood.

1. The conditional is formed by adding the endings **-ía, -ías, -ía, -íamos, -ían** to the entire infinitive, not just the stem. These endings are the same for all three conjugations. Note that they are also the same personal endings as those used for the imperfect of **-er** and **-ir** verbs.

hablaría	hablaríamos
hablarías	
hablaría	hablarían
comería	comeríamos
comerías	
comería	comerían
viviría	viviríamos
vivirías	
viviría	vivirían

2. Use the conditional to express conjecture or probability, referring to the past.

María estaría enferma.
Mary was probably ill.
Llegarían anoche.
They probably arrived last night.

REFLEXIVE VERBS
A reflexive verb is one whose subject and object are the same. The subject acts upon itself. The verb is always used with some form of the reflexive pronoun. In Spanish a reflexive verb is indicated by the pronoun **se** *(singular:* oneself, yourself, himself, herself, itself; *plural:* yourselves, themselves) attached to the infinitive.

1. The reflexive verb **lavarse** (to wash oneself) is often used as the model reflexive verb. Here we conjugate it in the present

tense.

me lavo	I wash myself
te lavas	you wash yourself
se lava	you wash yourself he washes himself she washes herself it washes itself
nos lavamos	we wash ourselves
se lavan	you wash yourselves they wash themselves

**NOTE:* Reflexives, like other object pronouns, often precede the verb. When used with the infinitive, they follow the verb and are attached to it.

Quiero lavarme. I want to wash myself.
¿Quieres lavarte?
Do you want to wash yourself?

Voy a acostarme. I'm going to bed.

2. A reflexive verb is called a reciprocal when the action passes from one person or thing to another, or from one group to another. It is only used in the first and third persons plural.

Se miran. They look at each other.
Nos ayudamos. We help each other.

THE SUBJUNCTIVE
There are four tenses of the subjunctive in common use. The present subjunctive and the past subjunctive are by far the most common.

1. The **present subjunctive** of all three verb types (-ar, -er, -ir) is formed by adding the endings to the stem of the present indicative first person singular. Drop the final -o and add the following endings:

-ar verbs	-e, -es, -e, -emos, -en
-er verbs	-a, -as, -a, -amos, -an
-ir verbs	-a, -as, -a, -amos, -an

hablar (and regular -ar verbs)

hable	hablemos
hables	
hable	hablen

comer (and regular -er verbs)

coma	comamos
comas	
coma	coman

vivir (and regular -ir verbs)

viva	vivamos
vivas	
viva	vivan

A few common verbs often used with the subjunctive:
querer estar contento esperar
preferir temer sentir
Yo quiero que ustedes hablen inglés.
I want you to speak English.
Ella prefiere que comamos en casa.
She prefers that we eat at home.

NOTE:* The present subjunctive can be translated in many ways according to how it is used. Many times it is translated as *may...*, expressing possibility or uncertainty. The present subjunctive is also used in commands with **usted and **ustedes** With **tú**, it is used only in negative commands.

Hable usted español.
Speak Spanish.
No hables tú. (Negative)
Don't talk.
Quizas me escriba.
Perhaps he'll write to me.

2. The past subjunctive is formed on the stem of the preterite of the third person plural (ellos). For -ar verbs, add these endings to the stem: -ara, -aras, -ara, -áramos, -aran.

hablara	habláramos
hablaras	
hablara	hablaran

Te dije que te lavaras las manos.
I told you to wash your hands.
Le di el dinero para que comprara el libro.
I gave him the money so that he might buy the book.

For -er and -ir verbs, find the stem in the same way (the preterite of the third person plural [ellos]) and add the following endings: -iera, -ieras, -iera, -iéramos, -ieran.

comiera	comiéramos
comieras	
comiera	comieran

viviera	viviéramos
vivieras	
viviera	vivieran

Si recibiera el dinero, yo pagaría la cuenta.
If I should receive the money, I would pay the bill.

Esperábamos que comieran temprano.
We were hoping that they would eat early.

3. The **present perfect subjunctive** is formed with the present subjunctive of the auxiliary verb **haber** and the past participle of the main verb.
haya hablado
haya comido
hayas hablado
hayas comido
haya hablado
haya comido
hayamos hablado
hayamos comido
hayan hablado
hayan comido
haya vivido
hayas vivido

haya vivido
hayamos vivido
hayan vivido

No creo que hayamos pagado
la cuenta todavía.
I don't think we have paid the bill yet.

Espero que por lo menos su ayudante
los haya visto.
I hope at least that your assistant has seen them.

4. The **past perfect subjunctive** is formed with the imperfect subjunctive of **haber** plus a past participle.

hubiera hablado	hubiera comido
hubieras hablado	hubieras comido
hubiera hablado	hubiera comido
hubiéramos hablado	hubiéramos comido
hubieran hablado	hubieran comido

hubiera vivido
hubieras vivido
hubiera vivido
hubiéramos vivido
hubieran vivido

Yo temía que Carlos no hubiera hablado con ella.
I feared that Carlos might not have spoken with her.
Ellos querían que hubiéramos llegado antes.
They wanted us to have arrived earlier.

USES OF THE SUBJUNCTIVE

In Spanish the subjunctive mood is used almost always in subordinate clauses to designate events that the speaker sees as not part of reality or not part of his or her own experience. It is used to express doubt, uncertainty, or when a contrary-to-fact supposition is made. It is also used in the following situations:

1. The present subjunctive is used in direct and implied commands, both affirmative and negative.

Hable usted
Hablen ustedes } Speak.

No hable usted
No hablen ustedes
No hables tú. } Do not speak.

2. The subjunctive is used with verbs of volition: some common volition verbs are **querer, aconsejar, sugerir, preferir recomender**, etc.
Te aconsejo que estudies.
I advise you to study.
Ella quiere que yo le escriba.
She wants me to write to her.
Yo les sugiero que no se muden hasta fines de junio.
I suggest that you don't move until the end of June.

3. The subjunctive is also required after many impersonal expressions that denote an element of subjectivity.

es necesario	
es preciso	it is necessary
es menester	it is necessary
es posible	it is possible
es imposible	it is impossible
es probable	it is probable
es bueno	it is good
es malo	it is bad
es mejor	it is better
es una lástima	it is a pity
es raro	it is rare
es importante	it is important
es fácil	it is easy
es difícil	it is difficult
es triste	it is sad
puede ser que	it may be that

Es necesario que llegues a tiempo.
It is necessary that you arrive on time.
Es importante que ella lo prepare.
It is important that she prepare it.
Es una lástima que estés enfermo.
It's a pity that you are ill.
Quiero que se lave las manos.
I want him to wash his hands.

4. Use the subjunctive with expressions of doubt.

no creer	not to believe
dudar	to doubt
es dudoso	it is doubtful
es incierto	it is uncertain
no es cierto	it is not certain

No creo que ella pueda venir.
I don't believe she will be able to come.
Es dudoso que Juan escriba.
It is doubtful that John will write.

5. The subjunctive is used when one person tells (**decir**) or asks (**pedir**) another person to do something.
Dígale que lo escriba.
Tell him to write it.
Me dijo que lo escribiera.
He told me to write it.
Nos piden que salgamos.
They are asking us to leave.

THE PROGRESSIVE TENSES

The progressive tenses in Spanish show that the action of the verb is in the process of taking place. The progressive forms are most commonly used with the present and the imperfect. It is on occasion also used with the future. **Estar, seguir, ir,** or **andar** are used along with the present participle to form the progressive tenses. You will find that the most commonly used auxiliary is **estar**.

1. The **present progressive** describes an action that is taking place at the moment that we are talking. In Spanish, it is formed with the present tense of **estar** and the equivalent of the *-ing* form of the conjugated verb. The *-ing* form endings in Spanish are **-ando** for the -**ar** (**hablar**) verbs and **-iendo** for the -**er** (**comer**) and -**ir** (**vivir**) verbs.

   hablar (FIRST CONJUGATION VERB)
   estoy hablando
   estás hablando
   está hablando
   estamos hablando
   están hablando
   comer (SECOND CONJUGATION VERB)
   estoy comiendo
   estás comiendo
   está comiendo
   estamos comiendo
   están comiendo

   vivir (THIRD CONJUGATION VERB)
   estoy viviendo
   estás viviendo
   está viviendo
   estamos viviendo
   están viviendo

   Estoy estudiando mi lección.
   I am studying my lesson.
   María está comiendo. Mary is eating.
   ¿Qué estás tomando?
   What are you drinking?
   ¿Dónde estás viviendo?
   Where are you living?

**NOTE:* The present progressive is never used in Spanish to refer to a future action:
Salgo mañana.
I'm leaving tomorrow. (I leave tomorrow.)

2. The **past (imperfect) progressive** indicates an action in progress in the past. It is formed with the imperfect (simple past) tense of the verb **estar** and the -**ando**, or -iendo form of the verb.

   estaba hablando
   estabas hablando
   estaba hablando
   estábamos hablando
   estaban hablando

   estaba comiendo
   estabas comiendo
   estaba comiendo
   estábamos comiendo
   estaban comiendo

   estaba viviendo
   estabas viviendo
   estaba viviendo
   estábamos viviendo
   estaban viviendo

   ¿En qué estabas pensando?
   What were you thinking about?
   ¿Qué estabas haciendo?
   What were you doing?

3. **Seguir** (instead of **estar**) is often used to form a progressive tense to imply that an action is continuing (not yet finished).

   Ellos siguen trabajando.
   They are still working.

IRREGULAR VERBS

1. The verbs **ir**, **dar**, and **estar** are considered irregular in the present tense. Note, however, that the only irregularity exists in the first person singular (**yo**). All other forms are the same as those for a regular -**ar** verb.

IR	DAR	ESTAR
voy	doy	estoy
vas	das	estás
va	da	está
vamos	damos	estamos
van	dan	están

2. **Poner**, **hacer**, **valer**, **traer** and **salir** are considered irregular in the present tense. Again, the only irregular form is the first person singular **yo**.

PONER	HACER	VALER
pongo	hago	valgo
pones	haces	vales
pone	hace	vale
ponemos	hacemos	valemos
ponen	hacen	valen

TRAER	SALIR
traigo	salgo
traes	sales
trae	sale
traemos	salimos
traen	salen

3. Most verbs that end in -**cer** or -**cir** are also irregular in the present tense. Again, they are irregular only in the first person singular.

APARECER	CONOCER
aparezco	conozco
apareces	conoces
aparece	conoce
aparecemos	conocemos
aparecen	conocen

CONDUCIR	DECIR
conduzco	digo
conduces	dices
conduce	dice
conducimos	decimos
conducen	dicen

4. **Saber** is also irregular in the present tense. The only irregularity is the first person singular, (**yo**):**sé, sabes, sabe, sabemos, saben.**

Spanish Grammar At A Glance

IRREGULAR VERBS:

PAST TENSE

Some verbs are irregular in the preterite (simple past) tense.

ANDAR	CAER	DAR
anduve	caí	di
anduviste	caíste	diste
anduvo	cayó	dio
anduvimos	caímos	dimos
anduvieron	cayeron	dieron

SER AND ESTAR

There are two verbs in Spanish which have the English meaning *to be:* **ser** and **estar**.

1. **Ser** is used to express origin, possession and material. The preposition **de** is added.

   Es de España. He is from Spain.
   Es el libro de Rosa. It is Rosa's book.
   La casa es de madera.
   The house is made of wood.

2. **Ser** is used for description.
   El auto es rojo. The car is red.
   La casa es grande. The house is big.

   Use **ser** with expressions of time.

   Es la una.
   It is one o'clock.
   Hoy es martes.
   Today is Tuesday.

3. **Ser** is used with marital status.

   ¿Es usted casada?
   Are you married?

4. **Estar** is used to express location or position. Note that the verb estar is always used whether the location is permanent or temporary.

   Ellos están en Los Ángeles.
   They are in Los Angeles.

   Madrid está en España.
   Madrid is in Spain.
   El hotel está en la Avenida Colón.
   The hotel is on Columbus Avenue.

5. **Estar** is used to describe a current condition.
   ¿Cómo está su esposa?
   How is your wife?
   María está enferma. Mary is ill.

6. **Estar** is used to form the progressive tenses.
   Estoy escribiendo. I am writing.

   Estamos jugando al béisbol.
   We are playing baseball.

PEDIR AND PREGUNTAR

The verbs **pedir** and **preguntar** mean *to ask*.

1. **Pedir** means to ask for or to request something:

   ¿Qué le piden los muchachos?
   What do the boys ask you for?
   ¿Vas a pedirle dinero a Juan?
   Are you going to ask Juan for money?

2. **Preguntar** means to ask a question:

   ¿Qué vas a preguntarle a María?
   What are you going to ask Mary?
   Le voy a preguntar a María si quiere ir al cine.
   I'm going to ask Mary if she wants to go to the movies.

INDEX BY SECTION

CONTRACTS 688

CRIMINAL LAW 561

IMMIGRATION 650

Made in the USA
Monee, IL
18 October 2026

66039192R00427